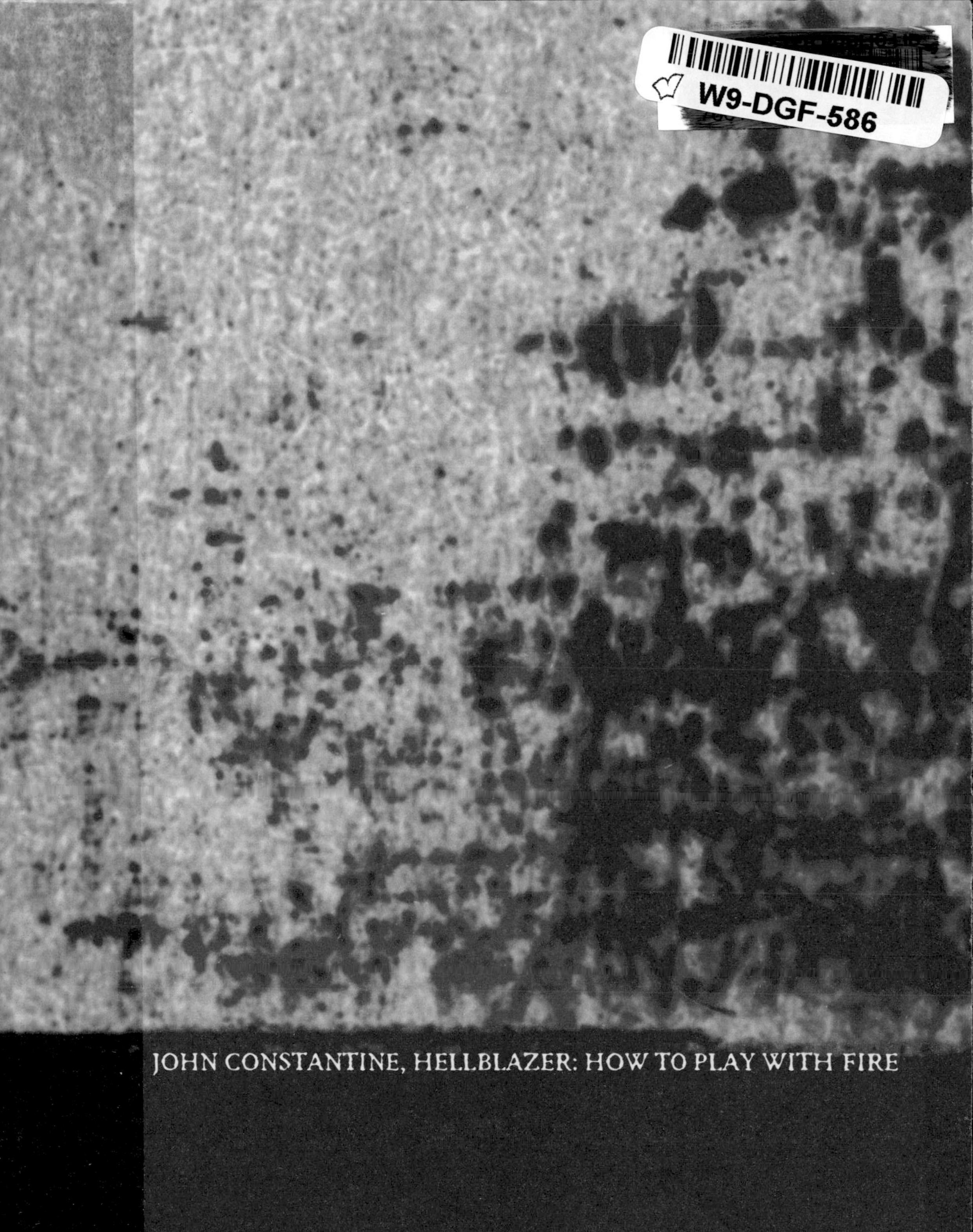

JOHN CONSTANTINE, HELLBLAZER: HOW TO PLAY WITH FIRE

JOHN CONSTANTINE, HELLBLAZER: HOW TO PLAY WITH FIRE

PAUL JENKINS GARTH ENNIS WRITERS

WARREN PLEECE JOHN HIGGINS ARTISTS

JAMES SINCLAIR COLORIST

CLEM ROBINS LETTERER

MING DOYLE COVER ART

SEAN PHILLIPS GLENN FABRY ORIGINAL SERIES COVERS

Axel Alonso Editor – Original Series
Jeb Woodard Group Editor – Collected Editions
Scott Nybakken Editor – Collected Edition
Louis Prandi Publication Design

Shelly Bond VP & Executive Editor – Vertigo

Diane Nelson President
Dan DiDio and Jim Lee Co-Publishers
Geoff Johns Chief Creative Officer
Amit Desai Senior VP – Marketing and
Global Franchise Management
Nairi Gardiner Senior VP – Finance
Sam Ades VP – Digital Marketing
Bobbie Chase VP – Talent Development
Mark Chiarello Senior VP – Art, Design
and Collected Editions
John Cunningham VP – Content Strategy
Anne DePies VP – Strategy Planning and Reporting
Don Falletti VP – Manufacturing Operations
Lawrence Ganem VP – Editorial Administration
and Talent Relations
Alison Gill Senior VP – Manufacturing and Operations
Hank Kanalz Senior VP – Editorial Strategy
and Administration
Jay Kogan VP – Legal Affairs

Derek Maddalena Senior VP – Sales and Business Development
Jack Mahan VP – Business Affairs
Dan Miron VP – Sales Planning and Trade Development
Nick Napolitano VP – Manufacturing Administration
Carol Roeder VP – Marketing
Eddie Scannell VP – Mass Account and Digital Sales
Courtney Simmons Senior VP – Publicity and Communications
Jim (Ski) Sokolowski VP – Comic Book Specialty
and Newsstand Sales
Sandy Yi Senior VP – Global Franchise Management

JOHN CONSTANTINE, HELLBLAZER VOL. 12: HOW TO PLAY WITH FIRE

DC Comics
2900 West Alameda Avenue
Burbank, CA 91505
Printed in the USA. First Printing.
ISBN: 978-1-4012-5810-8.

Jenkins, Paul, 1965-
   John Constantine, Hellblazer. Volume 12, How to play with fire / Paul Jenkins, Warren Pleece, Sean Phillips.
      pages cm
   ISBN 978-1-4012-5810-8 (paperback)
   1. Graphic novels. I. Pleece, Warren, illustrator. II. Phillips, Sean, illustrator. III. Title. IV.
Title: How to play with fire.
   PN6728.H383J49 2016
   741.5'973---dc23
                    2015034656

UP THE DOWN STAIRCASE, PART 1   7
FROM HELLBLAZER #121
COVER ART BY SEAN PHILLIPS

UP THE DOWN STAIRCASE, PART 2   31
FROM HELLBLAZER #122
COVER ART BY SEAN PHILLIPS

UP THE DOWN STAIRCASE, PART 3   55
FROM HELLBLAZER #123
COVER ART BY SEAN PHILLIPS

UP THE DOWN STAIRCASE, PART 4   79
FROM HELLBLAZER #124
COVER ART BY SEAN PHILLIPS

HOW TO PLAY WITH FIRE, PART 1:
BLOWING ON THE EMBERS   103
FROM HELLBLAZER #125
COVER ART BY SEAN PHILLIPS

HOW TO PLAY WITH FIRE, PART 2:
FANNING THE FLAMES   127
FROM HELLBLAZER #126
COVER ART BY SEAN PHILLIPS

HOW TO PLAY WITH FIRE, PART 3:
BURNING DOWN THE HOUSE   150
FROM HELLBLAZER #127
COVER ART BY SEAN PHILLIPS

HOW TO PLAY WITH FIRE, PART 4:
SIFTING THROUGH THE ASHES   173
FROM HELLBLAZER #128
COVER ART BY SEAN PHILLIPS

SON OF MAN, PART 1   197
FROM HELLBLAZER #129
COVER ART BY GLENN FABRY

SON OF MAN, PART 2   221
FROM HELLBLAZER #130
COVER ART BY GLENN FABRY

SON OF MAN, PART 3   245
FROM HELLBLAZER #131
COVER ART BY GLENN FABRY

SON OF MAN, PART 4   269
FROM HELLBLAZER #132
COVER ART BY GLENN FABRY

SON OF MAN, PART 5   293
FROM HELLBLAZER #133
COVER ART BY GLENN FABRY

JOHN CONSTANTINE, HELLBLAZER: HOW TO PLAY WITH FIRE

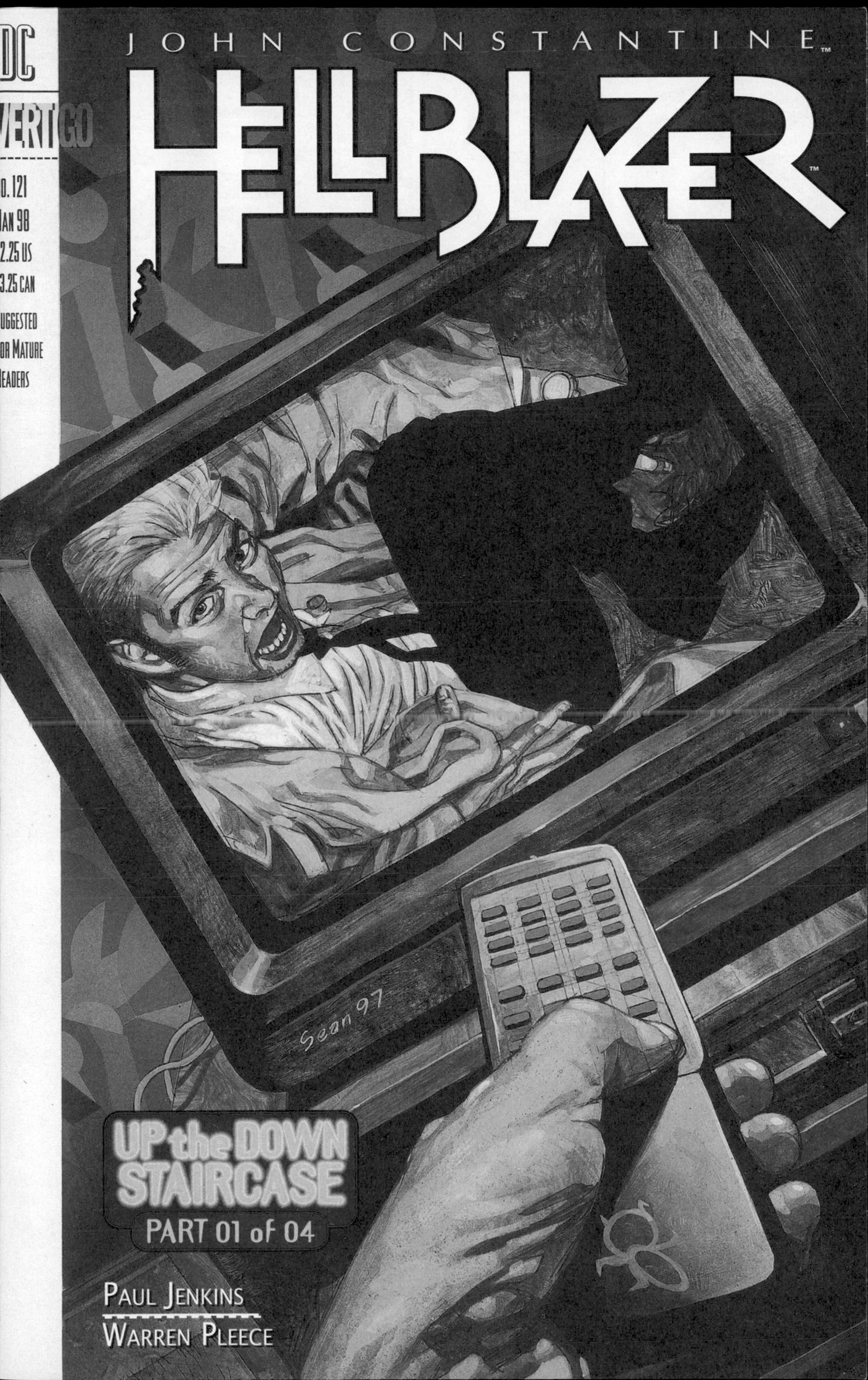
DC
VERTIGO
JOHN CONSTANTINE
HELLBLAZER
No. 121
JAN 98
$2.25 US
$3.25 CAN
SUGGESTED FOR MATURE READERS
Sean 97
UP the DOWN STAIRCASE
PART 01 of 04
PAUL JENKINS
WARREN PLEECE

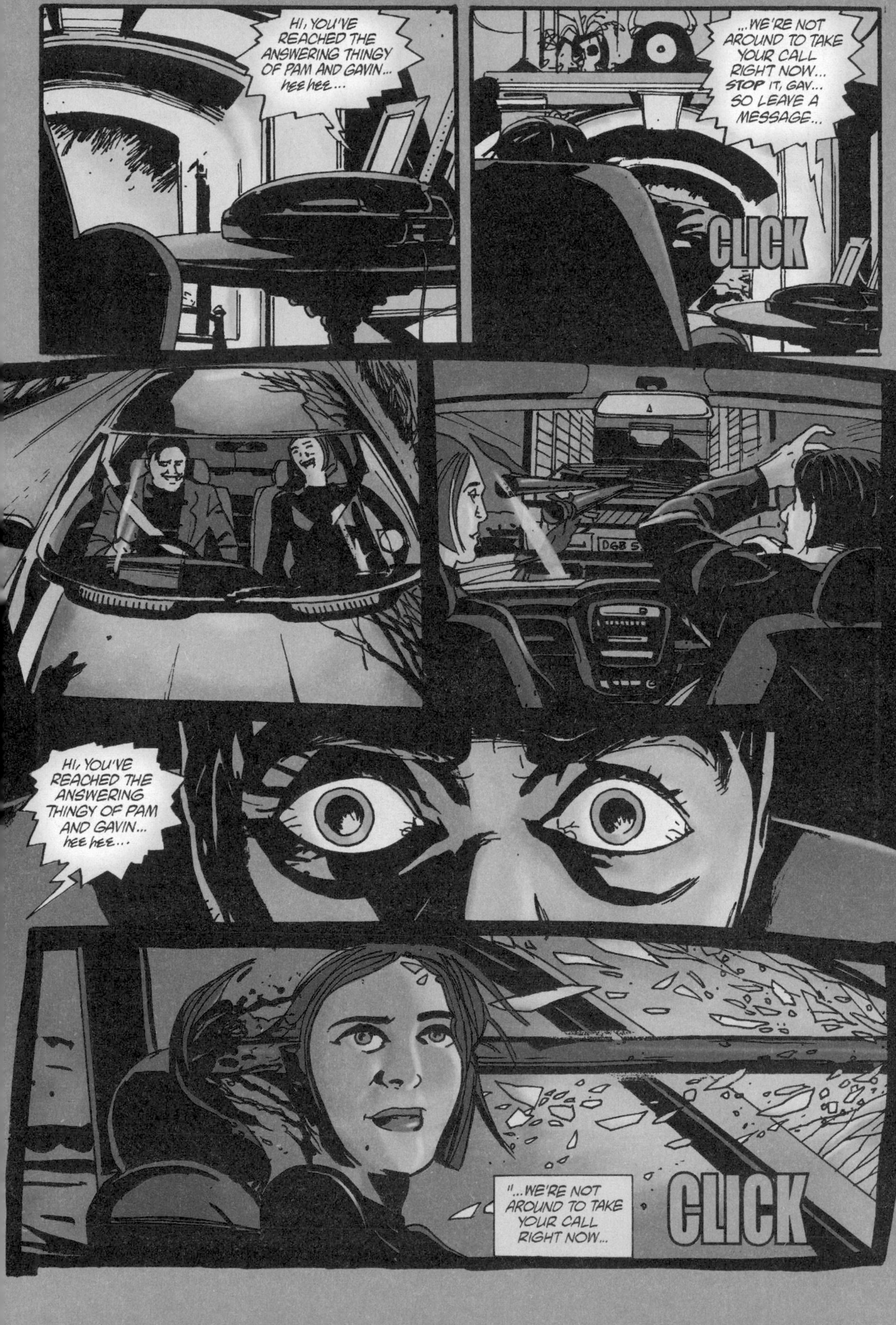
HI, YOU'VE REACHED THE ANSWERING THINGY OF PAM AND GAVIN... hee hee...
...WE'RE NOT AROUND TO TAKE YOUR CALL RIGHT NOW... STOP IT, GAV... SO LEAVE A MESSAGE...
CLICK
DGB 5
HI, YOU'VE REACHED THE ANSWERING THINGY OF PAM AND GAVIN... hee hee...
"...WE'RE NOT AROUND TO TAKE YOUR CALL RIGHT NOW...
CLICK

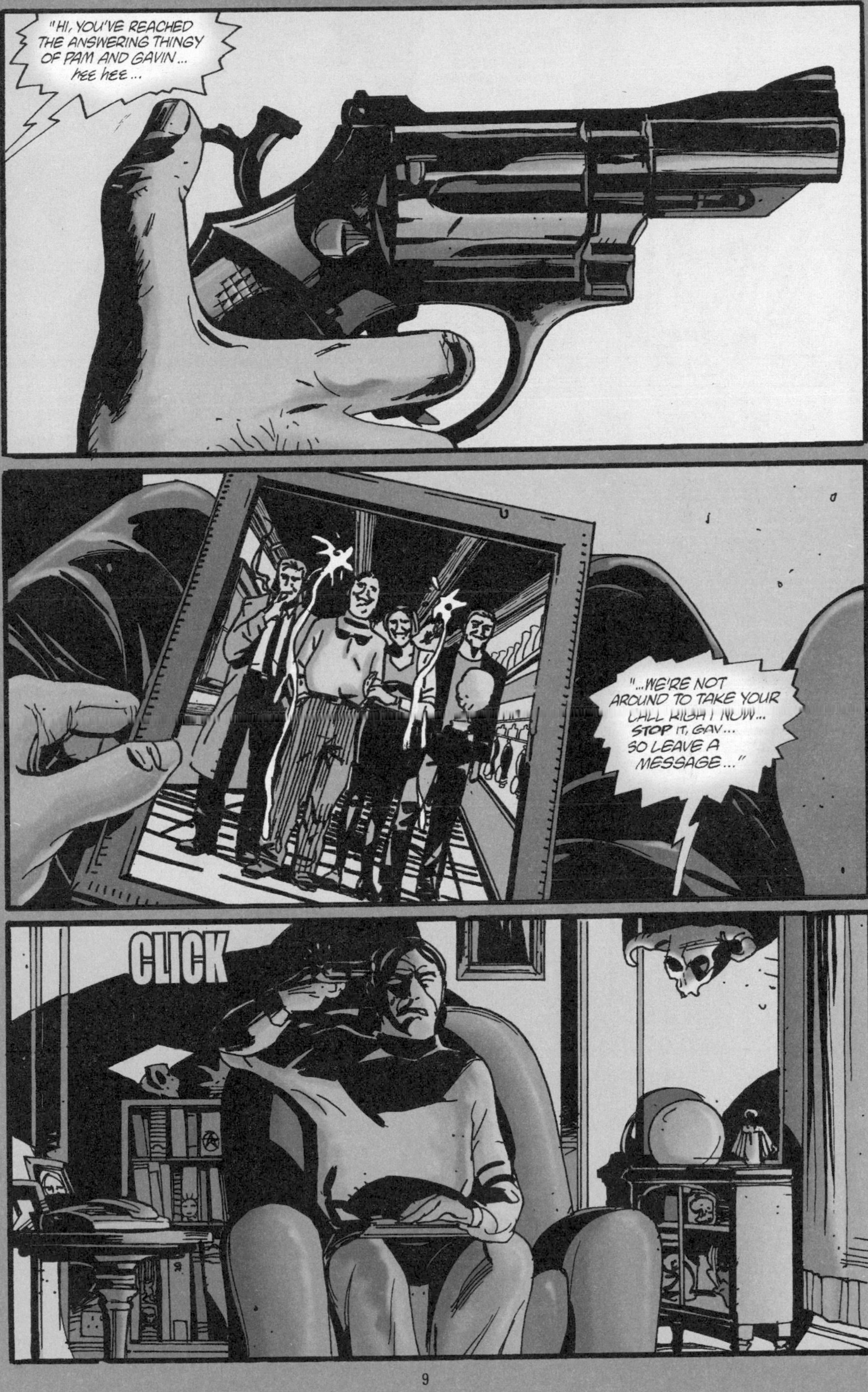
"HI, YOU'VE REACHED THE ANSWERING THINGY OF PAM AND GAVIN... hee hee...
"...WE'RE NOT AROUND TO TAKE YOUR CALL RIGHT NOW... STOP IT, GAV... SO LEAVE A MESSAGE..."
CLICK

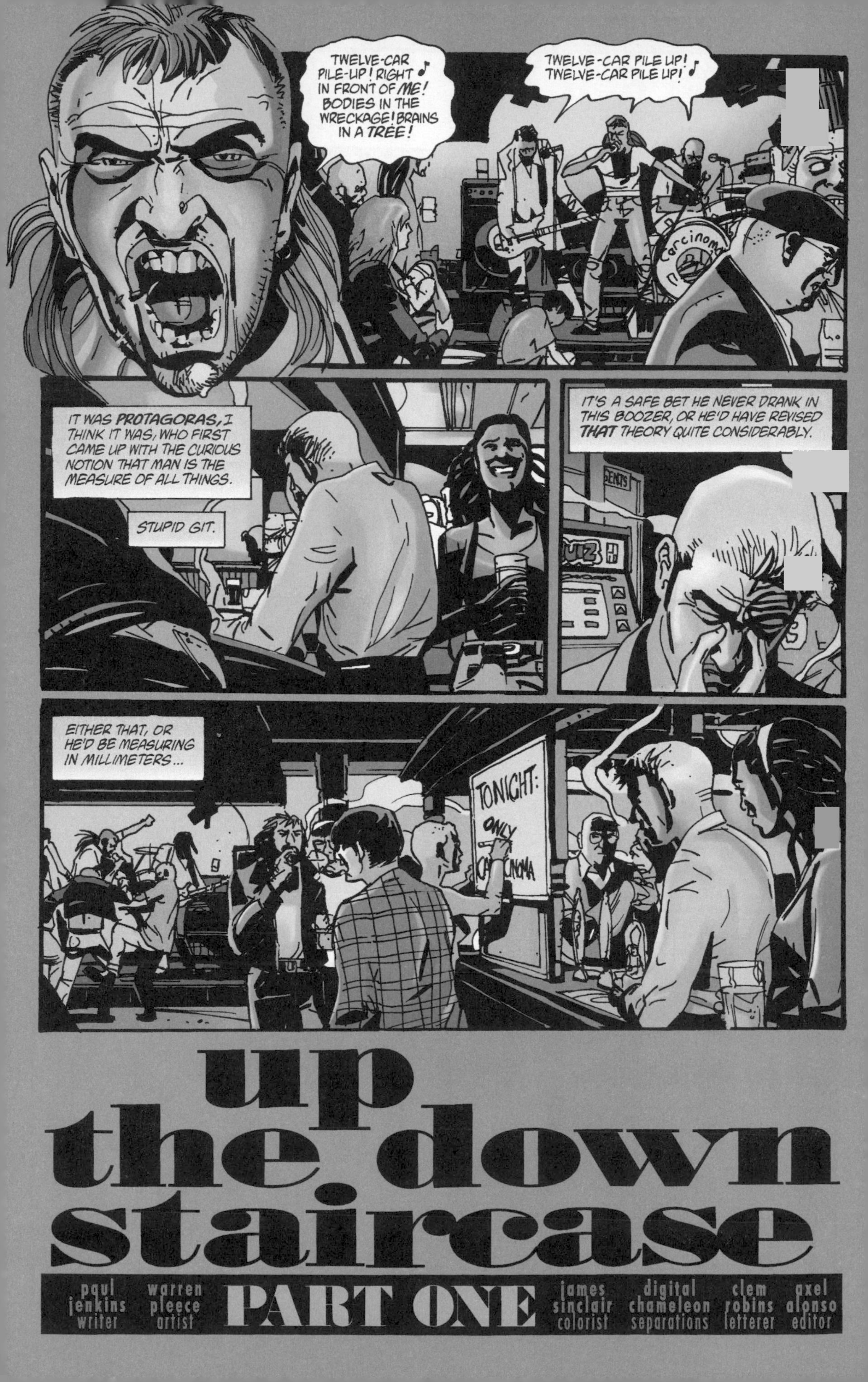
TWELVE-CAR PILE-UP! RIGHT IN FRONT OF ME! BODIES IN THE WRECKAGE! BRAINS IN A TREE!
TWELVE-CAR PILE UP! TWELVE-CAR PILE UP!
CARCINOMA
IT WAS PROTAGORAS, I THINK IT WAS, WHO FIRST CAME UP WITH THE CURIOUS NOTION THAT MAN IS THE MEASURE OF ALL THINGS.
STUPID GIT.
IT'S A SAFE BET HE NEVER DRANK IN THIS BOOZER, OR HE'D HAVE REVISED THAT THEORY QUITE CONSIDERABLY.
GENTS
EITHER THAT, OR HE'D BE MEASURING IN MILLIMETERS...
TONIGHT: ONLY CARCINOMA

up the down staircase

PART ONE

paul jenkins writer · warren pleece artist · james sinclair colorist · digital chameleon separations · clem robins letterer · axel alonso editor

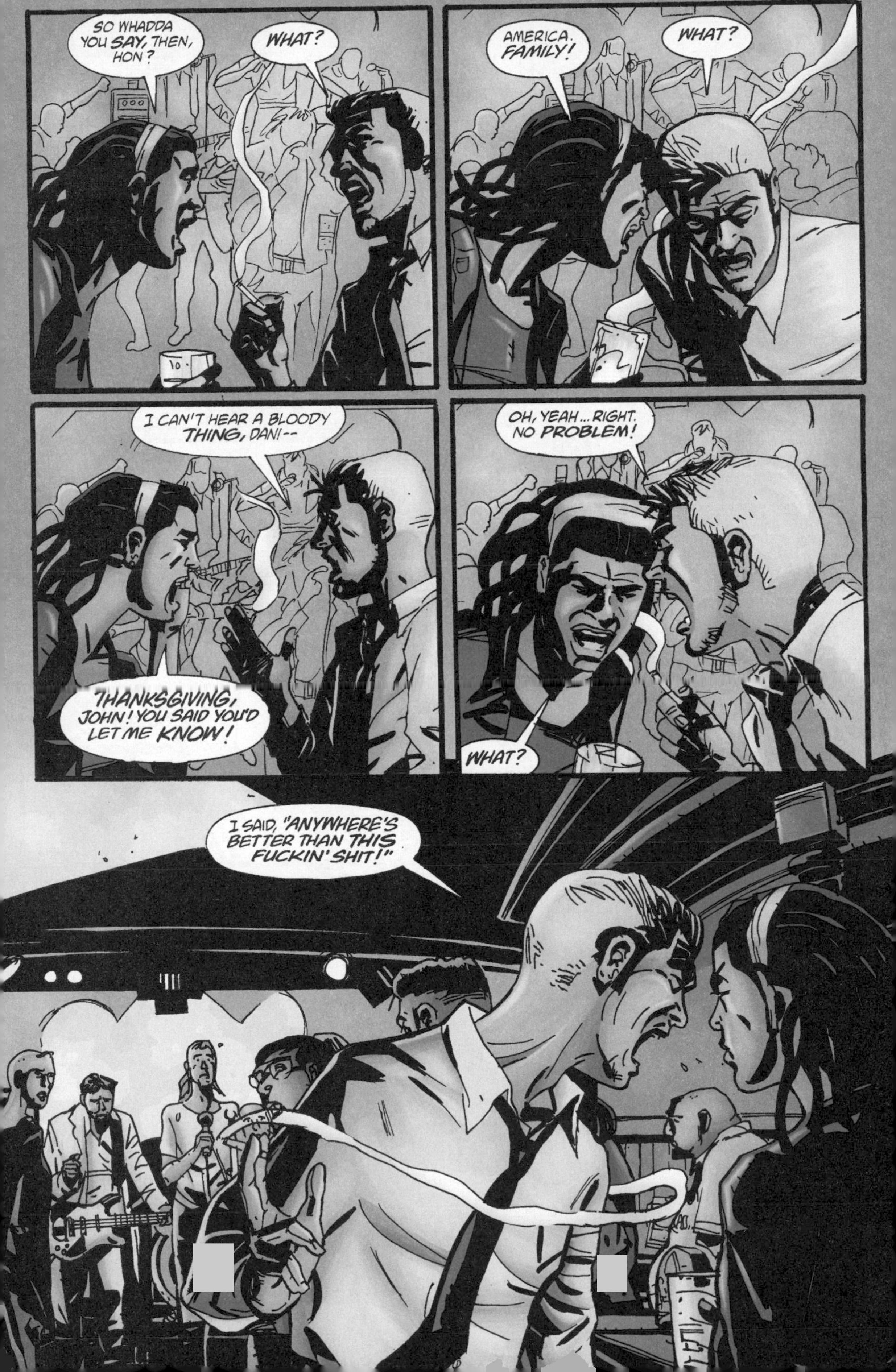
SO WHADDA YOU SAY, THEN, HON?
WHAT?
AMERICA. FAMILY!
WHAT?
I CAN'T HEAR A BLOODY THING, DANI--
THANKSGIVING, JOHN! YOU SAID YOU'D LET ME KNOW!
OH, YEAH... RIGHT. NO PROBLEM!
WHAT?
I SAID, "ANYWHERE'S BETTER THAN THIS FUCKIN' SHIT!"

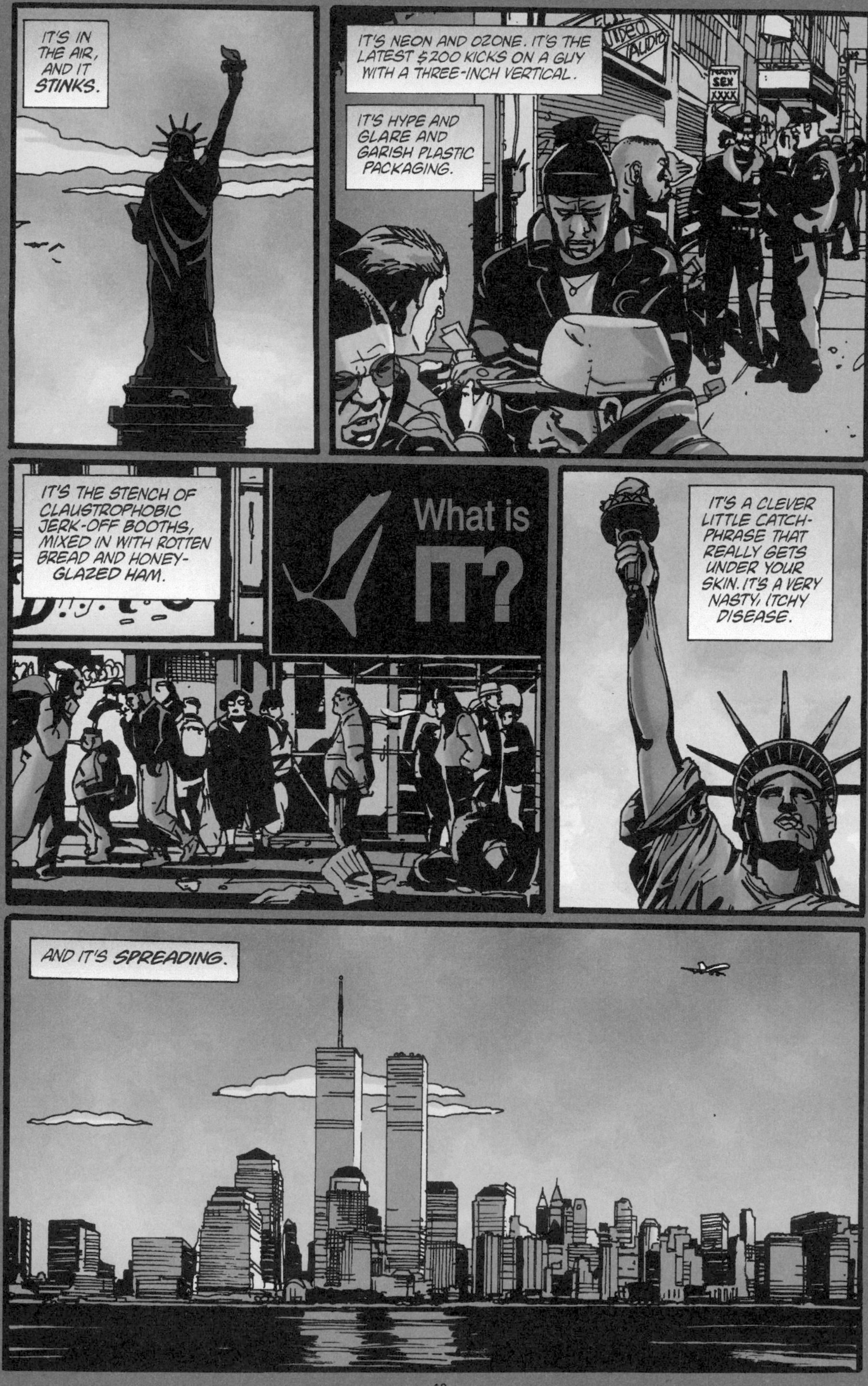
IT'S IN THE AIR, AND IT STINKS.
IT'S NEON AND OZONE. IT'S THE LATEST $200 KICKS ON A GUY WITH A THREE-INCH VERTICAL.
IT'S HYPE AND GLARE AND GARISH PLASTIC PACKAGING.
VIDEO
AUDIO
SEX
XXXX
IT'S THE STENCH OF CLAUSTROPHOBIC JERK-OFF BOOTHS, MIXED IN WITH ROTTEN BREAD AND HONEY-GLAZED HAM.
What is IT?
IT'S A CLEVER LITTLE CATCH-PHRASE THAT REALLY GETS UNDER YOUR SKIN. IT'S A VERY NASTY, ITCHY DISEASE.
AND IT'S SPREADING.

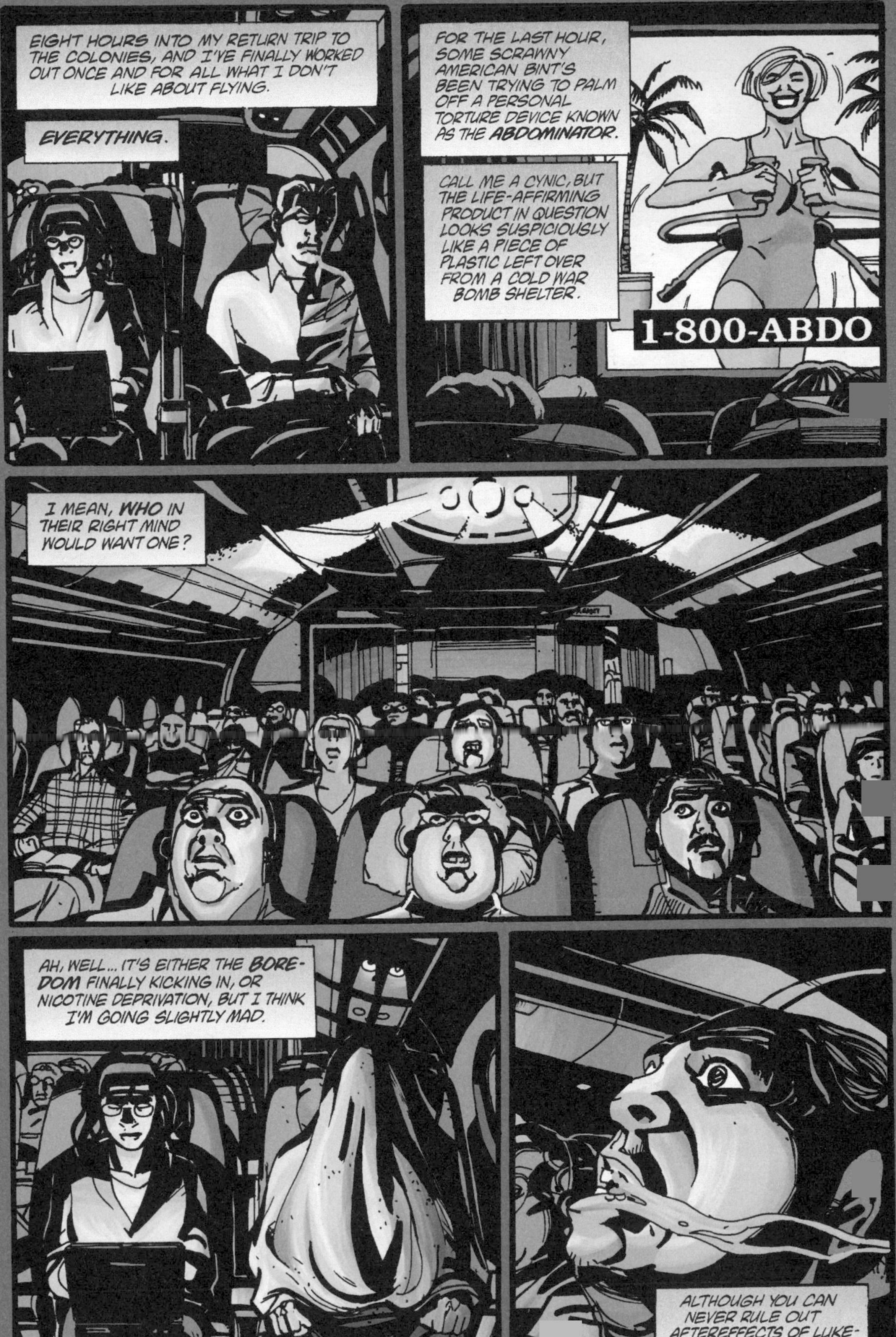
EIGHT HOURS INTO MY RETURN TRIP TO THE COLONIES, AND I'VE FINALLY WORKED OUT ONCE AND FOR ALL WHAT I DON'T LIKE ABOUT FLYING.
EVERYTHING.
FOR THE LAST HOUR, SOME SCRAWNY AMERICAN BINT'S BEEN TRYING TO PALM OFF A PERSONAL TORTURE DEVICE KNOWN AS THE ABDOMINATOR.
CALL ME A CYNIC, BUT THE LIFE-AFFIRMING PRODUCT IN QUESTION LOOKS SUSPICIOUSLY LIKE A PIECE OF PLASTIC LEFT OVER FROM A COLD WAR BOMB SHELTER.
1-800-ABDO
I MEAN, WHO IN THEIR RIGHT MIND WOULD WANT ONE?
AH, WELL... IT'S EITHER THE BOREDOM FINALLY KICKING IN, OR NICOTINE DEPRIVATION, BUT I THINK I'M GOING SLIGHTLY MAD.
ALTHOUGH YOU CAN NEVER RULE OUT AFTEREFFECTS OF LUKEWARM AIRLINE FOOD.

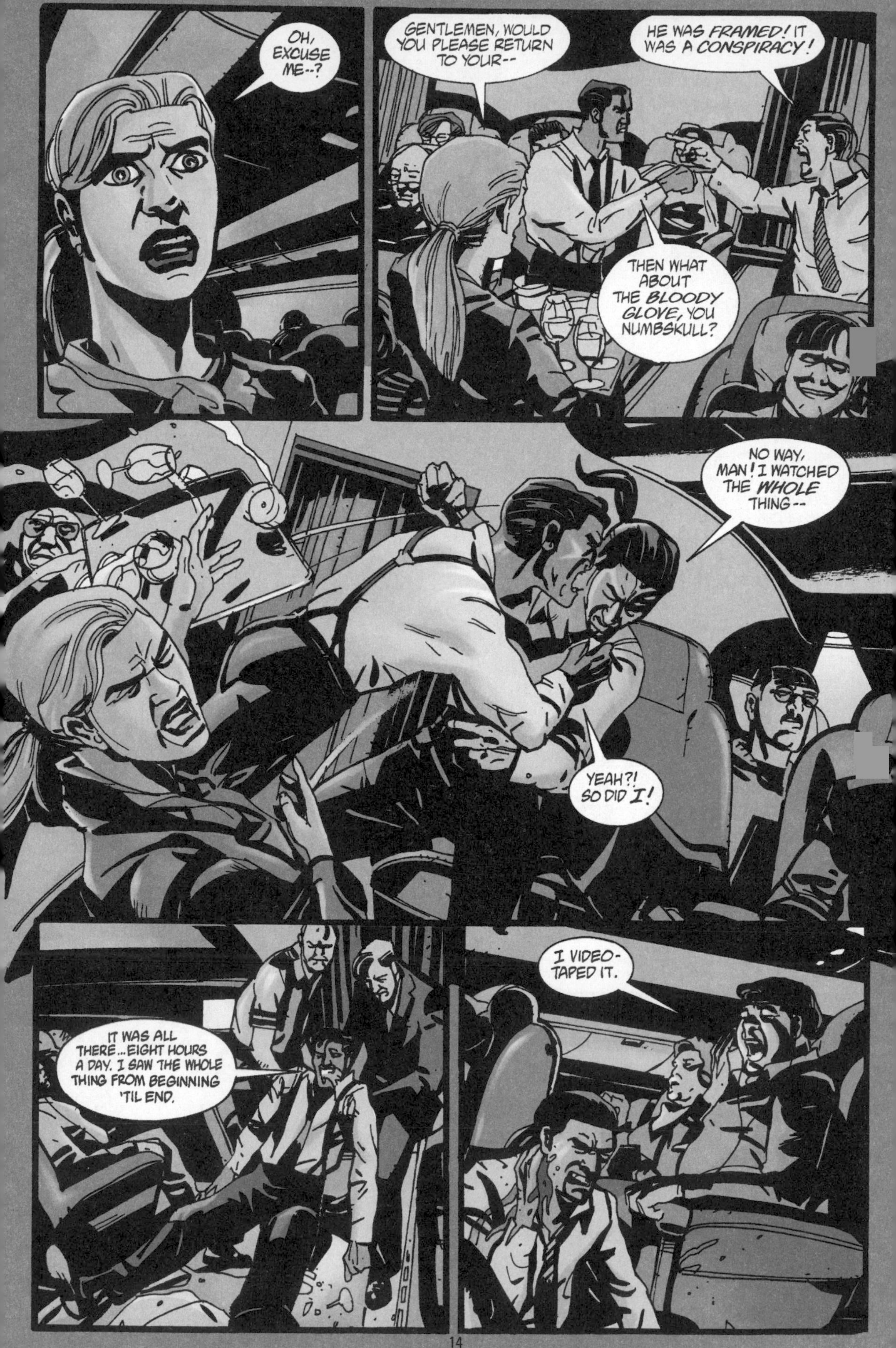
OH, EXCUSE ME--?
GENTLEMEN, WOULD YOU PLEASE RETURN TO YOUR--
HE WAS FRAMED! IT WAS A CONSPIRACY!
THEN WHAT ABOUT THE BLOODY GLOVE, YOU NUMBSKULL?
NO WAY, MAN! I WATCHED THE WHOLE THING--
YEAH?! SO DID I!
IT WAS ALL THERE...EIGHT HOURS A DAY. I SAW THE WHOLE THING FROM BEGINNING 'TIL END.
I VIDEO-TAPED IT.

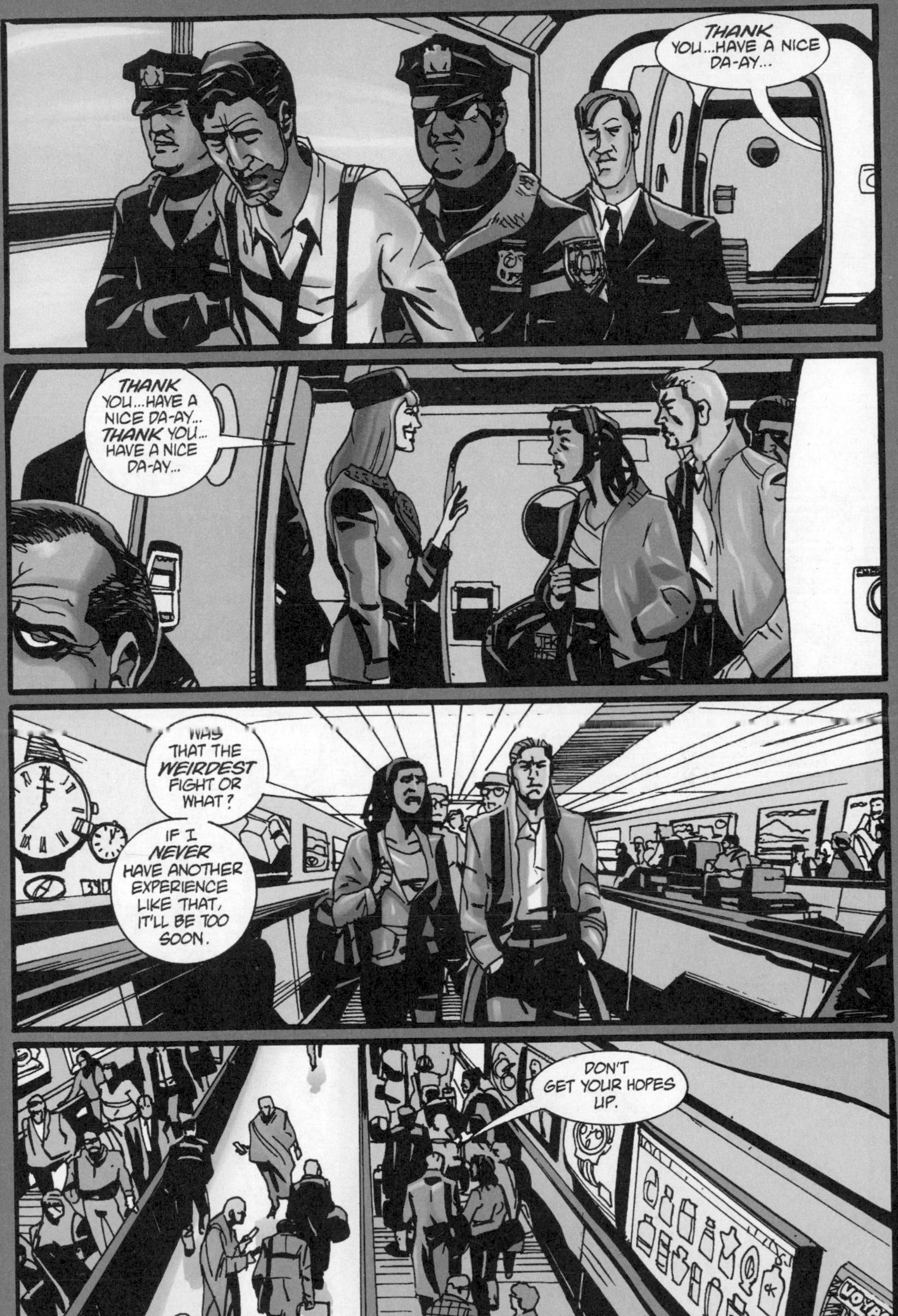
THANK YOU...HAVE A NICE DA-AY...
THANK YOU...HAVE A NICE DA-AY... THANK YOU... HAVE A NICE DA-AY...
WAS THAT THE WEIRDEST FIGHT OR WHAT?
IF I NEVER HAVE ANOTHER EXPERIENCE LIKE THAT, IT'LL BE TOO SOON.
DON'T GET YOUR HOPES UP.
VOYAG

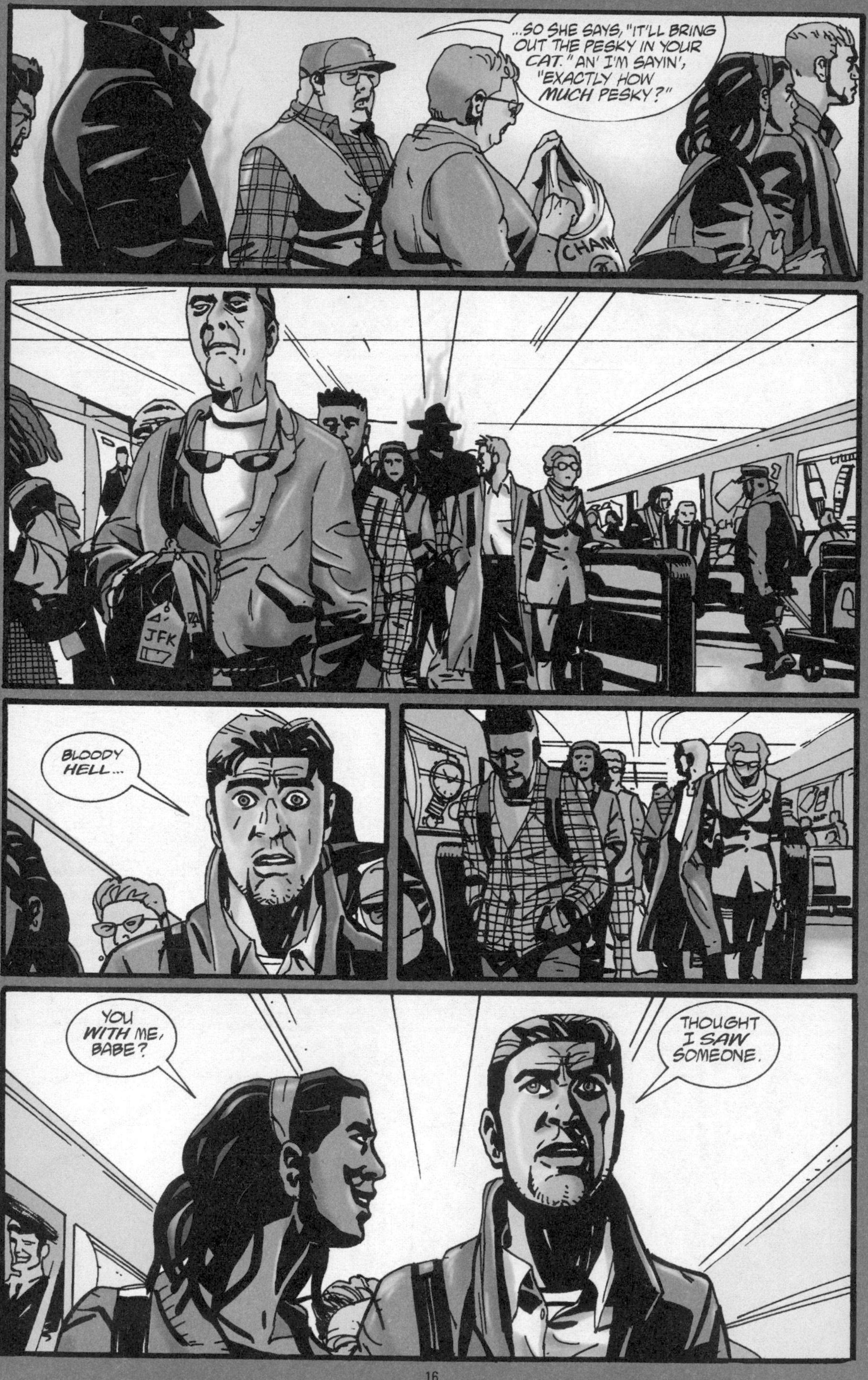
...SO SHE SAYS, "IT'LL BRING OUT THE PESKY IN YOUR CAT." AN' I'M SAYIN', "EXACTLY HOW MUCH PESKY?"
CHAN
JFK
BLOODY HELL...
YOU WITH ME, BABE?
THOUGHT I SAW SOMEONE.

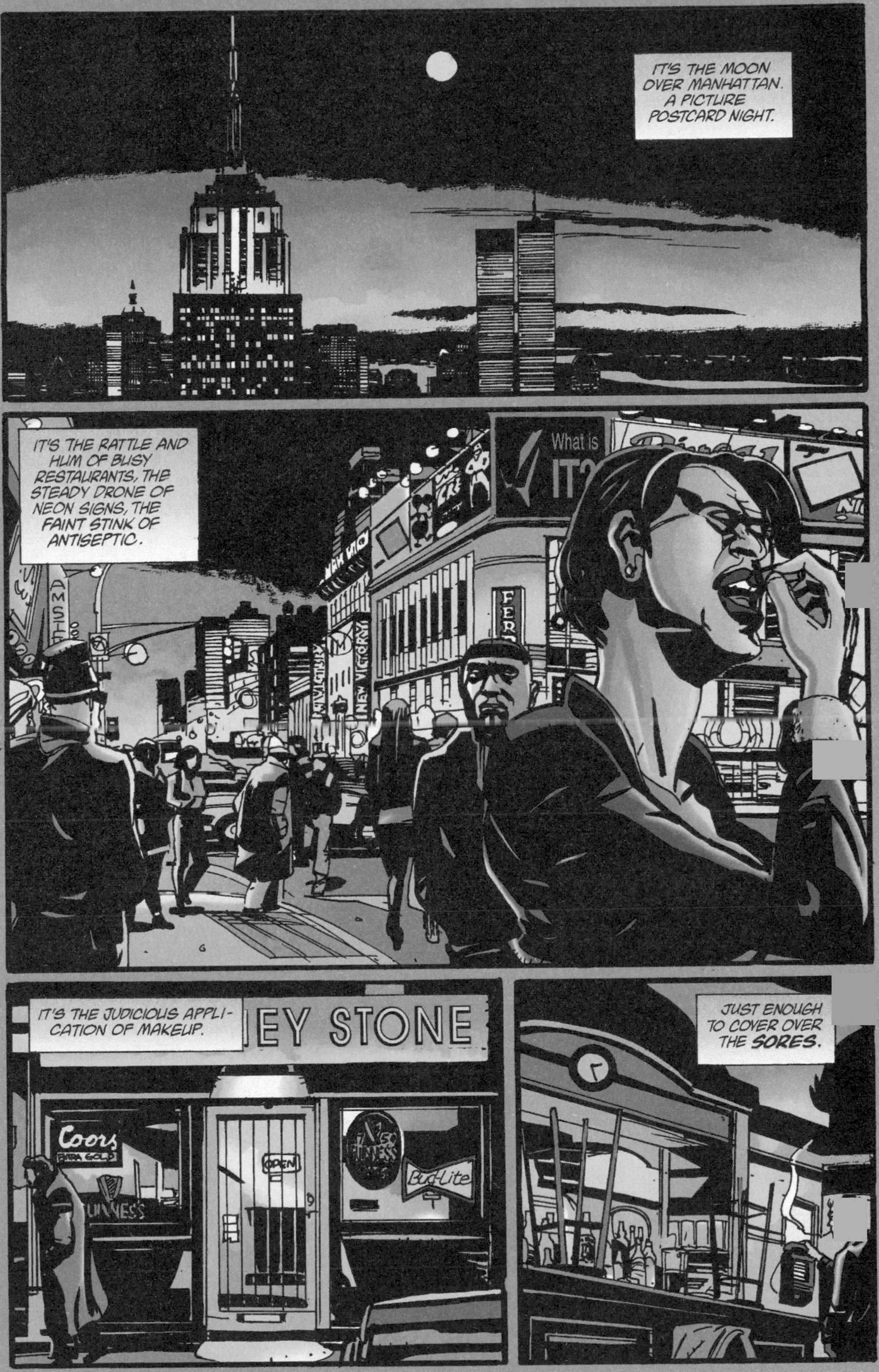
IT'S THE MOON OVER MANHATTAN. A PICTURE POSTCARD NIGHT.
IT'S THE RATTLE AND HUM OF BUSY RESTAURANTS, THE STEADY DRONE OF NEON SIGNS, THE FAINT STINK OF ANTISEPTIC.
What is
NEW VICTORY
IT'S THE JUDICIOUS APPLI-CATION OF MAKEUP.
EY STONE
Coors
OPEN
Bud-Lite
JUST ENOUGH TO COVER OVER THE **SORES**.

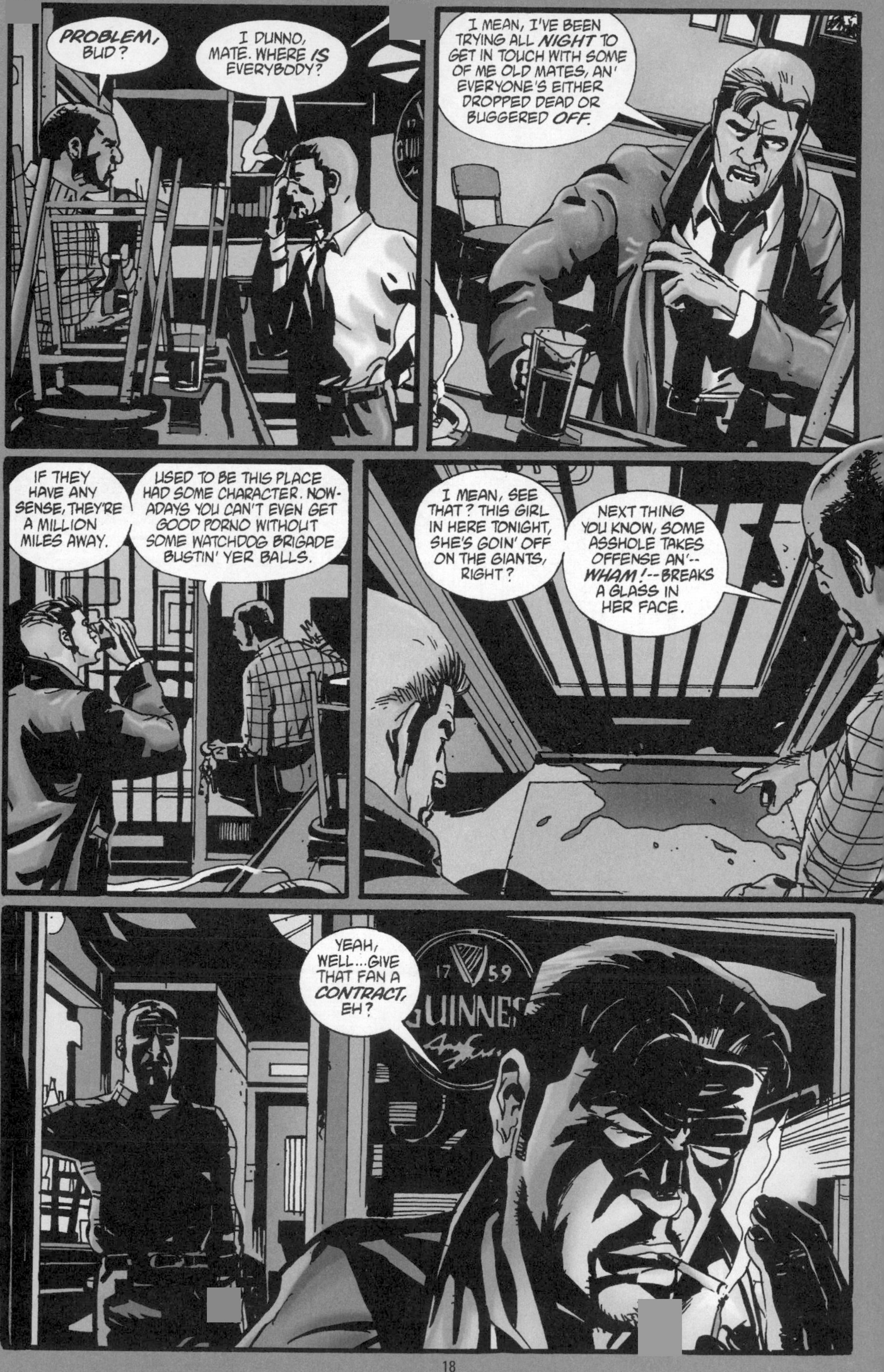
PROBLEM, BUD?
I DUNNO, MATE. WHERE IS EVERYBODY?
I MEAN, I'VE BEEN TRYING ALL NIGHT TO GET IN TOUCH WITH SOME OF ME OLD MATES, AN' EVERYONE'S EITHER DROPPED DEAD OR BUGGERED OFF.
IF THEY HAVE ANY SENSE, THEY'RE A MILLION MILES AWAY.
USED TO BE THIS PLACE HAD SOME CHARACTER. NOW-ADAYS YOU CAN'T EVEN GET GOOD PORNO WITHOUT SOME WATCHDOG BRIGADE BUSTIN' YER BALLS.
I MEAN, SEE THAT? THIS GIRL IN HERE TONIGHT, SHE'S GOIN' OFF ON THE GIANTS, RIGHT?
NEXT THING YOU KNOW, SOME ASSHOLE TAKES OFFENSE AN'-- WHAM!--BREAKS A GLASS IN HER FACE.
YEAH, WELL...GIVE THAT FAN A CONTRACT, EH?
17 59
GUINNES

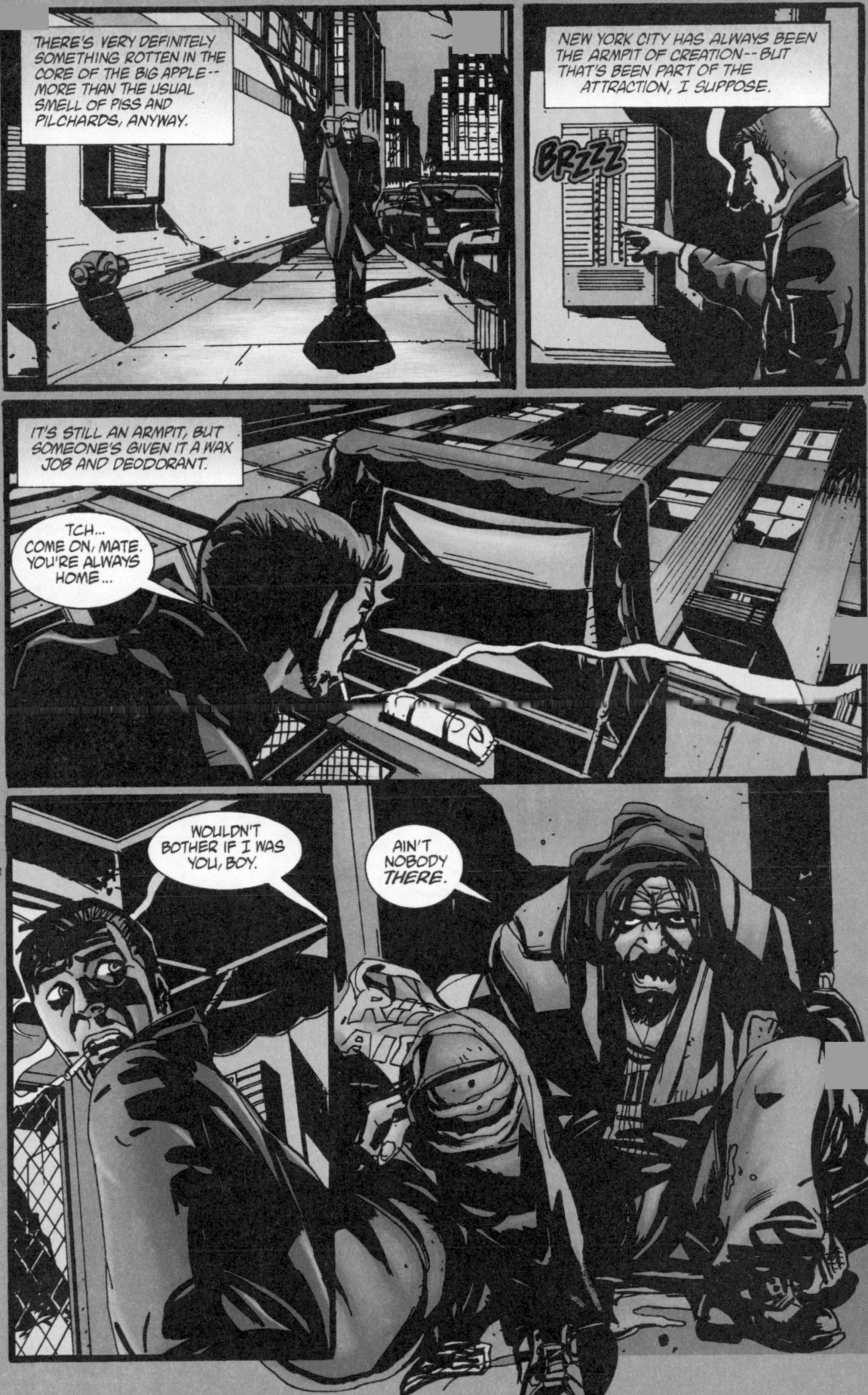
THERE'S VERY DEFINITELY SOMETHING ROTTEN IN THE CORE OF THE BIG APPLE-- MORE THAN THE USUAL SMELL OF PISS AND PILCHARDS, ANYWAY.
NEW YORK CITY HAS ALWAYS BEEN THE ARMPIT OF CREATION-- BUT THAT'S BEEN PART OF THE ATTRACTION, I SUPPOSE.
BRZZZ
IT'S STILL AN ARMPIT, BUT SOMEONE'S GIVEN IT A WAX JOB AND DEODORANT.
TCH... COME ON, MATE. YOU'RE ALWAYS HOME...
WOULDN'T BOTHER IF I WAS YOU, BOY.
AIN'T NOBODY THERE.

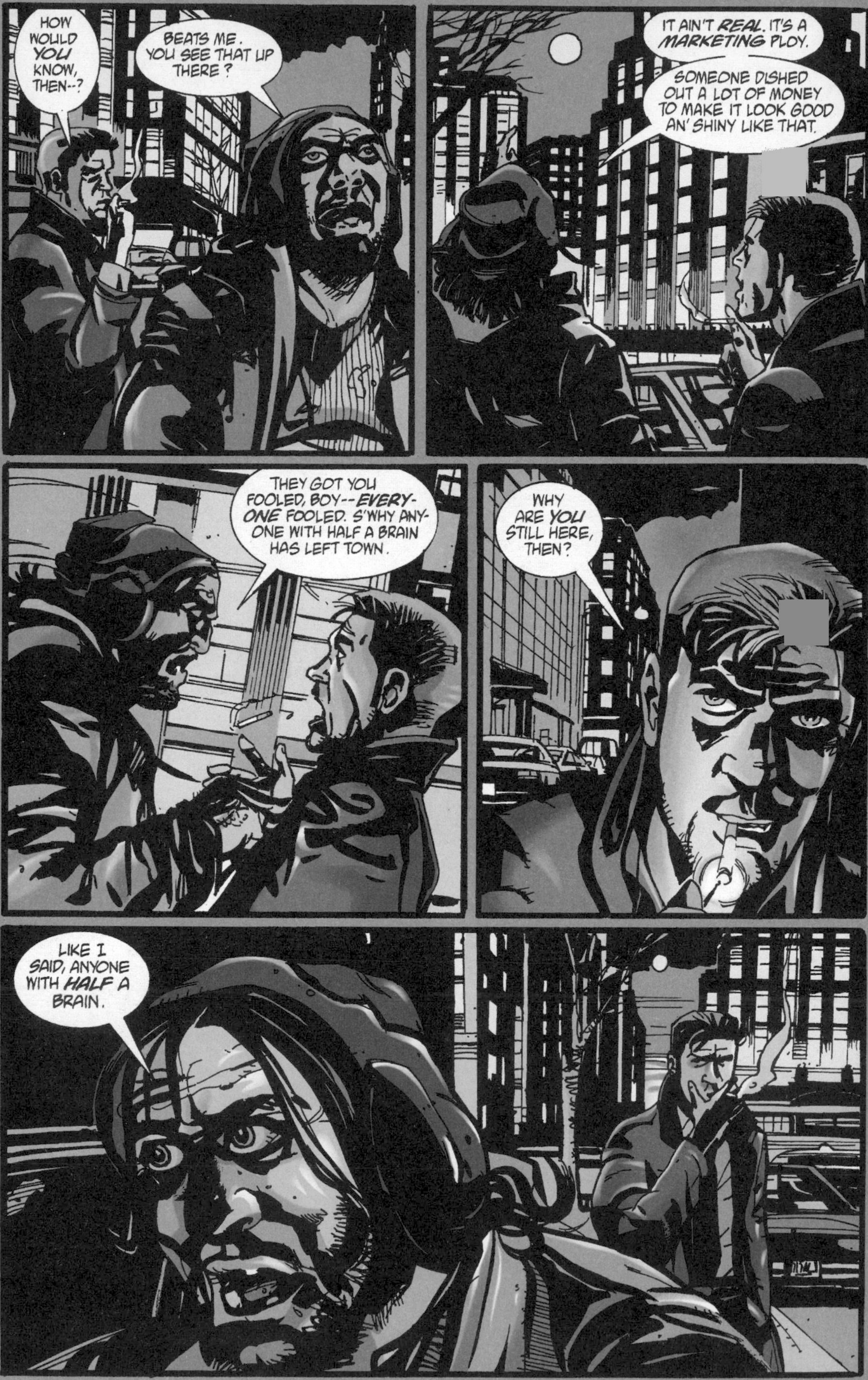
HOW WOULD YOU KNOW, THEN--?
BEATS ME. YOU SEE THAT UP THERE?
IT AIN'T REAL. IT'S A MARKETING PLOY.
SOMEONE DISHED OUT A LOT OF MONEY TO MAKE IT LOOK GOOD AN' SHINY LIKE THAT.
THEY GOT YOU FOOLED, BOY--EVERY-ONE FOOLED. S'WHY ANY-ONE WITH HALF A BRAIN HAS LEFT TOWN.
WHY ARE YOU STILL HERE, THEN?
LIKE I SAID, ANYONE WITH HALF A BRAIN.

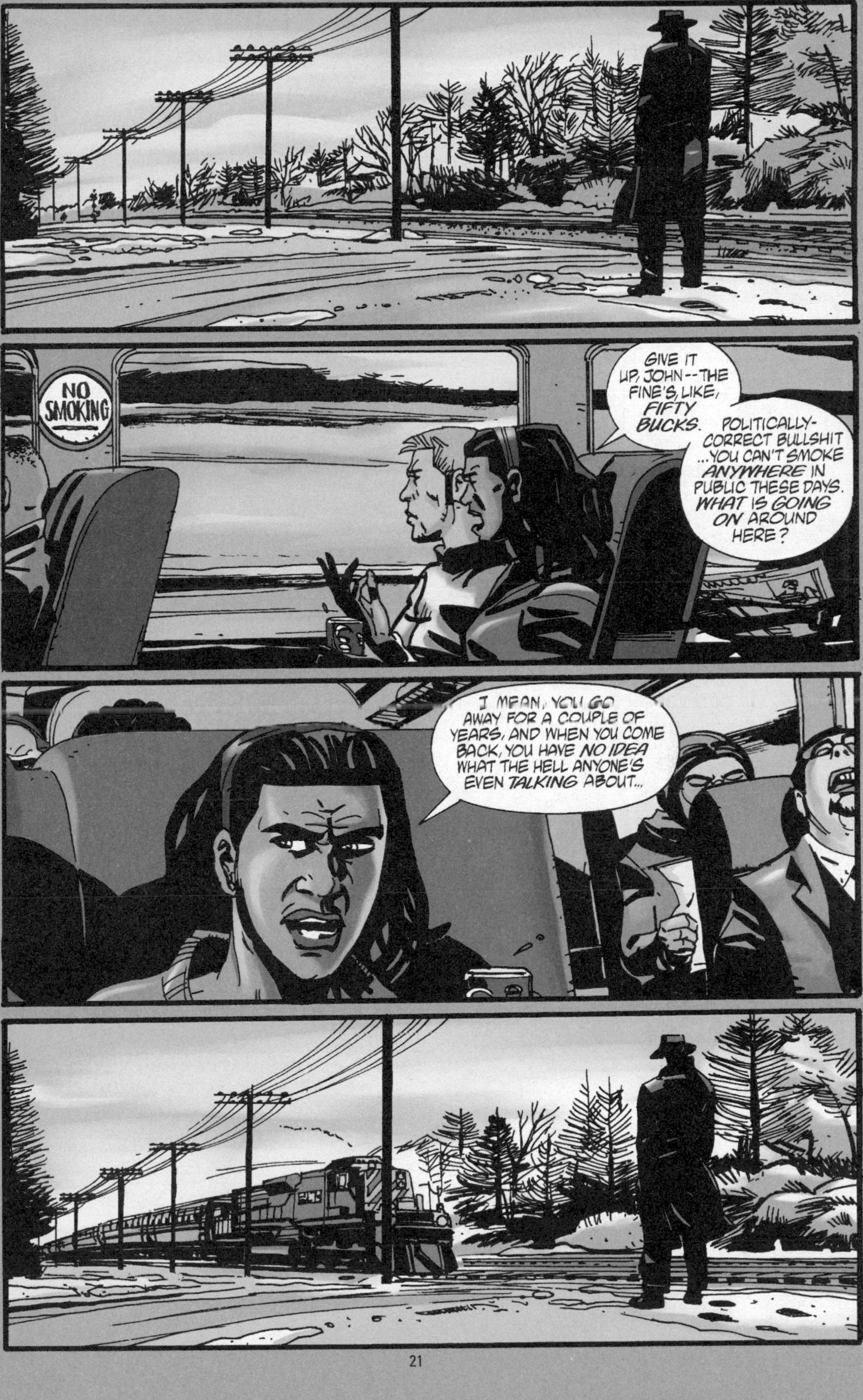
NO SMOKING
GIVE IT UP, JOHN--THE FINE'S, LIKE, FIFTY BUCKS.
POLITICALLY-CORRECT BULLSHIT ...YOU CAN'T SMOKE ANYWHERE IN PUBLIC THESE DAYS. WHAT IS GOING ON AROUND HERE?
I MEAN, YOU GO AWAY FOR A COUPLE OF YEARS, AND WHEN YOU COME BACK, YOU HAVE NO IDEA WHAT THE HELL ANYONE'S EVEN TALKING ABOUT...

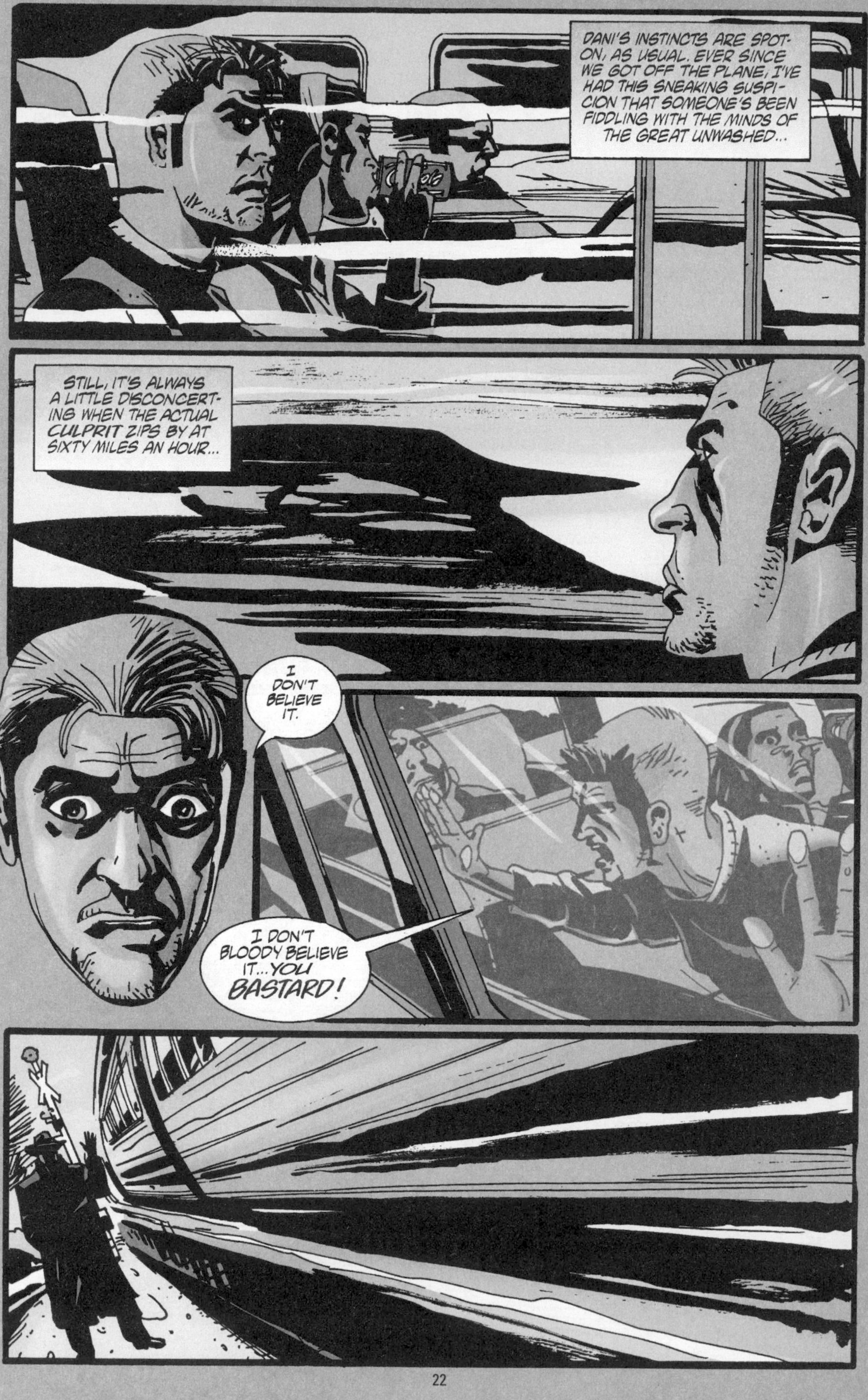

DANI'S INSTINCTS ARE SPOT-ON, AS USUAL. EVER SINCE WE GOT OFF THE PLANE, I'VE HAD THIS SNEAKING SUSPICION THAT SOMEONE'S BEEN FIDDLING WITH THE MINDS OF THE GREAT UNWASHED...
STILL, IT'S ALWAYS A LITTLE DISCONCERTING WHEN THE ACTUAL CULPRIT ZIPS BY AT SIXTY MILES AN HOUR...
I DON'T BELIEVE IT.
I DON'T BLOODY BELIEVE IT... YOU BASTARD!

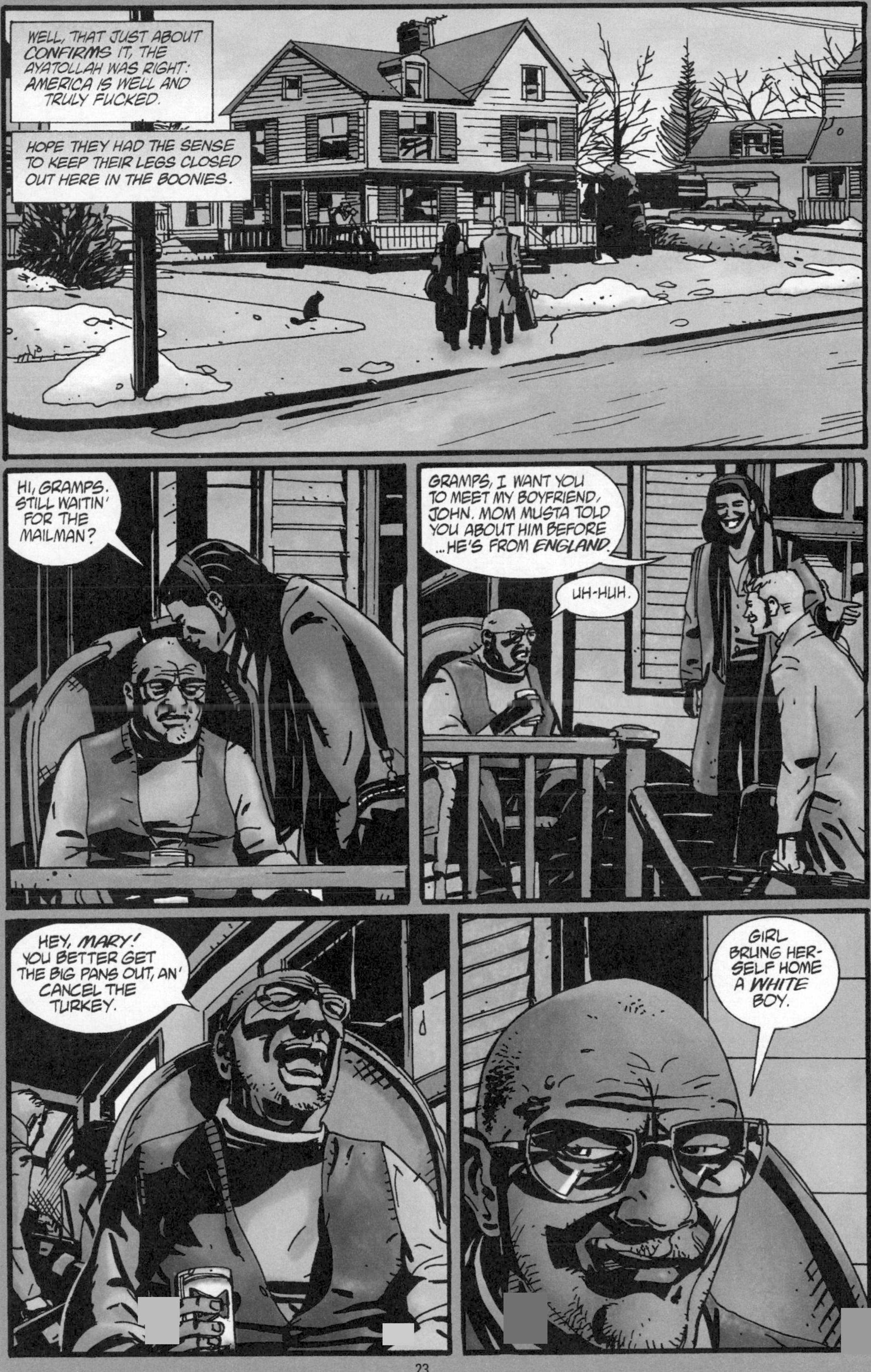
WELL, THAT JUST ABOUT CONFIRMS IT, THE AYATOLLAH WAS RIGHT: AMERICA IS WELL AND TRULY FUCKED.
HOPE THEY HAD THE SENSE TO KEEP THEIR LEGS CLOSED OUT HERE IN THE BOONIES.
HI, GRAMPS. STILL WAITIN' FOR THE MAILMAN?
GRAMPS, I WANT YOU TO MEET MY BOYFRIEND, JOHN. MOM MUSTA TOLD YOU ABOUT HIM BEFORE ...HE'S FROM ENGLAND.
UH-HUH.
HEY, MARY! YOU BETTER GET THE BIG PANS OUT, AN' CANCEL THE TURKEY.
GIRL BRUNG HER-SELF HOME A WHITE BOY.

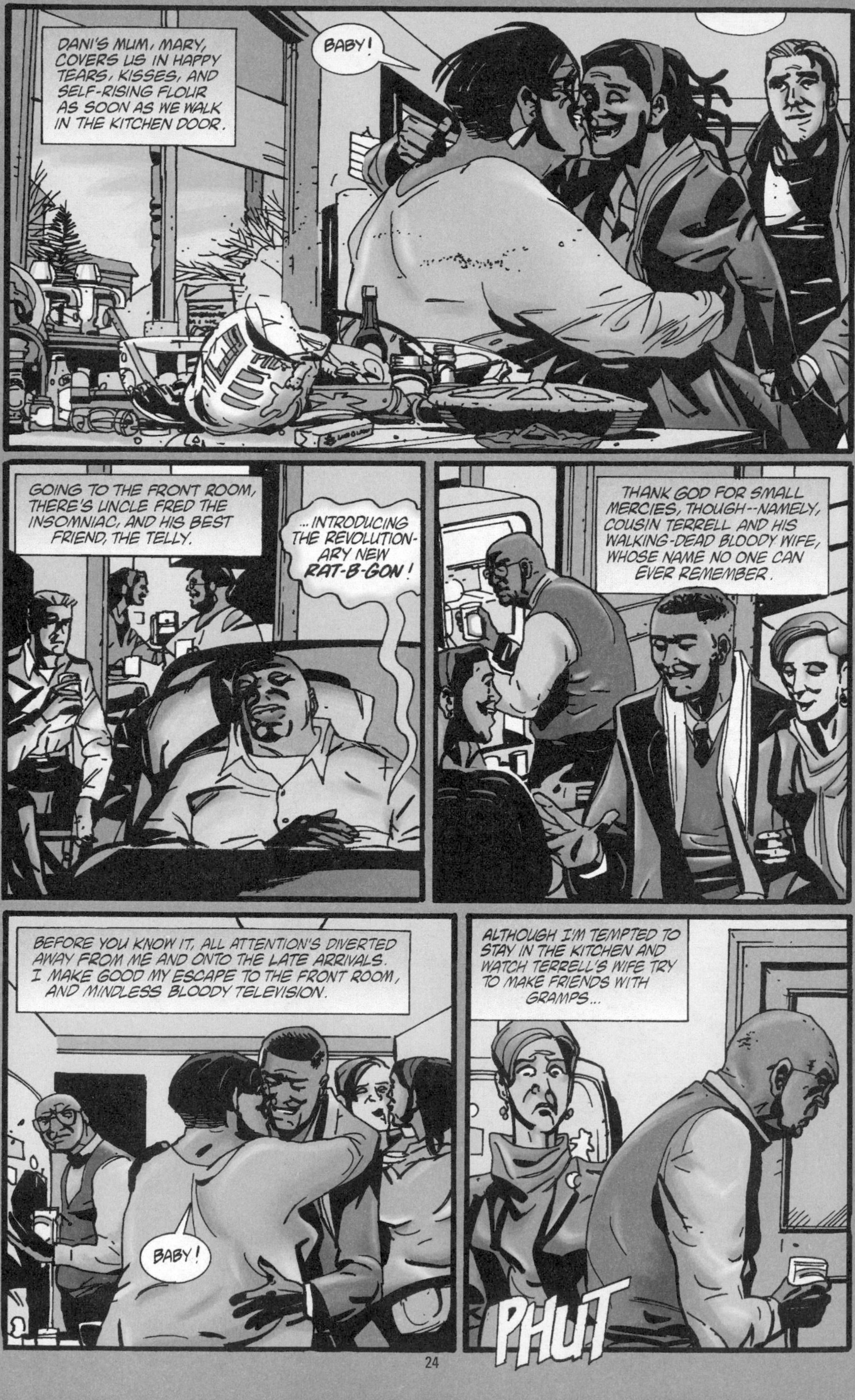
DANI'S MUM, MARY, COVERS US IN HAPPY TEARS, KISSES, AND SELF-RISING FLOUR AS SOON AS WE WALK IN THE KITCHEN DOOR.
BABY!
GOING TO THE FRONT ROOM, THERE'S UNCLE FRED THE INSOMNIAC, AND HIS BEST FRIEND, THE TELLY.
...INTRODUCING THE REVOLUTIONARY NEW RAT-B-GON!
THANK GOD FOR SMALL MERCIES, THOUGH--NAMELY, COUSIN TERRELL AND HIS WALKING-DEAD BLOODY WIFE, WHOSE NAME NO ONE CAN EVER REMEMBER.
BEFORE YOU KNOW IT, ALL ATTENTION'S DIVERTED AWAY FROM ME AND ONTO THE LATE ARRIVALS. I MAKE GOOD MY ESCAPE TO THE FRONT ROOM, AND MINDLESS BLOODY TELEVISION.
BABY!
ALTHOUGH I'M TEMPTED TO STAY IN THE KITCHEN AND WATCH TERRELL'S WIFE TRY TO MAKE FRIENDS WITH GRAMPS...
PHUT

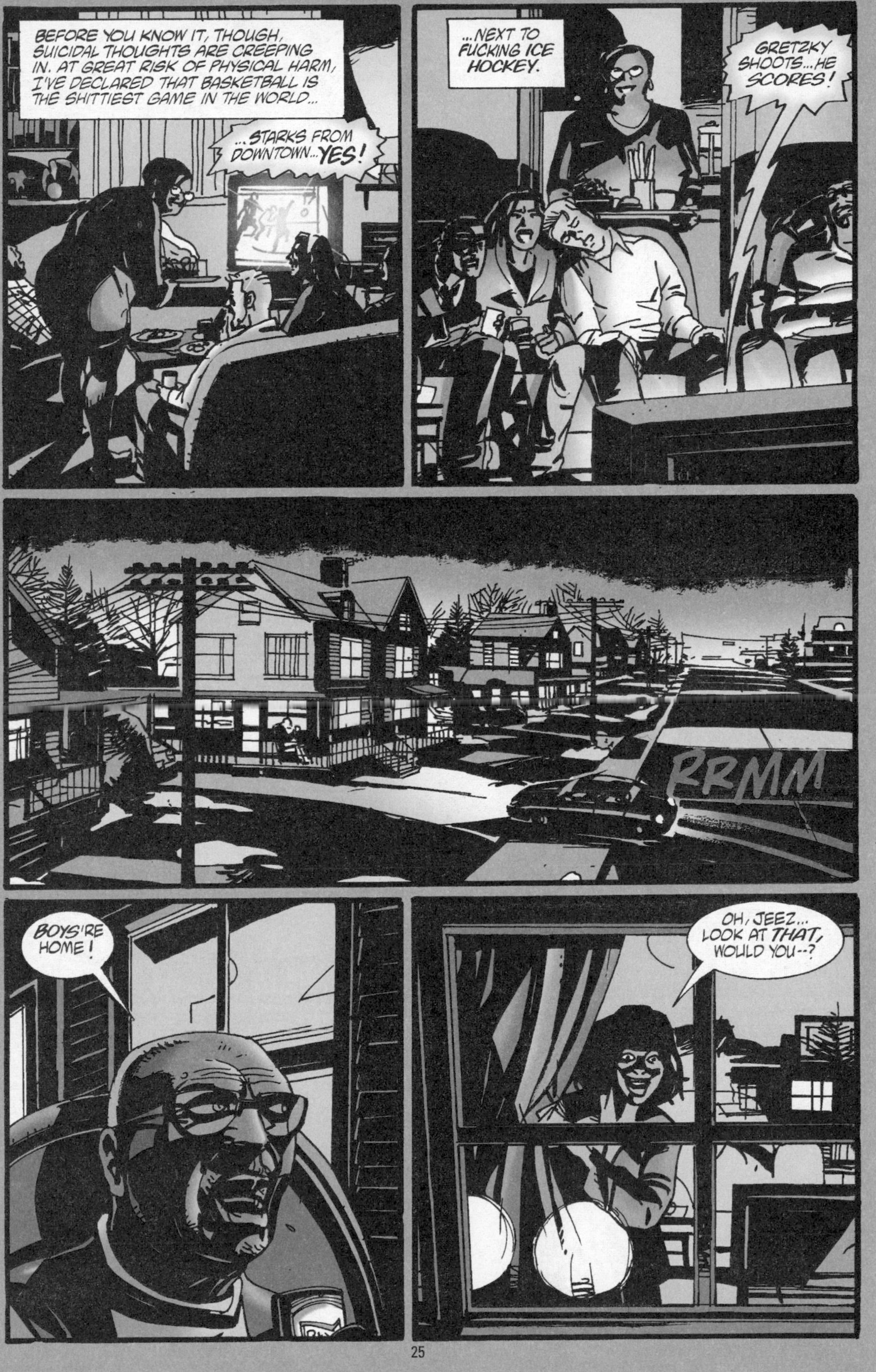
BEFORE YOU KNOW IT, THOUGH, SUICIDAL THOUGHTS ARE CREEPING IN. AT GREAT RISK OF PHYSICAL HARM, I'VE DECLARED THAT BASKETBALL IS THE SHITTIEST GAME IN THE WORLD...
...STARKS FROM DOWNTOWN...YES!
...NEXT TO FUCKING ICE HOCKEY.
GRETZKY SHOOTS...HE SCORES!
RRMM
BOYS'RE HOME!
OH, JEEZ... LOOK AT THAT, WOULD YOU--?

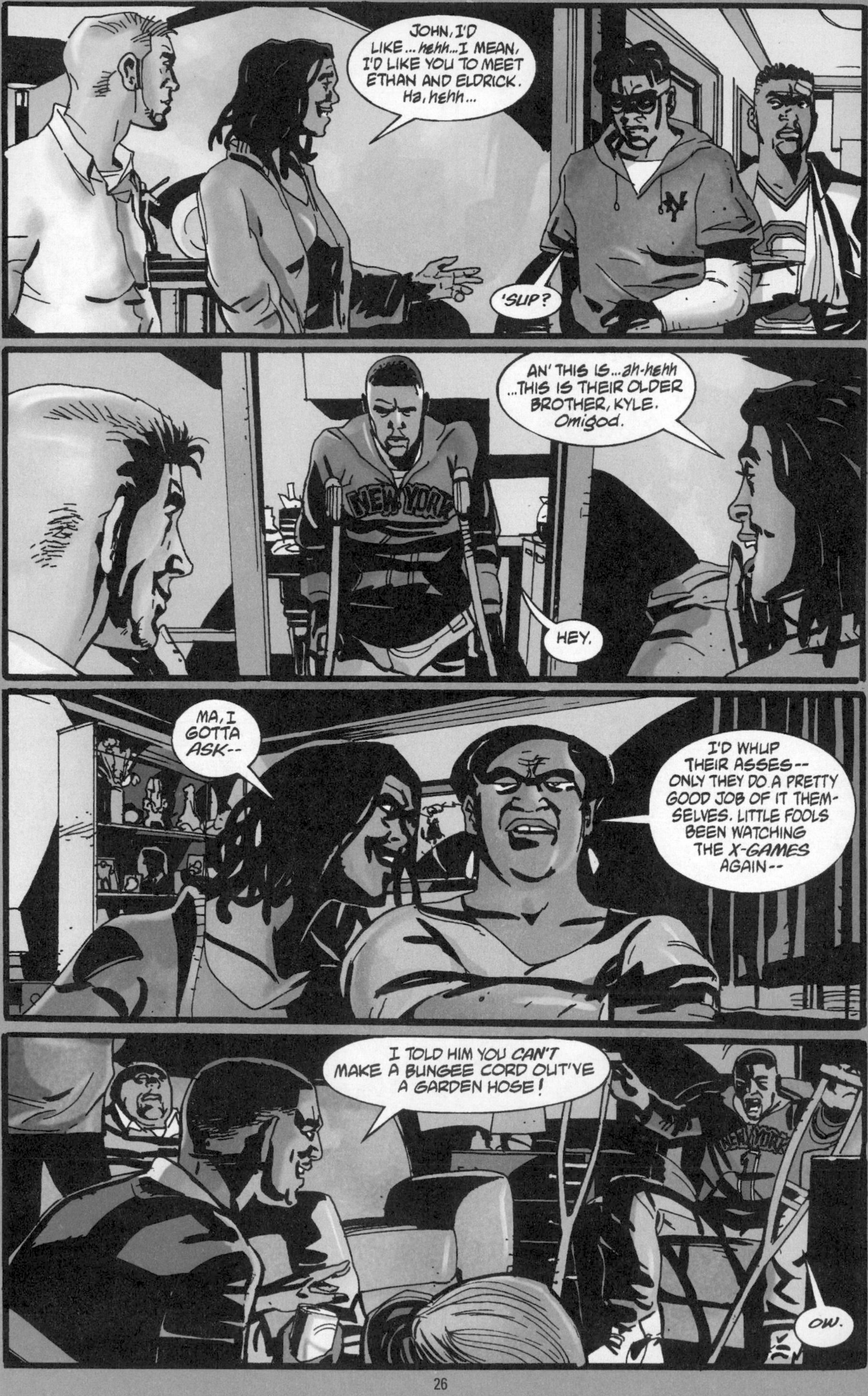
JOHN, I'D LIKE... hehh... I MEAN, I'D LIKE YOU TO MEET ETHAN AND ELDRICK. Ha, hehh...
'SUP?
AN' THIS IS... ah-hehh ...THIS IS THEIR OLDER BROTHER, KYLE. Omigod.
HEY.
MA, I GOTTA ASK--
I'D WHUP THEIR ASSES-- ONLY THEY DO A PRETTY GOOD JOB OF IT THEMSELVES. LITTLE FOOLS BEEN WATCHING THE X-GAMES AGAIN--
I TOLD HIM YOU CAN'T MAKE A BUNGEE CORD OUT'VE A GARDEN HOSE!
OW.

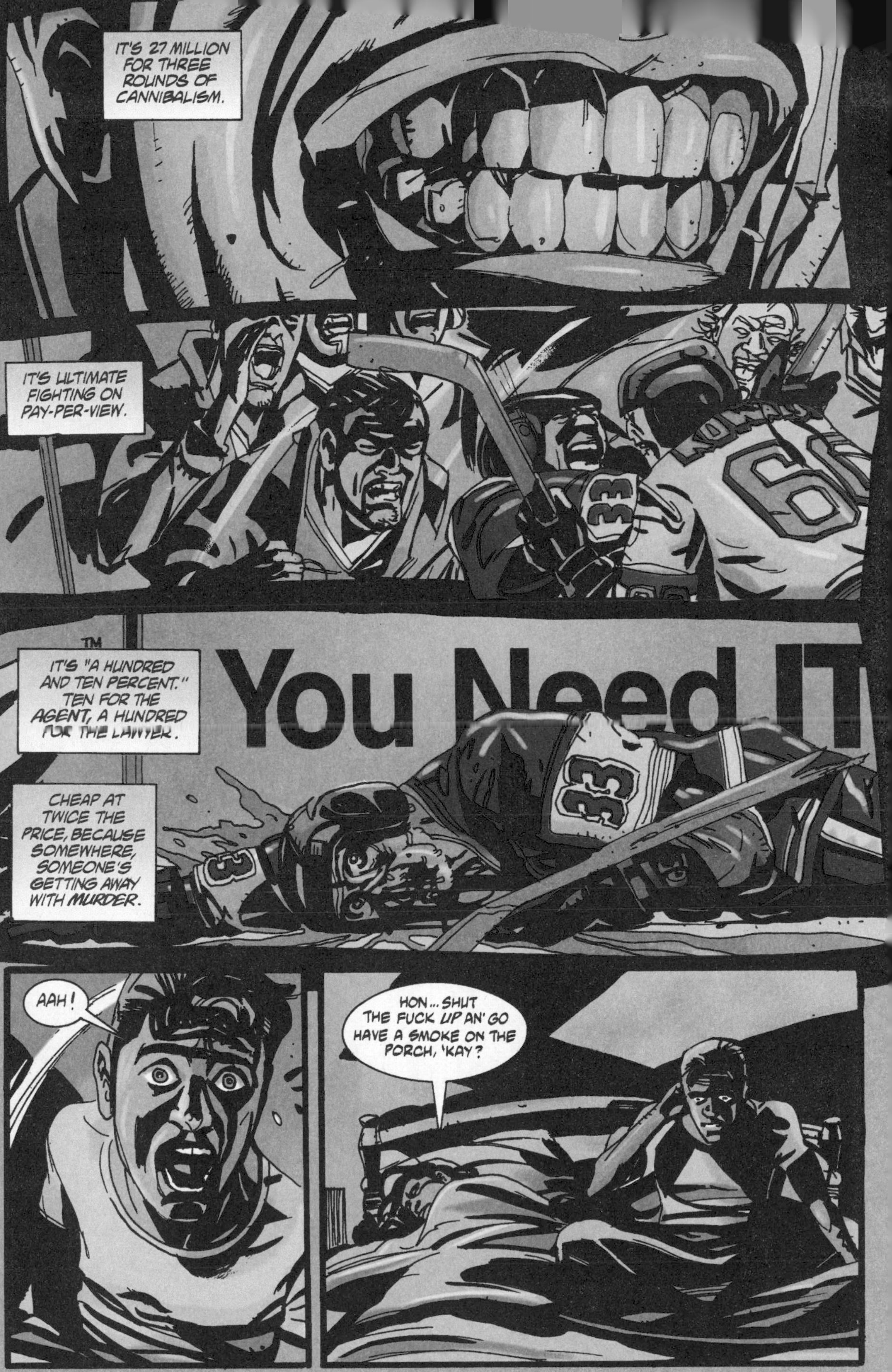

IT'S 27 MILLION FOR THREE ROUNDS OF CANNIBALISM.
IT'S ULTIMATE FIGHTING ON PAY-PER-VIEW.
IT'S "A HUNDRED AND TEN PERCENT." TEN FOR THE AGENT, A HUNDRED FOR THE LAWYER.
You Need IT
CHEAP AT TWICE THE PRICE, BECAUSE SOMEWHERE, SOMEONE'S GETTING AWAY WITH MURDER.
AAH!
HON... SHUT THE FUCK UP AN' GO HAVE A SMOKE ON THE PORCH, 'KAY?

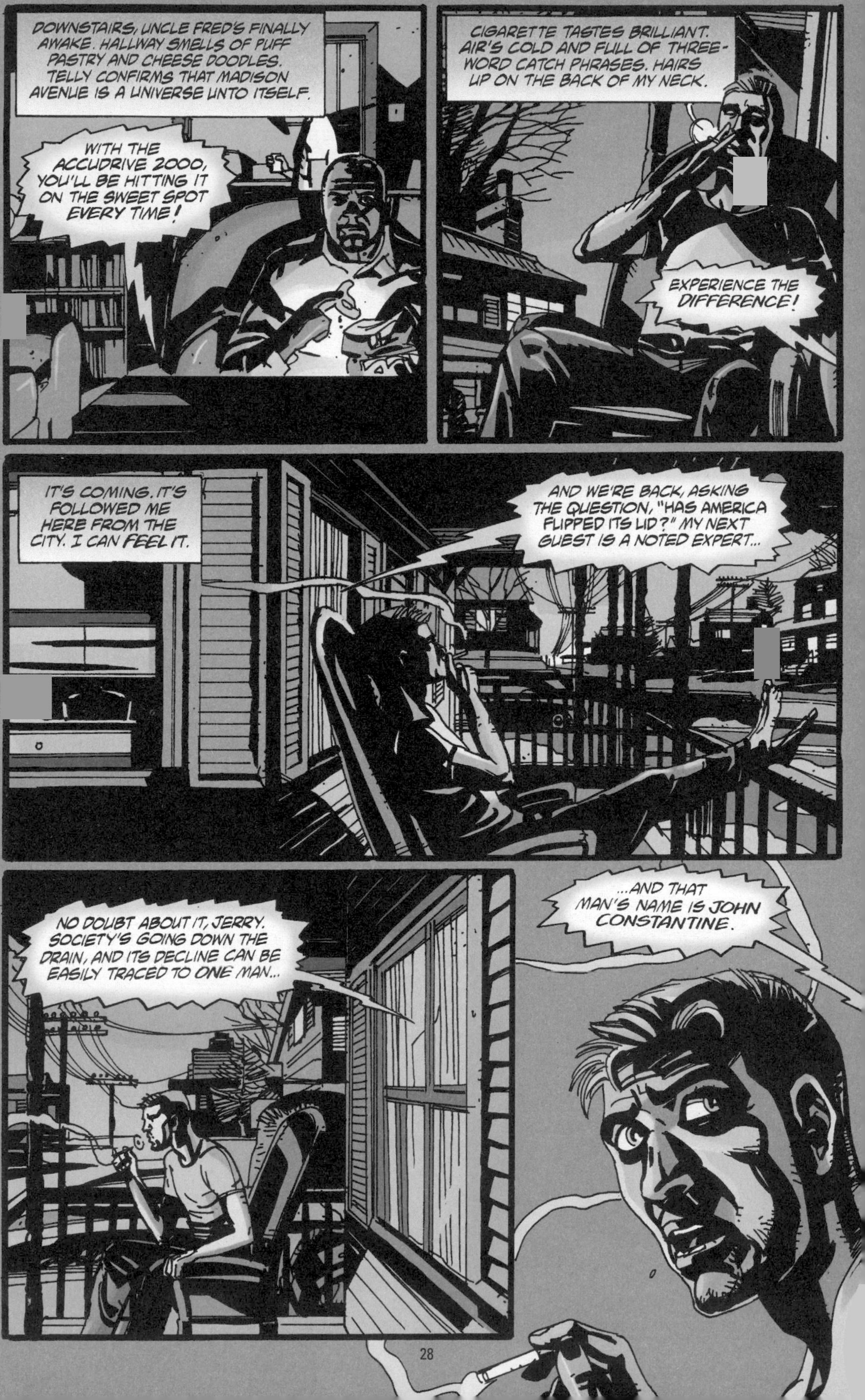
DOWNSTAIRS, UNCLE FRED'S FINALLY AWAKE. HALLWAY SMELLS OF PUFF PASTRY AND CHEESE DOODLES. TELLY CONFIRMS THAT MADISON AVENUE IS A UNIVERSE UNTO ITSELF.
WITH THE ACCUDRIVE 2000, YOU'LL BE HITTING IT ON THE SWEET SPOT EVERY TIME!
CIGARETTE TASTES BRILLIANT. AIR'S COLD AND FULL OF THREE-WORD CATCH PHRASES. HAIRS UP ON THE BACK OF MY NECK.
EXPERIENCE THE DIFFERENCE!
IT'S COMING. IT'S FOLLOWED ME HERE FROM THE CITY. I CAN FEEL IT.
AND WE'RE BACK, ASKING THE QUESTION, "HAS AMERICA FLIPPED ITS LID?" MY NEXT GUEST IS A NOTED EXPERT...
NO DOUBT ABOUT IT, JERRY. SOCIETY'S GOING DOWN THE DRAIN, AND ITS DECLINE CAN BE EASILY TRACED TO ONE MAN...
...AND THAT MAN'S NAME IS JOHN CONSTANTINE.

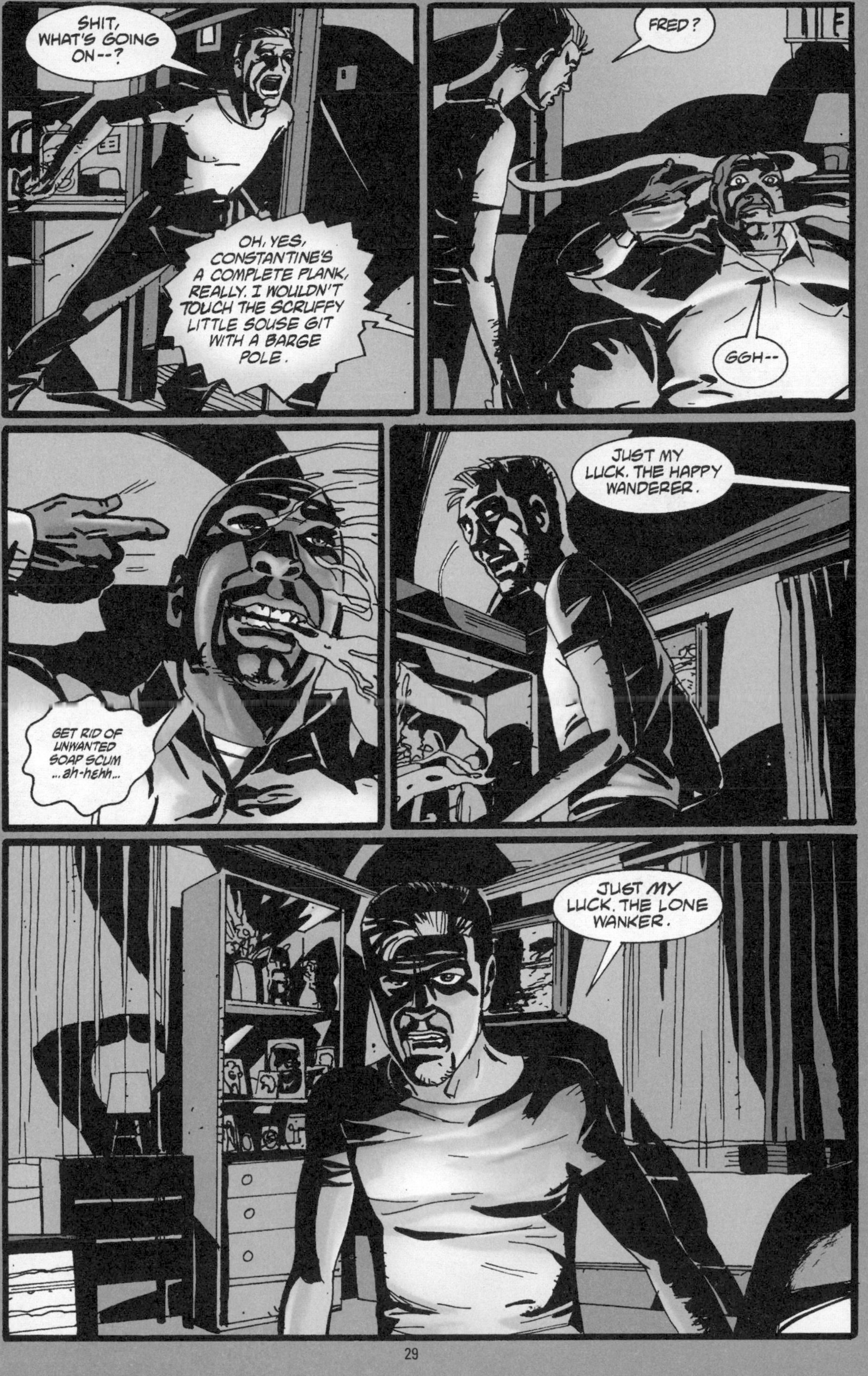
SHIT, WHAT'S GOING ON--?
OH, YES, CONSTANTINE'S A COMPLETE PLANK, REALLY. I WOULDN'T TOUCH THE SCRUFFY LITTLE SOUSE GIT WITH A BARGE POLE.
FRED?
GGH--
GET RID OF UNWANTED SOAP SCUM ...ah-hehh...
JUST MY LUCK. THE HAPPY WANDERER.
JUST MY LUCK. THE LONE WANKER.

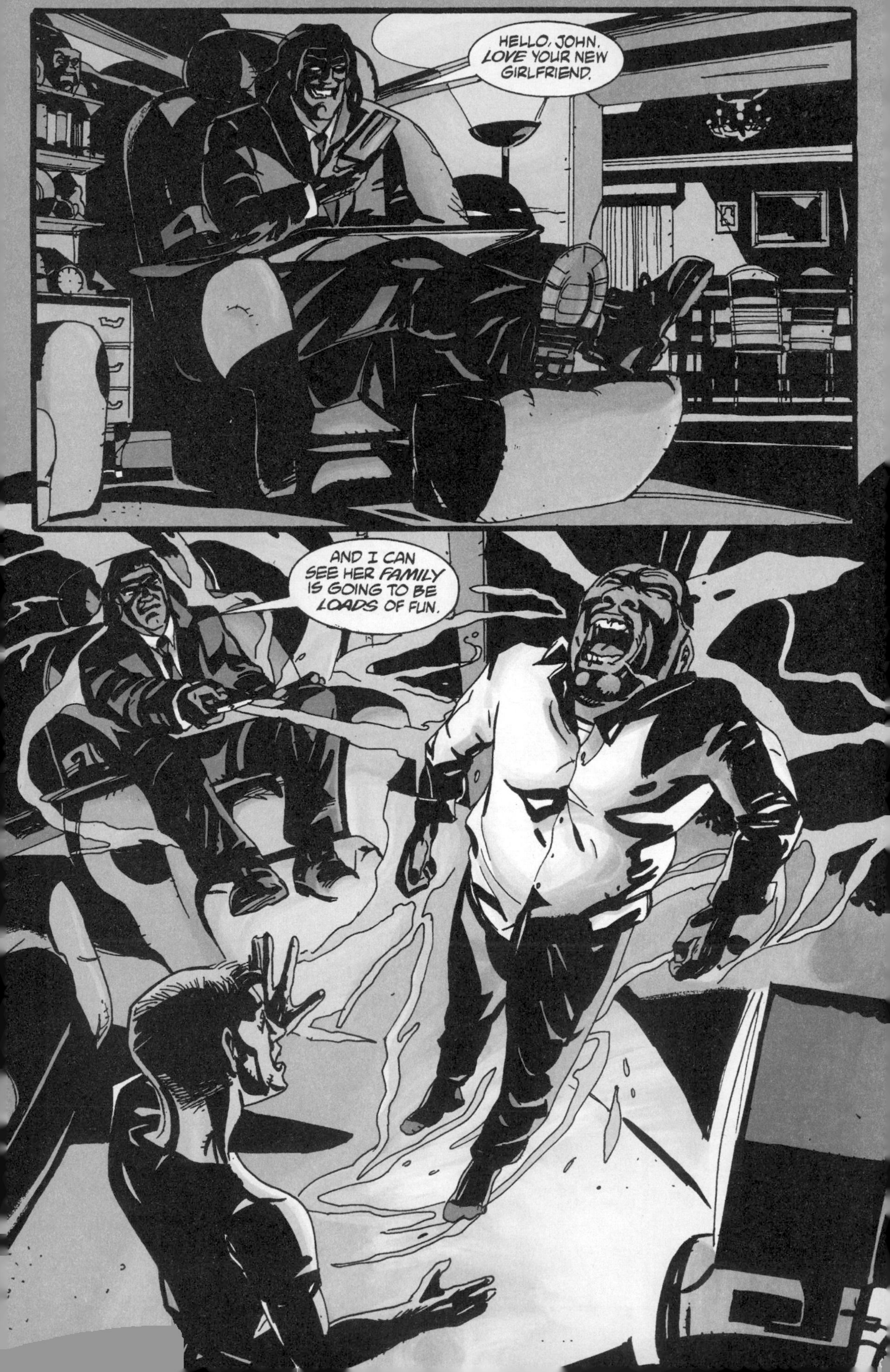
HELLO, JOHN. LOVE YOUR NEW GIRLFRIEND.
AND I CAN SEE HER FAMILY IS GOING TO BE LOADS OF FUN.

JOHN CONSTANTINE
HELLBLAZER
UP the DOWN STAIRCASE
PART 02 of 04
PAUL JENKINS • WARREN PLEECE

IT WASN'T MY FAULT.

TELL ME WHAT HAPPENED. FROM THE BEGINNING.

W-WELL...WE'D HAD SUCH A LOVELY *DAY*, YOU SEE?

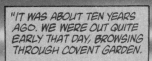

"IT WAS ABOUT TEN YEARS AGO. WE WERE OUT QUITE EARLY THAT DAY, BROWSING THROUGH COVENT GARDEN.

"IT WAS AN AWFULLY BLUSTERY MORNING. WE, hehh...WE USED IT AS AN EXCUSE TO DO A BIT OF SNUGGLING ON THE SLY.

"I...I REMEMBER WE SPLIT UP FOR A COUPLE OF HOURS. I WENT TRAIPSING AROUND THE LOCAL ANTIQUE BOOK STORES IN SEARCH OF A FIND.

"AND WHAT A FIND I MADE! A VIRTUALLY COMPLETE COPY OF MacADAM'S TREATISE ON TERROR MAGICK, WITH GUNPOWDER ILLUSTRATIONS. I WAS EVER SO PROUD.

"IN FACT, WE WERE BOTH SO GIDDY AFTERWARDS THAT WE WENT ON TO CELEBRATE WITH SOME OF THE CHAPS..."

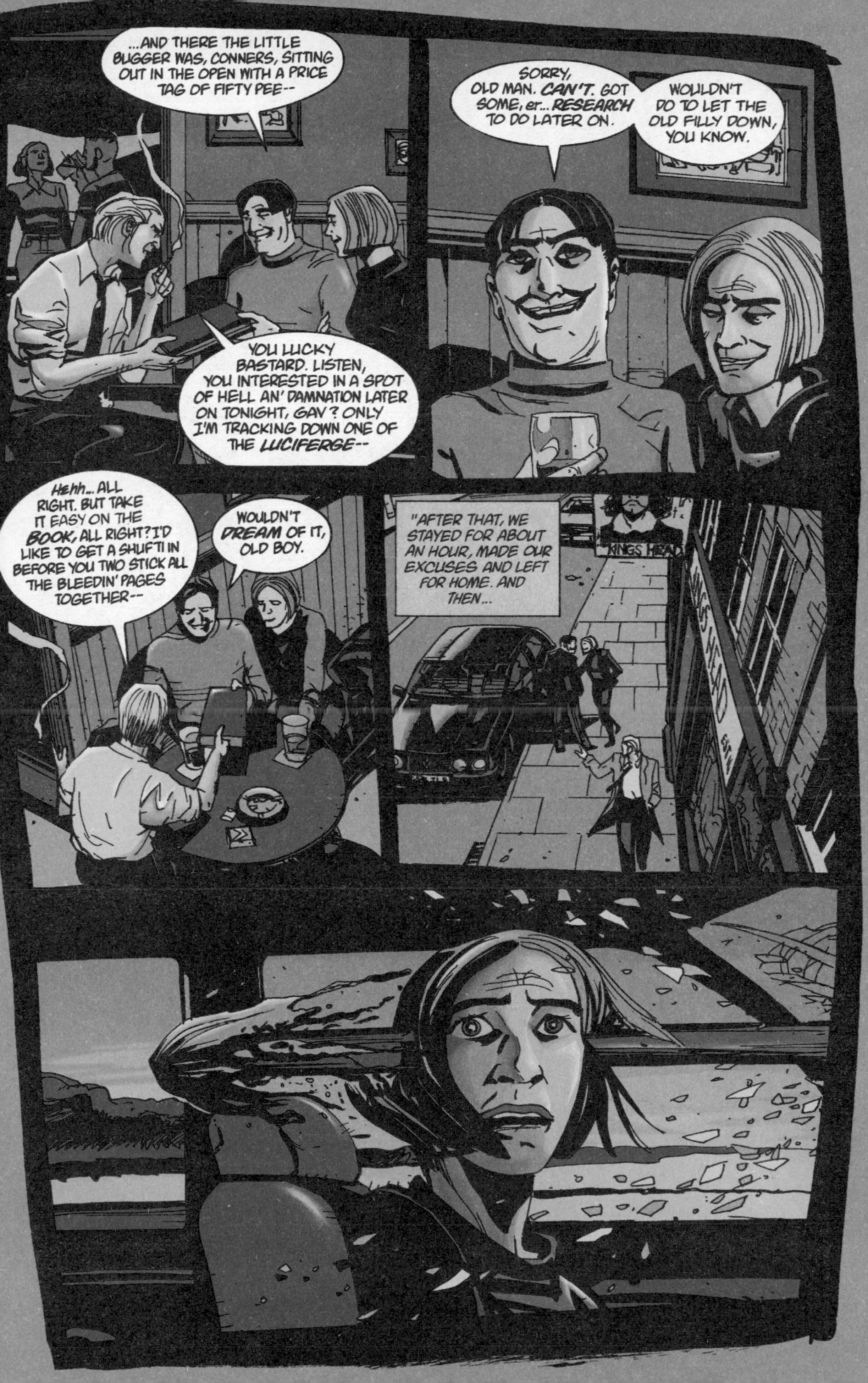
...AND THERE THE LITTLE BUGGER WAS, CONNERS, SITTING OUT IN THE OPEN WITH A PRICE TAG OF FIFTY PEE--
YOU LUCKY BASTARD. LISTEN, YOU INTERESTED IN A SPOT OF HELL AN' DAMNATION LATER ON TONIGHT, GAV? ONLY I'M TRACKING DOWN ONE OF THE LUCIFERGE--
SORRY, OLD MAN. CAN'T. GOT SOME, er... RESEARCH TO DO LATER ON.
WOULDN'T DO TO LET THE OLD FILLY DOWN, YOU KNOW.
Hehh... ALL RIGHT. BUT TAKE IT EASY ON THE BOOK, ALL RIGHT? I'D LIKE TO GET A SHUFTI IN BEFORE YOU TWO STICK ALL THE BLEEDIN' PAGES TOGETHER--
WOULDN'T DREAM OF IT, OLD BOY.
"AFTER THAT, WE STAYED FOR ABOUT AN HOUR, MADE OUR EXCUSES AND LEFT FOR HOME. AND THEN...
KINGS HEAD
KINGS HEAD

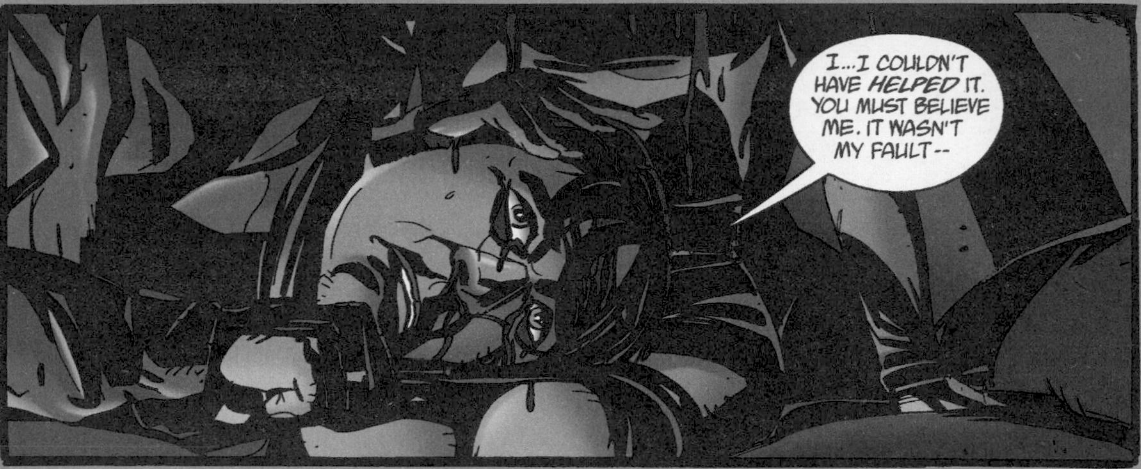
I...I COULDN'T HAVE *HELPED* IT. YOU MUST BELIEVE ME. IT WASN'T MY FAULT--

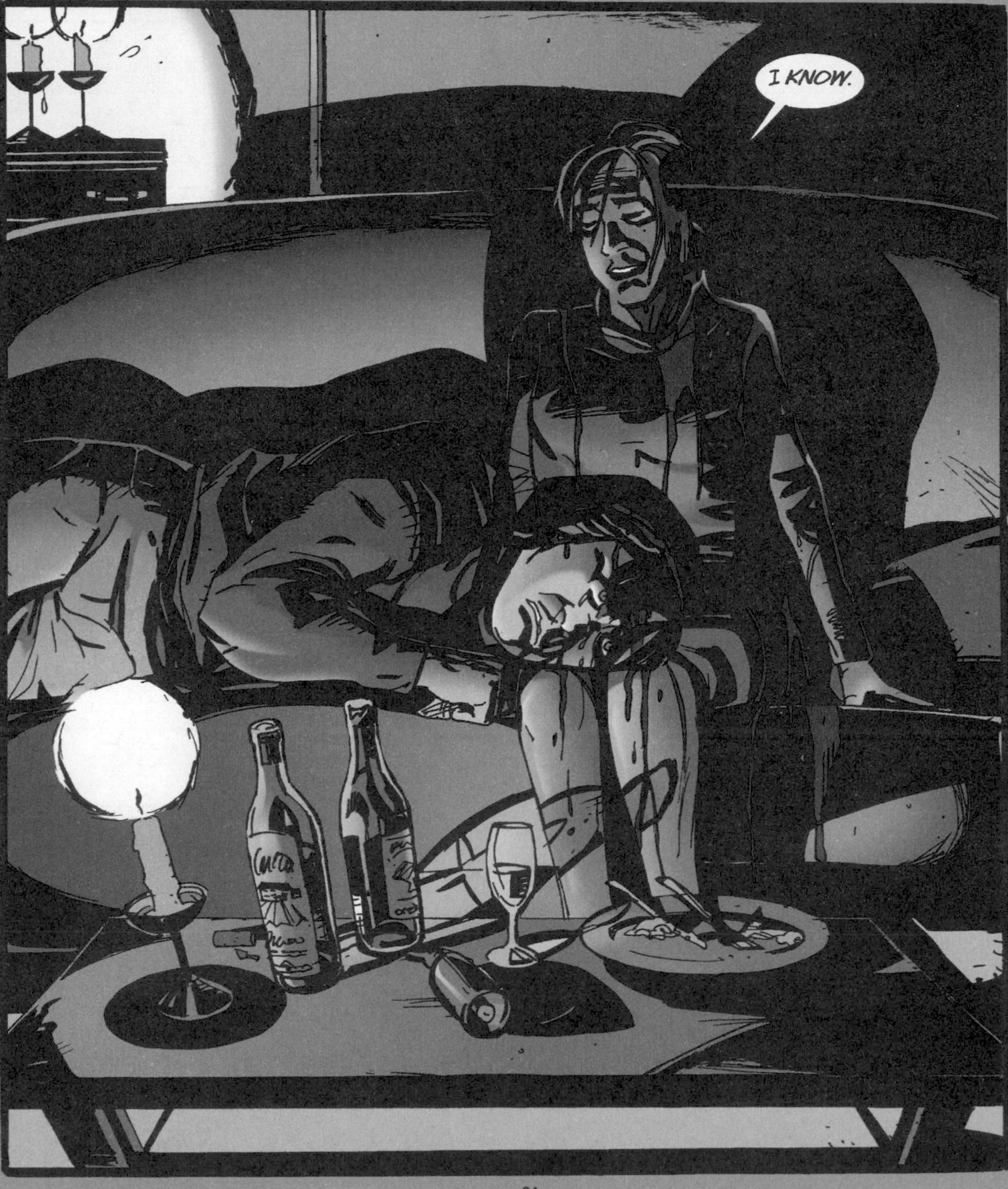
I KNOW.

up
staircase

PAUL JENKINS writer | WARREN PLEECE artist | JAMES SINCLAIR colorist | **part two** | DIGITAL CHAMELEON separations | CLEM ROBINS letterer | AXEL ALONSO editor

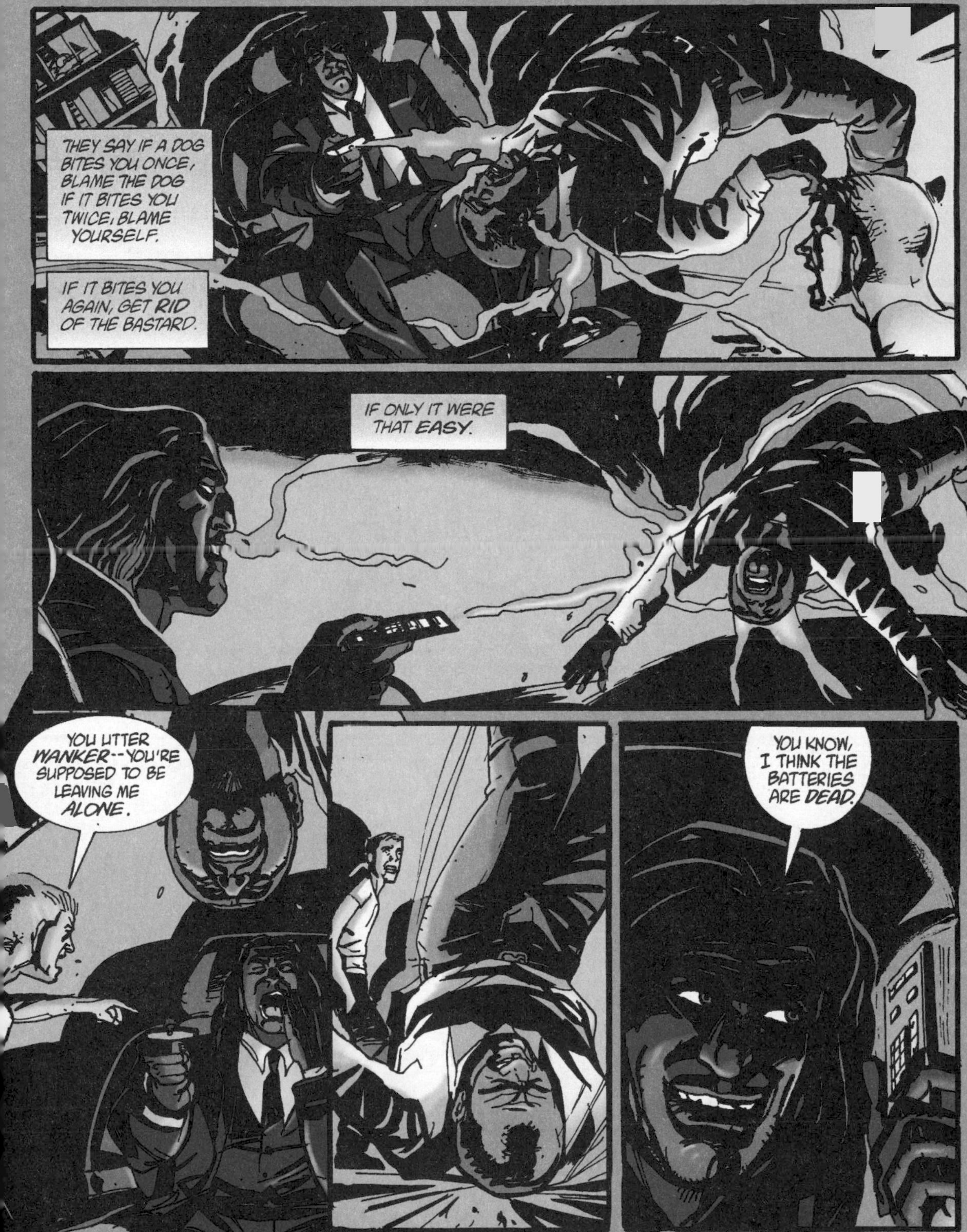
THEY SAY IF A DOG BITES YOU ONCE, BLAME THE DOG IF IT BITES YOU TWICE, BLAME YOURSELF.
IF IT BITES YOU AGAIN, GET RID OF THE BASTARD.
IF ONLY IT WERE THAT EASY.
YOU UTTER WANKER-- YOU'RE SUPPOSED TO BE LEAVING ME ALONE.
YOU KNOW, I THINK THE BATTERIES ARE DEAD.

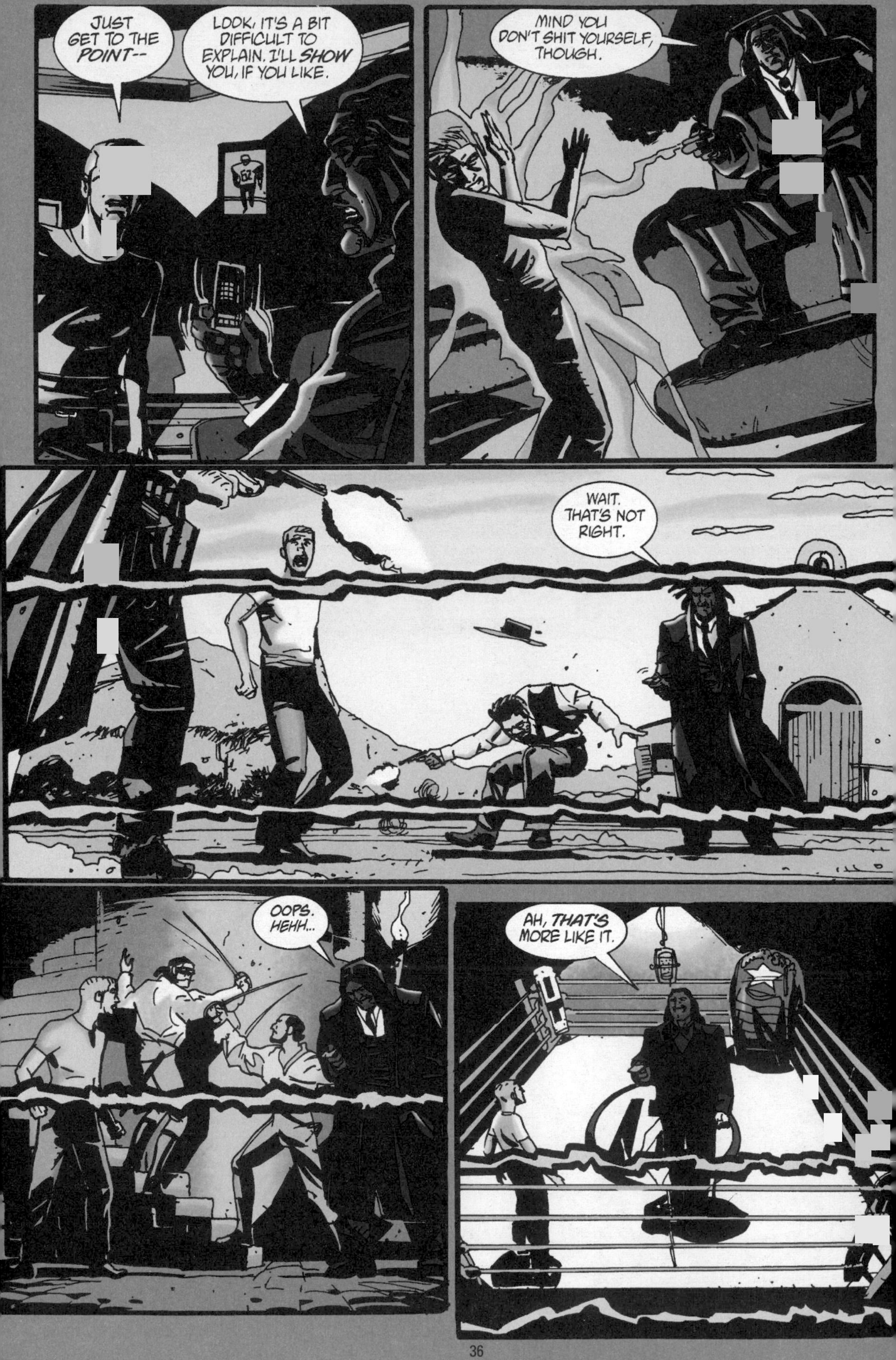
JUST GET TO THE *POINT*--
LOOK, IT'S A BIT DIFFICULT TO EXPLAIN. I'LL *SHOW* YOU, IF YOU LIKE.
MIND YOU DON'T SHIT YOURSELF, THOUGH.
WAIT. THAT'S NOT RIGHT.
OOPS. HEHH...
AH, *THAT'S* MORE LIKE IT.

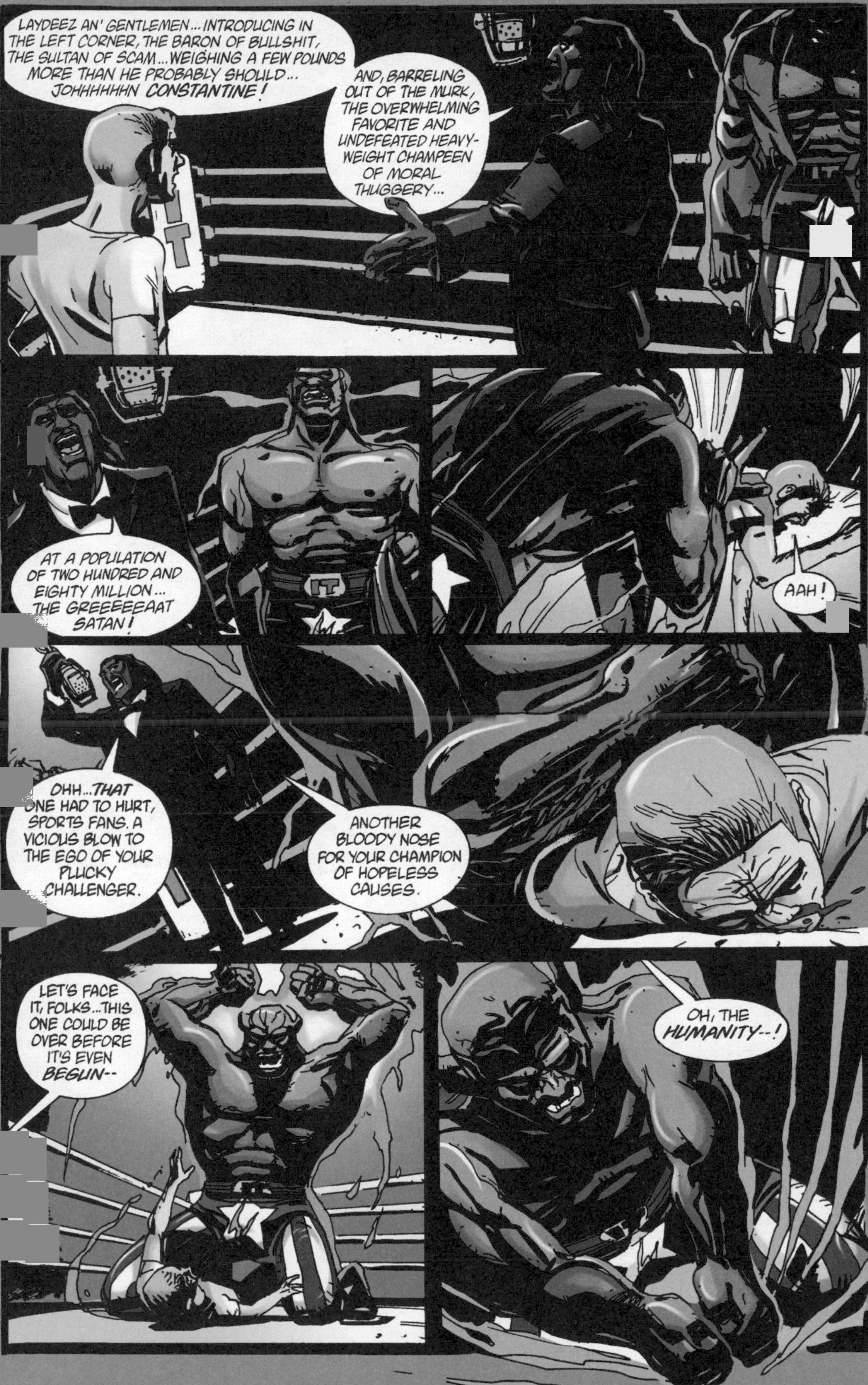
LAYDEEZ AN' GENTLEMEN... INTRODUCING IN THE LEFT CORNER, THE BARON OF BULLSHIT, THE SULTAN OF SCAM... WEIGHING A FEW POUNDS MORE THAN HE PROBABLY SHOULD... JOHHHHHHN CONSTANTINE!
AND, BARRELING OUT OF THE MURK, THE OVERWHELMING FAVORITE AND UNDEFEATED HEAVY-WEIGHT CHAMPEEN OF MORAL THUGGERY...
AT A POPULATION OF TWO HUNDRED AND EIGHTY MILLION... THE GREEEEEAAT SATAN!
AAH!
OHH...THAT ONE HAD TO HURT, SPORTS FANS. A VICIOUS BLOW TO THE EGO OF YOUR PLUCKY CHALLENGER.
ANOTHER BLOODY NOSE FOR YOUR CHAMPION OF HOPELESS CAUSES.
LET'S FACE IT, FOLKS...THIS ONE COULD BE OVER BEFORE IT'S EVEN BEGUN--
OH, THE HUMANITY--!

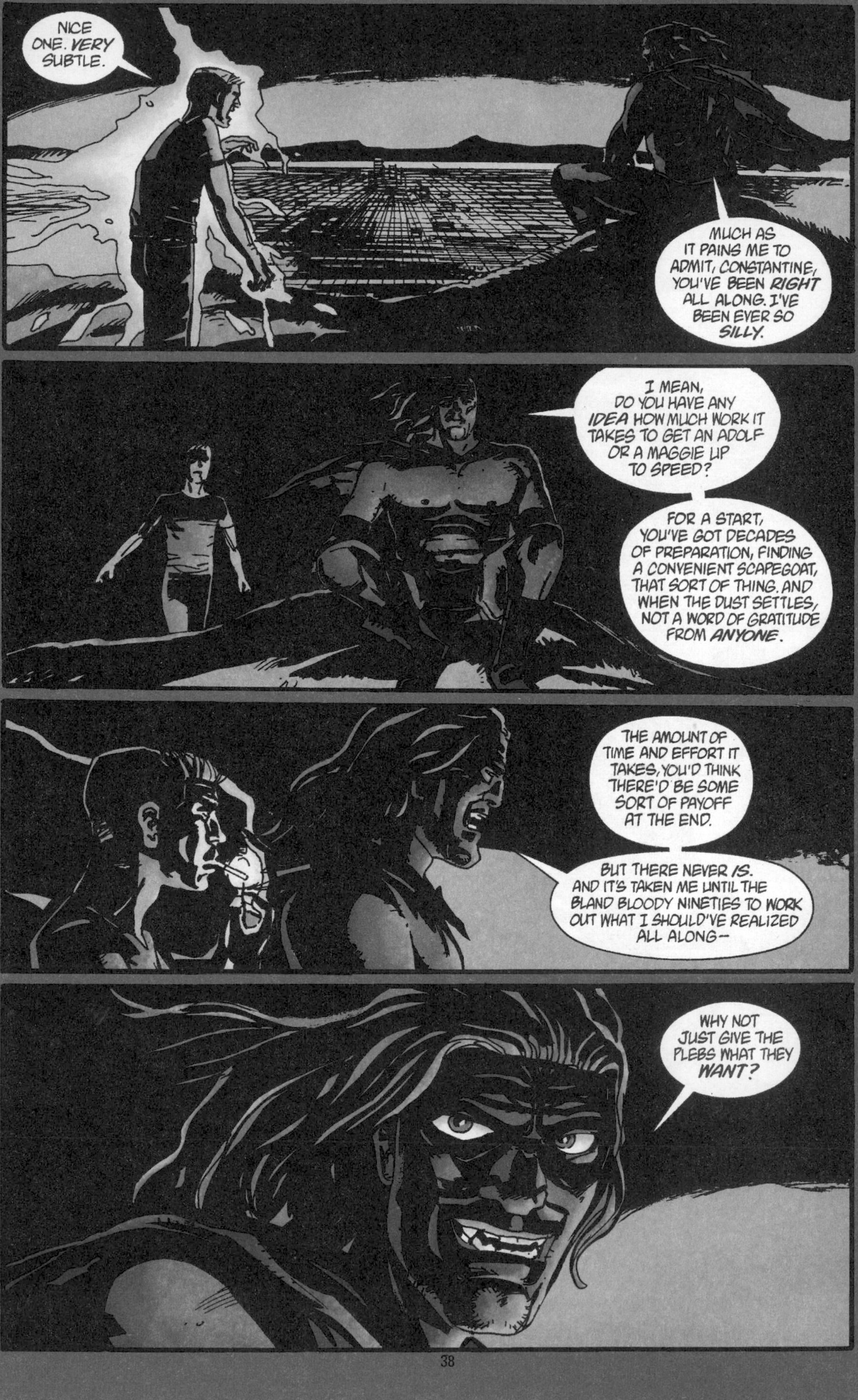
NICE ONE. VERY SUBTLE.
MUCH AS IT PAINS ME TO ADMIT, CONSTANTINE, YOU'VE BEEN RIGHT ALL ALONG. I'VE BEEN EVER SO SILLY.
I MEAN, DO YOU HAVE ANY IDEA HOW MUCH WORK IT TAKES TO GET AN ADOLF OR A MAGGIE UP TO SPEED?
FOR A START, YOU'VE GOT DECADES OF PREPARATION, FINDING A CONVENIENT SCAPEGOAT, THAT SORT OF THING. AND WHEN THE DUST SETTLES, NOT A WORD OF GRATITUDE FROM ANYONE.
THE AMOUNT OF TIME AND EFFORT IT TAKES, YOU'D THINK THERE'D BE SOME SORT OF PAYOFF AT THE END.
BUT THERE NEVER IS. AND IT'S TAKEN ME UNTIL THE BLAND BLOODY NINETIES TO WORK OUT WHAT I SHOULD'VE REALIZED ALL ALONG--
WHY NOT JUST GIVE THE PLEBS WHAT THEY WANT?

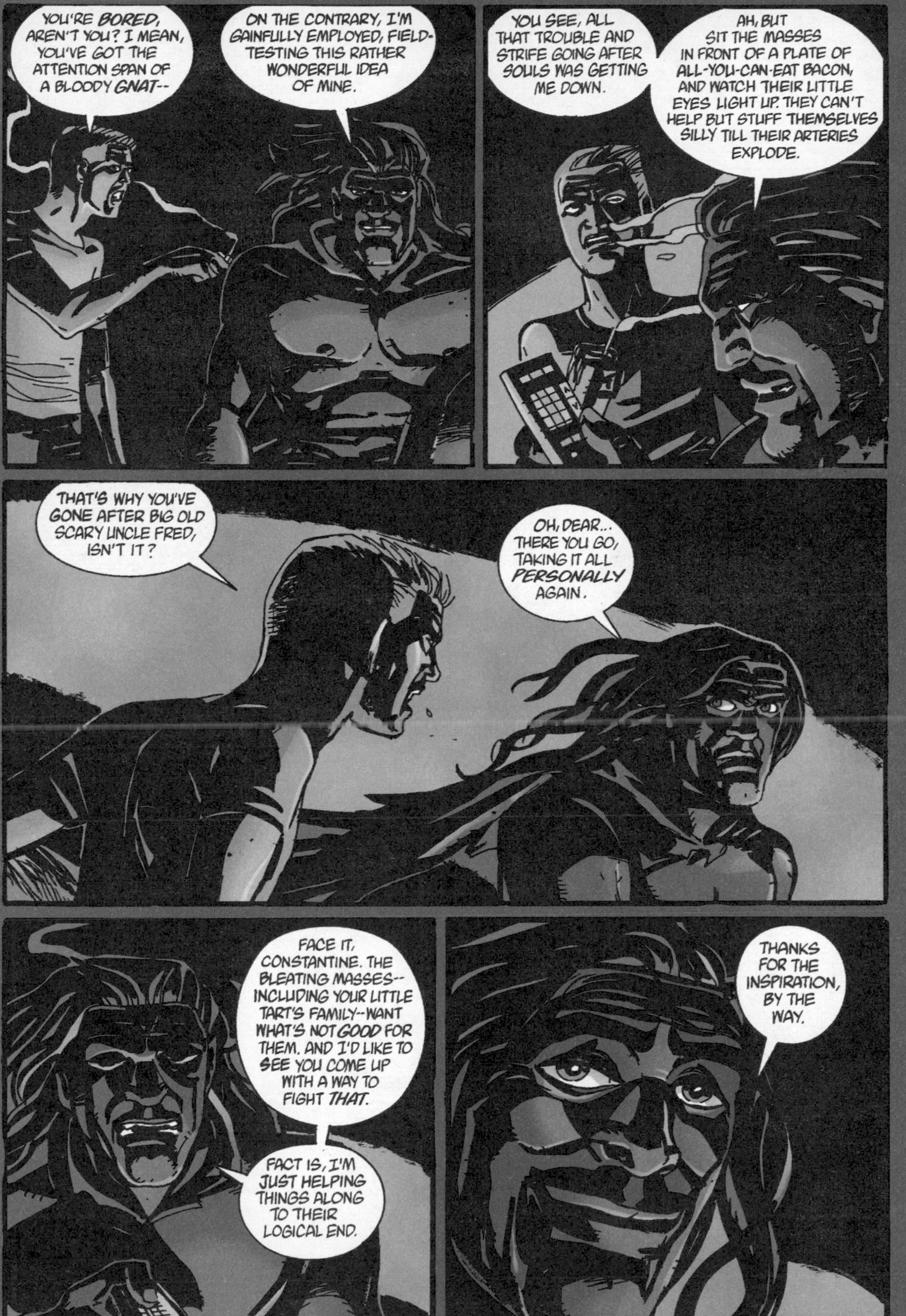
YOU'RE BORED, AREN'T YOU? I MEAN, YOU'VE GOT THE ATTENTION SPAN OF A BLOODY GNAT--
ON THE CONTRARY, I'M GAINFULLY EMPLOYED, FIELD-TESTING THIS RATHER WONDERFUL IDEA OF MINE.
YOU SEE, ALL THAT TROUBLE AND STRIFE GOING AFTER SOULS WAS GETTING ME DOWN.
AH, BUT SIT THE MASSES IN FRONT OF A PLATE OF ALL-YOU-CAN-EAT BACON, AND WATCH THEIR LITTLE EYES LIGHT UP. THEY CAN'T HELP BUT STUFF THEMSELVES SILLY TILL THEIR ARTERIES EXPLODE.
THAT'S WHY YOU'VE GONE AFTER BIG OLD SCARY UNCLE FRED, ISN'T IT?
OH, DEAR... THERE YOU GO, TAKING IT ALL PERSONALLY AGAIN.
FACE IT, CONSTANTINE. THE BLEATING MASSES--INCLUDING YOUR LITTLE TART'S FAMILY--WANT WHAT'S NOT GOOD FOR THEM. AND I'D LIKE TO SEE YOU COME UP WITH A WAY TO FIGHT THAT.
FACT IS, I'M JUST HELPING THINGS ALONG TO THEIR LOGICAL END.
THANKS FOR THE INSPIRATION, BY THE WAY.

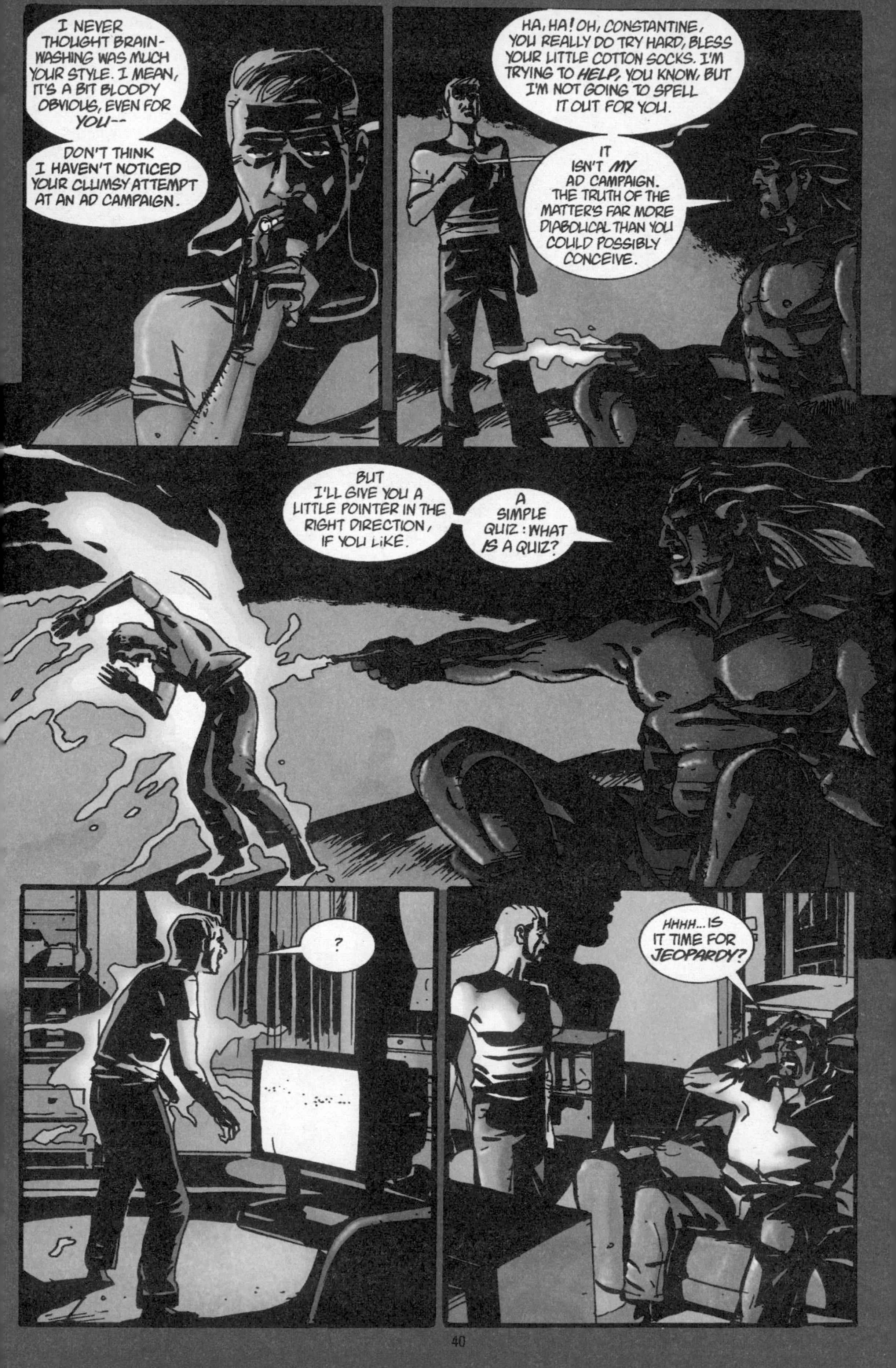
I NEVER THOUGHT BRAIN-WASHING WAS MUCH YOUR STYLE. I MEAN, IT'S A BIT BLOODY OBVIOUS, EVEN FOR YOU--
DON'T THINK I HAVEN'T NOTICED YOUR CLUMSY ATTEMPT AT AN AD CAMPAIGN.
HA, HA! OH, CONSTANTINE, YOU REALLY DO TRY HARD, BLESS YOUR LITTLE COTTON SOCKS. I'M TRYING TO HELP, YOU KNOW, BUT I'M NOT GOING TO SPELL IT OUT FOR YOU.
IT ISN'T MY AD CAMPAIGN. THE TRUTH OF THE MATTER'S FAR MORE DIABOLICAL THAN YOU COULD POSSIBLY CONCEIVE.
BUT I'LL GIVE YOU A LITTLE POINTER IN THE RIGHT DIRECTION, IF YOU LIKE.
A SIMPLE QUIZ: WHAT IS A QUIZ?
?
HHHH... IS IT TIME FOR JEOPARDY?

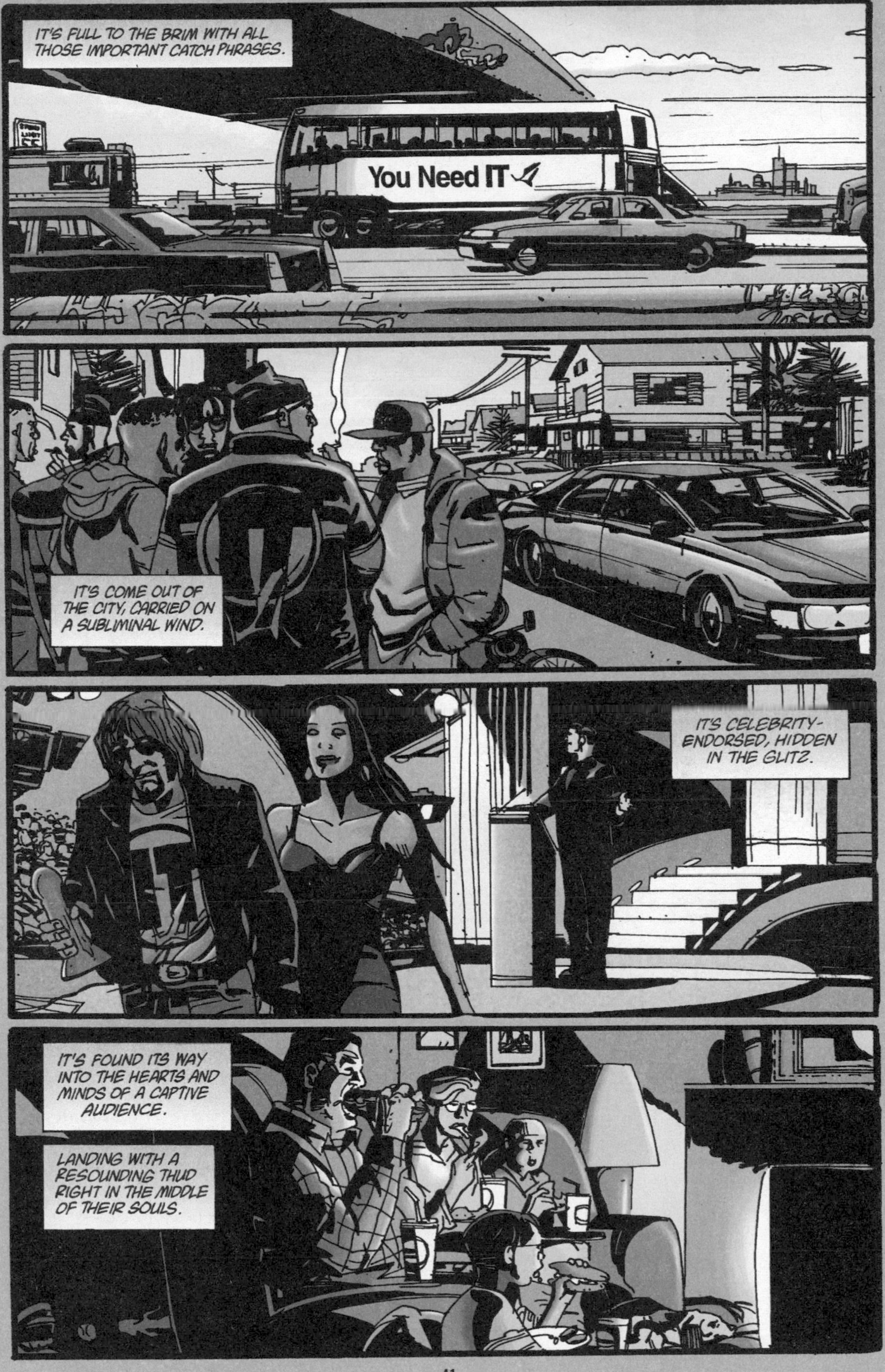
IT'S FULL TO THE BRIM WITH ALL THOSE IMPORTANT CATCH PHRASES.
You Need IT
IT'S COME OUT OF THE CITY, CARRIED ON A SUBLIMINAL WIND.
IT'S CELEBRITY-ENDORSED, HIDDEN IN THE GLITZ.
IT'S FOUND ITS WAY INTO THE HEARTS AND MINDS OF A CAPTIVE AUDIENCE.
LANDING WITH A RESOUNDING THUD RIGHT IN THE MIDDLE OF THEIR SOULS.

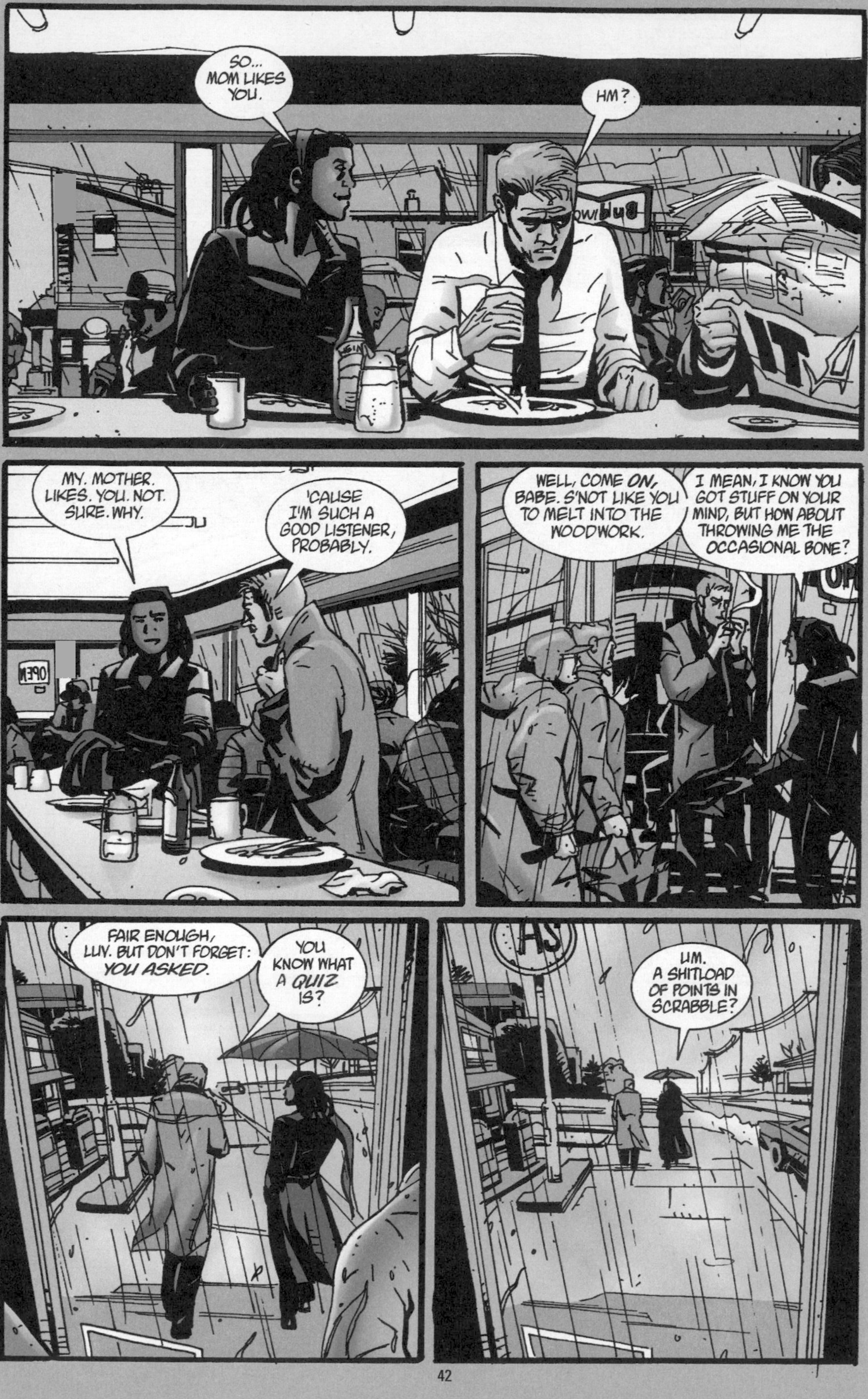
SO... MOM LIKES YOU.
HM?
MY. MOTHER. LIKES. YOU. NOT. SURE. WHY.
'CAUSE I'M SUCH A GOOD LISTENER, PROBABLY.
WELL, COME ON, BABE. S'NOT LIKE YOU TO MELT INTO THE WOODWORK.
I MEAN, I KNOW YOU GOT STUFF ON YOUR MIND, BUT HOW ABOUT THROWING ME THE OCCASIONAL BONE?
FAIR ENOUGH, LUV. BUT DON'T FORGET: YOU ASKED.
YOU KNOW WHAT A QUIZ IS?
UM. A SHITLOAD OF POINTS IN SCRABBLE?

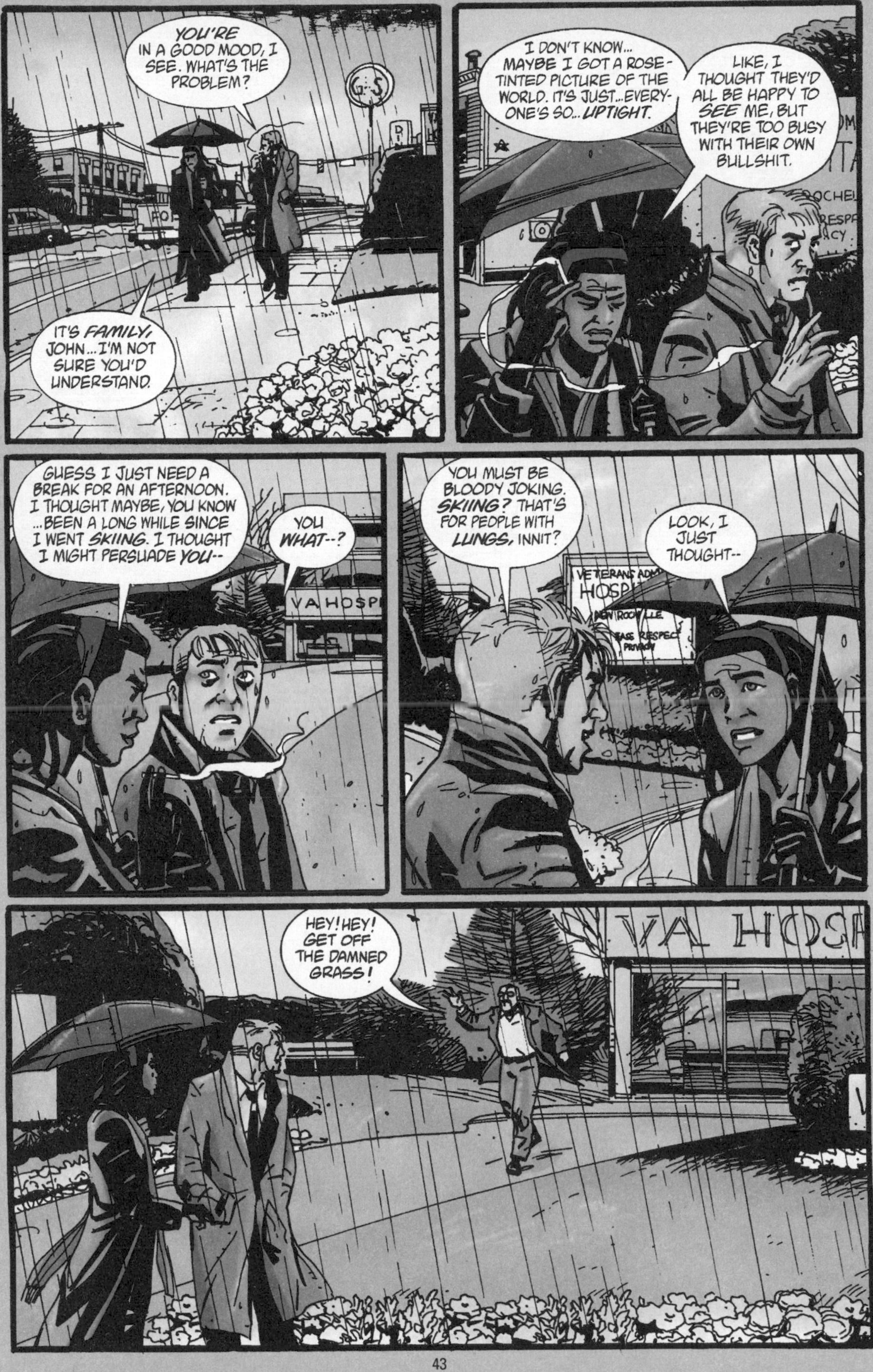
YOU'RE IN A GOOD MOOD, I SEE. WHAT'S THE PROBLEM?
IT'S FAMILY, JOHN... I'M NOT SURE YOU'D UNDERSTAND.
I DON'T KNOW... MAYBE I GOT A ROSE-TINTED PICTURE OF THE WORLD. IT'S JUST... EVERYONE'S SO... UPTIGHT.
LIKE, I THOUGHT THEY'D ALL BE HAPPY TO SEE ME, BUT THEY'RE TOO BUSY WITH THEIR OWN BULLSHIT.
GUESS I JUST NEED A BREAK FOR AN AFTERNOON. I THOUGHT MAYBE, YOU KNOW ...BEEN A LONG WHILE SINCE I WENT SKIING. I THOUGHT I MIGHT PERSUADE YOU--
YOU WHAT--?
VA HOSP
YOU MUST BE BLOODY JOKING. SKIING? THAT'S FOR PEOPLE WITH LUNGS, INNIT?
LOOK, I JUST THOUGHT--
HEY! HEY! GET OFF THE DAMNED GRASS!
VA HOS

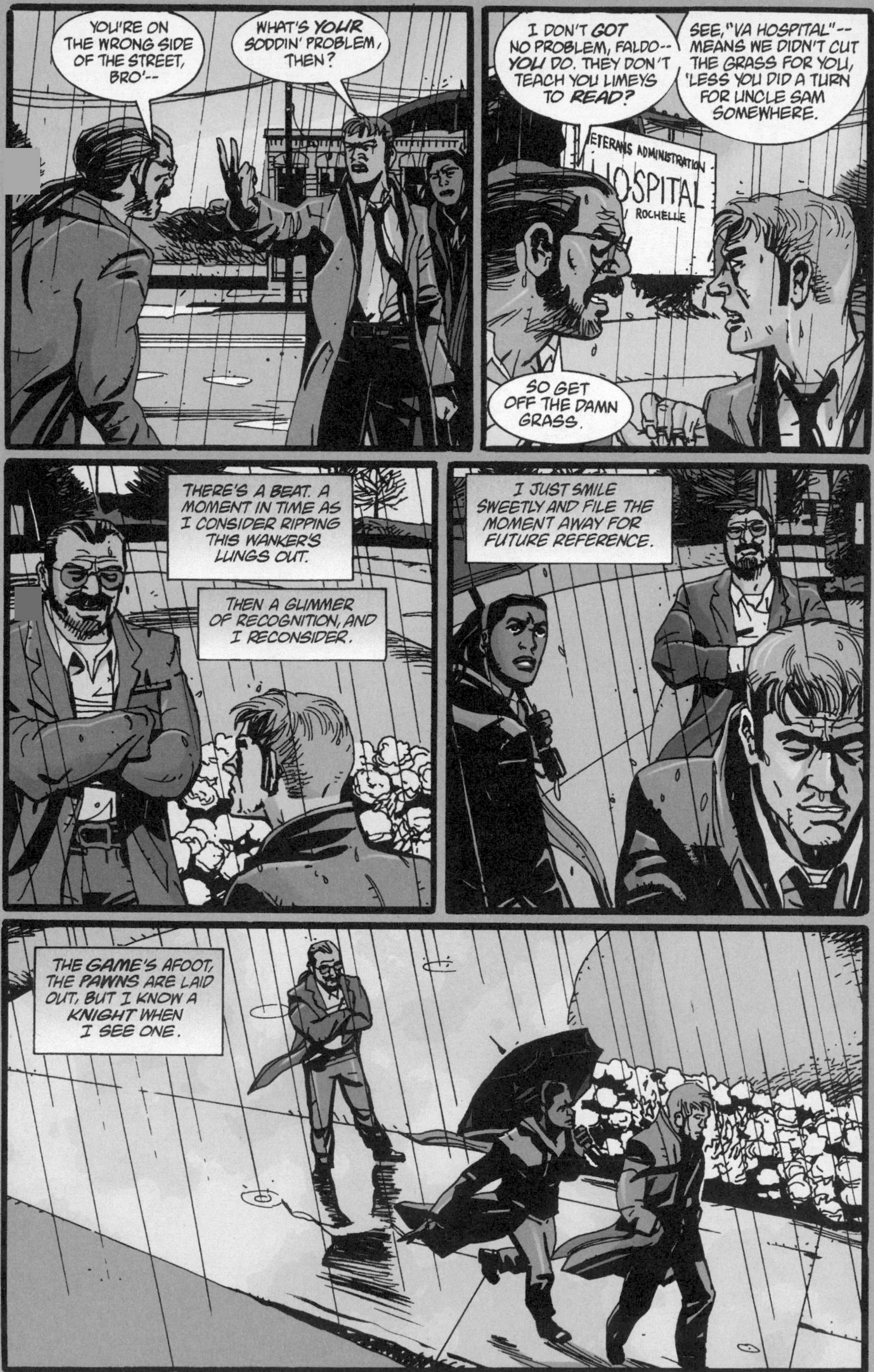
YOU'RE ON THE WRONG SIDE OF THE STREET, BRO'--
WHAT'S YOUR SODDIN' PROBLEM, THEN?
I DON'T GOT NO PROBLEM, FALDO-- YOU DO. THEY DON'T TEACH YOU LIMEYS TO READ?
SEE, "VA HOSPITAL"-- MEANS WE DIDN'T CUT THE GRASS FOR YOU, 'LESS YOU DID A TURN FOR UNCLE SAM SOMEWHERE.
VETERANS ADMINISTRATION
HOSPITAL
ROCHELLE
SO GET OFF THE DAMN GRASS.
THERE'S A BEAT. A MOMENT IN TIME AS I CONSIDER RIPPING THIS WANKER'S LUNGS OUT.
THEN A GLIMMER OF RECOGNITION, AND I RECONSIDER.
I JUST SMILE SWEETLY AND FILE THE MOMENT AWAY FOR FUTURE REFERENCE.
THE GAME'S AFOOT, THE PAWNS ARE LAID OUT, BUT I KNOW A KNIGHT WHEN I SEE ONE.

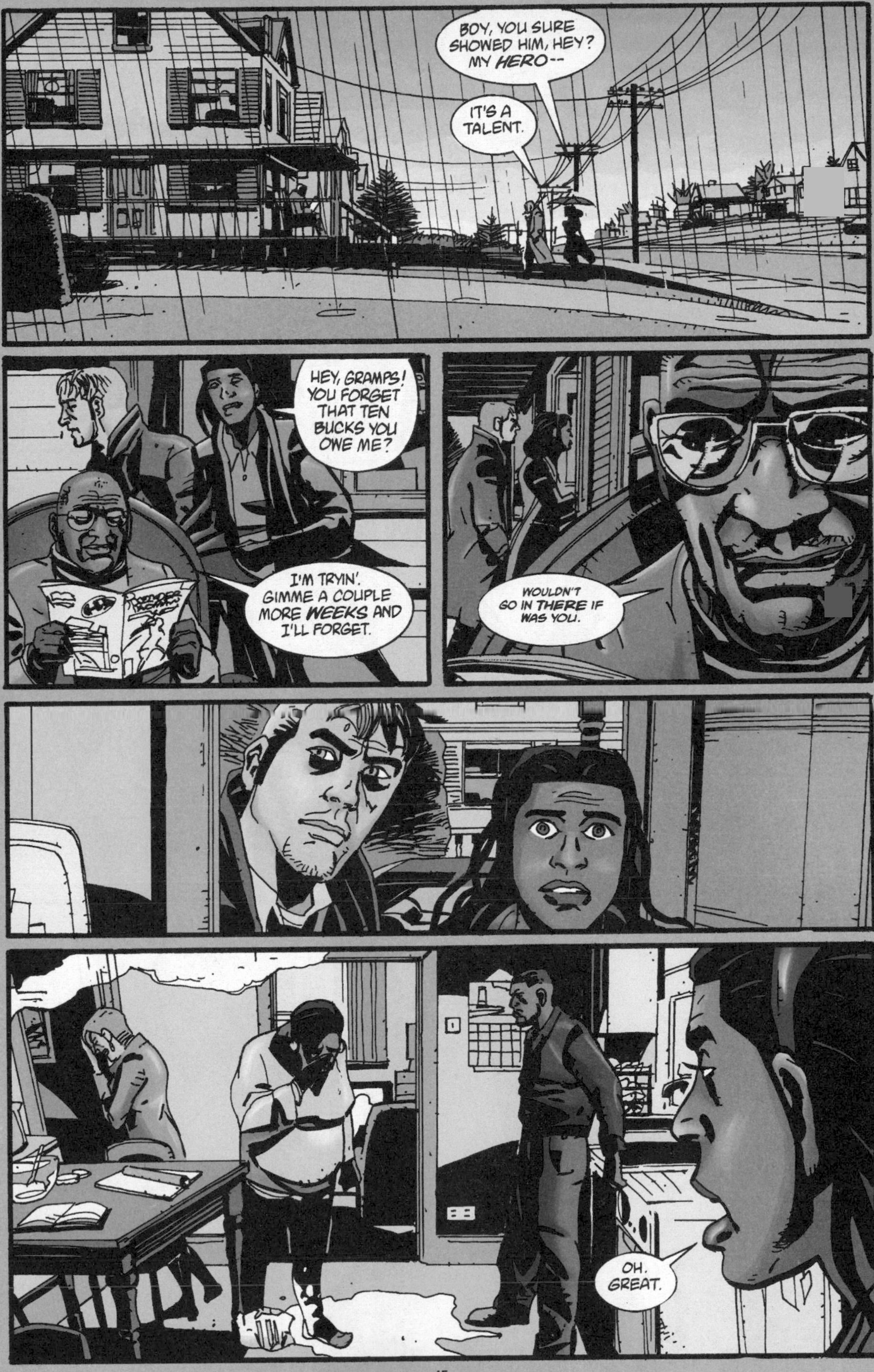
BOY, YOU SURE SHOWED HIM, HEY? MY HERO--
IT'S A TALENT.
HEY, GRAMPS! YOU FORGET THAT TEN BUCKS YOU OWE ME?
I'M TRYIN'. GIMME A COUPLE MORE WEEKS AND I'LL FORGET.
WOULDN'T GO IN THERE IF WAS YOU.
OH. GREAT.

GOOD OLD UNCLE FRED IMMEDIATELY ADDS TO THE FUN. IN A BOLD BID FOR AN EARLY GRAVE, HE GETS CAUGHT ORDERING A HUNDRED DOLLAR JUICE SQUEEZER FROM SOME NAFF MIDNIGHT INFOMERCIAL.

A GIFT FOR MARY'S BIRTHDAY, MIND, BUT HE USED *HER* CREDIT CARD.

AH, THE MERRIMENT AND MIRTH THAT IS THANKSGIVING--A TIME FOR THE FAMILY TO COME TOGETHER, GORGE THEMSELVES SILLY, AND SIT AROUND FARTING AND BELCHING IN FRONT OF THE FOOTBALL.

THE PERFECT OPPORTUNITY FOR COUSIN TERRELL AND ZOMBIE GIRL TO ANNOUNCE THEY'RE GETTING A *DIVORCE*.

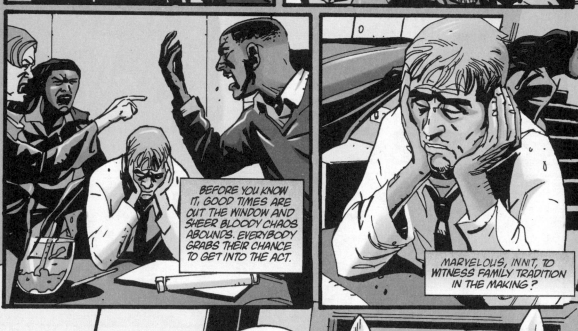

BEFORE YOU KNOW IT, GOOD TIMES ARE OUT THE WINDOW AND SHEER BLOODY CHAOS ABOUNDS. EVERYBODY GRABS THEIR CHANCE TO GET INTO THE ACT.

MARVELOUS, INNIT, TO WITNESS FAMILY TRADITION IN THE MAKING?

YOU COMING OR NOT?

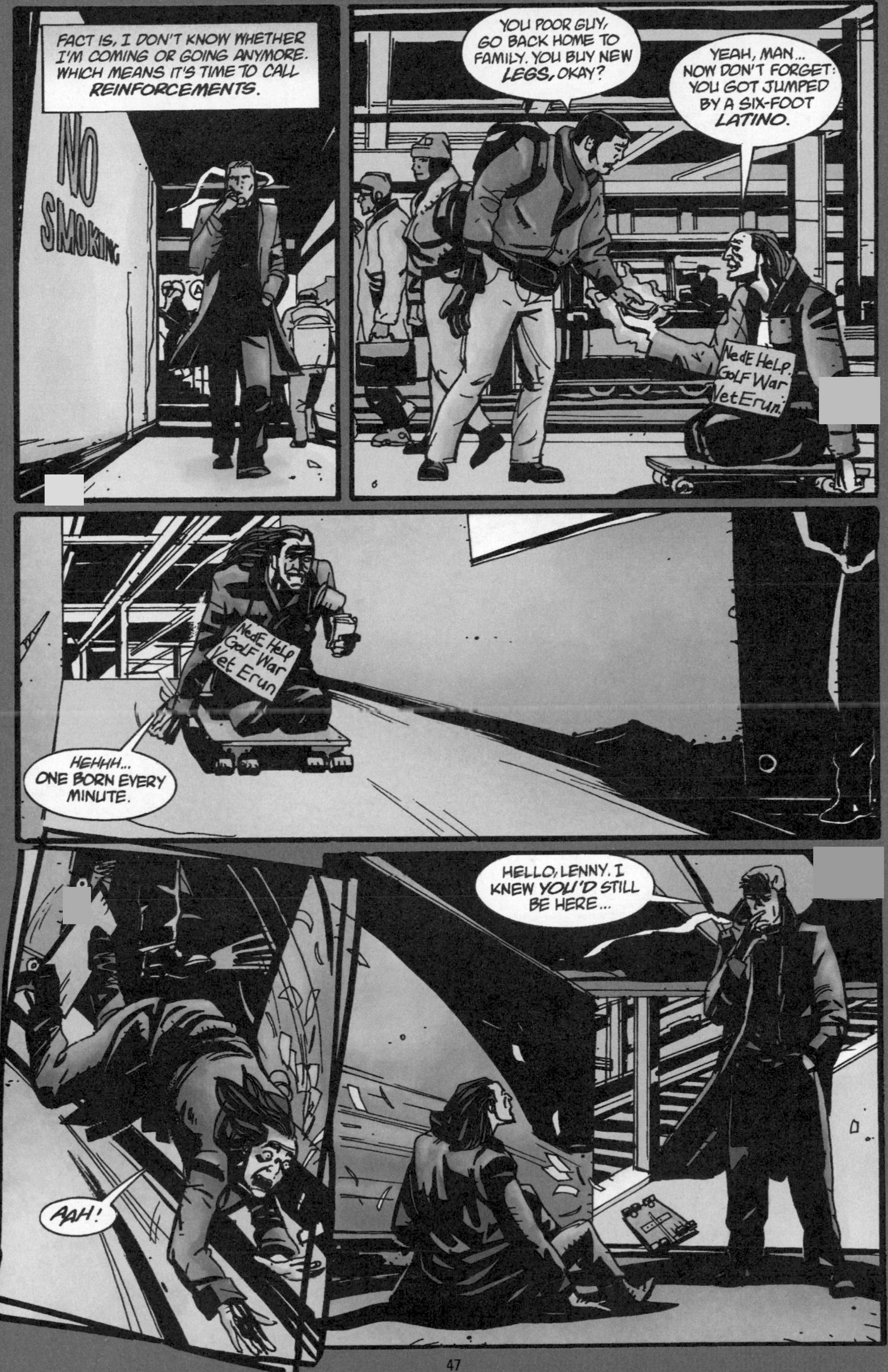
FACT IS, I DON'T KNOW WHETHER I'M COMING OR GOING ANYMORE. WHICH MEANS IT'S TIME TO CALL REINFORCEMENTS.
NO SMOKING
YOU POOR GUY, GO BACK HOME TO FAMILY. YOU BUY NEW LEGS, OKAY?
YEAH, MAN... NOW DON'T FORGET: YOU GOT JUMPED BY A SIX-FOOT LATINO.
NedE Help. GoLF War VetErun.
NedE Help GoLF War Vet Erun
HEHHH... ONE BORN EVERY MINUTE.
AAH!
HELLO, LENNY. I KNEW YOU'D STILL BE HERE...

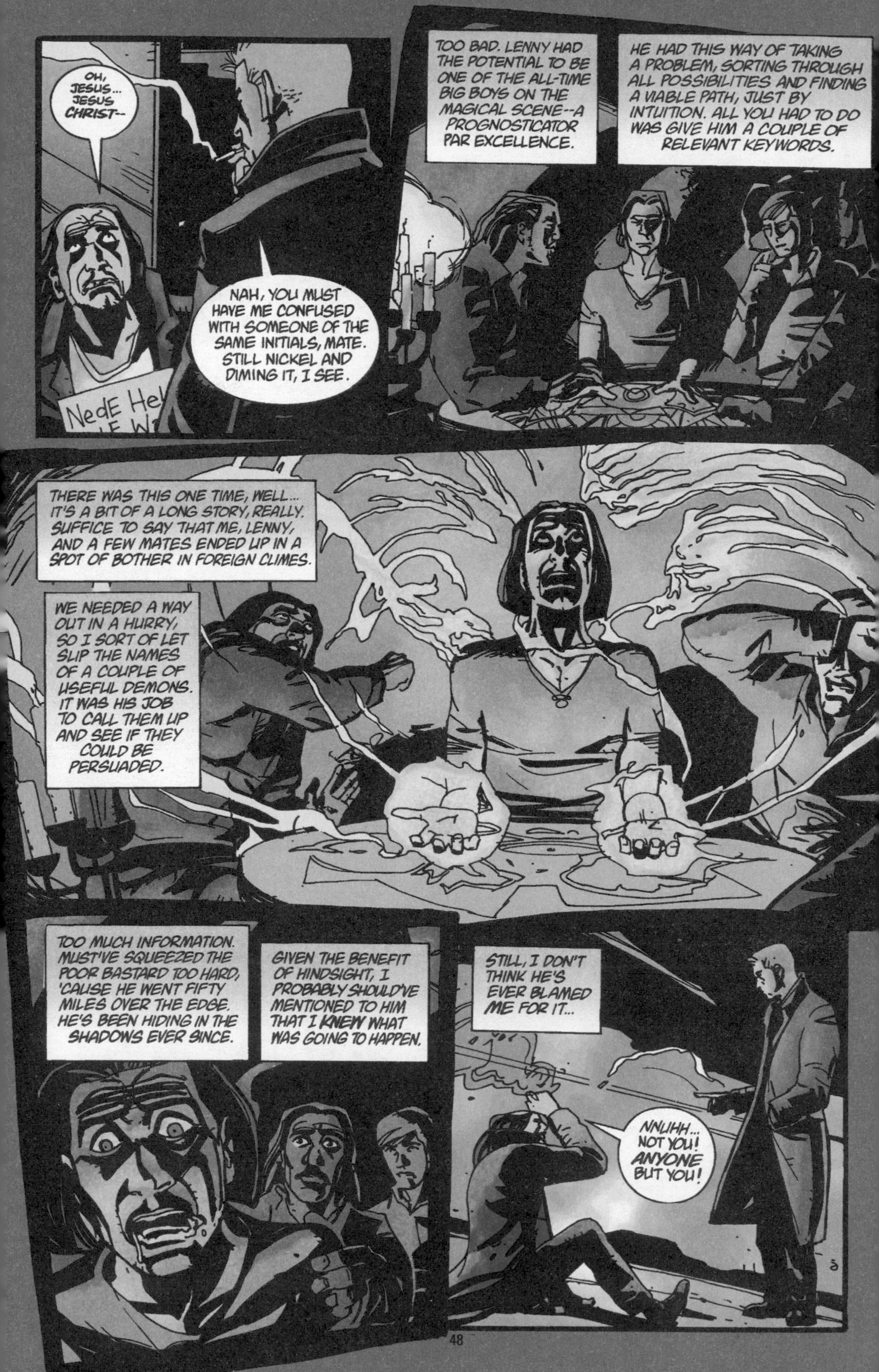
OH, JESUS... JESUS CHRIST--
NAH, YOU MUST HAVE ME CONFUSED WITH SOMEONE OF THE SAME INITIALS, MATE. STILL NICKEL AND DIMING IT, I SEE.
NedE Hel
TOO BAD. LENNY HAD THE POTENTIAL TO BE ONE OF THE ALL-TIME BIG BOYS ON THE MAGICAL SCENE--A PROGNOSTICATOR PAR EXCELLENCE.
HE HAD THIS WAY OF TAKING A PROBLEM, SORTING THROUGH ALL POSSIBILITIES AND FINDING A VIABLE PATH, JUST BY INTUITION. ALL YOU HAD TO DO WAS GIVE HIM A COUPLE OF RELEVANT KEYWORDS.
THERE WAS THIS ONE TIME, WELL... IT'S A BIT OF A LONG STORY, REALLY. SUFFICE TO SAY THAT ME, LENNY, AND A FEW MATES ENDED UP IN A SPOT OF BOTHER IN FOREIGN CLIMES.
WE NEEDED A WAY OUT IN A HURRY, SO I SORT OF LET SLIP THE NAMES OF A COUPLE OF USEFUL DEMONS. IT WAS HIS JOB TO CALL THEM UP AND SEE IF THEY COULD BE PERSUADED.
TOO MUCH INFORMATION. MUST'VE SQUEEZED THE POOR BASTARD TOO HARD, 'CAUSE HE WENT FIFTY MILES OVER THE EDGE. HE'S BEEN HIDING IN THE SHADOWS EVER SINCE.
GIVEN THE BENEFIT OF HINDSIGHT, I PROBABLY SHOULD'VE MENTIONED TO HIM THAT I KNEW WHAT WAS GOING TO HAPPEN.
STILL, I DON'T THINK HE'S EVER BLAMED ME FOR IT...
NNUHH... NOT YOU! ANYONE BUT YOU!

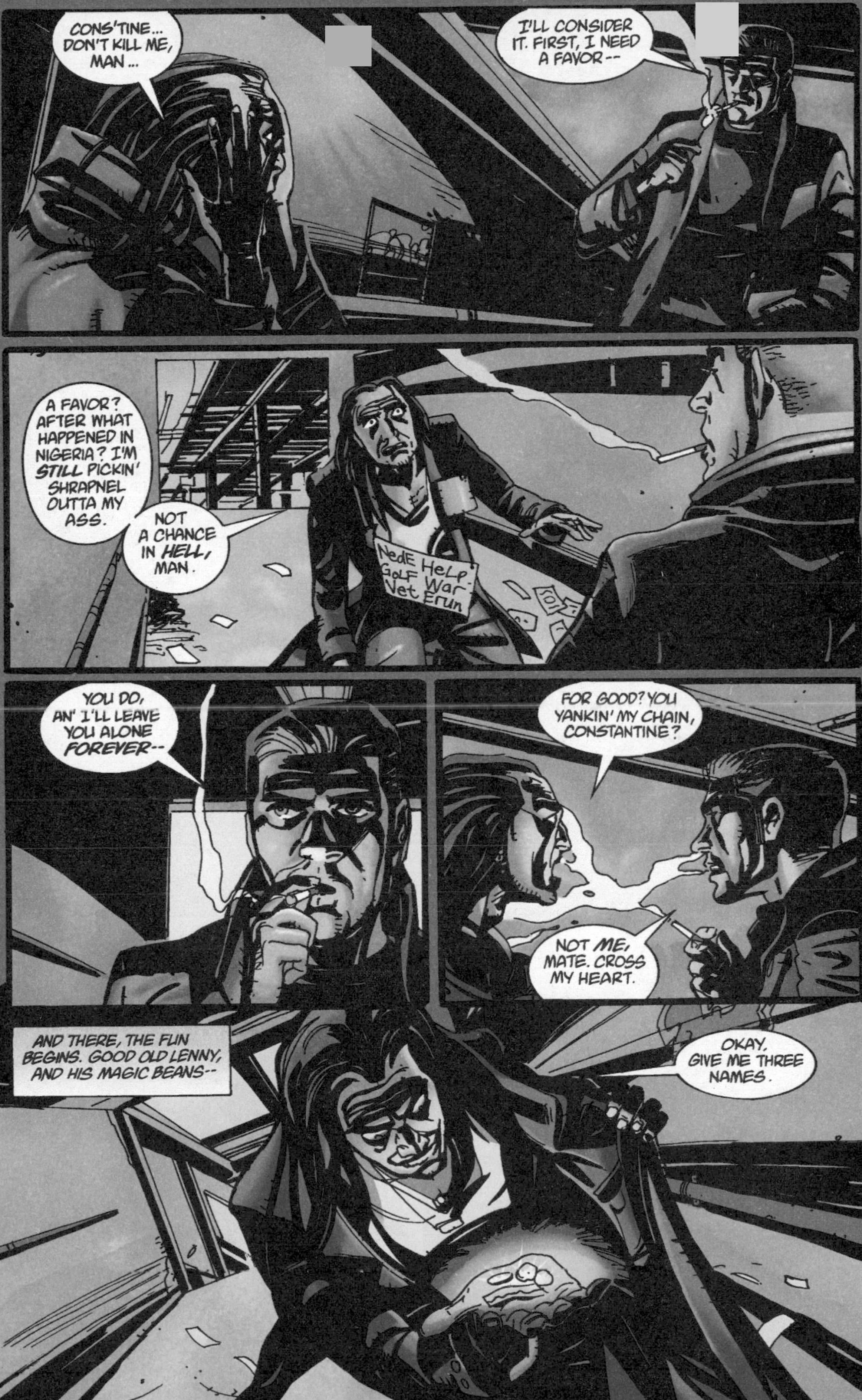
CONS'TINE... DON'T KILL ME, MAN...
I'LL CONSIDER IT. FIRST, I NEED A FAVOR--
A FAVOR? AFTER WHAT HAPPENED IN NIGERIA? I'M STILL PICKIN' SHRAPNEL OUTTA MY ASS.
NOT A CHANCE IN HELL, MAN.
NedE HelP GoLF War Vet Erun
YOU DO, AN' I'LL LEAVE YOU ALONE FOREVER--
FOR GOOD? YOU YANKIN' MY CHAIN, CONSTANTINE?
NOT ME, MATE. CROSS MY HEART.
AND THERE, THE FUN BEGINS. GOOD OLD LENNY, AND HIS MAGIC BEANS--
OKAY, GIVE ME THREE NAMES.

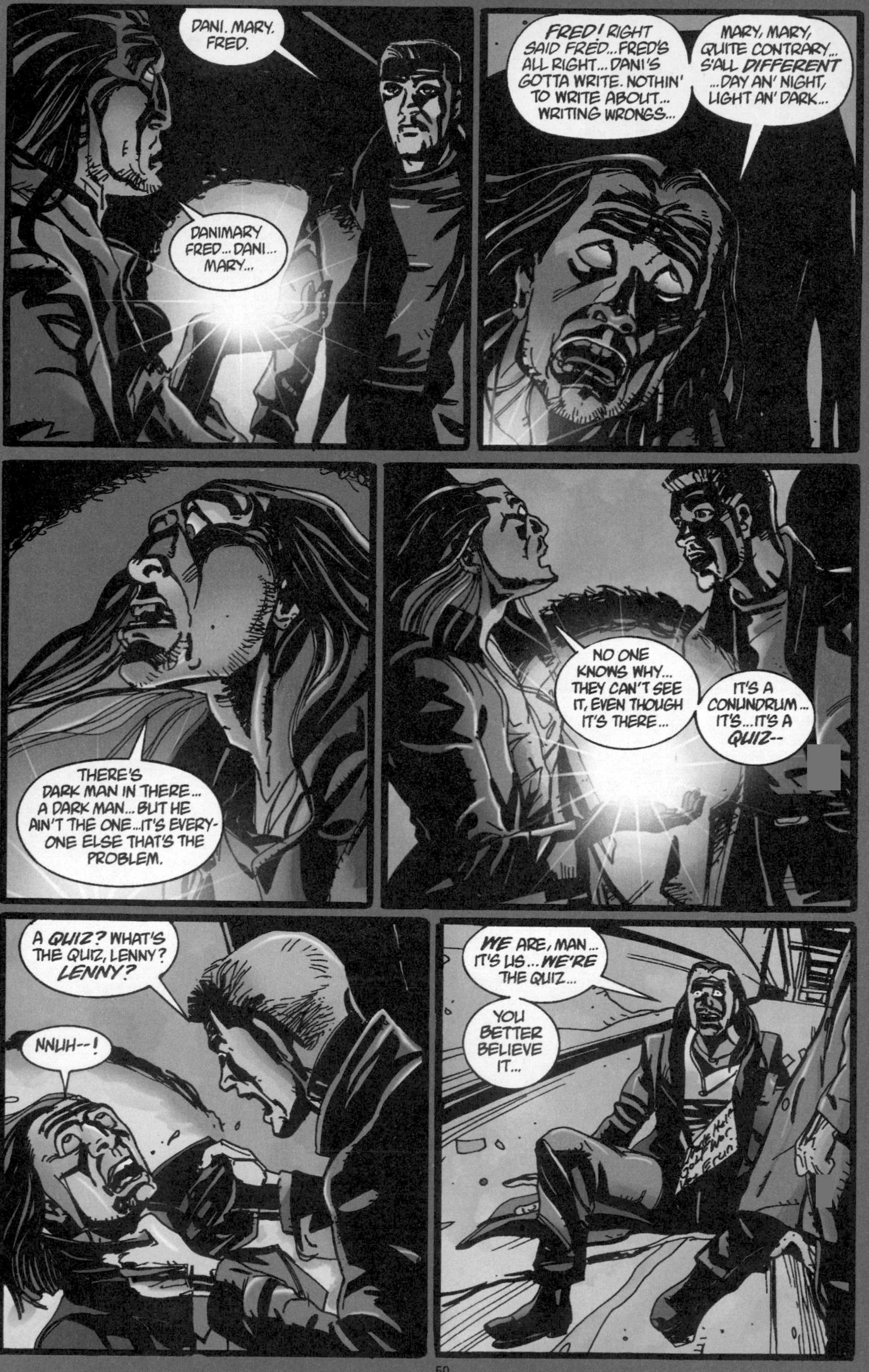
DANI. MARY. FRED.
DANIMARY FRED... DANI... MARY...
FRED! RIGHT SAID FRED... FRED'S ALL RIGHT... DANI'S GOTTA WRITE. NOTHIN' TO WRITE ABOUT... WRITING WRONGS...
MARY, MARY, QUITE CONTRARY... S'ALL DIFFERENT ...DAY AN' NIGHT, LIGHT AN' DARK...
THERE'S DARK MAN IN THERE... A DARK MAN... BUT HE AIN'T THE ONE... IT'S EVERY-ONE ELSE THAT'S THE PROBLEM.
NO ONE KNOWS WHY... THEY CAN'T SEE IT, EVEN THOUGH IT'S THERE...
IT'S A CONUNDRUM... IT'S... IT'S A QUIZ--
A QUIZ? WHAT'S THE QUIZ, LENNY? LENNY?
NNUH--!
WE ARE, MAN... IT'S US... WE'RE THE QUIZ...
YOU BETTER BELIEVE IT...

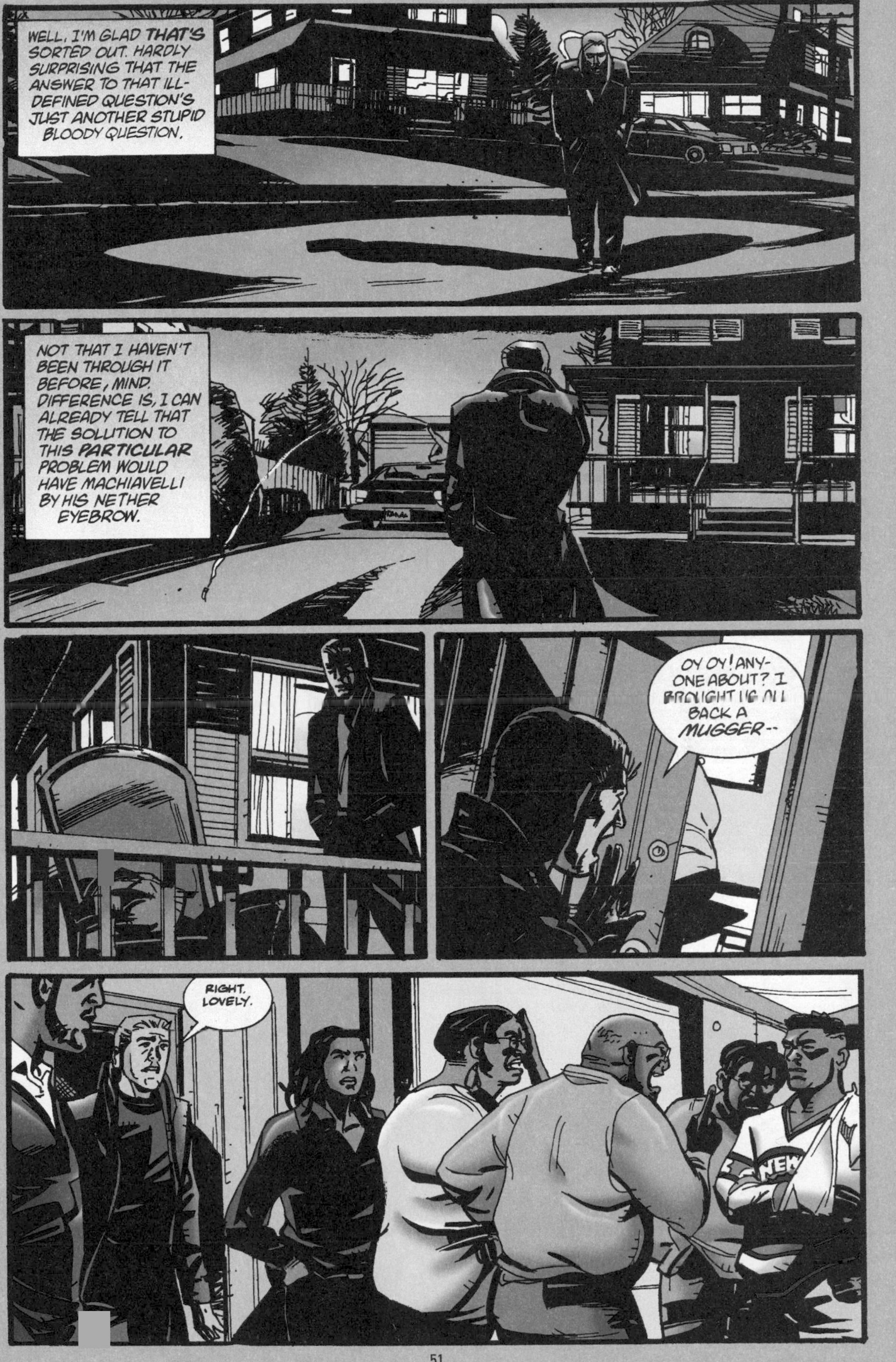
WELL, I'M GLAD THAT'S SORTED OUT. HARDLY SURPRISING THAT THE ANSWER TO THAT ILL-DEFINED QUESTION'S JUST ANOTHER STUPID BLOODY QUESTION.
NOT THAT I HAVEN'T BEEN THROUGH IT BEFORE, MIND. DIFFERENCE IS, I CAN ALREADY TELL THAT THE SOLUTION TO THIS PARTICULAR PROBLEM WOULD HAVE MACHIAVELLI BY HIS NETHER EYEBROW.
OY OY! ANYONE ABOUT? I BROUGHT US ALL BACK A MUGGER--
RIGHT. LOVELY.

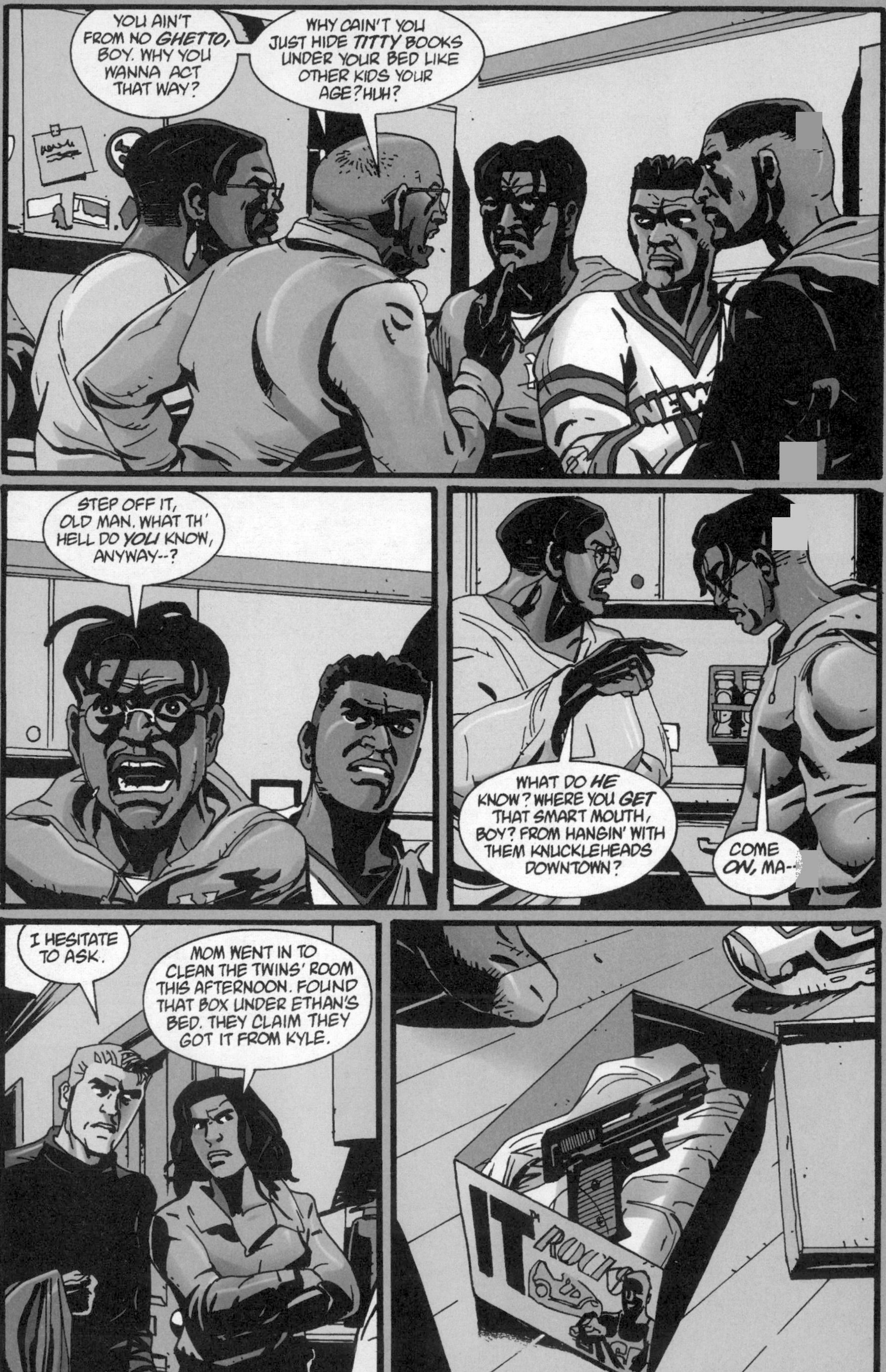
YOU AIN'T FROM NO GHETTO, BOY. WHY YOU WANNA ACT THAT WAY?
WHY CAIN'T YOU JUST HIDE TITTY BOOKS UNDER YOUR BED LIKE OTHER KIDS YOUR AGE? HUH?
STEP OFF IT, OLD MAN. WHAT TH' HELL DO YOU KNOW, ANYWAY--?
WHAT DO HE KNOW? WHERE YOU GET THAT SMART MOUTH, BOY? FROM HANGIN' WITH THEM KNUCKLEHEADS DOWNTOWN?
COME ON, MA-
I HESITATE TO ASK.
MOM WENT IN TO CLEAN THE TWINS' ROOM THIS AFTERNOON. FOUND THAT BOX UNDER ETHAN'S BED. THEY CLAIM THEY GOT IT FROM KYLE.
IT ROCKS

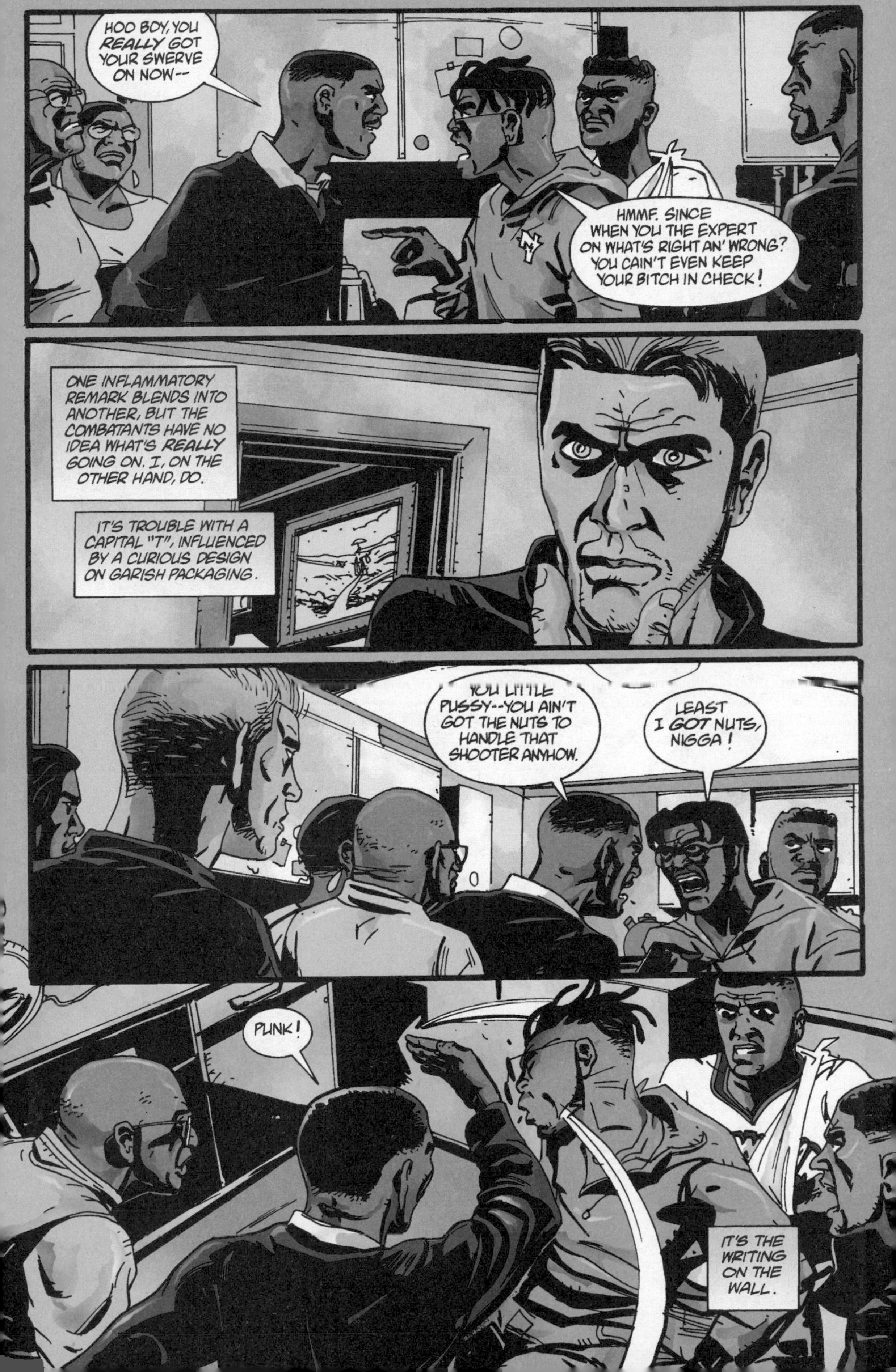
HOO BOY, YOU REALLY GOT YOUR SWERVE ON NOW--
HMMF. SINCE WHEN YOU THE EXPERT ON WHAT'S RIGHT AN' WRONG? YOU CAIN'T EVEN KEEP YOUR BITCH IN CHECK!
ONE INFLAMMATORY REMARK BLENDS INTO ANOTHER, BUT THE COMBATANTS HAVE NO IDEA WHAT'S REALLY GOING ON. I, ON THE OTHER HAND, DO.
IT'S TROUBLE WITH A CAPITAL "T", INFLUENCED BY A CURIOUS DESIGN ON GARISH PACKAGING.
YOU LITTLE PUSSY--YOU AIN'T GOT THE NUTS TO HANDLE THAT SHOOTER ANYHOW.
LEAST I GOT NUTS, NIGGA!
PUNK!
IT'S THE WRITING ON THE WALL.

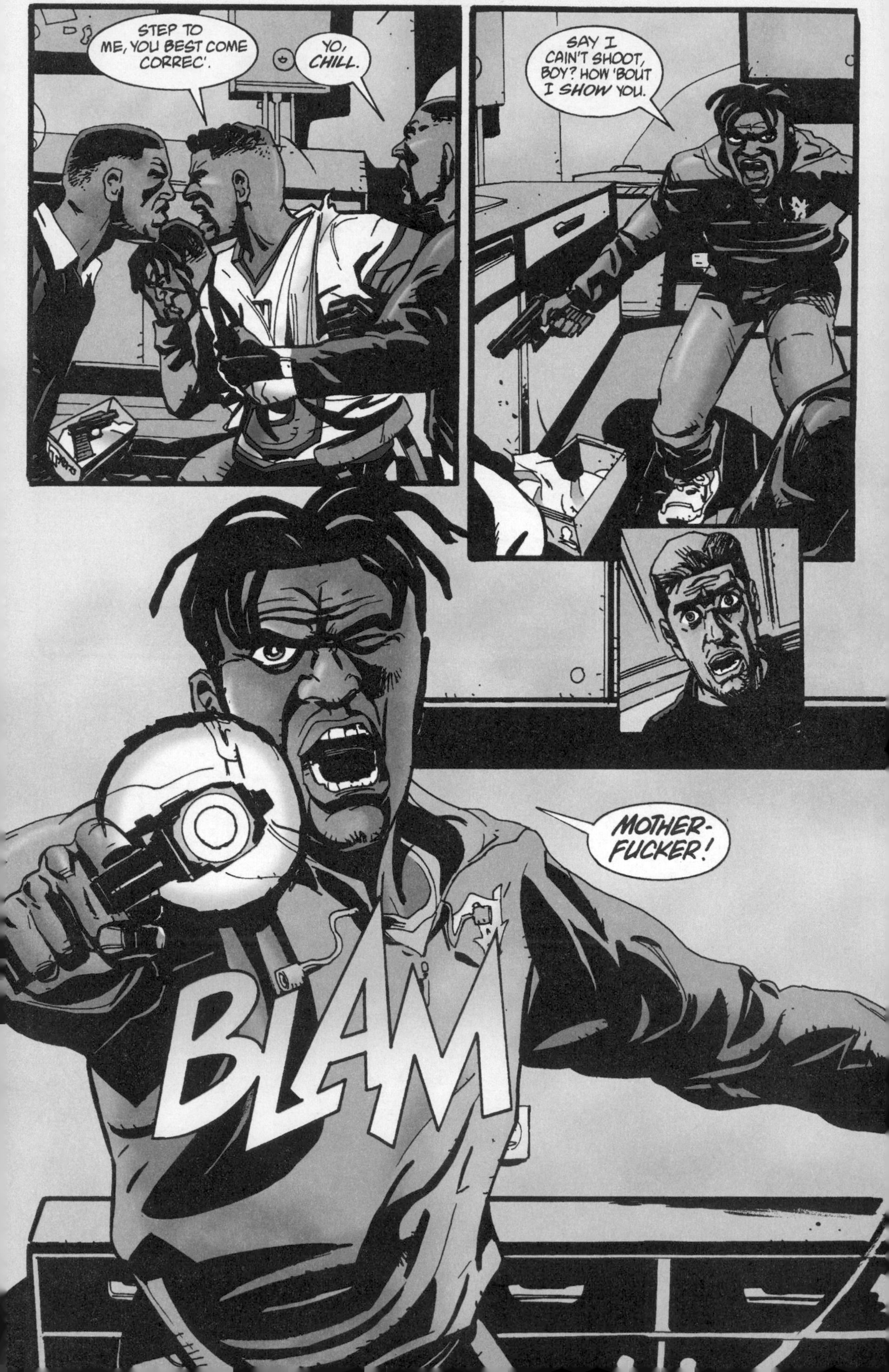
STEP TO ME, YOU BEST COME CORREC'.
YO, CHILL.
SAY I CAIN'T SHOOT, BOY? HOW 'BOUT I SHOW YOU.
MOTHER-FUCKER!
BLAM

JOHN CONSTANTINE

JC

VERTIGO

123
'98
5 US
5 CAN
GESTED
MATURE
DERS

HELLBLAZER

UP the DOWN STAIRCASE

PART 03 of 04

PAUL JENKINS

WARREN PLEECE

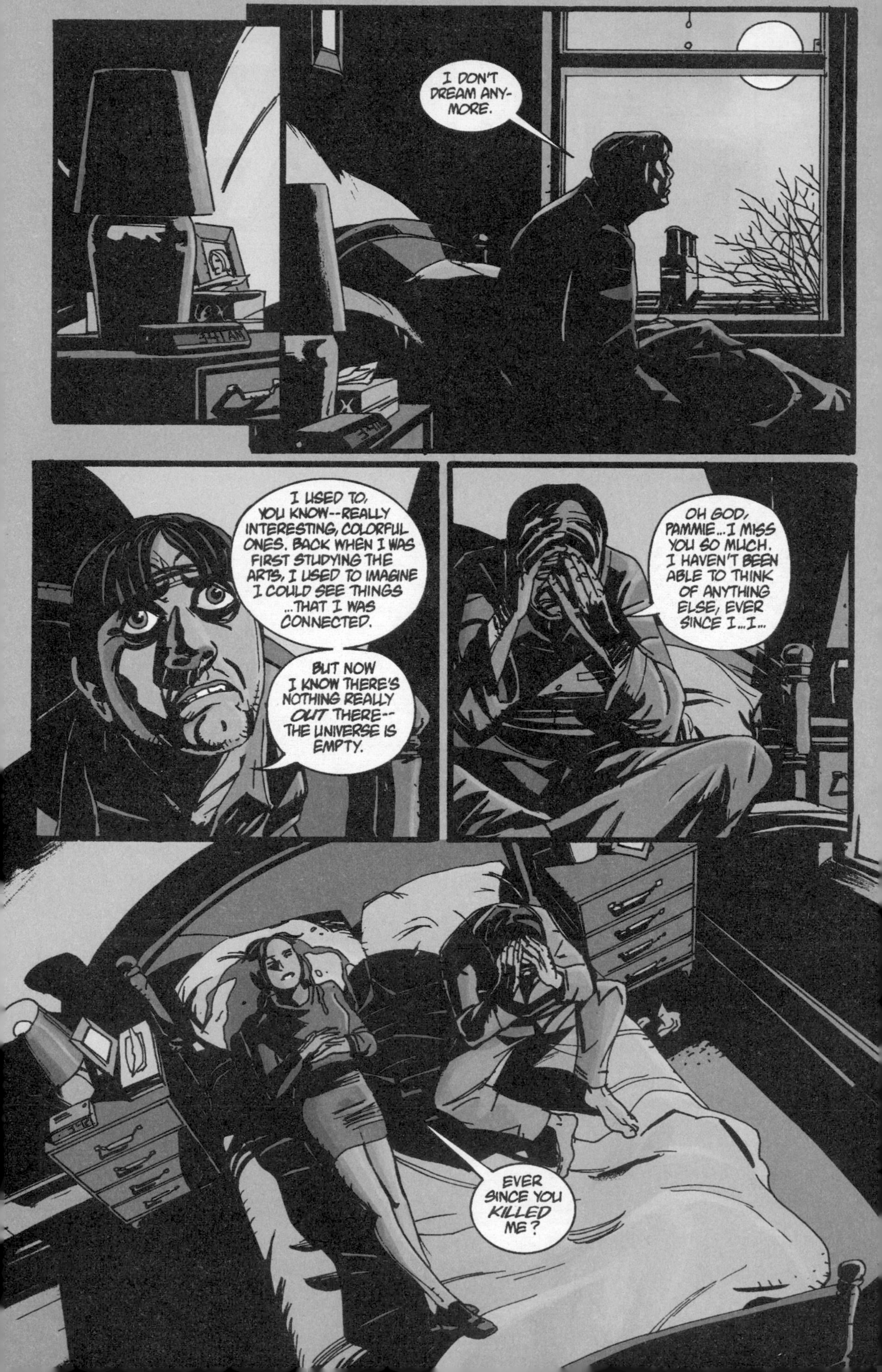
I DON'T DREAM ANYMORE.
I USED TO, YOU KNOW--REALLY INTERESTING, COLORFUL ONES. BACK WHEN I WAS FIRST STUDYING THE ARTS, I USED TO IMAGINE I COULD SEE THINGS ...THAT I WAS CONNECTED.
BUT NOW I KNOW THERE'S NOTHING REALLY OUT THERE-- THE UNIVERSE IS EMPTY.
OH GOD, PAMMIE...I MISS YOU SO MUCH. I HAVEN'T BEEN ABLE TO THINK OF ANYTHING ELSE, EVER SINCE I...I...
EVER SINCE YOU KILLED ME?

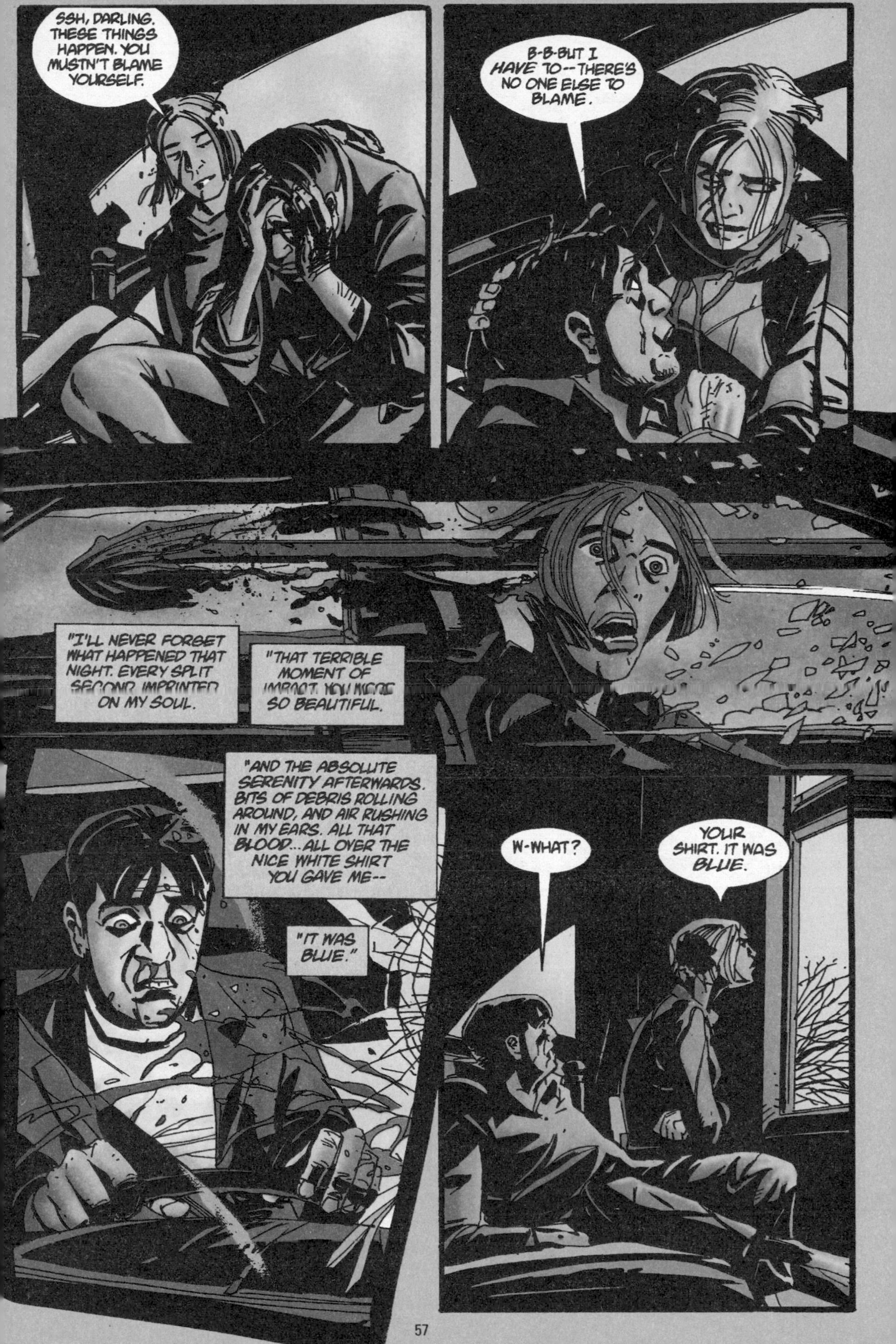
SSH, DARLING. THESE THINGS HAPPEN. YOU MUSTN'T BLAME YOURSELF.
B-B-BUT I *HAVE* TO--THERE'S NO ONE ELSE TO BLAME.
"I'LL NEVER FORGET WHAT HAPPENED THAT NIGHT. EVERY SPLIT SECOND IMPRINTED ON MY SOUL.
"THAT TERRIBLE MOMENT OF IMPACT. YOU WERE SO BEAUTIFUL.
"AND THE ABSOLUTE SERENITY AFTERWARDS. BITS OF DEBRIS ROLLING AROUND, AND AIR RUSHING IN MY EARS. ALL THAT BLOOD...ALL OVER THE NICE WHITE SHIRT YOU GAVE ME--
"IT WAS BLUE."
W-WHAT?
YOUR SHIRT. IT WAS BLUE.

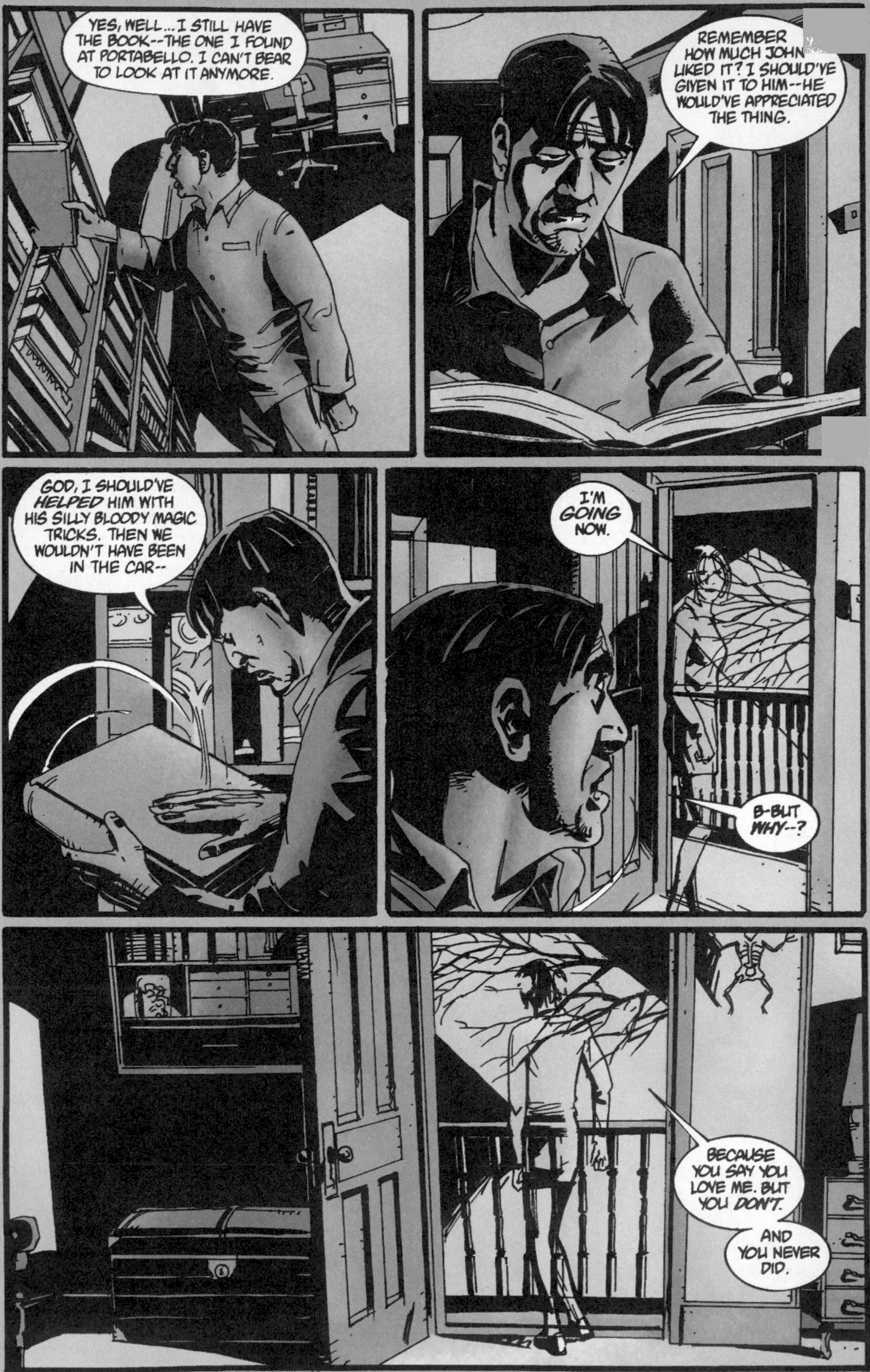
YES, WELL... I STILL HAVE THE BOOK--THE ONE I FOUND AT PORTABELLO. I CAN'T BEAR TO LOOK AT IT ANYMORE.
REMEMBER HOW MUCH JOHN LIKED IT? I SHOULD'VE GIVEN IT TO HIM--HE WOULD'VE APPRECIATED THE THING.
GOD, I SHOULD'VE HELPED HIM WITH HIS SILLY BLOODY MAGIC TRICKS. THEN WE WOULDN'T HAVE BEEN IN THE CAR--
I'M GOING NOW.
B-BUT WHY--?
BECAUSE YOU SAY YOU LOVE ME. BUT YOU DON'T.
AND YOU NEVER DID.

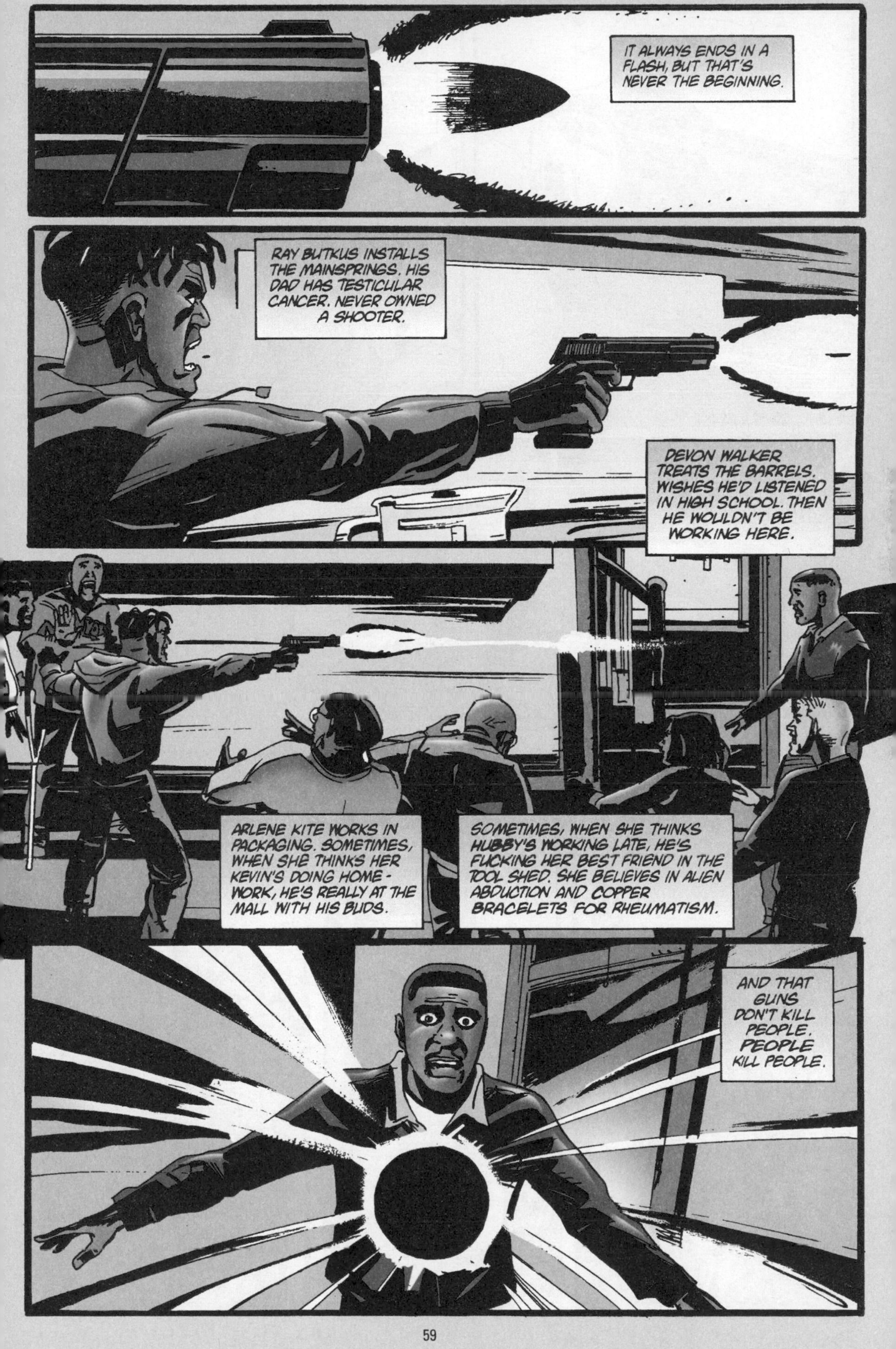
IT ALWAYS ENDS IN A FLASH, BUT THAT'S NEVER THE BEGINNING.
RAY BUTKUS INSTALLS THE MAINSPRINGS. HIS DAD HAS TESTICULAR CANCER. NEVER OWNED A SHOOTER.
DEVON WALKER TREATS THE BARRELS. WISHES HE'D LISTENED IN HIGH SCHOOL. THEN HE WOULDN'T BE WORKING HERE.
ARLENE KITE WORKS IN PACKAGING. SOMETIMES, WHEN SHE THINKS HER KEVIN'S DOING HOME-WORK, HE'S REALLY AT THE MALL WITH HIS BUDS.
SOMETIMES, WHEN SHE THINKS HUBBY'S WORKING LATE, HE'S FUCKING HER BEST FRIEND IN THE TOOL SHED. SHE BELIEVES IN ALIEN ABDUCTION AND COPPER BRACELETS FOR RHEUMATISM.
AND THAT GUNS DON'T KILL PEOPLE. PEOPLE KILL PEOPLE.

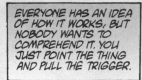
EVERYONE HAS AN IDEA OF HOW IT WORKS, BUT NOBODY WANTS TO COMPREHEND IT. YOU JUST POINT THE THING AND PULL THE TRIGGER.

HAMMER COMES DOWN, FIRING PIN HITS PRIMER, BULLET COMES OUT.

AND THEN EVERYONE TRUSTS TO LUCK.

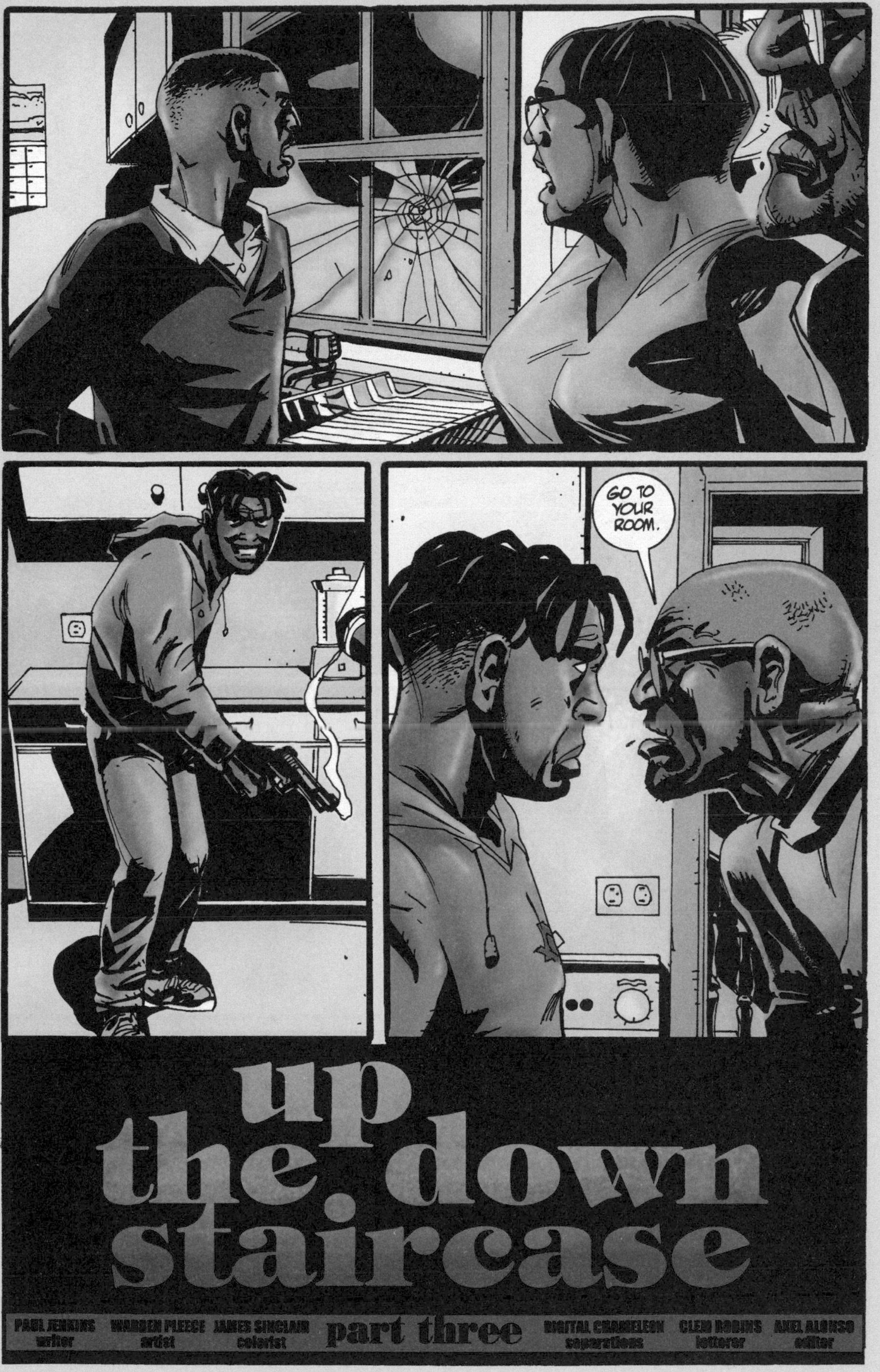
GO TO YOUR ROOM.
up the down staircase
PAUL JENKINS writer
WARREN PLEECE artist
JAMES SINCLAIR colorist
part three
DIGITAL CHAMELEON separations
CLEM ROBINS letterer
AXEL ALONSO editor

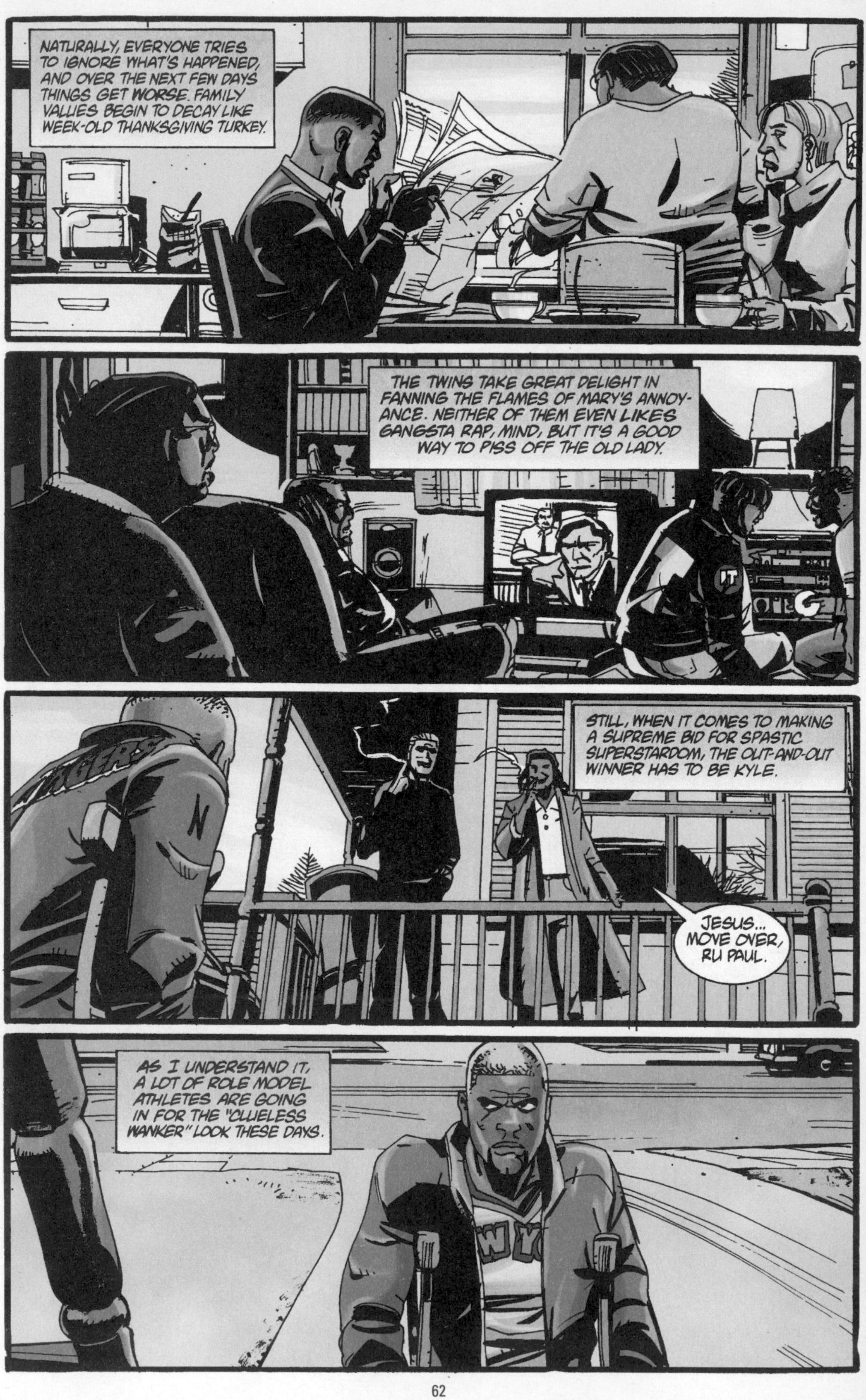
NATURALLY, EVERYONE TRIES TO IGNORE WHAT'S HAPPENED, AND OVER THE NEXT FEW DAYS THINGS GET WORSE. FAMILY VALUES BEGIN TO DECAY LIKE WEEK-OLD THANKSGIVING TURKEY.
THE TWINS TAKE GREAT DELIGHT IN FANNING THE FLAMES OF MARY'S ANNOYANCE. NEITHER OF THEM EVEN LIKES GANGSTA RAP, MIND, BUT IT'S A GOOD WAY TO PISS OFF THE OLD LADY.
STILL, WHEN IT COMES TO MAKING A SUPREME BID FOR SPASTIC SUPERSTARDOM, THE OUT-AND-OUT WINNER HAS TO BE KYLE.
JESUS... MOVE OVER, RU PAUL.
AS I UNDERSTAND IT, A LOT OF ROLE MODEL ATHLETES ARE GOING IN FOR THE "CLUELESS WANKER" LOOK THESE DAYS.

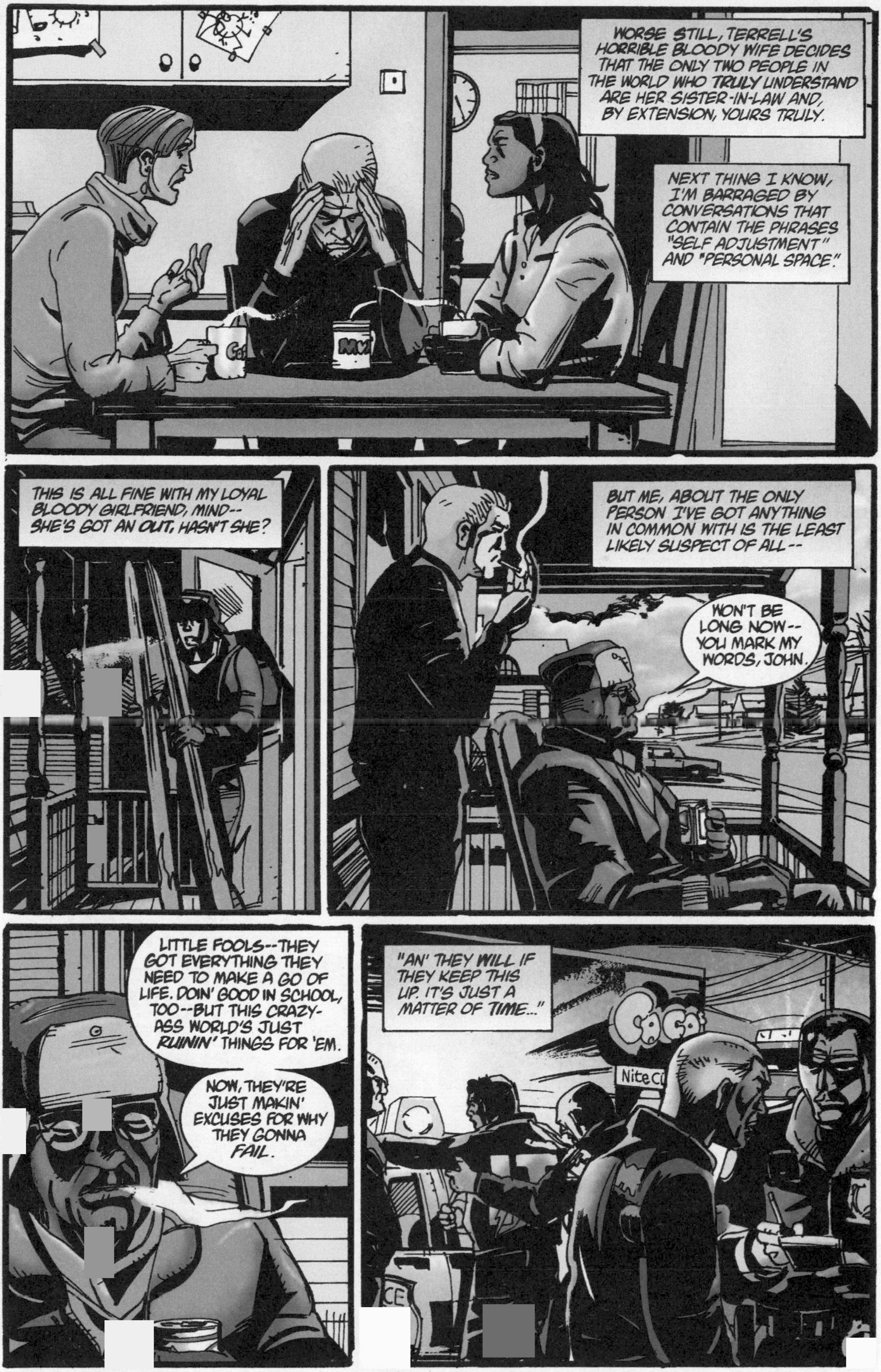
WORSE STILL, TERRELL'S HORRIBLE BLOODY WIFE DECIDES THAT THE ONLY TWO PEOPLE IN THE WORLD WHO TRULY UNDERSTAND ARE HER SISTER-IN-LAW AND, BY EXTENSION, YOURS TRULY.
NEXT THING I KNOW, I'M BARRAGED BY CONVERSATIONS THAT CONTAIN THE PHRASES "SELF ADJUSTMENT" AND "PERSONAL SPACE."
THIS IS ALL FINE WITH MY LOYAL BLOODY GIRLFRIEND, MIND-- SHE'S GOT AN OUT, HASN'T SHE?
BUT ME, ABOUT THE ONLY PERSON I'VE GOT ANYTHING IN COMMON WITH IS THE LEAST LIKELY SUSPECT OF ALL--
WON'T BE LONG NOW-- YOU MARK MY WORDS, JOHN.
LITTLE FOOLS--THEY GOT EVERYTHING THEY NEED TO MAKE A GO OF LIFE. DOIN' GOOD IN SCHOOL, TOO--BUT THIS CRAZY-ASS WORLD'S JUST RUININ' THINGS FOR 'EM.
NOW, THEY'RE JUST MAKIN' EXCUSES FOR WHY THEY GONNA FAIL.
"AN' THEY WILL IF THEY KEEP THIS UP. IT'S JUST A MATTER OF TIME..."
Nite Ci

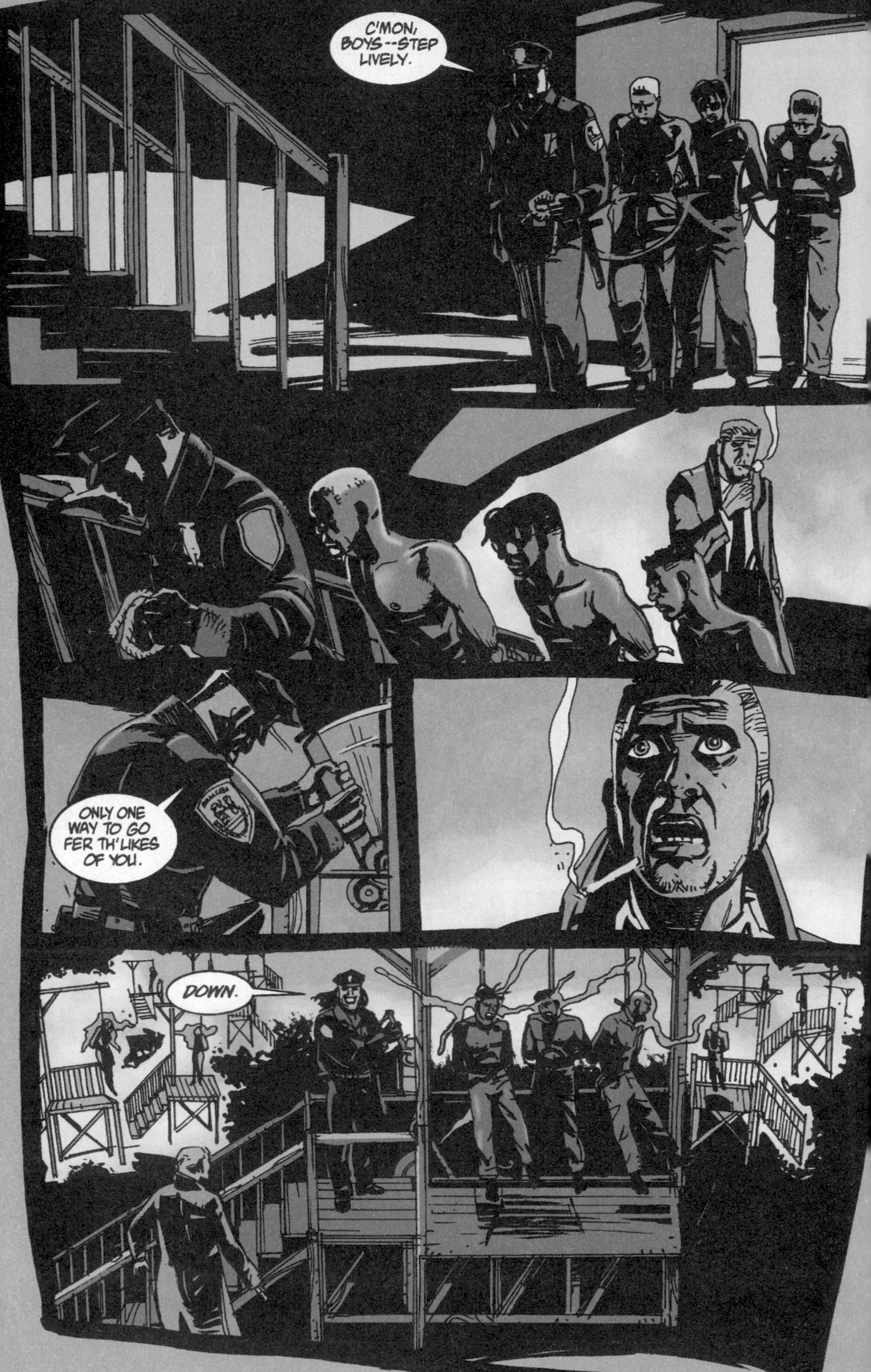
C'MON, BOYS--STEP LIVELY.
ONLY ONE WAY TO GO FER TH' LIKES OF YOU.
DOWN.

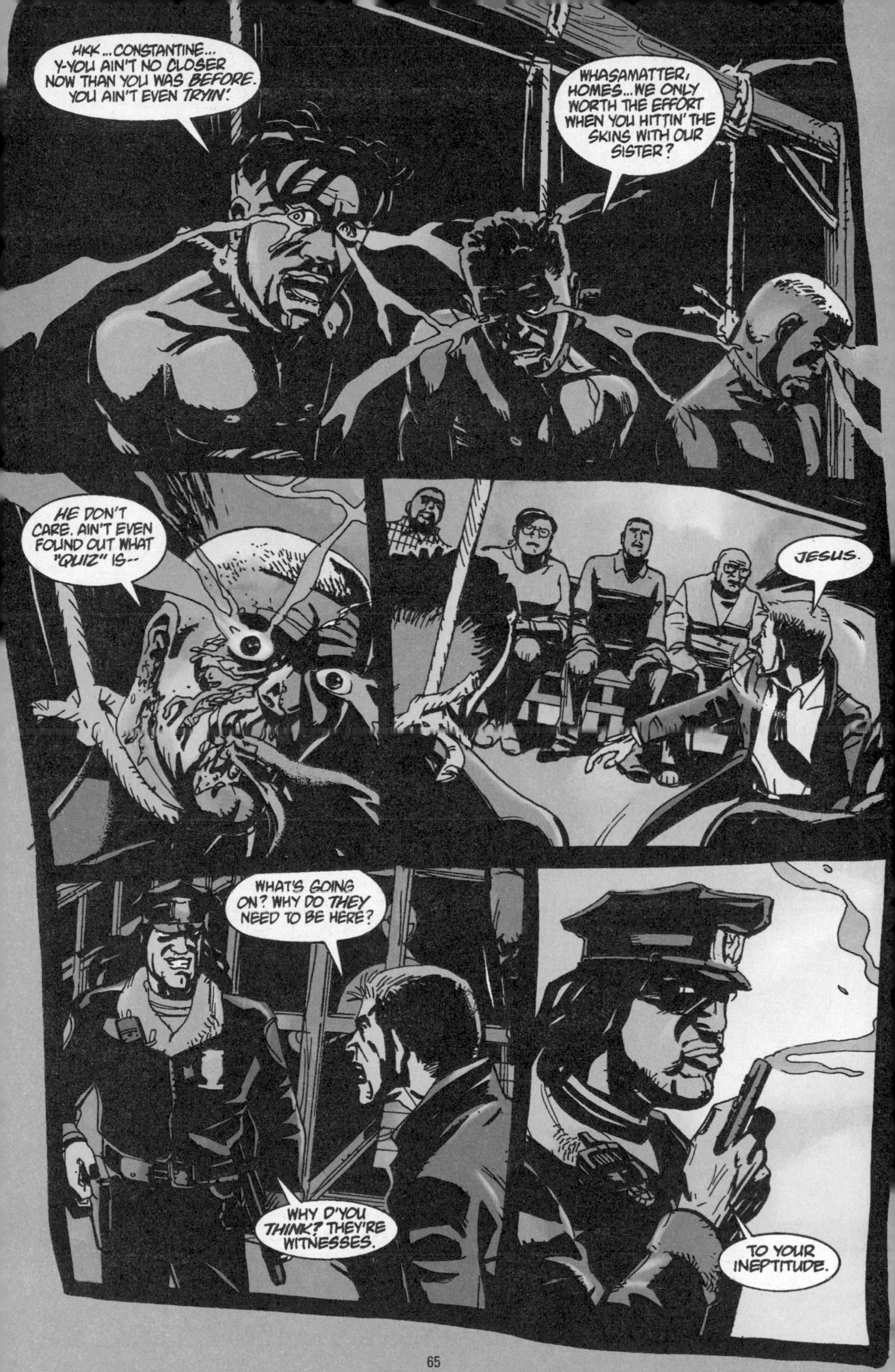
HKK...CONSTANTINE... Y-YOU AIN'T NO CLOSER NOW THAN YOU WAS BEFORE. YOU AIN'T EVEN TRYIN'.
WHASAMATTER, HOMES...WE ONLY WORTH THE EFFORT WHEN YOU HITTIN' THE SKINS WITH OUR SISTER?
HE DON'T CARE. AIN'T EVEN FOUND OUT WHAT "QUIZ" IS--
JESUS.
WHAT'S GOING ON? WHY DO THEY NEED TO BE HERE?
WHY D'YOU THINK? THEY'RE WITNESSES.
TO YOUR INEPTITUDE.

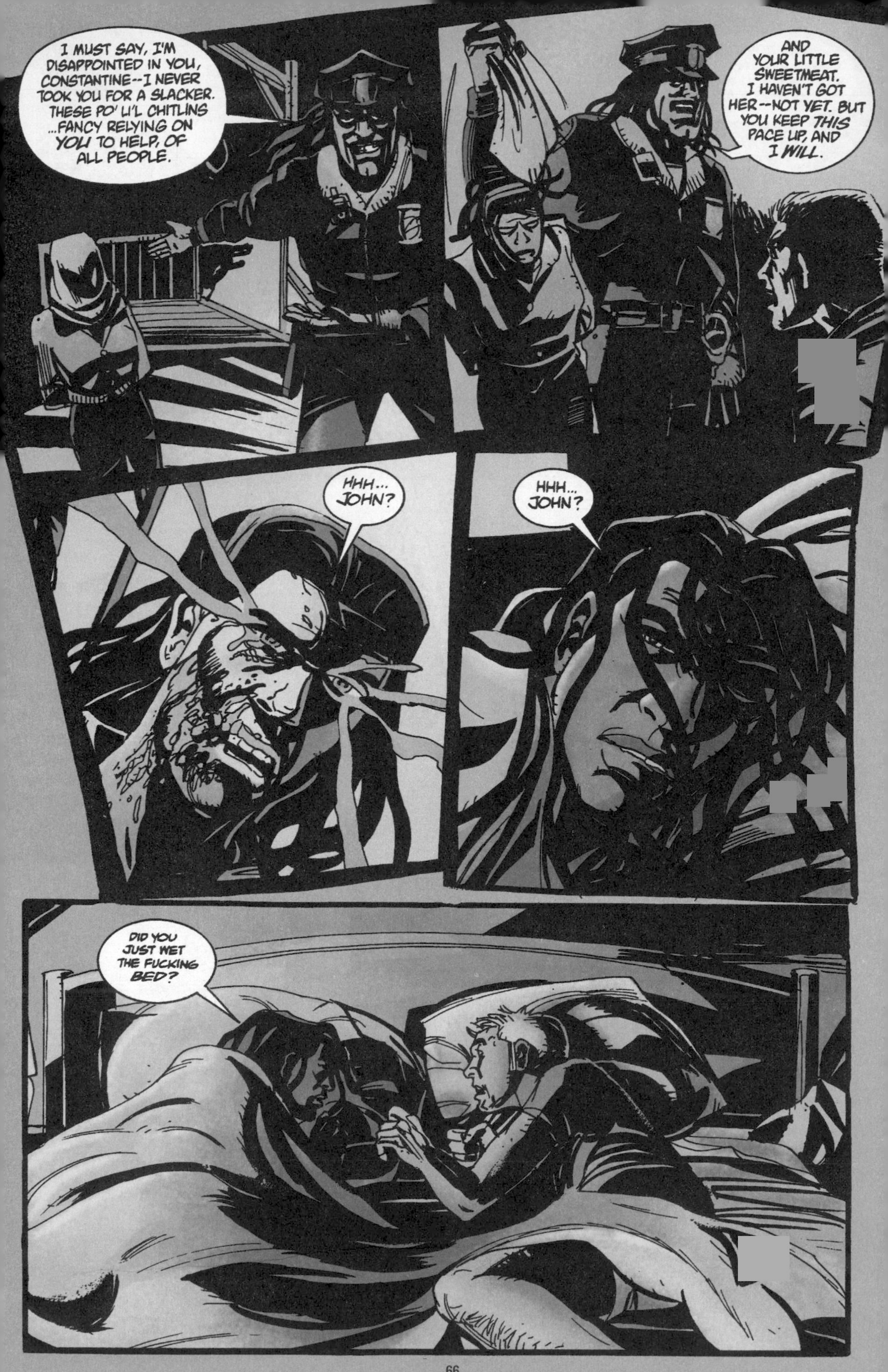
I MUST SAY, I'M DISAPPOINTED IN YOU, CONSTANTINE--I NEVER TOOK YOU FOR A SLACKER. THESE PO' LI'L CHITLINS ...FANCY RELYING ON YOU TO HELP, OF ALL PEOPLE.
AND YOUR LITTLE SWEETMEAT. I HAVEN'T GOT HER--NOT YET. BUT YOU KEEP THIS PACE UP, AND I WILL.
HHH... JOHN?
HHH... JOHN?
DID YOU JUST WET THE FUCKING BED?

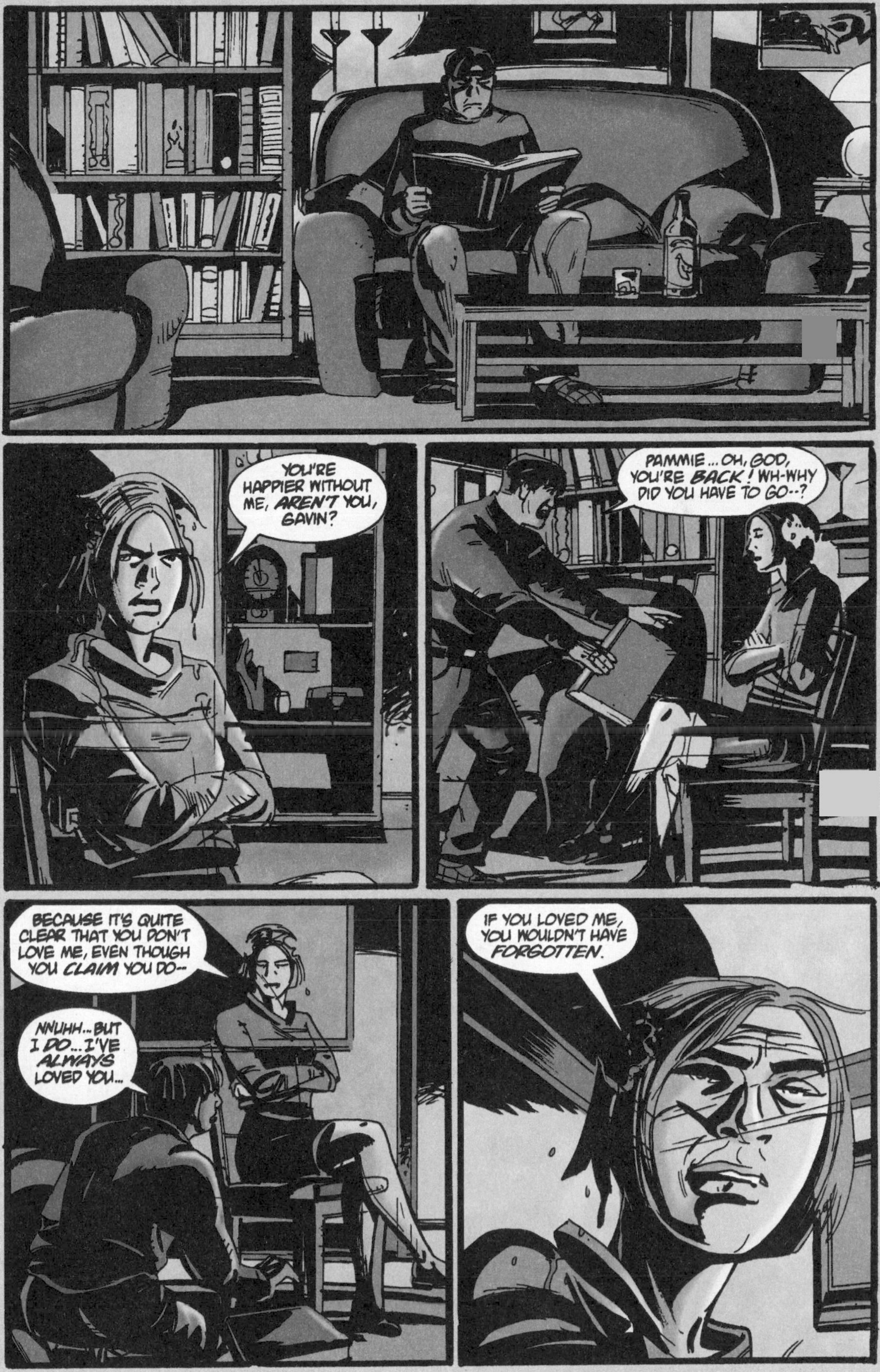
YOU'RE HAPPIER WITHOUT ME, AREN'T YOU, GAVIN?
PAMMIE... OH, GOD, YOU'RE BACK! WH-WHY DID YOU HAVE TO GO--?
BECAUSE IT'S QUITE CLEAR THAT YOU DON'T LOVE ME, EVEN THOUGH YOU CLAIM YOU DO--
NNUHH... BUT I DO... I'VE ALWAYS LOVED YOU...
IF YOU LOVED ME, YOU WOULDN'T HAVE FORGOTTEN.

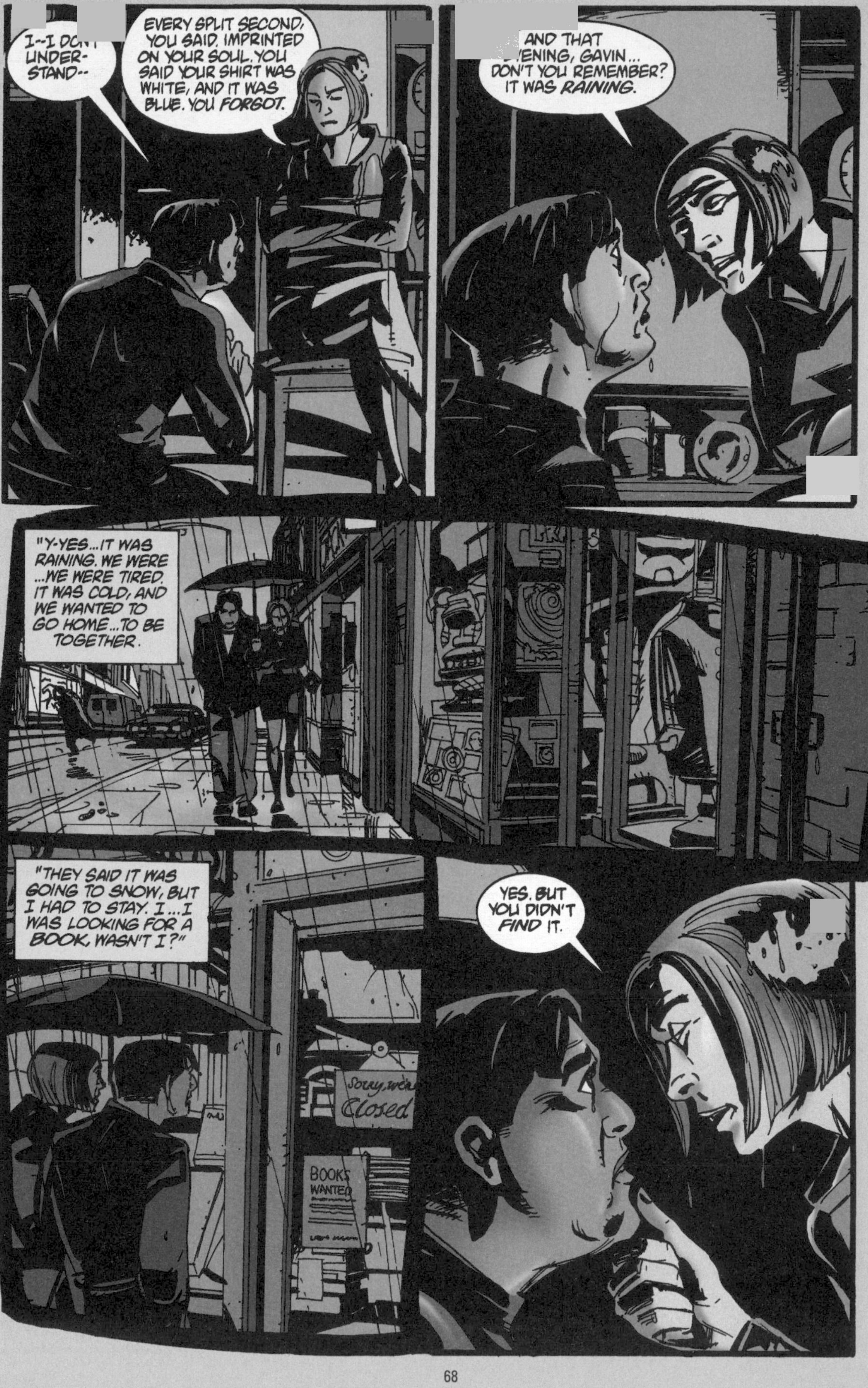
I--I DON'T UNDER-STAND--
EVERY SPLIT SECOND, YOU SAID, IMPRINTED ON YOUR SOUL. YOU SAID YOUR SHIRT WAS WHITE, AND IT WAS BLUE. YOU FORGOT.
AND THAT EVENING, GAVIN... DON'T YOU REMEMBER? IT WAS RAINING.
"Y-YES...IT WAS RAINING. WE WERE ...WE WERE TIRED. IT WAS COLD, AND WE WANTED TO GO HOME...TO BE TOGETHER.
"THEY SAID IT WAS GOING TO SNOW, BUT I HAD TO STAY. I...I WAS LOOKING FOR A BOOK, WASN'T I?"
Sorry, we're Closed
BOOKS WANTED
YES. BUT YOU DIDN'T FIND IT.

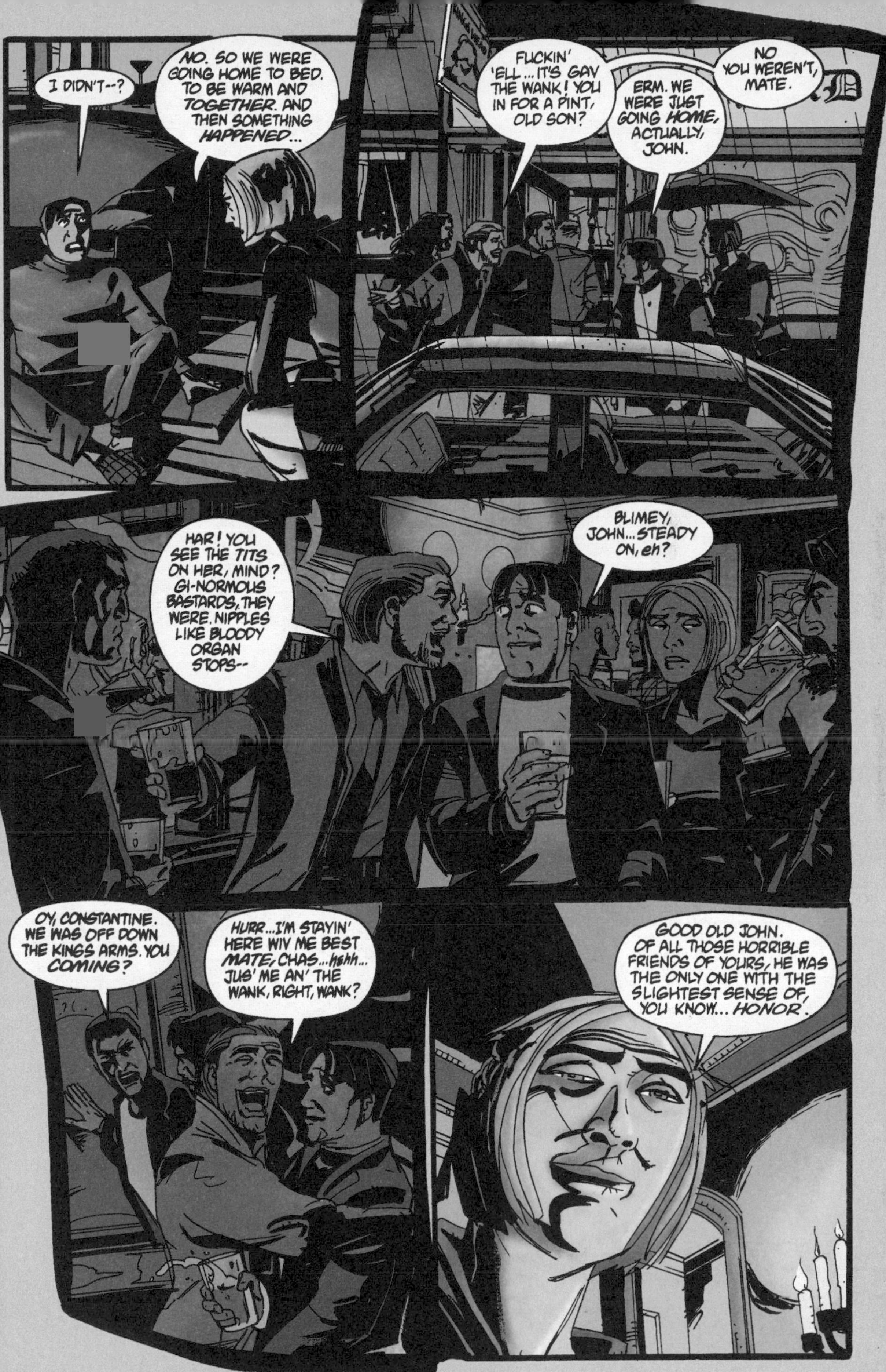
I DIDN'T--?
NO. SO WE WERE GOING HOME TO BED. TO BE WARM AND TOGETHER. AND THEN SOMETHING HAPPENED...
FUCKIN' 'ELL... IT'S GAV THE WANK! YOU IN FOR A PINT, OLD SON?
ERM. WE WERE JUST GOING HOME, ACTUALLY, JOHN.
NO YOU WEREN'T, MATE.
HAR! YOU SEE THE TITS ON HER, MIND? GI-NORMOUS BASTARDS, THEY WERE. NIPPLES LIKE BLOODY ORGAN STOPS--
BLIMEY, JOHN... STEADY ON, eh?
OY, CONSTANTINE. WE WAS OFF DOWN THE KINGS ARMS. YOU COMING?
HURR... I'M STAYIN' HERE WIV ME BEST MATE, CHAS... hehh... JUS' ME AN' THE WANK, RIGHT, WANK?
GOOD OLD JOHN. OF ALL THOSE HORRIBLE FRIENDS OF YOURS, HE WAS THE ONLY ONE WITH THE SLIGHTEST SENSE OF, YOU KNOW... HONOR.

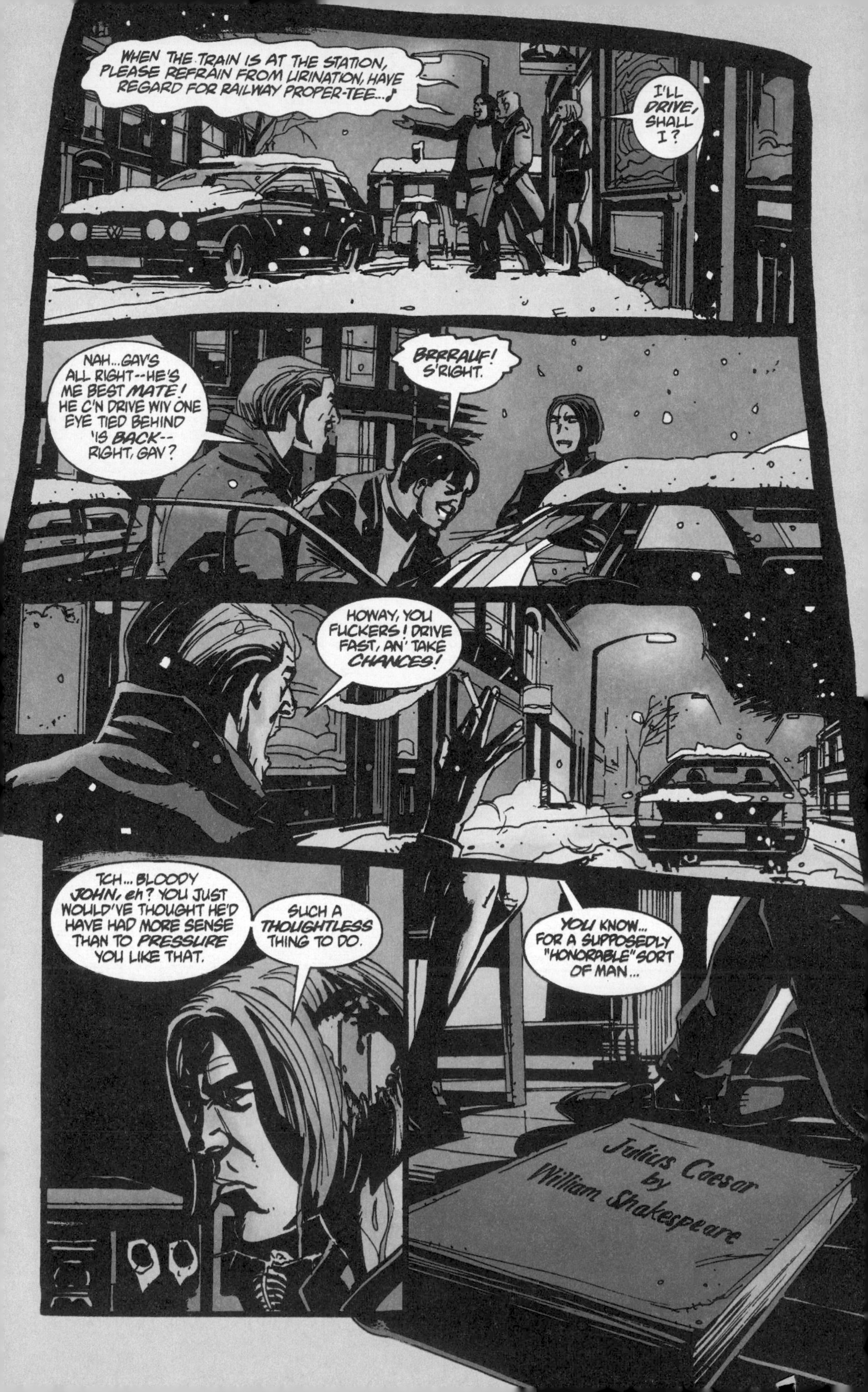
WHEN THE TRAIN IS AT THE STATION, PLEASE REFRAIN FROM URINATION, HAVE REGARD FOR RAILWAY PROPER-TEE...♪
I'LL DRIVE, SHALL I?
NAH...GAV'S ALL RIGHT--HE'S ME BEST MATE! HE C'N DRIVE WIV ONE EYE TIED BEHIND 'IS BACK--RIGHT, GAV?
BRRRAUF! S'RIGHT.
HOWAY, YOU FUCKERS! DRIVE FAST, AN' TAKE CHANCES!
TCH... BLOODY JOHN, eh? YOU JUST WOULD'VE THOUGHT HE'D HAVE HAD MORE SENSE THAN TO PRESSURE YOU LIKE THAT.
SUCH A THOUGHTLESS THING TO DO.
YOU KNOW... FOR A SUPPOSEDLY "HONORABLE" SORT OF MAN...
Julius Caesar by William Shakespeare

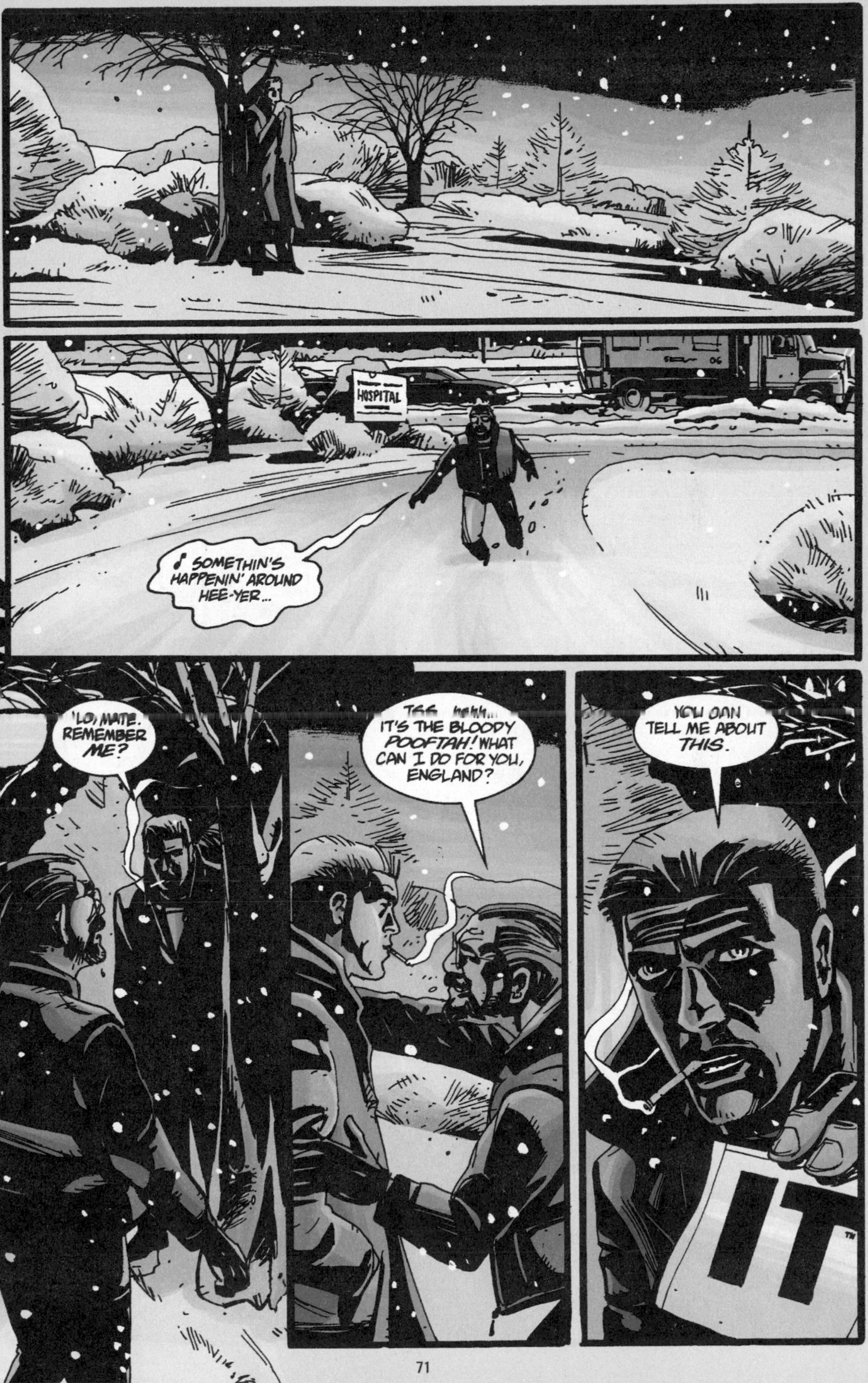
HOSPITAL
♪ SOMETHIN'S HAPPENIN' AROUND HEE-YER...
'LO, MATE. REMEMBER *ME*?
IT'S THE BLOODY *POOFTAH!* WHAT CAN I DO FOR YOU, ENGLAND?
YOU CAN TELL ME ABOUT *THIS*.
IT

HUH? WHAT'S THIS SUPPOSED TO BE?

I'M ASKING YOU.

WHAT THE FUCK WOULD I KNOW ABOUT IT, ENGLISH, AN' WHY WOULD I CARE?

AN' IF I DID KNOW ANYTHING, WHY THE FUCK WOULD I TELL YOU ABOUT IT? I DON'T EVEN KNOW YOU.

V.A. HOSPITAL

VETERANS ADMINISTRATION
HOSPITAL

'CAUSE I'M UP SHIT CREEK, AND I DON'T KNOW WHAT THE FUCK TO DO ABOUT IT.

'CAUSE THERE'S SOMETHING FUCKING 'WEIRD GOIN' ON, AN' MY BIRD'S FAMILY IS IN IT UP TO THEIR TITS. AN' IF I DON'T SORT IT OUT SOON, IT'S GONNA BE A BLOOD BATH, MATE.

LOOK--I CAN'T PUT MY FINGER ON IT, BUT I GET A SENSE OUT OF YOU, ALL RIGHT? I MEAN, EVERYONE AROUND HERE'S GOT SOME "EXPLOIT ME" SIGN PINNED TO THEIR BACK. THE FACT THAT YOU DON'T SEEM TO GIVE A BOLLOCK IS THE PRECISE REASON I'M HERE.

FIVE MINUTES OF YOUR TIME.

JACK DANIEL'S
Jennessee
WHISKEY

72

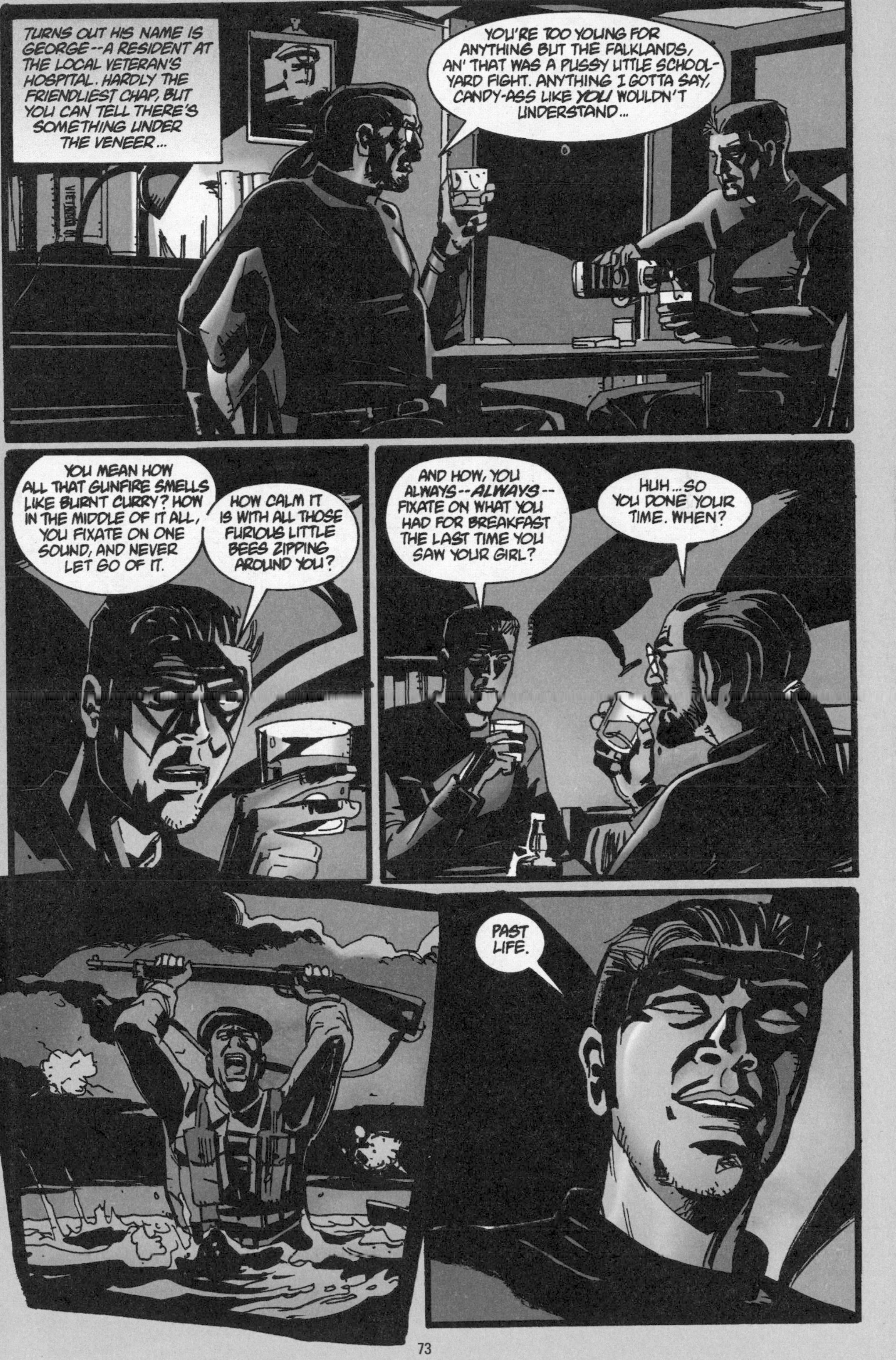
TURNS OUT HIS NAME IS GEORGE--A RESIDENT AT THE LOCAL VETERAN'S HOSPITAL. HARDLY THE FRIENDLIEST CHAP, BUT YOU CAN TELL THERE'S SOMETHING UNDER THE VENEER...
YOU'RE TOO YOUNG FOR ANYTHING BUT THE FALKLANDS, AN' THAT WAS A PUSSY LITTLE SCHOOL-YARD FIGHT. ANYTHING I GOTTA SAY, CANDY-ASS LIKE YOU WOULDN'T UNDERSTAND...
YOU MEAN HOW ALL THAT GUNFIRE SMELLS LIKE BURNT CURRY? HOW IN THE MIDDLE OF IT ALL, YOU FIXATE ON ONE SOUND, AND NEVER LET GO OF IT.
HOW CALM IT IS WITH ALL THOSE FURIOUS LITTLE BEES ZIPPING AROUND YOU?
AND HOW, YOU ALWAYS--ALWAYS--FIXATE ON WHAT YOU HAD FOR BREAKFAST THE LAST TIME YOU SAW YOUR GIRL?
HUH...SO YOU DONE YOUR TIME. WHEN?
PAST LIFE.

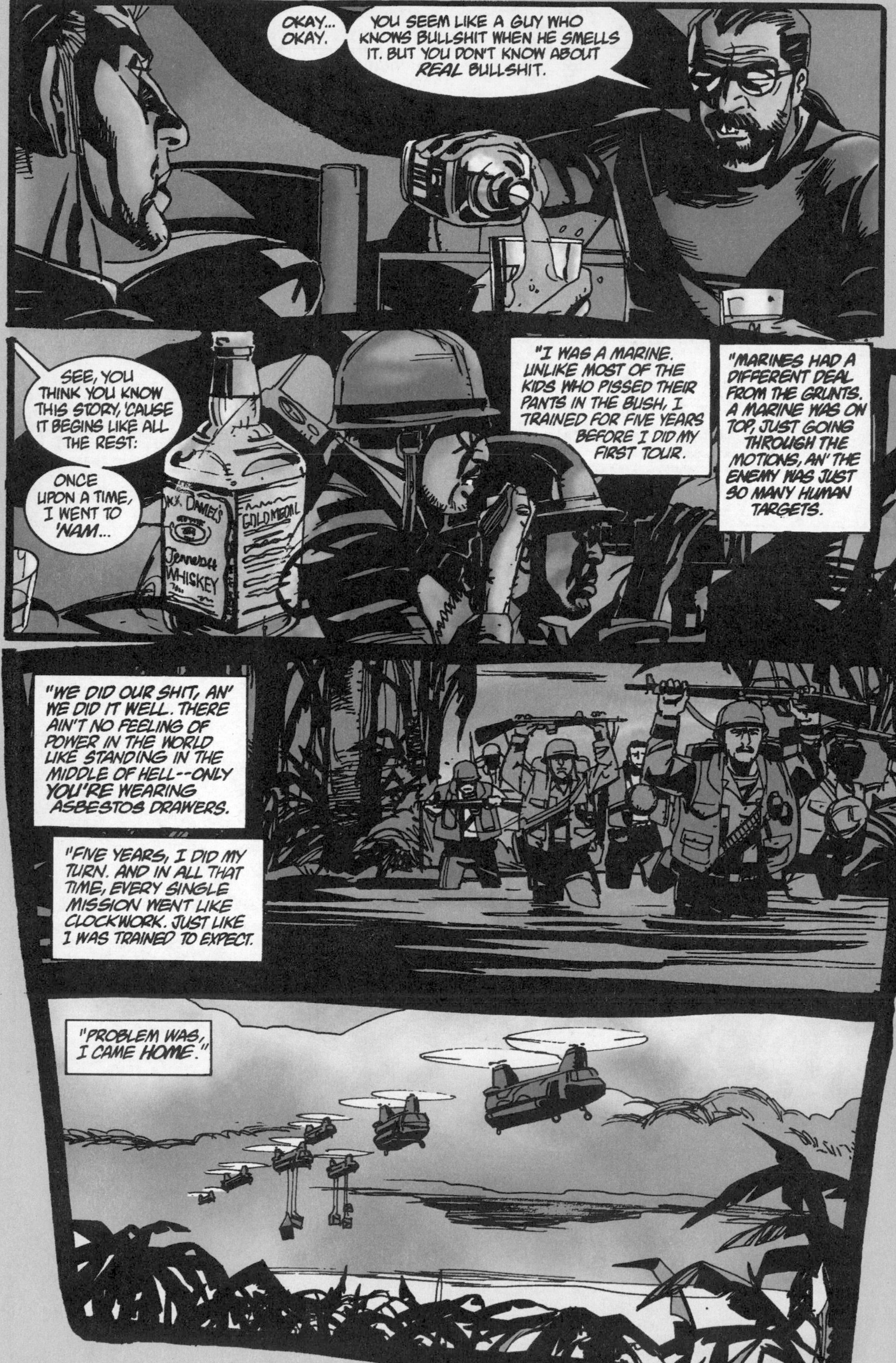
OKAY... OKAY.
YOU SEEM LIKE A GUY WHO KNOWS BULLSHIT WHEN HE SMELLS IT. BUT YOU DON'T KNOW ABOUT REAL BULLSHIT.
SEE, YOU THINK YOU KNOW THIS STORY, 'CAUSE IT BEGINS LIKE ALL THE REST:
ONCE UPON A TIME, I WENT TO 'NAM...
"I WAS A MARINE. UNLIKE MOST OF THE KIDS WHO PISSED THEIR PANTS IN THE BUSH, I TRAINED FOR FIVE YEARS BEFORE I DID MY FIRST TOUR.
"MARINES HAD A DIFFERENT DEAL FROM THE GRUNTS. A MARINE WAS ON TOP, JUST GOING THROUGH THE MOTIONS, AN' THE ENEMY WAS JUST SO MANY HUMAN TARGETS.
"WE DID OUR SHIT, AN' WE DID IT WELL. THERE AIN'T NO FEELING OF POWER IN THE WORLD LIKE STANDING IN THE MIDDLE OF HELL--ONLY YOU'RE WEARING ASBESTOS DRAWERS.
"FIVE YEARS, I DID MY TURN. AND IN ALL THAT TIME, EVERY SINGLE MISSION WENT LIKE CLOCKWORK. JUST LIKE I WAS TRAINED TO EXPECT.
"PROBLEM WAS, I CAME HOME."

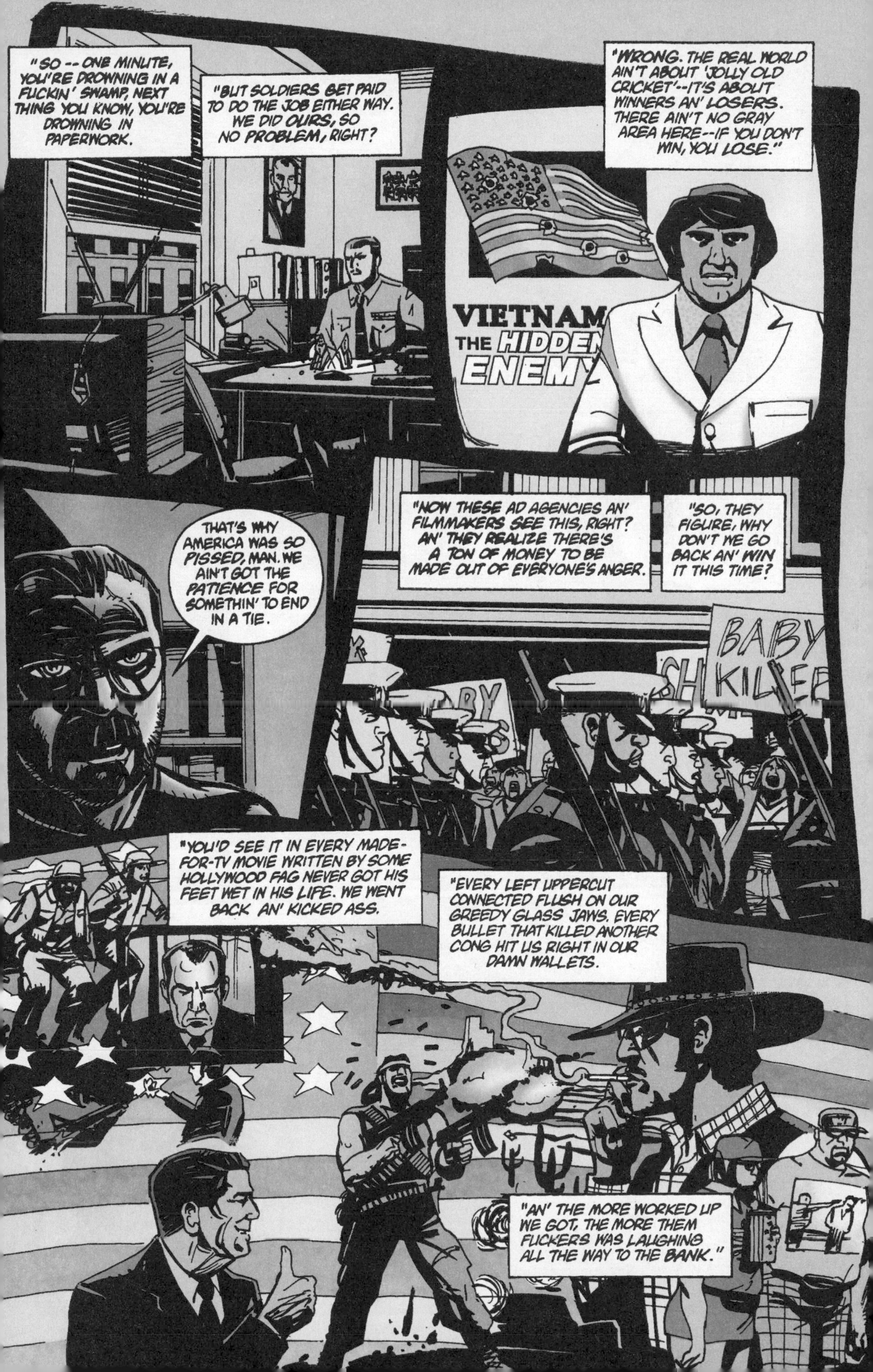
"SO -- ONE MINUTE, YOU'RE DROWNING IN A FUCKIN' SWAMP, NEXT THING YOU KNOW, YOU'RE DROWNING IN PAPERWORK.
"BUT SOLDIERS GET PAID TO DO THE JOB EITHER WAY. WE DID OURS, SO NO PROBLEM, RIGHT?
"WRONG. THE REAL WORLD AIN'T ABOUT 'JOLLY OLD CRICKET'--IT'S ABOUT WINNERS AN' LOSERS. THERE AIN'T NO GRAY AREA HERE--IF YOU DON'T WIN, YOU LOSE."
VIETNAM THE HIDDEN ENEMY
THAT'S WHY AMERICA WAS SO PISSED, MAN. WE AIN'T GOT THE PATIENCE FOR SOMETHIN' TO END IN A TIE.
"NOW THESE AD AGENCIES AN' FILMMAKERS SEE THIS, RIGHT? AN' THEY REALIZE THERE'S A TON OF MONEY TO BE MADE OUT OF EVERYONE'S ANGER.
"SO, THEY FIGURE, WHY DON'T WE GO BACK AN' WIN IT THIS TIME?
BABY KILLE
"YOU'D SEE IT IN EVERY MADE-FOR-TV MOVIE WRITTEN BY SOME HOLLYWOOD FAG NEVER GOT HIS FEET WET IN HIS LIFE. WE WENT BACK AN' KICKED ASS.
"EVERY LEFT UPPERCUT CONNECTED FLUSH ON OUR GREEDY GLASS JAWS. EVERY BULLET THAT KILLED ANOTHER CONG HIT US RIGHT IN OUR DAMN WALLETS.
"AN' THE MORE WORKED UP WE GOT, THE MORE THEM FUCKERS WAS LAUGHING ALL THE WAY TO THE BANK."

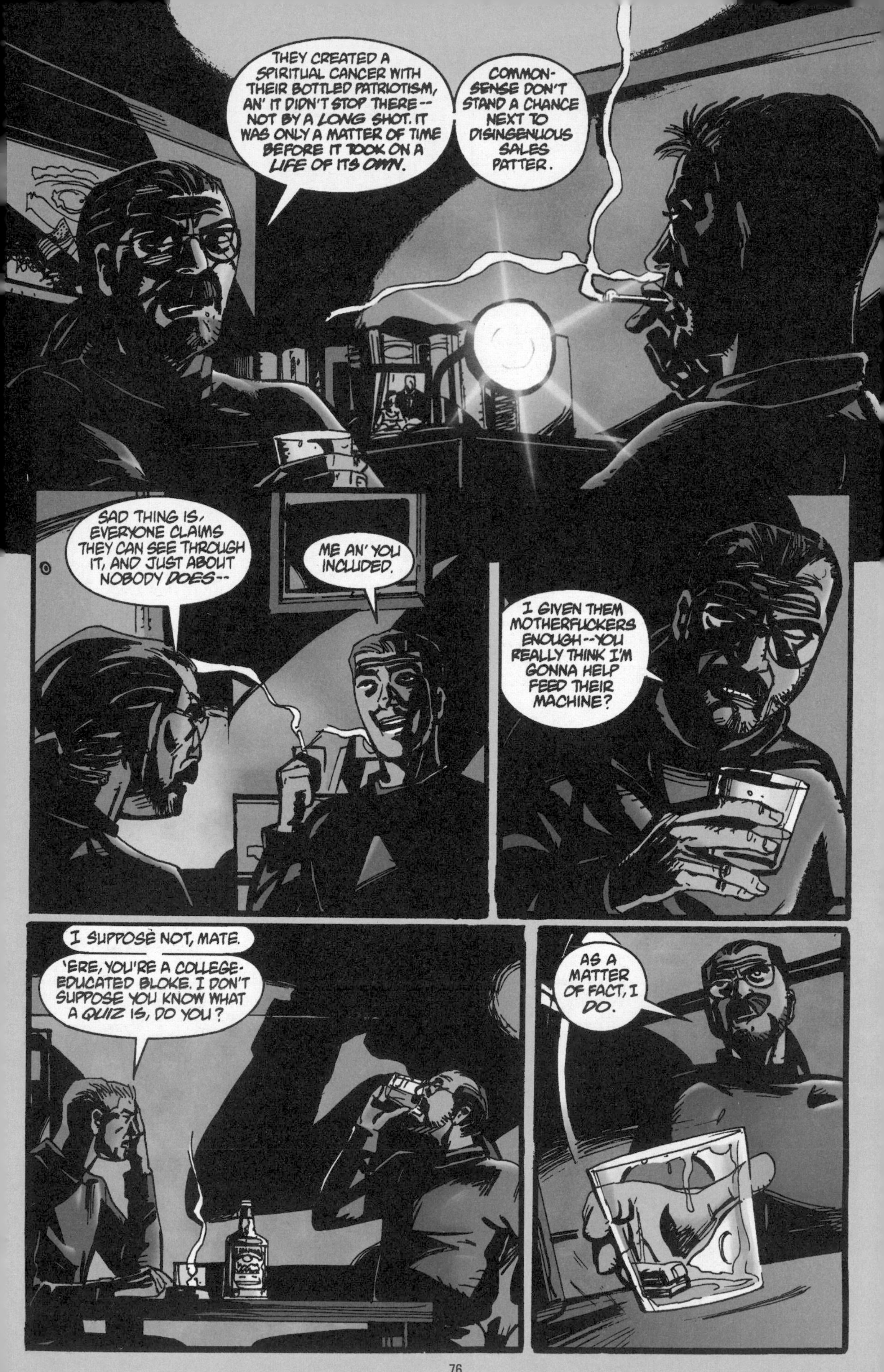
THEY CREATED A SPIRITUAL CANCER WITH THEIR BOTTLED PATRIOTISM, AN' IT DIDN'T STOP THERE-- NOT BY A LONG SHOT. IT WAS ONLY A MATTER OF TIME BEFORE IT TOOK ON A LIFE OF ITS OWN.
COMMON-SENSE DON'T STAND A CHANCE NEXT TO DISINGENUOUS SALES PATTER.
SAD THING IS, EVERYONE CLAIMS THEY CAN SEE THROUGH IT, AND JUST ABOUT NOBODY DOES--
ME AN' YOU INCLUDED.
I GIVEN THEM MOTHERFUCKERS ENOUGH--YOU REALLY THINK I'M GONNA HELP FEED THEIR MACHINE?
I SUPPOSE NOT, MATE.
'ERE, YOU'RE A COLLEGE-EDUCATED BLOKE. I DON'T SUPPOSE YOU KNOW WHAT A QUIZ IS, DO YOU?
AS A MATTER OF FACT, I DO.

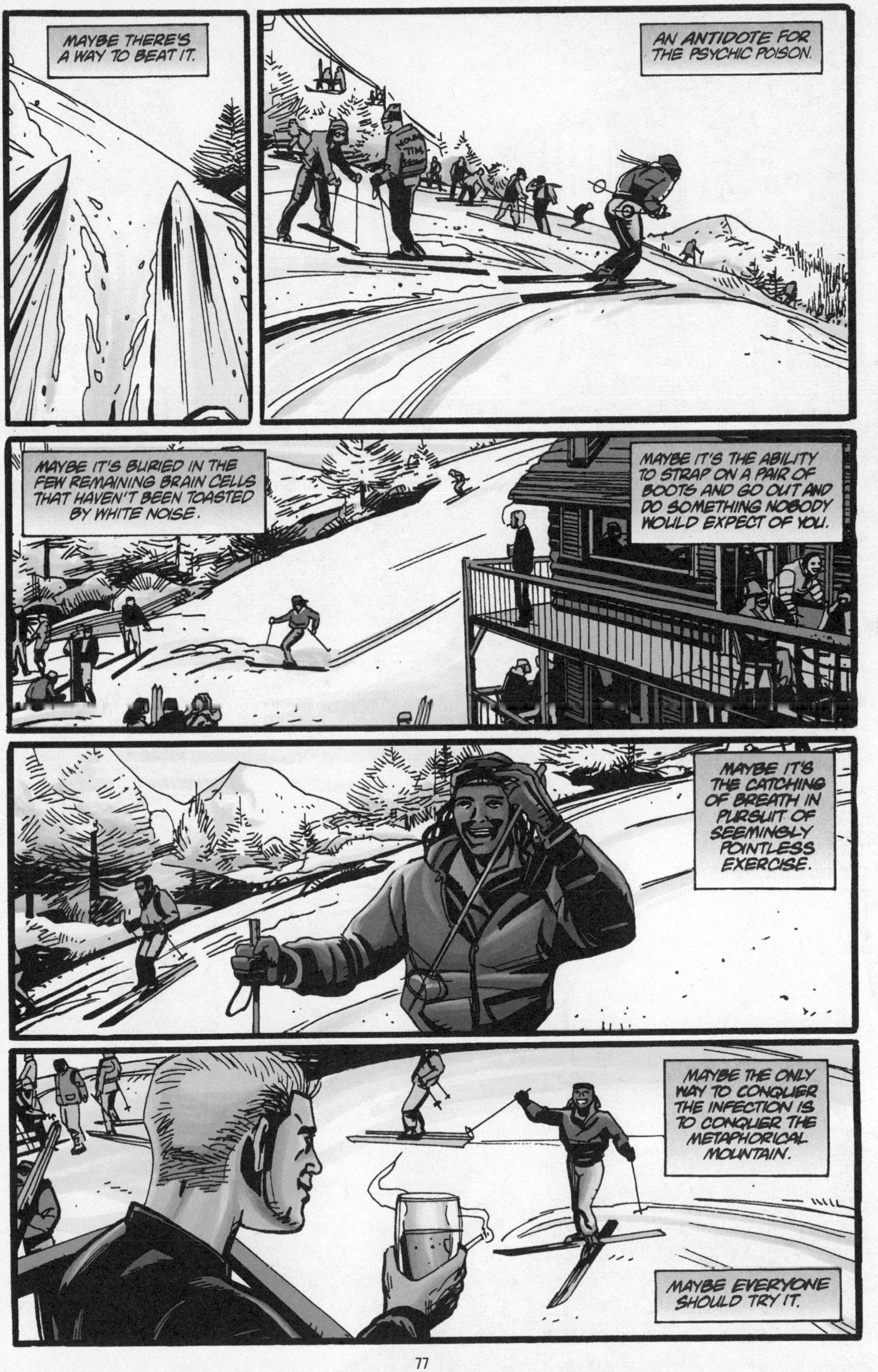
MAYBE THERE'S A WAY TO BEAT IT.
AN ANTIDOTE FOR THE PSYCHIC POISON.
MAYBE IT'S BURIED IN THE FEW REMAINING BRAIN CELLS THAT HAVEN'T BEEN TOASTED BY WHITE NOISE.
MAYBE IT'S THE ABILITY TO STRAP ON A PAIR OF BOOTS AND GO OUT AND DO SOMETHING NOBODY WOULD EXPECT OF YOU.
MAYBE IT'S THE CATCHING OF BREATH IN PURSUIT OF SEEMINGLY POINTLESS EXERCISE.
MAYBE THE ONLY WAY TO CONQUER THE INFECTION IS TO CONQUER THE METAPHORICAL MOUNTAIN.
MAYBE EVERYONE SHOULD TRY IT.

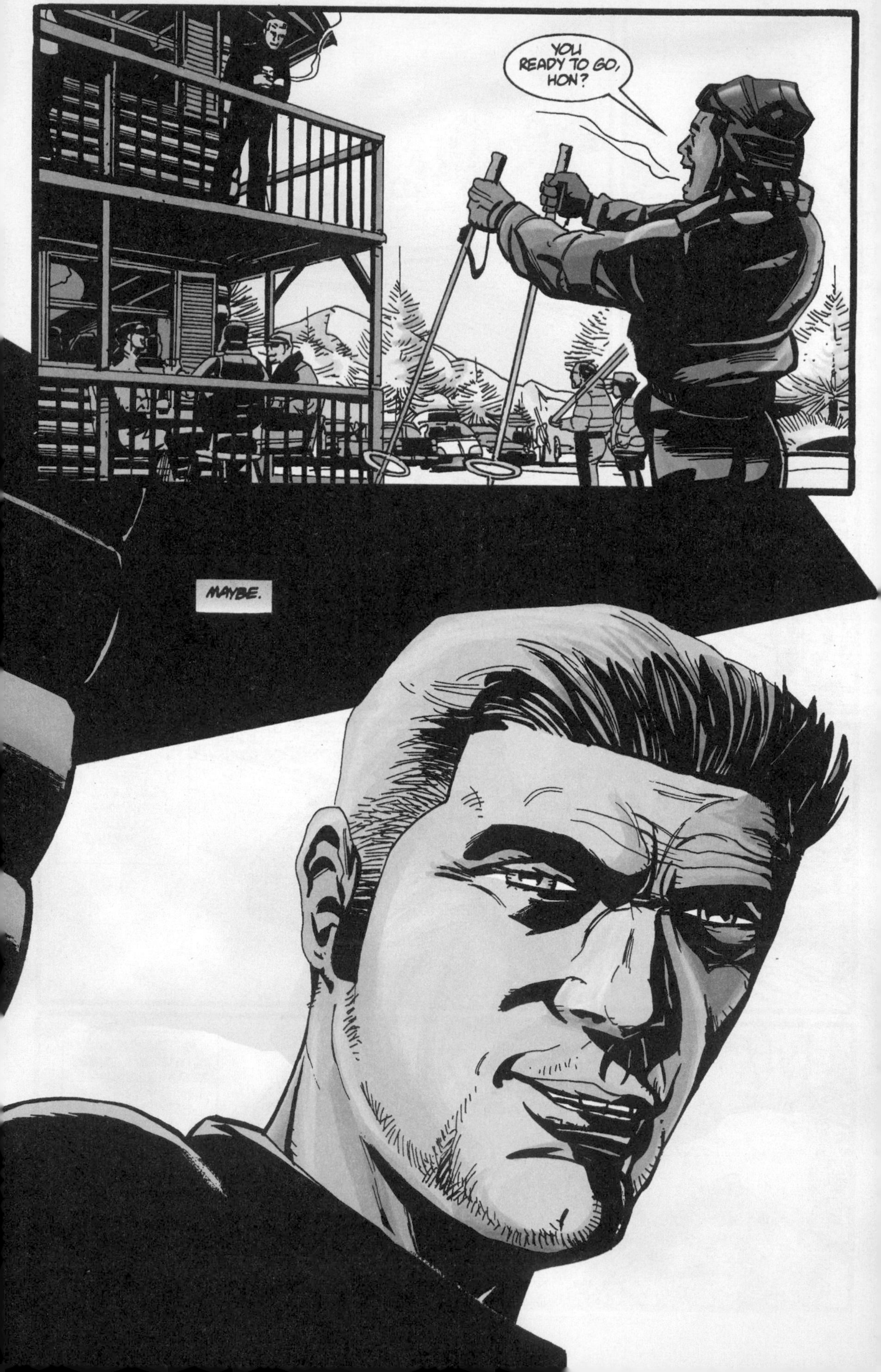
YOU READY TO GO, HON?
MAYBE.

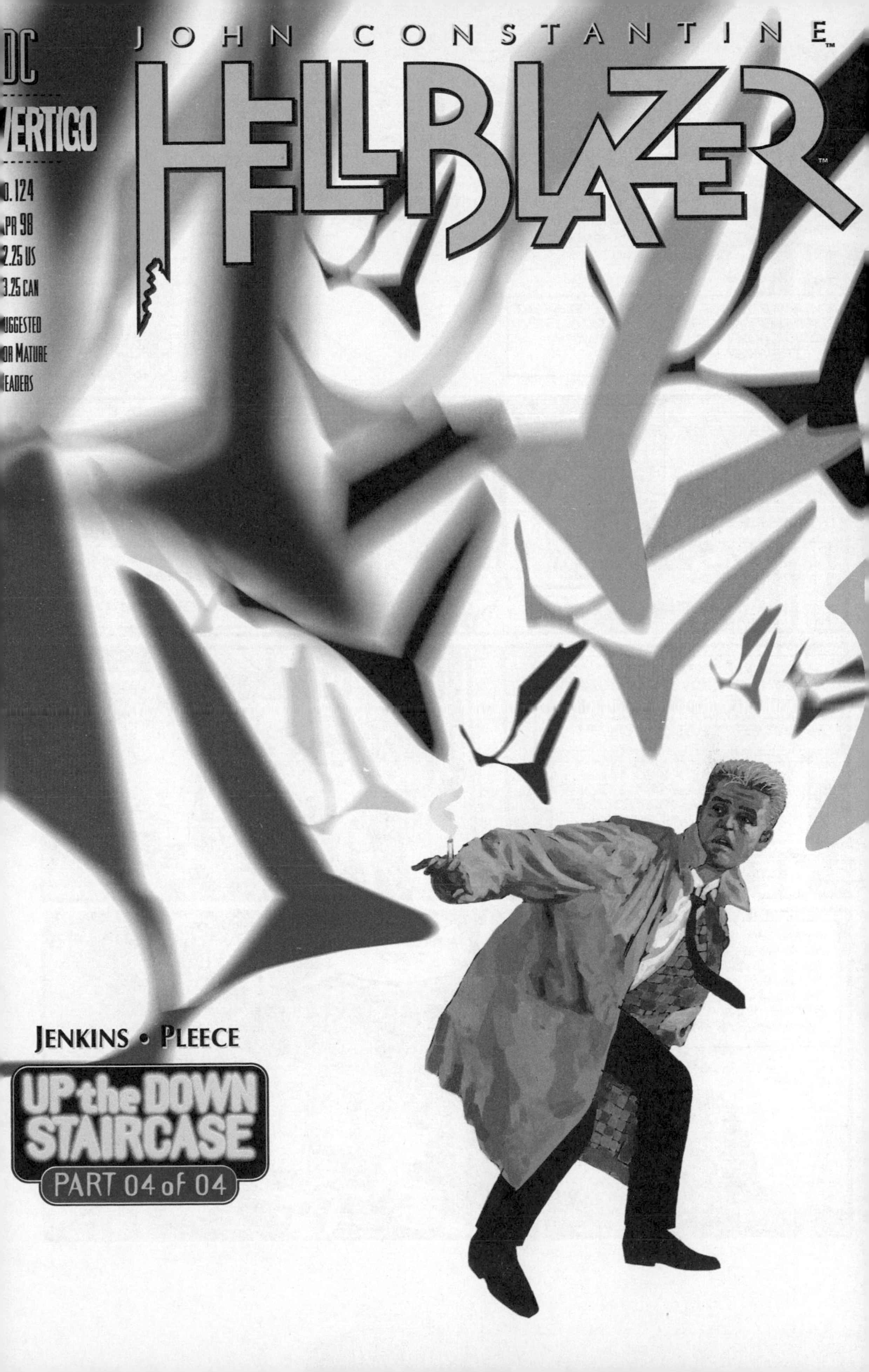
DC
VERTIGO
JOHN CONSTANTINE
HELLBLAZER
o.124
PR 98
2.25 US
3.25 CAN
UGGESTED
OR MATURE
EADERS
JENKINS • PLEECE
UP the DOWN STAIRCASE
PART 04 of 04

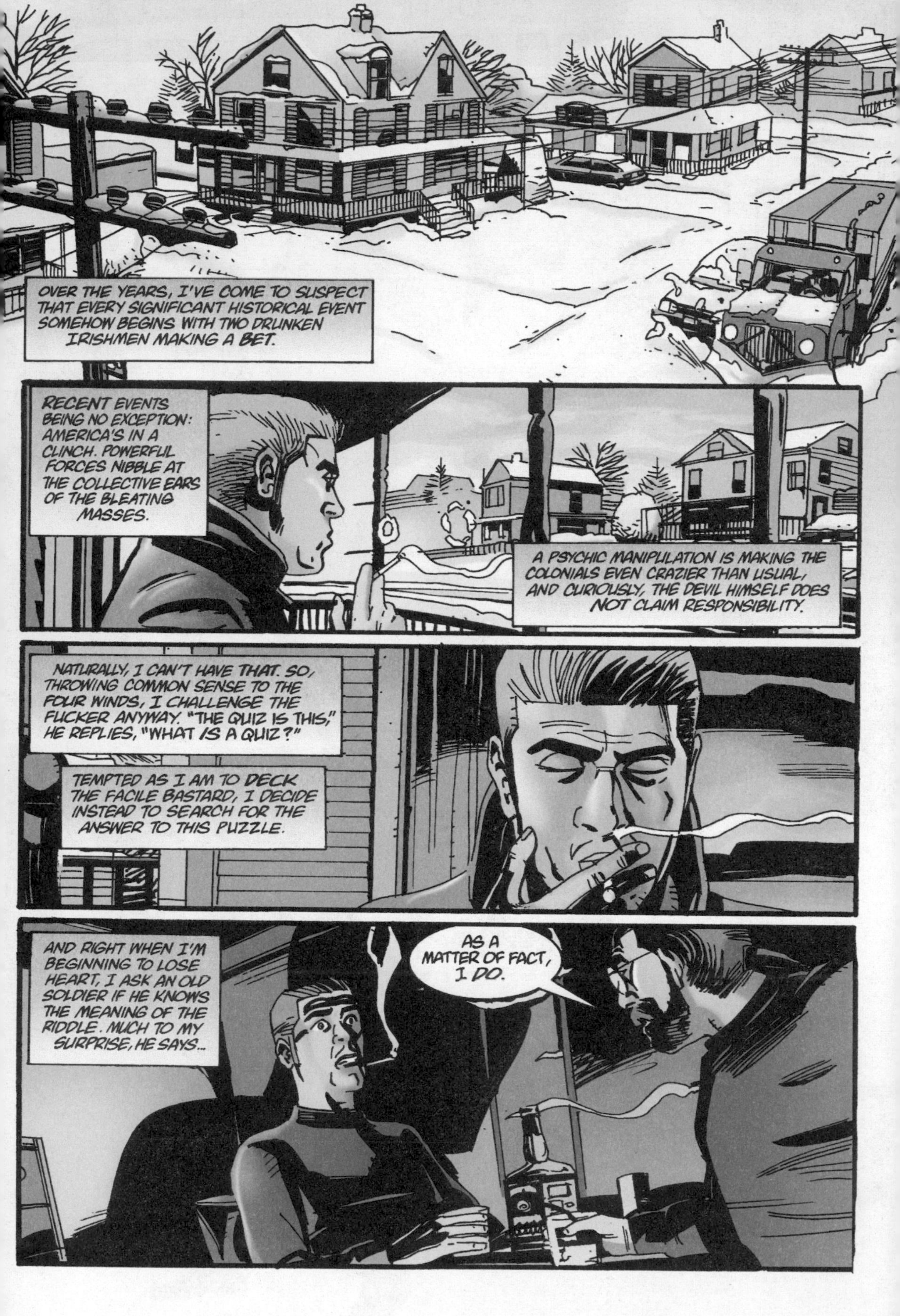

OVER THE YEARS, I'VE COME TO SUSPECT THAT EVERY SIGNIFICANT HISTORICAL EVENT SOMEHOW BEGINS WITH TWO DRUNKEN IRISHMEN MAKING A BET.
RECENT EVENTS BEING NO EXCEPTION: AMERICA'S IN A CLINCH. POWERFUL FORCES NIBBLE AT THE COLLECTIVE EARS OF THE BLEATING MASSES.
A PSYCHIC MANIPULATION IS MAKING THE COLONIALS EVEN CRAZIER THAN USUAL, AND CURIOUSLY, THE DEVIL HIMSELF DOES NOT CLAIM RESPONSIBILITY.
NATURALLY, I CAN'T HAVE THAT. SO, THROWING COMMON SENSE TO THE FOUR WINDS, I CHALLENGE THE FUCKER ANYWAY. "THE QUIZ IS THIS," HE REPLIES, "WHAT IS A QUIZ?"
TEMPTED AS I AM TO DECK THE FACILE BASTARD, I DECIDE INSTEAD TO SEARCH FOR THE ANSWER TO THIS PUZZLE.
AND RIGHT WHEN I'M BEGINNING TO LOSE HEART, I ASK AN OLD SOLDIER IF HE KNOWS THE MEANING OF THE RIDDLE. MUCH TO MY SURPRISE, HE SAYS...
AS A MATTER OF FACT, I DO.

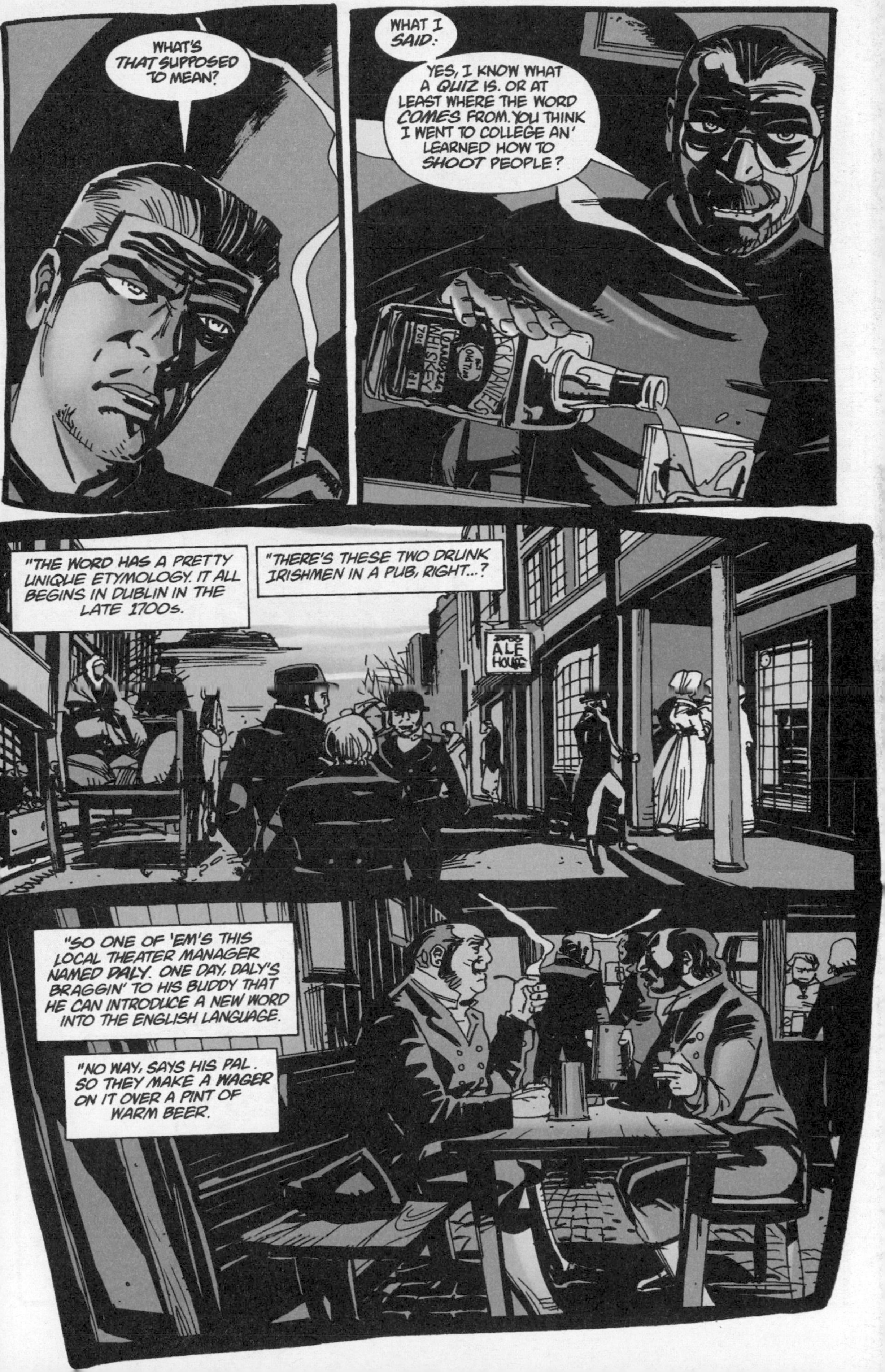
WHAT'S THAT SUPPOSED TO MEAN?
WHAT I SAID:
YES, I KNOW WHAT A QUIZ IS. OR AT LEAST WHERE THE WORD COMES FROM. YOU THINK I WENT TO COLLEGE AN' LEARNED HOW TO SHOOT PEOPLE?
JACK DANIEL'S
"THE WORD HAS A PRETTY UNIQUE ETYMOLOGY. IT ALL BEGINS IN DUBLIN IN THE LATE 1700s.
"THERE'S THESE TWO DRUNK IRISHMEN IN A PUB, RIGHT...?
ALE HOUSE
"SO ONE OF 'EM'S THIS LOCAL THEATER MANAGER NAMED DALY. ONE DAY, DALY'S BRAGGIN' TO HIS BUDDY THAT HE CAN INTRODUCE A NEW WORD INTO THE ENGLISH LANGUAGE.
"NO WAY, SAYS HIS PAL. SO THEY MAKE A WAGER ON IT OVER A PINT OF WARM BEER.

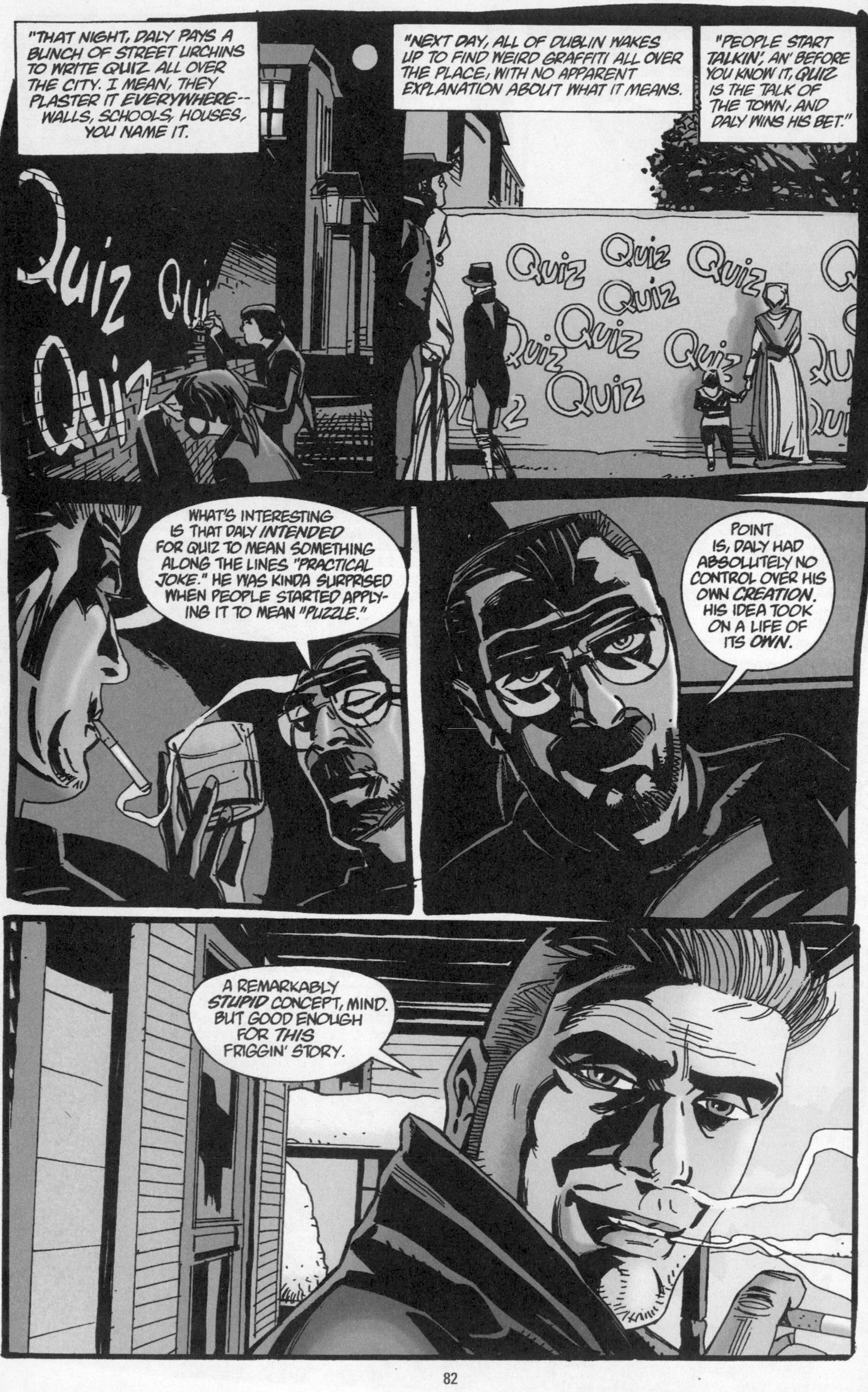
"THAT NIGHT, DALY PAYS A BUNCH OF STREET URCHINS TO WRITE QUIZ ALL OVER THE CITY. I MEAN, THEY PLASTER IT EVERYWHERE-- WALLS, SCHOOLS, HOUSES, YOU NAME IT.
Quiz Quiz Quiz
"NEXT DAY, ALL OF DUBLIN WAKES UP TO FIND WEIRD GRAFFITI ALL OVER THE PLACE, WITH NO APPARENT EXPLANATION ABOUT WHAT IT MEANS.
"PEOPLE START TALKIN', AN' BEFORE YOU KNOW IT, QUIZ IS THE TALK OF THE TOWN, AND DALY WINS HIS BET."
Quiz Quiz Quiz Quiz Quiz Quiz Quiz Quiz
WHAT'S INTERESTING IS THAT DALY INTENDED FOR QUIZ TO MEAN SOMETHING ALONG THE LINES "PRACTICAL JOKE." HE WAS KINDA SURPRISED WHEN PEOPLE STARTED APPLYING IT TO MEAN "PUZZLE."
POINT IS, DALY HAD ABSOLUTELY NO CONTROL OVER HIS OWN CREATION. HIS IDEA TOOK ON A LIFE OF ITS OWN.
A REMARKABLY STUPID CONCEPT, MIND. BUT GOOD ENOUGH FOR THIS FRIGGIN' STORY.

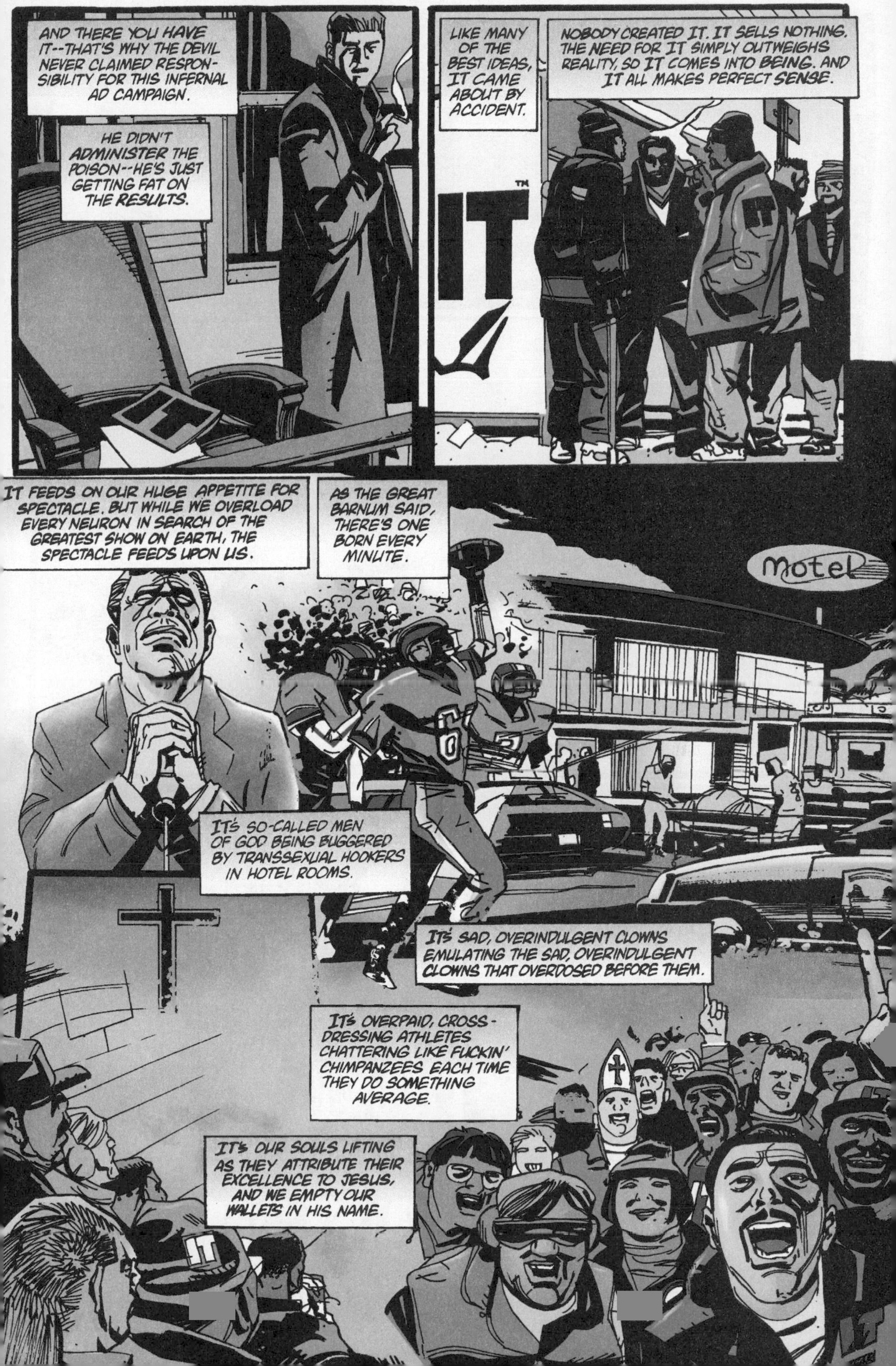
AND THERE YOU HAVE IT--THAT'S WHY THE DEVIL NEVER CLAIMED RESPONSIBILITY FOR THIS INFERNAL AD CAMPAIGN.
HE DIDN'T ADMINISTER THE POISON--HE'S JUST GETTING FAT ON THE RESULTS.
LIKE MANY OF THE BEST IDEAS, IT CAME ABOUT BY ACCIDENT.
NOBODY CREATED IT. IT SELLS NOTHING. THE NEED FOR IT SIMPLY OUTWEIGHS REALITY, SO IT COMES INTO BEING. AND IT ALL MAKES PERFECT SENSE.
IT™
IT FEEDS ON OUR HUGE APPETITE FOR SPECTACLE. BUT WHILE WE OVERLOAD EVERY NEURON IN SEARCH OF THE GREATEST SHOW ON EARTH, THE SPECTACLE FEEDS UPON US.
AS THE GREAT BARNUM SAID, THERE'S ONE BORN EVERY MINUTE.
Motel
IT'S SO-CALLED MEN OF GOD BEING BUGGERED BY TRANSSEXUAL HOOKERS IN HOTEL ROOMS.
IT'S SAD, OVERINDULGENT CLOWNS EMULATING THE SAD, OVERINDULGENT CLOWNS THAT OVERDOSED BEFORE THEM.
IT'S OVERPAID, CROSS-DRESSING ATHLETES CHATTERING LIKE FUCKIN' CHIMPANZEES EACH TIME THEY DO SOMETHING AVERAGE.
IT'S OUR SOULS LIFTING AS THEY ATTRIBUTE THEIR EXCELLENCE TO JESUS, AND WE EMPTY OUR WALLETS IN HIS NAME.

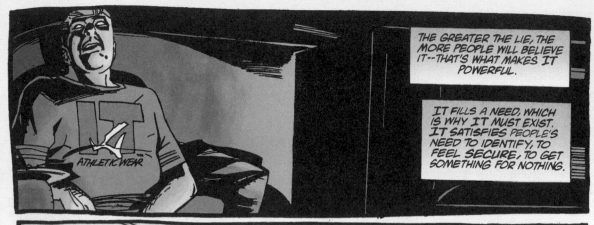

THE GREATER THE LIE, THE MORE PEOPLE WILL BELIEVE IT--THAT'S WHAT MAKES IT POWERFUL.

IT FILLS A NEED, WHICH IS WHY IT MUST EXIST. IT SATISFIES PEOPLE'S NEED TO IDENTIFY, TO FEEL SECURE, TO GET SOMETHING FOR NOTHING.

BUT SOME ARE AFFECTED TO A LESSER DEGREE-- THE ONES WHO ACTUALLY LIKE TO GO THROUGH THE PROCESS OF FALLING DOWN.

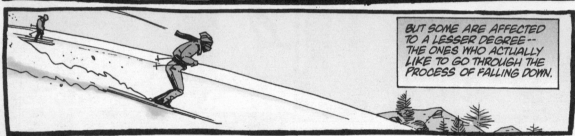

IT'S NOT A MATTER OF WATCHING IT ON THE BLOODY TELLY, IS IT? IT'S A MATTER OF GOING OUT AND ACTUALLY DOING IT.

IT'S LANDING ON YOUR ARSE, AND GETTING COLD AND WET AND TIRED. AND ENJOYING IT.

AND MAYBE THAT'S THE WAY YOU COUNTERACT THE POISON.

YOU INTRODUCE A MAVERICK IDEA.

up the down staircase

PAUL JENKINS
writer

WARREN PLEECE
artist

JAMES SINCLAIR
colorist

part four

DIGITAL CHAMELEON
separations

CLEM ROBINS
letterer

AXEL ALONSO
editor

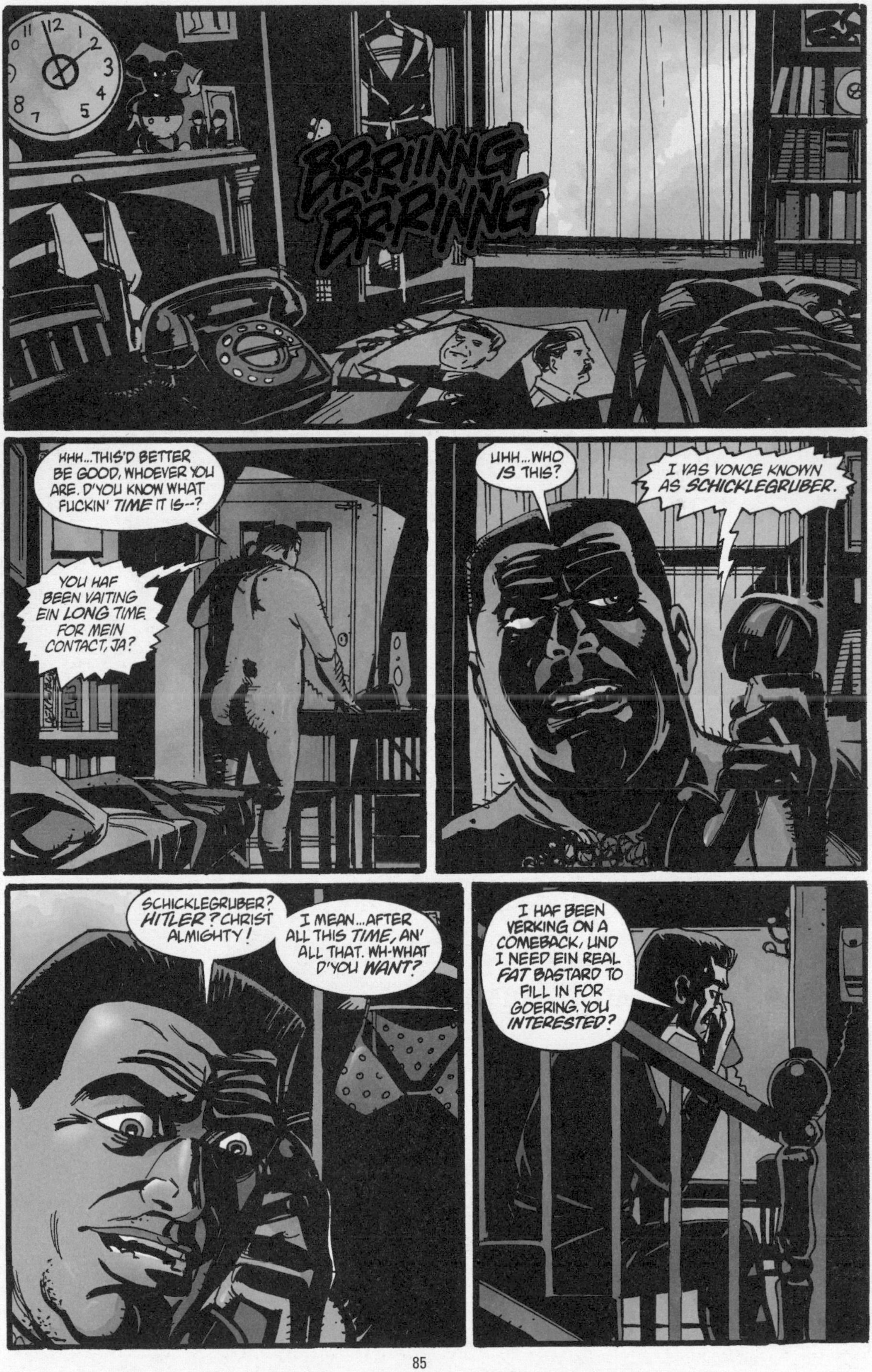
BRRIINNG
BRRINNG
KHH...THIS'D BETTER BE GOOD, WHOEVER YOU ARE. D'YOU KNOW WHAT FUCKIN' TIME IT IS--?
YOU HAF BEEN VAITING EIN LONG TIME. FOR MEIN CONTACT, JA?
UHH...WHO IS THIS?
I VAS VONCE KNOWN AS SCHICKLEGRUBER.
SCHICKLEGRUBER? HITLER? CHRIST ALMIGHTY!
I MEAN...AFTER ALL THIS TIME, AN' ALL THAT. WH-WHAT D'YOU WANT?
I HAF BEEN VERKING ON A COMEBACK, UND I NEED EIN REAL FAT BASTARD TO FILL IN FOR GOERING. YOU INTERESTED?

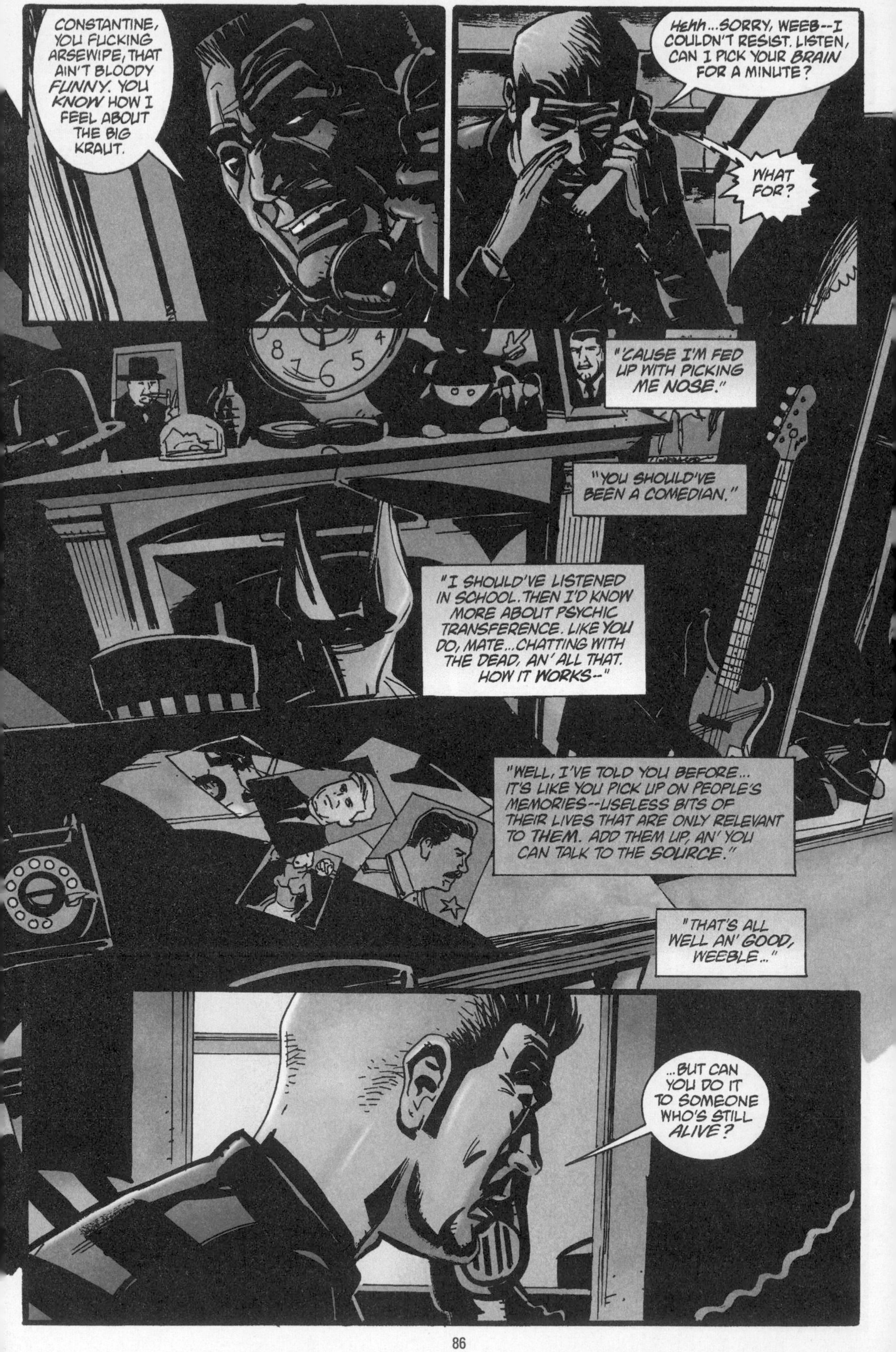
CONSTANTINE, YOU FUCKING ARSEWIPE, THAT AIN'T BLOODY FUNNY. YOU KNOW HOW I FEEL ABOUT THE BIG KRAUT.
Hehh...SORRY, WEEB--I COULDN'T RESIST. LISTEN, CAN I PICK YOUR BRAIN FOR A MINUTE?
WHAT FOR?
"'CAUSE I'M FED UP WITH PICKING ME NOSE."
"YOU SHOULD'VE BEEN A COMEDIAN."
"I SHOULD'VE LISTENED IN SCHOOL. THEN I'D KNOW MORE ABOUT PSYCHIC TRANSFERENCE. LIKE YOU DO, MATE...CHATTING WITH THE DEAD, AN' ALL THAT. HOW IT WORKS--"
"WELL, I'VE TOLD YOU BEFORE... IT'S LIKE YOU PICK UP ON PEOPLE'S MEMORIES--USELESS BITS OF THEIR LIVES THAT ARE ONLY RELEVANT TO THEM. ADD THEM UP, AN' YOU CAN TALK TO THE SOURCE."
"THAT'S ALL WELL AN' GOOD, WEEBLE..."
...BUT CAN YOU DO IT TO SOMEONE WHO'S STILL ALIVE?

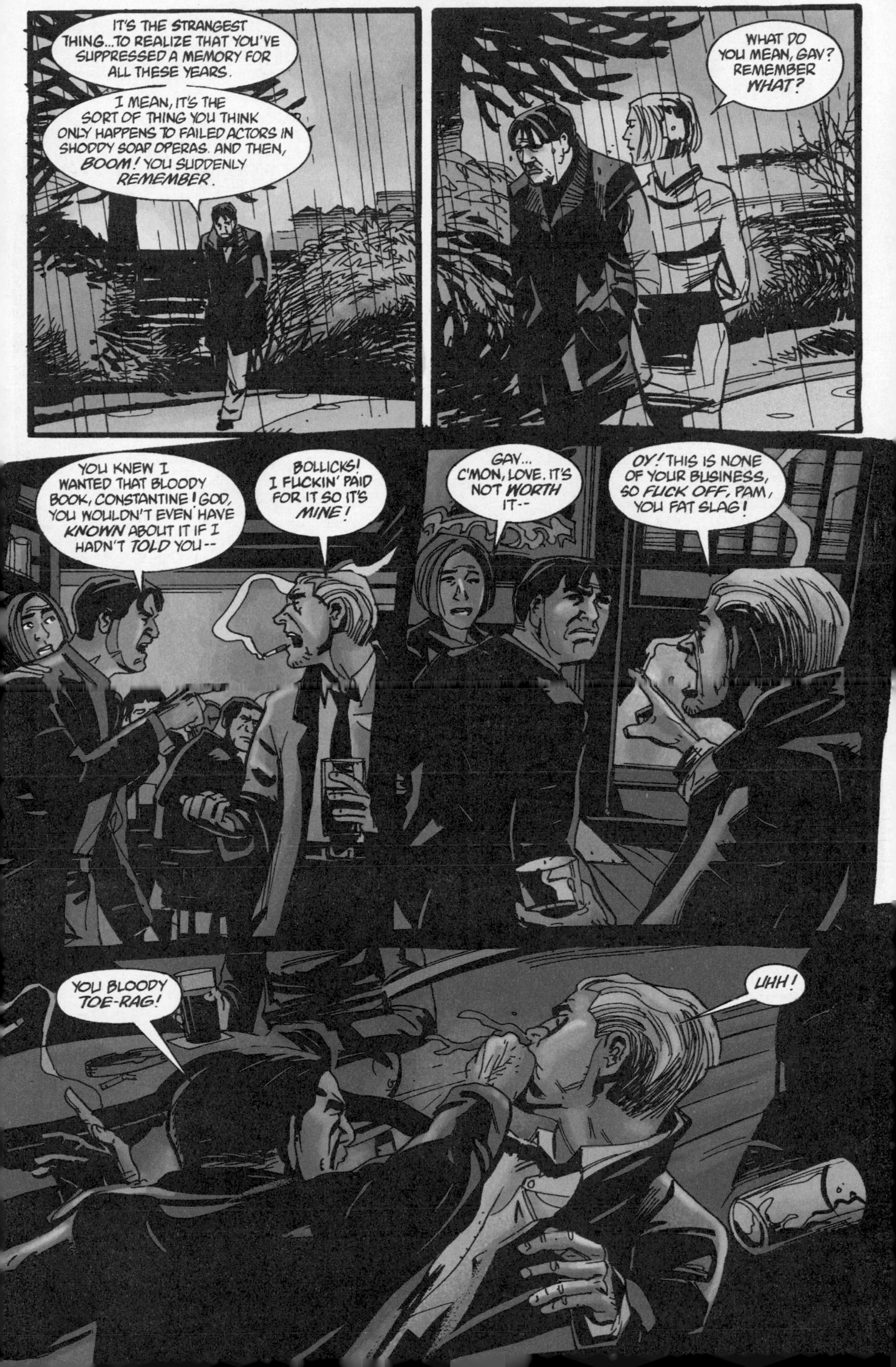
IT'S THE STRANGEST THING...TO REALIZE THAT YOU'VE SUPPRESSED A MEMORY FOR ALL THESE YEARS.
I MEAN, IT'S THE SORT OF THING YOU THINK ONLY HAPPENS TO FAILED ACTORS IN SHODDY SOAP OPERAS. AND THEN, BOOM! YOU SUDDENLY REMEMBER.
WHAT DO YOU MEAN, GAV? REMEMBER WHAT?
YOU KNEW I WANTED THAT BLOODY BOOK, CONSTANTINE! GOD, YOU WOULDN'T EVEN HAVE KNOWN ABOUT IT IF I HADN'T TOLD YOU--
BOLLICKS! I FUCKIN' PAID FOR IT SO IT'S MINE!
GAV... C'MON, LOVE. IT'S NOT WORTH IT--
OY! THIS IS NONE OF YOUR BUSINESS, SO FUCK OFF, PAM, YOU FAT SLAG!
YOU BLOODY TOE-RAG!
UHH!

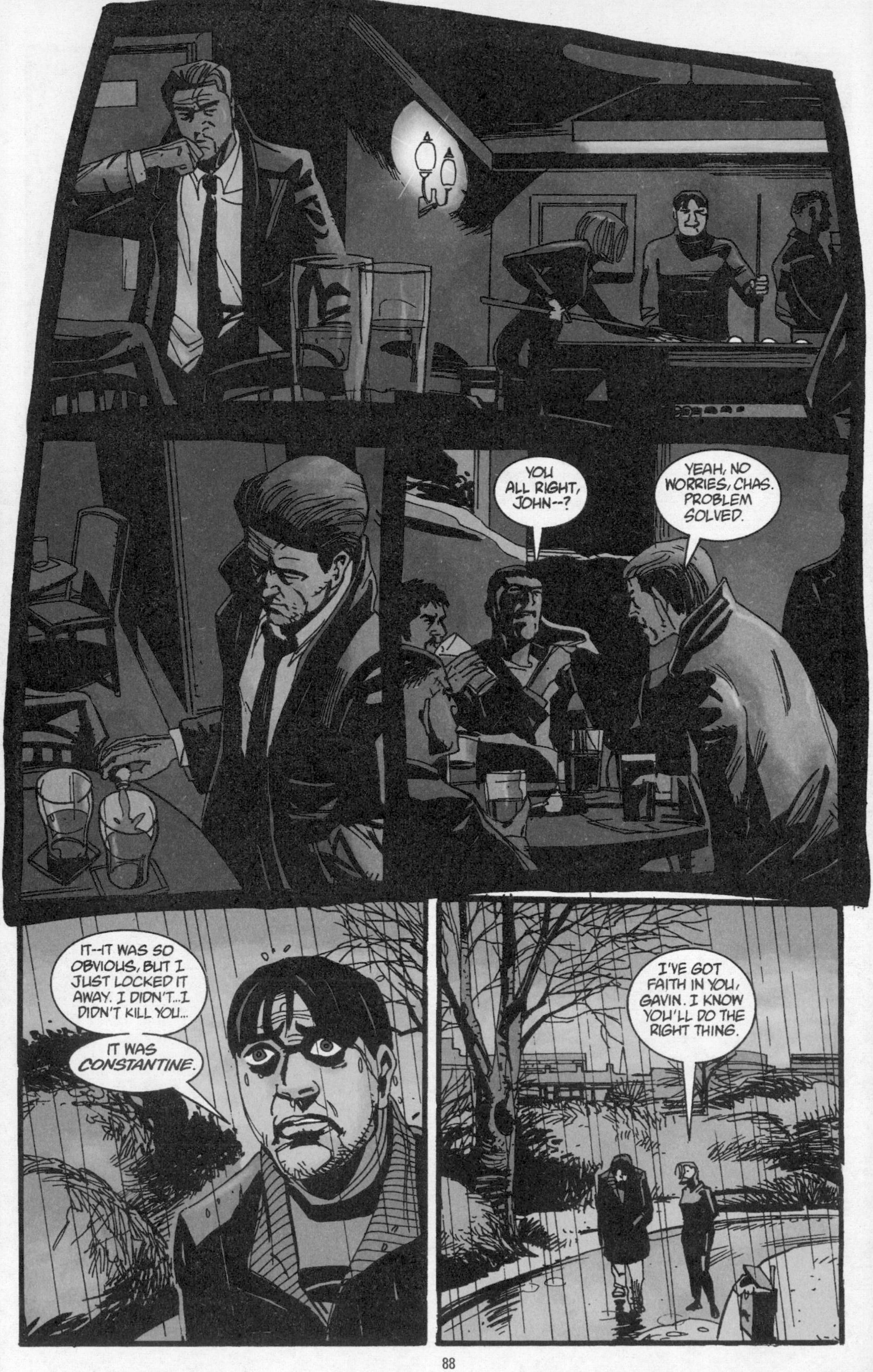

YOU ALL RIGHT, JOHN--?
YEAH, NO WORRIES, CHAS. PROBLEM SOLVED.
IT--IT WAS SO OBVIOUS, BUT I JUST LOCKED IT AWAY. I DIDN'T...I DIDN'T KILL YOU...
IT WAS CONSTANTINE.
I'VE GOT FAITH IN YOU, GAVIN. I KNOW YOU'LL DO THE RIGHT THING.

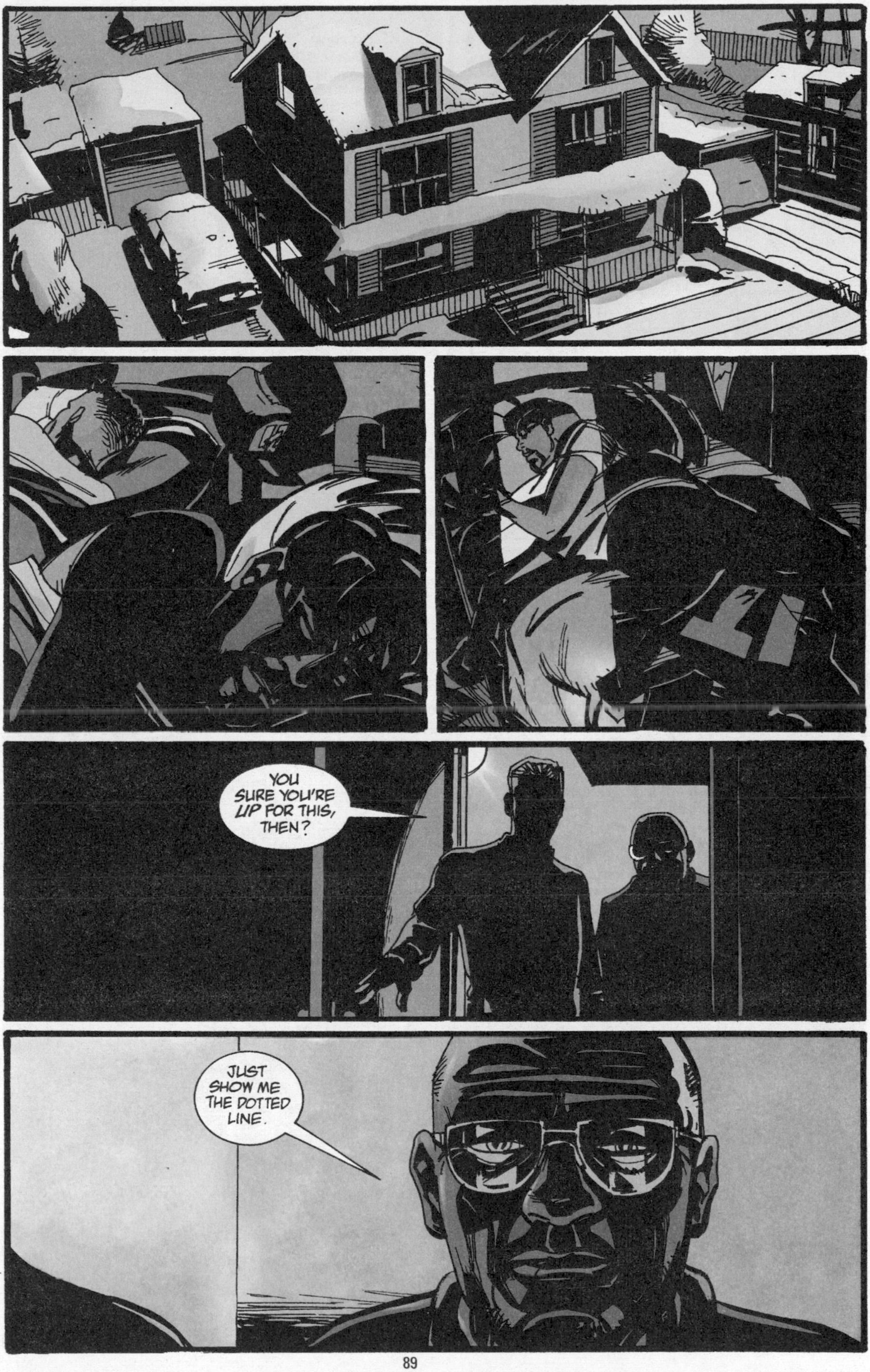
YOU SURE YOU'RE UP FOR THIS, THEN?
JUST SHOW ME THE DOTTED LINE.

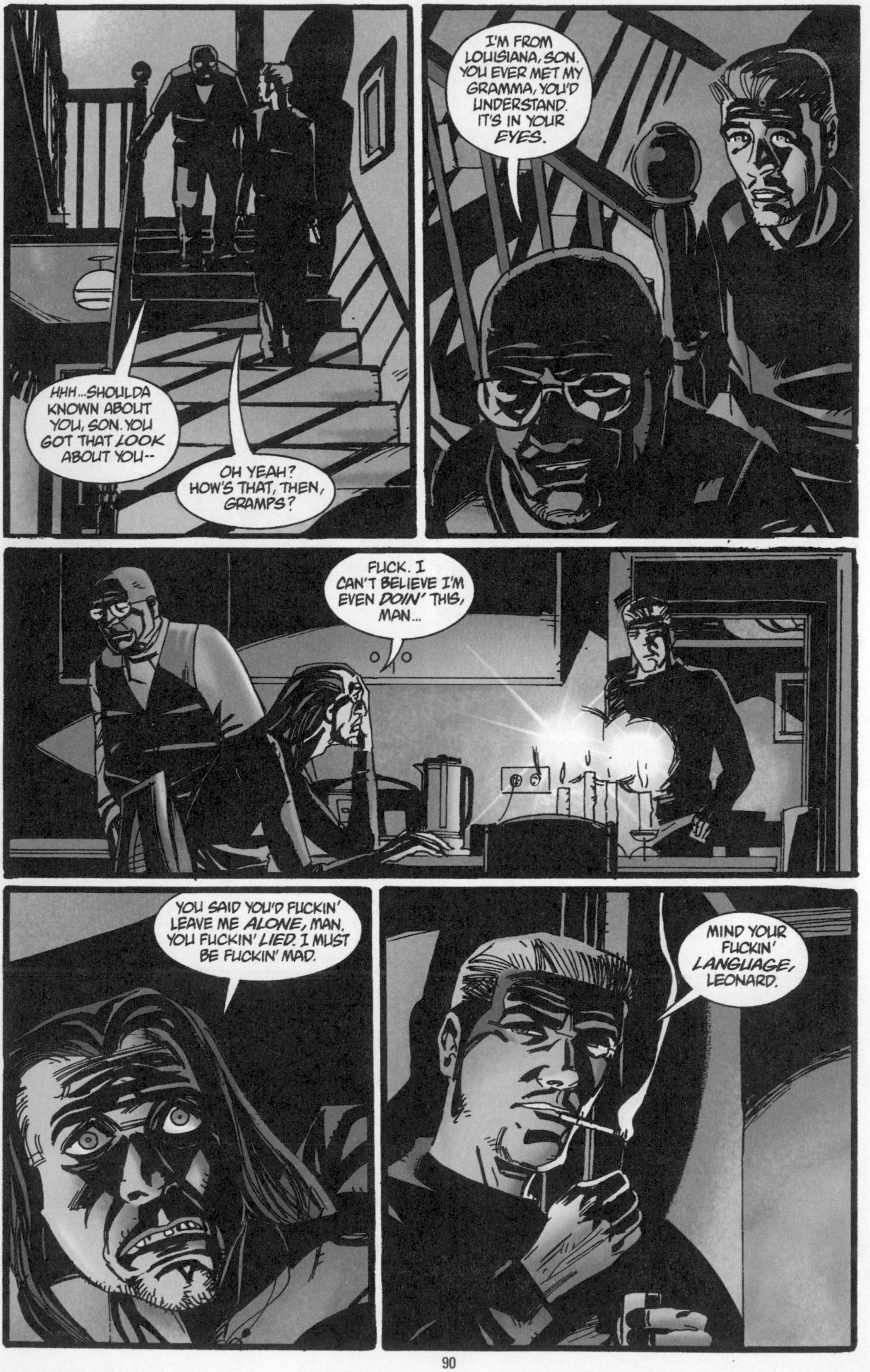
HHH...SHOULDA KNOWN ABOUT YOU, SON. YOU GOT THAT LOOK ABOUT YOU--
OH YEAH? HOW'S THAT, THEN, GRAMPS?
I'M FROM LOUISIANA, SON. YOU EVER MET MY GRAMMA, YOU'D UNDERSTAND. IT'S IN YOUR EYES.
FUCK. I CAN'T BELIEVE I'M EVEN DOIN' THIS, MAN...
YOU SAID YOU'D FUCKIN' LEAVE ME ALONE, MAN, YOU FUCKIN' LIED. I MUST BE FUCKIN' MAD.
MIND YOUR FUCKIN' LANGUAGE, LEONARD.

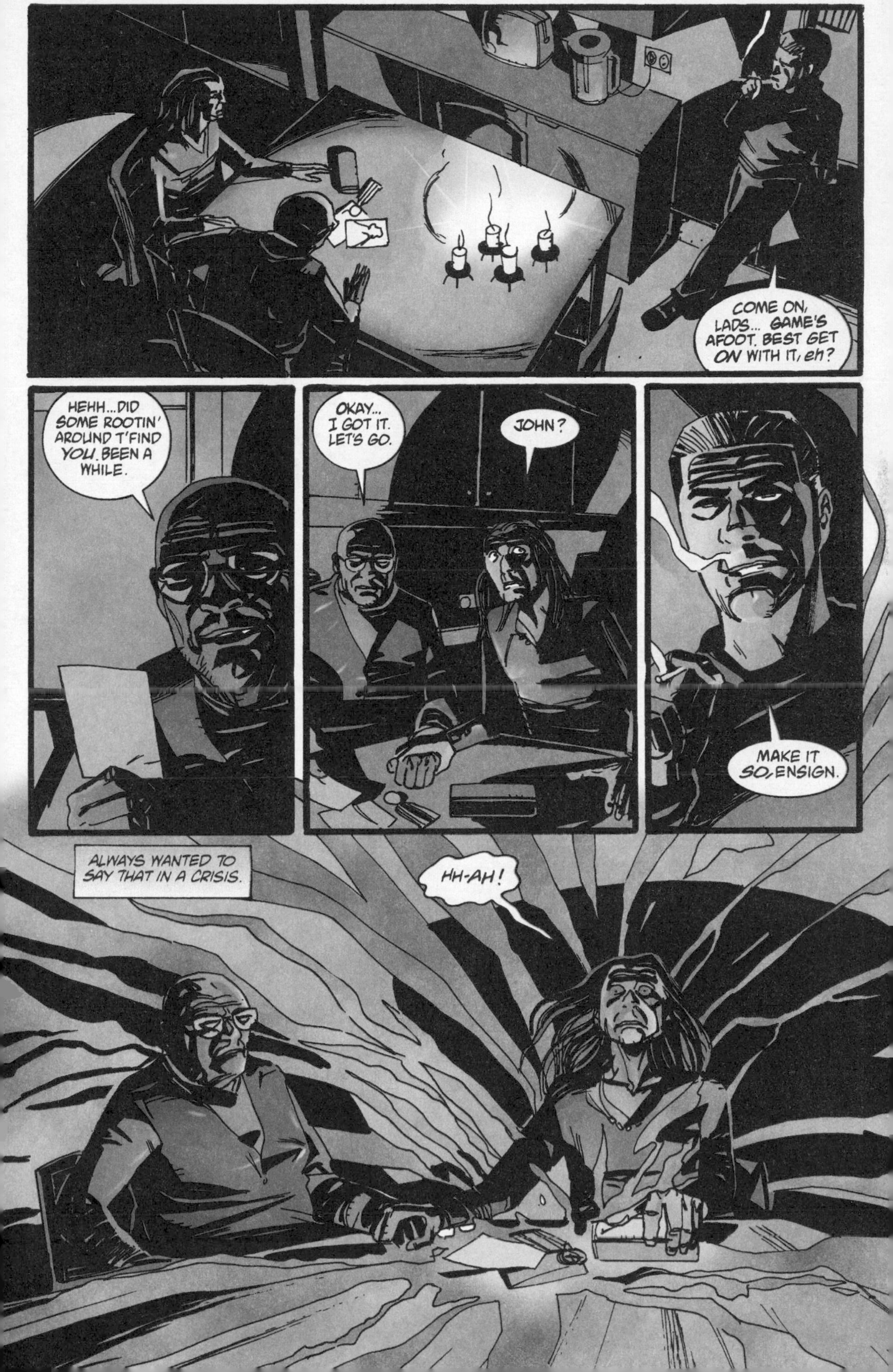
COME ON, LADS... GAME'S AFOOT. BEST GET ON WITH IT, eh?
HEHH...DID SOME ROOTIN' AROUND T'FIND YOU. BEEN A WHILE.
OKAY... I GOT IT. LET'S GO.
JOHN?
MAKE IT SO, ENSIGN.
ALWAYS WANTED TO SAY THAT IN A CRISIS.
HH-AH!

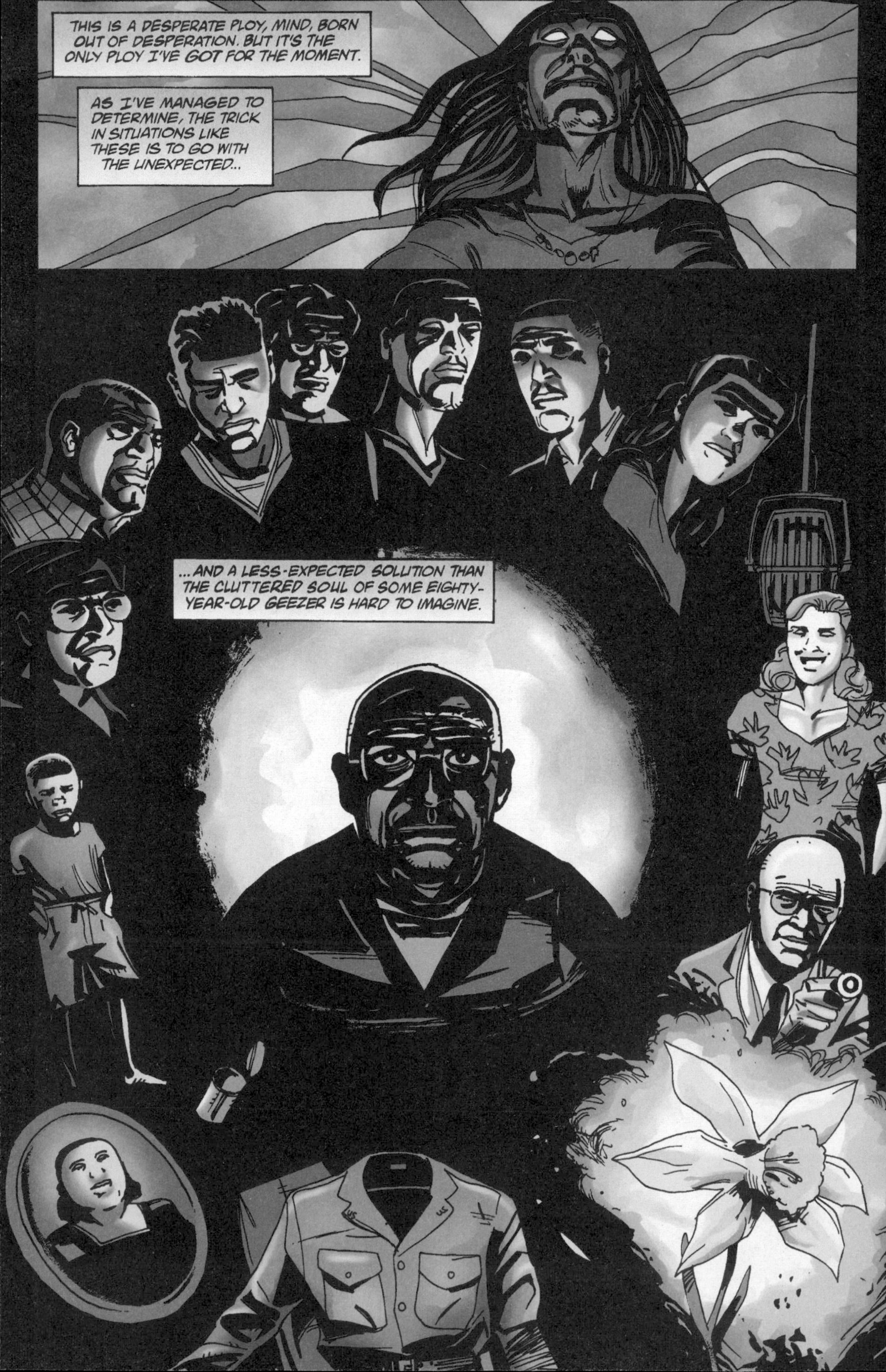
THIS IS A DESPERATE PLOY, MIND, BORN OUT OF DESPERATION. BUT IT'S THE ONLY PLOY I'VE GOT FOR THE MOMENT.
AS I'VE MANAGED TO DETERMINE, THE TRICK IN SITUATIONS LIKE THESE IS TO GO WITH THE UNEXPECTED...
...AND A LESS-EXPECTED SOLUTION THAN THE CLUTTERED SOUL OF SOME EIGHTY-YEAR-OLD GEEZER IS HARD TO IMAGINE.

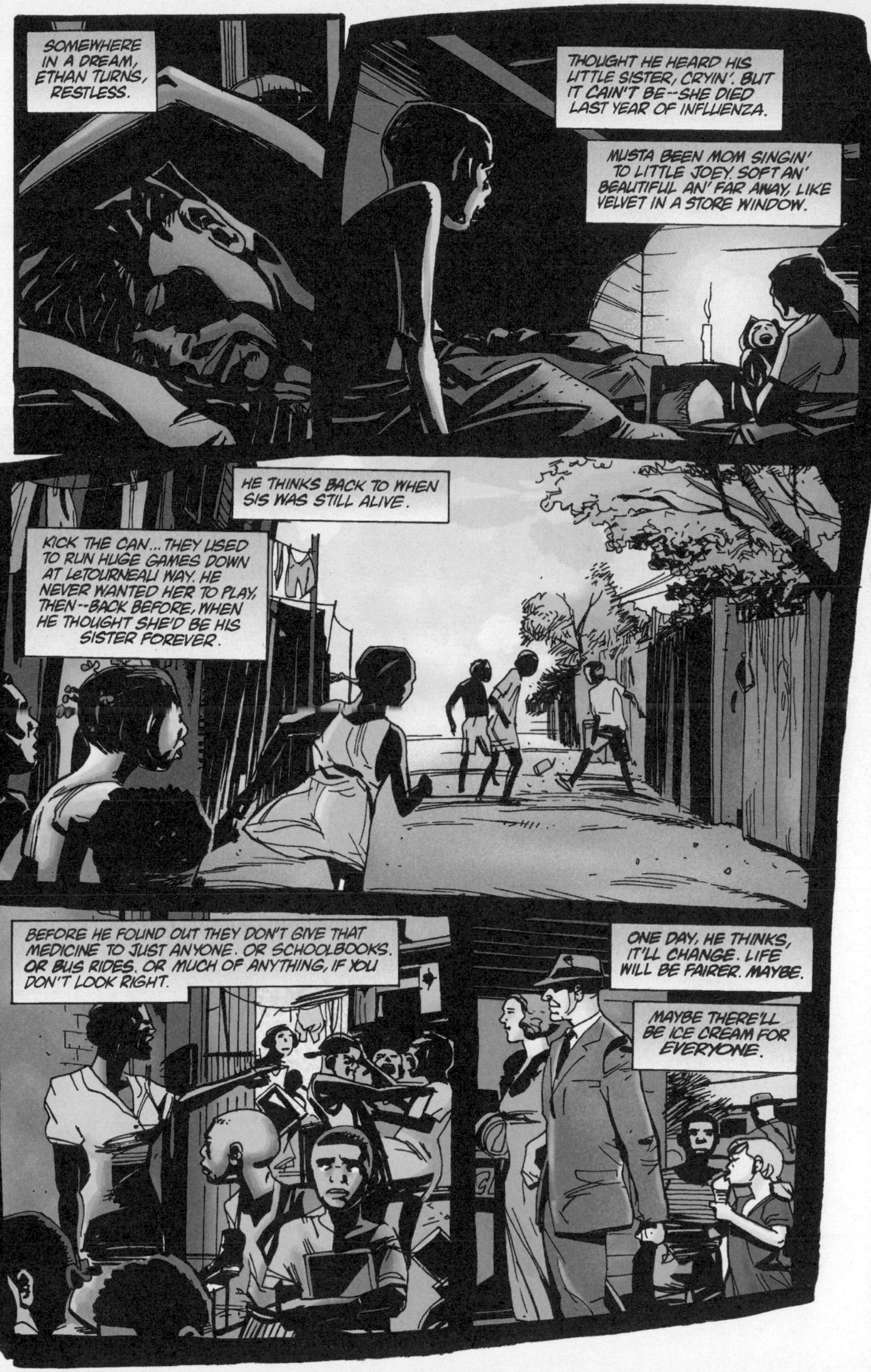
SOMEWHERE IN A DREAM, ETHAN TURNS, RESTLESS.
THOUGHT HE HEARD HIS LITTLE SISTER, CRYIN'. BUT IT CAIN'T BE--SHE DIED LAST YEAR OF INFLUENZA.
MUSTA BEEN MOM SINGIN' TO LITTLE JOEY. SOFT AN' BEAUTIFUL AN' FAR AWAY, LIKE VELVET IN A STORE WINDOW.
HE THINKS BACK TO WHEN SIS WAS STILL ALIVE.
KICK THE CAN... THEY USED TO RUN HUGE GAMES DOWN AT LeTOURNEAU WAY. HE NEVER WANTED HER TO PLAY, THEN--BACK BEFORE, WHEN HE THOUGHT SHE'D BE HIS SISTER FOREVER.
BEFORE HE FOUND OUT THEY DON'T GIVE THAT MEDICINE TO JUST ANYONE. OR SCHOOLBOOKS. OR BUS RIDES. OR MUCH OF ANYTHING, IF YOU DON'T LOOK RIGHT.
ONE DAY, HE THINKS, IT'LL CHANGE. LIFE WILL BE FAIRER. MAYBE.
MAYBE THERE'LL BE ICE CREAM FOR EVERYONE.

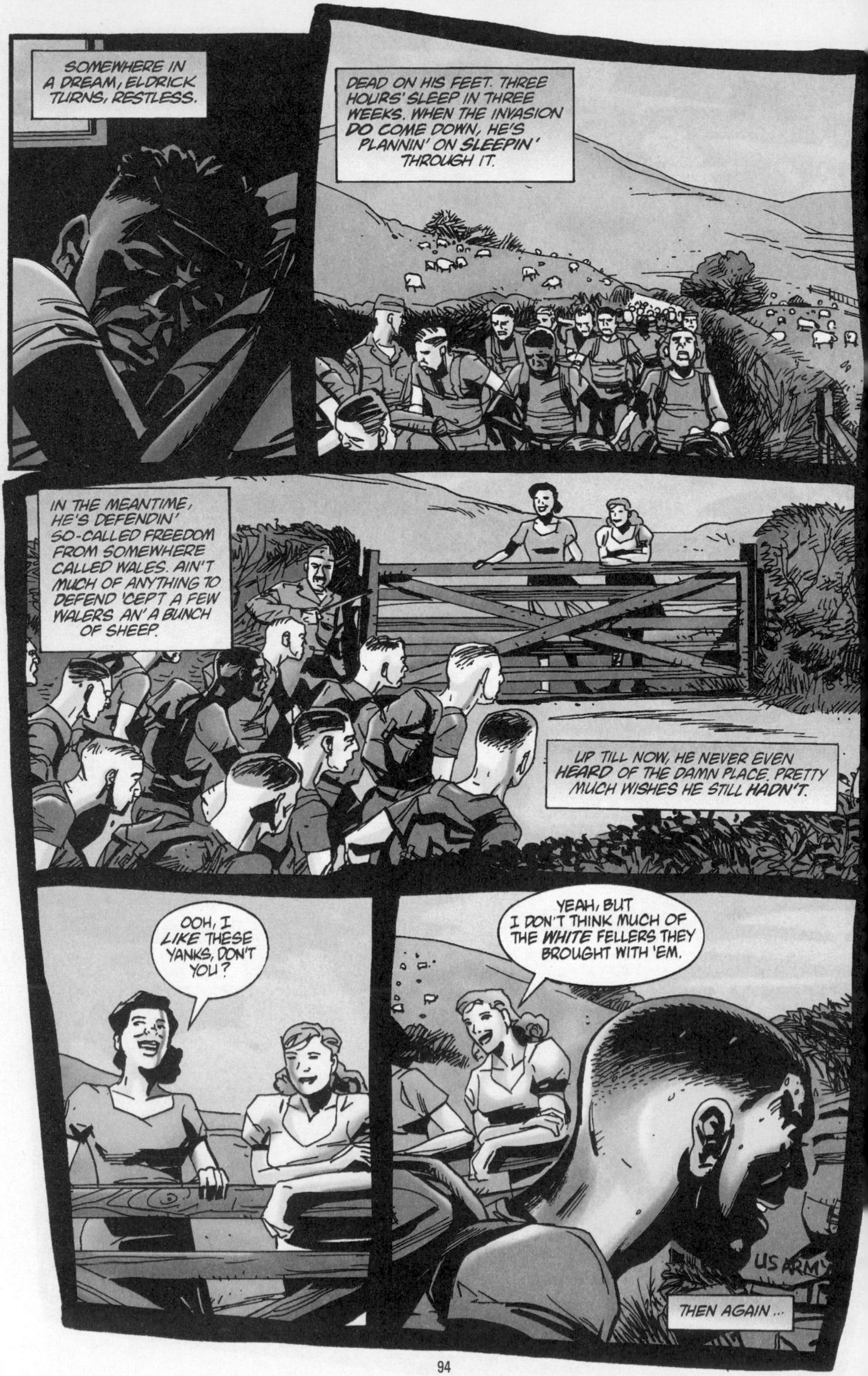
SOMEWHERE IN A DREAM, ELDRICK TURNS, RESTLESS.
DEAD ON HIS FEET. THREE HOURS' SLEEP IN THREE WEEKS. WHEN THE INVASION DO COME DOWN, HE'S PLANNIN' ON SLEEPIN' THROUGH IT.
IN THE MEANTIME, HE'S DEFENDIN' SO-CALLED FREEDOM FROM SOMEWHERE CALLED WALES. AIN'T MUCH OF ANYTHING TO DEFEND 'CEPT A FEW WALERS AN' A BUNCH OF SHEEP.
UP TILL NOW, HE NEVER EVEN HEARD OF THE DAMN PLACE. PRETTY MUCH WISHES HE STILL HADN'T.
OOH, I LIKE THESE YANKS, DON'T YOU?
YEAH, BUT I DON'T THINK MUCH OF THE WHITE FELLERS THEY BROUGHT WITH 'EM.
US ARMY
THEN AGAIN...

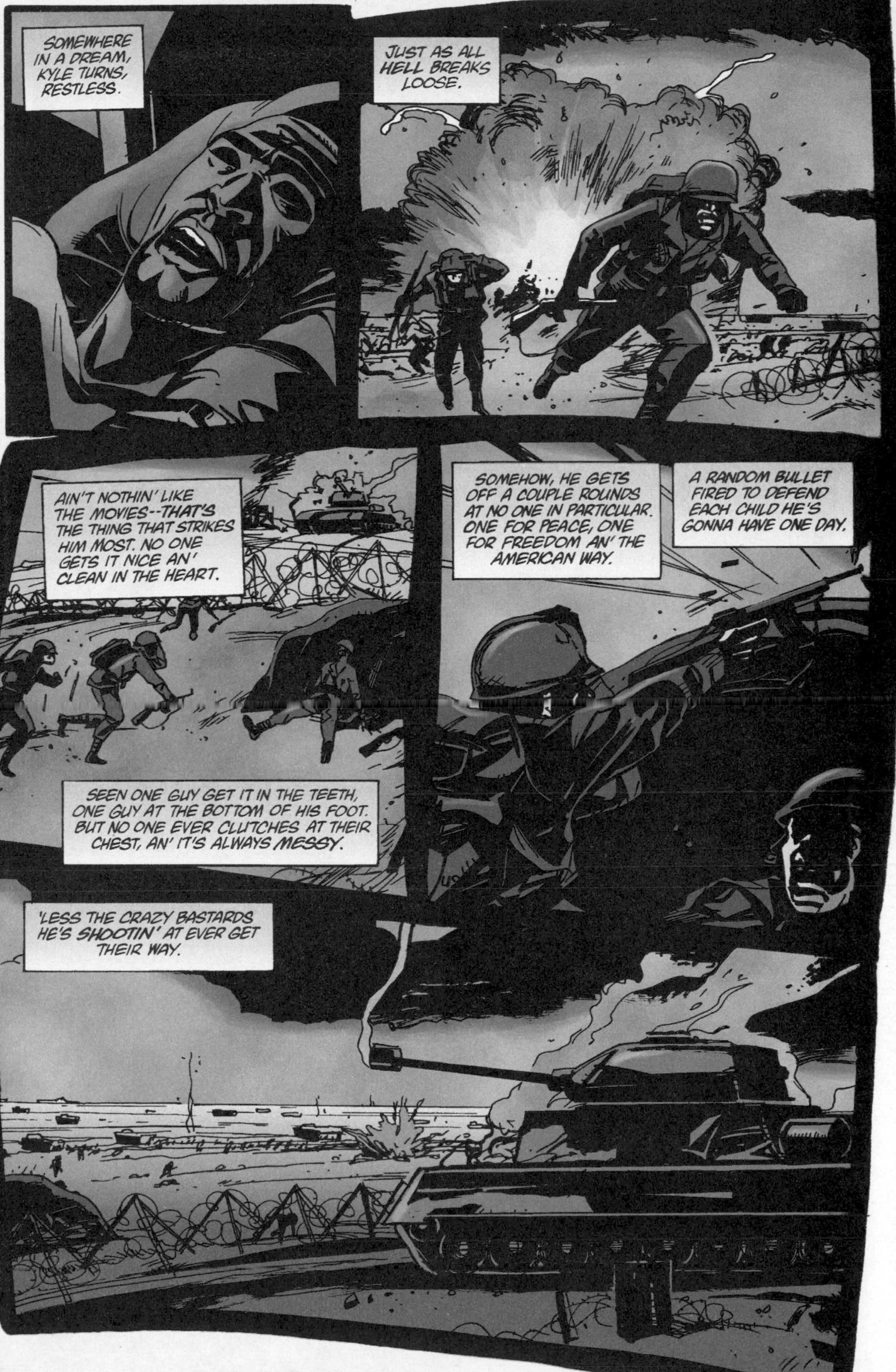
SOMEWHERE IN A DREAM, KYLE TURNS, RESTLESS.
JUST AS ALL HELL BREAKS LOOSE.
AIN'T NOTHIN' LIKE THE MOVIES--THAT'S THE THING THAT STRIKES HIM MOST. NO ONE GETS IT NICE AN' CLEAN IN THE HEART.
SEEN ONE GUY GET IT IN THE TEETH, ONE GUY AT THE BOTTOM OF HIS FOOT. BUT NO ONE EVER CLUTCHES AT THEIR CHEST, AN' IT'S ALWAYS MESSY.
SOMEHOW, HE GETS OFF A COUPLE ROUNDS AT NO ONE IN PARTICULAR. ONE FOR PEACE, ONE FOR FREEDOM AN' THE AMERICAN WAY.
A RANDOM BULLET FIRED TO DEFEND EACH CHILD HE'S GONNA HAVE ONE DAY.
'LESS THE CRAZY BASTARDS HE'S SHOOTIN' AT EVER GET THEIR WAY.

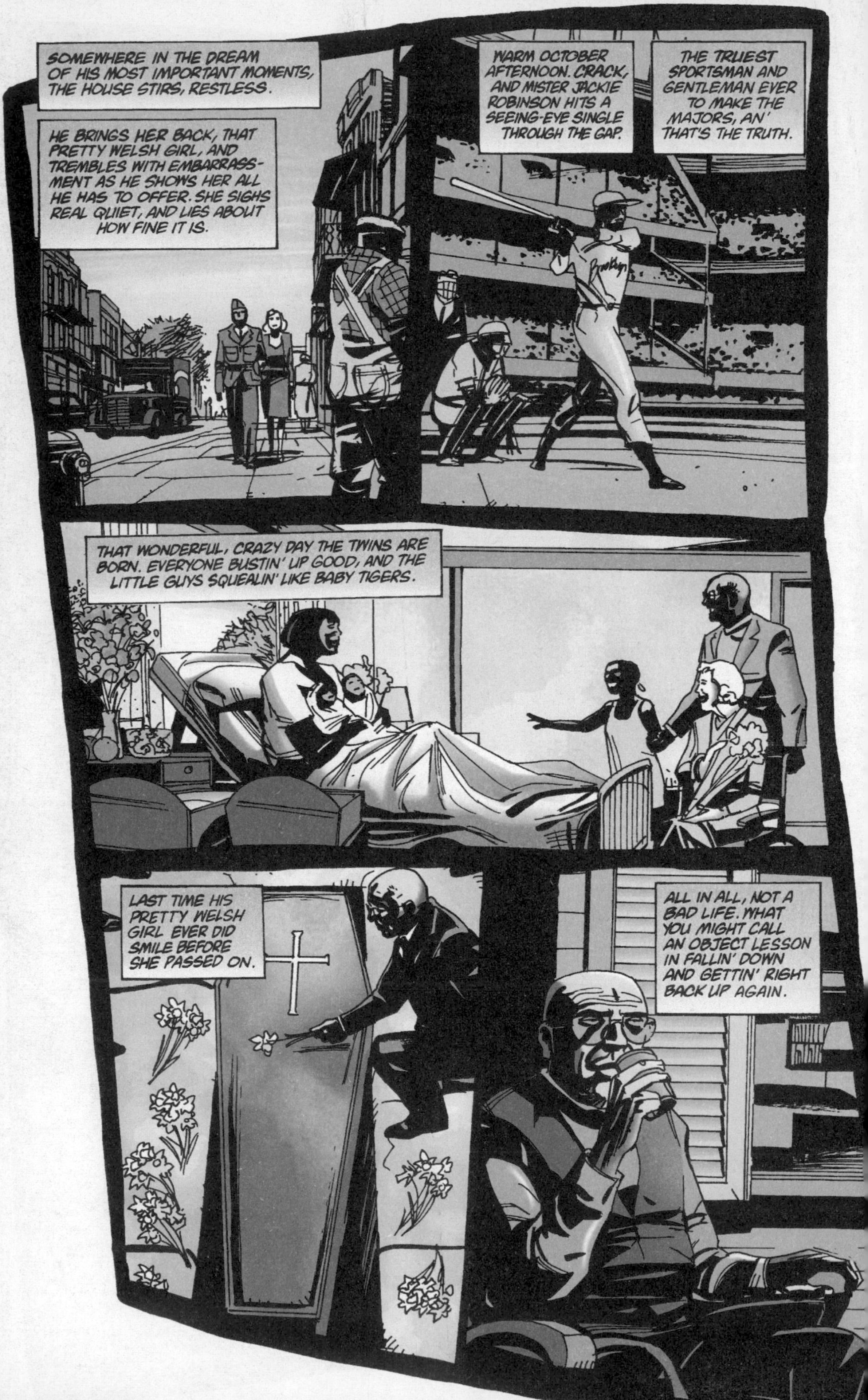
SOMEWHERE IN THE DREAM OF HIS MOST IMPORTANT MOMENTS, THE HOUSE STIRS, RESTLESS.
HE BRINGS HER BACK, THAT PRETTY WELSH GIRL, AND TREMBLES WITH EMBARRASS-MENT AS HE SHOWS HER ALL HE HAS TO OFFER. SHE SIGHS REAL QUIET, AND LIES ABOUT HOW FINE IT IS.
WARM OCTOBER AFTERNOON. CRACK, AND MISTER JACKIE ROBINSON HITS A SEEING-EYE SINGLE THROUGH THE GAP.
THE TRUEST SPORTSMAN AND GENTLEMAN EVER TO MAKE THE MAJORS, AN' THAT'S THE TRUTH.
THAT WONDERFUL, CRAZY DAY THE TWINS ARE BORN. EVERYONE BUSTIN' UP GOOD, AND THE LITTLE GUYS SQUEALIN' LIKE BABY TIGERS.
LAST TIME HIS PRETTY WELSH GIRL EVER DID SMILE BEFORE SHE PASSED ON.
ALL IN ALL, NOT A BAD LIFE. WHAT YOU MIGHT CALL AN OBJECT LESSON IN FALLIN' DOWN AND GETTIN' RIGHT BACK UP AGAIN.

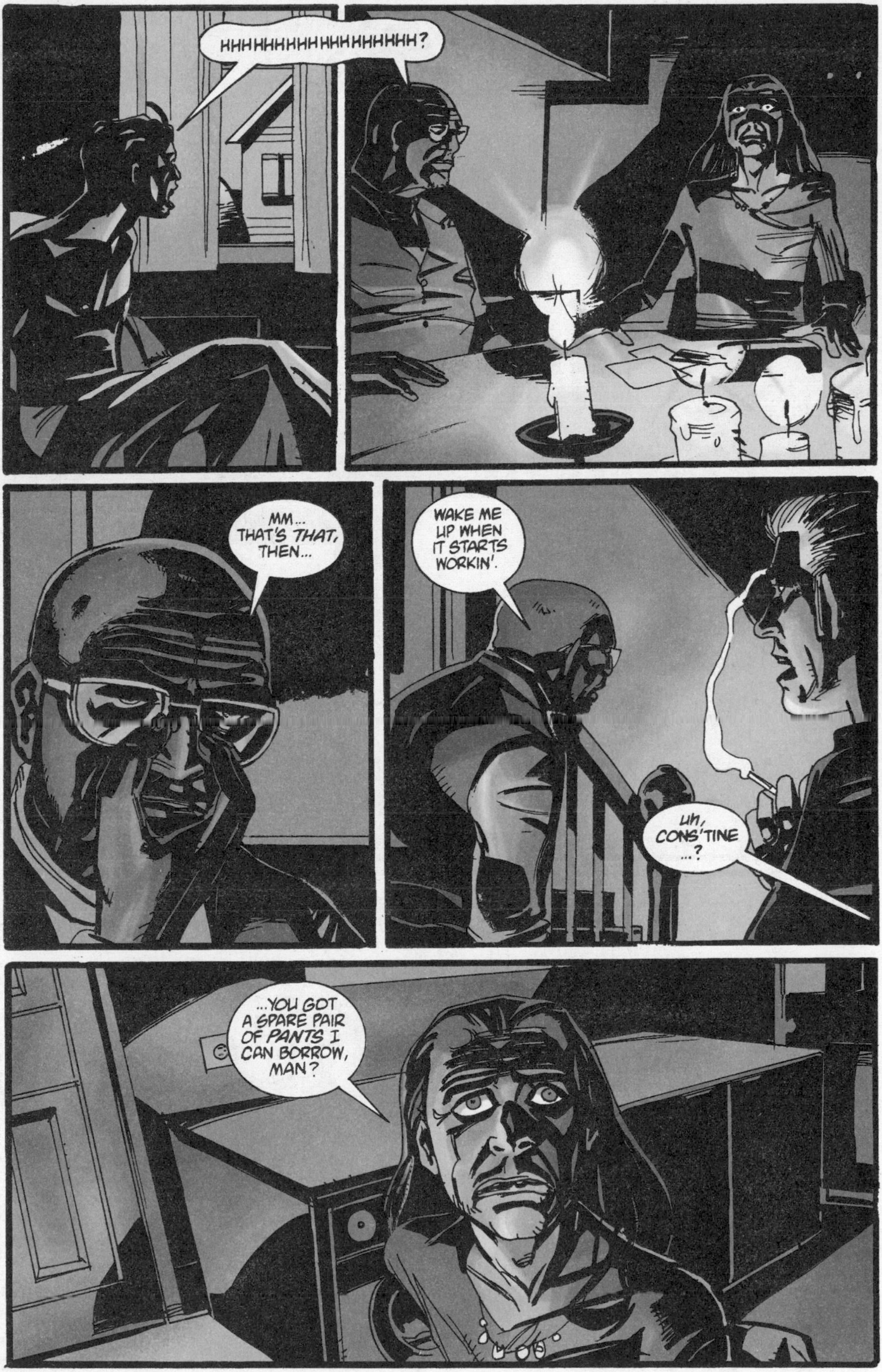
HHHHHHHHHHHHHHHHHH?
MM... THAT'S *THAT*, THEN...
WAKE ME UP WHEN IT STARTS WORKIN'.
UH, CONS'TINE ...?
...YOU GOT A SPARE PAIR OF *PANTS* I CAN BORROW, MAN?

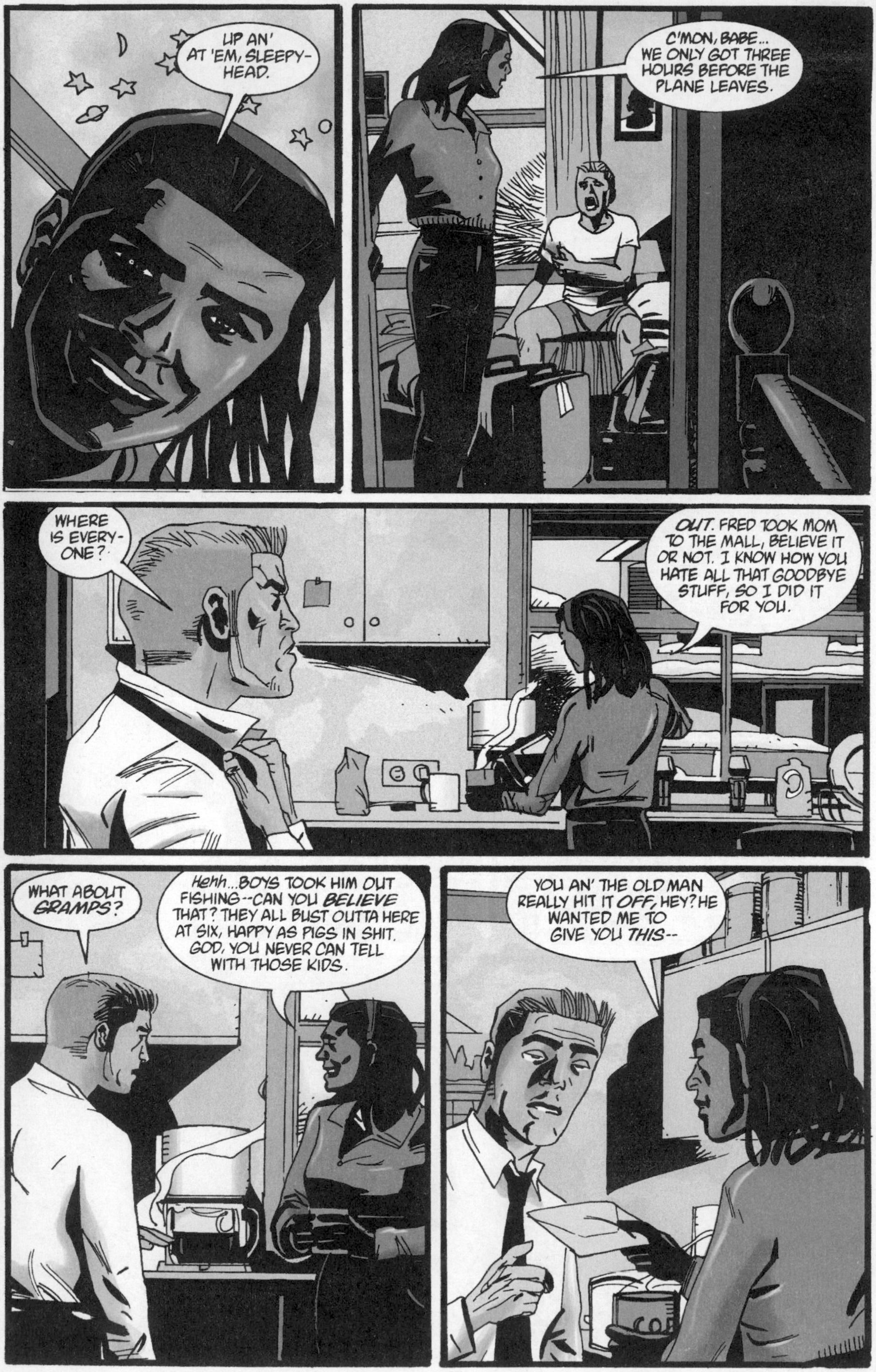
UP AN' AT 'EM, SLEEPY-HEAD.
C'MON, BABE... WE ONLY GOT THREE HOURS BEFORE THE PLANE LEAVES.
WHERE IS EVERY-ONE?
OUT. FRED TOOK MOM TO THE MALL, BELIEVE IT OR NOT. I KNOW HOW YOU HATE ALL THAT GOODBYE STUFF, SO I DID IT FOR YOU.
WHAT ABOUT GRAMPS?
Hehh...BOYS TOOK HIM OUT FISHING--CAN YOU BELIEVE THAT? THEY ALL BUST OUTTA HERE AT SIX, HAPPY AS PIGS IN SHIT. GOD, YOU NEVER CAN TELL WITH THOSE KIDS.
YOU AN' THE OLD MAN REALLY HIT IT OFF, HEY? HE WANTED ME TO GIVE YOU THIS--

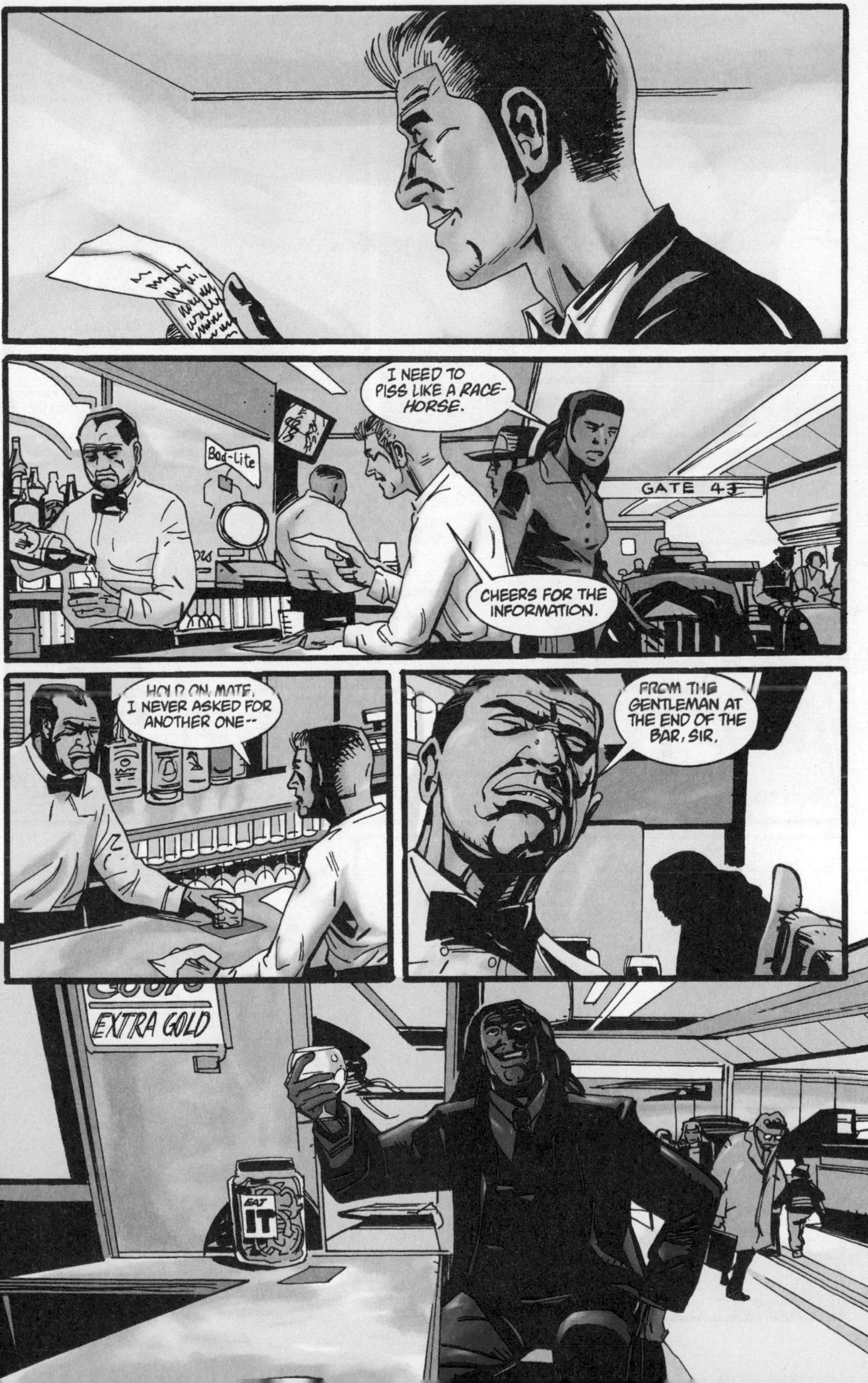
I NEED TO PISS LIKE A RACE-HORSE.
Bud-Lite
GATE 43
CHEERS FOR THE INFORMATION.
HOLD ON, MATE. I NEVER ASKED FOR ANOTHER ONE--
FROM THE GENTLEMAN AT THE END OF THE BAR, SIR.
EXTRA GOLD
EAT IT

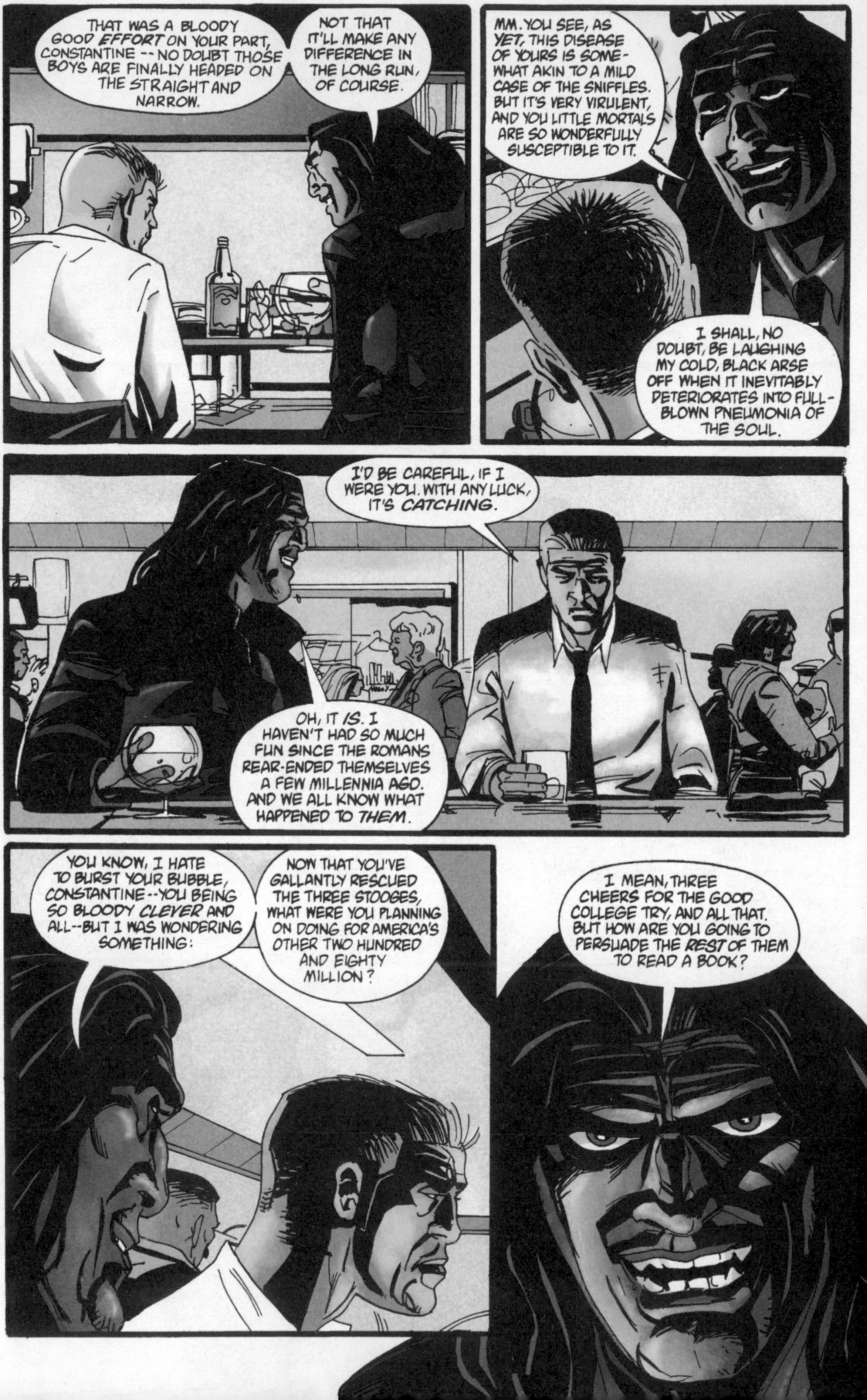
THAT WAS A BLOODY GOOD EFFORT ON YOUR PART, CONSTANTINE -- NO DOUBT THOSE BOYS ARE FINALLY HEADED ON THE STRAIGHT AND NARROW.
NOT THAT IT'LL MAKE ANY DIFFERENCE IN THE LONG RUN, OF COURSE.
MM. YOU SEE, AS YET, THIS DISEASE OF YOURS IS SOMEWHAT AKIN TO A MILD CASE OF THE SNIFFLES. BUT IT'S VERY VIRULENT, AND YOU LITTLE MORTALS ARE SO WONDERFULLY SUSCEPTIBLE TO IT.
I SHALL, NO DOUBT, BE LAUGHING MY COLD, BLACK ARSE OFF WHEN IT INEVITABLY DETERIORATES INTO FULL-BLOWN PNEUMONIA OF THE SOUL.
I'D BE CAREFUL, IF I WERE YOU. WITH ANY LUCK, IT'S CATCHING.
OH, IT IS. I HAVEN'T HAD SO MUCH FUN SINCE THE ROMANS REAR-ENDED THEMSELVES A FEW MILLENNIA AGO. AND WE ALL KNOW WHAT HAPPENED TO THEM.
YOU KNOW, I HATE TO BURST YOUR BUBBLE, CONSTANTINE--YOU BEING SO BLOODY CLEVER AND ALL--BUT I WAS WONDERING SOMETHING:
NOW THAT YOU'VE GALLANTLY RESCUED THE THREE STOOGES, WHAT WERE YOU PLANNING ON DOING FOR AMERICA'S OTHER TWO HUNDRED AND EIGHTY MILLION?
I MEAN, THREE CHEERS FOR THE GOOD COLLEGE TRY, AND ALL THAT. BUT HOW ARE YOU GOING TO PERSUADE THE REST OF THEM TO READ A BOOK?

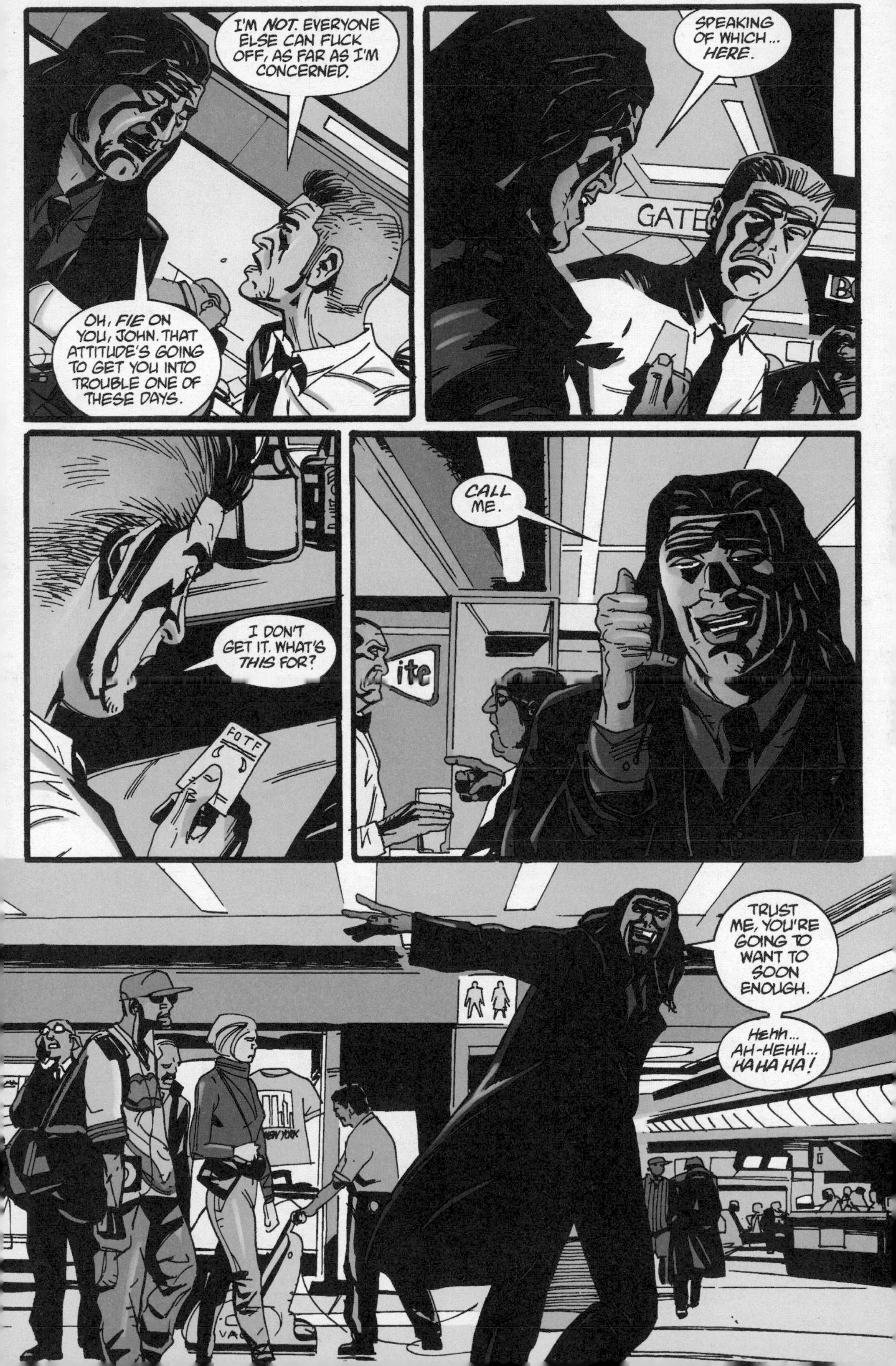
I'M NOT. EVERYONE ELSE CAN FUCK OFF, AS FAR AS I'M CONCERNED.
OH, FIE ON YOU, JOHN. THAT ATTITUDE'S GOING TO GET YOU INTO TROUBLE ONE OF THESE DAYS.
SPEAKING OF WHICH... HERE.
GATE
I DON'T GET IT. WHAT'S THIS FOR?
FOTF
CALL ME.
ite
TRUST ME, YOU'RE GOING TO WANT TO SOON ENOUGH.
Hehh... AH-HEHH... HA HA HA!
NEW YORK

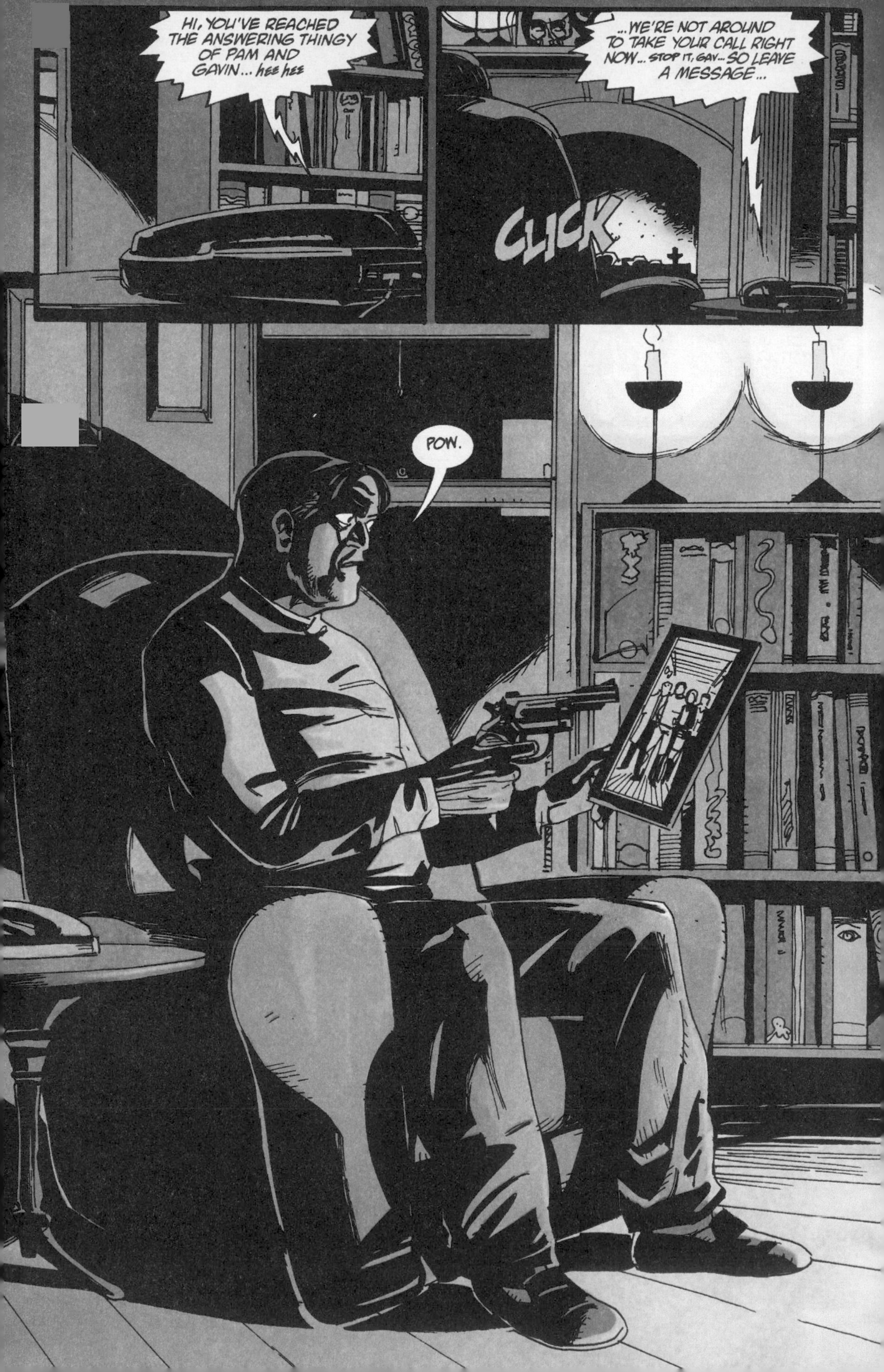
HI, YOU'VE REACHED THE ANSWERING THINGY OF PAM AND GAVIN... hee hee
...WE'RE NOT AROUND TO TAKE YOUR CALL RIGHT NOW... STOP IT, GAV... SO LEAVE A MESSAGE...
CLICK
POW.

JOHN CONSTANTINE

HELLBLAZER

C

VERTIGO

125

98

5 US

5 CAN

GESTED
MATURE
DERS

HOW TO PLAY WITH FIRE
- Part One of Four -
PAUL JENKINS / WARREN PLEECE

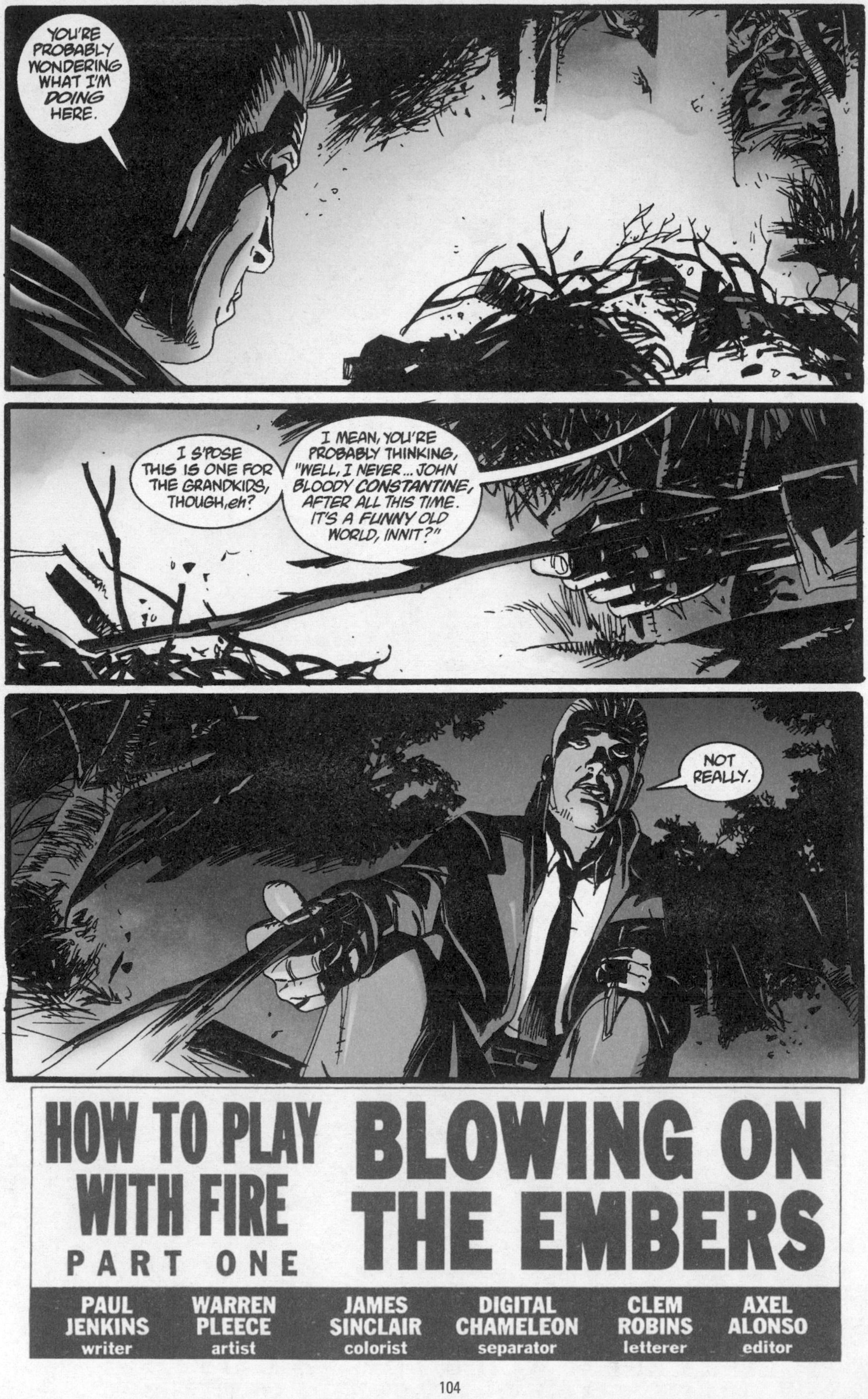

YOU'RE PROBABLY WONDERING WHAT I'M DOING HERE.
I S'POSE THIS IS ONE FOR THE GRANDKIDS, THOUGH, eh?
I MEAN, YOU'RE PROBABLY THINKING, "WELL, I NEVER... JOHN BLOODY CONSTANTINE, AFTER ALL THIS TIME. IT'S A FUNNY OLD WORLD, INNIT?"
NOT REALLY.

HOW TO PLAY WITH FIRE
PART ONE

BLOWING ON THE EMBERS

PAUL JENKINS	WARREN PLEECE	JAMES SINCLAIR	DIGITAL CHAMELEON	CLEM ROBINS	AXEL ALONSO
writer	artist	colorist	separator	letterer	editor

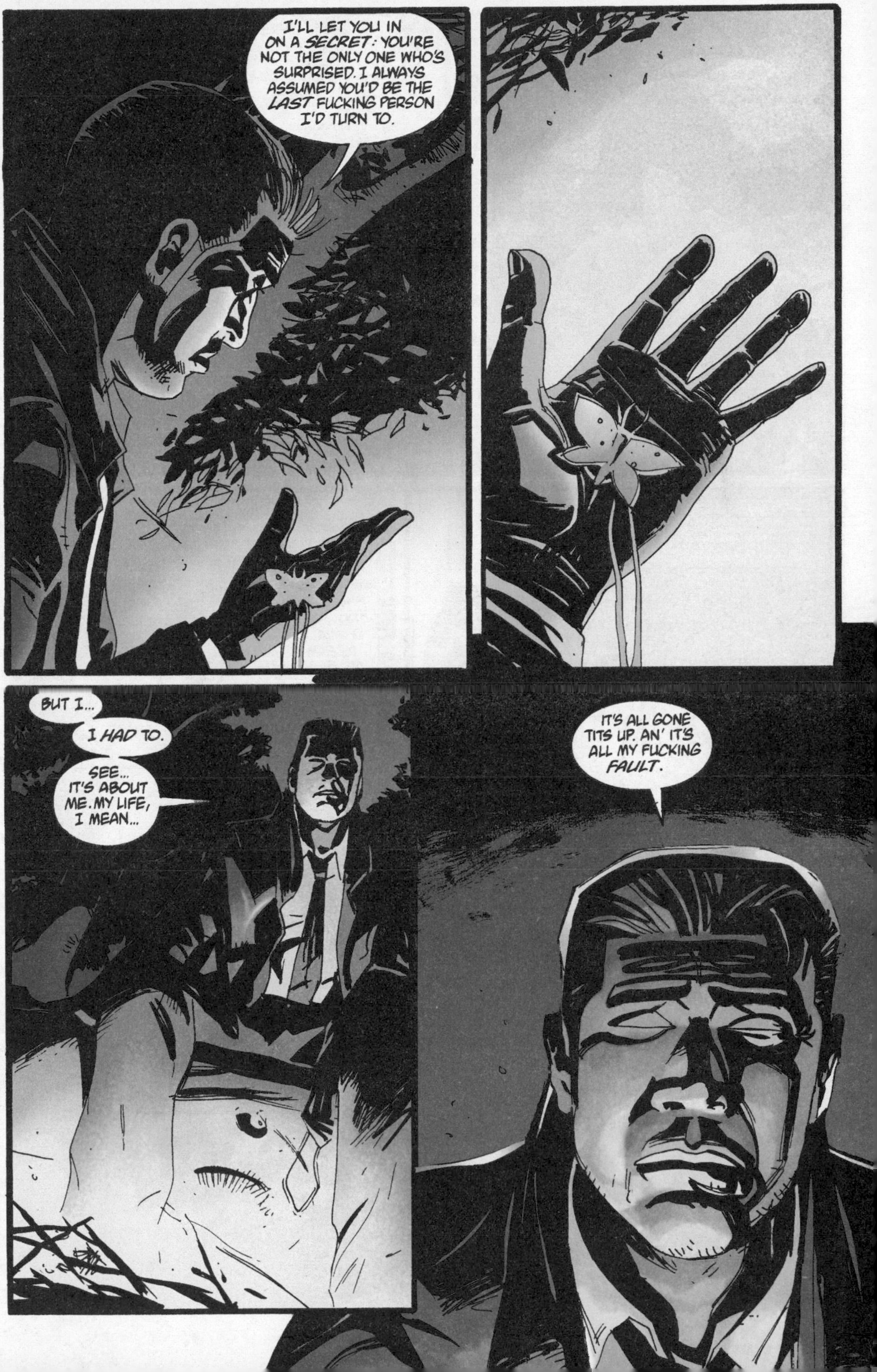
I'LL LET YOU IN ON A *SECRET*: YOU'RE NOT THE ONLY ONE WHO'S SURPRISED. I ALWAYS ASSUMED YOU'D BE THE *LAST* FUCKING PERSON I'D TURN TO.
BUT I...
I *HAD* TO.
SEE... IT'S ABOUT ME. MY LIFE, I MEAN...
IT'S ALL GONE TITS UP. AN' IT'S ALL MY FUCKING *FAULT*.

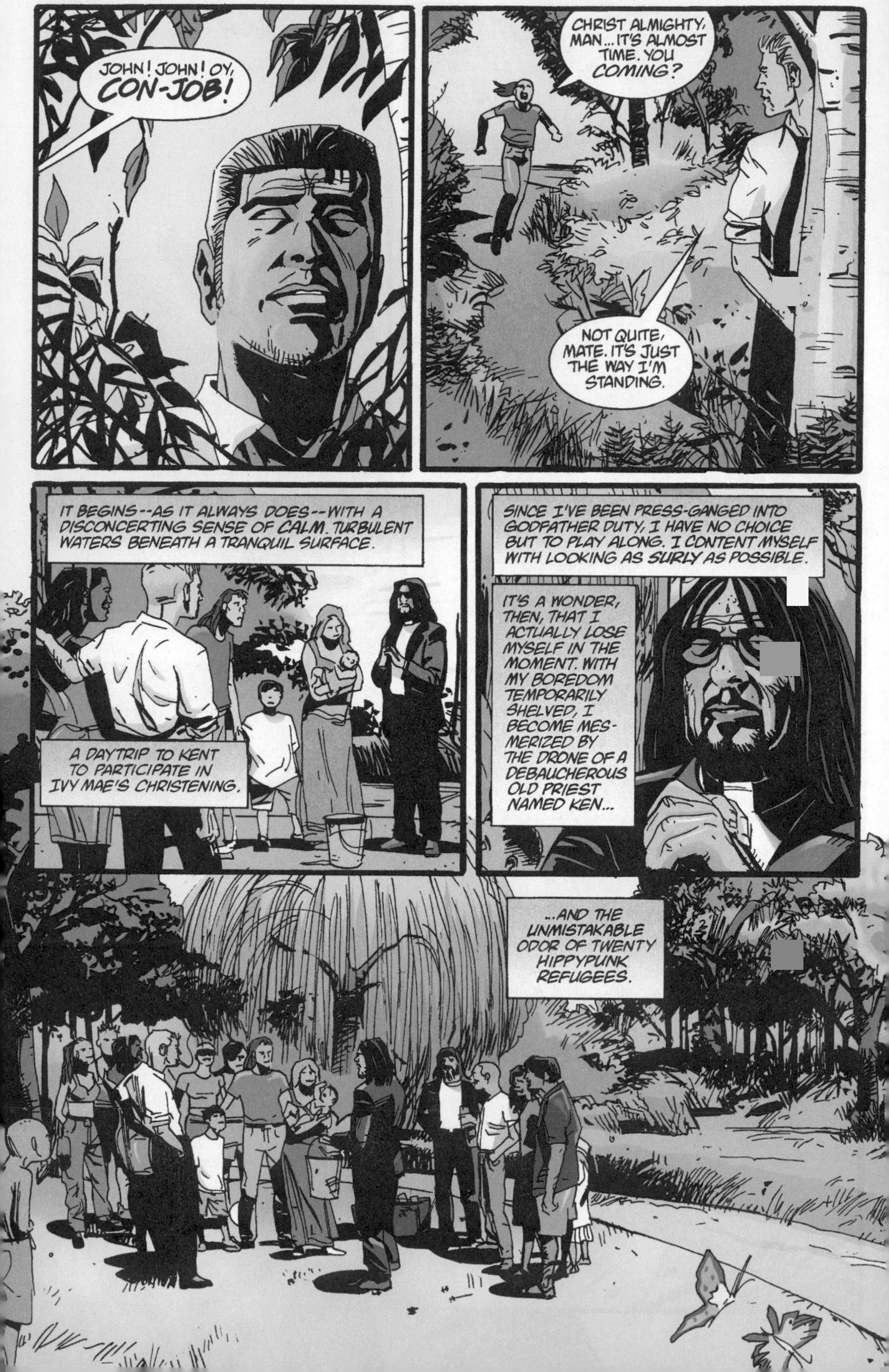
JOHN! JOHN! OY, CON-JOB!
CHRIST ALMIGHTY, MAN... IT'S ALMOST TIME. YOU COMING?
NOT QUITE, MATE. IT'S JUST THE WAY I'M STANDING.
IT BEGINS--AS IT ALWAYS DOES--WITH A DISCONCERTING SENSE OF CALM. TURBULENT WATERS BENEATH A TRANQUIL SURFACE.
A DAYTRIP TO KENT TO PARTICIPATE IN IVY MAE'S CHRISTENING.
SINCE I'VE BEEN PRESS-GANGED INTO GODFATHER DUTY, I HAVE NO CHOICE BUT TO PLAY ALONG. I CONTENT MYSELF WITH LOOKING AS SURLY AS POSSIBLE.
IT'S A WONDER, THEN, THAT I ACTUALLY LOSE MYSELF IN THE MOMENT. WITH MY BOREDOM TEMPORARILY SHELVED, I BECOME MES-MERIZED BY THE DRONE OF A DEBAUCHEROUS OLD PRIEST NAMED KEN...
...AND THE UNMISTAKABLE ODOR OF TWENTY HIPPYPUNK REFUGEES.

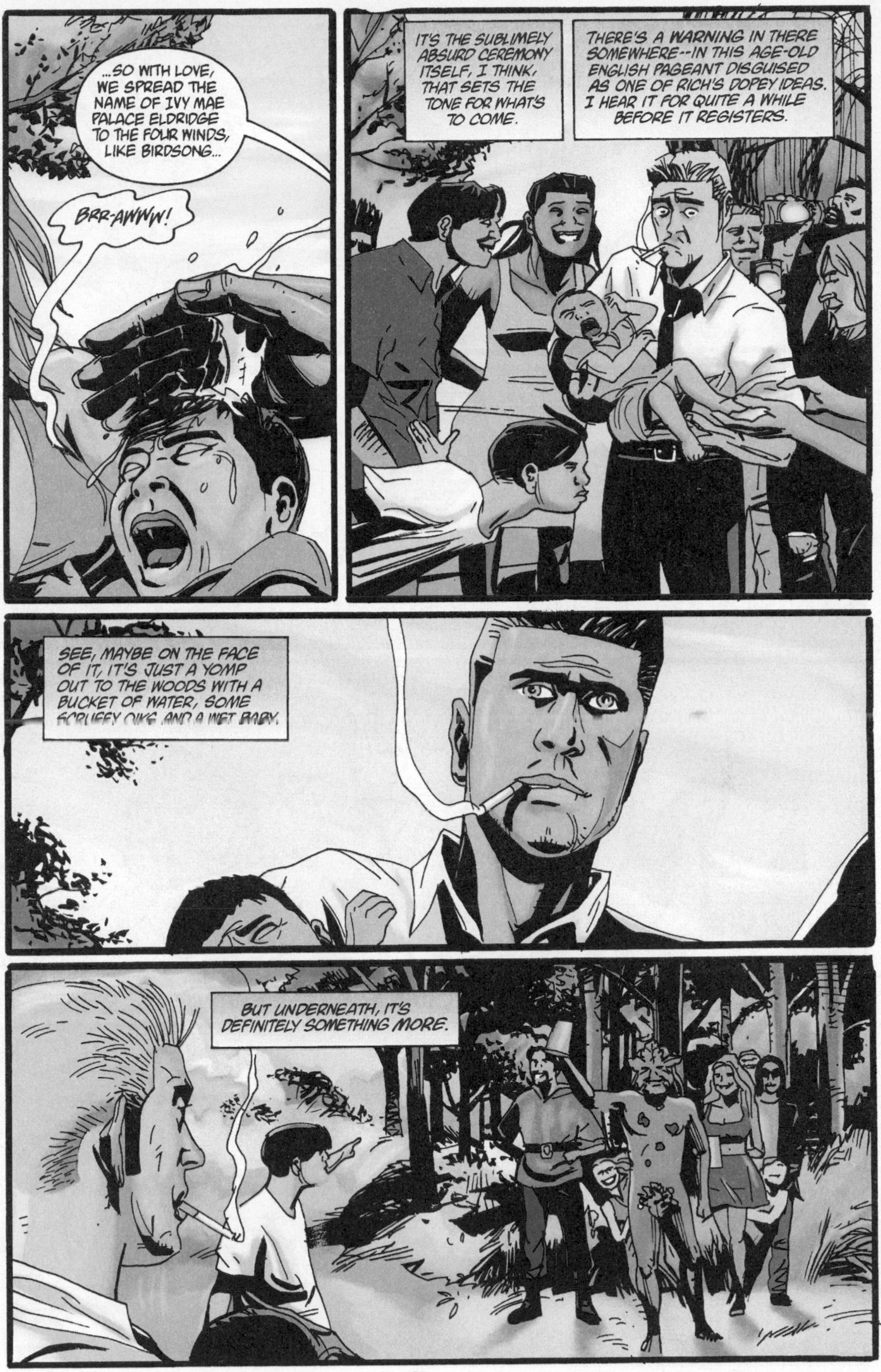
...SO WITH LOVE, WE SPREAD THE NAME OF IVY MAE PALACE ELDRIDGE TO THE FOUR WINDS, LIKE BIRDSONG...
BRR-AWWW!
IT'S THE SUBLIMELY ABSURD CEREMONY ITSELF, I THINK, THAT SETS THE TONE FOR WHAT'S TO COME.
THERE'S A WARNING IN THERE SOMEWHERE--IN THIS AGE-OLD ENGLISH PAGEANT DISGUISED AS ONE OF RICH'S DOPEY IDEAS. I HEAR IT FOR QUITE A WHILE BEFORE IT REGISTERS.
SEE, MAYBE ON THE FACE OF IT, IT'S JUST A YOMP OUT TO THE WOODS WITH A BUCKET OF WATER, SOME SCRUFFY OIKS AND A WET BABY.
BUT UNDERNEATH, IT'S DEFINITELY SOMETHING MORE.

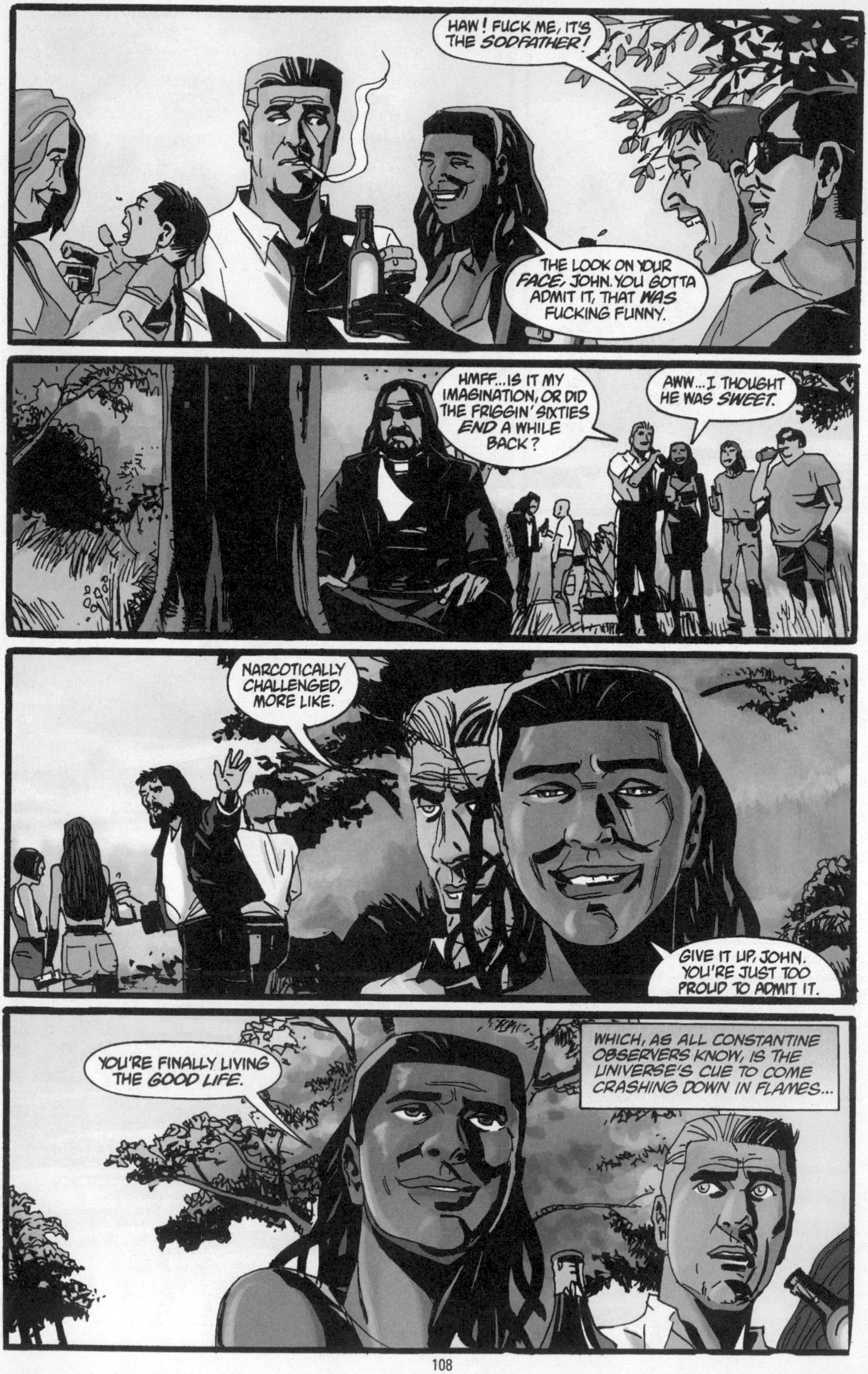
HAW! FUCK ME, IT'S THE SODFATHER!
THE LOOK ON YOUR FACE, JOHN. YOU GOTTA ADMIT IT, THAT WAS FUCKING FUNNY.
HMFF... IS IT MY IMAGINATION, OR DID THE FRIGGIN' SIXTIES END A WHILE BACK?
AWW... I THOUGHT HE WAS SWEET.
NARCOTICALLY CHALLENGED, MORE LIKE.
GIVE IT UP, JOHN. YOU'RE JUST TOO PROUD TO ADMIT IT.
YOU'RE FINALLY LIVING THE GOOD LIFE.
WHICH, AS ALL CONSTANTINE OBSERVERS KNOW, IS THE UNIVERSE'S CUE TO COME CRASHING DOWN IN FLAMES...

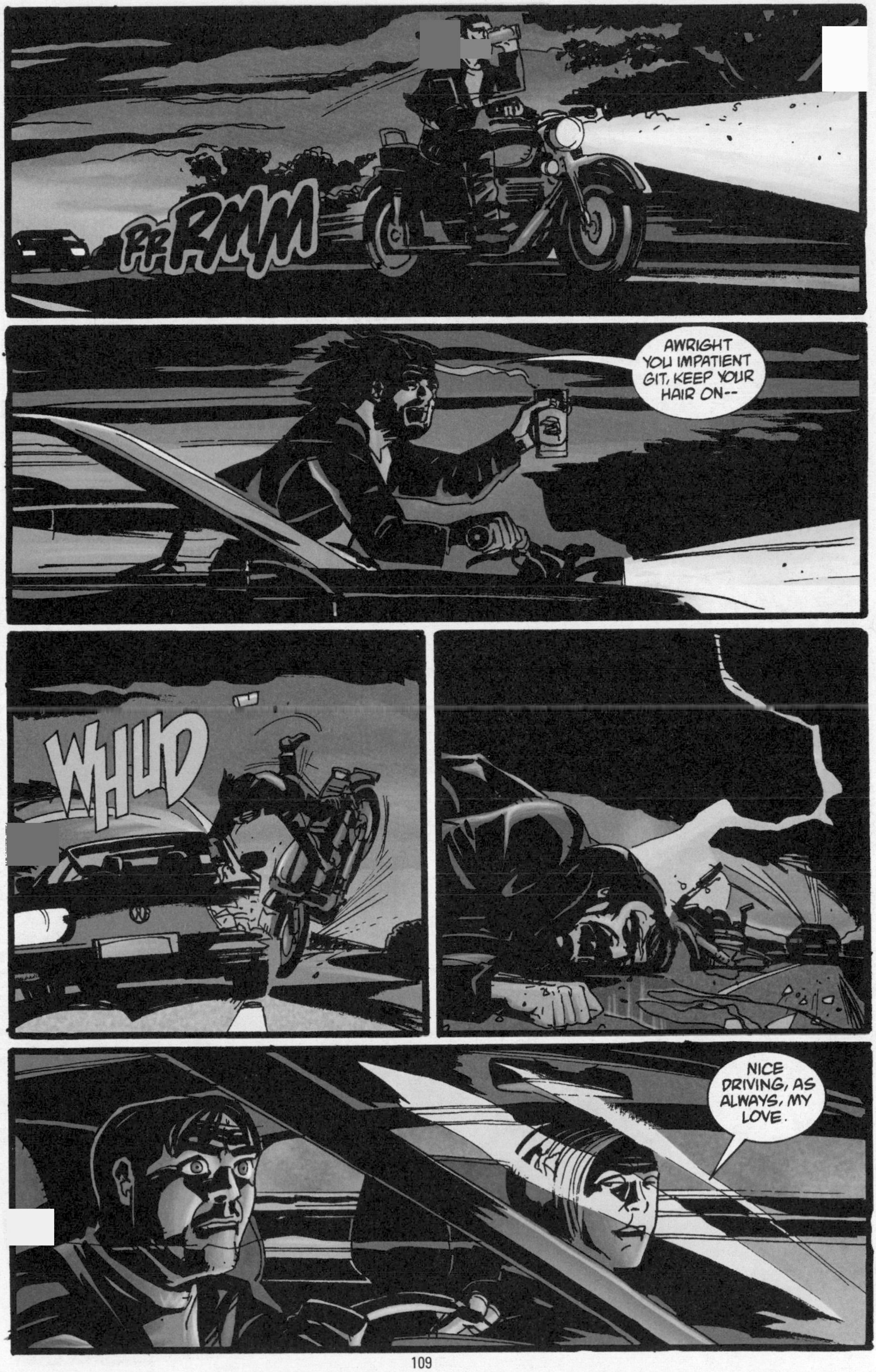

RRRMM
AWRIGHT YOU IMPATIENT GIT, KEEP YOUR HAIR ON--
WHUD
NICE DRIVING, AS ALWAYS, MY LOVE.

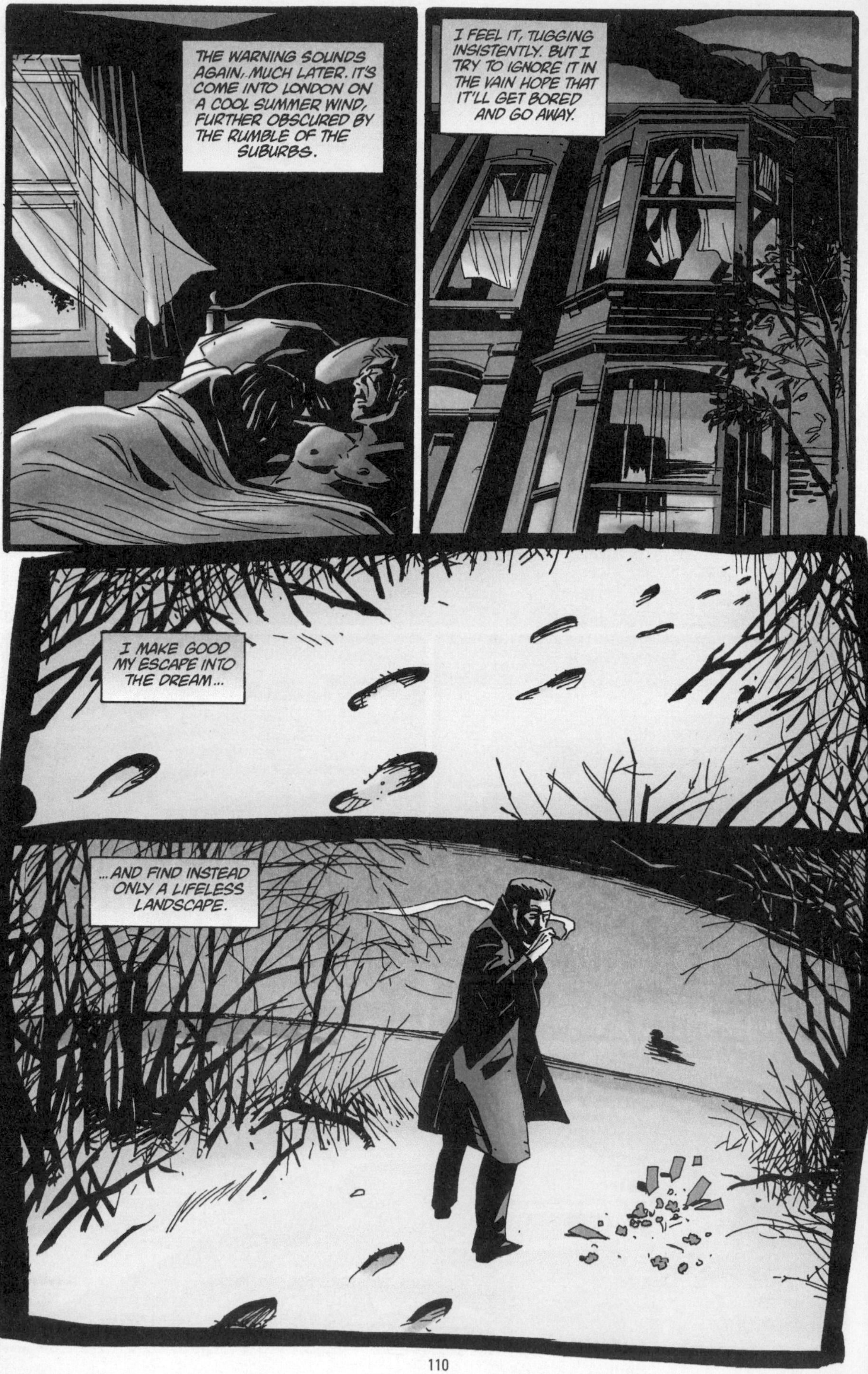

THE WARNING SOUNDS AGAIN, MUCH LATER. IT'S COME INTO LONDON ON A COOL SUMMER WIND, FURTHER OBSCURED BY THE RUMBLE OF THE SUBURBS.
I FEEL IT, TUGGING INSISTENTLY. BUT I TRY TO IGNORE IT IN THE VAIN HOPE THAT IT'LL GET BORED AND GO AWAY.
I MAKE GOOD MY ESCAPE INTO THE DREAM...
...AND FIND INSTEAD ONLY A LIFELESS LANDSCAPE.

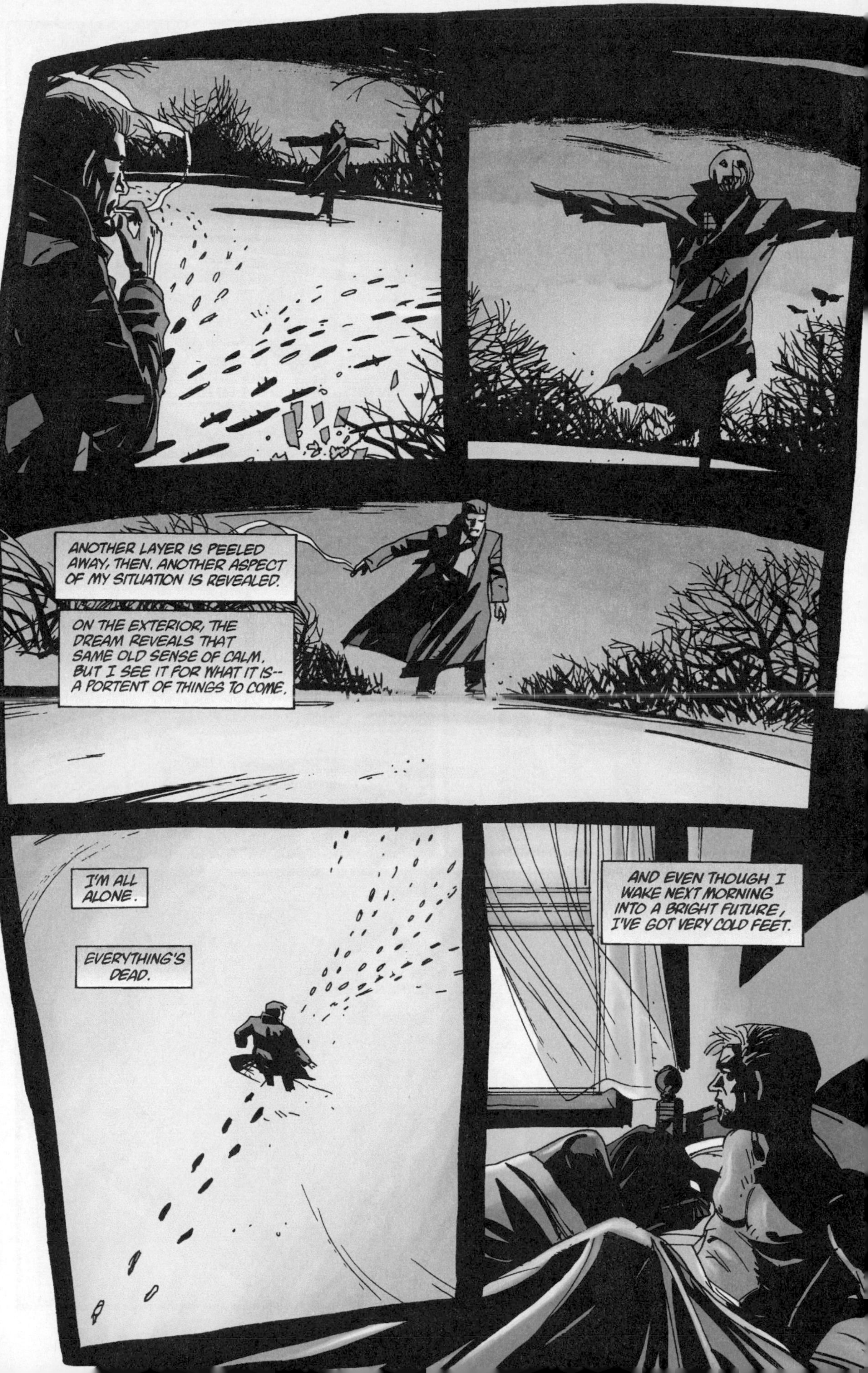
ANOTHER LAYER IS PEELED AWAY, THEN. ANOTHER ASPECT OF MY SITUATION IS REVEALED.
ON THE EXTERIOR, THE DREAM REVEALS THAT SAME OLD SENSE OF CALM. BUT I SEE IT FOR WHAT IT IS-- A PORTENT OF THINGS TO COME.
I'M ALL ALONE.
EVERYTHING'S DEAD.
AND EVEN THOUGH I WAKE NEXT MORNING INTO A BRIGHT FUTURE, I'VE GOT VERY COLD FEET.

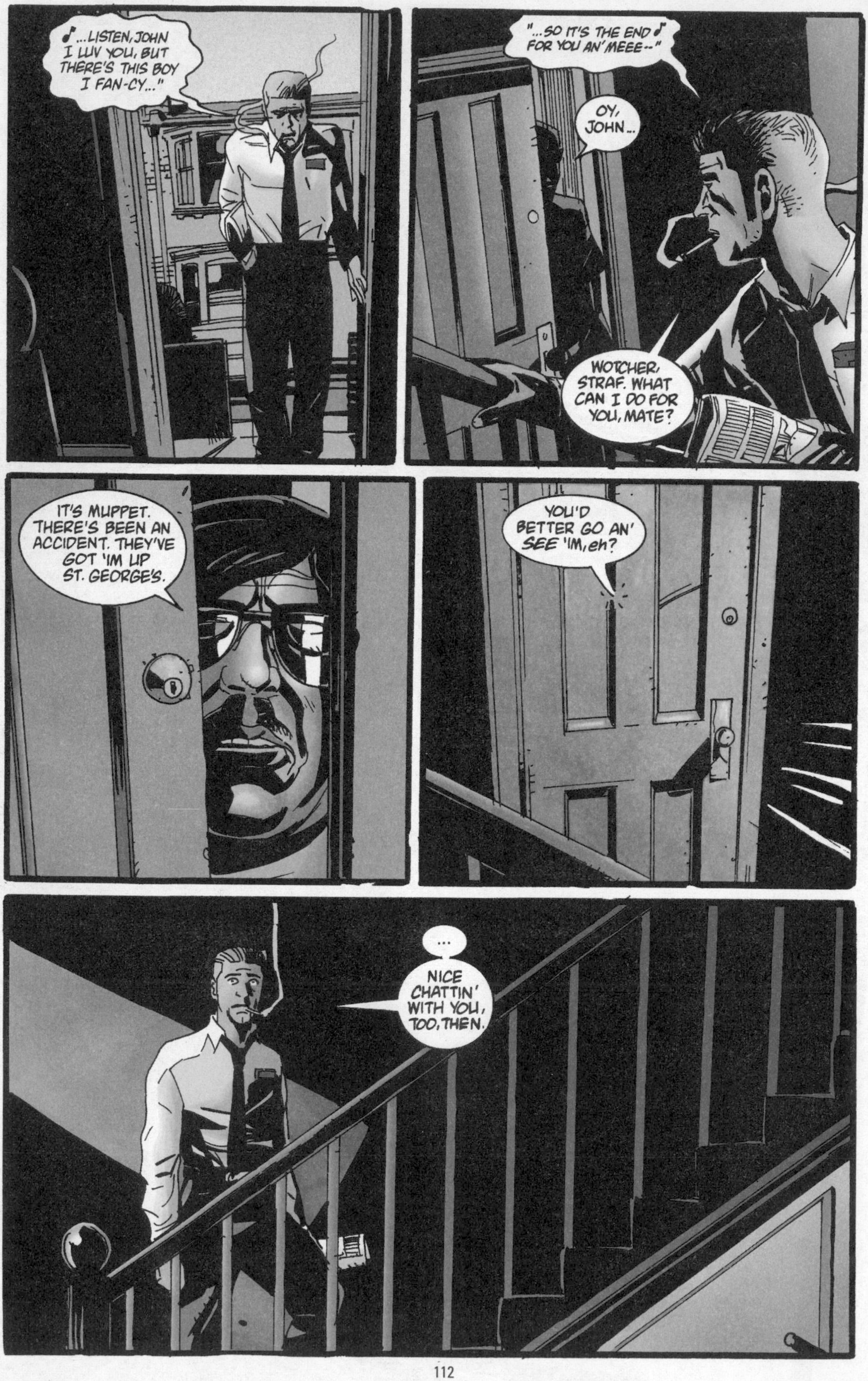
♪ ...LISTEN, JOHN I LUV YOU, BUT THERE'S THIS BOY I FAN-CY..."
"...SO IT'S THE END ♪ FOR YOU AN' MEEE--"
OY, JOHN...
WOTCHER, STRAF. WHAT CAN I DO FOR YOU, MATE?
IT'S MUPPET. THERE'S BEEN AN ACCIDENT. THEY'VE GOT 'IM UP ST. GEORGE'S.
YOU'D BETTER GO AN' SEE 'IM, eh?
...
NICE CHATTIN' WITH YOU, TOO, THEN.

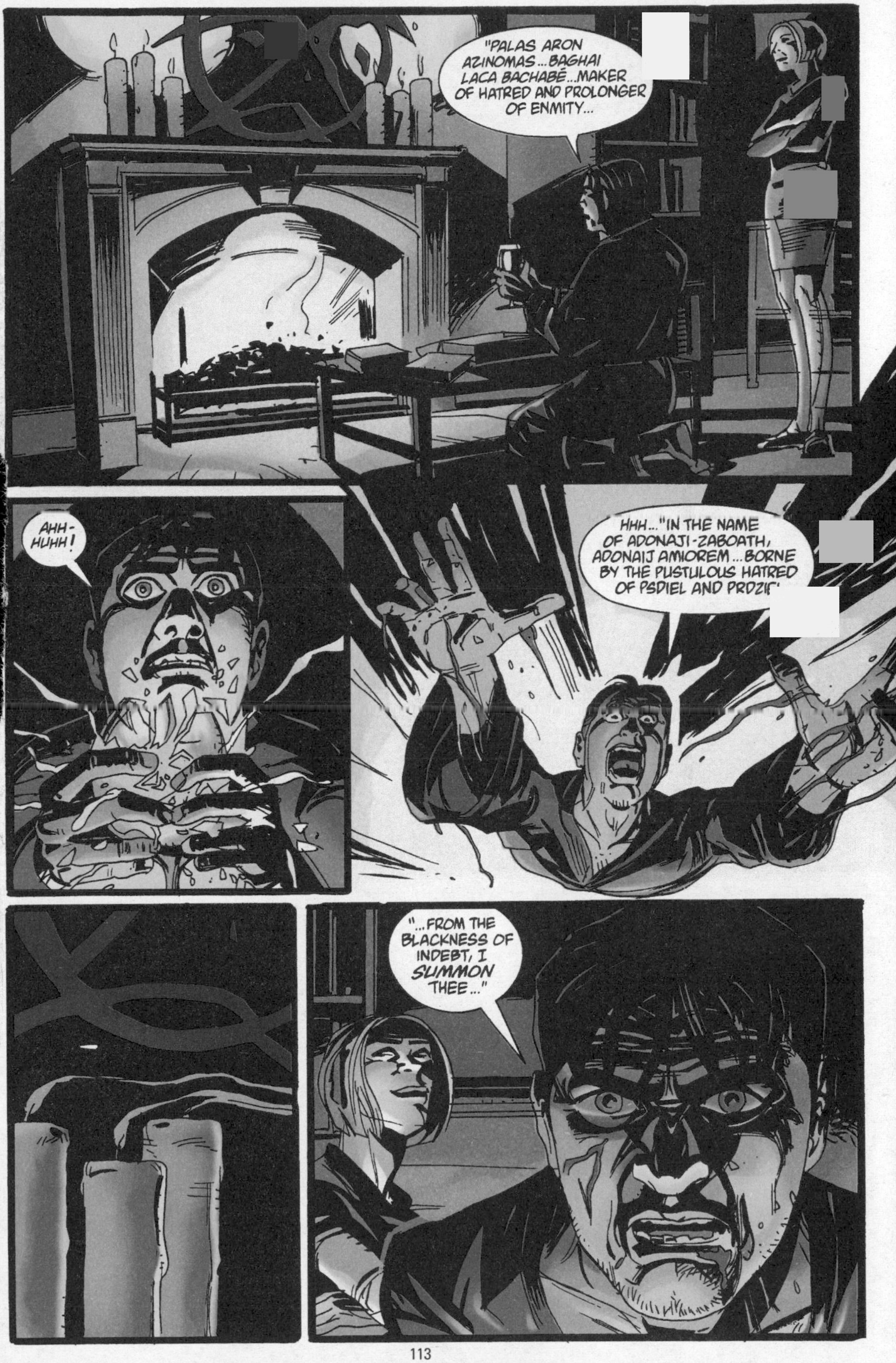
"PALAS ARON AZINOMAS...BAGHAI LACA BACHABÉ...MAKER OF HATRED AND PROLONGER OF ENMITY...
AHH-HUHH!
HHH..."IN THE NAME OF ADONAJI-ZABOATH, ADONAIJ AMIOREM...BORNE BY THE PUSTULOUS HATRED OF PSDIEL AND PROZI
"...FROM THE BLACKNESS OF INDEBT, I SUMMON THEE..."

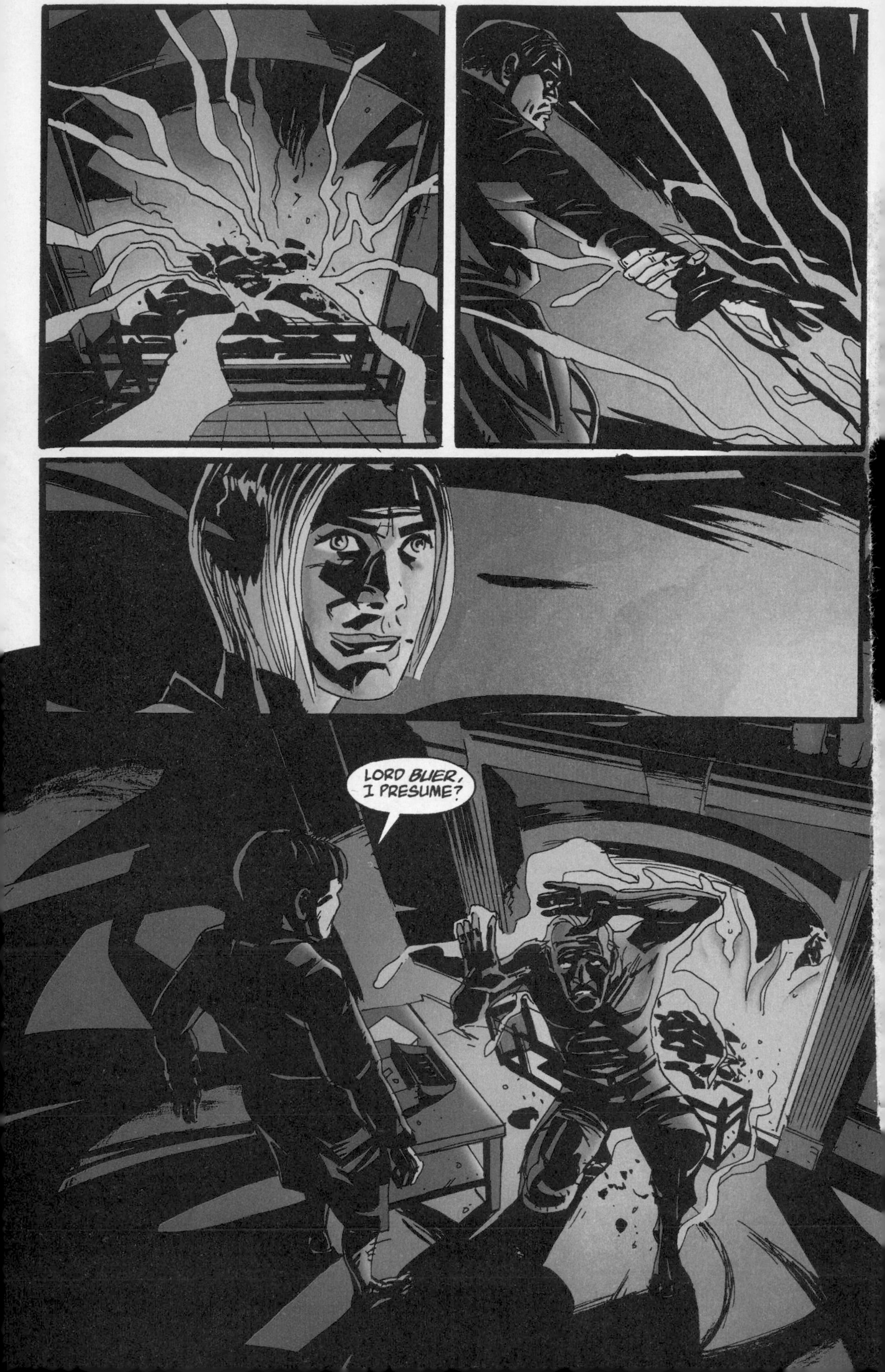
LORD BUER, I PRESUME?

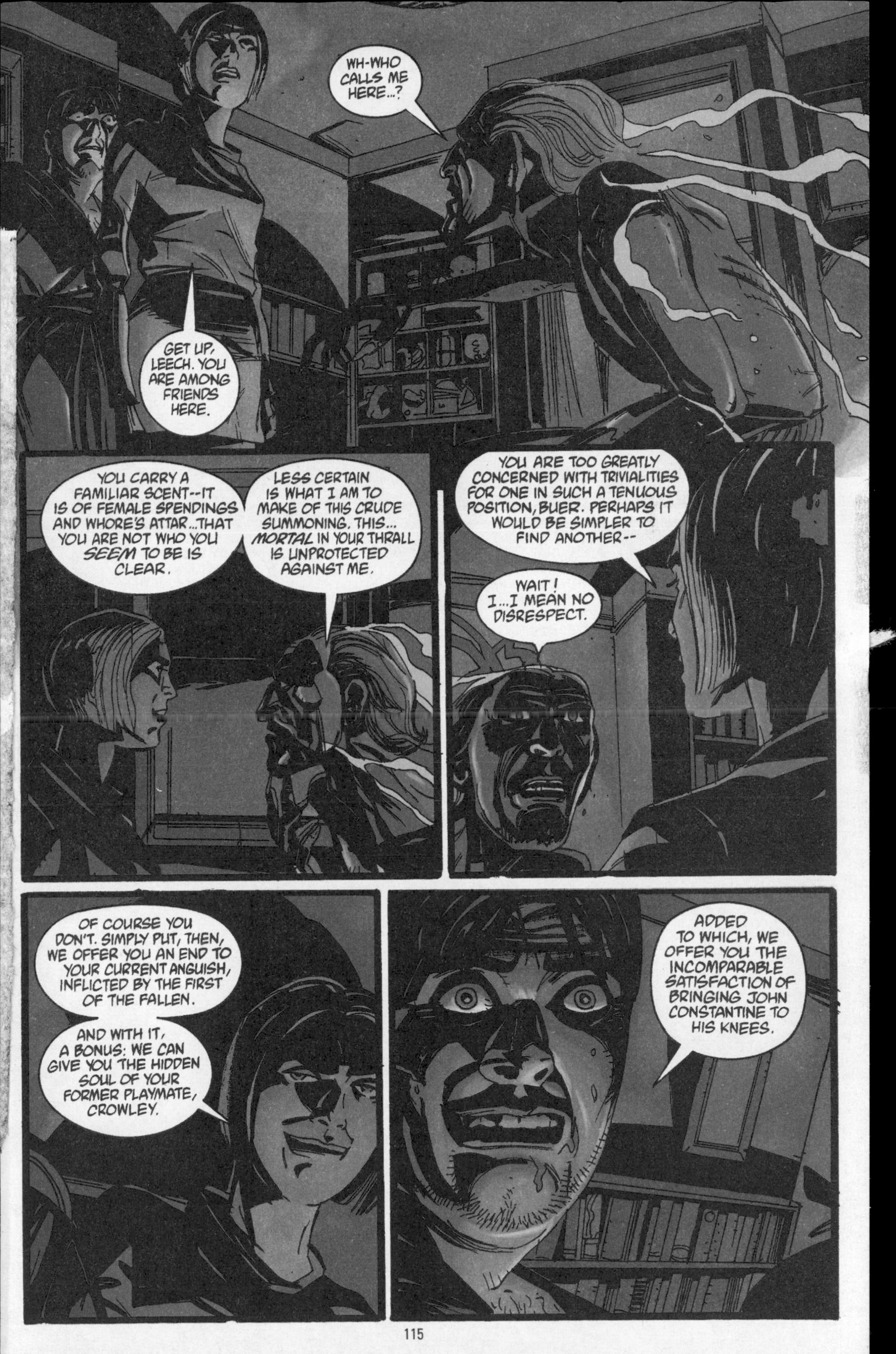
WH-WHO CALLS ME HERE...?
GET UP, LEECH. YOU ARE AMONG FRIENDS HERE.
YOU CARRY A FAMILIAR SCENT--IT IS OF FEMALE SPENDINGS AND WHORE'S ATTAR...THAT YOU ARE NOT WHO YOU *SEEM* TO BE IS CLEAR.
LESS CERTAIN IS WHAT I AM TO MAKE OF THIS CRUDE SUMMONING. THIS... *MORTAL* IN YOUR THRALL IS UNPROTECTED AGAINST ME.
YOU ARE TOO GREATLY CONCERNED WITH TRIVIALITIES FOR ONE IN SUCH A TENUOUS POSITION, BUER. PERHAPS IT WOULD BE SIMPLER TO FIND ANOTHER--
WAIT! I...I MEAN NO DISRESPECT.
OF COURSE YOU DON'T. SIMPLY PUT, THEN, WE OFFER YOU AN END TO YOUR CURRENT ANGUISH, INFLICTED BY THE FIRST OF THE FALLEN.
AND WITH IT, A BONUS: WE CAN GIVE YOU THE HIDDEN SOUL OF YOUR FORMER PLAYMATE, CROWLEY.
ADDED TO WHICH, WE OFFER YOU THE INCOMPARABLE SATISFACTION OF BRINGING JOHN CONSTANTINE TO HIS KNEES.

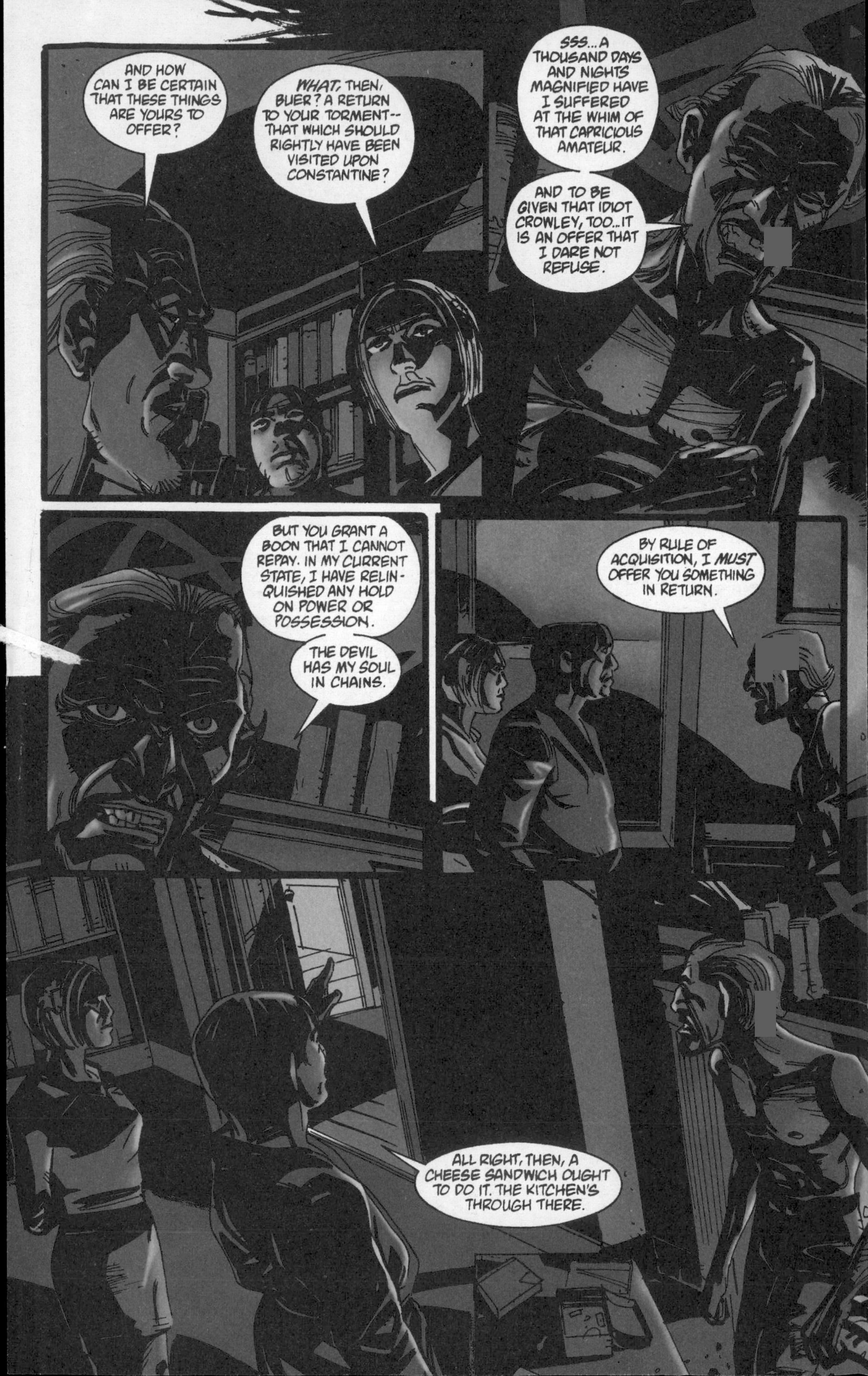
AND HOW CAN I BE CERTAIN THAT THESE THINGS ARE YOURS TO OFFER?
WHAT, THEN, BUER? A RETURN TO YOUR TORMENT-- THAT WHICH SHOULD RIGHTLY HAVE BEEN VISITED UPON CONSTANTINE?
SSS... A THOUSAND DAYS AND NIGHTS MAGNIFIED HAVE I SUFFERED AT THE WHIM OF THAT CAPRICIOUS AMATEUR.
AND TO BE GIVEN THAT IDIOT CROWLEY, TOO... IT IS AN OFFER THAT I DARE NOT REFUSE.
BUT YOU GRANT A BOON THAT I CANNOT REPAY. IN MY CURRENT STATE, I HAVE RELIN-QUISHED ANY HOLD ON POWER OR POSSESSION.
THE DEVIL HAS MY SOUL IN CHAINS.
BY RULE OF ACQUISITION, I MUST OFFER YOU SOMETHING IN RETURN.
ALL RIGHT, THEN, A CHEESE SANDWICH OUGHT TO DO IT. THE KITCHEN'S THROUGH THERE.

"I WON'T LIE TO YOU--THE SITUATION'S RATHER GRAVE, I'M AFRAID."

HOW GRAVE?

LOOK...WE'RE CONFIDENT WE'VE STEMMED ANY INTERNAL BLEEDING, BUT THAT DOESN'T MEAN HE'S OUT OF THE WOODS YET. THE IMPACT'S BRUISED HIS BRAIN, AND IT'S DANGEROUSLY *SWOLLEN*.

WHAT THAT MEANS IS THAT WE HAVE TO MONITOR...

NO SMOKING

CRITICAL

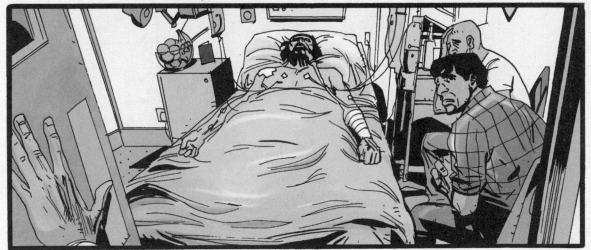

HMM...SOME PEOPLE CHOOSE A FUNNY WAY TO *EXPAND* THEIR FUCKIN' MINDS--

YOU WHAT? YOU FOOKIN' *WHAT*--? YOU THINK IT'S FOOKIN' *FUNNY*, CONSTANTINE? AH'LL SHOW YE WHA'S FOOKIN' *FUNNY*--

STEADY ON, LOFTY--

YE'VE ALLUS GOTTA *SHINE*, HAVEN'T YER? THA'S ME BEST FOOKIN' *MATE* LYIN' THERE, AN' YOU'RE TOO BUSY TAKIN' CENTER FOOKIN' *STAGE* T'KNOW WHEN T'SHUT YER STUPID GOB!

DON'T SAY SORRY OR ANYTHIN'--YEH'VE DONE ENOUGH. JUST FOOK OFF AN' LEAVE THE REST OF US *ALONE*, ALL RIGHT?

COME, LOFTUS...IS BEST WE *GO* NOW, YES?

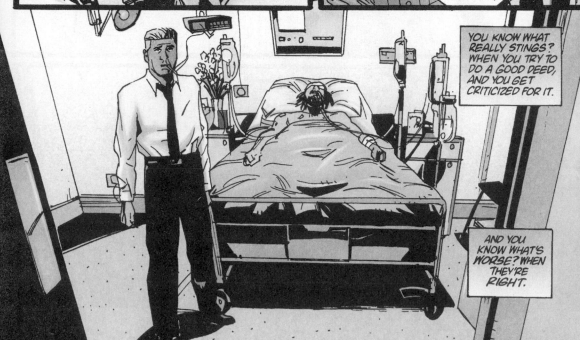

YOU KNOW WHAT REALLY STINGS? WHEN YOU TRY TO DO A GOOD DEED, AND YOU GET CRITICIZED FOR IT.

AND YOU KNOW WHAT'S *WORSE*? WHEN THEY'RE RIGHT.

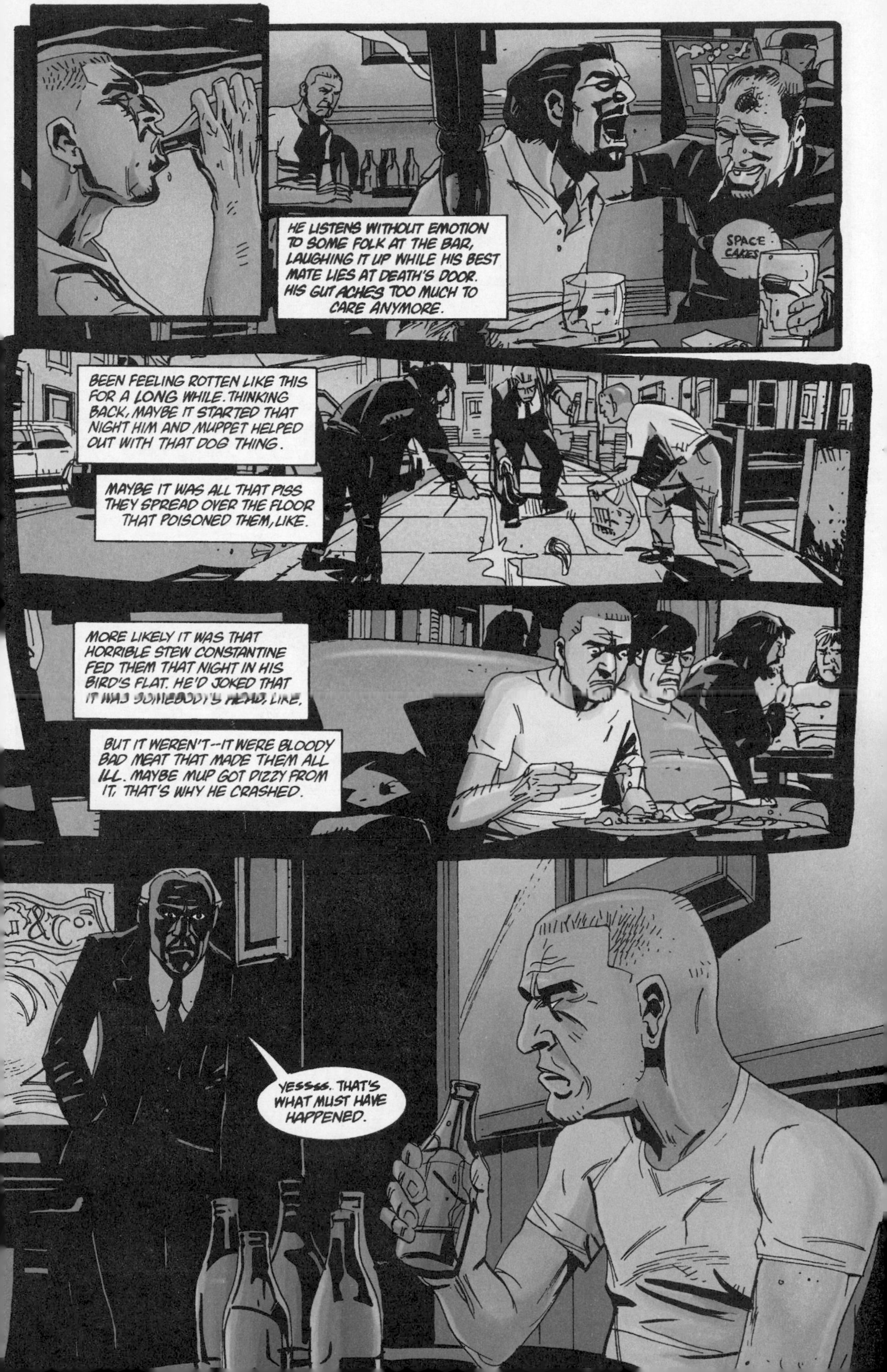

HE LISTENS WITHOUT EMOTION TO SOME FOLK AT THE BAR, LAUGHING IT UP WHILE HIS BEST MATE LIES AT DEATH'S DOOR. HIS GUT ACHES TOO MUCH TO CARE ANYMORE.
SPACE CAKES
BEEN FEELING ROTTEN LIKE THIS FOR A LONG WHILE. THINKING BACK, MAYBE IT STARTED THAT NIGHT HIM AND MUPPET HELPED OUT WITH THAT DOG THING.
MAYBE IT WAS ALL THAT PISS THEY SPREAD OVER THE FLOOR THAT POISONED THEM, LIKE.
MORE LIKELY IT WAS THAT HORRIBLE STEW CONSTANTINE FED THEM THAT NIGHT IN HIS BIRD'S FLAT. HE'D JOKED THAT IT WAS SOMEBODY'S HEAD, LIKE.
BUT IT WEREN'T--IT WERE BLOODY BAD MEAT THAT MADE THEM ALL ILL. MAYBE MUP GOT DIZZY FROM IT, THAT'S WHY HE CRASHED.
YESSSS. THAT'S WHAT MUST HAVE HAPPENED.

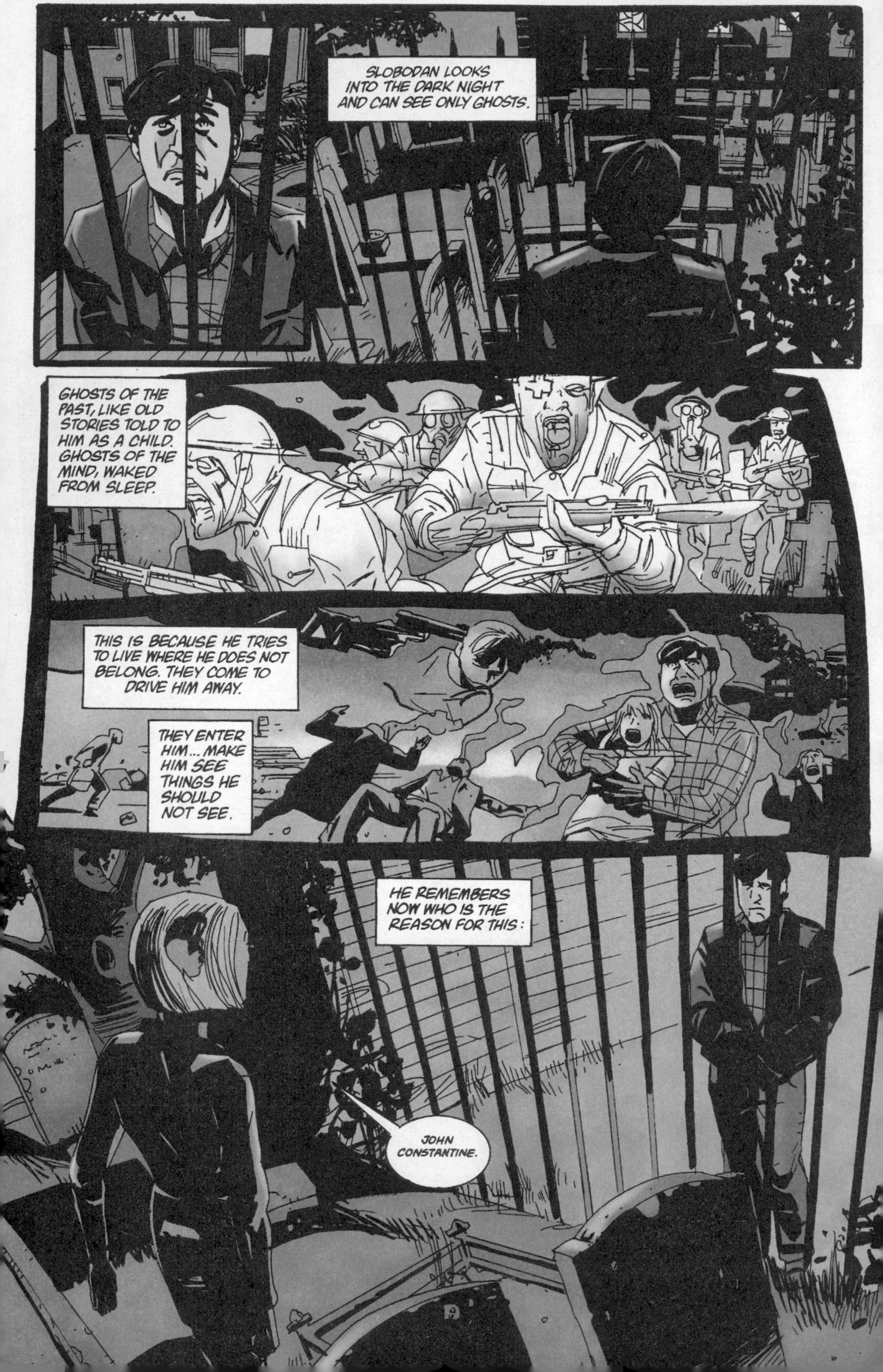
SLOBODAN LOOKS INTO THE DARK NIGHT AND CAN SEE ONLY GHOSTS.
GHOSTS OF THE PAST, LIKE OLD STORIES TOLD TO HIM AS A CHILD. GHOSTS OF THE MIND, WAKED FROM SLEEP.
THIS IS BECAUSE HE TRIES TO LIVE WHERE HE DOES NOT BELONG. THEY COME TO DRIVE HIM AWAY.
THEY ENTER HIM... MAKE HIM SEE THINGS HE SHOULD NOT SEE.
HE REMEMBERS NOW WHO IS THE REASON FOR THIS:
JOHN CONSTANTINE.

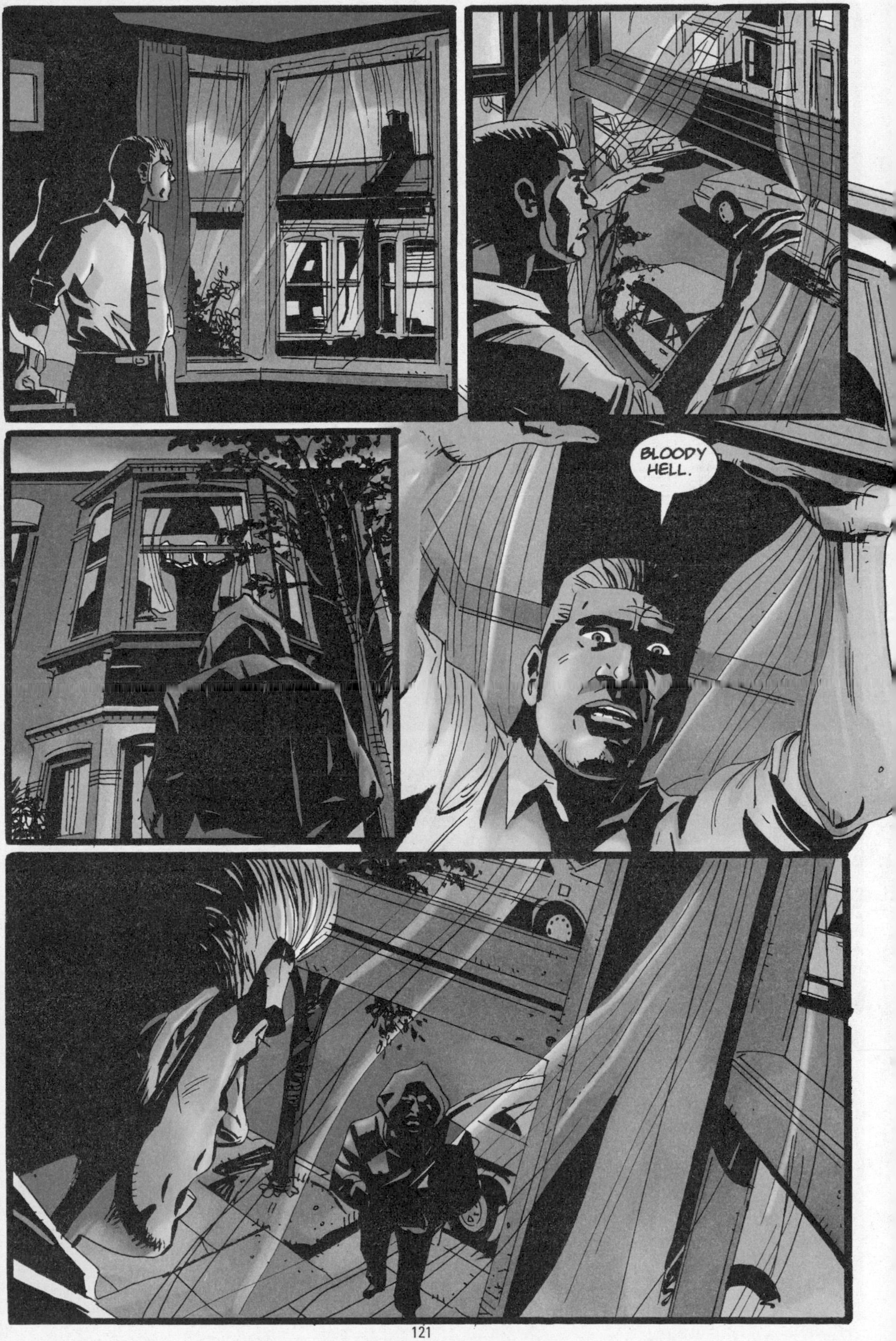
BLOODY HELL.

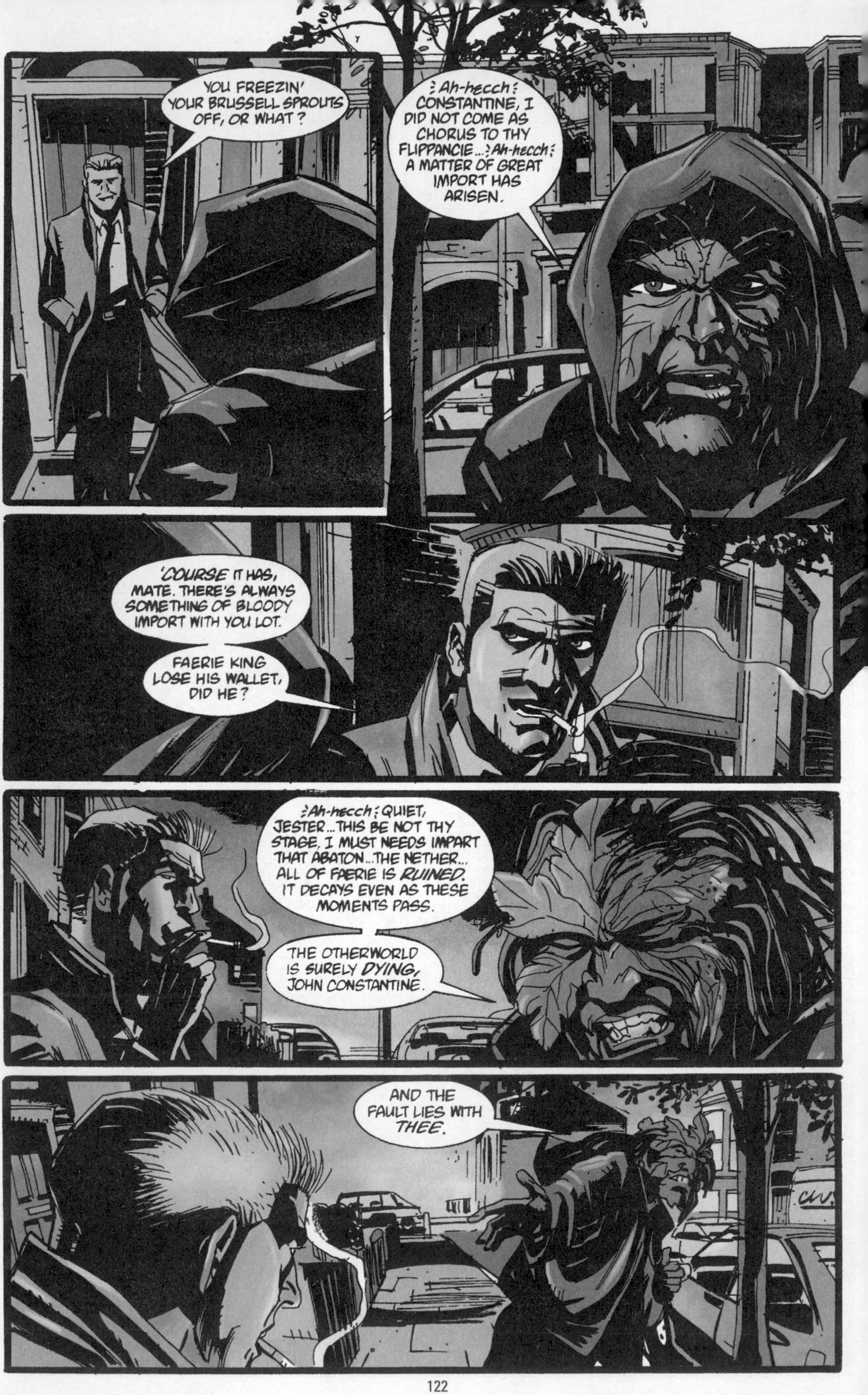
YOU FREEZIN' YOUR BRUSSELL SPROUTS OFF, OR WHAT?
¿Ah-hecch¿ CONSTANTINE, I DID NOT COME AS CHORUS TO THY FLIPPANCIE... ¿Ah-hecch¿ A MATTER OF GREAT IMPORT HAS ARISEN.
'COURSE IT HAS, MATE. THERE'S ALWAYS SOMETHING OF BLOODY IMPORT WITH YOU LOT.
FAERIE KING LOSE HIS WALLET, DID HE?
¿Ah-hecch¿ QUIET, JESTER... THIS BE NOT THY STAGE. I MUST NEEDS IMPART THAT ABATON... THE NETHER... ALL OF FAERIE IS RUINED. IT DECAYS EVEN AS THESE MOMENTS PASS.
THE OTHERWORLD IS SURELY DYING, JOHN CONSTANTINE.
AND THE FAULT LIES WITH THEE.

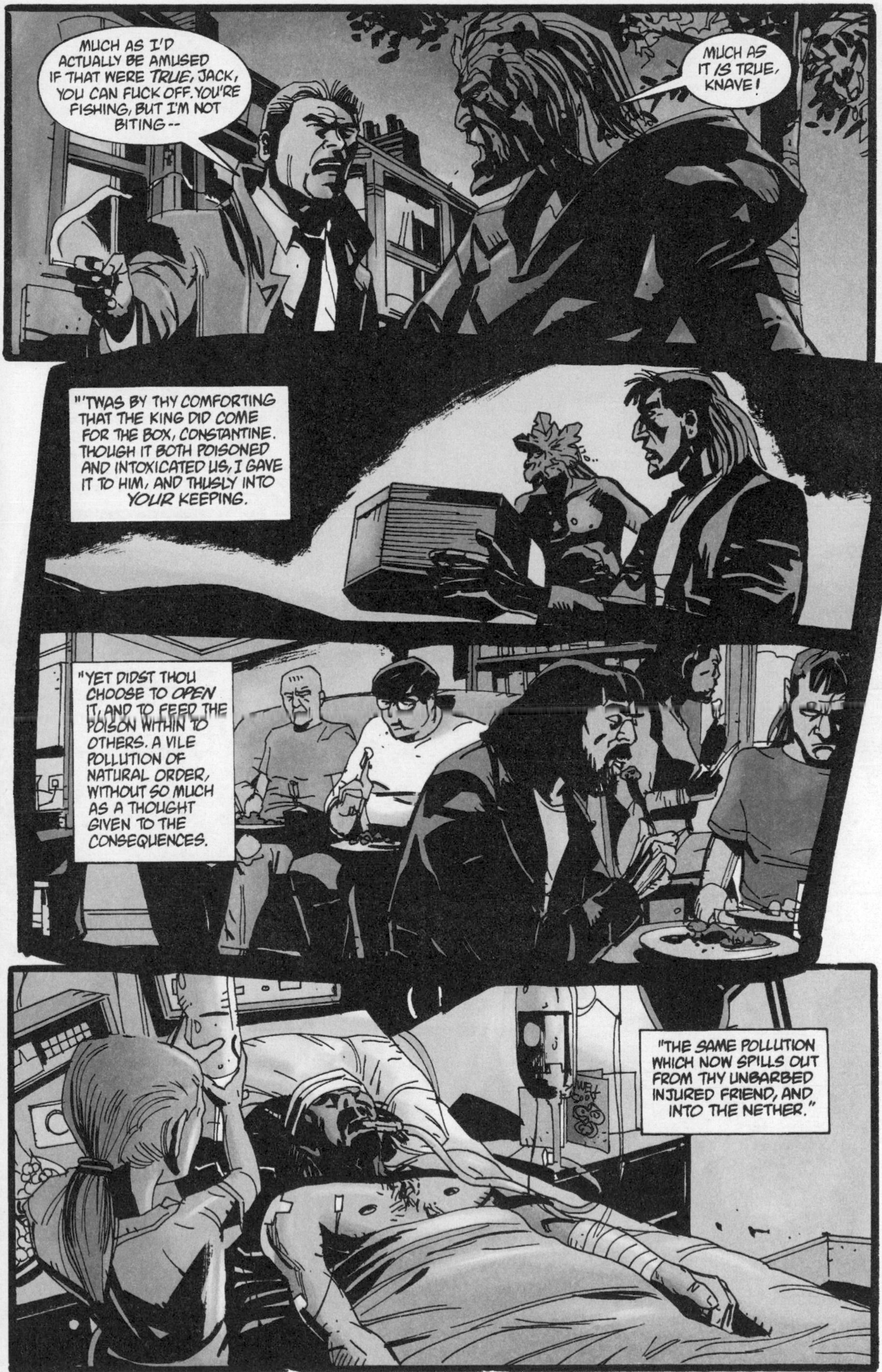
MUCH AS I'D ACTUALLY BE AMUSED IF THAT WERE TRUE, JACK, YOU CAN FUCK OFF. YOU'RE FISHING, BUT I'M NOT BITING--
MUCH AS IT IS TRUE, KNAVE!
"'TWAS BY THY COMFORTING THAT THE KING DID COME FOR THE BOX, CONSTANTINE. THOUGH IT BOTH POISONED AND INTOXICATED US, I GAVE IT TO HIM, AND THUSLY INTO YOUR KEEPING.
"YET DIDST THOU CHOOSE TO OPEN IT, AND TO FEED THE POISON WITHIN TO OTHERS. A VILE POLLUTION OF NATURAL ORDER, WITHOUT SO MUCH AS A THOUGHT GIVEN TO THE CONSEQUENCES.
"THE SAME POLLUTION WHICH NOW SPILLS OUT FROM THY UNBARBED INJURED FRIEND, AND INTO THE NETHER."

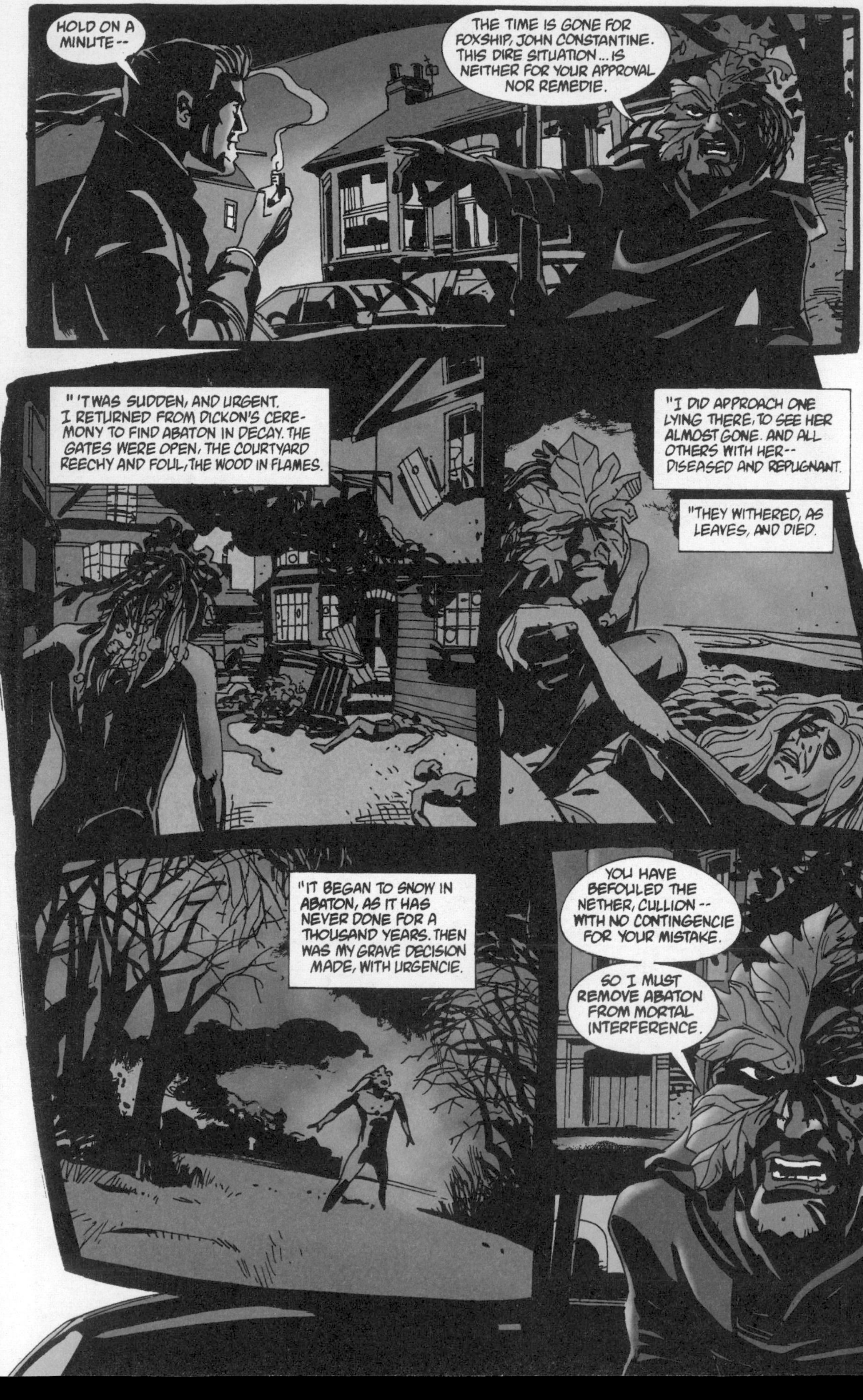
HOLD ON A MINUTE--
THE TIME IS GONE FOR FOXSHIP, JOHN CONSTANTINE. THIS DIRE SITUATION... IS NEITHER FOR YOUR APPROVAL NOR REMEDIE.
"'TWAS SUDDEN, AND URGENT. I RETURNED FROM DICKON'S CEREMONY TO FIND ABATON IN DECAY. THE GATES WERE OPEN, THE COURTYARD REECHY AND FOUL, THE WOOD IN FLAMES.
"I DID APPROACH ONE LYING THERE, TO SEE HER ALMOST GONE. AND ALL OTHERS WITH HER-- DISEASED AND REPUGNANT.
"THEY WITHERED, AS LEAVES, AND DIED.
"IT BEGAN TO SNOW IN ABATON, AS IT HAS NEVER DONE FOR A THOUSAND YEARS. THEN WAS MY GRAVE DECISION MADE, WITH URGENCIE.
YOU HAVE BEFOULED THE NETHER, CULLION-- WITH NO CONTINGENCIE FOR YOUR MISTAKE.
SO I MUST REMOVE ABATON FROM MORTAL INTERFERENCE.

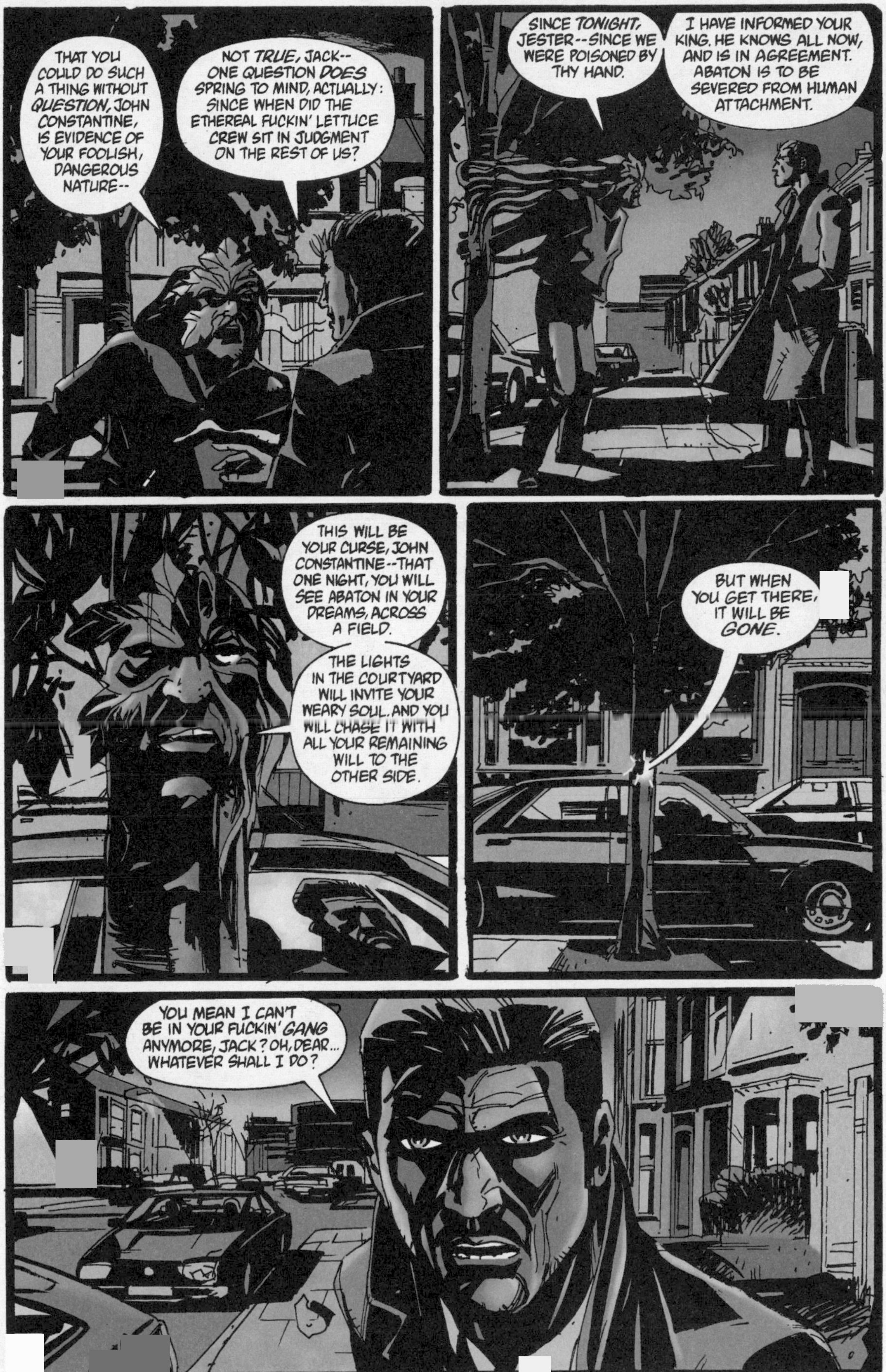
THAT YOU COULD DO SUCH A THING WITHOUT QUESTION, JOHN CONSTANTINE, IS EVIDENCE OF YOUR FOOLISH, DANGEROUS NATURE--
NOT TRUE, JACK--ONE QUESTION DOES SPRING TO MIND, ACTUALLY: SINCE WHEN DID THE ETHEREAL FUCKIN' LETTUCE CREW SIT IN JUDGMENT ON THE REST OF US?
SINCE TONIGHT, JESTER--SINCE WE WERE POISONED BY THY HAND.
I HAVE INFORMED YOUR KING. HE KNOWS ALL NOW, AND IS IN AGREEMENT. ABATON IS TO BE SEVERED FROM HUMAN ATTACHMENT.
THIS WILL BE YOUR CURSE, JOHN CONSTANTINE--THAT ONE NIGHT, YOU WILL SEE ABATON IN YOUR DREAMS, ACROSS A FIELD.
THE LIGHTS IN THE COURTYARD WILL INVITE YOUR WEARY SOUL, AND YOU WILL CHASE IT WITH ALL YOUR REMAINING WILL TO THE OTHER SIDE.
BUT WHEN YOU GET THERE, IT WILL BE GONE.
YOU MEAN I CAN'T BE IN YOUR FUCKIN' GANG ANYMORE, JACK? OH, DEAR... WHATEVER SHALL I DO?

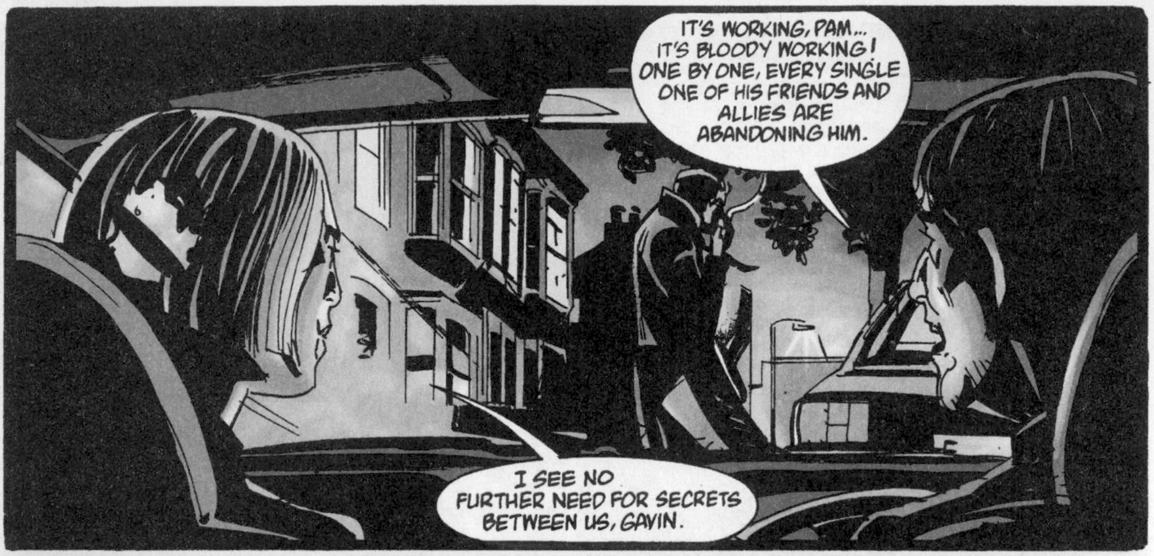
IT'S WORKING, PAM... IT'S BLOODY WORKING! ONE BY ONE, EVERY SINGLE ONE OF HIS FRIENDS AND ALLIES ARE ABANDONING HIM.
I SEE NO FURTHER NEED FOR SECRETS BETWEEN US, GAVIN.

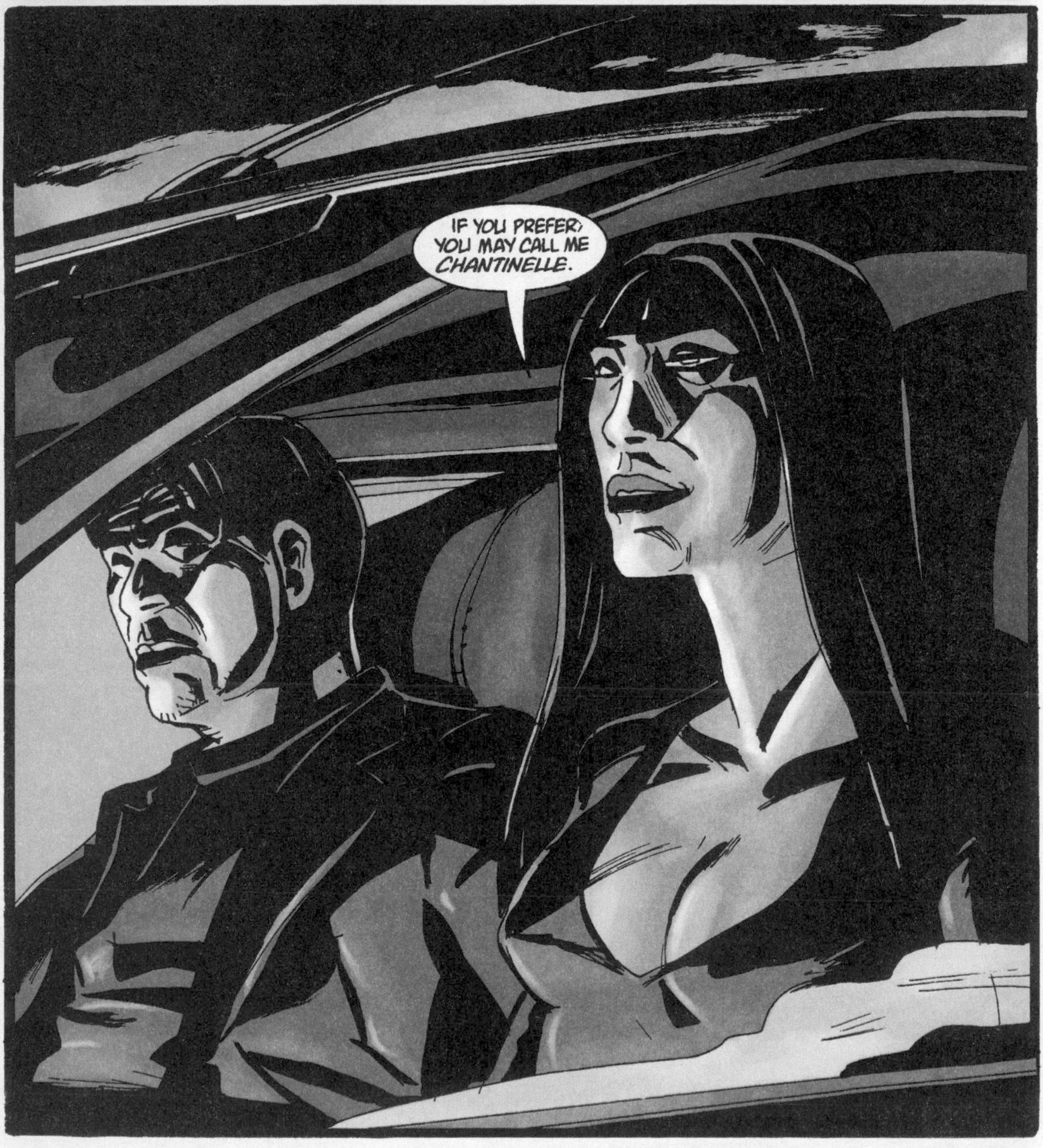
IF YOU PREFER, YOU MAY CALL ME CHANTINELLE.

JOHN CONSTANTINE
HELLBLAZER
PAUL JENKINS • WARREN PLEECE
Sean 98
HOW TO PLAY WITH FIRE
Part Two of Four

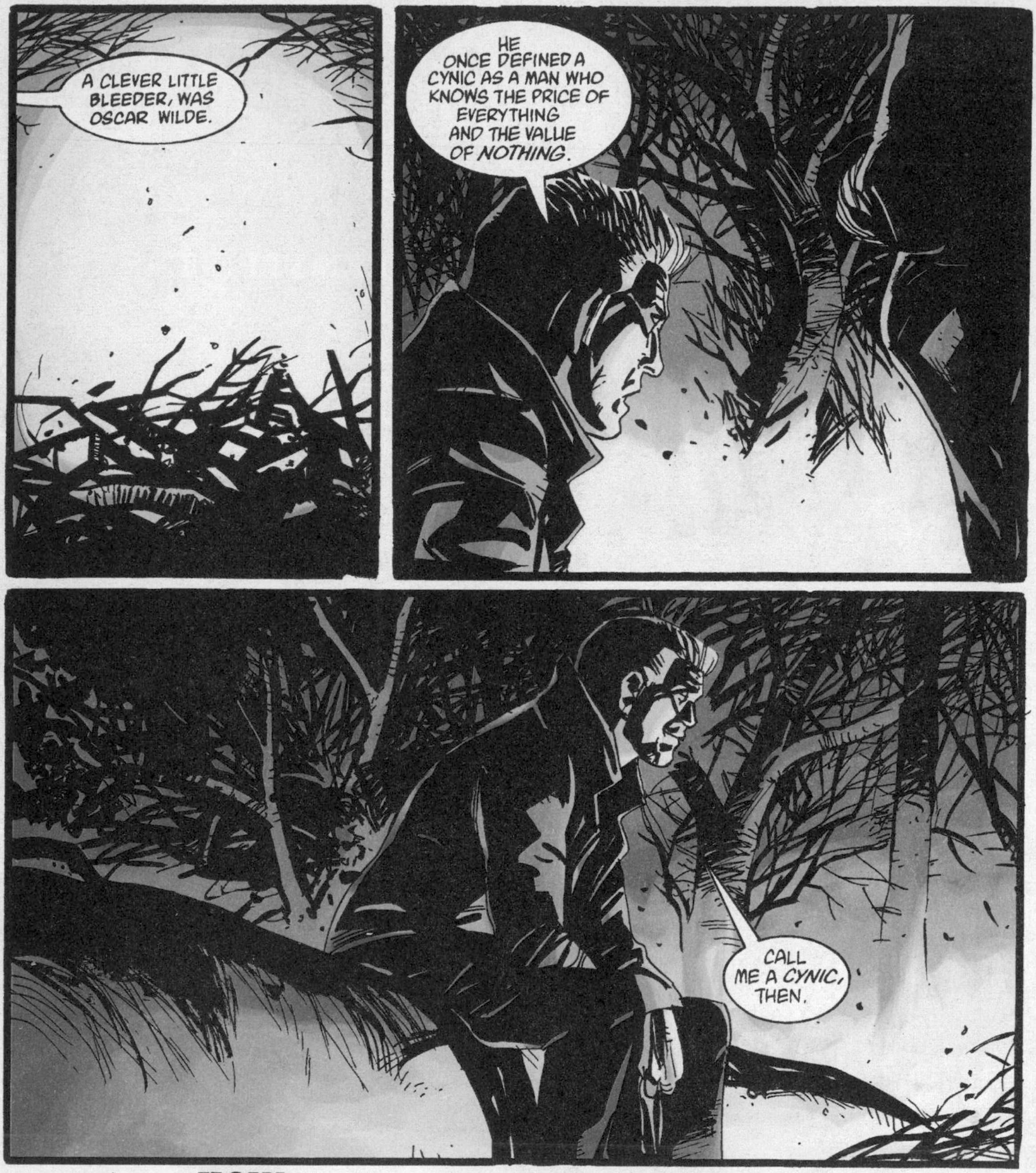
A CLEVER LITTLE BLEEDER, WAS OSCAR WILDE.
HE ONCE DEFINED A CYNIC AS A MAN WHO KNOWS THE PRICE OF EVERYTHING AND THE VALUE OF *NOTHING*.
CALL ME A *CYNIC*, THEN.

HOW TO PLAY WITH FIRE PART TWO

FANNING THE FLAMES

PAUL JENKINS writer · WARREN PLEECE artist · JAMES SINCLAIR colorist · DIGITAL CHAMELEON separations · CLEM ROBINS letterer · AXEL ALONSO editor

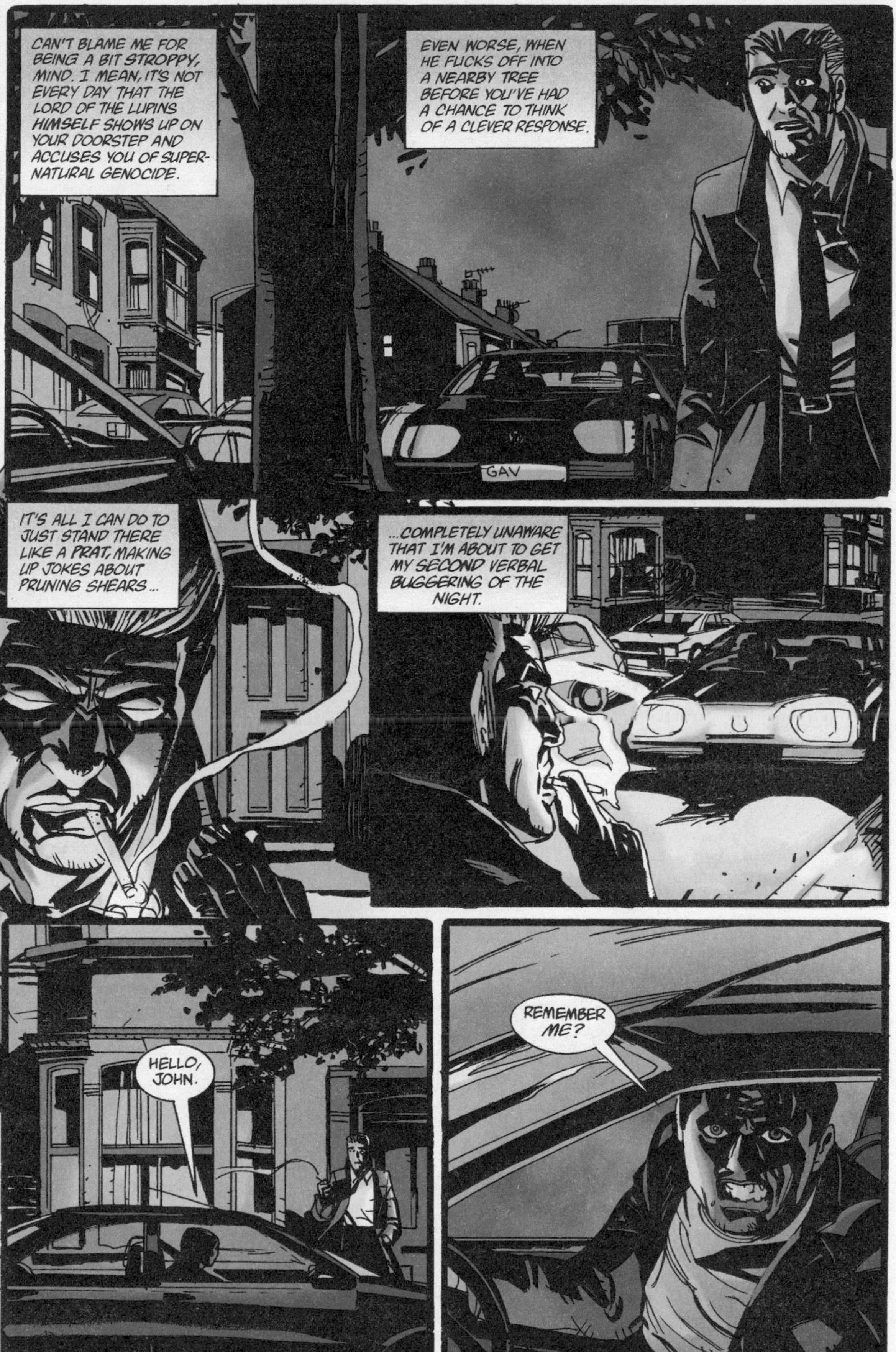

CAN'T BLAME ME FOR BEING A BIT STROPPY, MIND. I MEAN, IT'S NOT EVERY DAY THAT THE LORD OF THE LUPINS HIMSELF SHOWS UP ON YOUR DOORSTEP AND ACCUSES YOU OF SUPER-NATURAL GENOCIDE.
EVEN WORSE, WHEN HE FUCKS OFF INTO A NEARBY TREE BEFORE YOU'VE HAD A CHANCE TO THINK OF A CLEVER RESPONSE.
GAV
IT'S ALL I CAN DO TO JUST STAND THERE LIKE A PRAT, MAKING UP JOKES ABOUT PRUNING SHEARS...
...COMPLETELY UNAWARE THAT I'M ABOUT TO GET MY SECOND VERBAL BUGGERING OF THE NIGHT.
HELLO, JOHN.
REMEMBER ME?

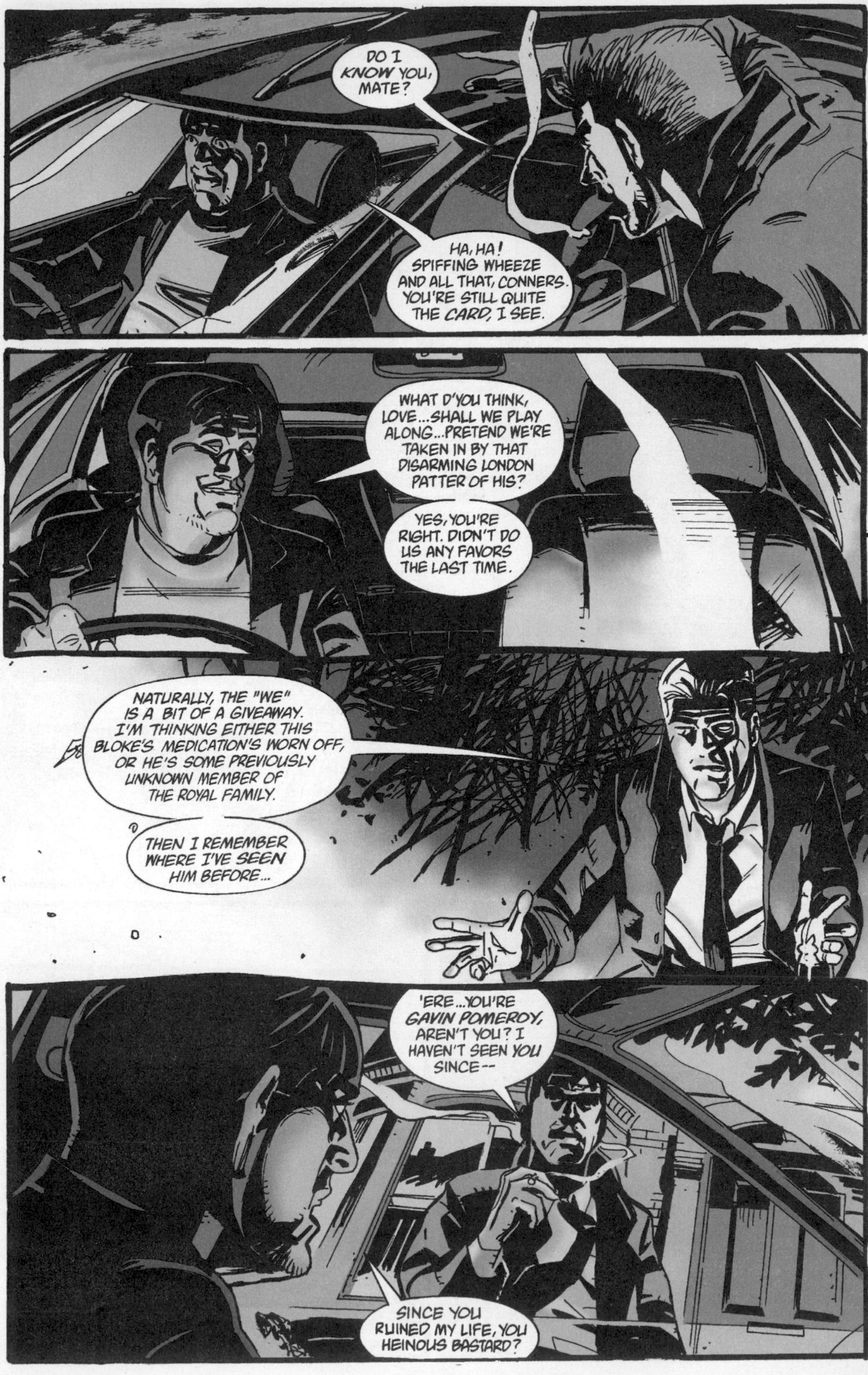
DO I KNOW YOU, MATE?
HA, HA! SPIFFING WHEEZE AND ALL THAT, CONNERS. YOU'RE STILL QUITE THE CARD, I SEE.
WHAT D'YOU THINK, LOVE...SHALL WE PLAY ALONG...PRETEND WE'RE TAKEN IN BY THAT DISARMING LONDON PATTER OF HIS?
YES, YOU'RE RIGHT. DIDN'T DO US ANY FAVORS THE LAST TIME.
NATURALLY, THE "WE" IS A BIT OF A GIVEAWAY. I'M THINKING EITHER THIS BLOKE'S MEDICATION'S WORN OFF, OR HE'S SOME PREVIOUSLY UNKNOWN MEMBER OF THE ROYAL FAMILY.
THEN I REMEMBER WHERE I'VE SEEN HIM BEFORE...
'ERE...YOU'RE GAVIN POMEROY, AREN'T YOU? I HAVEN'T SEEN YOU SINCE--
SINCE YOU RUINED MY LIFE, YOU HEINOUS BASTARD?

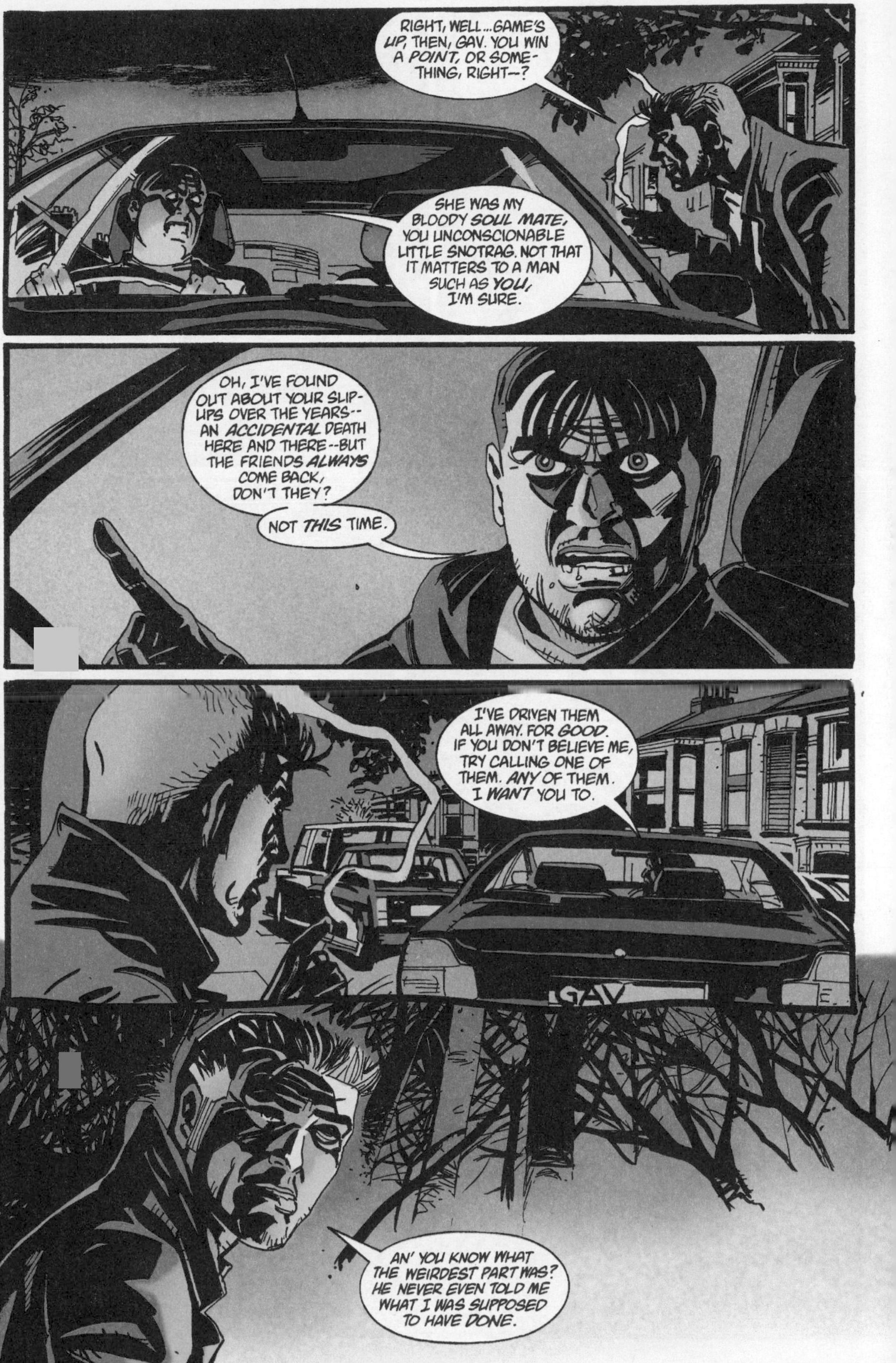
RIGHT, WELL...GAME'S UP, THEN, GAV. YOU WIN A POINT, OR SOMETHING, RIGHT--?
SHE WAS MY BLOODY SOUL MATE, YOU UNCONSCIONABLE LITTLE SNOTRAG. NOT THAT IT MATTERS TO A MAN SUCH AS YOU, I'M SURE.
OH, I'VE FOUND OUT ABOUT YOUR SLIP-UPS OVER THE YEARS-- AN ACCIDENTAL DEATH HERE AND THERE--BUT THE FRIENDS ALWAYS COME BACK, DON'T THEY?
NOT THIS TIME.
I'VE DRIVEN THEM ALL AWAY. FOR GOOD. IF YOU DON'T BELIEVE ME, TRY CALLING ONE OF THEM. ANY OF THEM. I WANT YOU TO.
GAV
AN' YOU KNOW WHAT THE WEIRDEST PART WAS? HE NEVER EVEN TOLD ME WHAT I WAS SUPPOSED TO HAVE DONE.

SO, TELL US AGAIN, ALLY-- WHAT DOES IT LOOK LIKE?

IT DOESNAE LOOK LIKE FUCK ALL, YE DAFT BASTARD! IT'S A STATE OF MIND, FULL O' BIG, MEAN DEVILS AN' VATS OF SCALDIN' PORRIDGE.

YEAH, BUT WHAT'S THE LANDSCAPE LIKE? I MEAN, ARE THERE ANY BUILDINGS, OR CAVES 'N STUFF?

LOOK, YE BIG PLANK...WAIT...THERE'S SOMEONE HERE.

AW, CRIKEY...NOT HIM. NOT **HIM!**

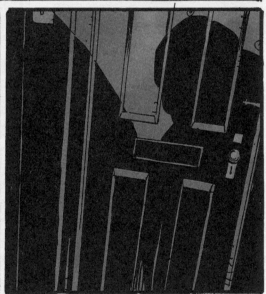

HELLO, CROWLEY. I WISH I COULD SAY IT'S A *PLEASURE* TO SEE YOU AGAIN.

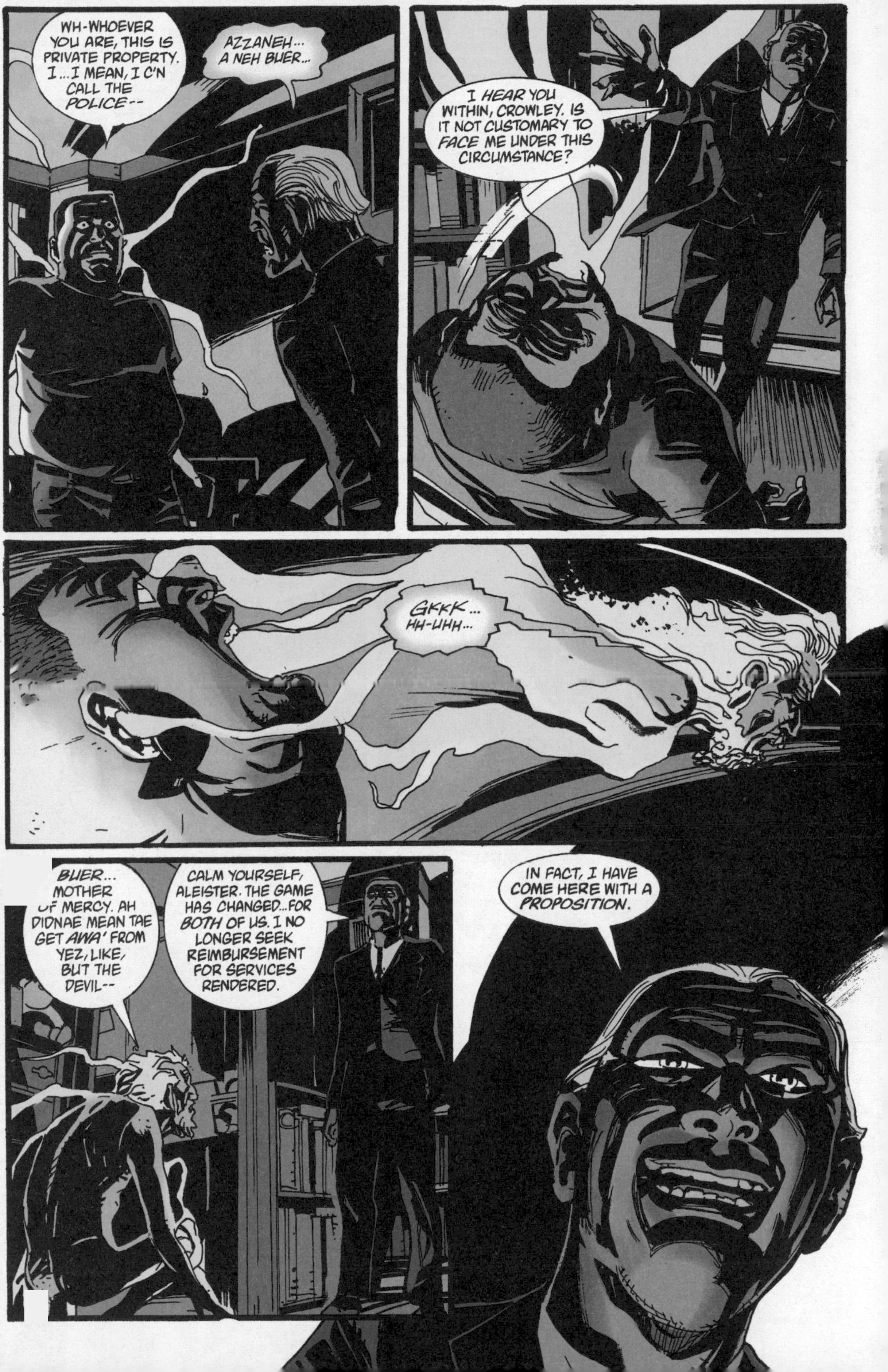
WH-WHOEVER YOU ARE, THIS IS PRIVATE PROPERTY. I...I MEAN, I C'N CALL THE POLICE--
AZZANEH... A NEH BUER...
I HEAR YOU WITHIN, CROWLEY. IS IT NOT CUSTOMARY TO FACE ME UNDER THIS CIRCUMSTANCE?
GKKK... HH-UHH...
BUER... MOTHER OF MERCY. AH DIDNAE MEAN TAE GET AWA' FROM YEZ, LIKE, BUT THE DEVIL--
CALM YOURSELF, ALEISTER. THE GAME HAS CHANGED...FOR BOTH OF US. I NO LONGER SEEK REIMBURSEMENT FOR SERVICES RENDERED.
IN FACT, I HAVE COME HERE WITH A PROPOSITION.

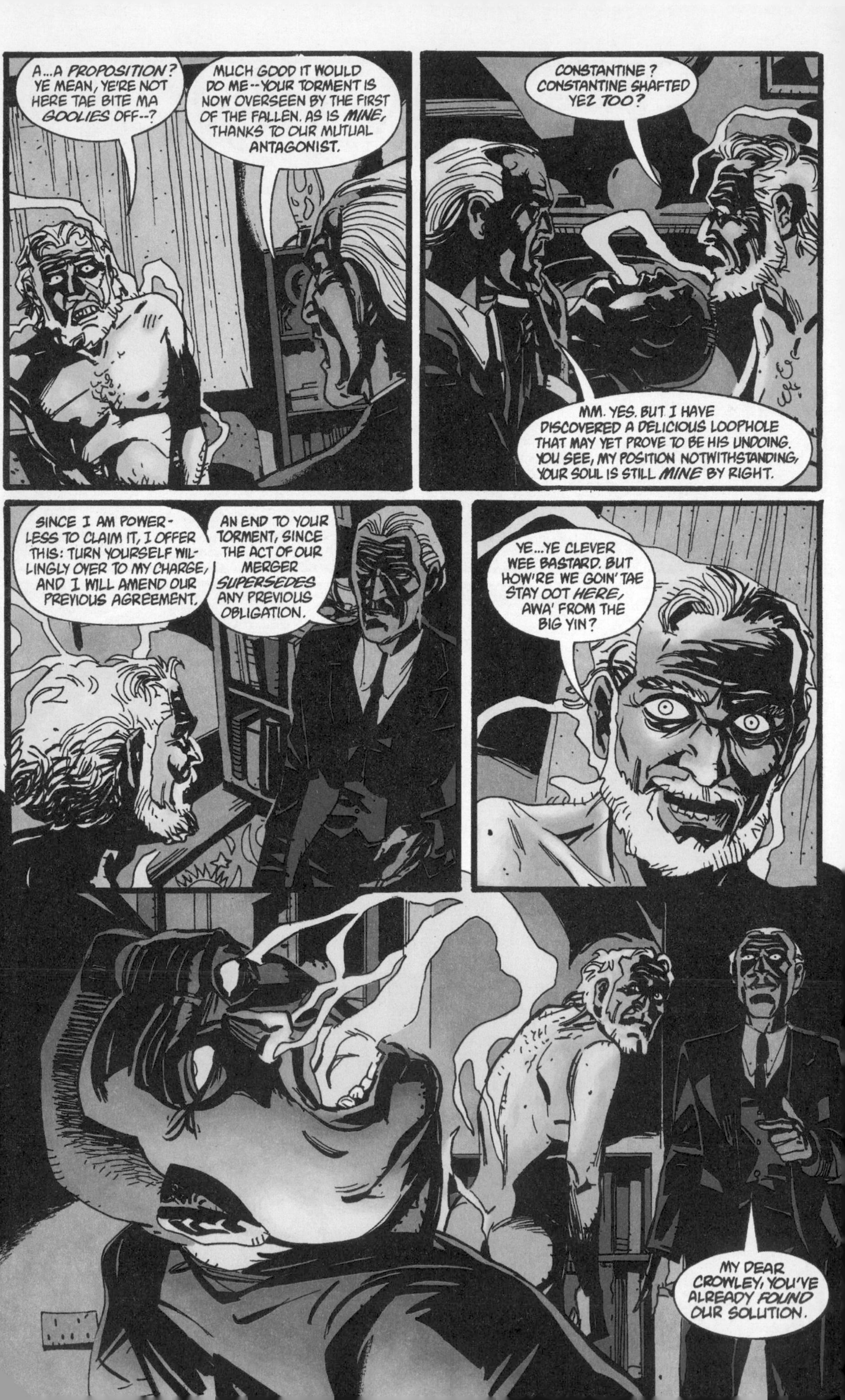
A...A *PROPOSITION*? YE MEAN, YE'RE NOT HERE TAE BITE MA *GOOLIES* OFF--?
MUCH GOOD IT WOULD DO ME--YOUR TORMENT IS NOW OVERSEEN BY THE FIRST OF THE FALLEN. AS IS *MINE*, THANKS TO OUR MUTUAL ANTAGONIST.
CONSTANTINE? CONSTANTINE SHAFTED YEZ *TOO*?
MM. YES. BUT I HAVE DISCOVERED A DELICIOUS LOOPHOLE THAT MAY YET PROVE TO BE HIS UNDOING. YOU SEE, MY POSITION NOTWITHSTANDING, YOUR SOUL IS STILL *MINE* BY RIGHT.
SINCE I AM POWERLESS TO CLAIM IT, I OFFER THIS: TURN YOURSELF WILLINGLY OVER TO MY CHARGE, AND I WILL AMEND OUR PREVIOUS AGREEMENT.
AN END TO YOUR TORMENT, SINCE THE ACT OF OUR MERGER *SUPERSEDES* ANY PREVIOUS OBLIGATION.
YE...YE CLEVER WEE BASTARD. BUT HOW'RE WE GOIN' TAE STAY OOT *HERE*, AWA' FROM THE BIG YIN?
MY DEAR CROWLEY, YOU'VE ALREADY *FOUND* OUR SOLUTION.

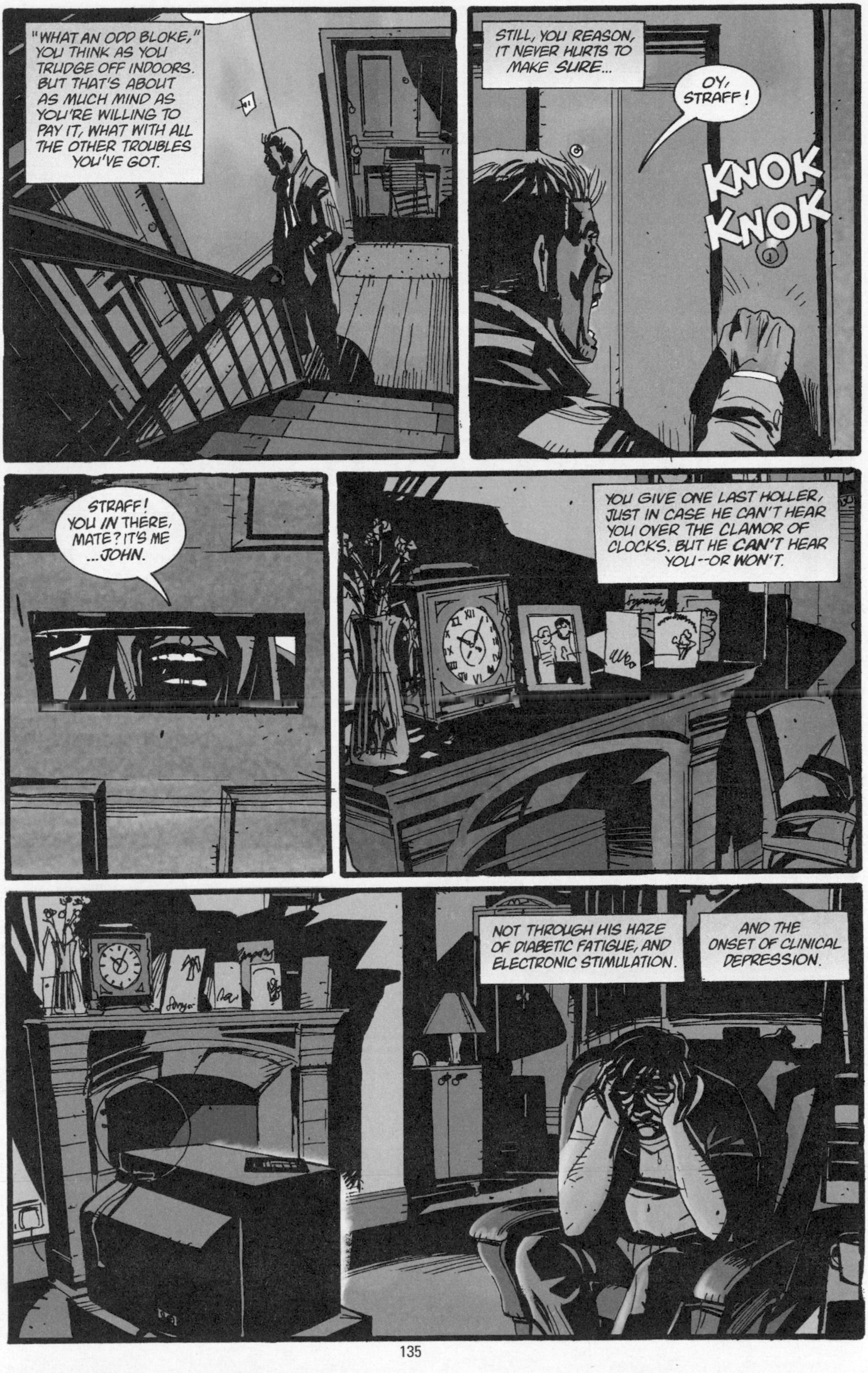
"WHAT AN ODD BLOKE," YOU THINK AS YOU TRUDGE OFF INDOORS. BUT THAT'S ABOUT AS MUCH MIND AS YOU'RE WILLING TO PAY IT, WHAT WITH ALL THE OTHER TROUBLES YOU'VE GOT.
STILL, YOU REASON, IT NEVER HURTS TO MAKE SURE...
OY, STRAFF!
KNOK KNOK
STRAFF! YOU IN THERE, MATE? IT'S ME ...JOHN.
YOU GIVE ONE LAST HOLLER, JUST IN CASE HE CAN'T HEAR YOU OVER THE CLAMOR OF CLOCKS. BUT HE CAN'T HEAR YOU--OR WON'T.
NOT THROUGH HIS HAZE OF DIABETIC FATIGUE, AND ELECTRONIC STIMULATION.
AND THE ONSET OF CLINICAL DEPRESSION.

"BEEN FAR TOO LONG," YOU LIE TO YOURSELF AS YOU WANDER UP WATER STREET; AS IF BY THINKING IT, YOU SOMEHOW JUSTIFY ALL THE YEARS YOU'VE NEVER BOTHERED TO VISIT.

AS IF THAT'S THE REAL REASON YOU'VE COME BACK.

AS IF YOU REALLY CARE.

WHAT DO YOU WANT?

CHRIST, TONY... IS IT TOO MUCH OF A STRETCH TO BELIEVE I CAME BY TO SAY HELLO?

NOT BLOODY LIKELY.

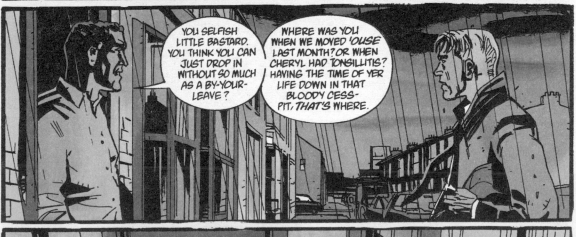

YOU SELFISH LITTLE BASTARD. YOU THINK YOU CAN JUST DROP IN WITHOUT SO MUCH AS A BY-YOUR-LEAVE?

WHERE WAS YOU WHEN WE MOVED 'OUSE LAST MONTH? OR WHEN CHERYL HAD TONSILLITIS? HAVING THE TIME OF YER LIFE DOWN IN THAT BLOODY CESS-PIT, THAT'S WHERE.

SO WHY DON'T YOU JUST FUCK OFF BACK THERE, WHERE YOU BELONG?

SLAM

THERE YOU ARE, UNCLE JOHN!

SORRY, I'VE BEEN GASPING FOR ONE...

OY! SINCE WHEN DID YOU PICK *THEM* UP?

SINCE I FOUND OUT THEY WERE *BAD* FOR ME. LOOK, I CAME HERE T'*TELL* YOU SOMETHIN'--DON'T BLAME ME DAD, ALL RIGHT? IT AIN'T 'IS *FAULT*.

SOMETHIN'S HAPPENIN', UNCLE JOHN--I WOULD'VE TOLD YER BEFORE, BUT MAM SAID *NOT* TO...SHE SAID YOU WAS BETTER OFF LEFT ALONE.

"IT STARTED A FEW DAYS AGO. WE ALL BEGAN TO HAVE THE SAME DREAM. DAD MENTIONED IT FIRST, AN' ME AN MUM WAS, LIKE... 'CHRIST! THAT 'APPENED TO *US*!'"

"BUT IT'S STILL GOING ON... NO ONE WANTS T'TALK ABOUT IT. BREAKFAST'S BEEN BLOODY 'ORRIBLE FOR DAYS NOW."

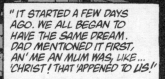

"IT'S GRANDAD."

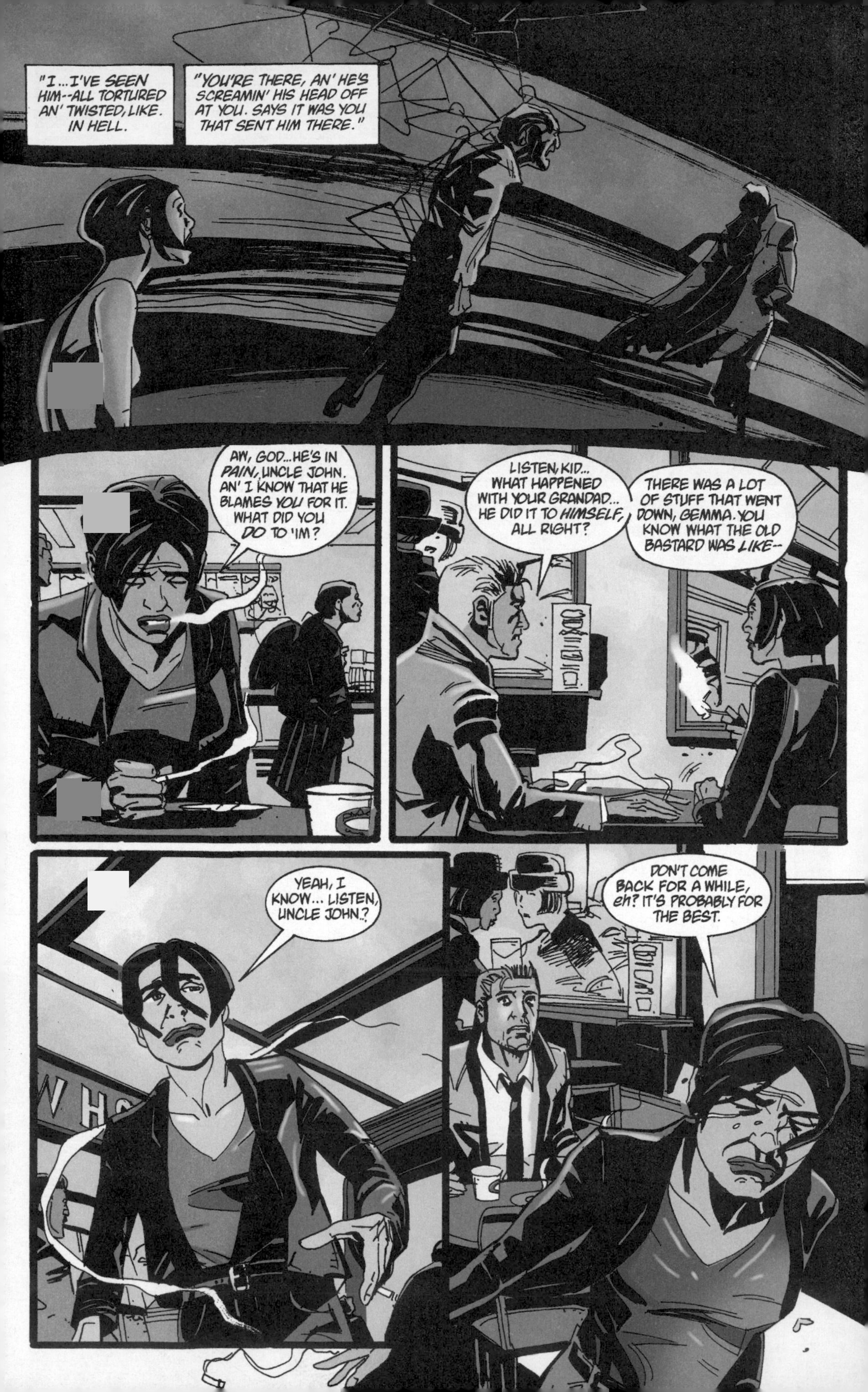
"I... I'VE SEEN HIM--ALL TORTURED AN' TWISTED, LIKE. IN HELL.
"YOU'RE THERE, AN' HE'S SCREAMIN' HIS HEAD OFF AT YOU. SAYS IT WAS YOU THAT SENT HIM THERE."
AW, GOD... HE'S IN PAIN, UNCLE JOHN. AN' I KNOW THAT HE BLAMES YOU FOR IT. WHAT DID YOU DO TO 'IM?
LISTEN, KID... WHAT HAPPENED WITH YOUR GRANDAD... HE DID IT TO HIMSELF, ALL RIGHT?
THERE WAS A LOT OF STUFF THAT WENT DOWN, GEMMA. YOU KNOW WHAT THE OLD BASTARD WAS LIKE--
YEAH, I KNOW... LISTEN, UNCLE JOHN.?
DON'T COME BACK FOR A WHILE, eh? IT'S PROBABLY FOR THE BEST.

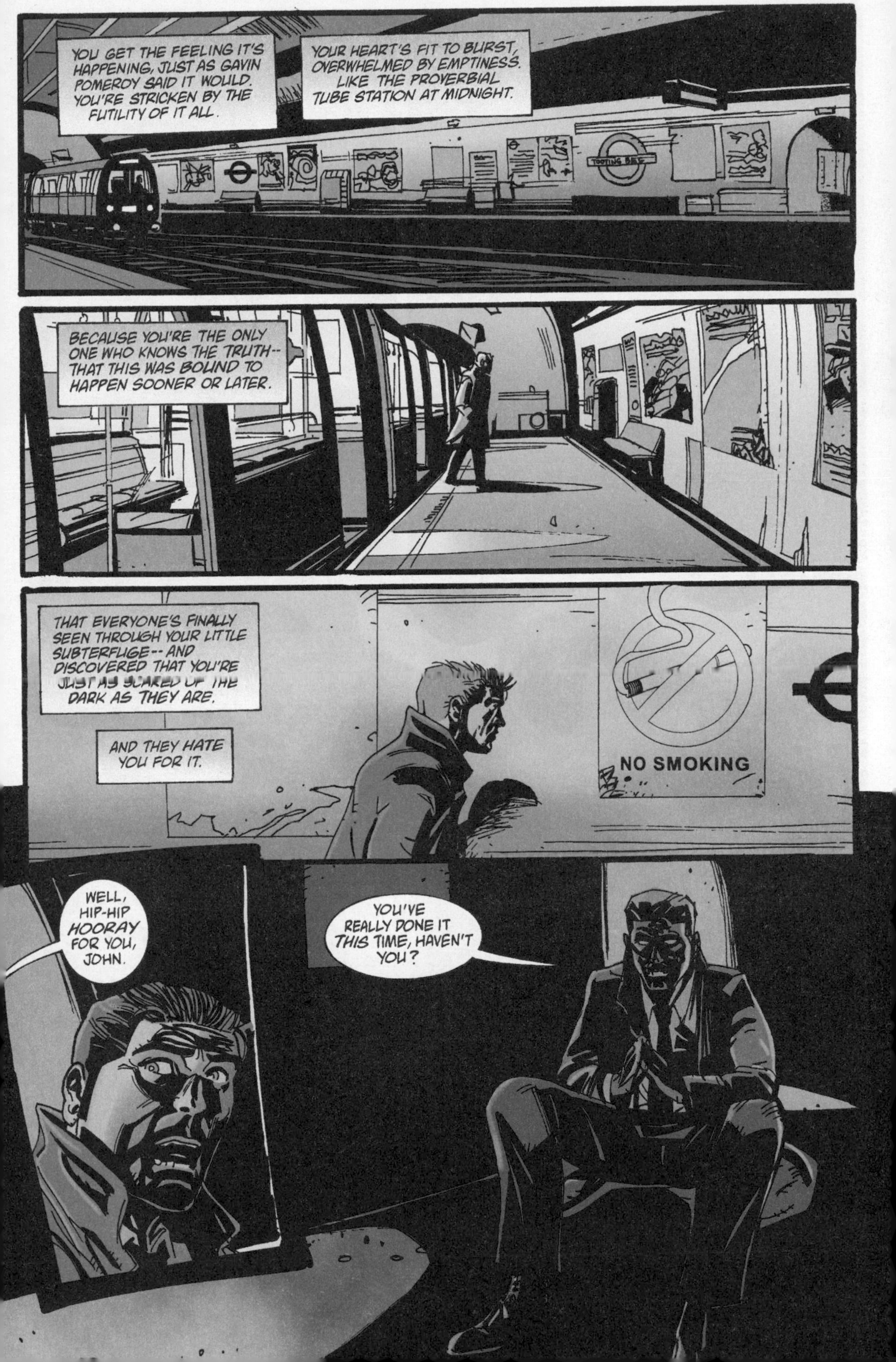
YOU GET THE FEELING IT'S HAPPENING, JUST AS GAVIN POMEROY SAID IT WOULD. YOU'RE STRICKEN BY THE FUTILITY OF IT ALL.
YOUR HEART'S FIT TO BURST, OVERWHELMED BY EMPTINESS. LIKE THE PROVERBIAL TUBE STATION AT MIDNIGHT.
TOOTING BEC
BECAUSE YOU'RE THE ONLY ONE WHO KNOWS THE TRUTH-- THAT THIS WAS BOUND TO HAPPEN SOONER OR LATER.
THAT EVERYONE'S FINALLY SEEN THROUGH YOUR LITTLE SUBTERFUGE-- AND DISCOVERED THAT YOU'RE JUST AS SCARED OF THE DARK AS THEY ARE.
AND THEY HATE YOU FOR IT.
NO SMOKING
WELL, HIP-HIP HOORAY FOR YOU, JOHN.
YOU'VE REALLY DONE IT THIS TIME, HAVEN'T YOU?

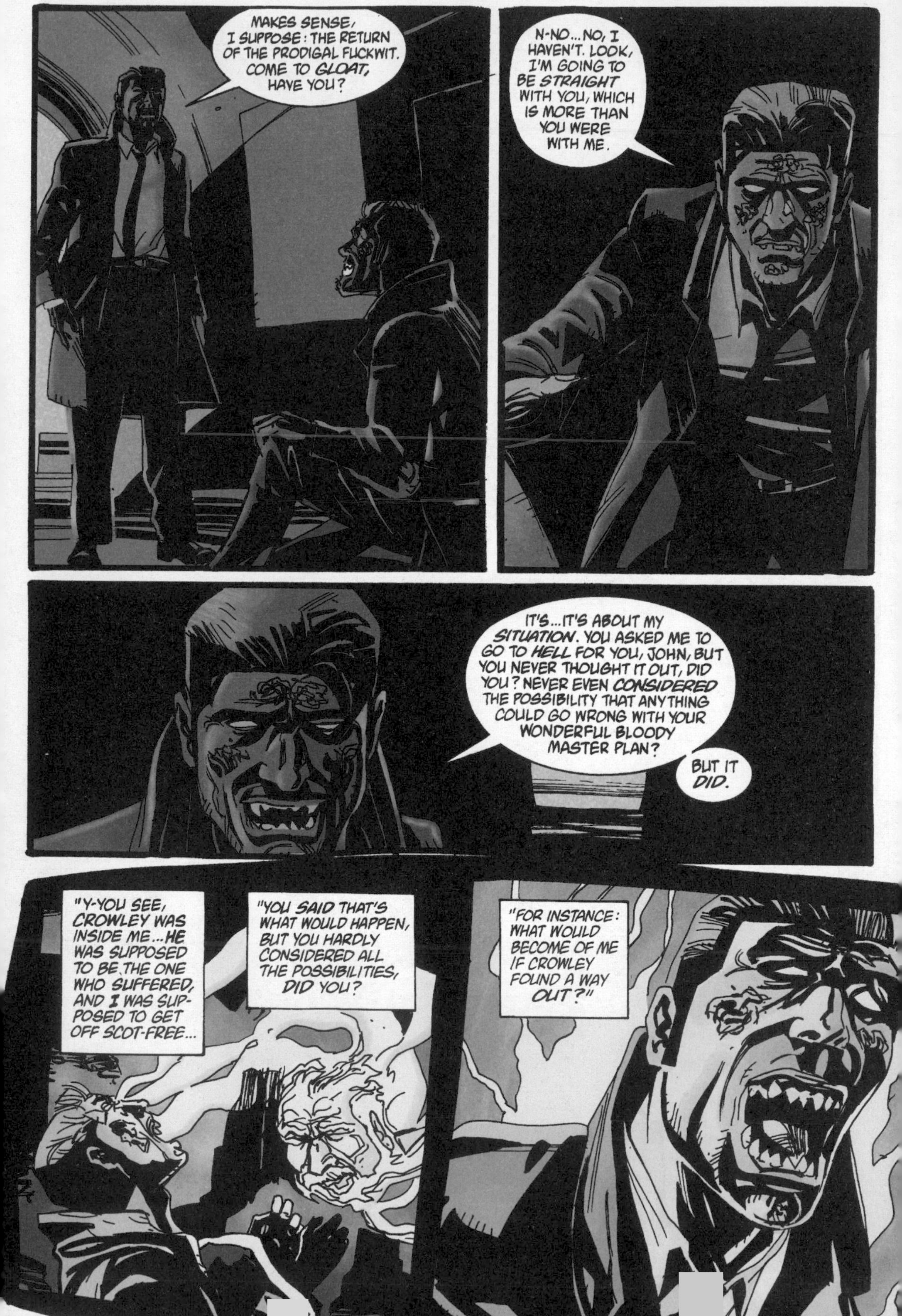
MAKES SENSE, I SUPPOSE: THE RETURN OF THE PRODIGAL FUCKWIT. COME TO GLOAT, HAVE YOU?
N-NO... NO, I HAVEN'T. LOOK, I'M GOING TO BE STRAIGHT WITH YOU, WHICH IS MORE THAN YOU WERE WITH ME.
IT'S... IT'S ABOUT MY SITUATION. YOU ASKED ME TO GO TO HELL FOR YOU, JOHN, BUT YOU NEVER THOUGHT IT OUT, DID YOU? NEVER EVEN CONSIDERED THE POSSIBILITY THAT ANYTHING COULD GO WRONG WITH YOUR WONDERFUL BLOODY MASTER PLAN?
BUT IT DID.
"Y-YOU SEE, CROWLEY WAS INSIDE ME... HE WAS SUPPOSED TO BE THE ONE WHO SUFFERED, AND I WAS SUPPOSED TO GET OFF SCOT-FREE...
"YOU SAID THAT'S WHAT WOULD HAPPEN, BUT YOU HARDLY CONSIDERED ALL THE POSSIBILITIES, DID YOU?
"FOR INSTANCE: WHAT WOULD BECOME OF ME IF CROWLEY FOUND A WAY OUT?"

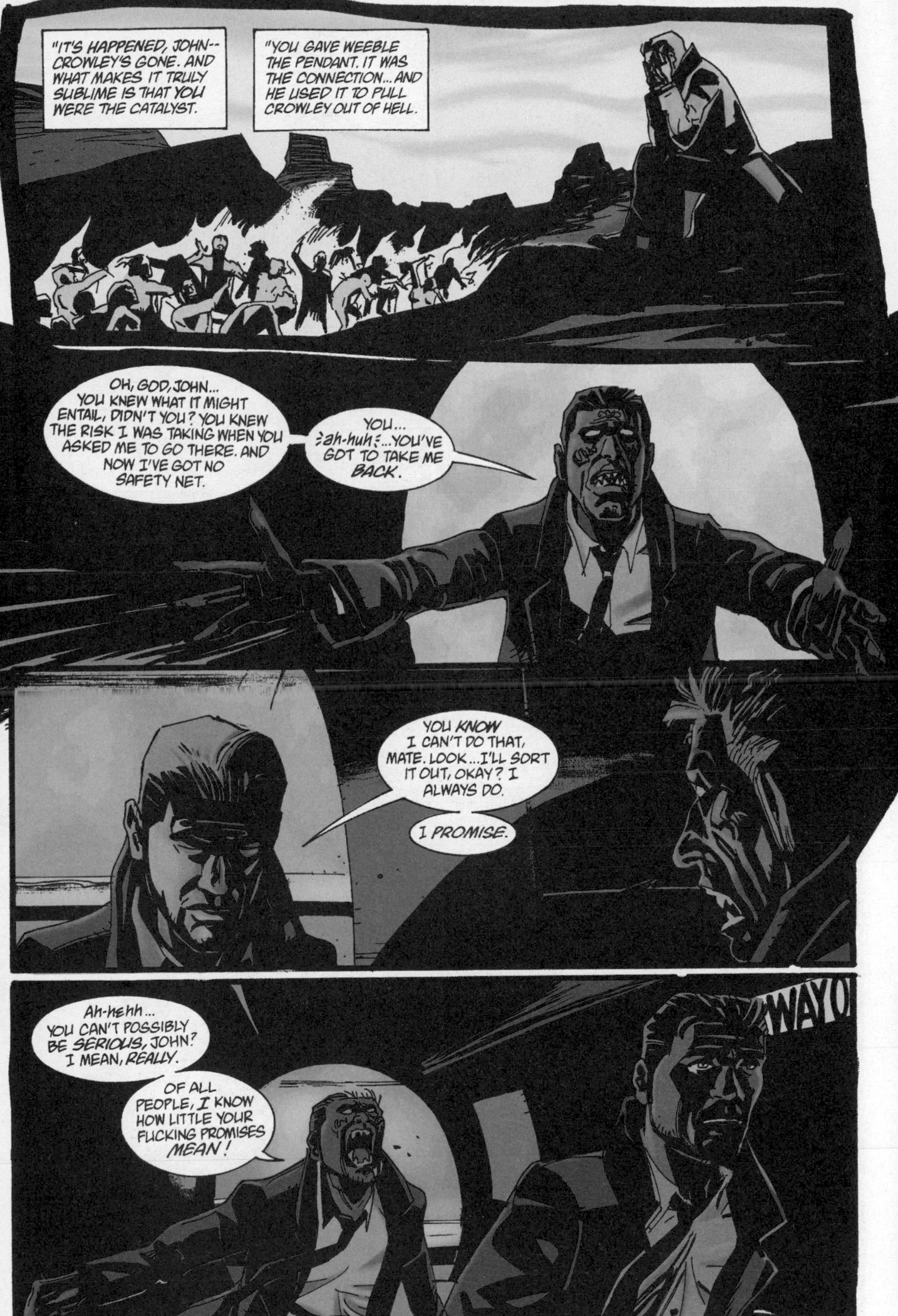
"IT'S HAPPENED, JOHN--CROWLEY'S GONE. AND WHAT MAKES IT TRULY SUBLIME IS THAT YOU WERE THE CATALYST.
"YOU GAVE WEEBLE THE PENDANT. IT WAS THE CONNECTION... AND HE USED IT TO PULL CROWLEY OUT OF HELL.
OH, GOD, JOHN... YOU KNEW WHAT IT MIGHT ENTAIL, DIDN'T YOU? YOU KNEW THE RISK I WAS TAKING WHEN YOU ASKED ME TO GO THERE. AND NOW I'VE GOT NO SAFETY NET.
YOU... ah-huh ...YOU'VE GOT TO TAKE ME BACK.
YOU KNOW I CAN'T DO THAT, MATE. LOOK... I'LL SORT IT OUT, OKAY? I ALWAYS DO.
I PROMISE.
Ah-hehh... YOU CAN'T POSSIBLY BE SERIOUS, JOHN? I MEAN, REALLY.
OF ALL PEOPLE, I KNOW HOW LITTLE YOUR FUCKING PROMISES MEAN!

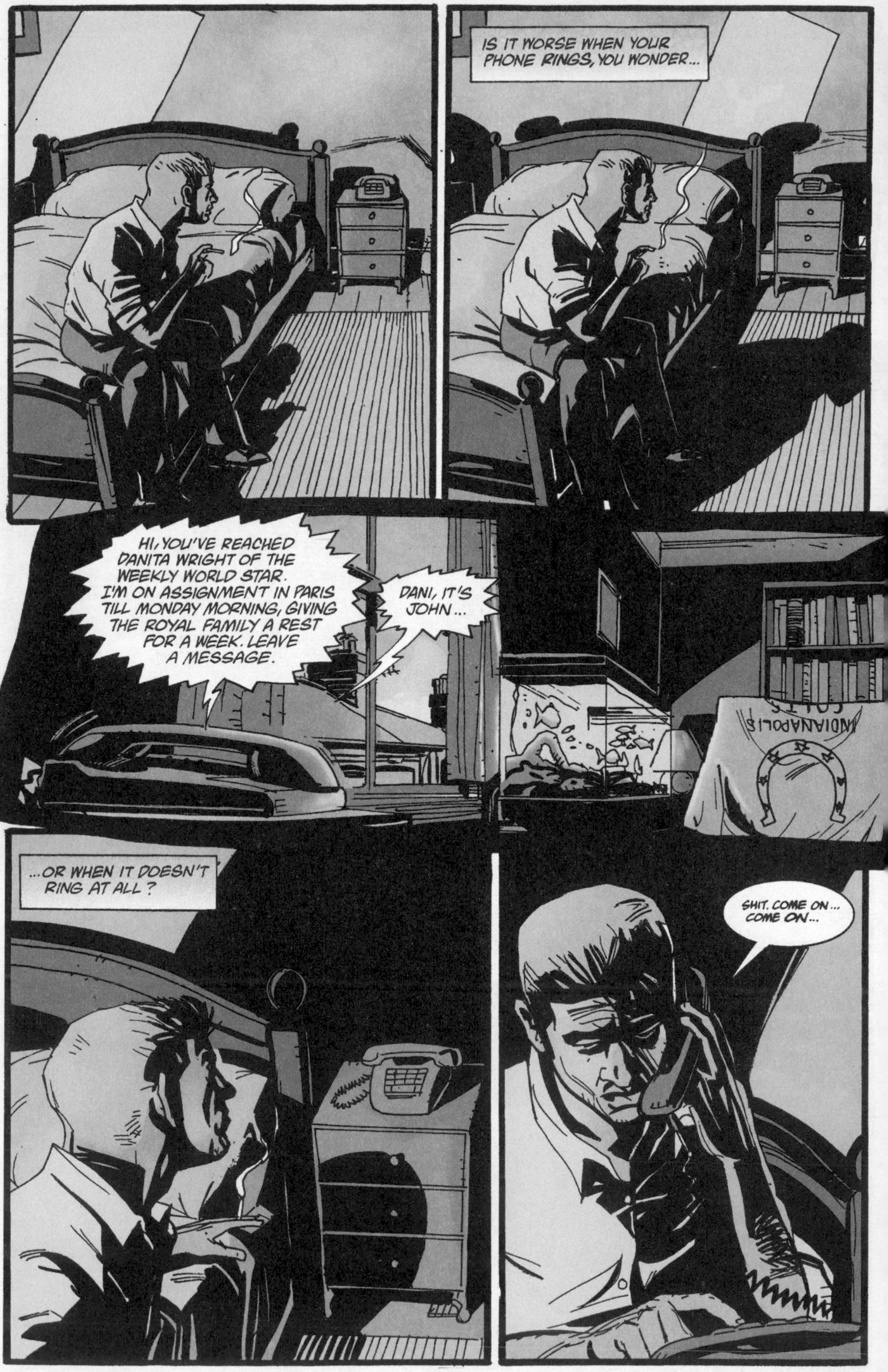
IS IT WORSE WHEN YOUR PHONE RINGS, YOU WONDER...
HI, YOU'VE REACHED DANITA WRIGHT OF THE WEEKLY WORLD STAR. I'M ON ASSIGNMENT IN PARIS TILL MONDAY MORNING, GIVING THE ROYAL FAMILY A REST FOR A WEEK. LEAVE A MESSAGE.
DANI, IT'S JOHN...
INDIANAPOLIS COLTS
...OR WHEN IT DOESN'T RING AT ALL?
SHIT. COME ON... COME ON...

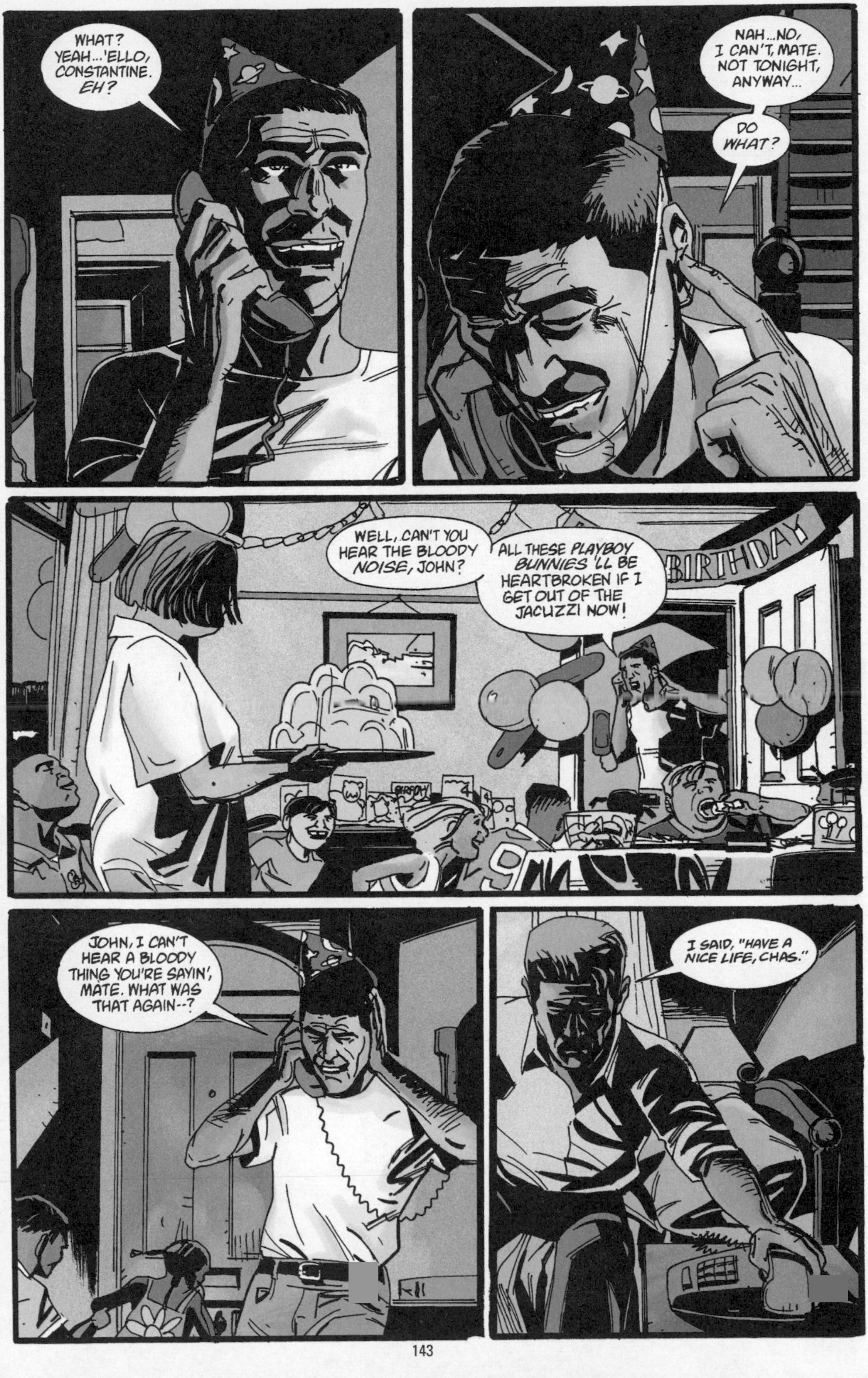
WHAT? YEAH...'ELLO, CONSTANTINE. *EH?*
NAH...NO, I CAN'T, MATE. NOT TONIGHT, ANYWAY...
DO *WHAT?*
WELL, CAN'T YOU HEAR THE BLOODY *NOISE*, JOHN?
ALL THESE *PLAYBOY BUNNIES* 'LL BE HEARTBROKEN IF I GET OUT OF THE JACUZZI NOW!
BIRTHDAY
JOHN, I CAN'T HEAR A BLOODY THING YOU'RE SAYIN', MATE. WHAT WAS THAT AGAIN--?
I SAID, *"HAVE A NICE LIFE, CHAS."*

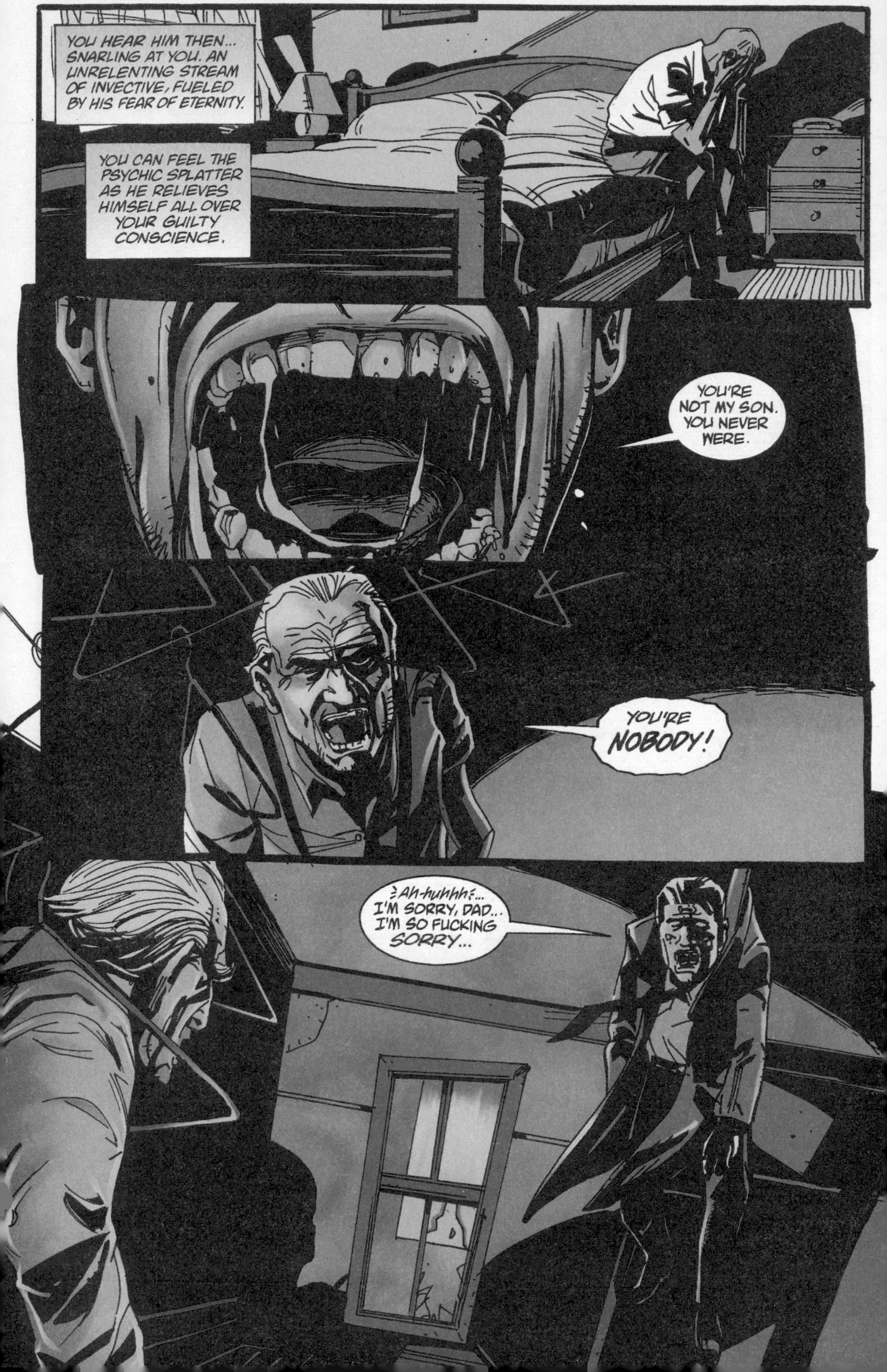
YOU HEAR HIM THEN... SNARLING AT YOU. AN UNRELENTING STREAM OF INVECTIVE, FUELED BY HIS FEAR OF ETERNITY.
YOU CAN FEEL THE PSYCHIC SPLATTER AS HE RELIEVES HIMSELF ALL OVER YOUR GUILTY CONSCIENCE.
YOU'RE NOT MY SON. YOU NEVER WERE.
YOU'RE NOBODY!
Ah-huhhh... I'M SORRY, DAD... I'M SO FUCKING SORRY...

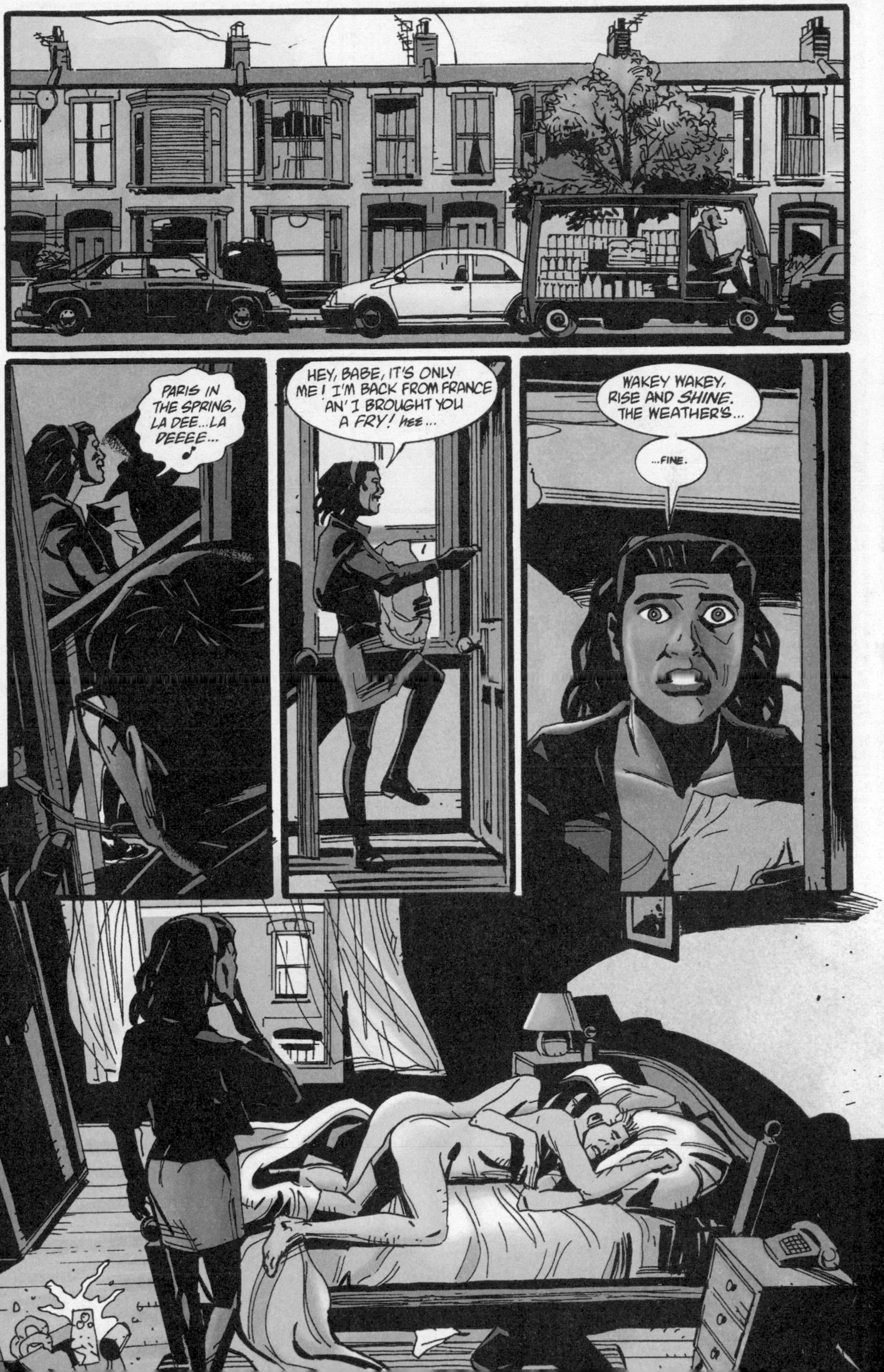
PARIS IN THE SPRING, LA DEE...LA DEEEE...
HEY, BABE, IT'S ONLY ME! I'M BACK FROM FRANCE AN' I BROUGHT YOU A FRY! hee...
WAKEY WAKEY, RISE AND SHINE. THE WEATHER'S...
...FINE.

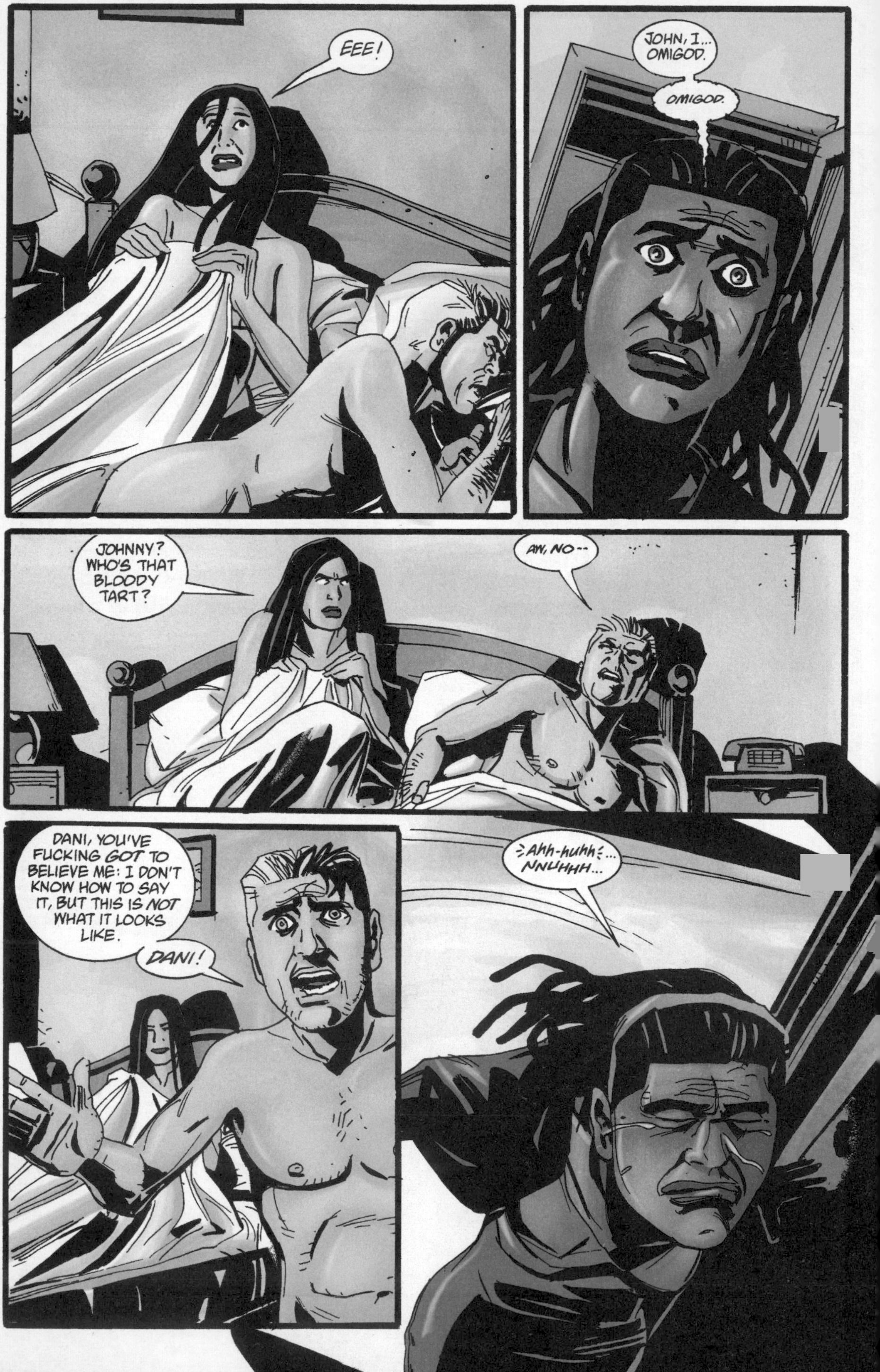
EEE!
JOHN, I... OMIGOD.
OMIGOD.
JOHNNY? WHO'S THAT BLOODY TART?
AW, NO--
DANI, YOU'VE FUCKING GOT TO BELIEVE ME: I DON'T KNOW HOW TO SAY IT, BUT THIS IS NOT WHAT IT LOOKS LIKE.
DANI!
Ahh-huhh... NNUHHH...

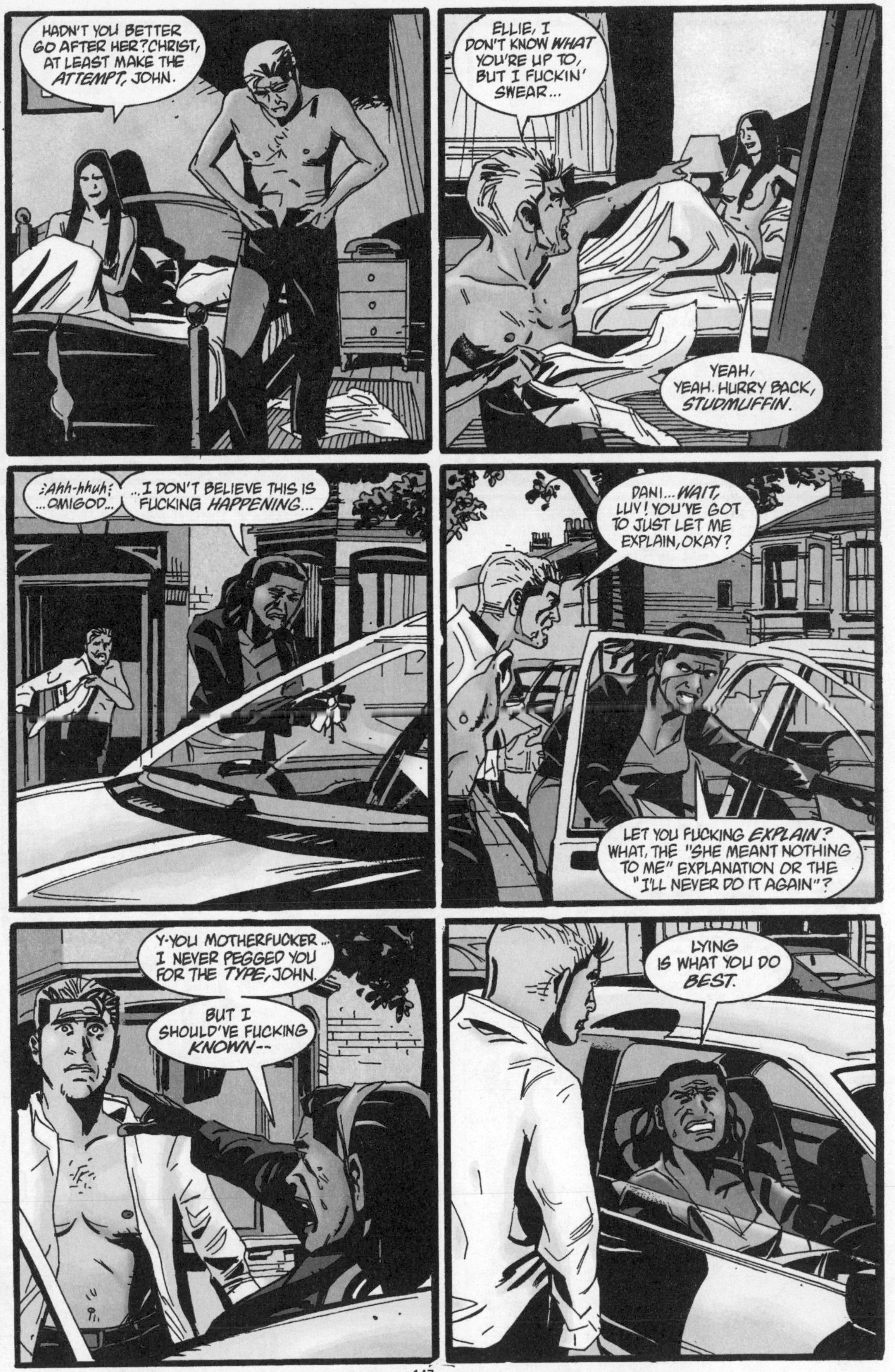
HADN'T YOU BETTER GO AFTER HER? CHRIST, AT LEAST MAKE THE *ATTEMPT*, JOHN.
ELLIE, I DON'T KNOW *WHAT* YOU'RE UP TO, BUT I FUCKIN' SWEAR...
YEAH, YEAH. HURRY BACK, *STUDMUFFIN*.
Ahh-hhuh ...OMIGOD...
...I DON'T BELIEVE THIS IS FUCKING *HAPPENING*...
DANI... *WAIT*, LUV! YOU'VE GOT TO JUST LET ME EXPLAIN, OKAY?
LET YOU FUCKING *EXPLAIN*? WHAT, THE "SHE MEANT NOTHING TO ME" EXPLANATION OR THE "I'LL NEVER DO IT AGAIN"?
Y-YOU MOTHERFUCKER... I NEVER PEGGED YOU FOR THE *TYPE*, JOHN.
BUT I SHOULD'VE FUCKING *KNOWN*--
LYING IS WHAT YOU DO *BEST*.

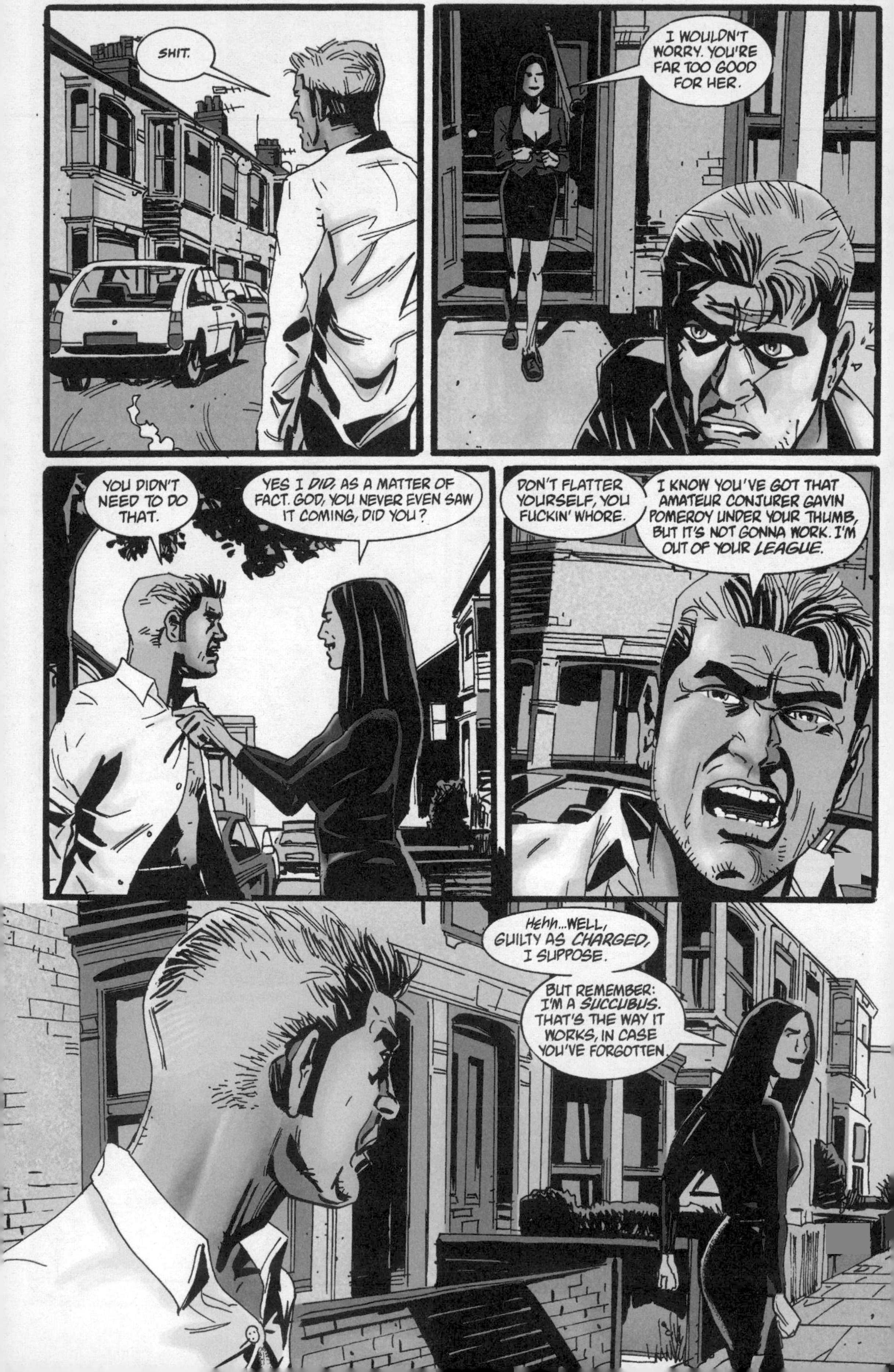
SHIT.
I WOULDN'T WORRY. YOU'RE FAR TOO GOOD FOR HER.
YOU DIDN'T NEED TO DO THAT.
YES I *DID*, AS A MATTER OF FACT. GOD, YOU NEVER EVEN SAW IT COMING, DID YOU?
DON'T FLATTER YOURSELF, YOU FUCKIN' WHORE.
I KNOW YOU'VE GOT THAT AMATEUR CONJURER GAVIN POMEROY UNDER YOUR THUMB, BUT IT'S NOT GONNA WORK. I'M OUT OF YOUR *LEAGUE*.
Hehh...WELL, GUILTY AS *CHARGED*, I SUPPOSE.
BUT REMEMBER: I'M A *SUCCUBUS*. THAT'S THE WAY IT WORKS, IN CASE YOU'VE FORGOTTEN.

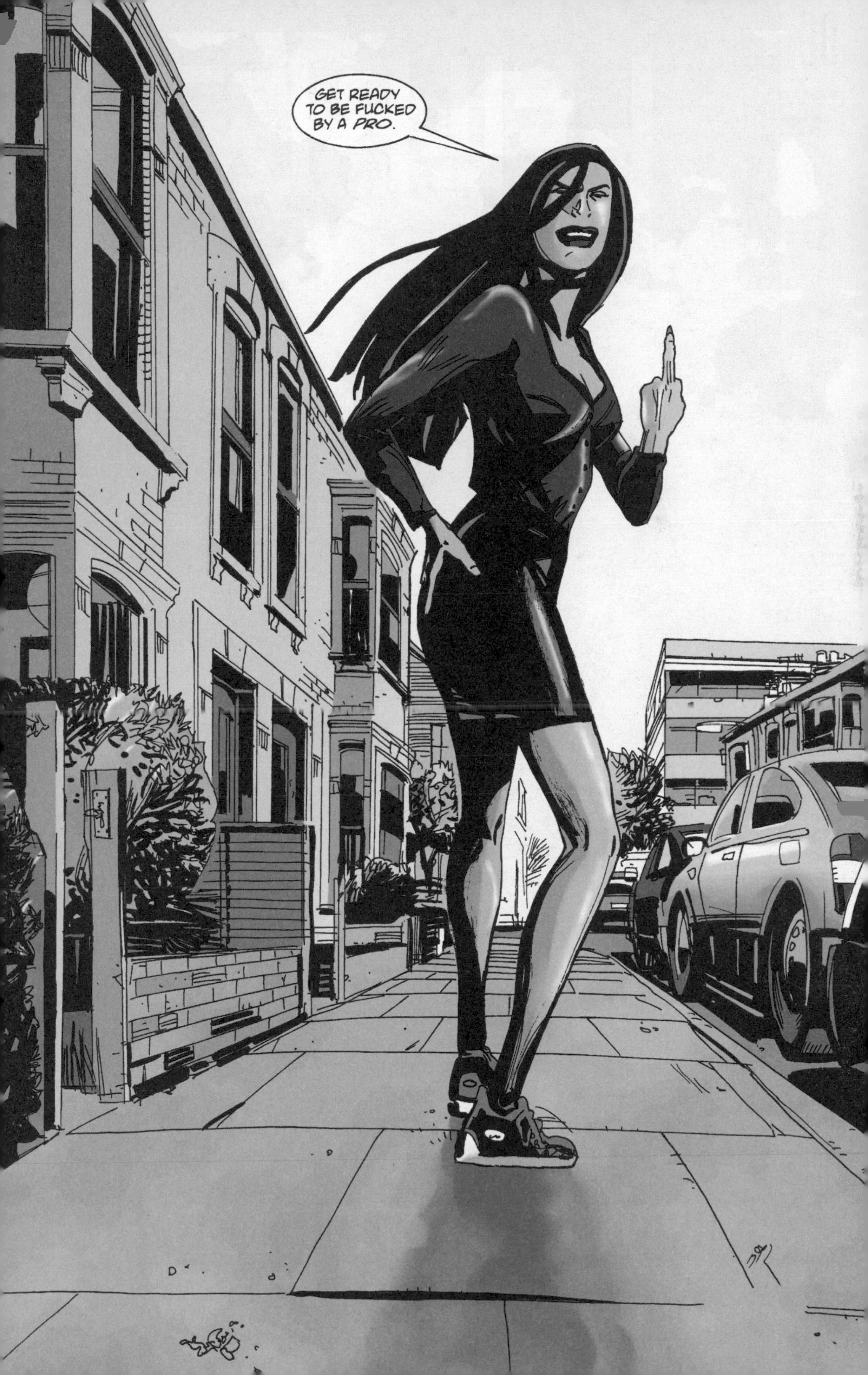
GET READY TO BE FUCKED BY A PRO.

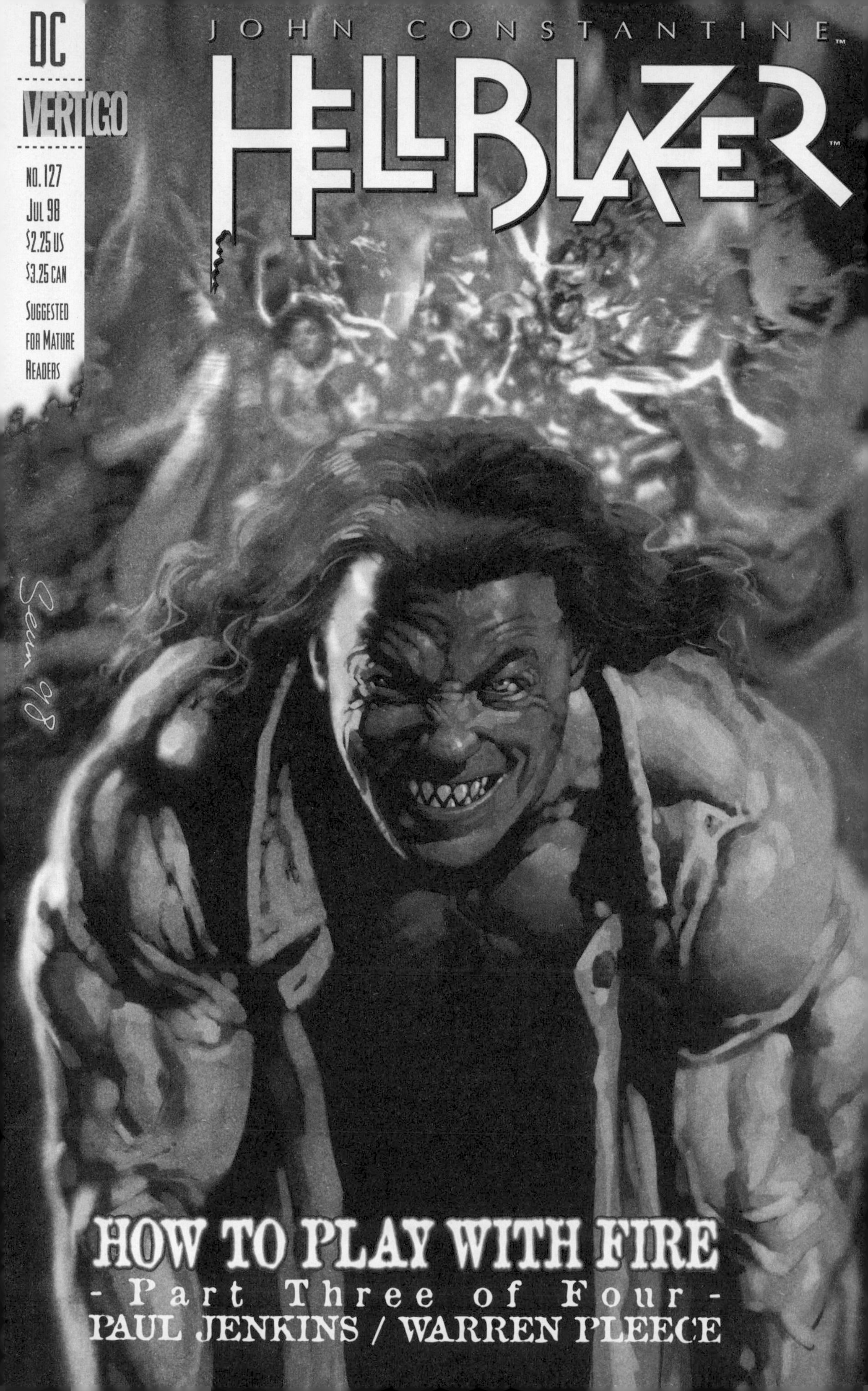
DC
VERTIGO
NO. 127
JUL 98
$2.25 US
$3.25 CAN
SUGGESTED FOR MATURE READERS
JOHN CONSTANTINE
HELLBLAZER
HOW TO PLAY WITH FIRE
- Part Three of Four -
PAUL JENKINS / WARREN PLEECE

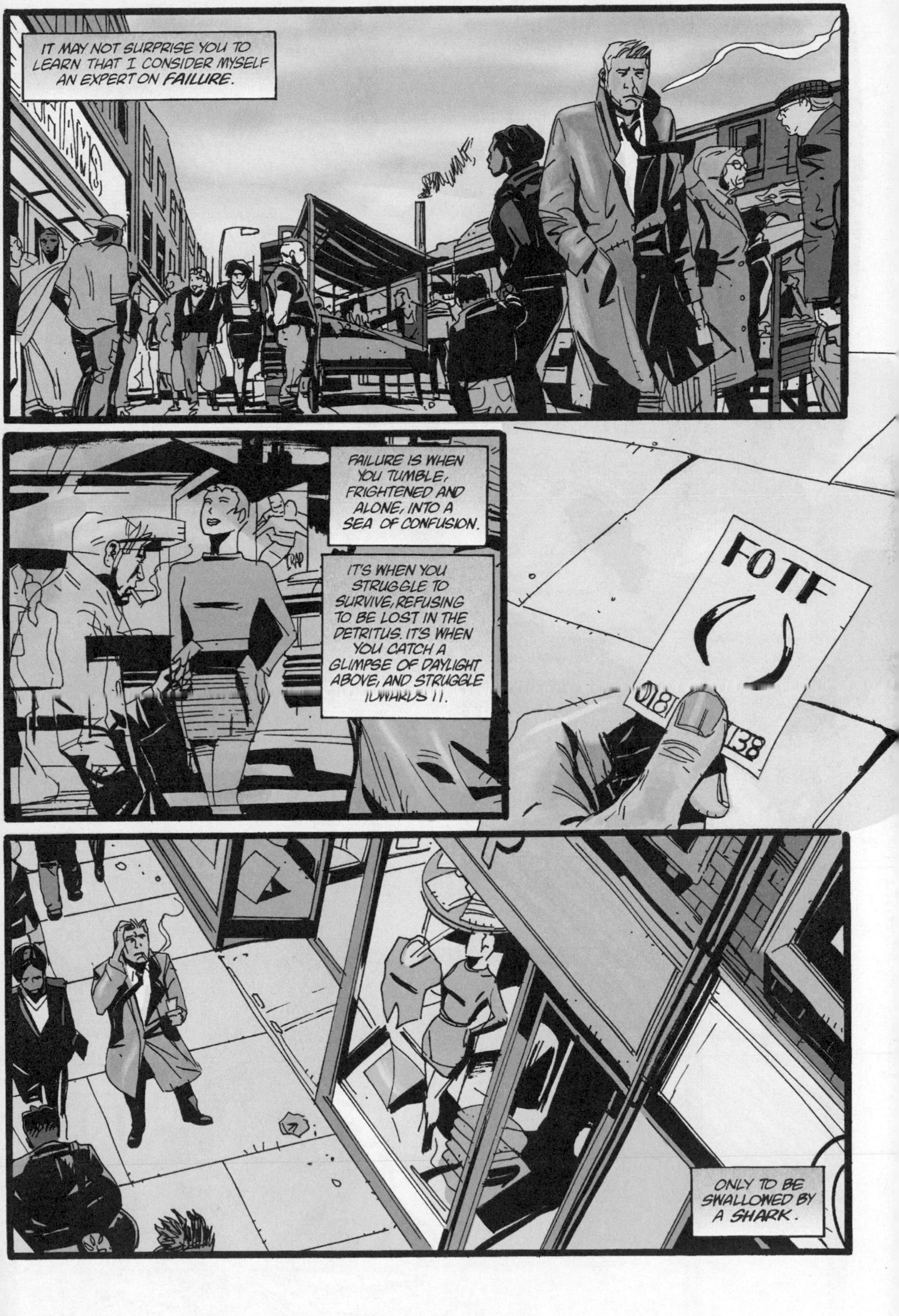
IT MAY NOT SURPRISE YOU TO LEARN THAT I CONSIDER MYSELF AN EXPERT ON FAILURE.
FAILURE IS WHEN YOU TUMBLE, FRIGHTENED AND ALONE, INTO A SEA OF CONFUSION.
IT'S WHEN YOU STRUGGLE TO SURVIVE, REFUSING TO BE LOST IN THE DETRITUS. IT'S WHEN YOU CATCH A GLIMPSE OF DAYLIGHT ABOVE, AND STRUGGLE TOWARDS IT.
FOTF
018
138
ONLY TO BE SWALLOWED BY A SHARK.

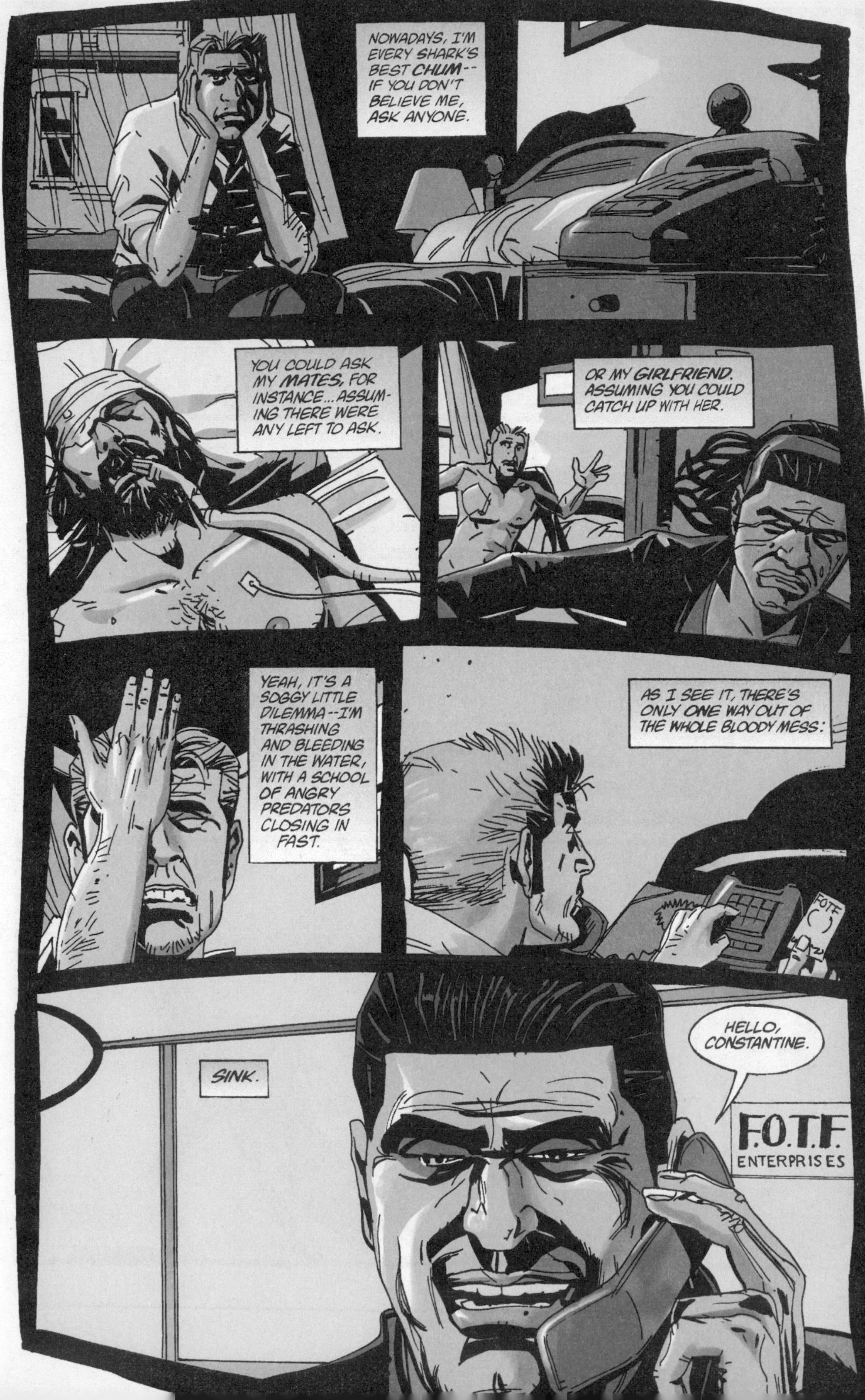
NOWADAYS, I'M EVERY SHARK'S BEST CHUM-- IF YOU DON'T BELIEVE ME, ASK ANYONE.
YOU COULD ASK MY MATES, FOR INSTANCE... ASSUMING THERE WERE ANY LEFT TO ASK.
OR MY GIRLFRIEND. ASSUMING YOU COULD CATCH UP WITH HER.
YEAH, IT'S A SOGGY LITTLE DILEMMA--I'M THRASHING AND BLEEDING IN THE WATER, WITH A SCHOOL OF ANGRY PREDATORS CLOSING IN FAST.
AS I SEE IT, THERE'S ONLY ONE WAY OUT OF THE WHOLE BLOODY MESS:
FOTF
SINK.
HELLO, CONSTANTINE.
F.O.T.F. ENTERPRISES

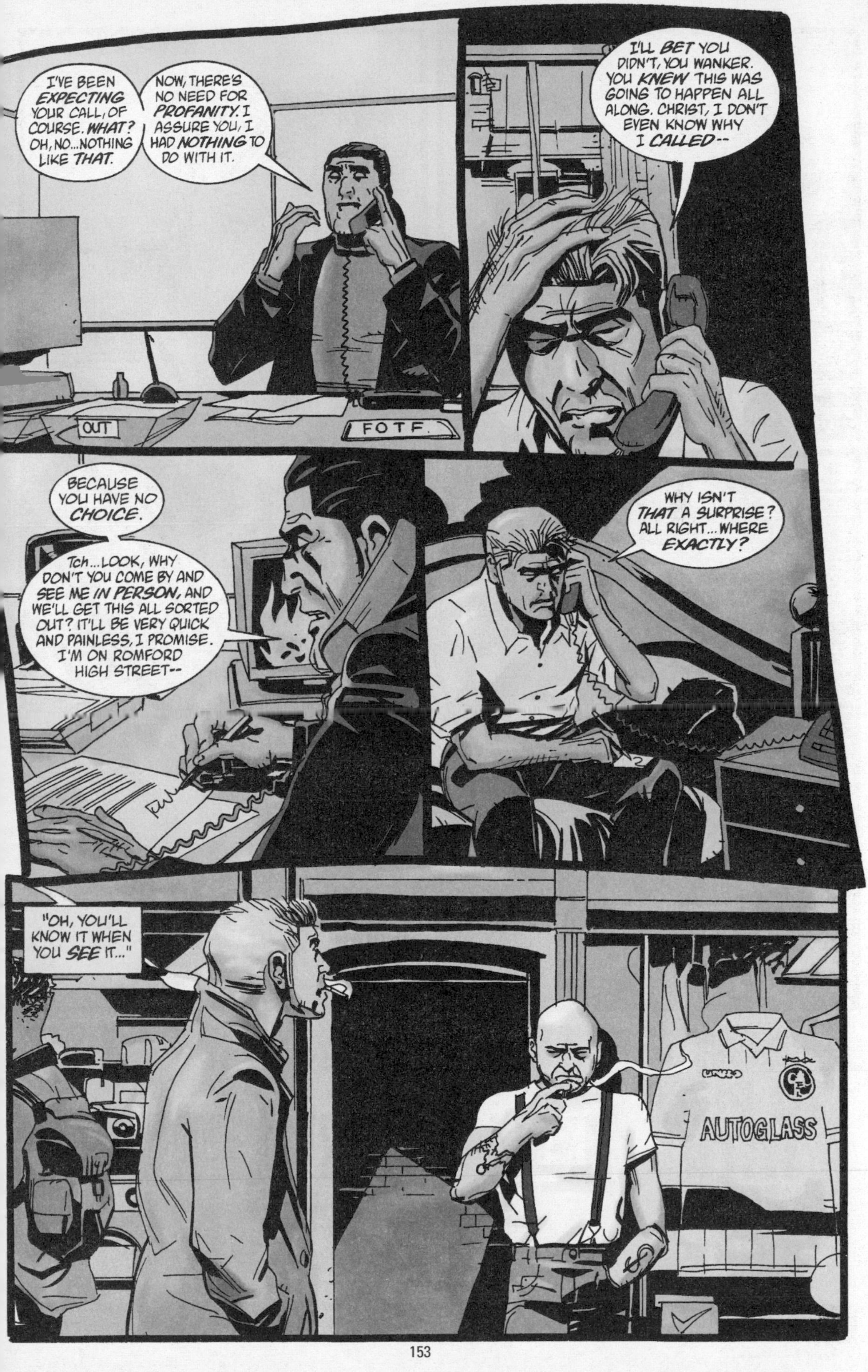
I'VE BEEN EXPECTING YOUR CALL, OF COURSE. WHAT? OH, NO...NOTHING LIKE THAT.
NOW, THERE'S NO NEED FOR PROFANITY. I ASSURE YOU, I HAD NOTHING TO DO WITH IT.
OUT
F.O.T.F.
I'LL BET YOU DIDN'T, YOU WANKER. YOU KNEW THIS WAS GOING TO HAPPEN ALL ALONG. CHRIST, I DON'T EVEN KNOW WHY I CALLED--
BECAUSE YOU HAVE NO CHOICE.
Tch...LOOK, WHY DON'T YOU COME BY AND SEE ME IN PERSON, AND WE'LL GET THIS ALL SORTED OUT? IT'LL BE VERY QUICK AND PAINLESS, I PROMISE. I'M ON ROMFORD HIGH STREET--
WHY ISN'T THAT A SURPRISE? ALL RIGHT...WHERE EXACTLY?
"OH, YOU'LL KNOW IT WHEN YOU SEE IT..."
AUTOGLASS

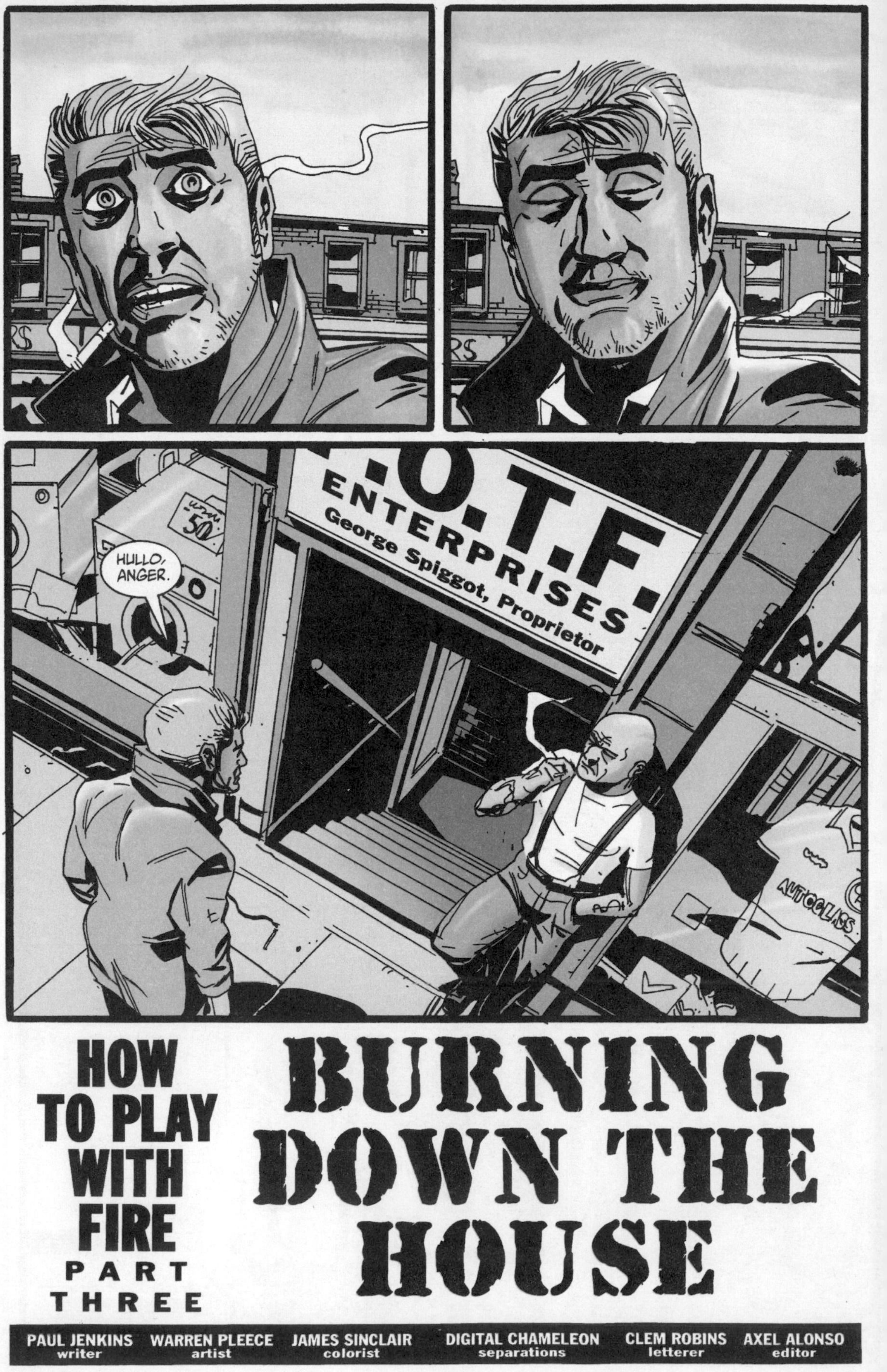
HULLO, ANGER.
O.T.F.
ENTERPRISES
George Spiggot, Proprietor
AUTOGLASS

HOW TO PLAY WITH FIRE PART THREE

BURNING DOWN THE HOUSE

PAUL JENKINS writer · WARREN PLEECE artist · JAMES SINCLAIR colorist · DIGITAL CHAMELEON separations · CLEM ROBINS letterer · AXEL ALONSO editor

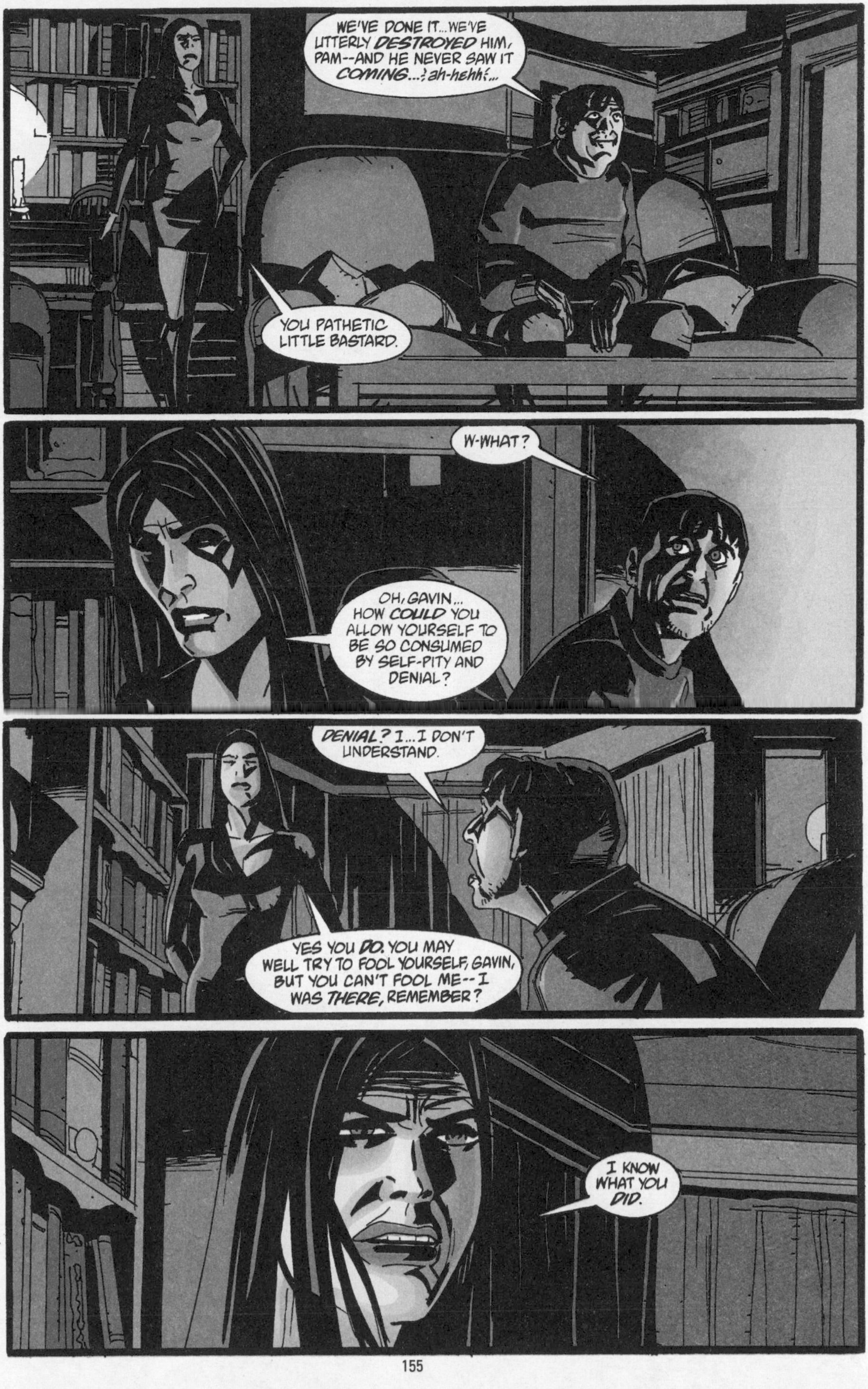
WE'VE DONE IT...WE'VE UTTERLY DESTROYED HIM, PAM--AND HE NEVER SAW IT COMING...ah-hehh...
YOU PATHETIC LITTLE BASTARD.
W-WHAT?
OH, GAVIN... HOW COULD YOU ALLOW YOURSELF TO BE SO CONSUMED BY SELF-PITY AND DENIAL?
DENIAL? I...I DON'T UNDERSTAND.
YES YOU DO. YOU MAY WELL TRY TO FOOL YOURSELF, GAVIN, BUT YOU CAN'T FOOL ME--I WAS THERE, REMEMBER?
I KNOW WHAT YOU DID.

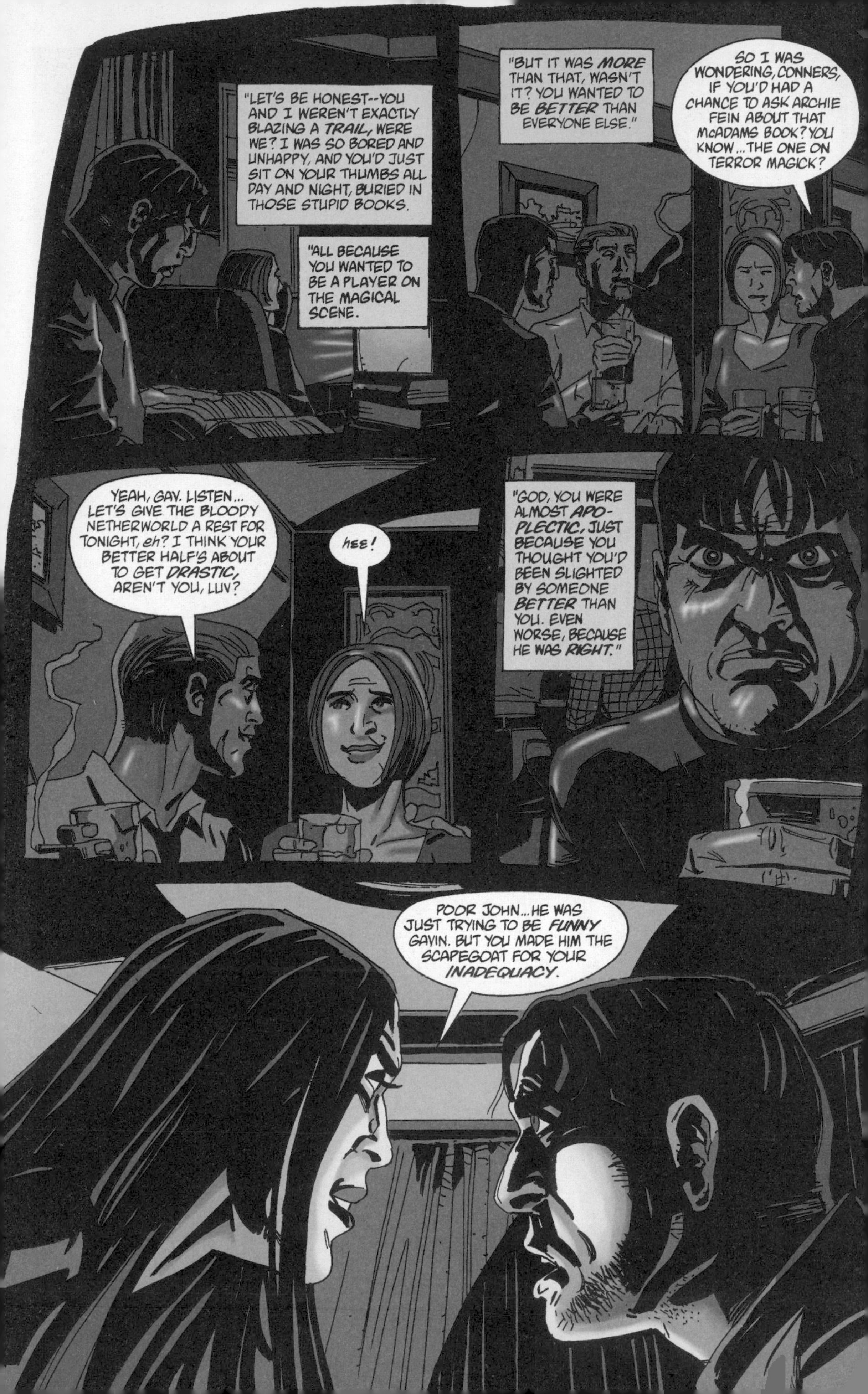
"LET'S BE HONEST--YOU AND I WEREN'T EXACTLY BLAZING A TRAIL, WERE WE? I WAS SO BORED AND UNHAPPY, AND YOU'D JUST SIT ON YOUR THUMBS ALL DAY AND NIGHT, BURIED IN THOSE STUPID BOOKS.
"ALL BECAUSE YOU WANTED TO BE A PLAYER ON THE MAGICAL SCENE.
"BUT IT WAS MORE THAN THAT, WASN'T IT? YOU WANTED TO BE BETTER THAN EVERYONE ELSE."
SO I WAS WONDERING, CONNERS, IF YOU'D HAD A CHANCE TO ASK ARCHIE FEIN ABOUT THAT McADAMS BOOK? YOU KNOW...THE ONE ON TERROR MAGICK?
YEAH, GAV. LISTEN... LET'S GIVE THE BLOODY NETHERWORLD A REST FOR TONIGHT, eh? I THINK YOUR BETTER HALF'S ABOUT TO GET DRASTIC, AREN'T YOU, LUV?
hee!
"GOD, YOU WERE ALMOST APO-PLECTIC, JUST BECAUSE YOU THOUGHT YOU'D BEEN SLIGHTED BY SOMEONE BETTER THAN YOU. EVEN WORSE, BECAUSE HE WAS RIGHT."
POOR JOHN...HE WAS JUST TRYING TO BE FUNNY GAVIN. BUT YOU MADE HIM THE SCAPEGOAT FOR YOUR INADEQUACY.

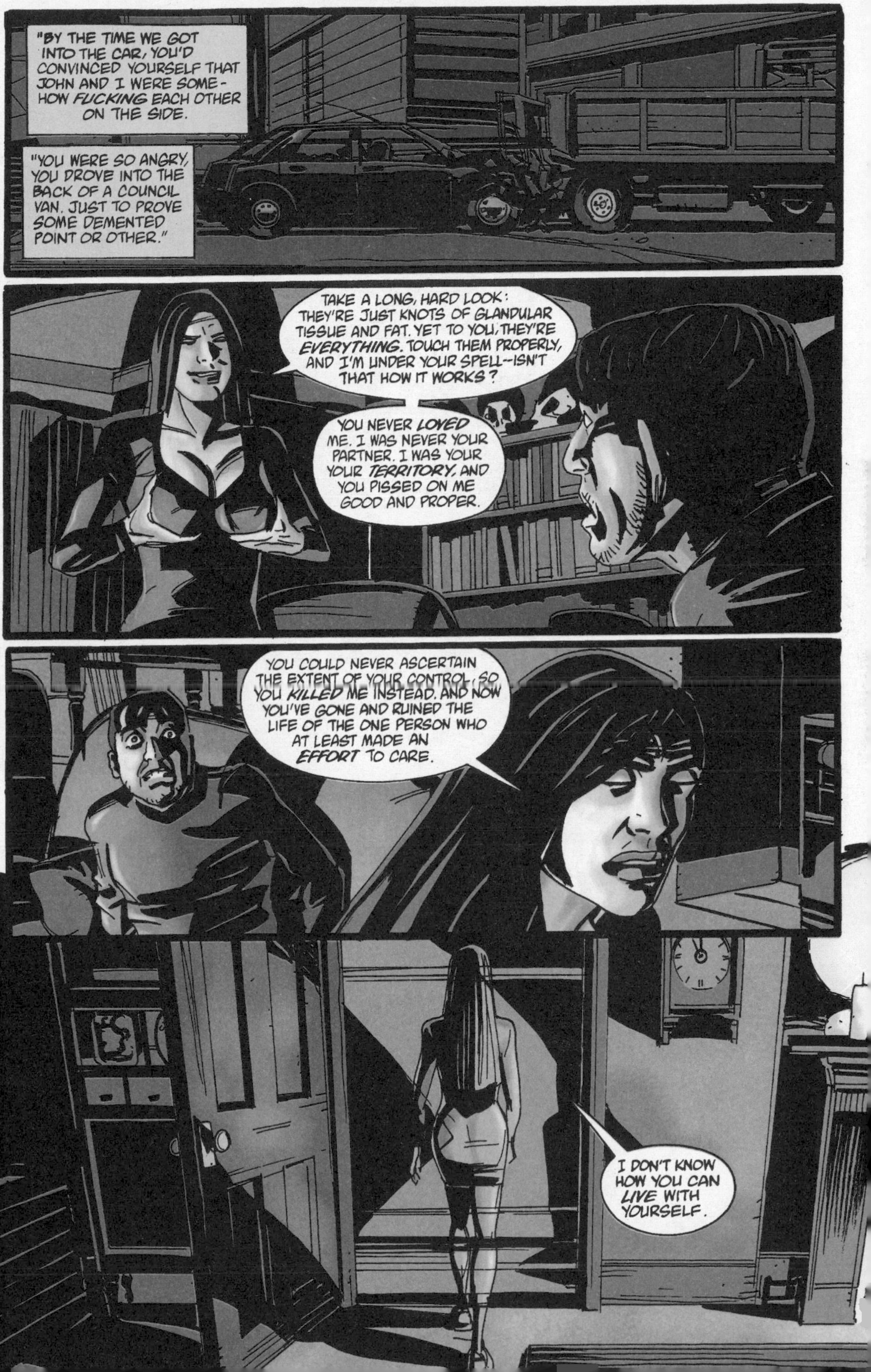
"BY THE TIME WE GOT INTO THE CAR, YOU'D CONVINCED YOURSELF THAT JOHN AND I WERE SOME-HOW FUCKING EACH OTHER ON THE SIDE.
"YOU WERE SO ANGRY, YOU DROVE INTO THE BACK OF A COUNCIL VAN. JUST TO PROVE SOME DEMENTED POINT OR OTHER."
TAKE A LONG, HARD LOOK: THEY'RE JUST KNOTS OF GLANDULAR TISSUE AND FAT. YET TO YOU, THEY'RE EVERYTHING. TOUCH THEM PROPERLY, AND I'M UNDER YOUR SPELL--ISN'T THAT HOW IT WORKS?
YOU NEVER LOVED ME. I WAS NEVER YOUR PARTNER. I WAS YOUR YOUR TERRITORY, AND YOU PISSED ON ME GOOD AND PROPER.
YOU COULD NEVER ASCERTAIN THE EXTENT OF YOUR CONTROL, SO YOU KILLED ME INSTEAD. AND NOW YOU'VE GONE AND RUINED THE LIFE OF THE ONE PERSON WHO AT LEAST MADE AN EFFORT TO CARE.
I DON'T KNOW HOW YOU CAN LIVE WITH YOURSELF.

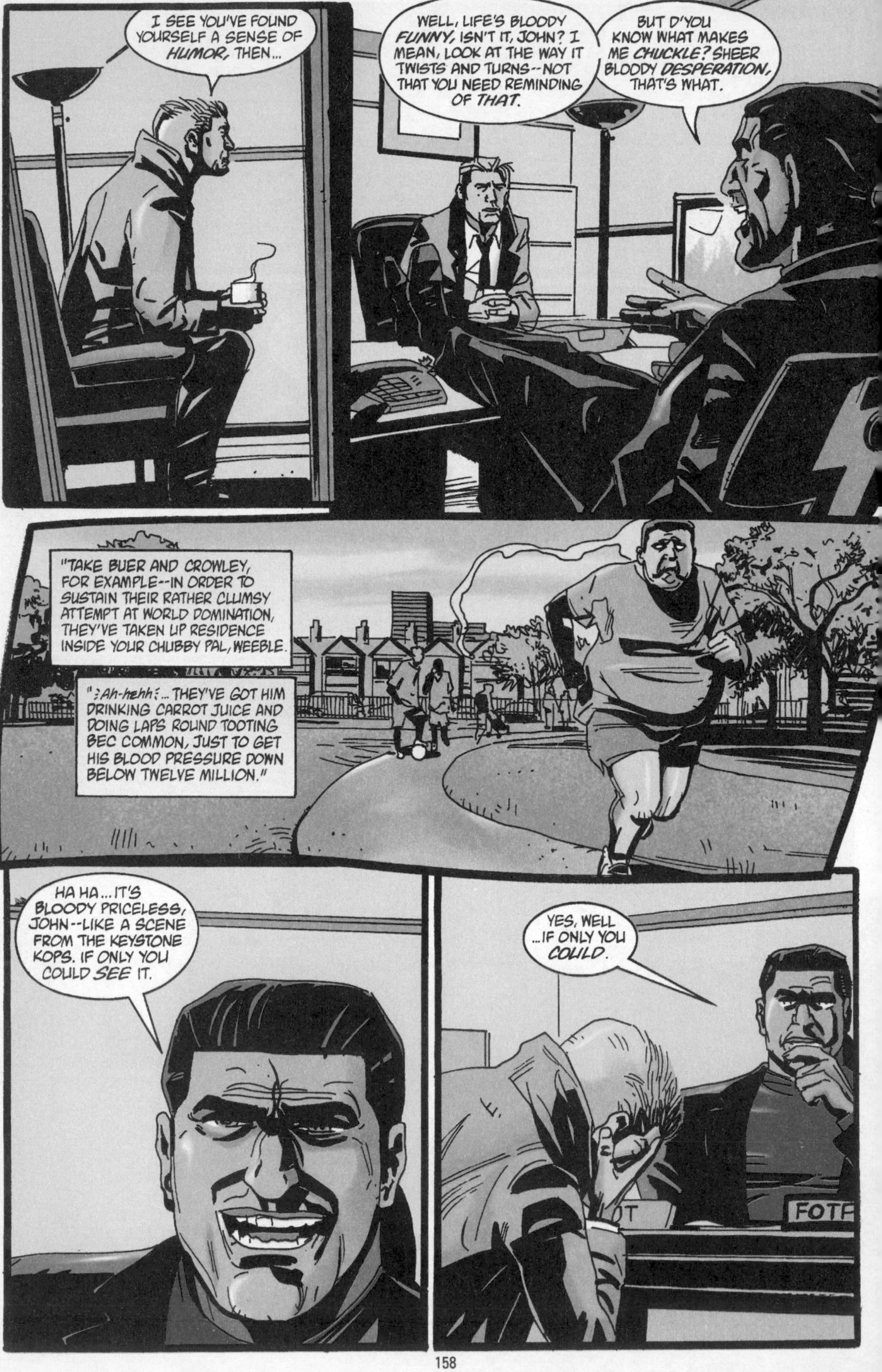
I SEE YOU'VE FOUND YOURSELF A SENSE OF *HUMOR,* THEN...
WELL, LIFE'S BLOODY *FUNNY,* ISN'T IT, JOHN? I MEAN, LOOK AT THE WAY IT TWISTS AND TURNS--NOT THAT YOU NEED REMINDING OF *THAT.*
BUT D'YOU KNOW WHAT MAKES ME *CHUCKLE?* SHEER BLOODY *DESPERATION,* THAT'S WHAT.
"TAKE BUER AND CROWLEY, FOR EXAMPLE--IN ORDER TO SUSTAIN THEIR RATHER CLUMSY ATTEMPT AT WORLD DOMINATION, THEY'VE TAKEN UP RESIDENCE INSIDE YOUR CHUBBY PAL, WEEBLE.
"*Ah-hehh*... THEY'VE GOT HIM DRINKING CARROT JUICE AND DOING LAPS ROUND TOOTING BEC COMMON, JUST TO GET HIS BLOOD PRESSURE DOWN BELOW TWELVE MILLION."
HA HA... IT'S BLOODY PRICELESS, JOHN--LIKE A SCENE FROM THE KEYSTONE KOPS. IF ONLY YOU COULD *SEE* IT.
YES, WELL ...IF ONLY YOU *COULD.*
FOTF

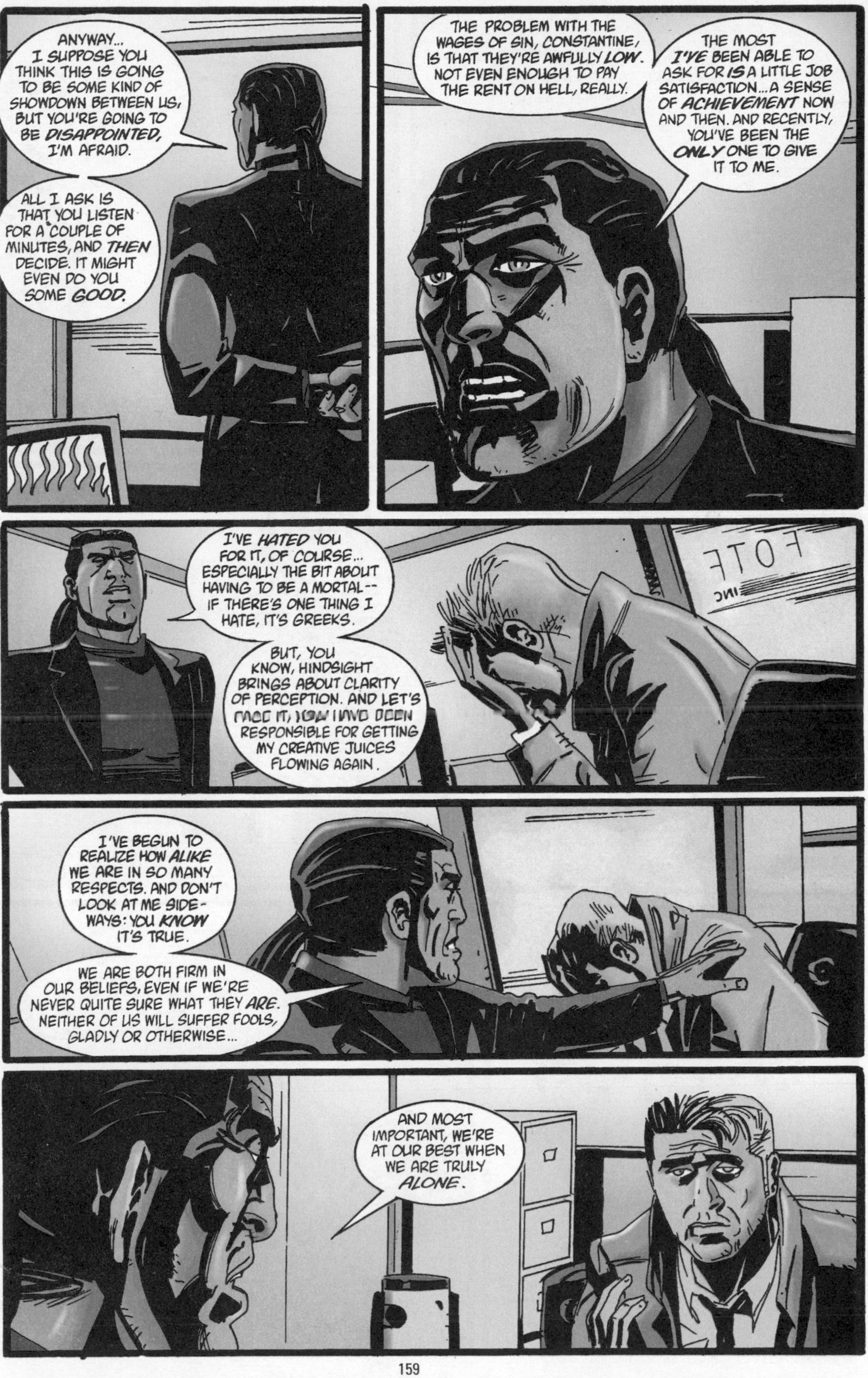
ANYWAY... I SUPPOSE YOU THINK THIS IS GOING TO BE SOME KIND OF SHOWDOWN BETWEEN US, BUT YOU'RE GOING TO BE *DISAPPOINTED*, I'M AFRAID.
ALL I ASK IS THAT YOU LISTEN FOR A COUPLE OF MINUTES, AND *THEN* DECIDE. IT MIGHT EVEN DO YOU SOME *GOOD*.
THE PROBLEM WITH THE WAGES OF SIN, CONSTANTINE, IS THAT THEY'RE AWFULLY *LOW*. NOT EVEN ENOUGH TO PAY THE RENT ON HELL, REALLY.
THE MOST *I'VE* BEEN ABLE TO ASK FOR *IS* A LITTLE JOB SATISFACTION... A SENSE OF *ACHIEVEMENT* NOW AND THEN. AND RECENTLY, YOU'VE BEEN THE *ONLY* ONE TO GIVE IT TO ME.
I'VE *HATED* YOU FOR IT, OF COURSE... ESPECIALLY THE BIT ABOUT HAVING TO BE A MORTAL-- IF THERE'S ONE THING I HATE, IT'S GREEKS.
BUT, YOU KNOW, HINDSIGHT BRINGS ABOUT CLARITY OF PERCEPTION. AND LET'S FACE IT, YOU HAVE BEEN RESPONSIBLE FOR GETTING MY CREATIVE JUICES FLOWING AGAIN.
I'VE BEGUN TO REALIZE HOW *ALIKE* WE ARE IN SO MANY RESPECTS. AND DON'T LOOK AT ME SIDE-WAYS: YOU *KNOW* IT'S TRUE.
WE ARE BOTH FIRM IN OUR BELIEFS, EVEN IF WE'RE NEVER QUITE SURE WHAT THEY *ARE*. NEITHER OF US WILL SUFFER FOOLS, GLADLY OR OTHERWISE...
AND MOST IMPORTANT, WE'RE AT OUR BEST WHEN WE ARE TRULY *ALONE*.

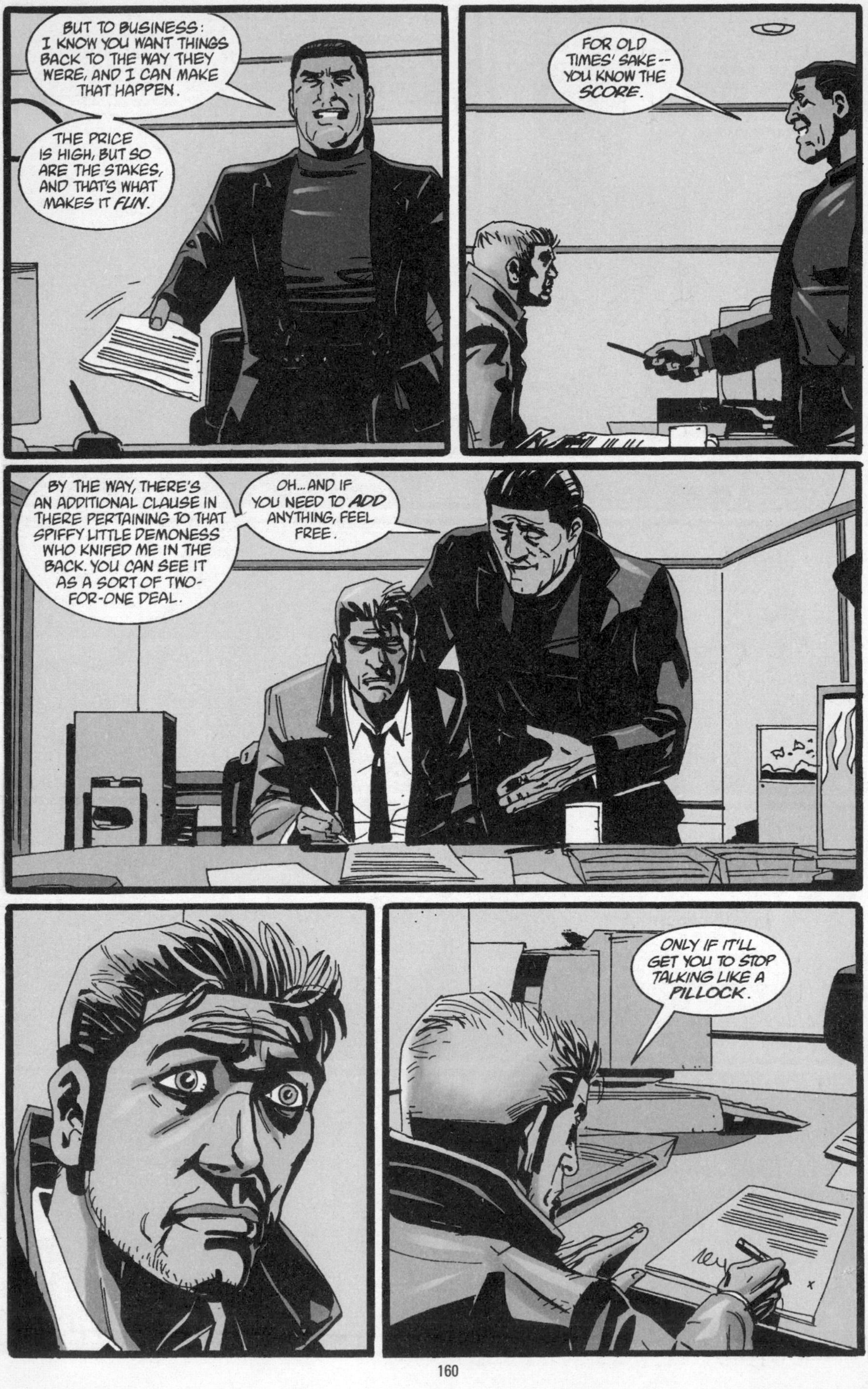
BUT TO BUSINESS: I KNOW YOU WANT THINGS BACK TO THE WAY THEY WERE, AND I CAN MAKE THAT HAPPEN.
THE PRICE IS HIGH, BUT SO ARE THE STAKES, AND THAT'S WHAT MAKES IT FUN.
FOR OLD TIMES' SAKE-- YOU KNOW THE SCORE.
BY THE WAY, THERE'S AN ADDITIONAL CLAUSE IN THERE PERTAINING TO THAT SPIFFY LITTLE DEMONESS WHO KNIFED ME IN THE BACK. YOU CAN SEE IT AS A SORT OF TWO-FOR-ONE DEAL.
OH...AND IF YOU NEED TO ADD ANYTHING, FEEL FREE.
ONLY IF IT'LL GET YOU TO STOP TALKING LIKE A PILLOCK.

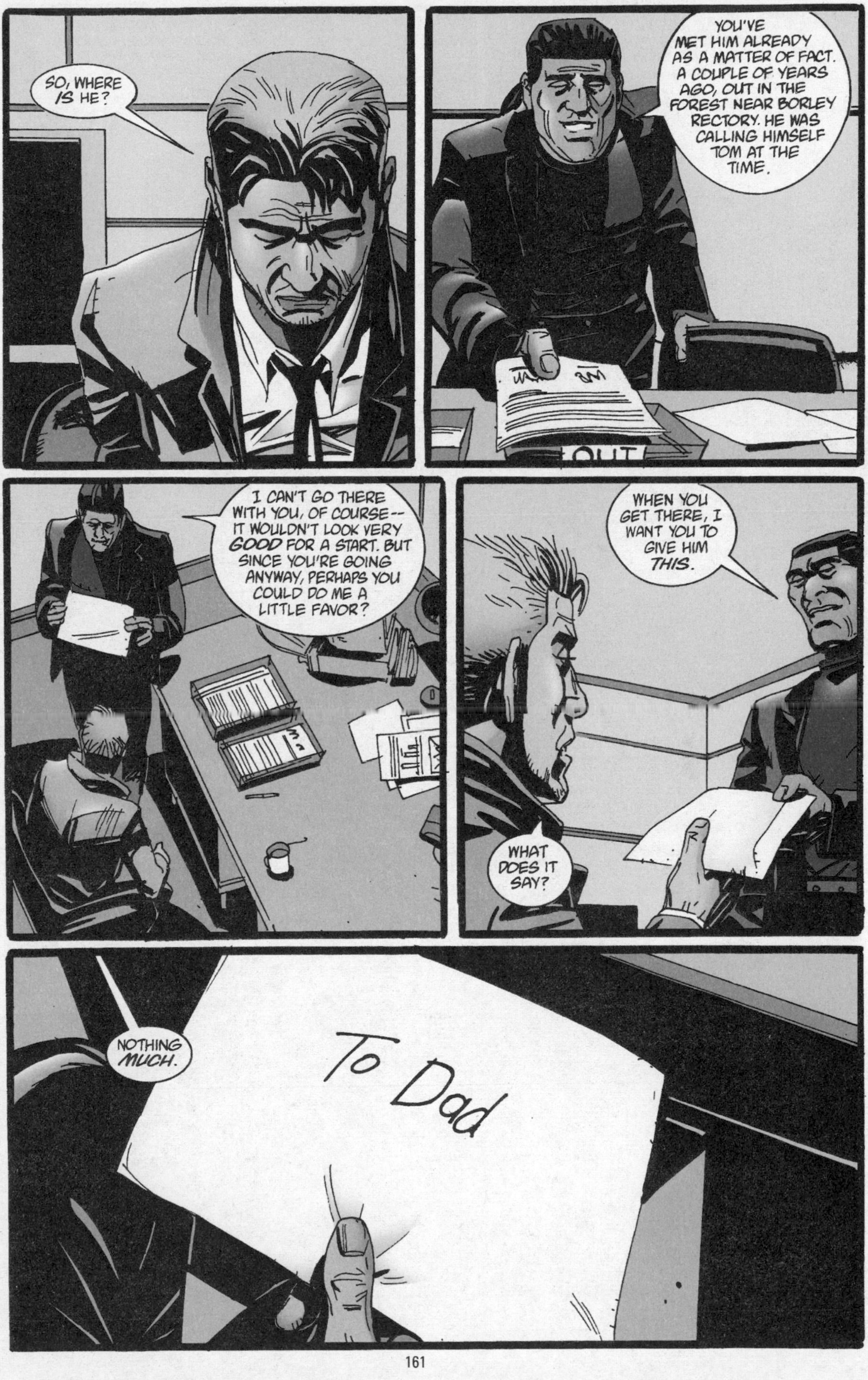
SO, WHERE IS HE?
YOU'VE MET HIM ALREADY AS A MATTER OF FACT. A COUPLE OF YEARS AGO, OUT IN THE FOREST NEAR BORLEY RECTORY. HE WAS CALLING HIMSELF TOM AT THE TIME.
OUT
I CAN'T GO THERE WITH YOU, OF COURSE-- IT WOULDN'T LOOK VERY GOOD FOR A START. BUT SINCE YOU'RE GOING ANYWAY, PERHAPS YOU COULD DO ME A LITTLE FAVOR?
WHEN YOU GET THERE, I WANT YOU TO GIVE HIM THIS.
WHAT DOES IT SAY?
NOTHING MUCH.
To Dad

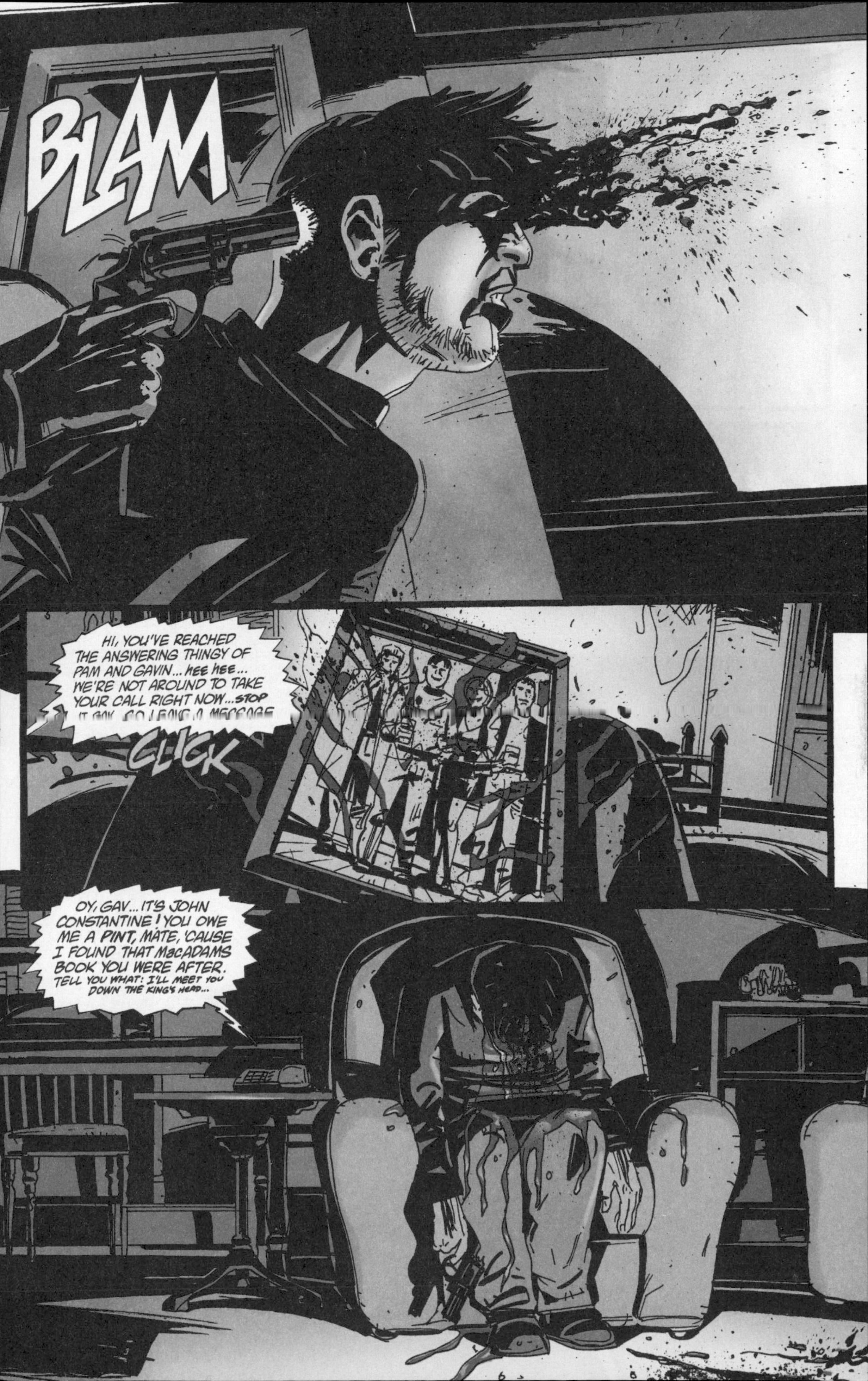
BLAM
HI, YOU'VE REACHED THE ANSWERING THINGY OF PAM AND GAVIN... hee hee... WE'RE NOT AROUND TO TAKE YOUR CALL RIGHT NOW...STOP
CLICK
OY, GAV... IT'S JOHN CONSTANTINE! YOU OWE ME A PINT, MATE, 'CAUSE I FOUND THAT MacADAMS BOOK YOU WERE AFTER. TELL YOU WHAT: I'LL MEET YOU DOWN THE KING'S HEAD...

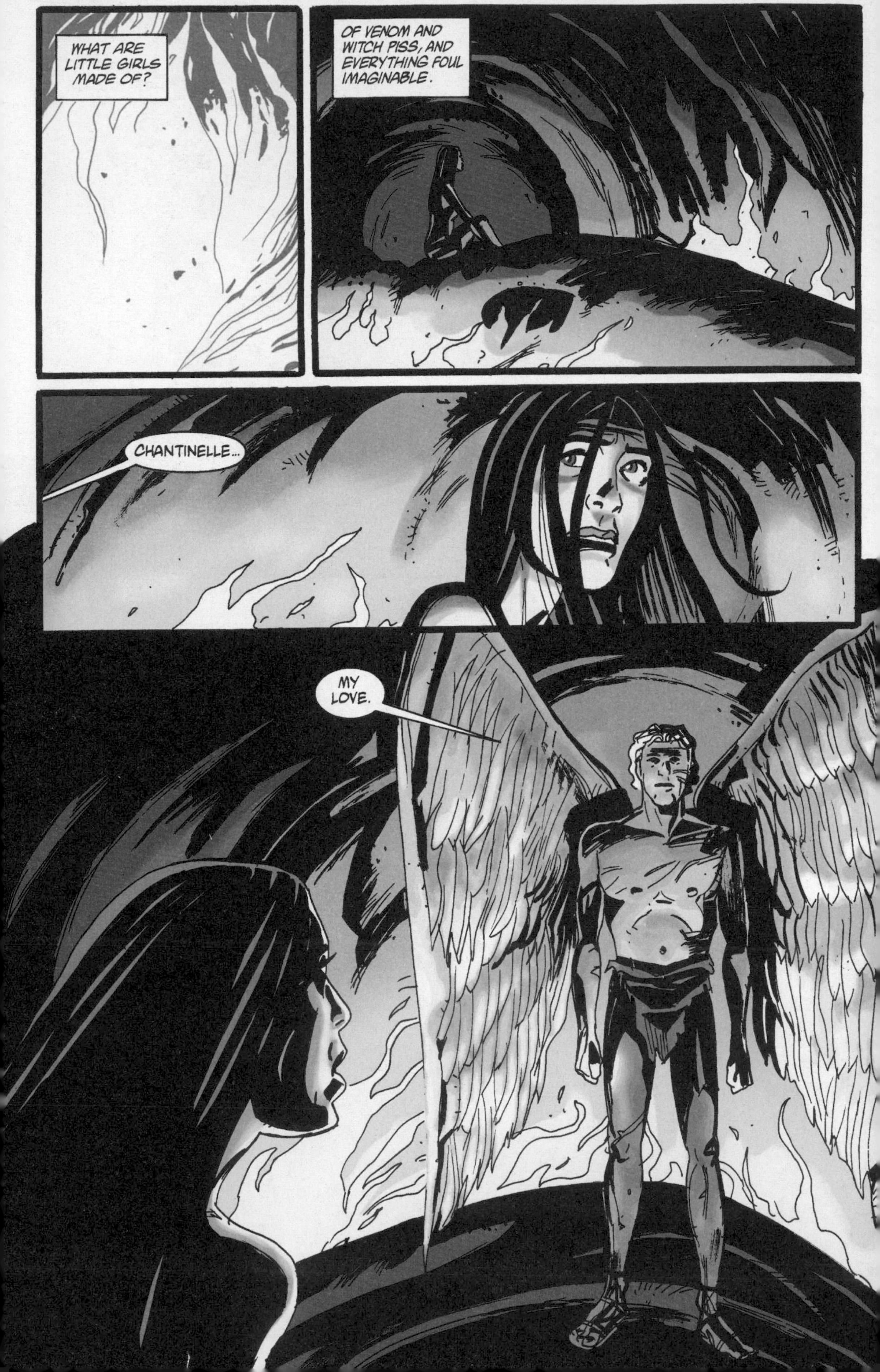
WHAT ARE LITTLE GIRLS MADE OF?
OF VENOM AND WITCH PISS, AND EVERYTHING FOUL IMAGINABLE.
CHANTINELLE...
MY LOVE.

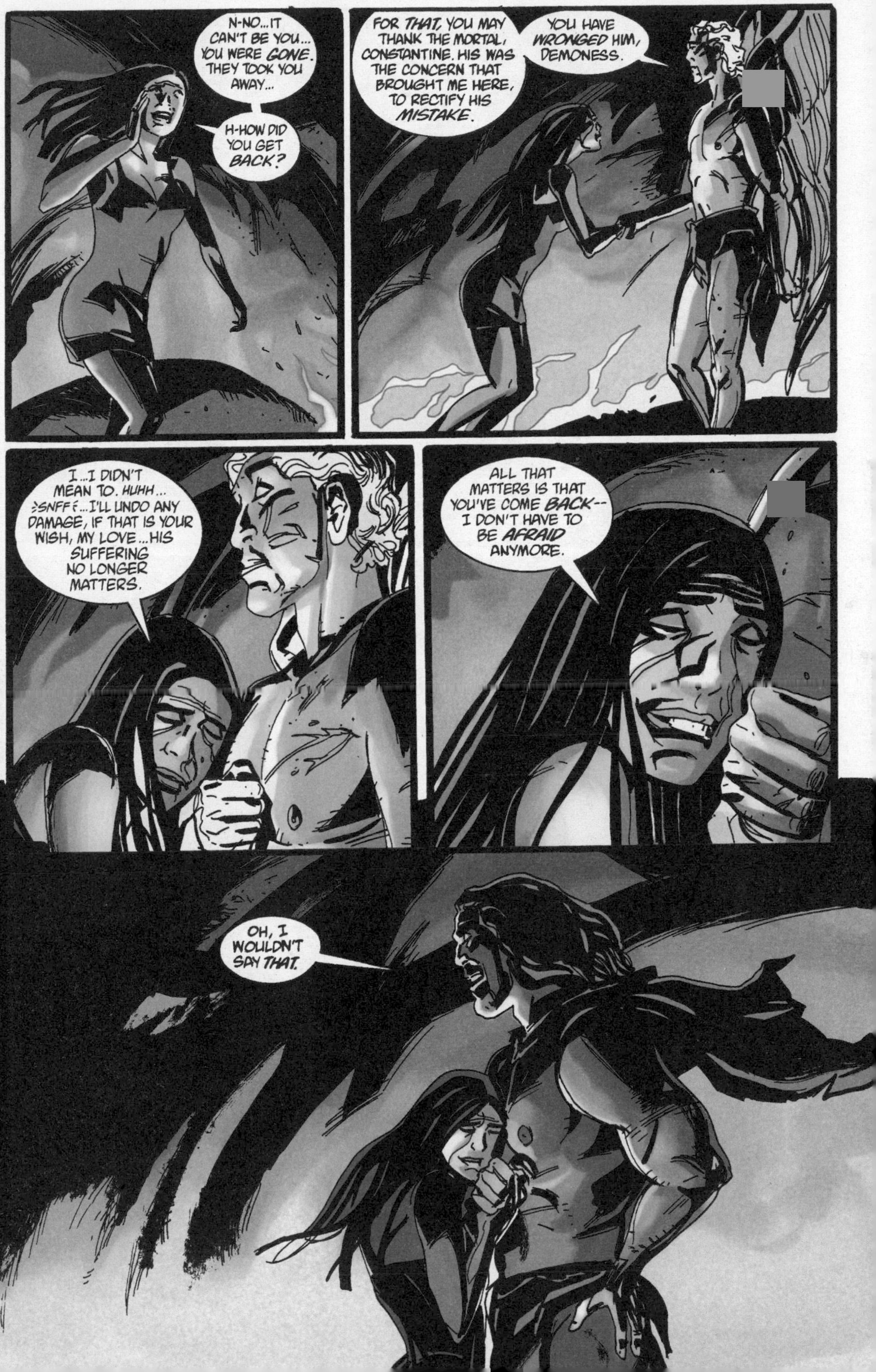
N-NO...IT CAN'T BE YOU... YOU WERE GONE. THEY TOOK YOU AWAY...
H-HOW DID YOU GET BACK?
YOU HAVE WRONGED HIM, DEMONESS.
FOR THAT, YOU MAY THANK THE MORTAL, CONSTANTINE. HIS WAS THE CONCERN THAT BROUGHT ME HERE, TO RECTIFY HIS MISTAKE.
I...I DIDN'T MEAN TO. HUHH... >SNFF<...I'LL UNDO ANY DAMAGE, IF THAT IS YOUR WISH, MY LOVE...HIS SUFFERING NO LONGER MATTERS.
ALL THAT MATTERS IS THAT YOU'VE COME BACK-- I DON'T HAVE TO BE AFRAID ANYMORE.
OH, I WOULDN'T SAY THAT.

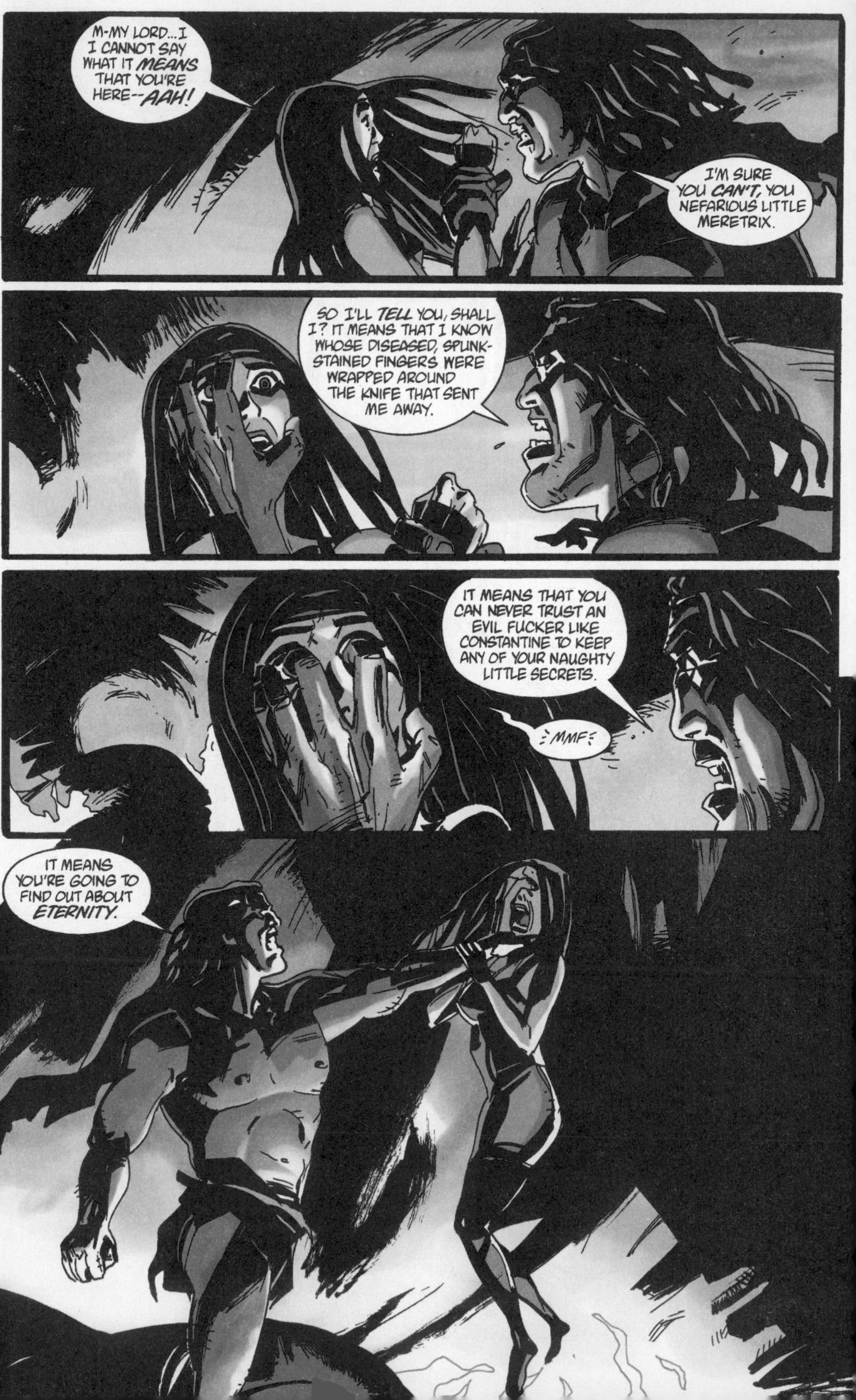
M-MY LORD... I I CANNOT SAY WHAT IT MEANS THAT YOU'RE HERE--AAH!
I'M SURE YOU CAN'T, YOU NEFARIOUS LITTLE MERETRIX.
SO I'LL TELL YOU, SHALL I? IT MEANS THAT I KNOW WHOSE DISEASED, SPUNK-STAINED FINGERS WERE WRAPPED AROUND THE KNIFE THAT SENT ME AWAY.
IT MEANS THAT YOU CAN NEVER TRUST AN EVIL FUCKER LIKE CONSTANTINE TO KEEP ANY OF YOUR NAUGHTY LITTLE SECRETS.
MMF
IT MEANS YOU'RE GOING TO FIND OUT ABOUT ETERNITY.

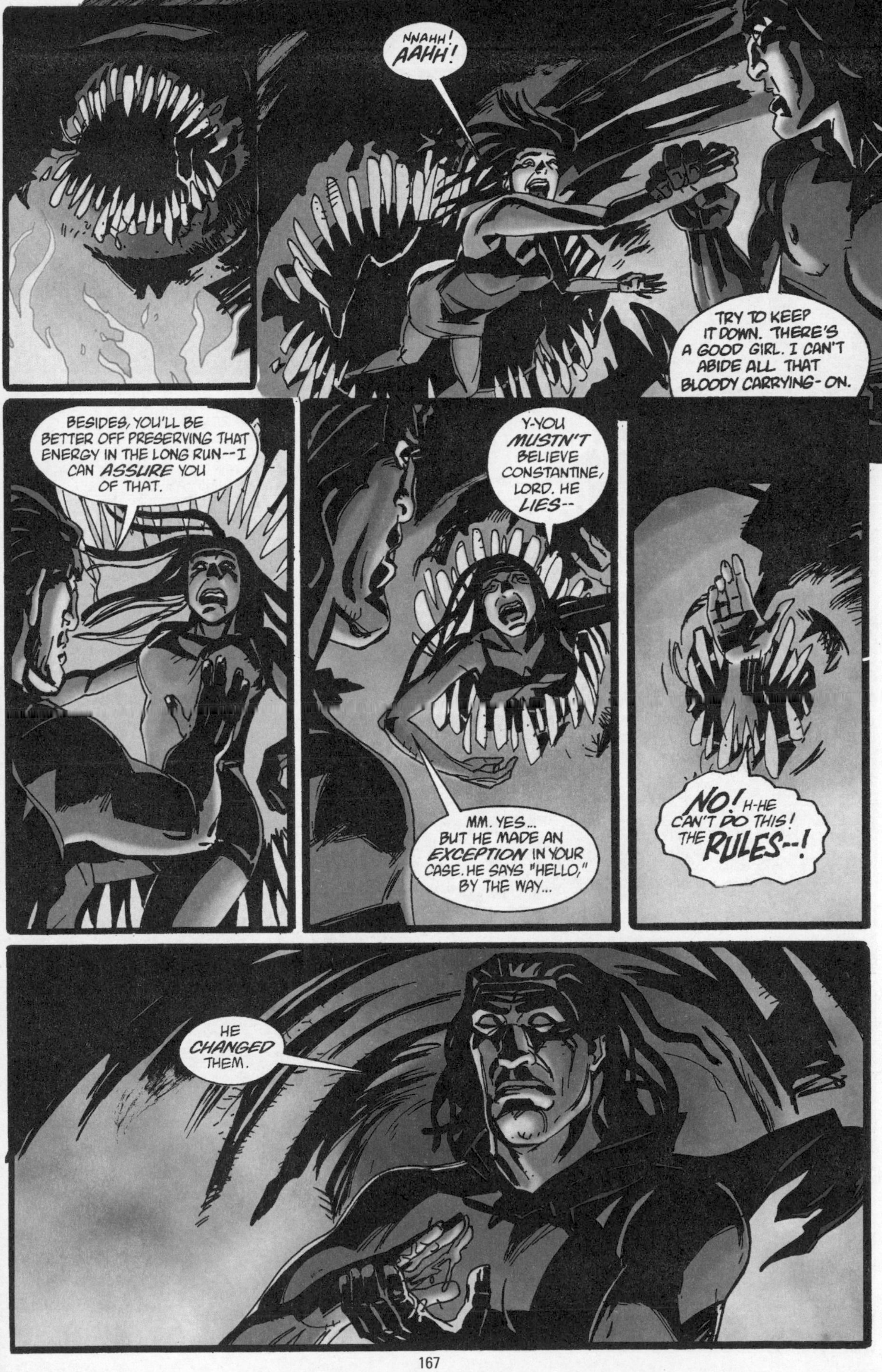
NNAHH! AAHH!
TRY TO KEEP IT DOWN. THERE'S A GOOD GIRL. I CAN'T ABIDE ALL THAT BLOODY CARRYING-ON.
BESIDES, YOU'LL BE BETTER OFF PRESERVING THAT ENERGY IN THE LONG RUN--I CAN ASSURE YOU OF THAT.
Y-YOU MUSTN'T BELIEVE CONSTANTINE, LORD. HE LIES--
MM. YES... BUT HE MADE AN EXCEPTION IN YOUR CASE. HE SAYS "HELLO," BY THE WAY...
NO! H-HE CAN'T DO THIS! THE RULES--!
HE CHANGED THEM.

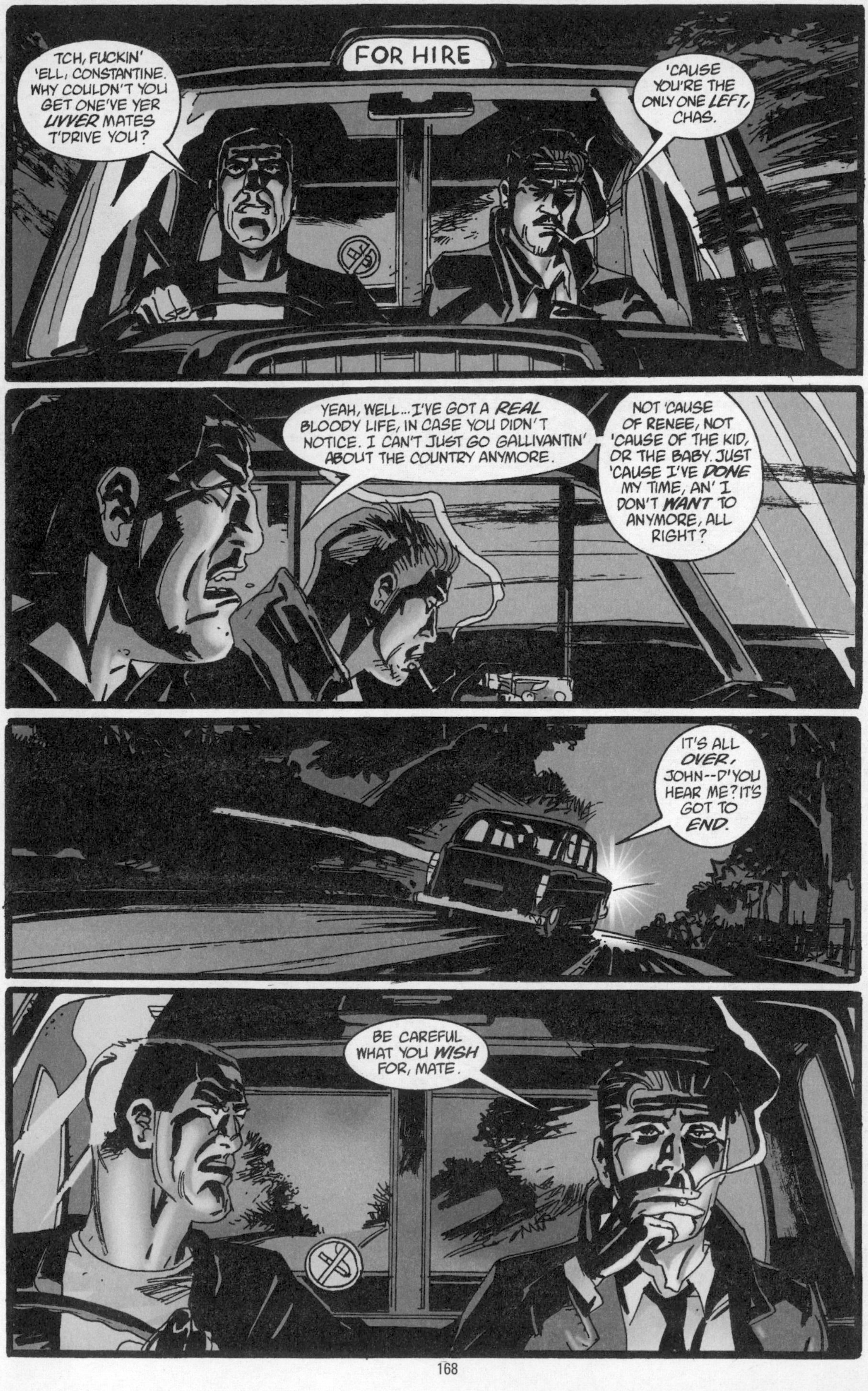
FOR HIRE
TCH, FUCKIN' 'ELL, CONSTANTINE. WHY COULDN'T YOU GET ONE'VE YER LIVVER MATES T'DRIVE YOU?
'CAUSE YOU'RE THE ONLY ONE LEFT, CHAS.
YEAH, WELL... I'VE GOT A REAL BLOODY LIFE, IN CASE YOU DIDN'T NOTICE. I CAN'T JUST GO GALLIVANTIN' ABOUT THE COUNTRY ANYMORE.
NOT 'CAUSE OF RENEE, NOT 'CAUSE OF THE KID, OR THE BABY. JUST 'CAUSE I'VE DONE MY TIME, AN' I DON'T WANT TO ANYMORE, ALL RIGHT?
IT'S ALL OVER, JOHN--D'YOU HEAR ME? IT'S GOT TO END.
BE CAREFUL WHAT YOU WISH FOR, MATE.

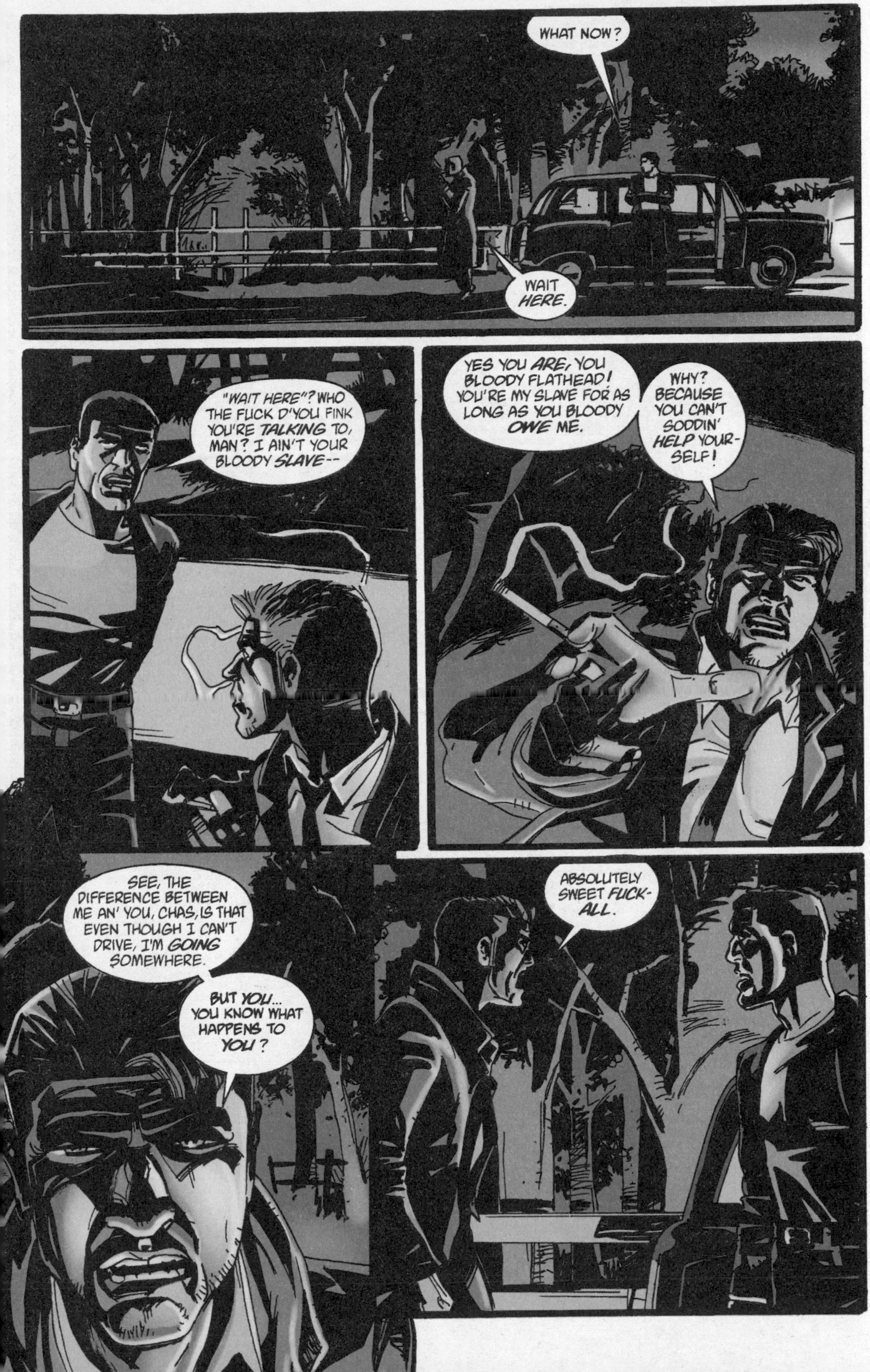
WHAT NOW?
WAIT HERE.
"WAIT HERE"? WHO THE FUCK D'YOU FINK YOU'RE TALKING TO, MAN? I AIN'T YOUR BLOODY SLAVE--
YES YOU ARE, YOU BLOODY FLATHEAD! YOU'RE MY SLAVE FOR AS LONG AS YOU BLOODY OWE ME.
WHY? BECAUSE YOU CAN'T SODDIN' HELP YOURSELF!
SEE, THE DIFFERENCE BETWEEN ME AN' YOU, CHAS, IS THAT EVEN THOUGH I CAN'T DRIVE, I'M GOING SOMEWHERE.
BUT YOU... YOU KNOW WHAT HAPPENS TO YOU?
ABSOLUTELY SWEET FUCK-ALL.

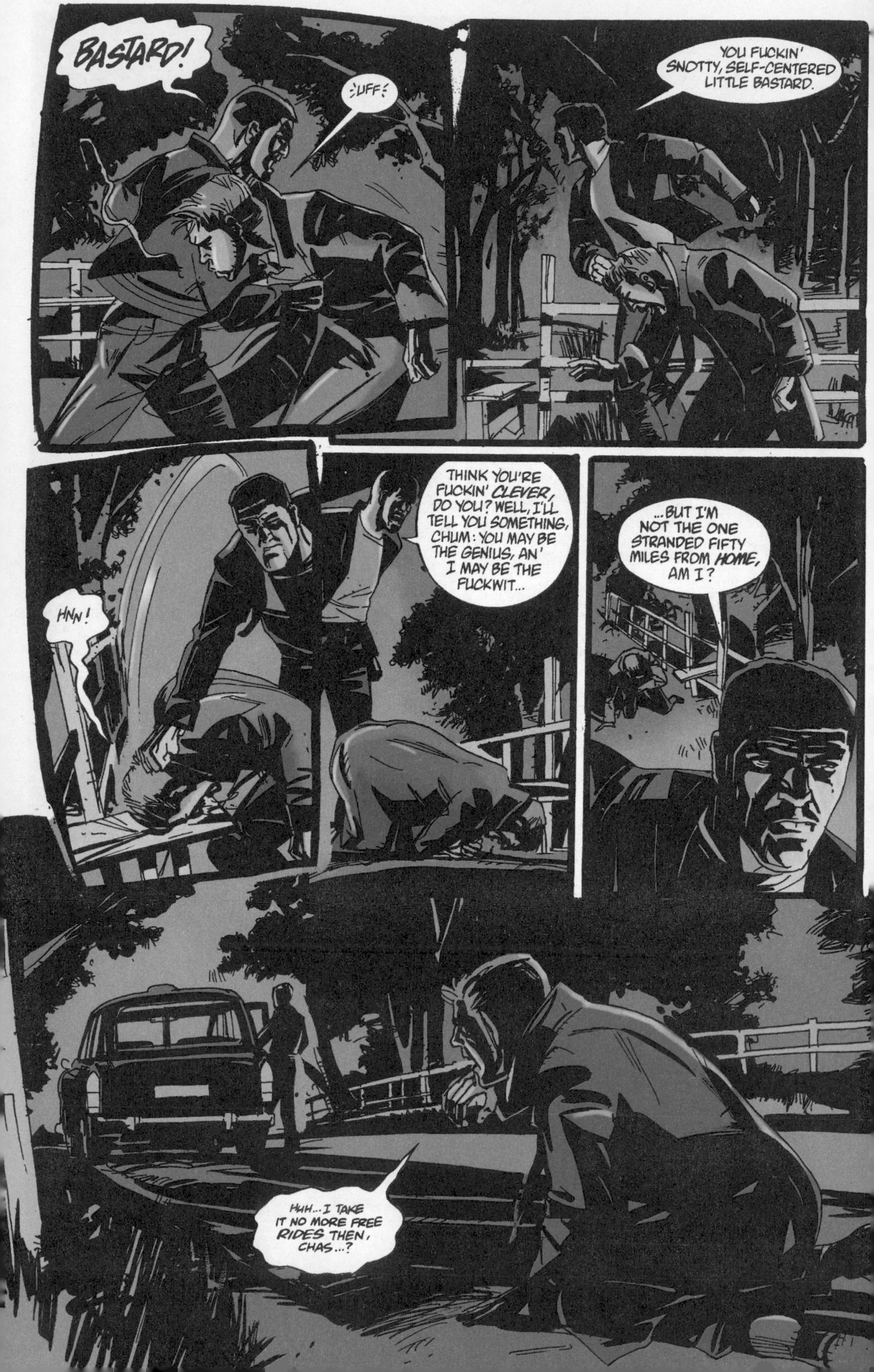
BASTARD!
UFF
YOU FUCKIN' SNOTTY, SELF-CENTERED LITTLE BASTARD.
HNN!
THINK YOU'RE FUCKIN' CLEVER, DO YOU? WELL, I'LL TELL YOU SOMETHING, CHUM: YOU MAY BE THE GENIUS, AN' I MAY BE THE FUCKWIT...
...BUT I'M NOT THE ONE STRANDED FIFTY MILES FROM HOME, AM I?
HUH... I TAKE IT NO MORE FREE RIDES THEN, CHAS...?

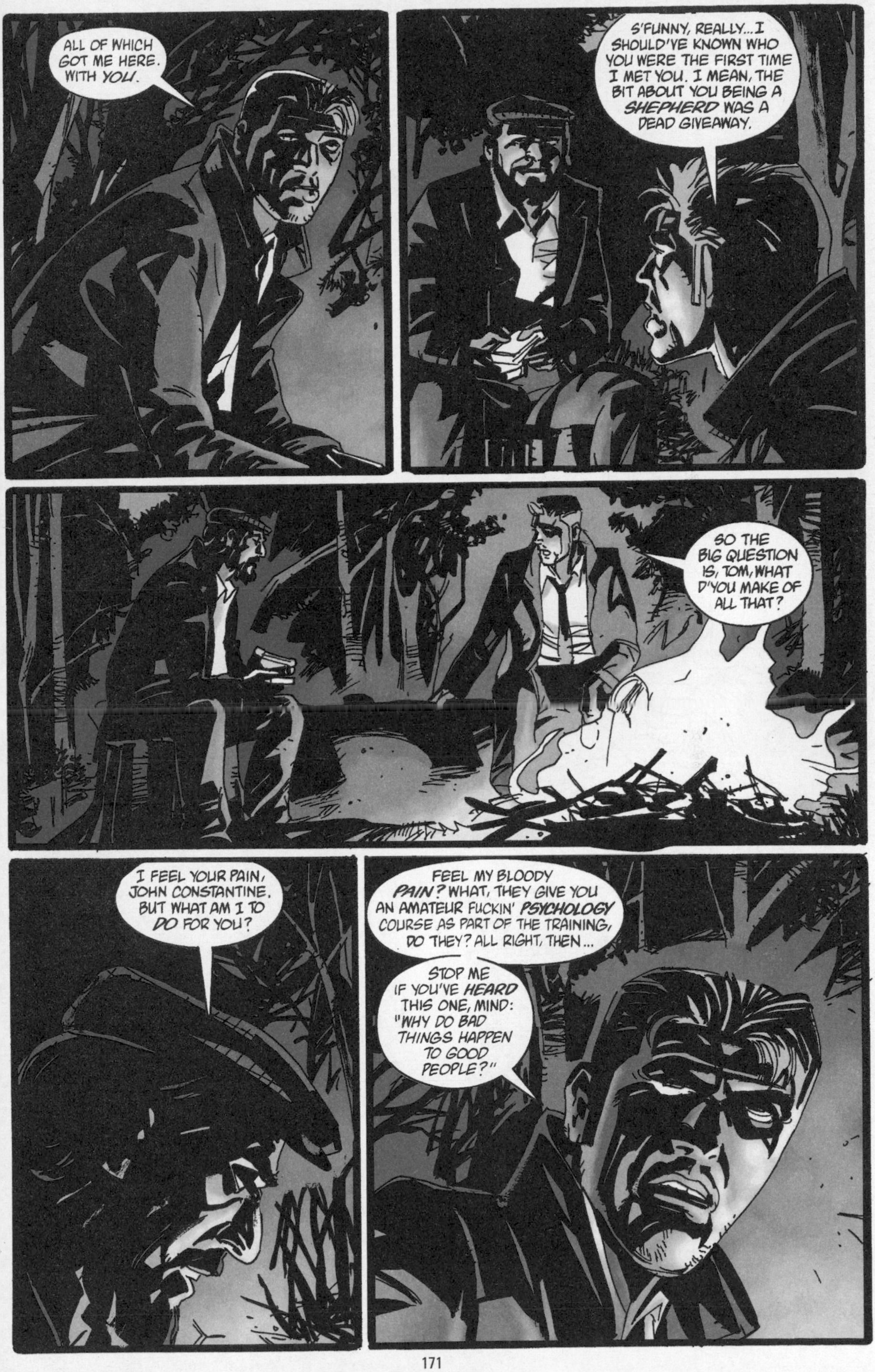
ALL OF WHICH GOT ME HERE. WITH YOU.
S'FUNNY, REALLY... I SHOULD'VE KNOWN WHO YOU WERE THE FIRST TIME I MET YOU. I MEAN, THE BIT ABOUT YOU BEING A SHEPHERD WAS A DEAD GIVEAWAY.
SO THE BIG QUESTION IS, TOM, WHAT D'YOU MAKE OF ALL THAT?
I FEEL YOUR PAIN, JOHN CONSTANTINE. BUT WHAT AM I TO DO FOR YOU?
FEEL MY BLOODY PAIN? WHAT, THEY GIVE YOU AN AMATEUR FUCKIN' PSYCHOLOGY COURSE AS PART OF THE TRAINING, DO THEY? ALL RIGHT, THEN...
STOP ME IF YOU'VE HEARD THIS ONE, MIND: "WHY DO BAD THINGS HAPPEN TO GOOD PEOPLE?"

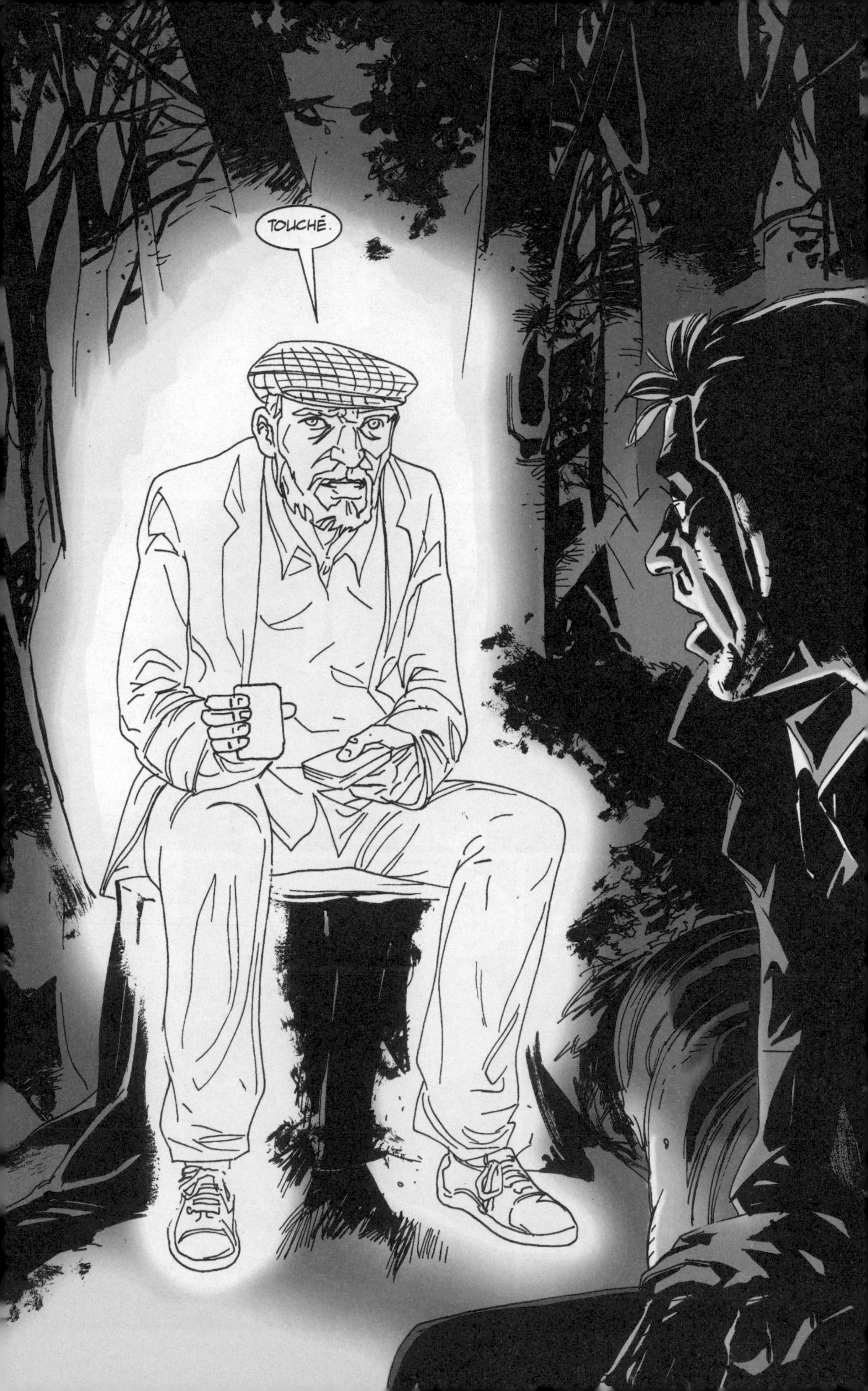
TOUCHÉ.

JOHN CONSTANTINE

HELLBLAZER ™

DC

VERTIGO

128

G 98

25 US

5 CAN

GESTED
MATURE
DERS

PAUL JENKINS
WARREN PLEECE

HOW TO
PLAY
WITH FIRE
Part Four
of Four

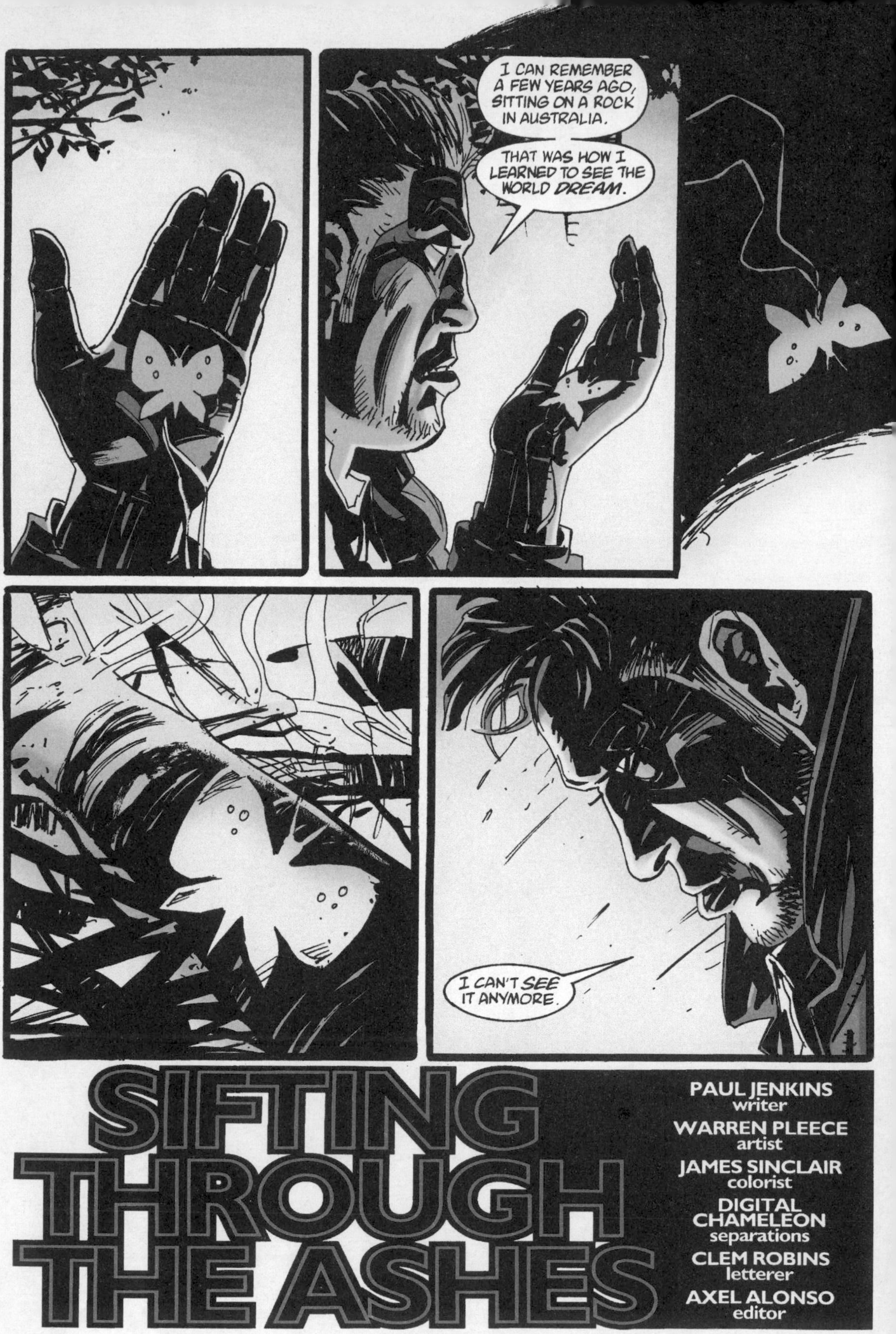
I CAN REMEMBER A FEW YEARS AGO, SITTING ON A ROCK IN AUSTRALIA.
THAT WAS HOW I LEARNED TO SEE THE WORLD *DREAM*.
I CAN'T *SEE* IT ANYMORE.

SIFTING THROUGH THE ASHES

PAUL JENKINS
writer

WARREN PLEECE
artist

JAMES SINCLAIR
colorist

DIGITAL CHAMELEON
separations

CLEM ROBINS
letterer

AXEL ALONSO
editor

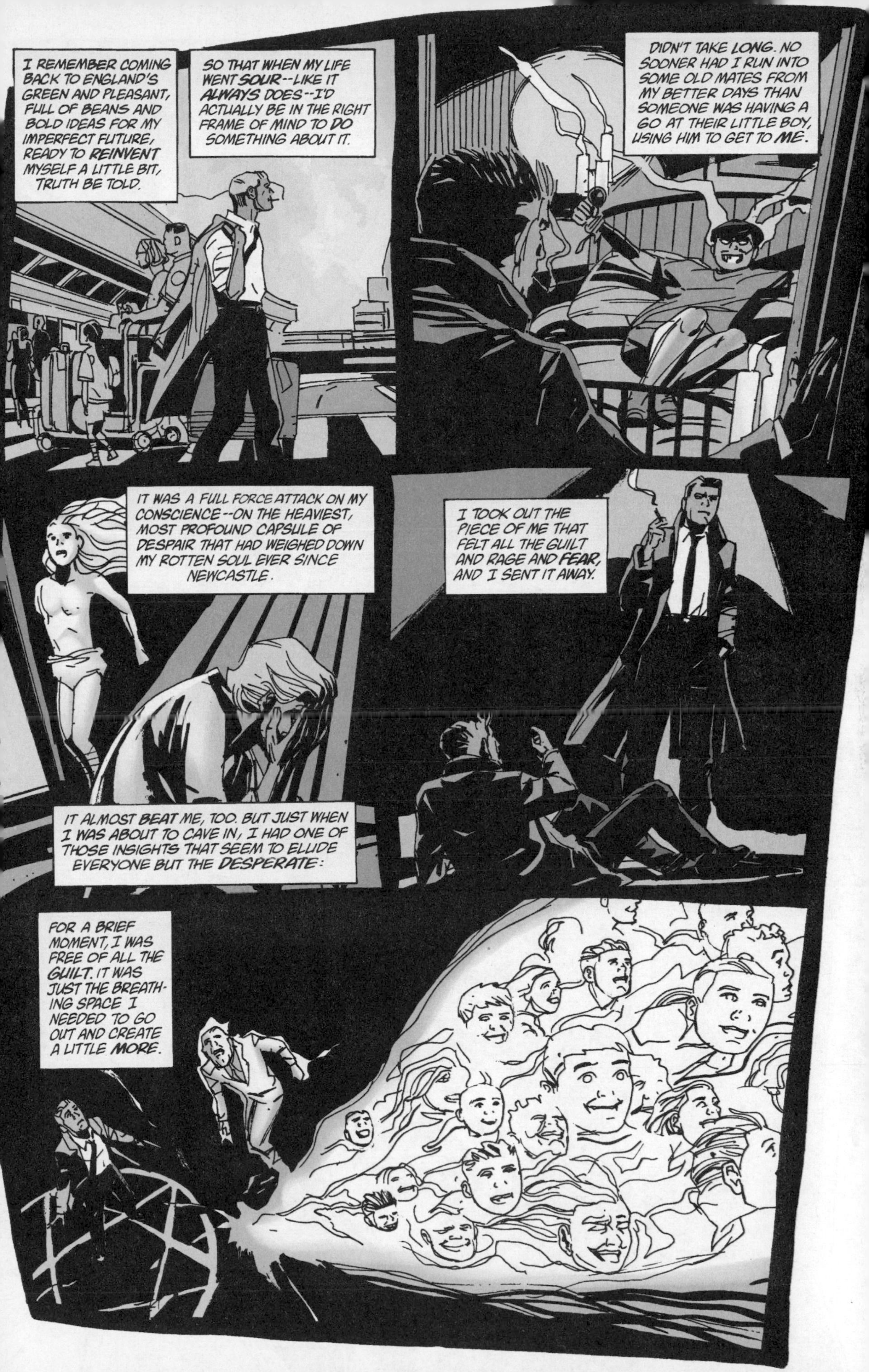
I REMEMBER COMING BACK TO ENGLAND'S GREEN AND PLEASANT, FULL OF BEANS AND BOLD IDEAS FOR MY IMPERFECT FUTURE, READY TO REINVENT MYSELF A LITTLE BIT, TRUTH BE TOLD.
SO THAT WHEN MY LIFE WENT SOUR--LIKE IT ALWAYS DOES--I'D ACTUALLY BE IN THE RIGHT FRAME OF MIND TO DO SOMETHING ABOUT IT.
DIDN'T TAKE LONG. NO SOONER HAD I RUN INTO SOME OLD MATES FROM MY BETTER DAYS THAN SOMEONE WAS HAVING A GO AT THEIR LITTLE BOY, USING HIM TO GET TO ME.
IT WAS A FULL FORCE ATTACK ON MY CONSCIENCE--ON THE HEAVIEST, MOST PROFOUND CAPSULE OF DESPAIR THAT HAD WEIGHED DOWN MY ROTTEN SOUL EVER SINCE NEWCASTLE.
IT ALMOST BEAT ME, TOO. BUT JUST WHEN I WAS ABOUT TO CAVE IN, I HAD ONE OF THOSE INSIGHTS THAT SEEM TO ELUDE EVERYONE BUT THE DESPERATE:
I TOOK OUT THE PIECE OF ME THAT FELT ALL THE GUILT AND RAGE AND FEAR, AND I SENT IT AWAY.
FOR A BRIEF MOMENT, I WAS FREE OF ALL THE GUILT. IT WAS JUST THE BREATHING SPACE I NEEDED TO GO OUT AND CREATE A LITTLE MORE.

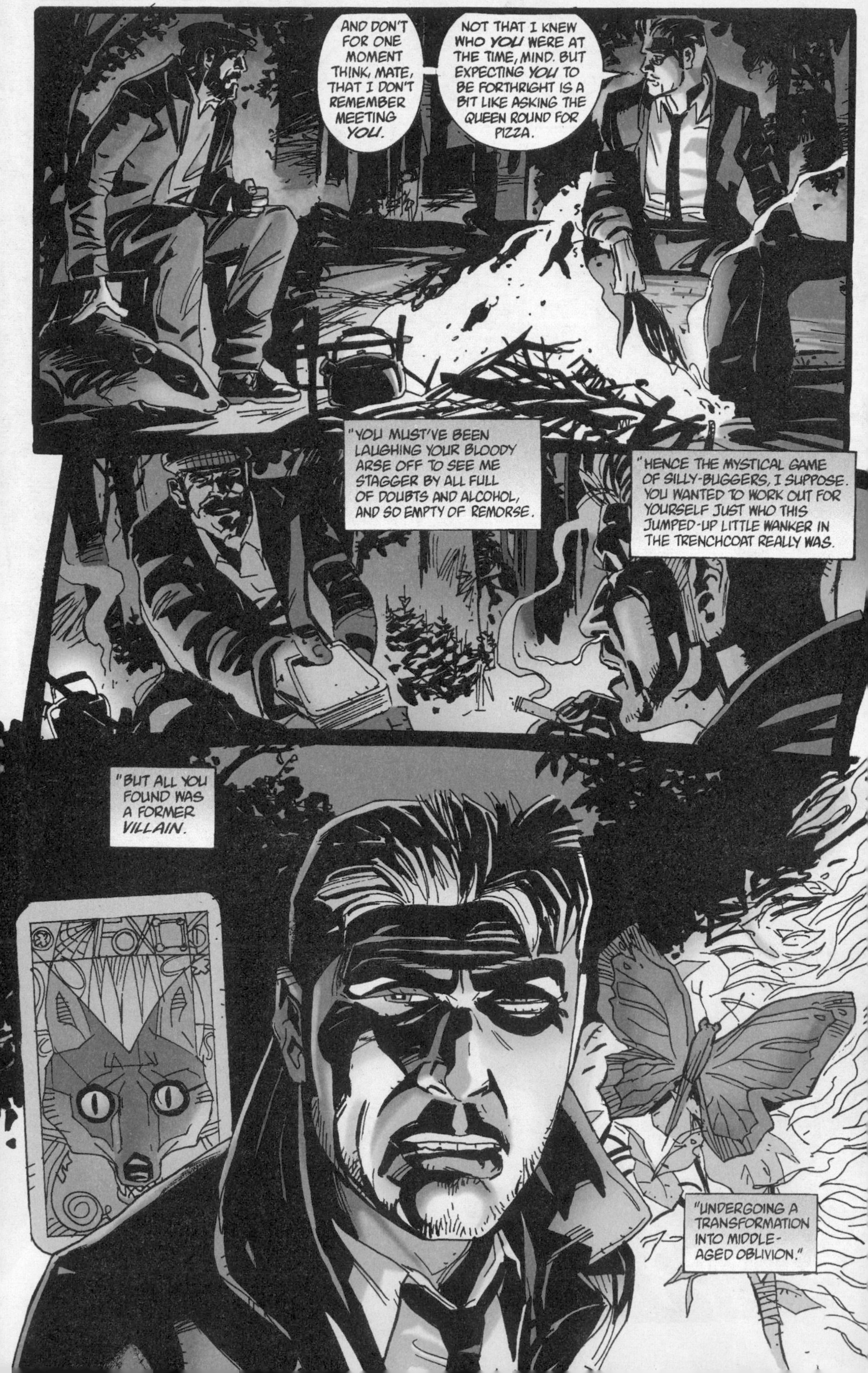
AND DON'T FOR ONE MOMENT THINK, MATE, THAT I DON'T REMEMBER MEETING *YOU*.
NOT THAT I KNEW WHO *YOU* WERE AT THE TIME, MIND. BUT EXPECTING *YOU* TO BE FORTHRIGHT IS A BIT LIKE ASKING THE QUEEN ROUND FOR PIZZA.
"YOU MUST'VE BEEN LAUGHING YOUR BLOODY ARSE OFF TO SEE ME STAGGER BY ALL FULL OF DOUBTS AND ALCOHOL, AND SO EMPTY OF REMORSE.
"HENCE THE MYSTICAL GAME OF SILLY-BUGGERS, I SUPPOSE. YOU WANTED TO WORK OUT FOR YOURSELF JUST WHO THIS JUMPED-UP LITTLE WANKER IN THE TRENCHCOAT REALLY WAS.
"BUT ALL YOU FOUND WAS A FORMER *VILLAIN*.
"UNDERGOING A TRANSFORMATION INTO MIDDLE-AGED OBLIVION."

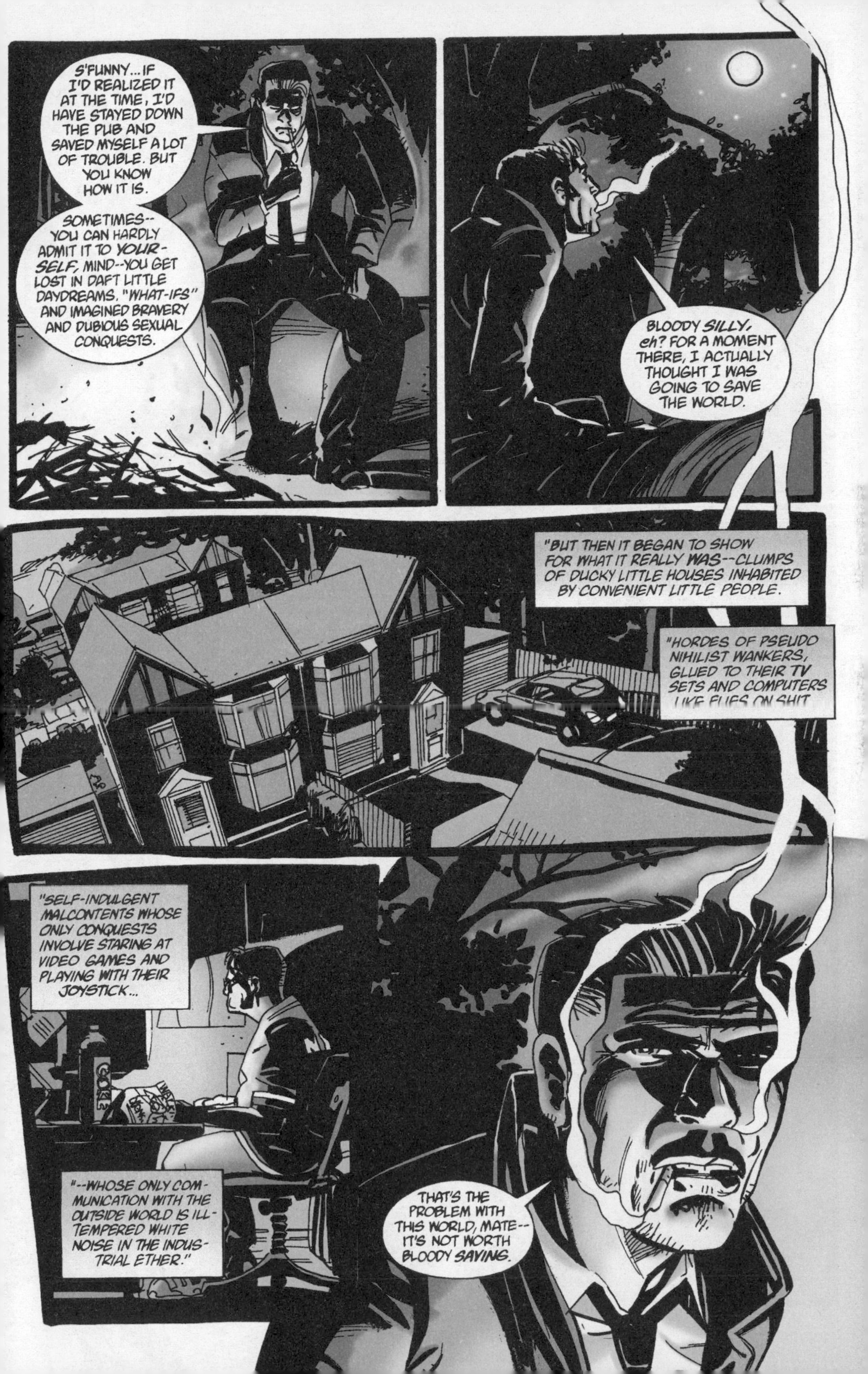
S'FUNNY... IF I'D REALIZED IT AT THE TIME, I'D HAVE STAYED DOWN THE PUB AND SAVED MYSELF A LOT OF TROUBLE. BUT YOU KNOW HOW IT IS.
SOMETIMES-- YOU CAN HARDLY ADMIT IT TO YOURSELF, MIND--YOU GET LOST IN DAFT LITTLE DAYDREAMS. "WHAT-IFS" AND IMAGINED BRAVERY AND DUBIOUS SEXUAL CONQUESTS.
BLOODY SILLY, eh? FOR A MOMENT THERE, I ACTUALLY THOUGHT I WAS GOING TO SAVE THE WORLD.
"BUT THEN IT BEGAN TO SHOW FOR WHAT IT REALLY WAS--CLUMPS OF DUCKY LITTLE HOUSES INHABITED BY CONVENIENT LITTLE PEOPLE.
"HORDES OF PSEUDO NIHILIST WANKERS, GLUED TO THEIR TV SETS AND COMPUTERS LIKE FLIES ON SHIT
"SELF-INDULGENT MALCONTENTS WHOSE ONLY CONQUESTS INVOLVE STARING AT VIDEO GAMES AND PLAYING WITH THEIR JOYSTICK...
"--WHOSE ONLY COMMUNICATION WITH THE OUTSIDE WORLD IS ILL-TEMPERED WHITE NOISE IN THE INDUSTRIAL ETHER."
THAT'S THE PROBLEM WITH THIS WORLD, MATE-- IT'S NOT WORTH BLOODY SAVING.

THEN WHY ARE YOU HERE?

FUCKED IF *I* KNOW. WHY ARE *YOU?*

BECAUSE THIS PLACE, WITH ALL ITS IMPERFECTIONS, IS STILL THE MOST WORTHY OF ALL CREATION.

OH YEAH...IT'S A FUCKIN' *CLASSIC*, MATE. SO WONDERFUL, IN FACT, THAT IT'S BEEN REWORKED ABOUT FIFTY SQUILLION TIMES.

NOT TO MENTION THE FACT THAT THE HIGHER POWERS-THAT-BE HAVE FARTED AROUND WITH PEOPLE'S FAITH, DAMNED THE POOR BLOODY NON-BELIEVERS, POISONED THE FAERIES, AND KILLED OFF ALL THE CABBAGES.

ALL UNDER THE GUISE OF SOME INDE-FATIGABLE SODDIN' *PLAN.* NOT THAT THE OLD BOY UPSTAIRS COULDN'T REMOVE HIS ESSENCE WITHOUT SO MUCH AS A SNAP OF HIS FIGURATIVE FINGERS, HE JUST CAN'T BE *ARSED* TO.

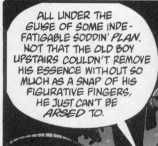

BECAUSE THAT IS NOT PART OF HIS *DESIGN*, JOHN CONSTANTINE.

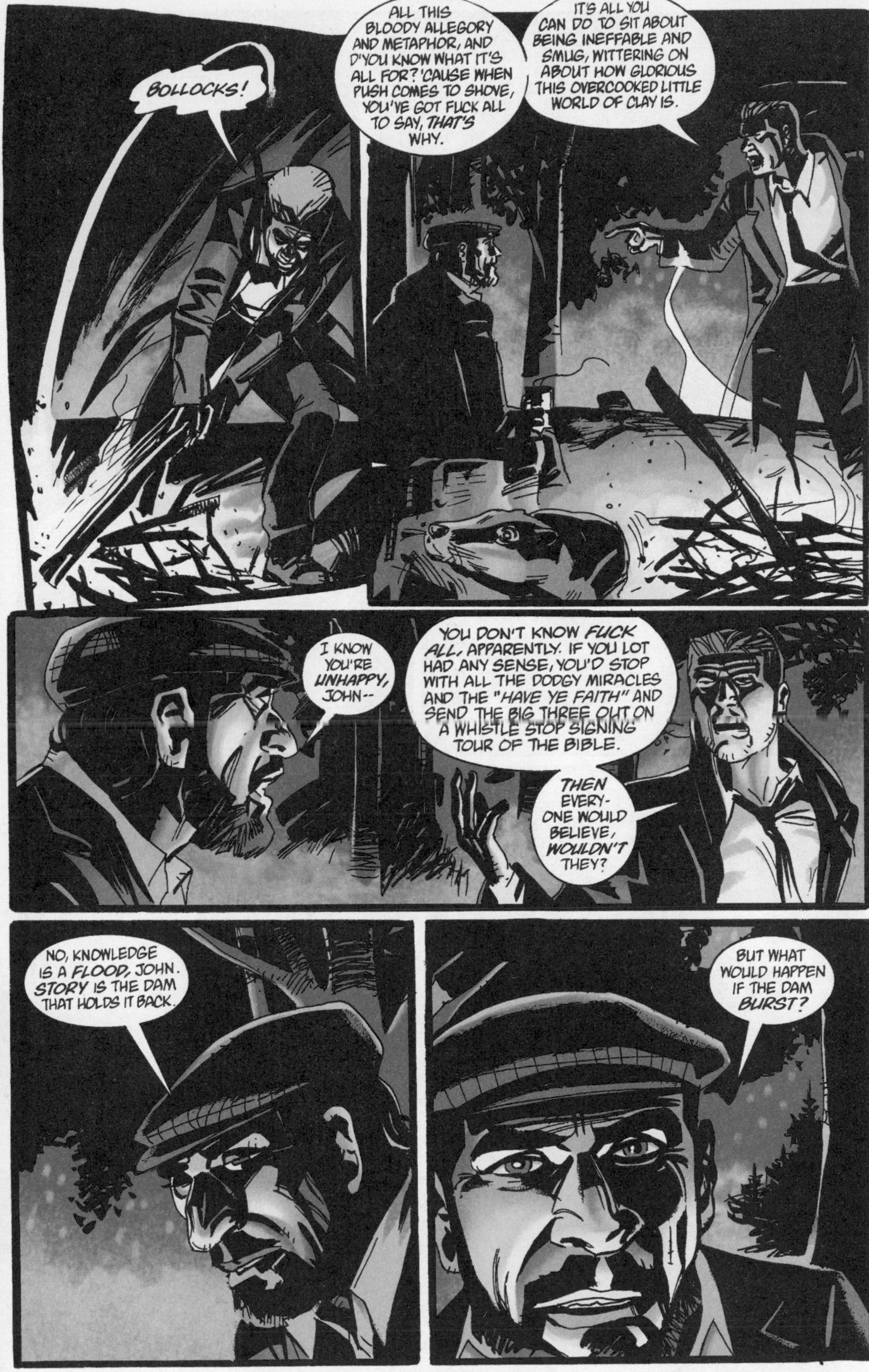
BOLLOCKS!
ALL THIS BLOODY ALLEGORY AND METAPHOR, AND D'YOU KNOW WHAT IT'S ALL FOR? 'CAUSE WHEN PUSH COMES TO SHOVE, YOU'VE GOT FUCK ALL TO SAY, THAT'S WHY.
IT'S ALL YOU CAN DO TO SIT ABOUT BEING INEFFABLE AND SMUG, WITTERING ON ABOUT HOW GLORIOUS THIS OVERCOOKED LITTLE WORLD OF CLAY IS.
I KNOW YOU'RE UNHAPPY, JOHN--
YOU DON'T KNOW FUCK ALL, APPARENTLY. IF YOU LOT HAD ANY SENSE, YOU'D STOP WITH ALL THE DODGY MIRACLES AND THE "HAVE YE FAITH" AND SEND THE BIG THREE OUT ON A WHISTLE STOP SIGNING TOUR OF THE BIBLE.
THEN EVERY-ONE WOULD BELIEVE, WOULDN'T THEY?
NO, KNOWLEDGE IS A FLOOD, JOHN. STORY IS THE DAM THAT HOLDS IT BACK.
BUT WHAT WOULD HAPPEN IF THE DAM BURST?

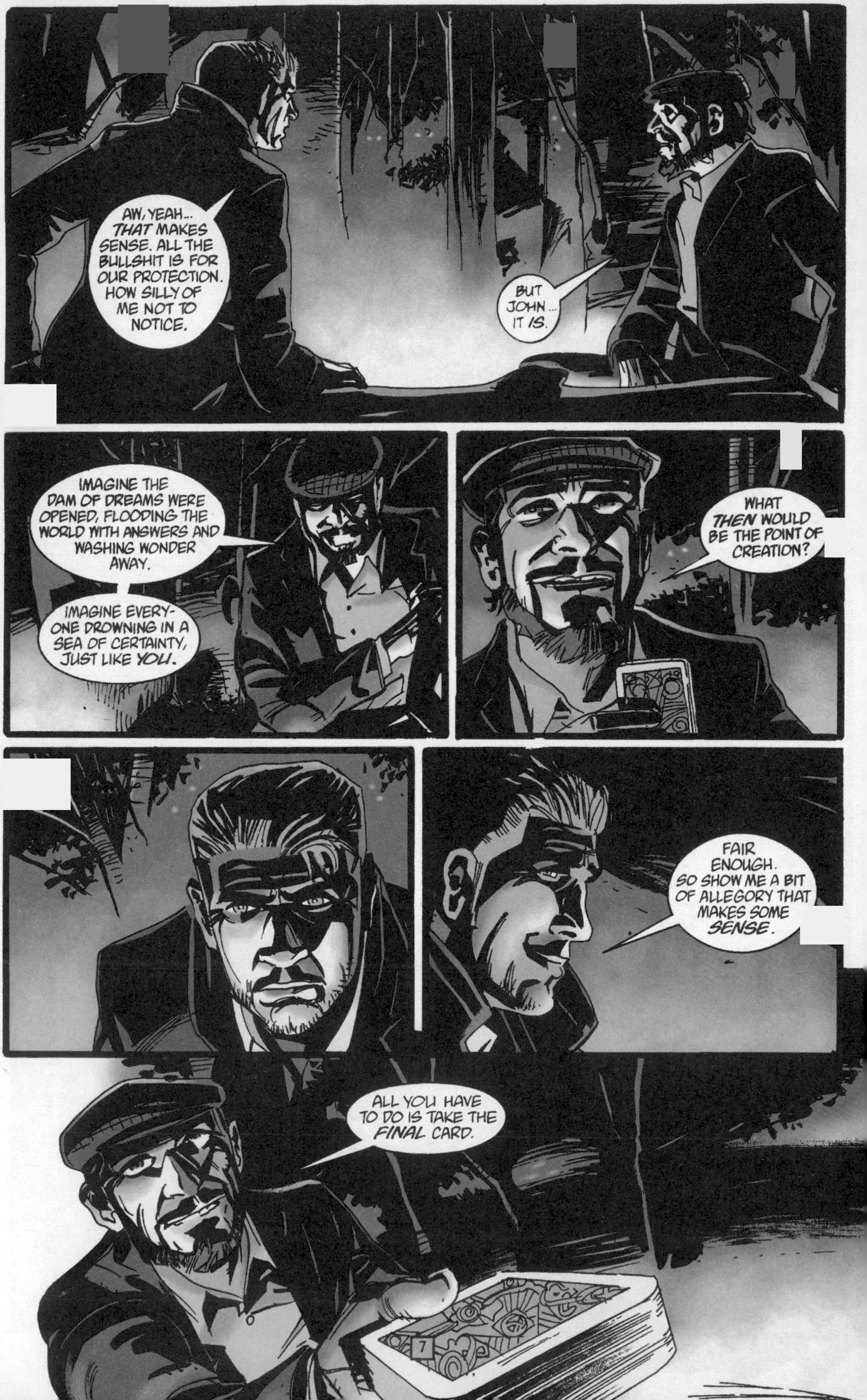
AW, YEAH... THAT MAKES SENSE. ALL THE BULLSHIT IS FOR OUR PROTECTION. HOW SILLY OF ME NOT TO NOTICE.
BUT JOHN... IT IS.
IMAGINE THE DAM OF DREAMS WERE OPENED, FLOODING THE WORLD WITH ANSWERS AND WASHING WONDER AWAY.
IMAGINE EVERY-ONE DROWNING IN A SEA OF CERTAINTY, JUST LIKE YOU.
WHAT THEN WOULD BE THE POINT OF CREATION?
FAIR ENOUGH. SO SHOW ME A BIT OF ALLEGORY THAT MAKES SOME SENSE.
ALL YOU HAVE TO DO IS TAKE THE FINAL CARD.

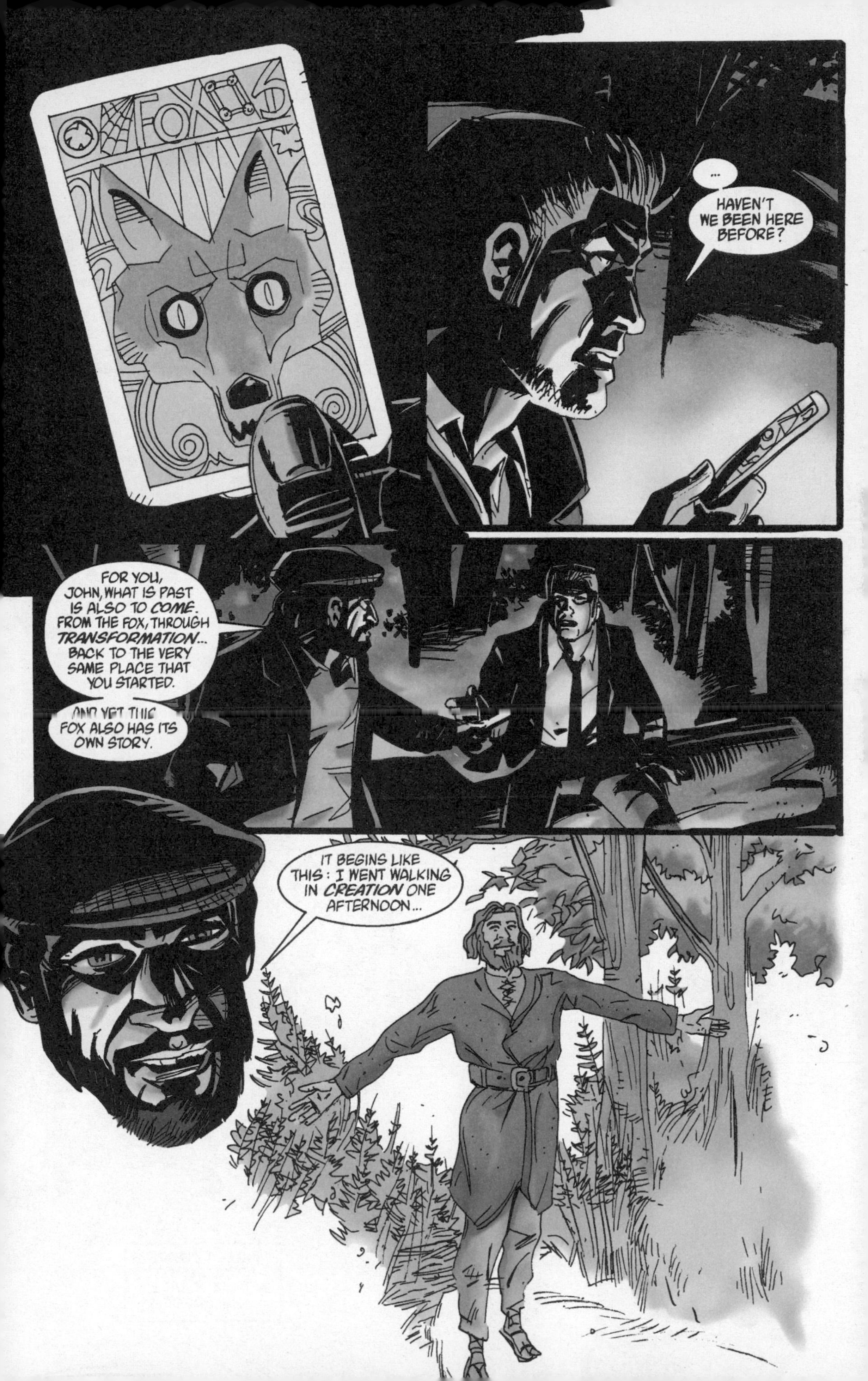
FOX
...
HAVEN'T WE BEEN HERE BEFORE?
FOR YOU, JOHN, WHAT IS PAST IS ALSO TO *COME*. FROM THE FOX, THROUGH ***TRANSFORMATION***... BACK TO THE VERY SAME PLACE THAT YOU STARTED.
AND YET THIS FOX ALSO HAS ITS OWN STORY.
IT BEGINS LIKE THIS : I WENT WALKING IN ***CREATION*** ONE AFTERNOON...

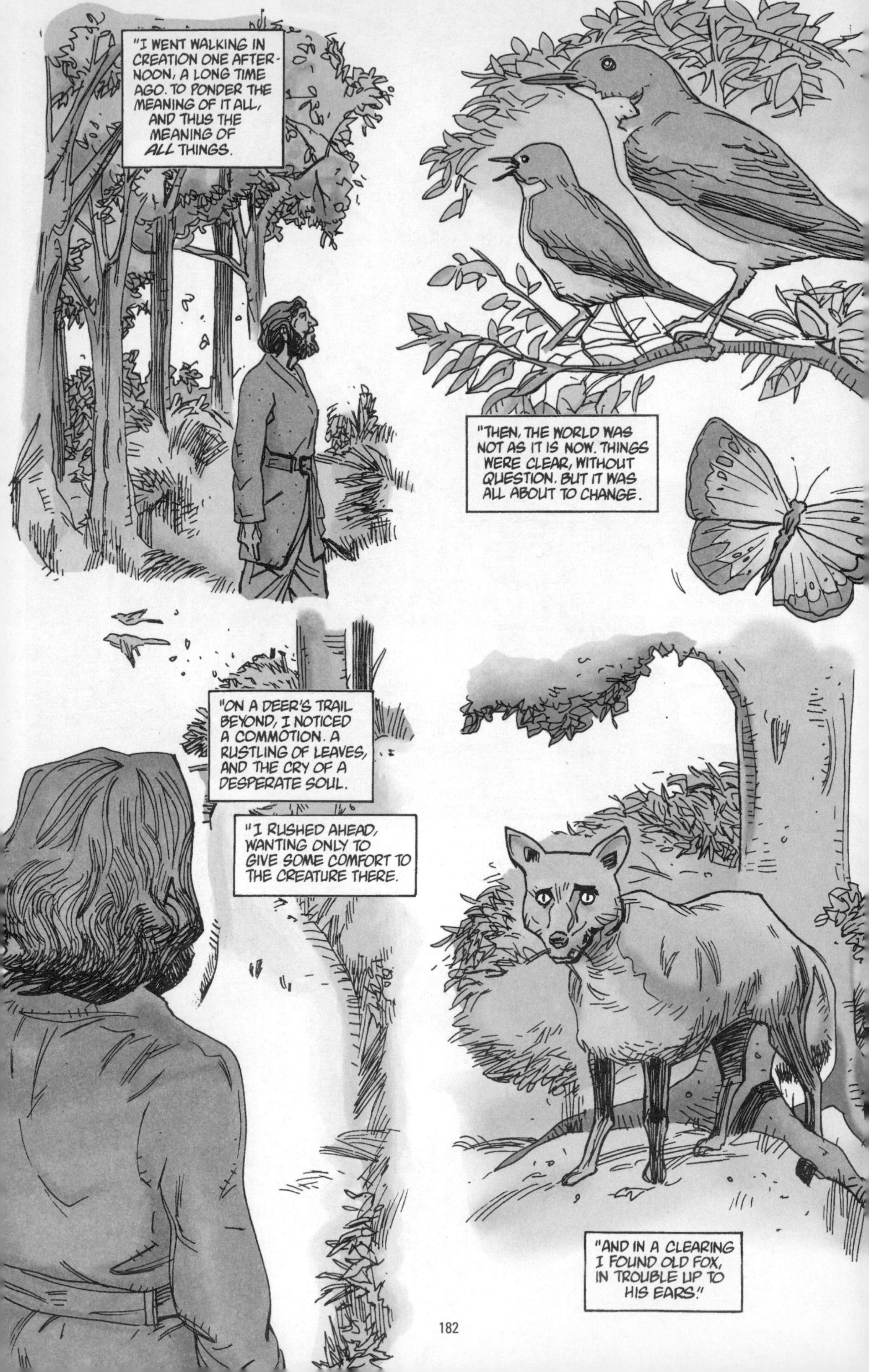
"I WENT WALKING IN CREATION ONE AFTER-NOON, A LONG TIME AGO. TO PONDER THE MEANING OF IT ALL, AND THUS THE MEANING OF *ALL* THINGS.
"THEN, THE WORLD WAS NOT AS IT IS NOW. THINGS WERE CLEAR, WITHOUT QUESTION. BUT IT WAS ALL ABOUT TO CHANGE.
"ON A DEER'S TRAIL BEYOND, I NOTICED A COMMOTION. A RUSTLING OF LEAVES, AND THE CRY OF A DESPERATE SOUL.
"I RUSHED AHEAD, WANTING ONLY TO GIVE SOME COMFORT TO THE CREATURE THERE.
"AND IN A CLEARING I FOUND OLD FOX, IN TROUBLE UP TO HIS EARS."

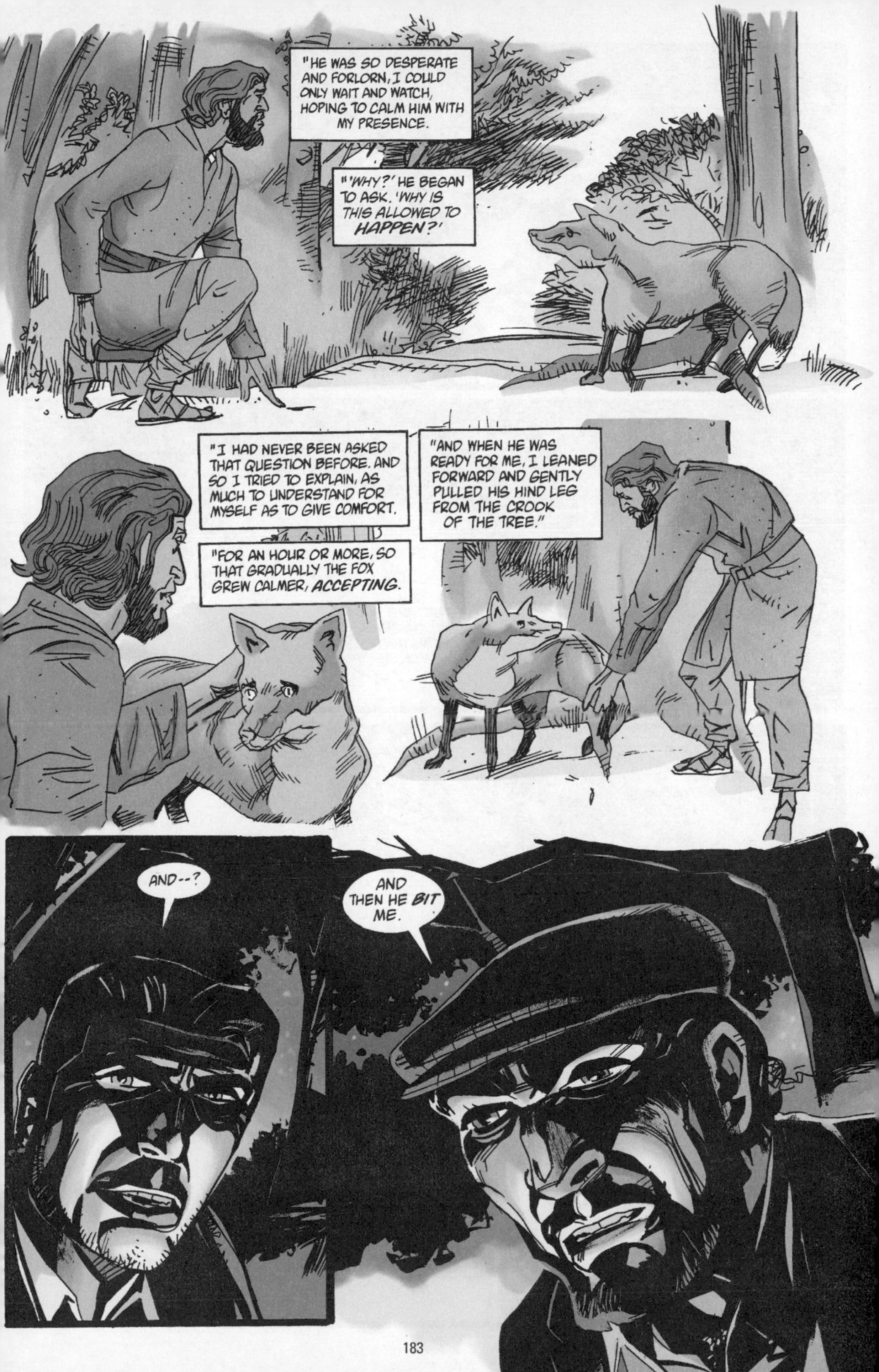
"HE WAS SO DESPERATE AND FORLORN, I COULD ONLY WAIT AND WATCH, HOPING TO CALM HIM WITH MY PRESENCE.
"'WHY?' HE BEGAN TO ASK. 'WHY IS THIS ALLOWED TO HAPPEN?'
"I HAD NEVER BEEN ASKED THAT QUESTION BEFORE. AND SO I TRIED TO EXPLAIN, AS MUCH TO UNDERSTAND FOR MYSELF AS TO GIVE COMFORT.
"FOR AN HOUR OR MORE, SO THAT GRADUALLY THE FOX GREW CALMER, ACCEPTING.
"AND WHEN HE WAS READY FOR ME, I LEANED FORWARD AND GENTLY PULLED HIS HIND LEG FROM THE CROOK OF THE TREE."
AND--?
AND THEN HE BIT ME.

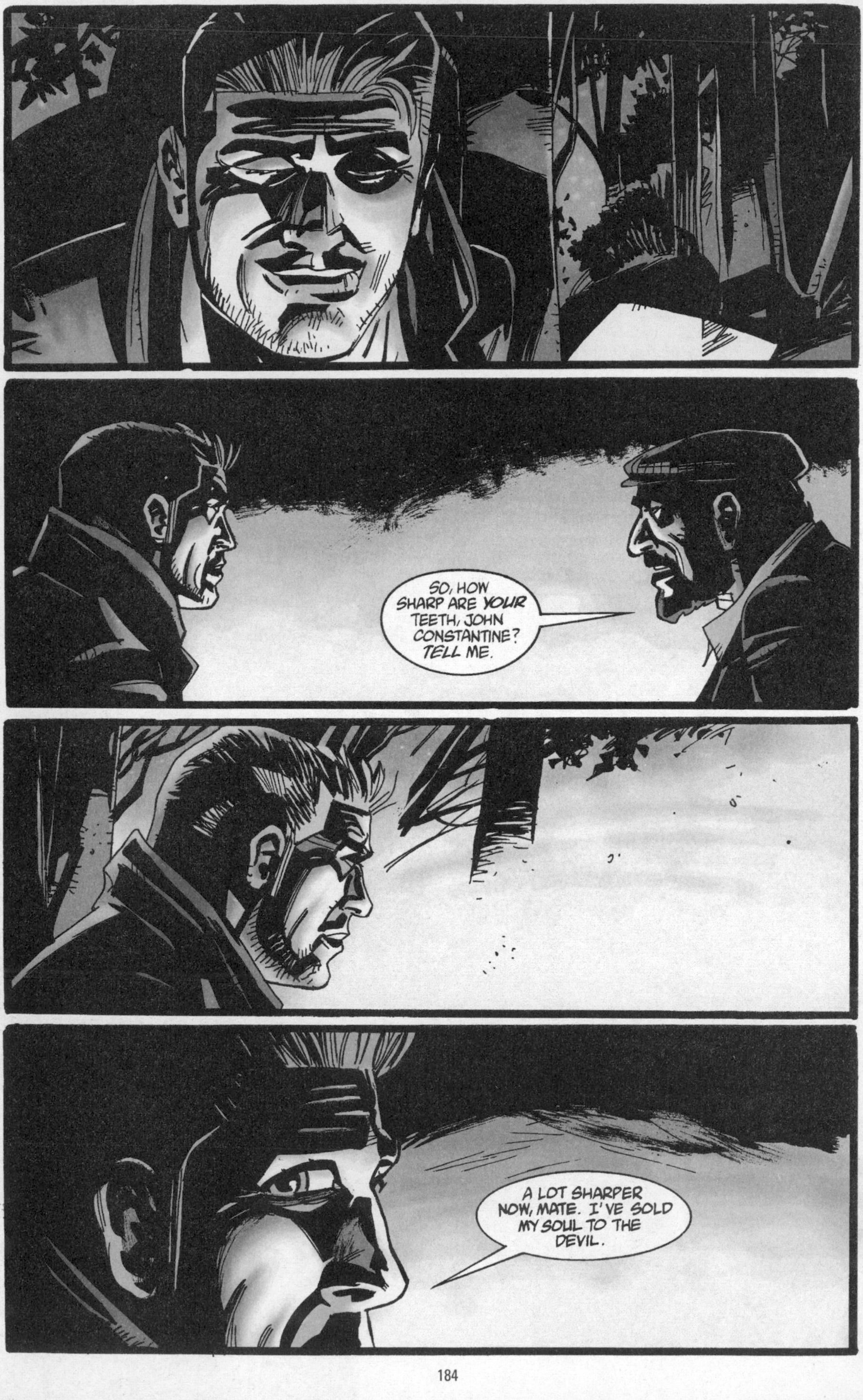
SO, HOW SHARP ARE YOUR TEETH, JOHN CONSTANTINE? TELL ME.
A LOT SHARPER NOW, MATE. I'VE SOLD MY SOUL TO THE DEVIL.

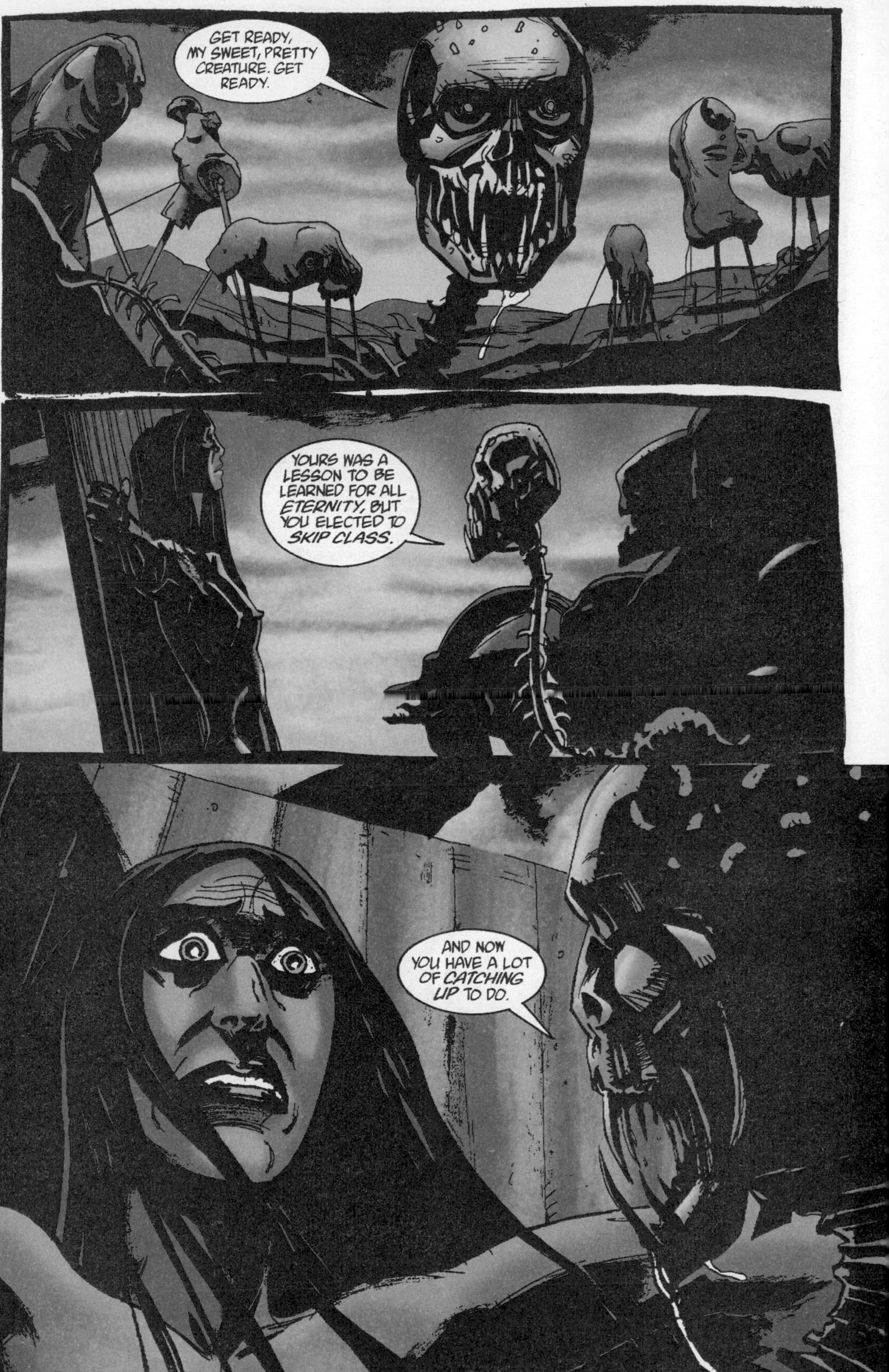
GET READY, MY SWEET, PRETTY CREATURE. GET READY.
YOURS WAS A LESSON TO BE LEARNED FOR ALL *ETERNITY*, BUT YOU ELECTED TO *SKIP CLASS*.
AND NOW YOU HAVE A LOT OF *CATCHING UP* TO DO.

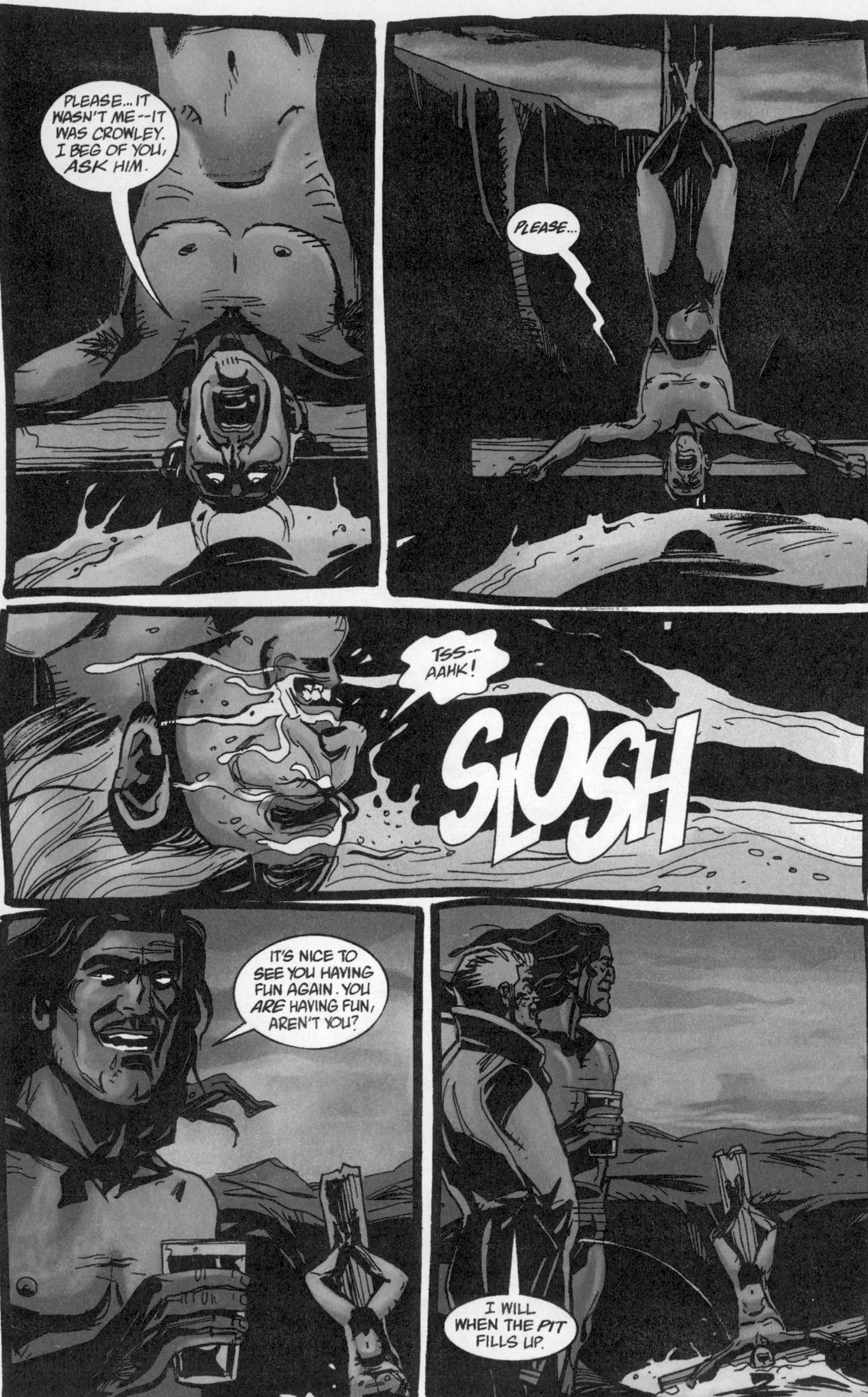

PLEASE... IT WASN'T ME--IT WAS CROWLEY. I BEG OF YOU, ASK HIM.
PLEASE...
TSS--AAHK!
SLOSH
IT'S NICE TO SEE YOU HAVING FUN AGAIN. YOU ARE HAVING FUN, AREN'T YOU?
I WILL WHEN THE PIT FILLS UP.

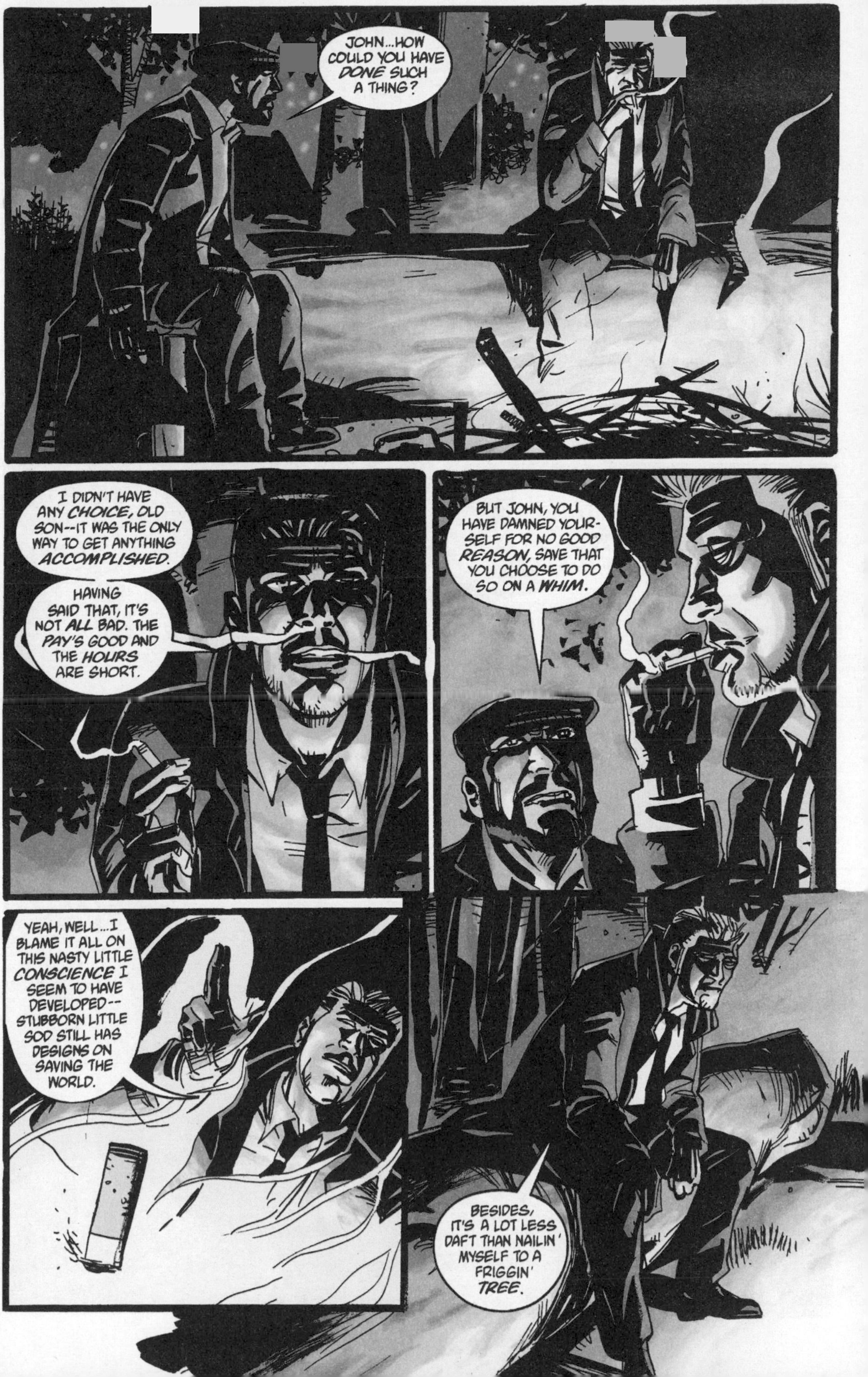
JOHN...HOW COULD YOU HAVE DONE SUCH A THING?
I DIDN'T HAVE ANY CHOICE, OLD SON--IT WAS THE ONLY WAY TO GET ANYTHING ACCOMPLISHED.
HAVING SAID THAT, IT'S NOT ALL BAD. THE PAY'S GOOD AND THE HOURS ARE SHORT.
BUT JOHN, YOU HAVE DAMNED YOURSELF FOR NO GOOD REASON, SAVE THAT YOU CHOOSE TO DO SO ON A WHIM.
YEAH, WELL...I BLAME IT ALL ON THIS NASTY LITTLE CONSCIENCE I SEEM TO HAVE DEVELOPED--STUBBORN LITTLE SOD STILL HAS DESIGNS ON SAVING THE WORLD.
BESIDES, IT'S A LOT LESS DAFT THAN NAILIN' MYSELF TO A FRIGGIN' TREE.

YOU DON'T KNOW WHAT YOU HAVE *DONE*--

YES I DO.

I'VE GOT THIS *GREAT* THREAT WORKED OUT, SEE? IT GOES LIKE THIS:

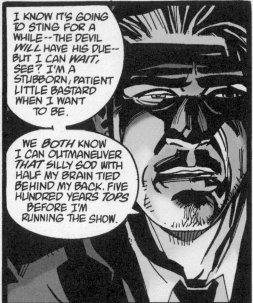

I KNOW IT'S GOING TO STING FOR A WHILE--THE DEVIL *WILL* HAVE HIS DUE-- BUT I CAN *WAIT*, SEE? I'M A STUBBORN, PATIENT LITTLE BASTARD WHEN I WANT TO BE.

WE *BOTH* KNOW I CAN OUTMANEUVER *THAT* SILLY SOD WITH HALF MY BRAIN TIED BEHIND MY BACK. FIVE HUNDRED YEARS *TOPS* BEFORE I'M RUNNING THE SHOW.

IMAGINE A SOD LIKE *ME* LET LOOSE ON GOD'S PRETTY LITTLE CREATION, ARMED WITH REIN- FORCEMENTS, ALL OF THEM *ORGANIZED*, FOR A CHANGE. WELL, IT'D BE A RIGHT BLOODY MESS, *WOULDN'T* IT?

'COURSE, IF HE AGREES TO STOP BLOODY INTER- FERING AND LEAVE MY MATES ALONE FOR GOOD, I MIGHT THINK ABOUT CHANGING MY MIND. *YOUR* CHOICE.

I'LL SEE WHAT I CAN *DO*.

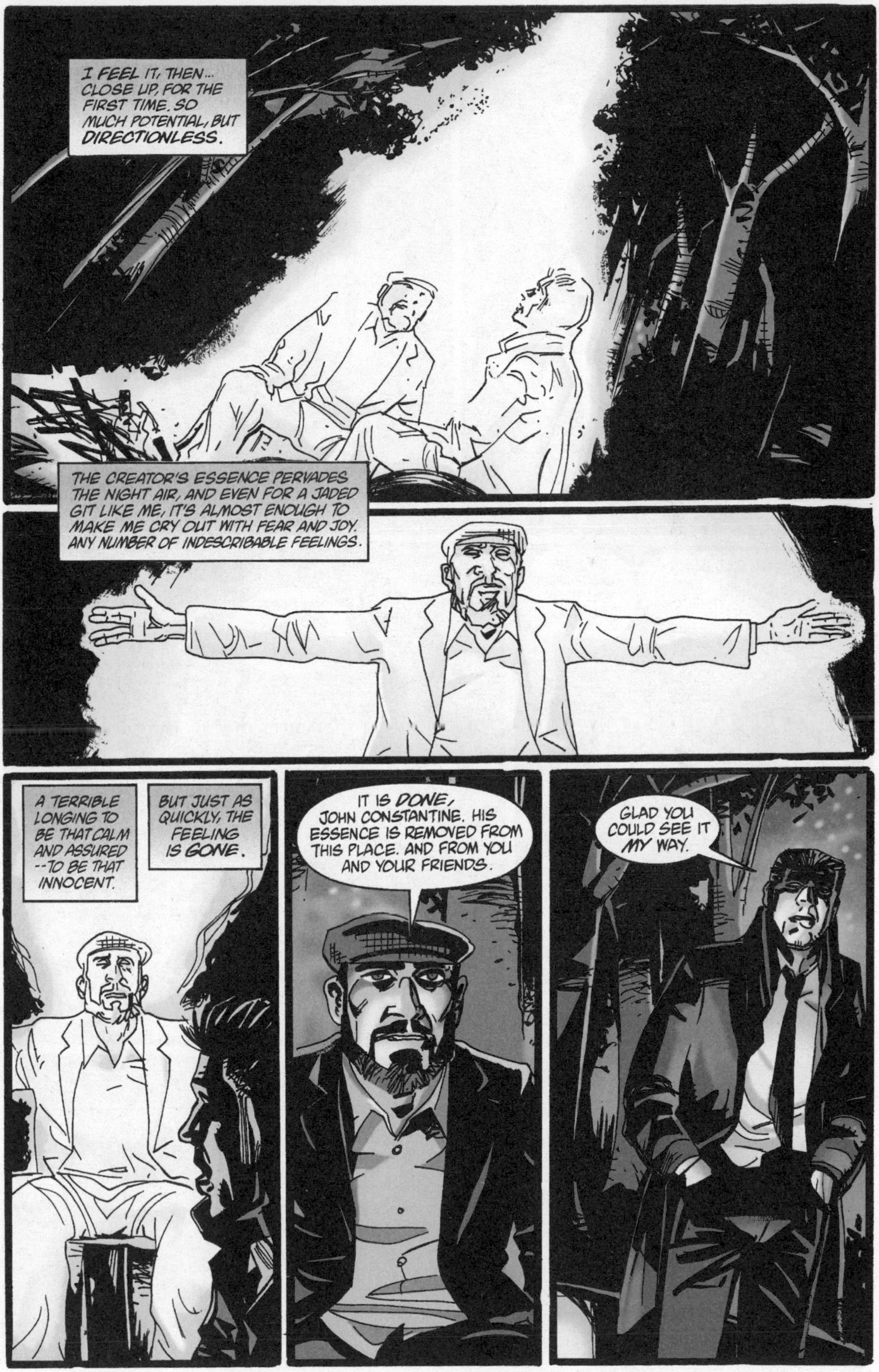
I FEEL IT, THEN... CLOSE UP, FOR THE FIRST TIME. SO MUCH POTENTIAL, BUT DIRECTIONLESS.
THE CREATOR'S ESSENCE PERVADES THE NIGHT AIR, AND EVEN FOR A JADED GIT LIKE ME, IT'S ALMOST ENOUGH TO MAKE ME CRY OUT WITH FEAR AND JOY. ANY NUMBER OF INDESCRIBABLE FEELINGS.
A TERRIBLE LONGING TO BE THAT CALM AND ASSURED --TO BE THAT INNOCENT.
BUT JUST AS QUICKLY, THE FEELING IS GONE.
IT IS DONE, JOHN CONSTANTINE. HIS ESSENCE IS REMOVED FROM THIS PLACE. AND FROM YOU AND YOUR FRIENDS.
GLAD YOU COULD SEE IT MY WAY.

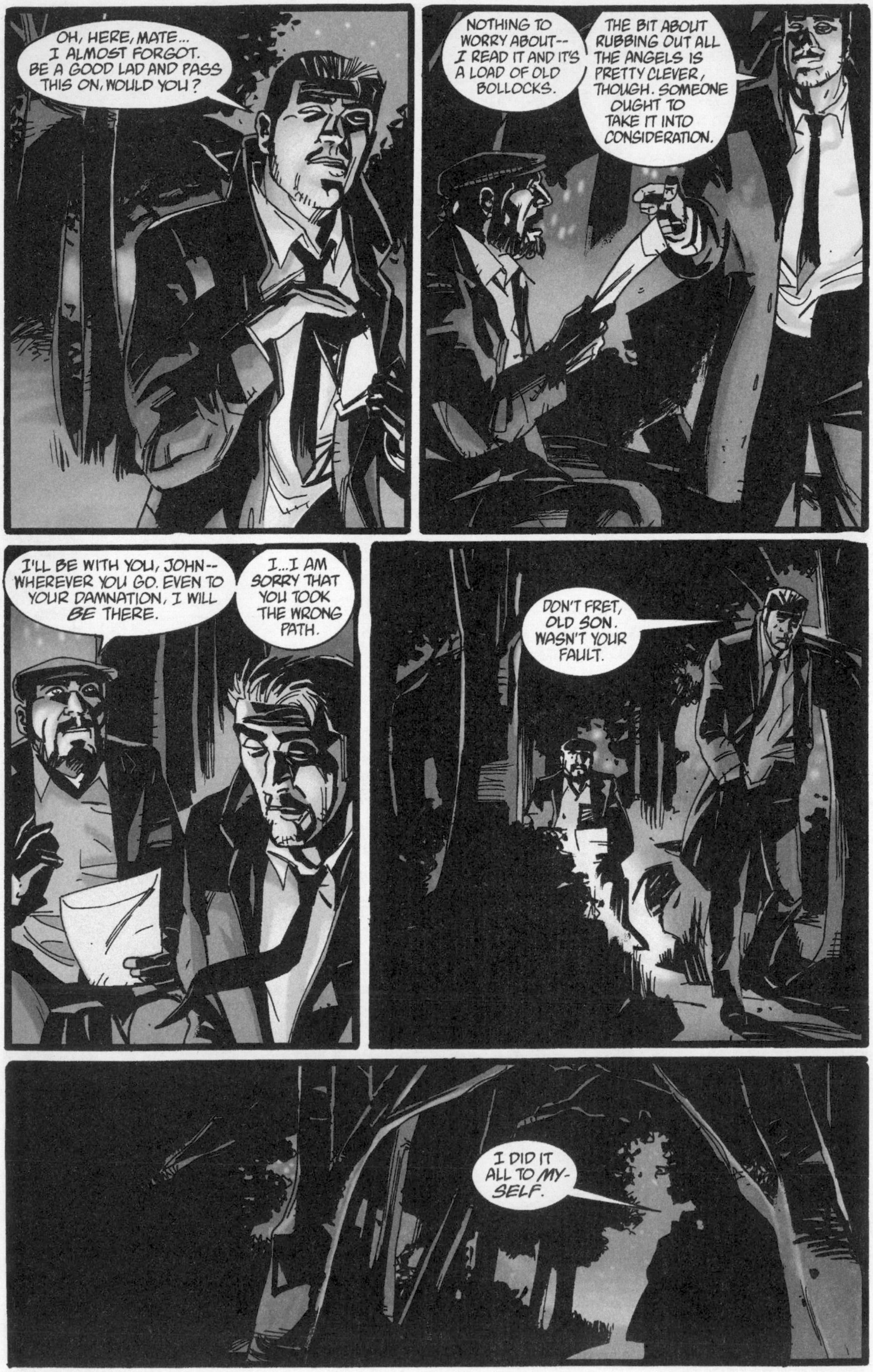
OH, HERE, MATE... I ALMOST FORGOT. BE A GOOD LAD AND PASS THIS ON, WOULD YOU?
NOTHING TO WORRY ABOUT-- I READ IT AND IT'S A LOAD OF OLD BOLLOCKS.
THE BIT ABOUT RUBBING OUT ALL THE ANGELS IS PRETTY CLEVER, THOUGH. SOMEONE OUGHT TO TAKE IT INTO CONSIDERATION.
I'LL BE WITH YOU, JOHN-- WHEREVER YOU GO. EVEN TO YOUR DAMNATION, I WILL BE THERE.
I...I AM SORRY THAT YOU TOOK THE WRONG PATH.
DON'T FRET, OLD SON. WASN'T YOUR FAULT.
I DID IT ALL TO MY-SELF.

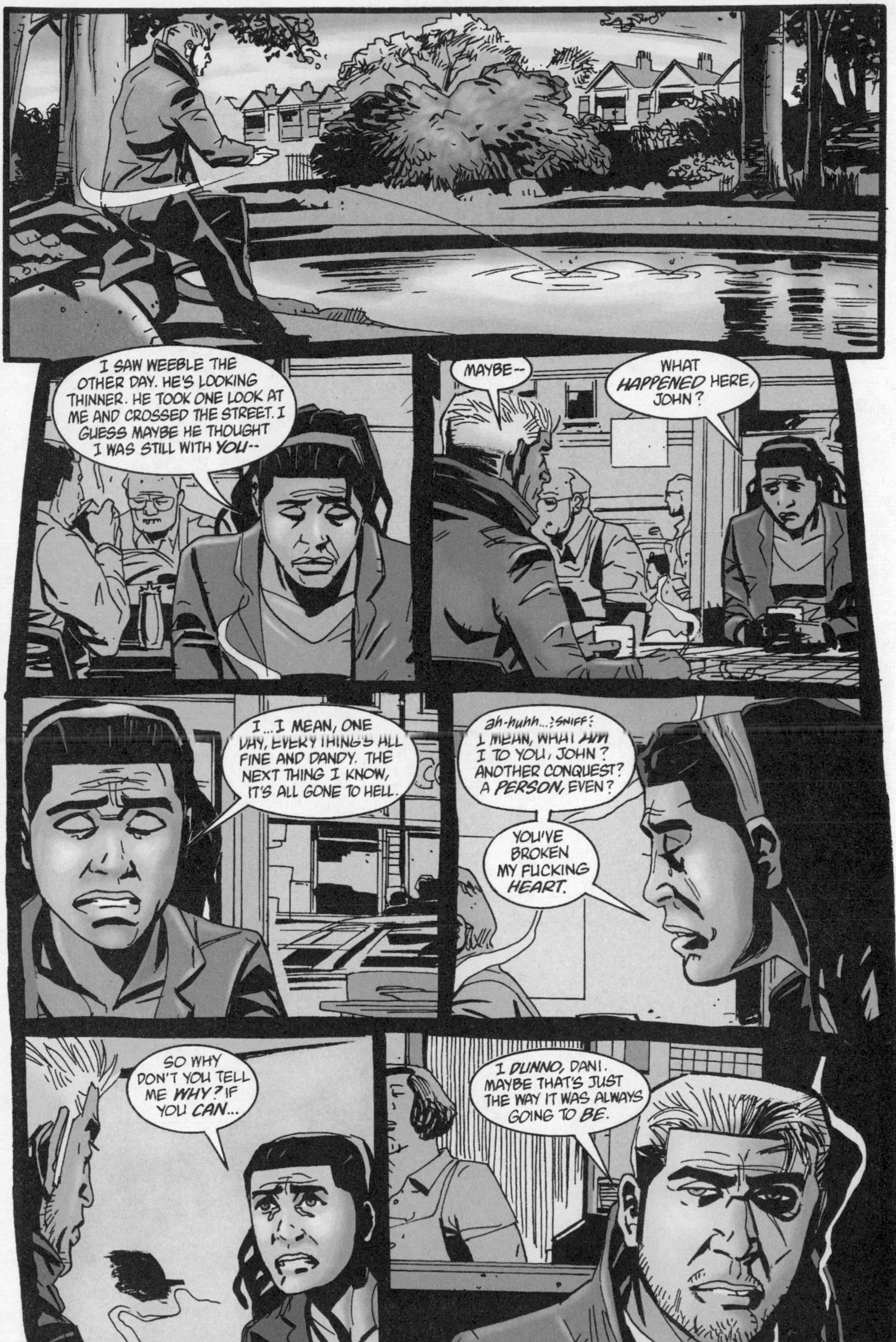
I SAW WEEBLE THE OTHER DAY. HE'S LOOKING THINNER. HE TOOK ONE LOOK AT ME AND CROSSED THE STREET. I GUESS MAYBE HE THOUGHT I WAS STILL WITH YOU--
MAYBE--
WHAT HAPPENED HERE, JOHN?
I...I MEAN, ONE DAY, EVERYTHING'S ALL FINE AND DANDY. THE NEXT THING I KNOW, IT'S ALL GONE TO HELL.
ah-huhh... SNIFF
I MEAN, WHAT AM I TO YOU, JOHN? ANOTHER CONQUEST? A PERSON, EVEN?
YOU'VE BROKEN MY FUCKING HEART.
SO WHY DON'T YOU TELL ME WHY? IF YOU CAN...
I DUNNO, DANI. MAYBE THAT'S JUST THE WAY IT WAS ALWAYS GOING TO BE.

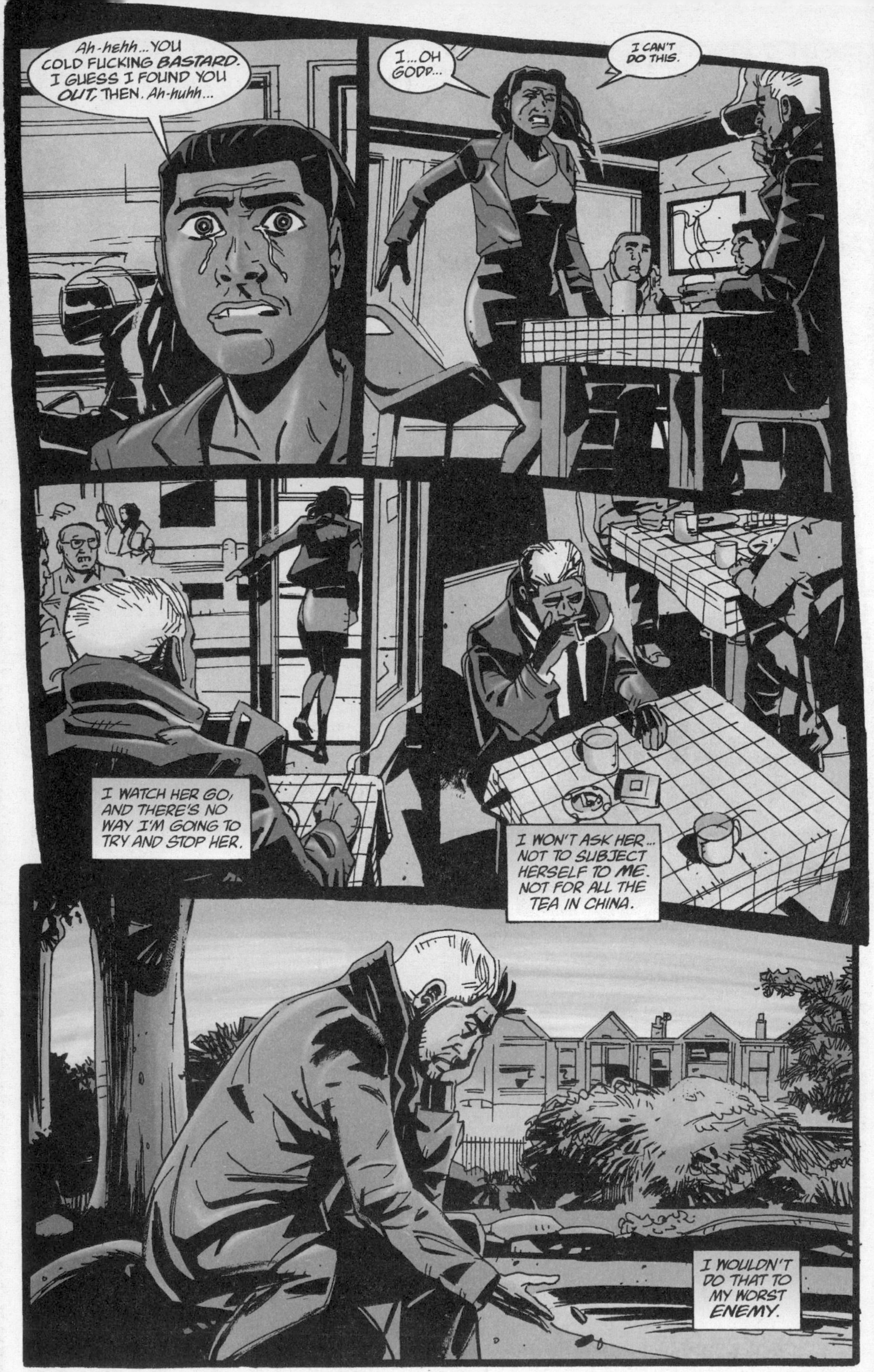
Ah-hehh... YOU COLD FUCKING BASTARD. I GUESS I FOUND YOU OUT, THEN. Ah-huhh...
I... OH GODD...
I CAN'T DO THIS.
I WATCH HER GO, AND THERE'S NO WAY I'M GOING TO TRY AND STOP HER.
I WON'T ASK HER... NOT TO SUBJECT HERSELF TO ME. NOT FOR ALL THE TEA IN CHINA.
I WOULDN'T DO THAT TO MY WORST ENEMY.

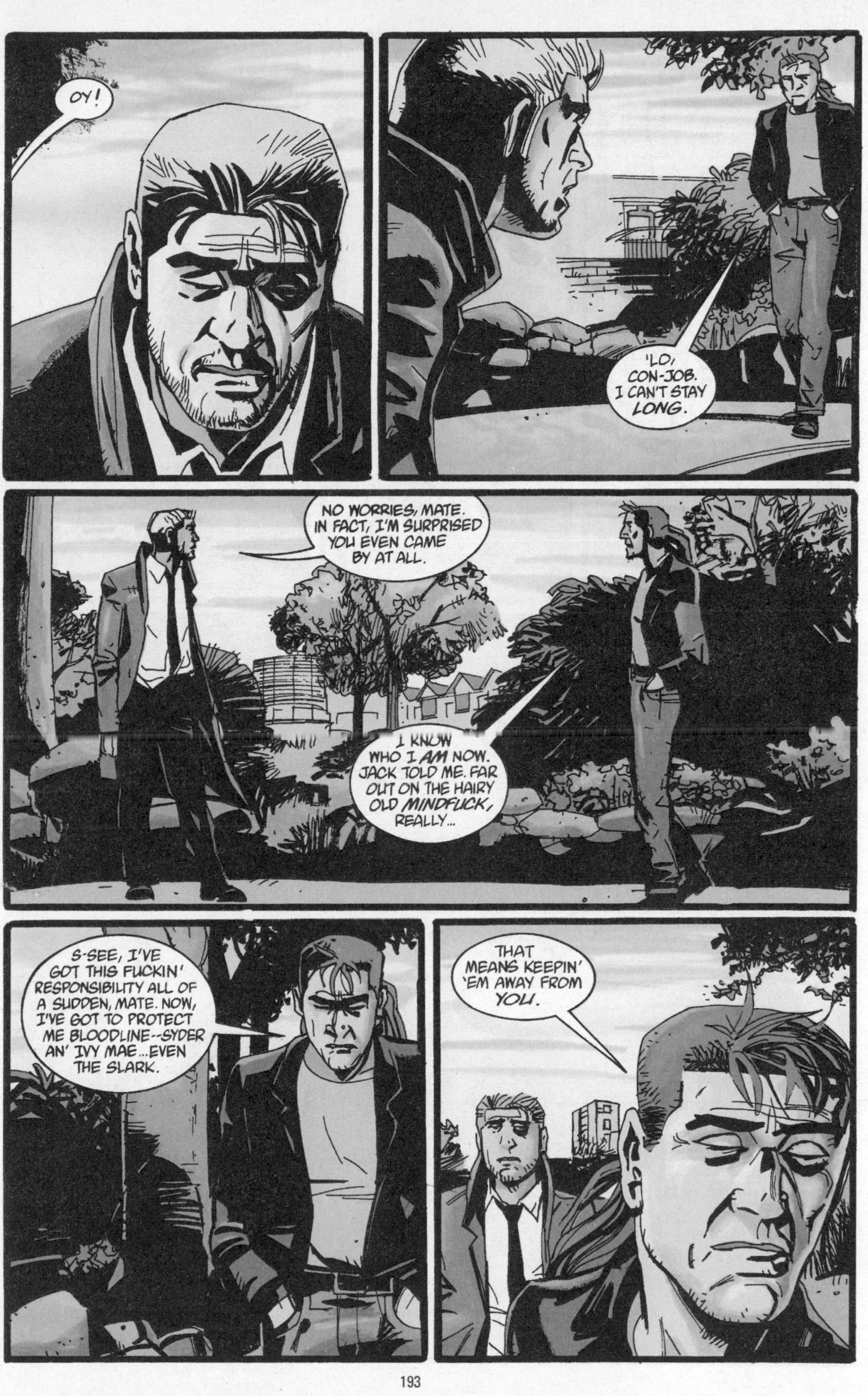
OY!
'LO, CON-JOB. I CAN'T STAY LONG.
NO WORRIES, MATE. IN FACT, I'M SURPRISED YOU EVEN CAME BY AT ALL.
I KNOW WHO I AM NOW. JACK TOLD ME. FAR OUT ON THE HAIRY OLD MINDFUCK, REALLY...
S-SEE, I'VE GOT THIS FUCKIN' RESPONSIBILITY ALL OF A SUDDEN, MATE. NOW, I'VE GOT TO PROTECT ME BLOODLINE--SYDER AN' IVY MAE...EVEN THE SLARK.
THAT MEANS KEEPIN' 'EM AWAY FROM YOU.

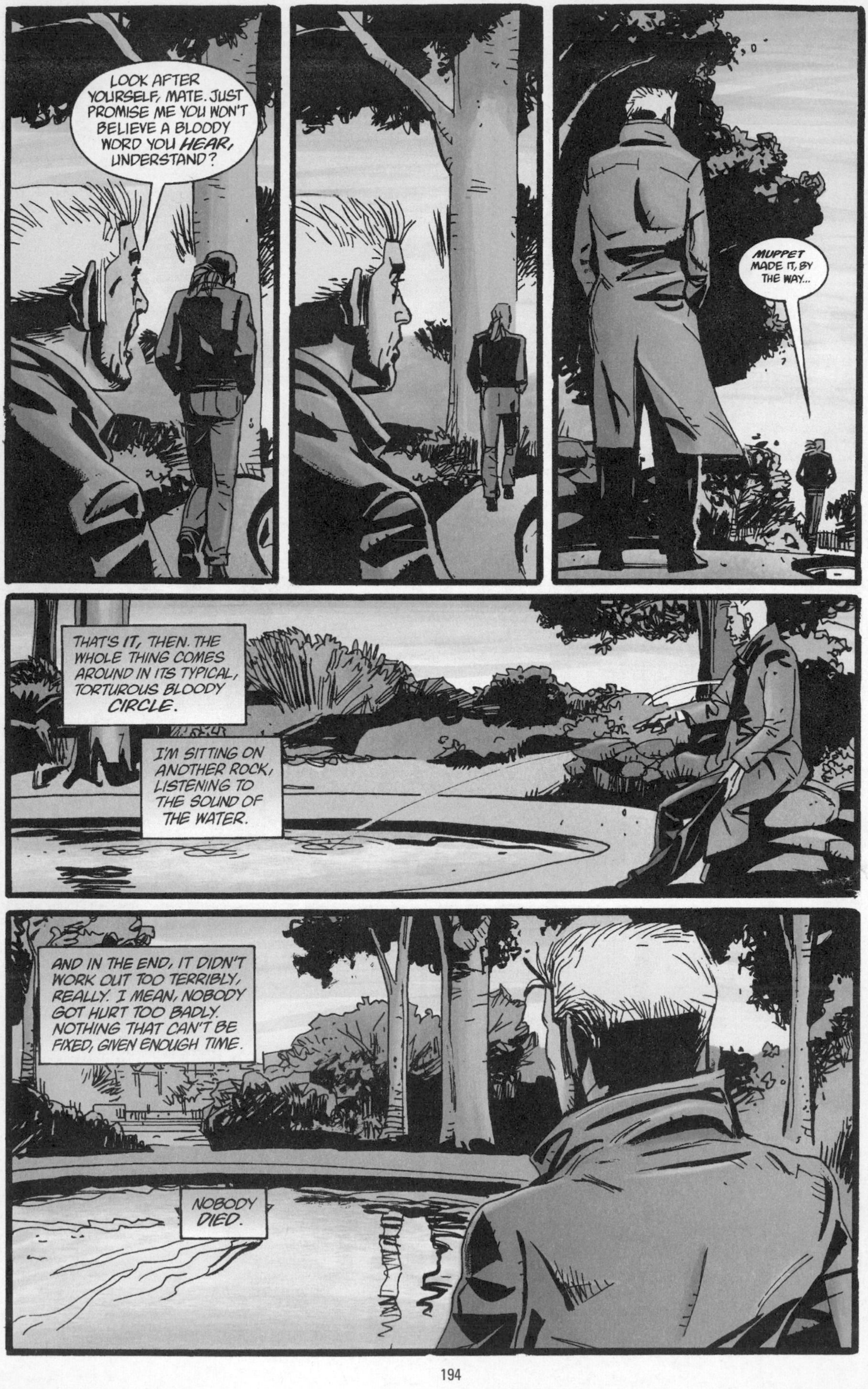
LOOK AFTER YOURSELF, MATE. JUST PROMISE ME YOU WON'T BELIEVE A BLOODY WORD YOU HEAR, UNDERSTAND?
MUPPET MADE IT, BY THE WAY...
THAT'S IT, THEN. THE WHOLE THING COMES AROUND IN ITS TYPICAL, TORTUROUS BLOODY CIRCLE.
I'M SITTING ON ANOTHER ROCK, LISTENING TO THE SOUND OF THE WATER.
AND IN THE END, IT DIDN'T WORK OUT TOO TERRIBLY, REALLY. I MEAN, NOBODY GOT HURT TOO BADLY. NOTHING THAT CAN'T BE FIXED, GIVEN ENOUGH TIME.
NOBODY DIED.

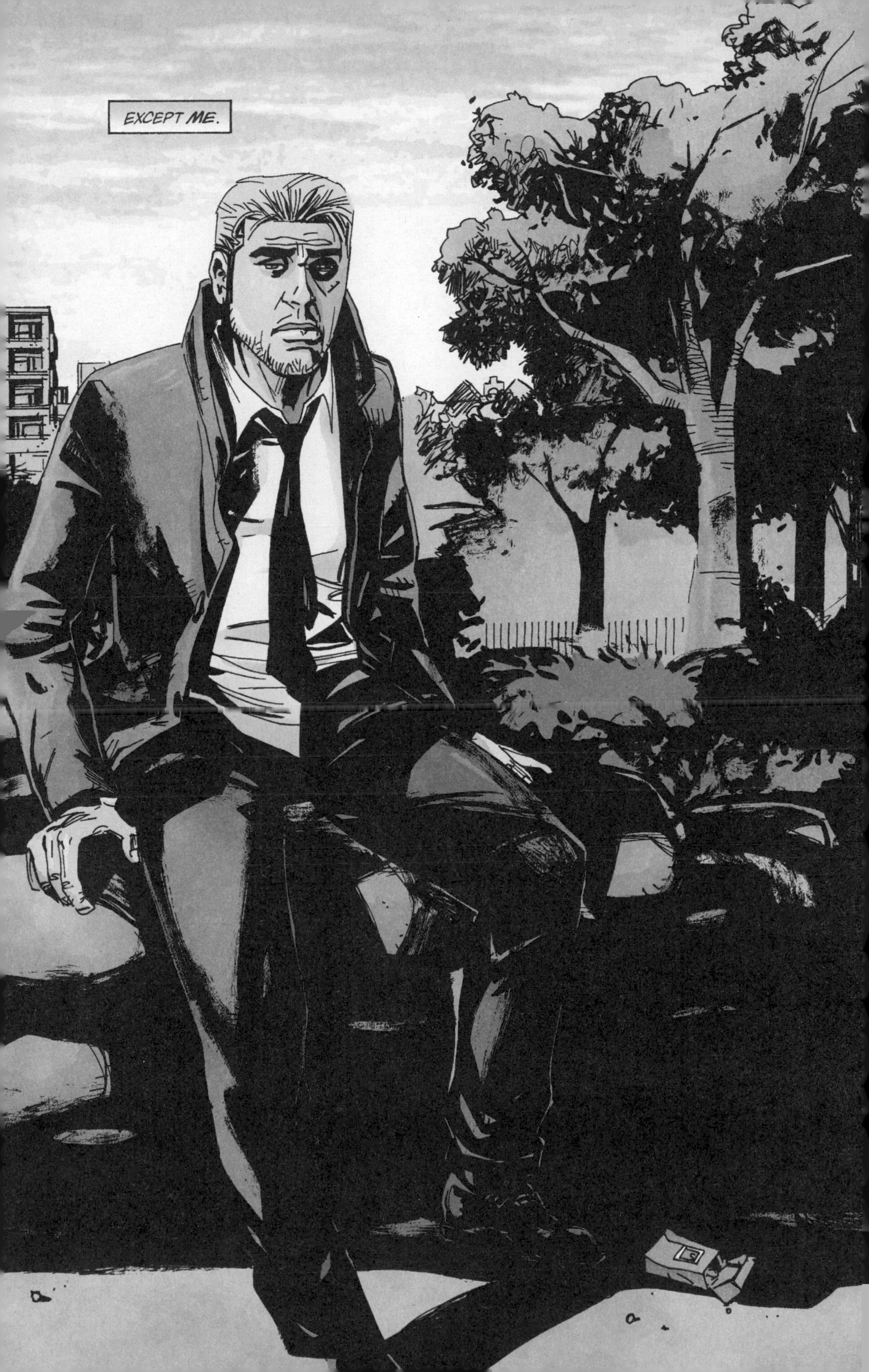
EXCEPT ME.

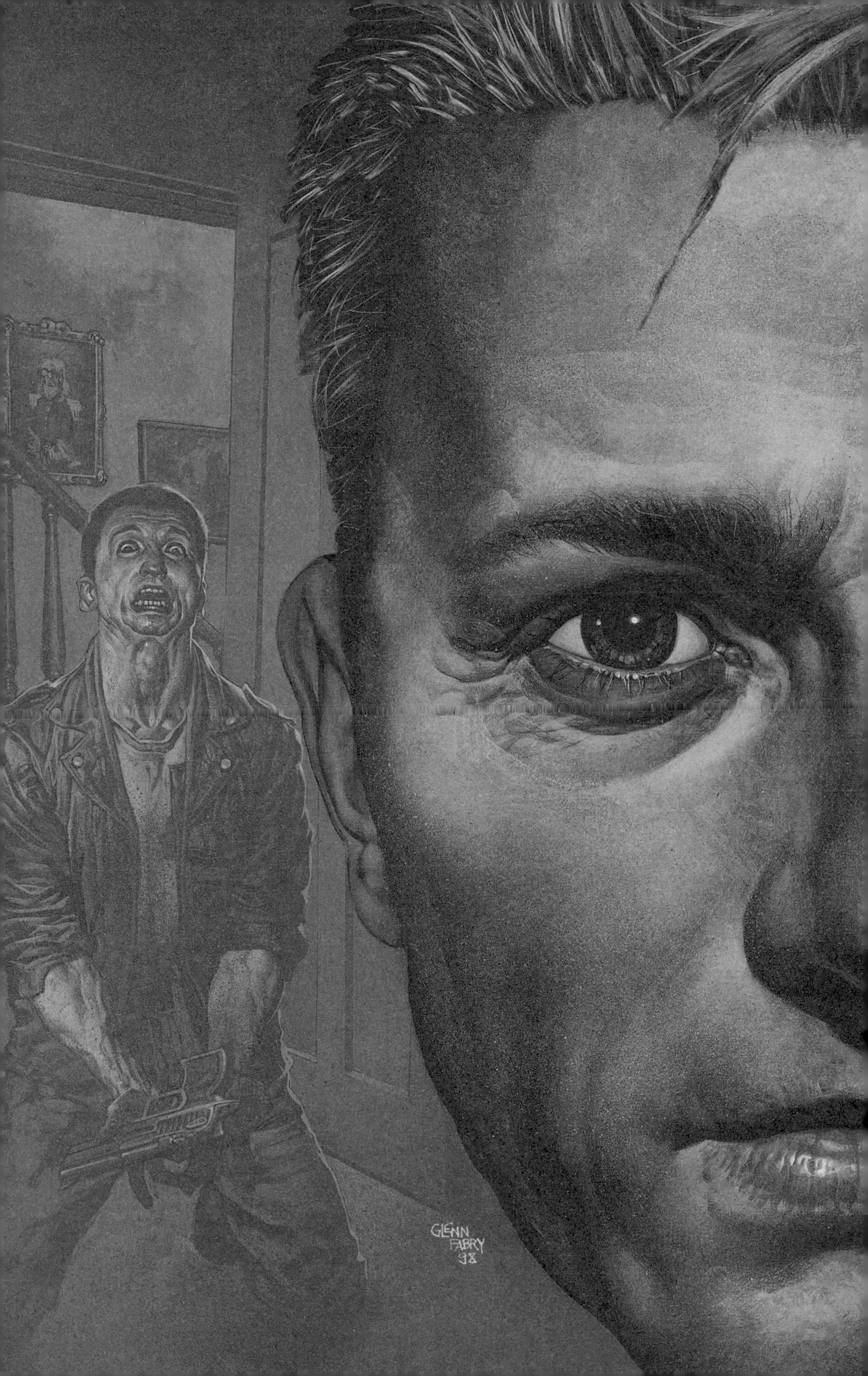
GLENN FABRY 98

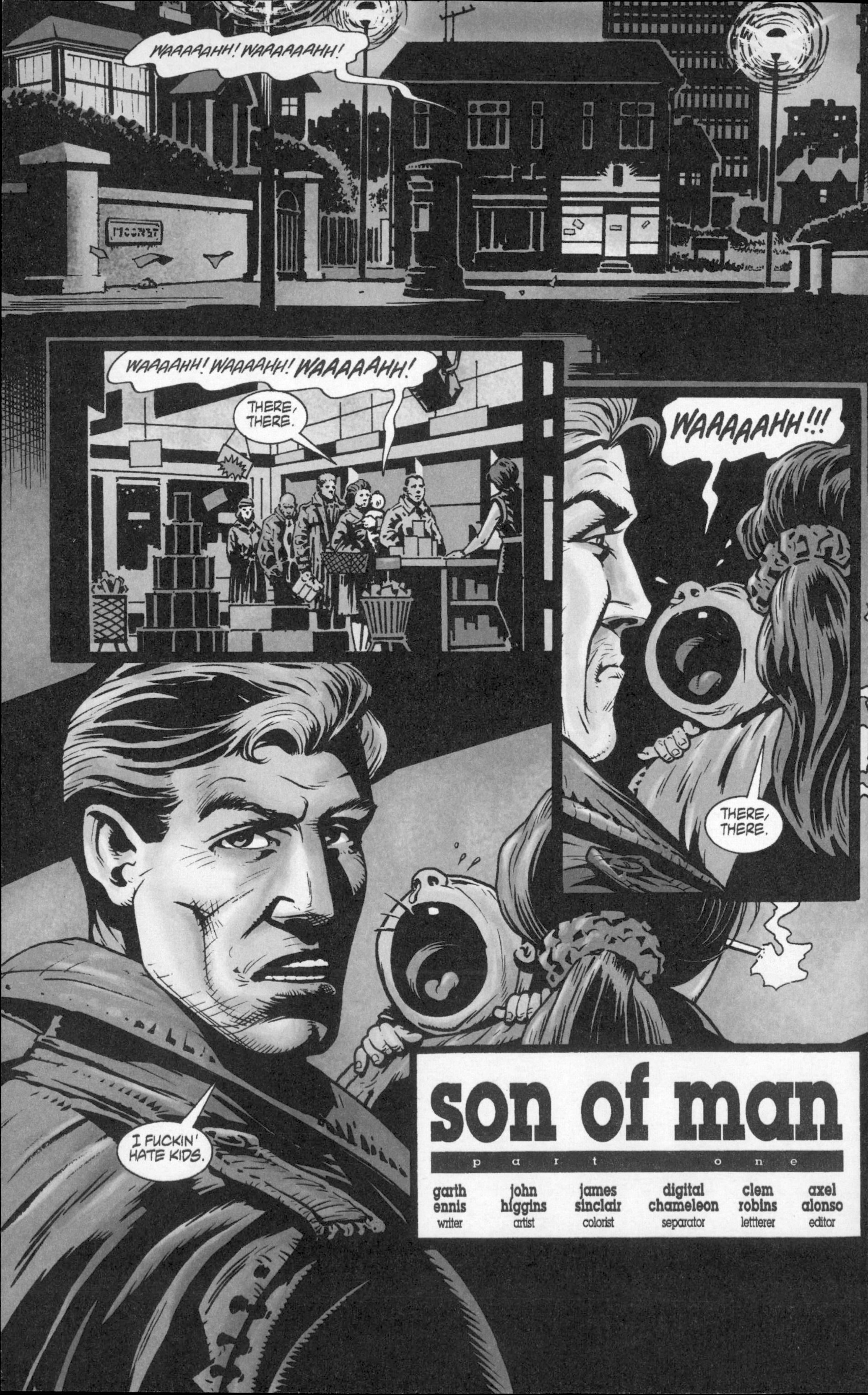
WAAAAAHH! WAAAAAAHH!
WAAAAHH! WAAAAHH! WAAAAAHH!
THERE, THERE.
WAAAAAHH!!!
THERE, THERE.
I FUCKIN' HATE KIDS.
son of man
part one
garth ennis writer
john higgins artist
james sinclair colorist
digital chameleon separator
clem robins letterer
axel alonso editor

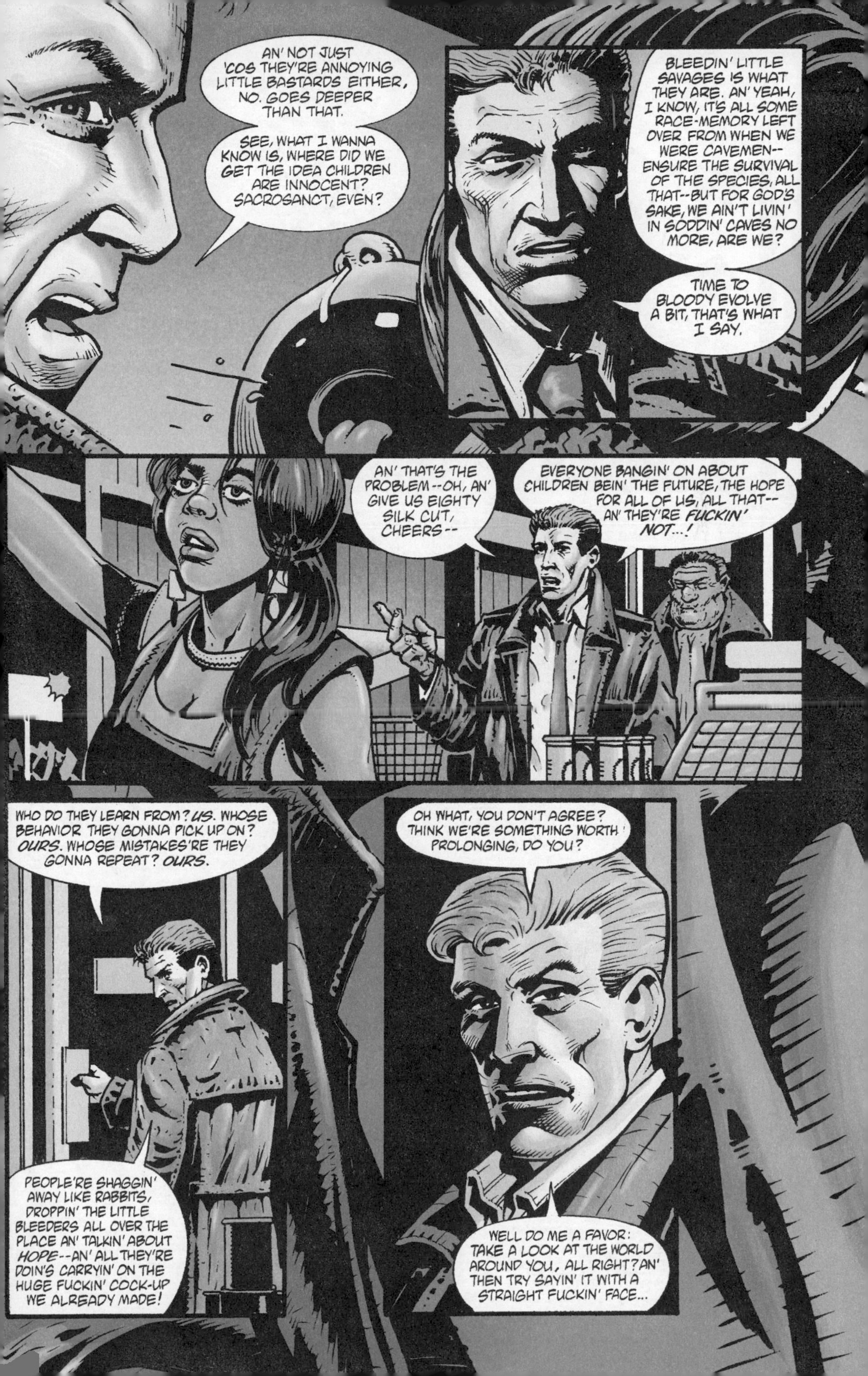
AN' NOT JUST 'COS THEY'RE ANNOYING LITTLE BASTARDS EITHER, NO. GOES DEEPER THAN THAT.
SEE, WHAT I WANNA KNOW IS, WHERE DID WE GET THE IDEA CHILDREN ARE INNOCENT? SACROSANCT, EVEN?
BLEEDIN' LITTLE SAVAGES IS WHAT THEY ARE. AN' YEAH, I KNOW, IT'S ALL SOME RACE-MEMORY LEFT OVER FROM WHEN WE WERE CAVEMEN-- ENSURE THE SURVIVAL OF THE SPECIES, ALL THAT--BUT FOR GOD'S SAKE, WE AIN'T LIVIN' IN SODDIN' CAVES NO MORE, ARE WE?
TIME TO BLOODY EVOLVE A BIT, THAT'S WHAT I SAY.
AN' THAT'S THE PROBLEM --OH, AN' GIVE US EIGHTY SILK CUT, CHEERS--
EVERYONE BANGIN' ON ABOUT CHILDREN BEIN' THE FUTURE, THE HOPE FOR ALL OF US, ALL THAT-- AN' THEY'RE FUCKIN' NOT...!
WHO DO THEY LEARN FROM? US. WHOSE BEHAVIOR THEY GONNA PICK UP ON? OURS. WHOSE MISTAKES'RE THEY GONNA REPEAT? OURS.
PEOPLE'RE SHAGGIN' AWAY LIKE RABBITS, DROPPIN' THE LITTLE BLEEDERS ALL OVER THE PLACE AN' TALKIN' ABOUT HOPE--AN' ALL THEY'RE DOIN'S CARRYIN' ON THE HUGE FUCKIN' COCK-UP WE ALREADY MADE!
OH WHAT, YOU DON'T AGREE? THINK WE'RE SOMETHING WORTH PROLONGING, DO YOU?
WELL DO ME A FAVOR: TAKE A LOOK AT THE WORLD AROUND YOU, ALL RIGHT? AN' THEN TRY SAYIN' IT WITH A STRAIGHT FUCKIN' FACE...

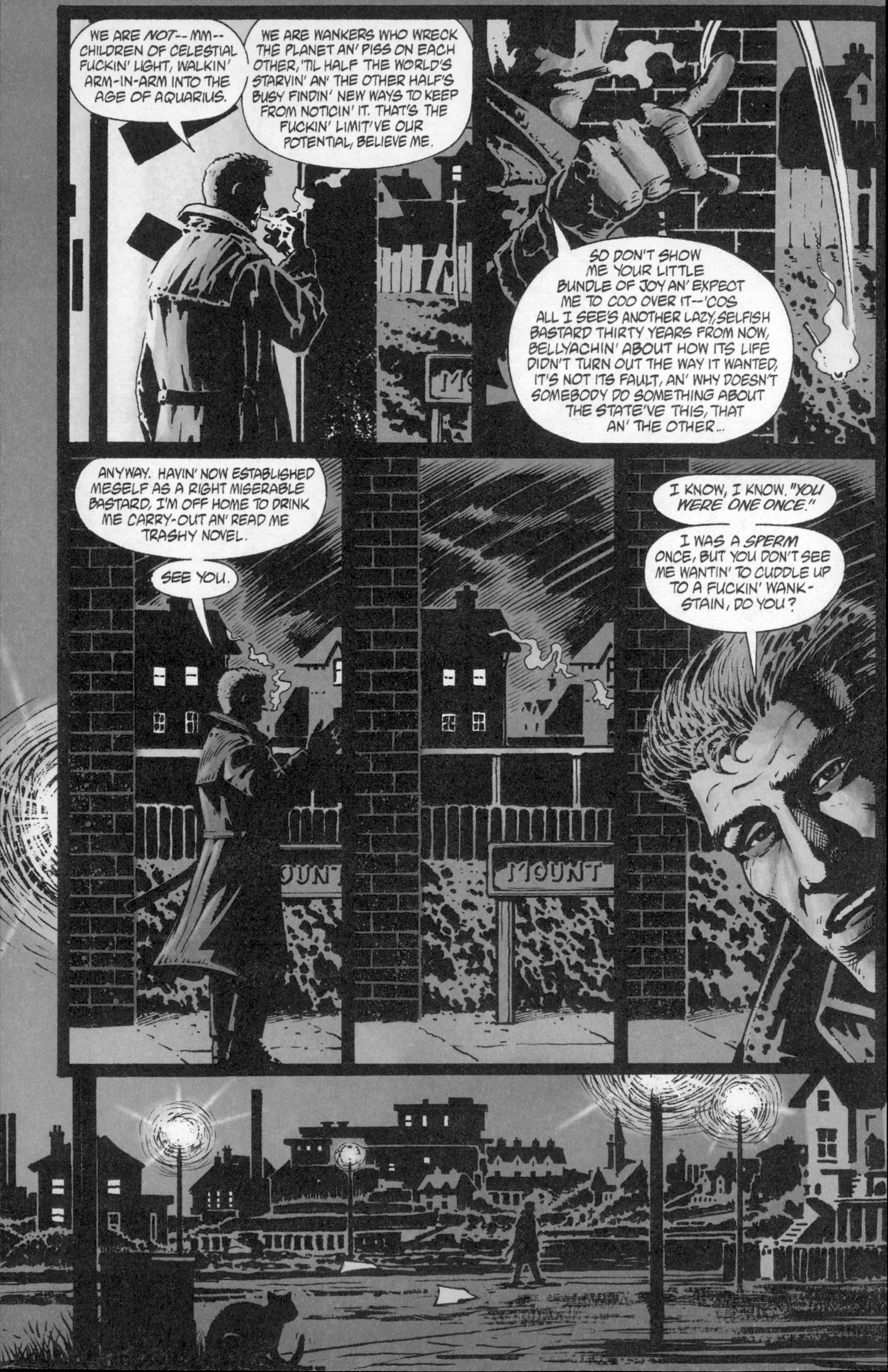
WE ARE *NOT*-- MM-- CHILDREN OF CELESTIAL FUCKIN' LIGHT, WALKIN' ARM-IN-ARM INTO THE AGE OF AQUARIUS.
WE ARE WANKERS WHO WRECK THE PLANET AN' PISS ON EACH OTHER, 'TIL HALF THE WORLD'S STARVIN' AN' THE OTHER HALF'S BUSY FINDIN' NEW WAYS TO KEEP FROM NOTICIN' IT. THAT'S THE FUCKIN' LIMIT'VE OUR POTENTIAL, BELIEVE ME.
SO DON'T SHOW ME YOUR LITTLE BUNDLE OF JOY AN' EXPECT ME TO COO OVER IT--'COS ALL I SEE'S ANOTHER LAZY, SELFISH BASTARD THIRTY YEARS FROM NOW, BELLYACHIN' ABOUT HOW ITS LIFE DIDN'T TURN OUT THE WAY IT WANTED, IT'S NOT ITS FAULT, AN' WHY DOESN'T SOMEBODY DO SOMETHING ABOUT THE STATE'VE THIS, THAT AN' THE OTHER...
ANYWAY. HAVIN' NOW ESTABLISHED MESELF AS A RIGHT MISERABLE BASTARD, I'M OFF HOME TO DRINK ME CARRY-OUT AN' READ ME TRASHY NOVEL.
SEE YOU.
MOUNT
I KNOW, I KNOW. "*YOU WERE ONE ONCE.*"
I WAS A *SPERM* ONCE, BUT YOU DON'T SEE ME WANTIN' TO CUDDLE UP TO A FUCKIN' WANK-STAIN, DO YOU?

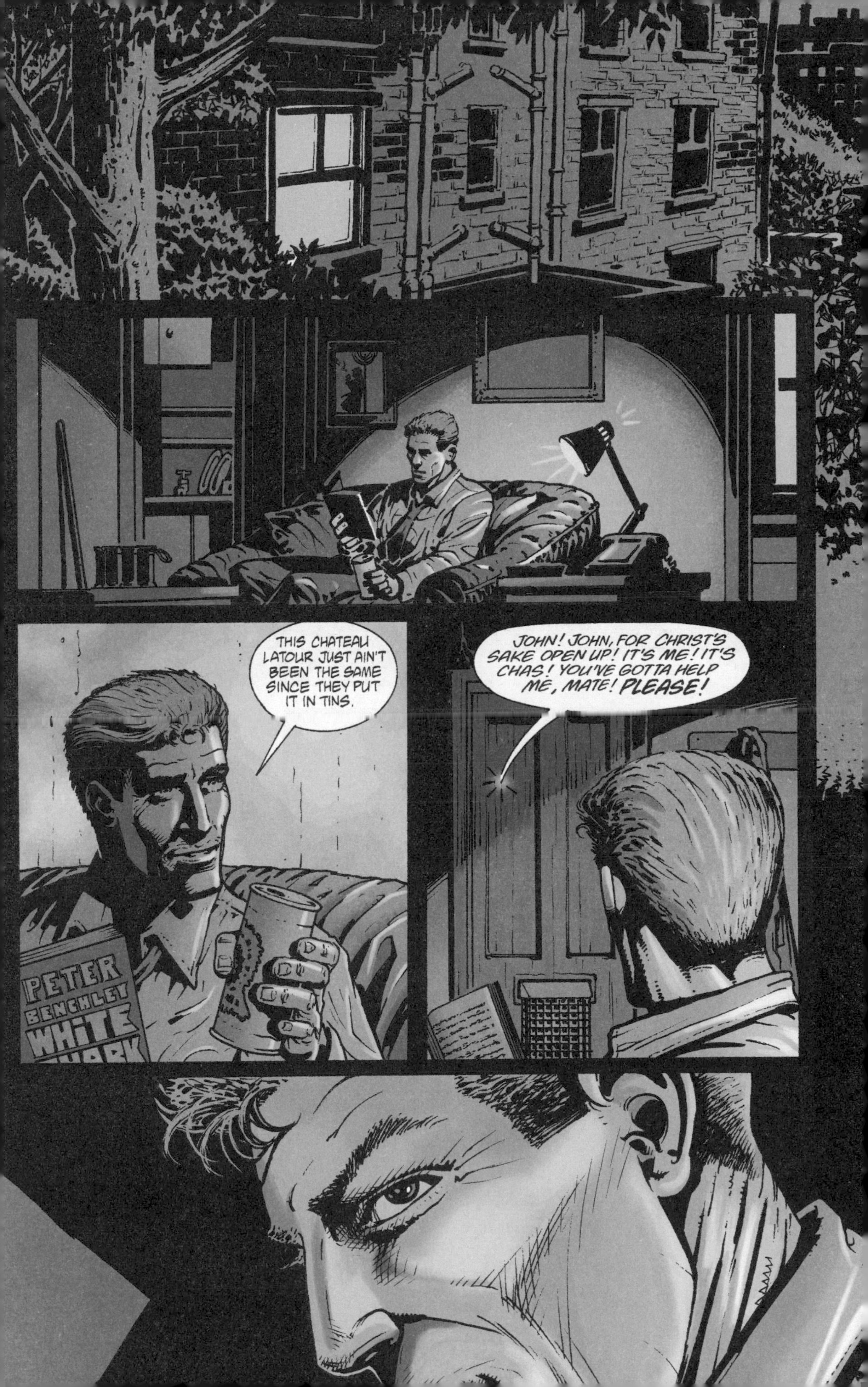
THIS CHATEAU LATOUR JUST AIN'T BEEN THE SAME SINCE THEY PUT IT IN TINS.
PETER BENCHLEY WHITE SHARK
JOHN! JOHN, FOR CHRIST'S SAKE OPEN UP! IT'S ME! IT'S CHAS! YOU'VE GOTTA HELP ME, MATE! PLEASE!

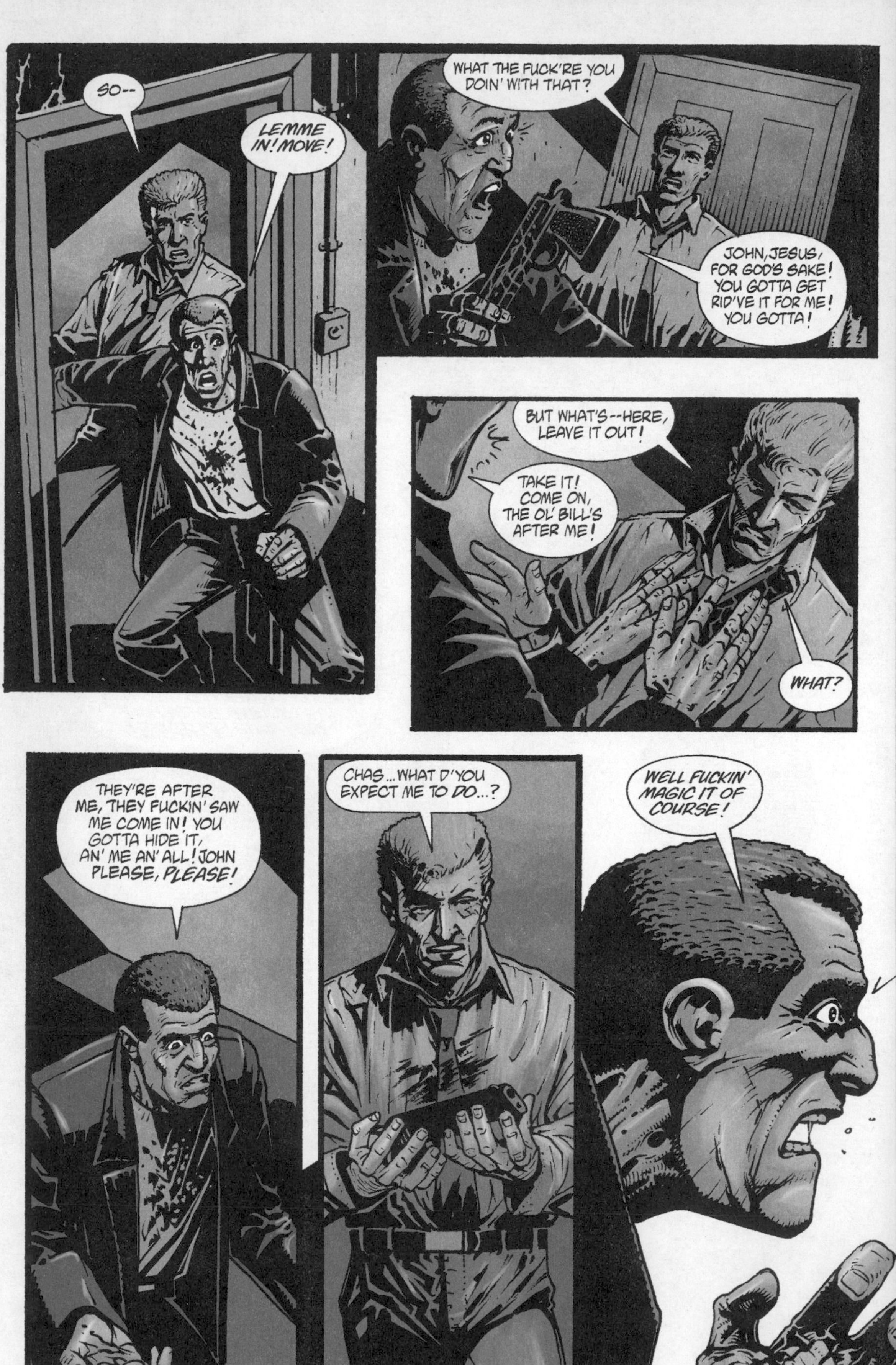
SO--
LEMME IN! MOVE!
WHAT THE FUCK'RE YOU DOIN' WITH THAT?
JOHN, JESUS, FOR GOD'S SAKE! YOU GOTTA GET RID'VE IT FOR ME! YOU GOTTA!
BUT WHAT'S--HERE, LEAVE IT OUT!
TAKE IT! COME ON, THE OL' BILL'S AFTER ME!
WHAT?
THEY'RE AFTER ME, THEY FUCKIN' SAW ME COME IN! YOU GOTTA HIDE IT, AN' ME AN' ALL! JOHN PLEASE, PLEASE!
CHAS... WHAT D'YOU EXPECT ME TO DO...?
WELL FUCKIN' MAGIC IT OF COURSE!

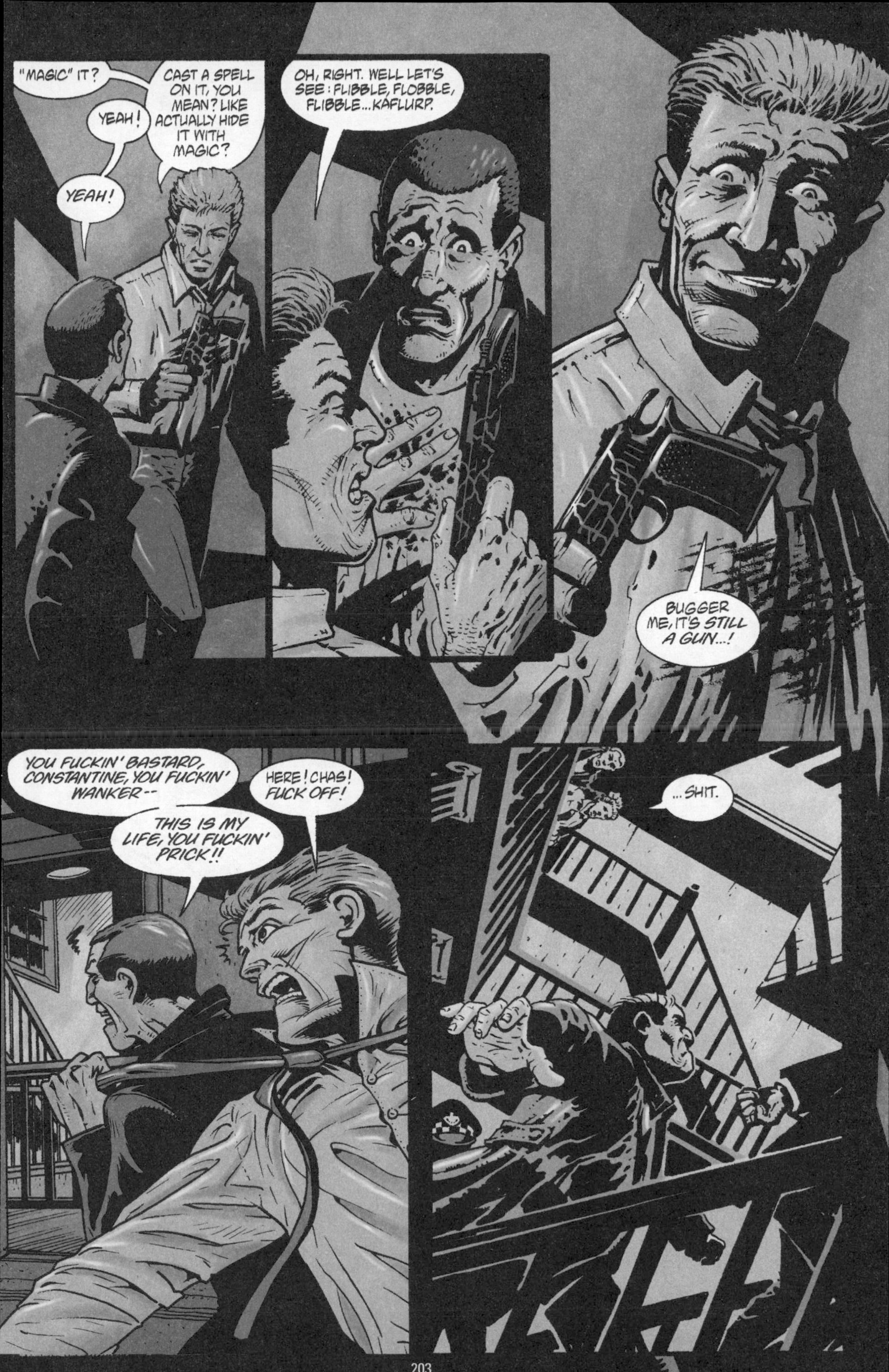
"MAGIC" IT?
CAST A SPELL ON IT, YOU MEAN? LIKE ACTUALLY HIDE IT WITH MAGIC?
YEAH!
YEAH!
OH, RIGHT. WELL LET'S SEE: FLIBBLE, FLOBBLE, FLIBBLE...KAFLURP.
BUGGER ME, IT'S STILL A GUN...!
YOU FUCKIN' BASTARD, CONSTANTINE, YOU FUCKIN' WANKER--
THIS IS MY LIFE, YOU FUCKIN' PRICK!!
HERE! CHAS! FUCK OFF!
...SHIT.

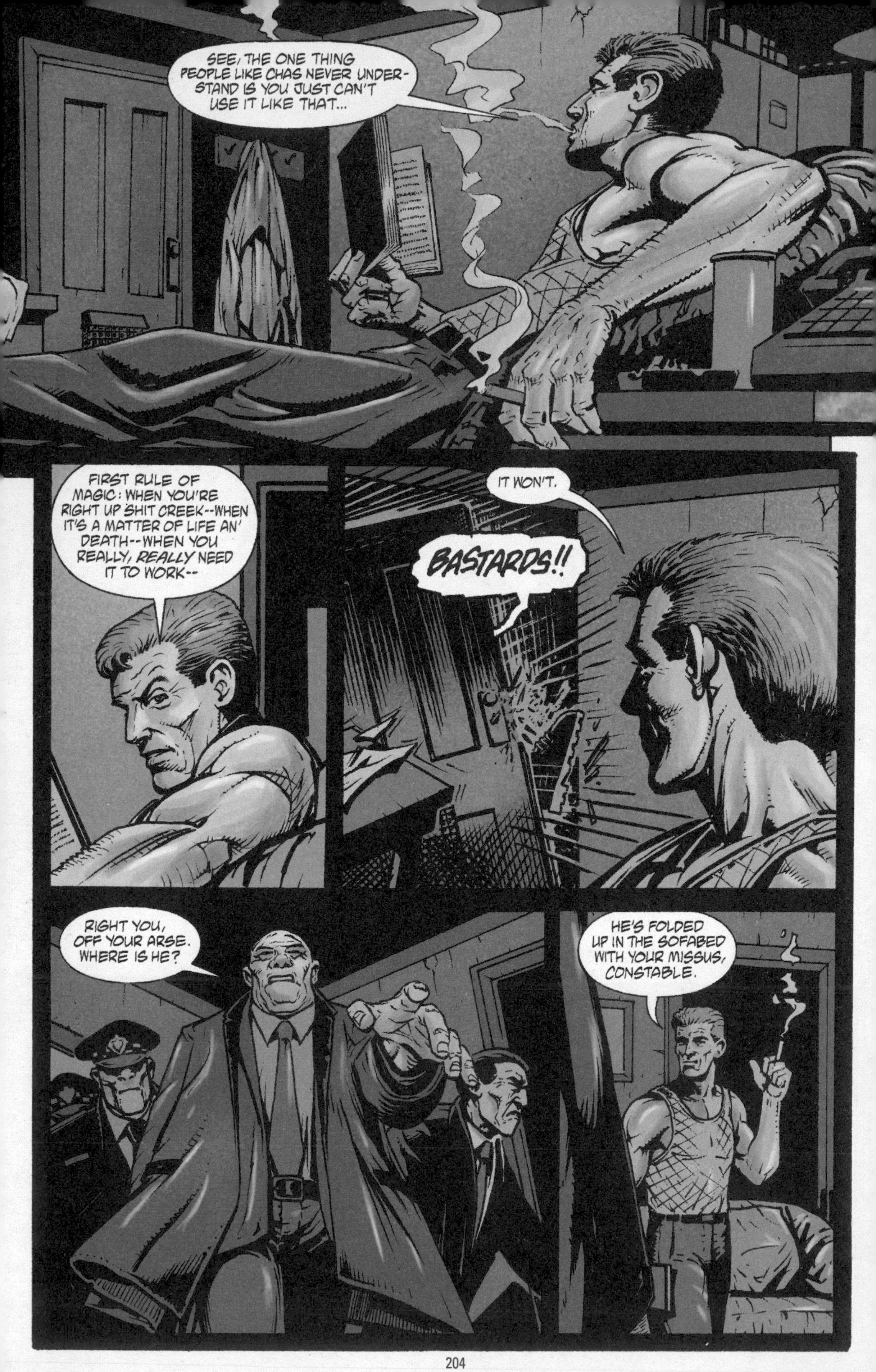
SEE, THE ONE THING PEOPLE LIKE CHAS NEVER UNDERSTAND IS YOU JUST CAN'T USE IT LIKE THAT...
FIRST RULE OF MAGIC: WHEN YOU'RE RIGHT UP SHIT CREEK--WHEN IT'S A MATTER OF LIFE AN' DEATH--WHEN YOU REALLY, REALLY NEED IT TO WORK--
IT WON'T.
BASTARDS!!
RIGHT YOU, OFF YOUR ARSE. WHERE IS HE?
HE'S FOLDED UP IN THE SOFABED WITH YOUR MISSUS, CONSTABLE.

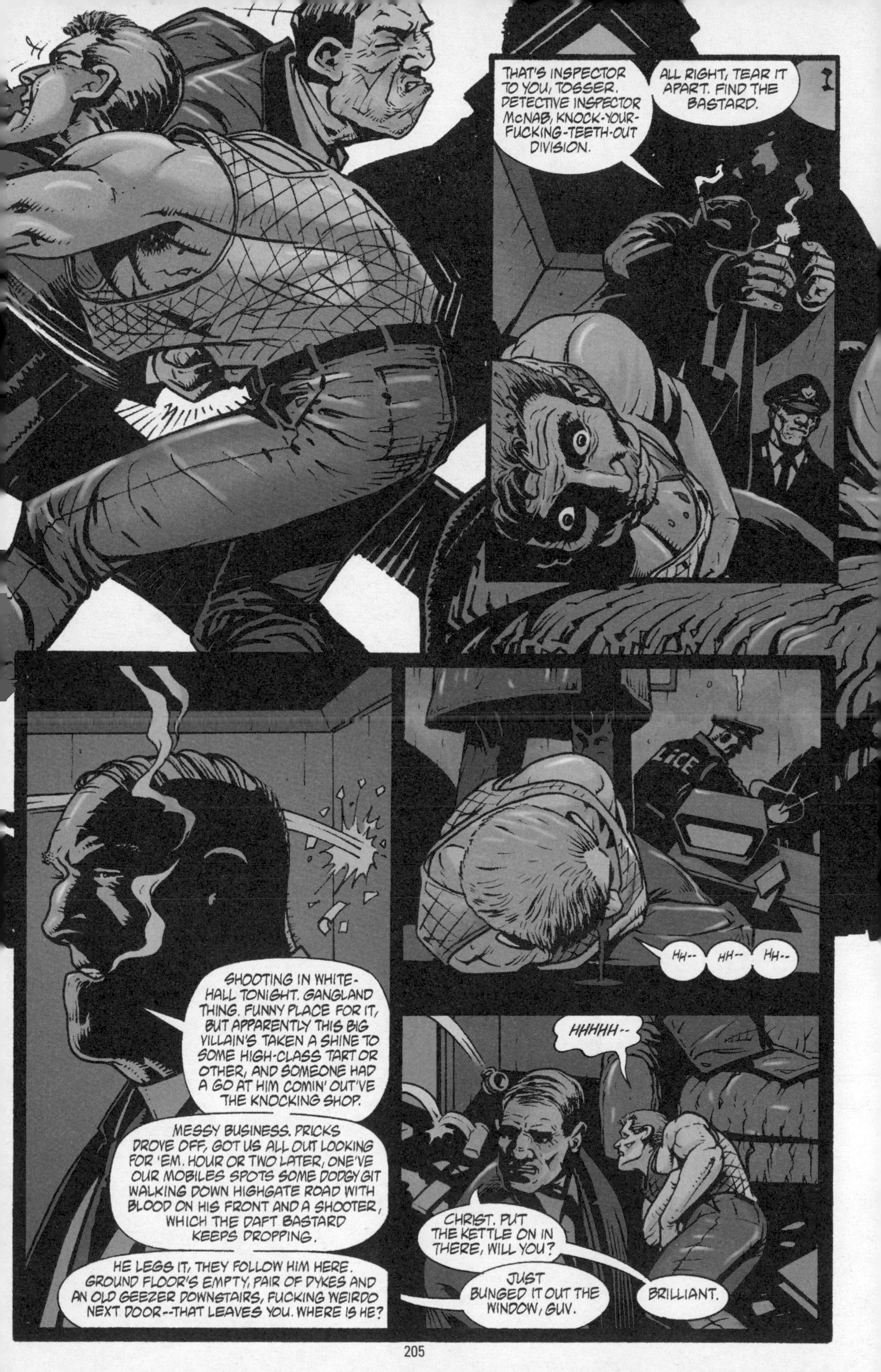
THAT'S INSPECTOR TO YOU, TOSSER. DETECTIVE INSPECTOR McNAB, KNOCK-YOUR-FUCKING-TEETH-OUT DIVISION.
ALL RIGHT, TEAR IT APART. FIND THE BASTARD.
SHOOTING IN WHITEHALL TONIGHT. GANGLAND THING. FUNNY PLACE FOR IT, BUT APPARENTLY THIS BIG VILLAIN'S TAKEN A SHINE TO SOME HIGH-CLASS TART OR OTHER, AND SOMEONE HAD A GO AT HIM COMIN' OUT'VE THE KNOCKING SHOP.
MESSY BUSINESS. PRICKS DROVE OFF, GOT US ALL OUT LOOKING FOR 'EM. HOUR OR TWO LATER, ONE'VE OUR MOBILES SPOTS SOME DODGY GIT WALKING DOWN HIGHGATE ROAD WITH BLOOD ON HIS FRONT AND A SHOOTER, WHICH THE DAFT BASTARD KEEPS DROPPING.
HE LEGS IT, THEY FOLLOW HIM HERE. GROUND FLOOR'S EMPTY, PAIR OF DYKES AND AN OLD GEEZER DOWNSTAIRS, FUCKING WEIRDO NEXT DOOR--THAT LEAVES YOU. WHERE IS HE?
HH-- HH-- HH--
HHHHH--
CHRIST. PUT THE KETTLE ON IN THERE, WILL YOU?
JUST BUNGED IT OUT THE WINDOW, GUV.
BRILLIANT.

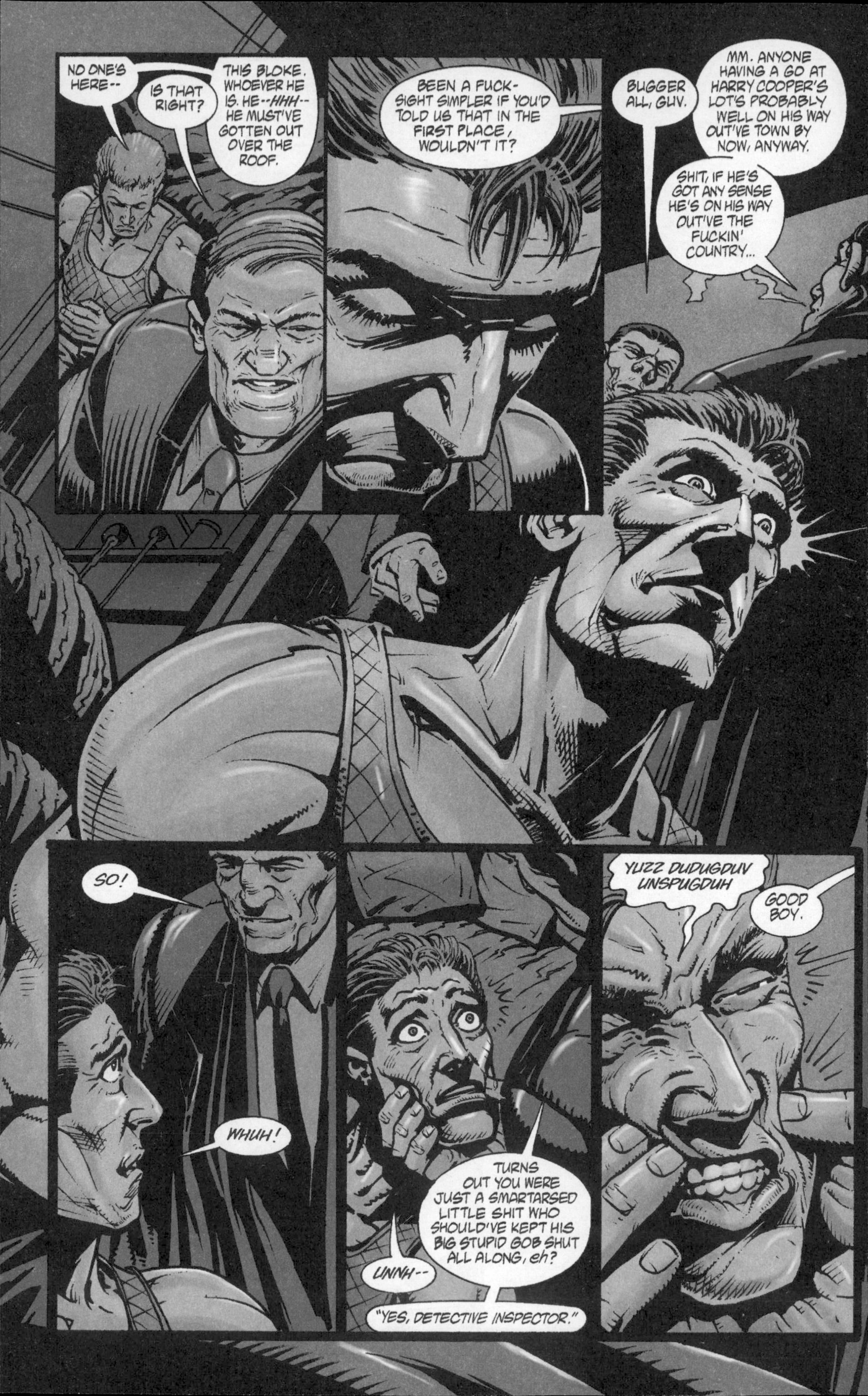
NO ONE'S HERE--
IS THAT RIGHT?
THIS BLOKE. WHOEVER HE IS. HE--HHH-- HE MUST'VE GOTTEN OUT OVER THE ROOF.
BEEN A FUCK-SIGHT SIMPLER IF YOU'D TOLD US THAT IN THE FIRST PLACE, WOULDN'T IT?
BUGGER ALL, GUV.
MM. ANYONE HAVING A GO AT HARRY COOPER'S LOT'S PROBABLY WELL ON HIS WAY OUT'VE TOWN BY NOW, ANYWAY.
SHIT, IF HE'S GOT ANY SENSE HE'S ON HIS WAY OUT'VE THE FUCKIN' COUNTRY...
SO!
WHUH!
TURNS OUT YOU WERE JUST A SMARTARSED LITTLE SHIT WHO SHOULD'VE KEPT HIS BIG STUPID GOB SHUT ALL ALONG, eh?
UNNH--
"YES, DETECTIVE INSPECTOR."
YUZZ DUDUGDUV UNSPUGDUH
GOOD BOY.

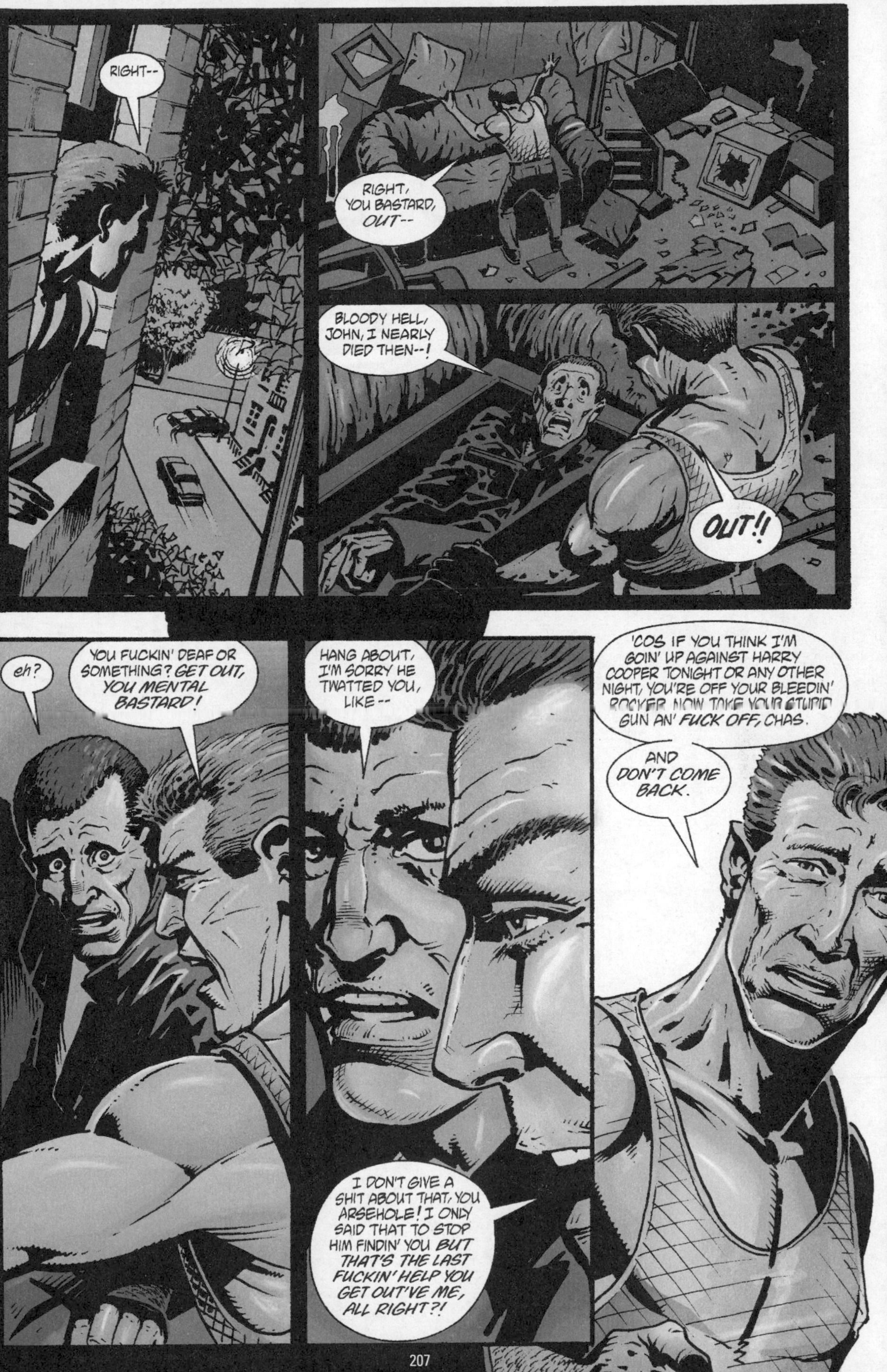
RIGHT--
RIGHT, YOU BASTARD, *OUT*--
BLOODY HELL, JOHN, I NEARLY DIED THEN--!
OUT!!
eh?
YOU FUCKIN' DEAF OR SOMETHING? *GET OUT, YOU MENTAL BASTARD!*
HANG ABOUT, I'M SORRY HE TWATTED YOU, LIKE --
I DON'T GIVE A SHIT ABOUT THAT, YOU ARSEHOLE! I ONLY SAID THAT TO STOP HIM FINDIN' YOU *BUT THAT'S THE LAST FUCKIN' HELP YOU GET OUT'VE ME, ALL RIGHT?!*
'COS IF YOU THINK I'M GOIN' UP AGAINST HARRY COOPER TONIGHT OR ANY OTHER NIGHT, YOU'RE OFF YOUR BLEEDIN' ROCKER NOW TAKE YOUR STUPID GUN AN' *FUCK OFF*, CHAS.
AND *DON'T COME BACK*.

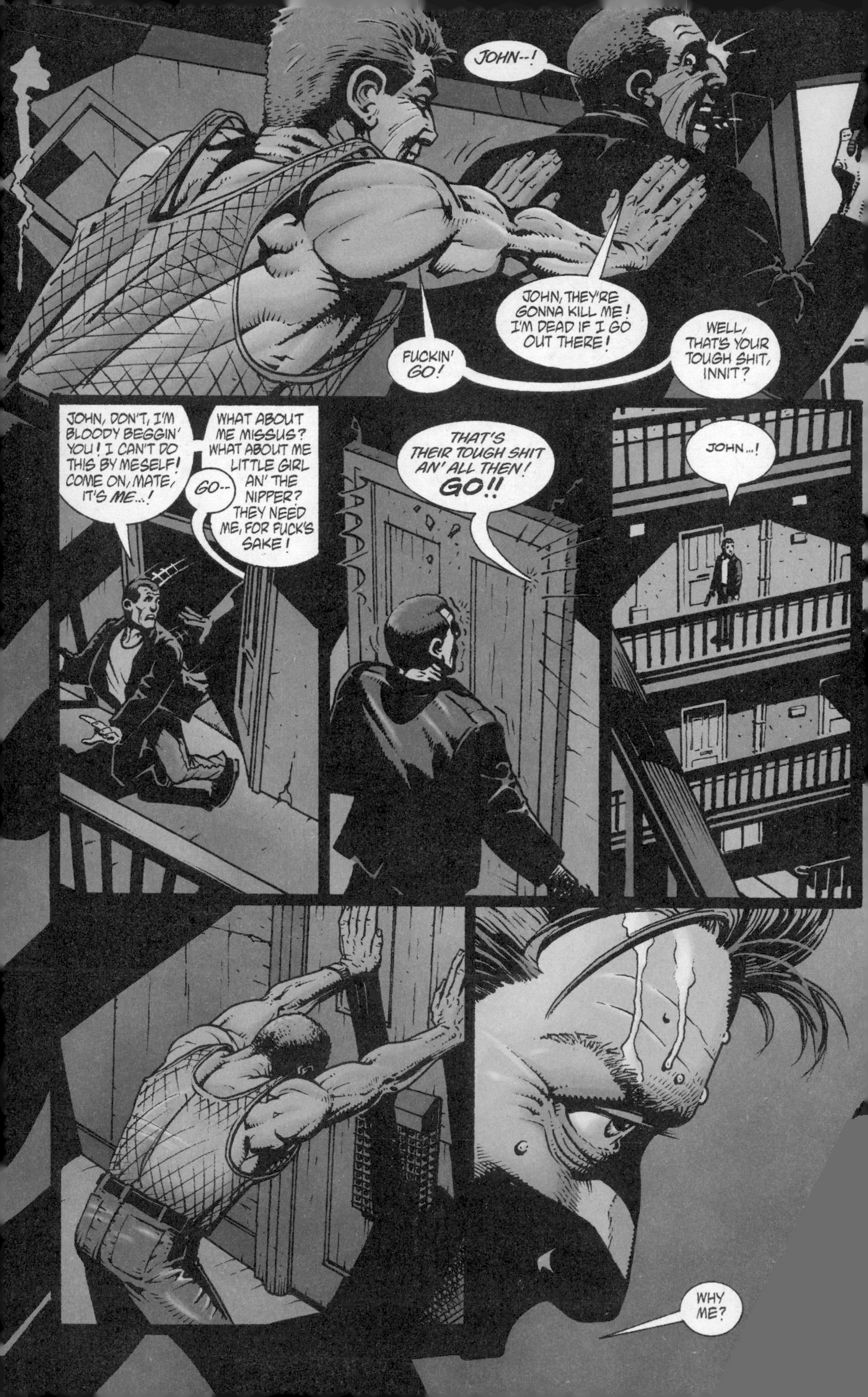
JOHN--!
JOHN, THEY'RE GONNA KILL ME! I'M DEAD IF I GO OUT THERE!
FUCKIN' GO!
WELL, THAT'S YOUR TOUGH SHIT, INNIT?
JOHN, DON'T, I'M BLOODY BEGGIN' YOU! I CAN'T DO THIS BY MESELF! COME ON, MATE, IT'S ME...!
GO--
WHAT ABOUT ME MISSUS? WHAT ABOUT ME LITTLE GIRL AN' THE NIPPER? THEY NEED ME, FOR FUCK'S SAKE!
THAT'S THEIR TOUGH SHIT AN' ALL THEN! GO!!
JOHN...!
WHY ME?

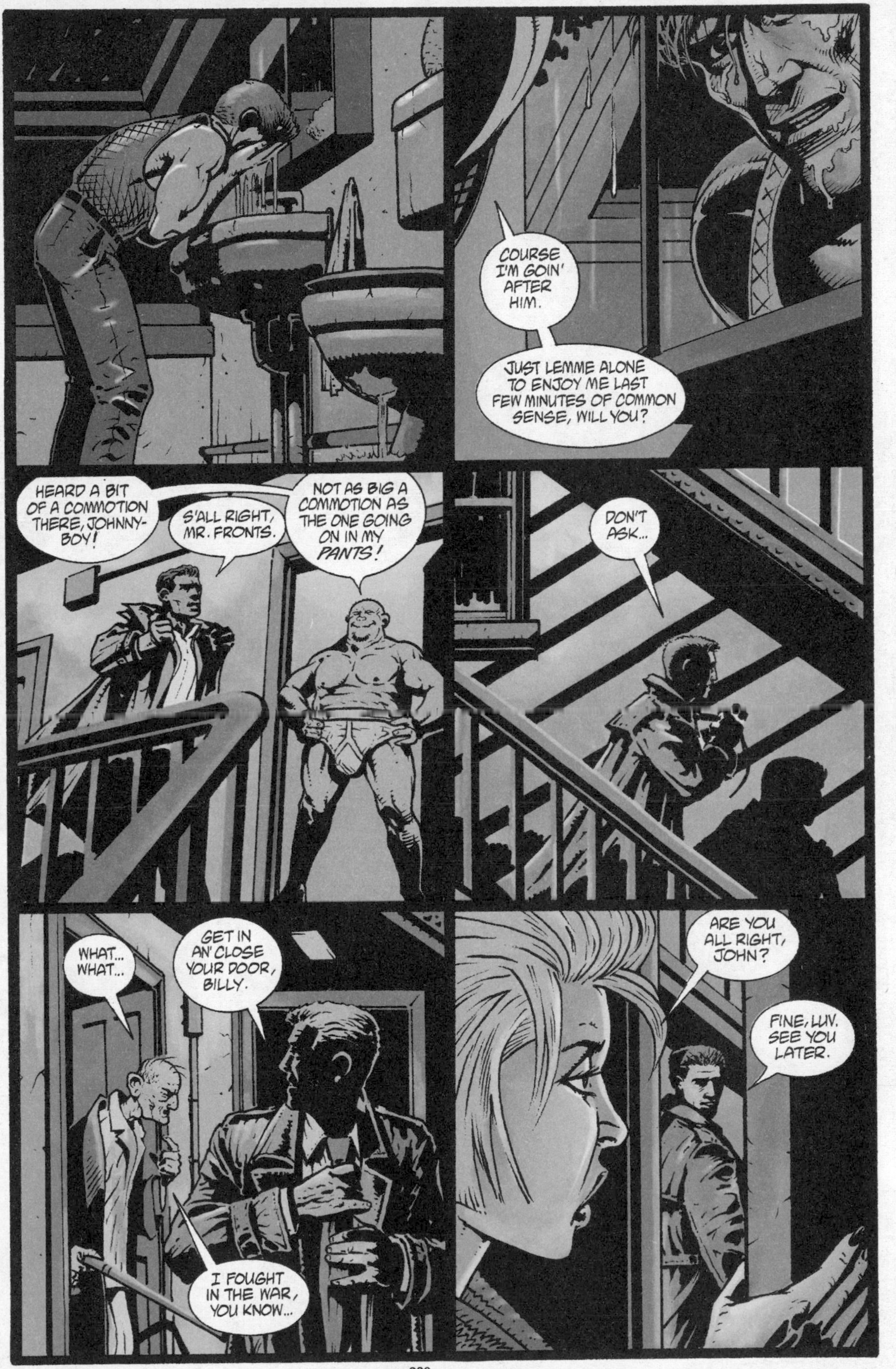
COURSE I'M GOIN' AFTER HIM.
JUST LEMME ALONE TO ENJOY ME LAST FEW MINUTES OF COMMON SENSE, WILL YOU?
HEARD A BIT OF A COMMOTION THERE, JOHNNY-BOY!
S'ALL RIGHT, MR. FRONTS.
NOT AS BIG A COMMOTION AS THE ONE GOING ON IN MY PANTS!
DON'T ASK...
WHAT... WHAT...
GET IN AN' CLOSE YOUR DOOR, BILLY.
I FOUGHT IN THE WAR, YOU KNOW...
ARE YOU ALL RIGHT, JOHN?
FINE, LUV. SEE YOU LATER.

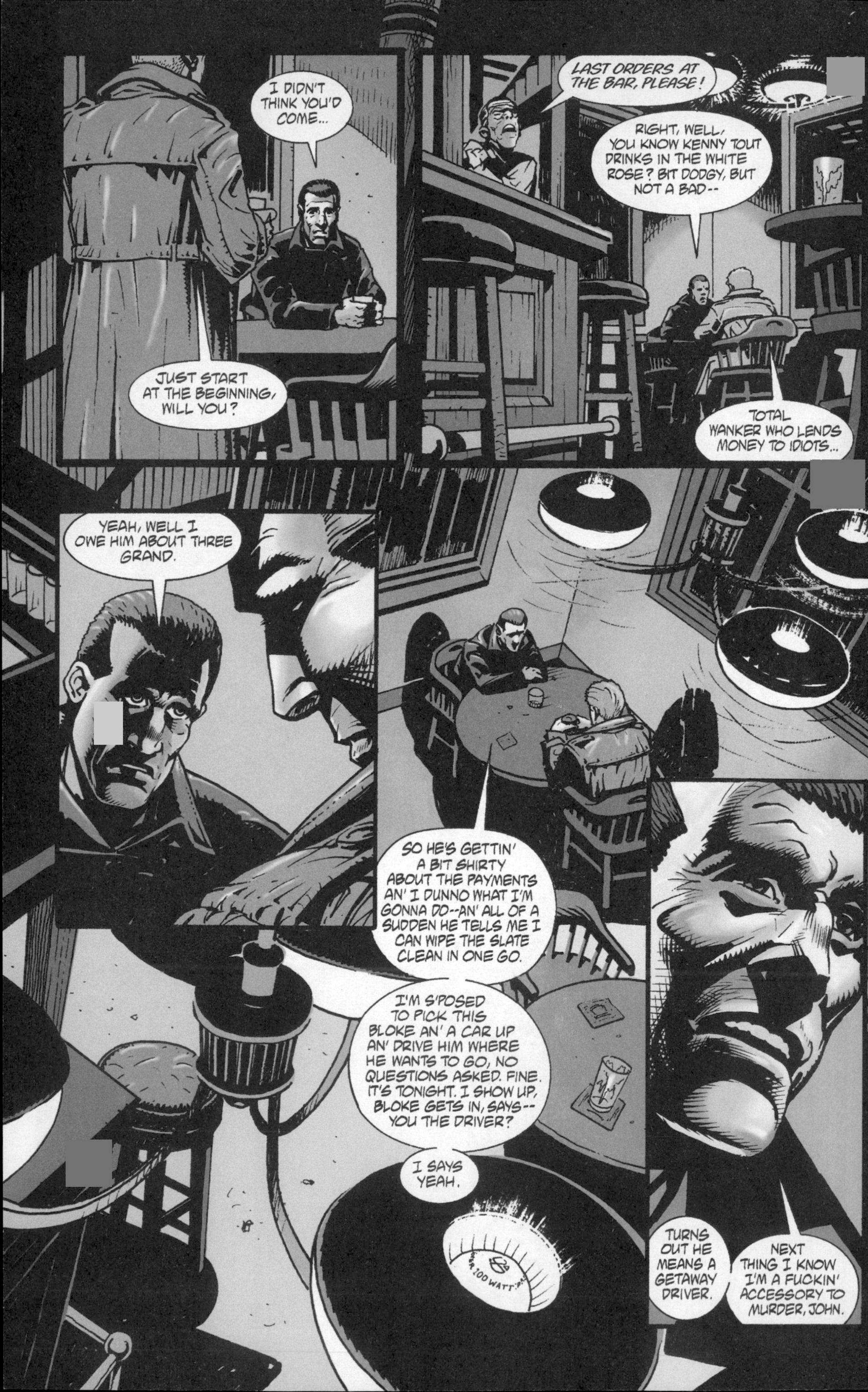
I DIDN'T THINK YOU'D COME...
JUST START AT THE BEGINNING, WILL YOU?
LAST ORDERS AT THE BAR, PLEASE!
RIGHT, WELL, YOU KNOW KENNY TOUT DRINKS IN THE WHITE ROSE? BIT DODGY, BUT NOT A BAD--
TOTAL WANKER WHO LENDS MONEY TO IDIOTS...
YEAH, WELL I OWE HIM ABOUT THREE GRAND.
SO HE'S GETTIN' A BIT SHIRTY ABOUT THE PAYMENTS AN' I DUNNO WHAT I'M GONNA DO--AN' ALL OF A SUDDEN HE TELLS ME I CAN WIPE THE SLATE CLEAN IN ONE GO.
I'M S'POSED TO PICK THIS BLOKE AN' A CAR UP AN' DRIVE HIM WHERE HE WANTS TO GO, NO QUESTIONS ASKED. FINE. IT'S TONIGHT. I SHOW UP, BLOKE GETS IN, SAYS-- YOU THE DRIVER?
I SAYS YEAH.
TURNS OUT HE MEANS A GETAWAY DRIVER.
NEXT THING I KNOW I'M A FUCKIN' ACCESSORY TO MURDER, JOHN.
100 WATT

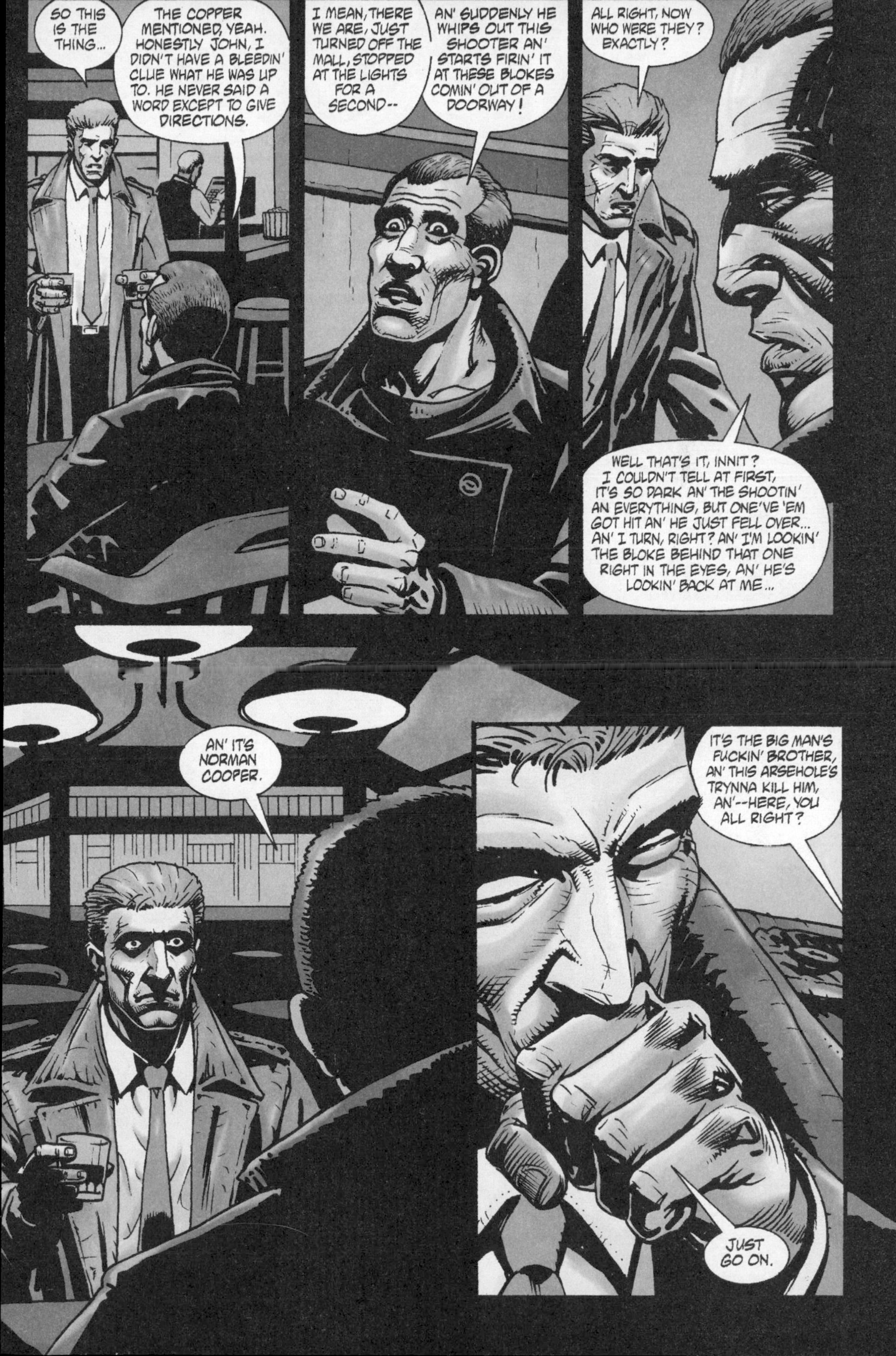
SO THIS IS THE THING...
THE COPPER MENTIONED, YEAH. HONESTLY JOHN, I DIDN'T HAVE A BLEEDIN' CLUE WHAT HE WAS UP TO. HE NEVER SAID A WORD EXCEPT TO GIVE DIRECTIONS.
I MEAN, THERE WE ARE, JUST TURNED OFF THE MALL, STOPPED AT THE LIGHTS FOR A SECOND--
AN' SUDDENLY HE WHIPS OUT THIS SHOOTER AN' STARTS FIRIN' IT AT THESE BLOKES COMIN' OUT OF A DOORWAY!
ALL RIGHT, NOW WHO WERE THEY? EXACTLY?
WELL THAT'S IT, INNIT? I COULDN'T TELL AT FIRST, IT'S SO DARK AN' THE SHOOTIN' AN EVERYTHING, BUT ONE'VE 'EM GOT HIT AN' HE JUST FELL OVER... AN' I TURN, RIGHT? AN' I'M LOOKIN' THE BLOKE BEHIND THAT ONE RIGHT IN THE EYES, AN' HE'S LOOKIN' BACK AT ME...
AN' IT'S NORMAN COOPER.
IT'S THE BIG MAN'S FUCKIN' BROTHER, AN' THIS ARSEHOLE'S TRYNNA KILL HIM, AN'--HERE, YOU ALL RIGHT?
JUST GO ON.

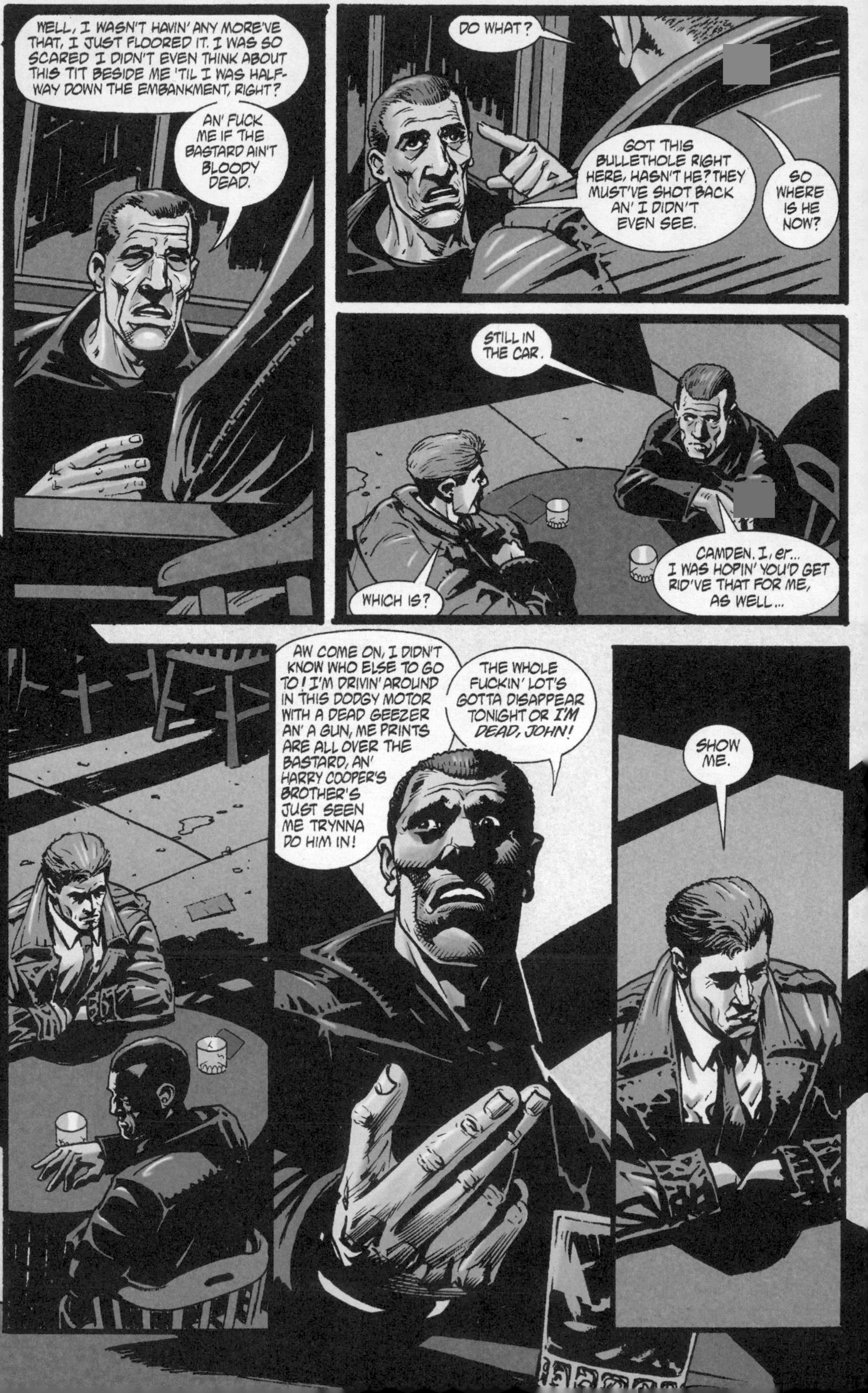
WELL, I WASN'T HAVIN' ANY MORE'VE THAT, I JUST FLOORED IT. I WAS SO SCARED I DIDN'T EVEN THINK ABOUT THIS TIT BESIDE ME 'TIL I WAS HALF-WAY DOWN THE EMBANKMENT, RIGHT?
AN' FUCK ME IF THE BASTARD AIN'T BLOODY DEAD.
DO WHAT?
GOT THIS BULLETHOLE RIGHT HERE, HASN'T HE? THEY MUST'VE SHOT BACK AN' I DIDN'T EVEN SEE.
SO WHERE IS HE NOW?
STILL IN THE CAR.
CAMDEN. I, er... I WAS HOPIN' YOU'D GET RID'VE THAT FOR ME, AS WELL...
WHICH IS?
AW COME ON, I DIDN'T KNOW WHO ELSE TO GO TO! I'M DRIVIN' AROUND IN THIS DODGY MOTOR WITH A DEAD GEEZER AN' A GUN, ME PRINTS ARE ALL OVER THE BASTARD, AN' HARRY COOPER'S BROTHER'S JUST SEEN ME TRYNNA DO HIM IN!
THE WHOLE FUCKIN' LOT'S GOTTA DISAPPEAR TONIGHT OR *I'M DEAD, JOHN!*
SHOW ME.

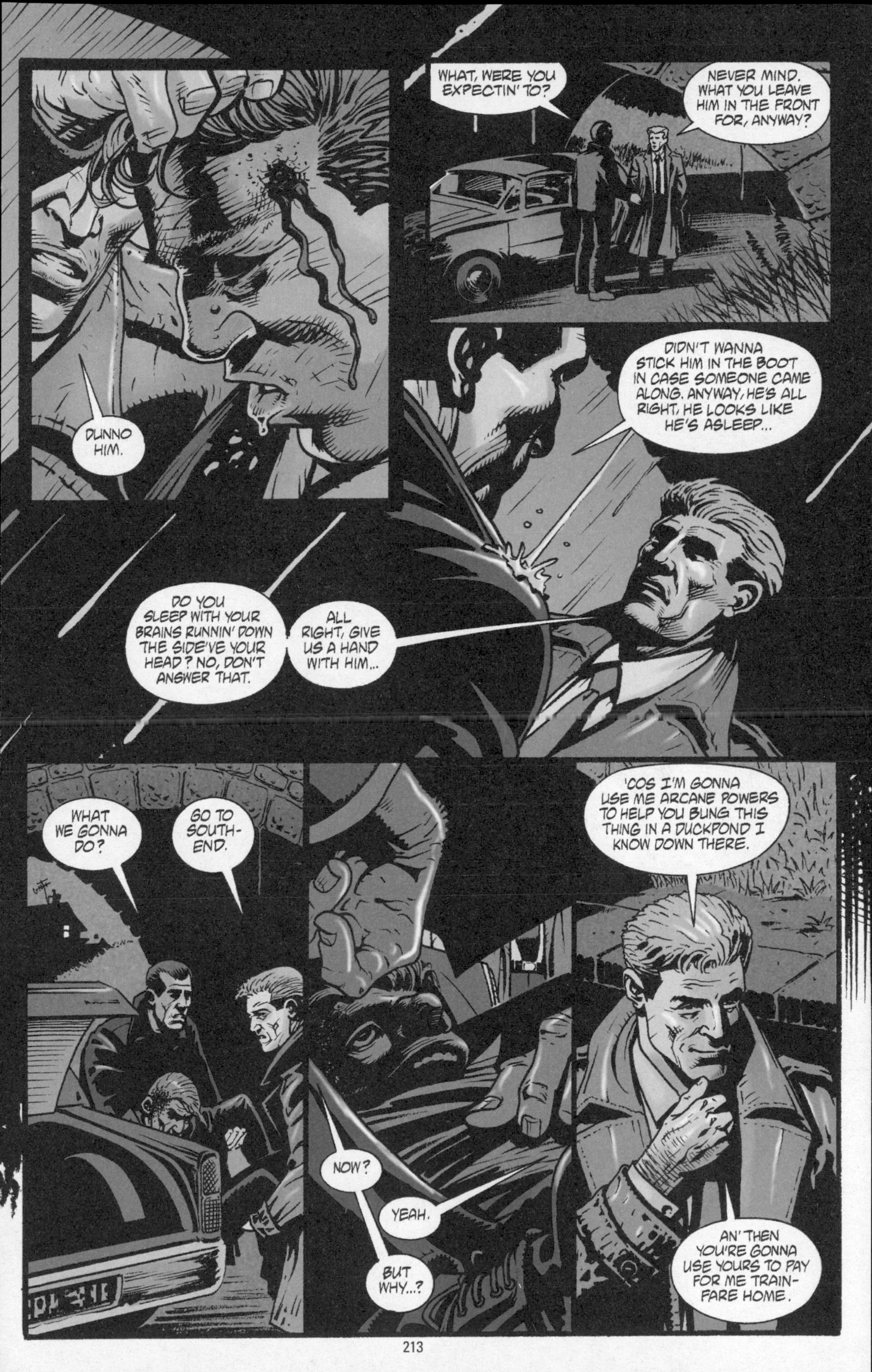
DUNNO HIM.
WHAT, WERE YOU EXPECTIN' TO?
NEVER MIND. WHAT YOU LEAVE HIM IN THE FRONT FOR, ANYWAY?
DIDN'T WANNA STICK HIM IN THE BOOT IN CASE SOMEONE CAME ALONG. ANYWAY, HE'S ALL RIGHT, HE LOOKS LIKE HE'S ASLEEP...
DO YOU SLEEP WITH YOUR BRAINS RUNNIN' DOWN THE SIDE'VE YOUR HEAD? NO, DON'T ANSWER THAT.
ALL RIGHT, GIVE US A HAND WITH HIM...
WHAT WE GONNA DO?
GO TO SOUTH-END.
NOW?
YEAH.
BUT WHY...?
'COS I'M GONNA USE ME ARCANE POWERS TO HELP YOU BUNG THIS THING IN A DUCKPOND I KNOW DOWN THERE.
AN' THEN YOU'RE GONNA USE YOURS TO PAY FOR ME TRAIN-FARE HOME.

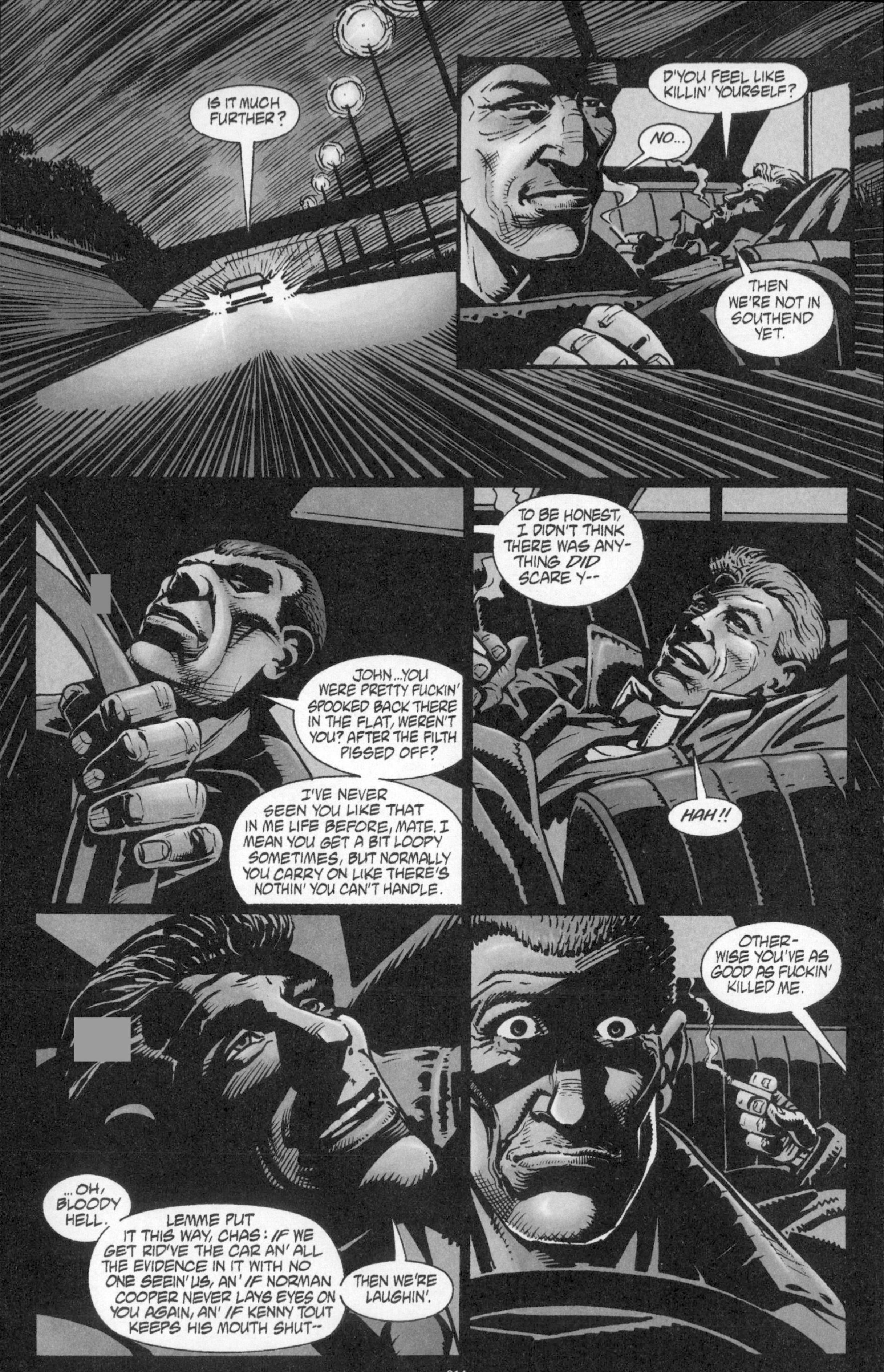
IS IT MUCH FURTHER?
D'YOU FEEL LIKE KILLIN' YOURSELF?
NO...
THEN WE'RE NOT IN SOUTHEND YET.
JOHN...YOU WERE PRETTY FUCKIN' SPOOKED BACK THERE IN THE FLAT, WEREN'T YOU? AFTER THE FILTH PISSED OFF?
I'VE NEVER SEEN YOU LIKE THAT IN ME LIFE BEFORE, MATE. I MEAN YOU GET A BIT LOOPY SOMETIMES, BUT NORMALLY YOU CARRY ON LIKE THERE'S NOTHIN' YOU CAN'T HANDLE.
TO BE HONEST, I DIDN'T THINK THERE WAS ANY-THING DID SCARE Y--
HAH!!
...OH, BLOODY HELL.
LEMME PUT IT THIS WAY, CHAS: IF WE GET RID'VE THE CAR AN' ALL THE EVIDENCE IN IT WITH NO ONE SEEIN' US, AN' IF NORMAN COOPER NEVER LAYS EYES ON YOU AGAIN, AN' IF KENNY TOUT KEEPS HIS MOUTH SHUT--
THEN WE'RE LAUGHIN'.
OTHER-WISE YOU'VE AS GOOD AS FUCKIN' KILLED ME.

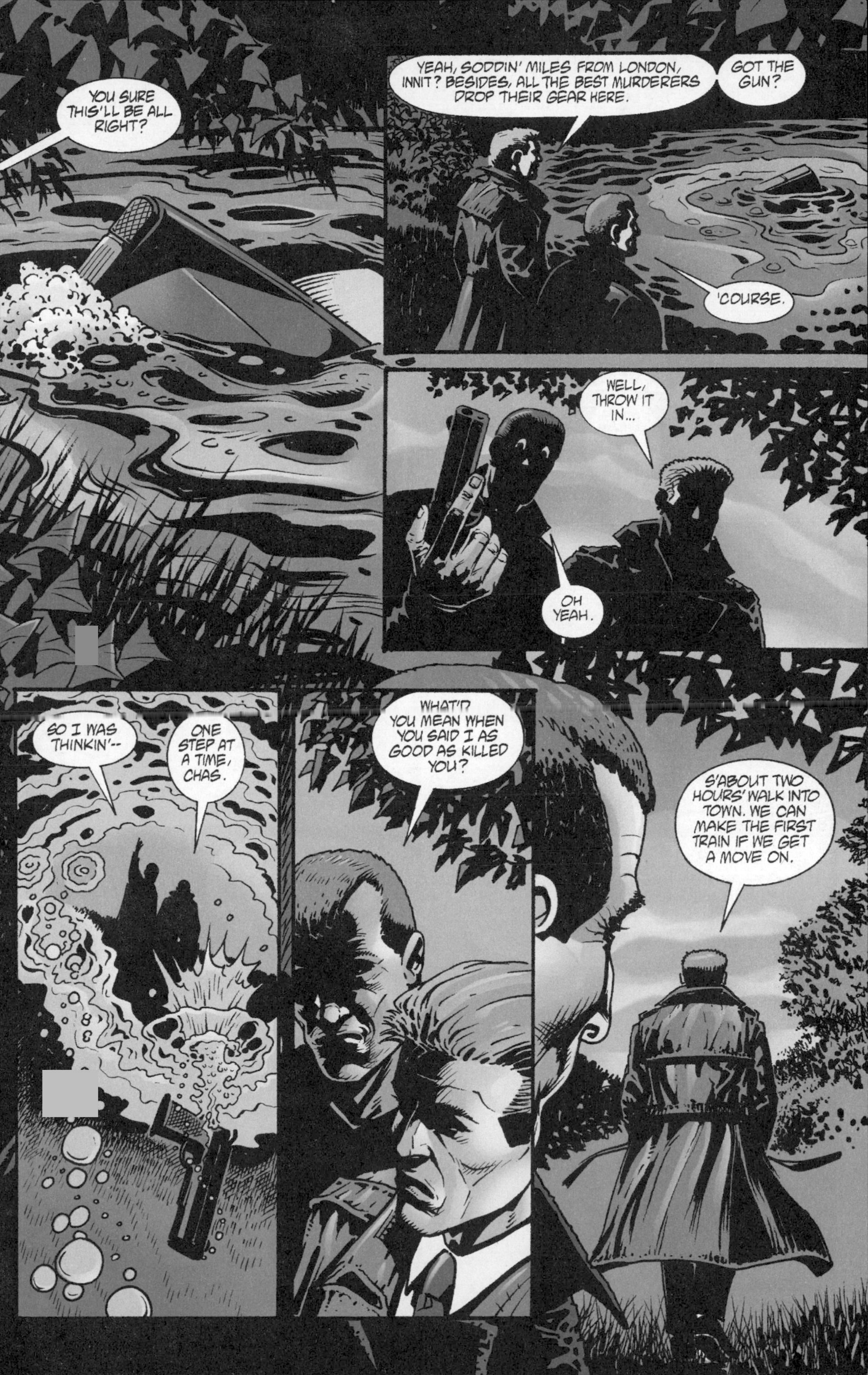
YOU SURE THIS'LL BE ALL RIGHT?
YEAH, SODDIN' MILES FROM LONDON, INNIT? BESIDES, ALL THE BEST MURDERERS DROP THEIR GEAR HERE.
GOT THE GUN?
'COURSE.
WELL, THROW IT IN...
OH YEAH.
SO I WAS THINKIN'--
ONE STEP AT A TIME, CHAS.
WHAT'D YOU MEAN WHEN YOU SAID I AS GOOD AS KILLED YOU?
S'ABOUT TWO HOURS' WALK INTO TOWN. WE CAN MAKE THE FIRST TRAIN IF WE GET A MOVE ON.

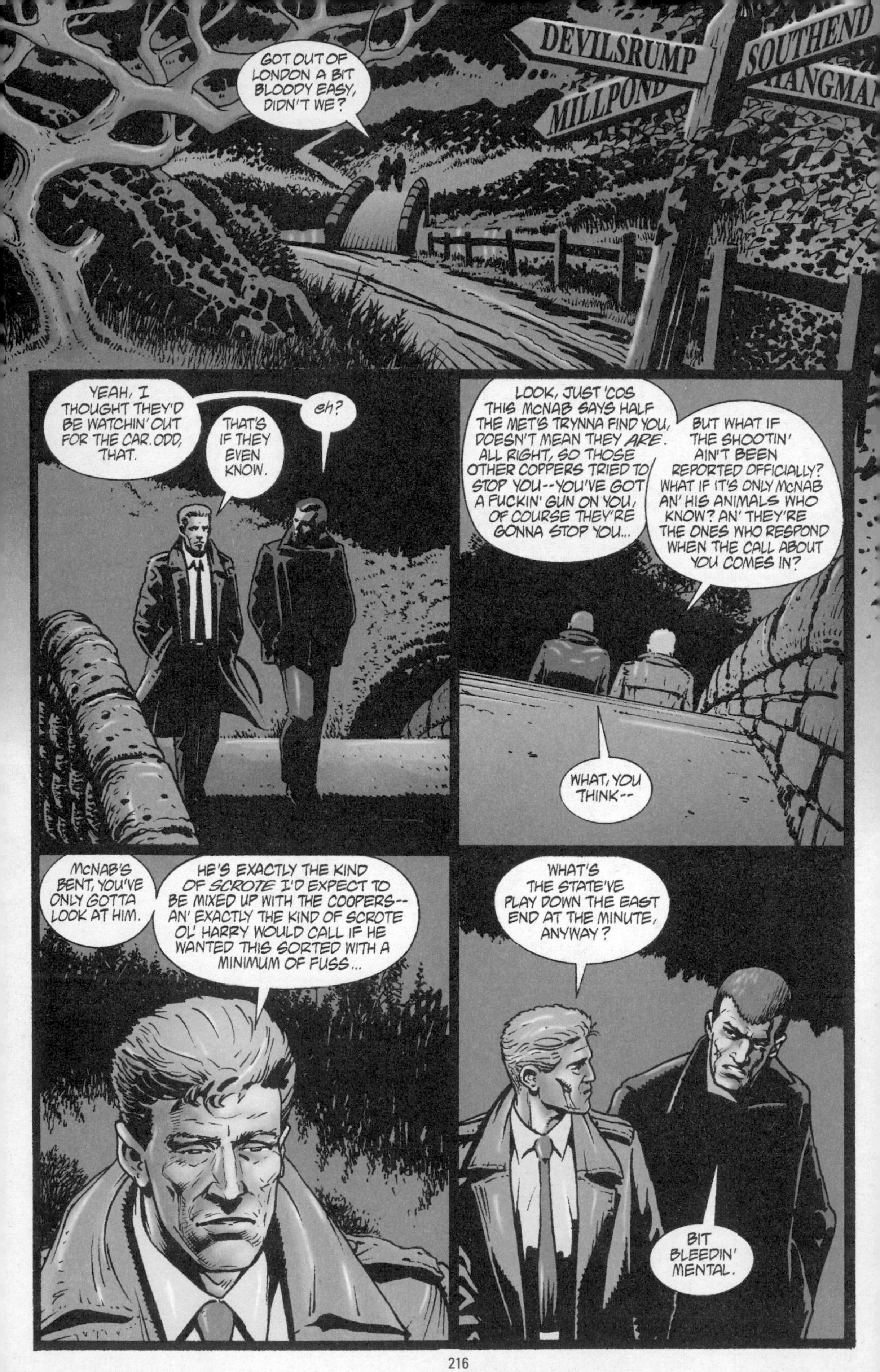
DEVILSRUMP
SOUTHEND
MILLPOND
GOT OUT OF LONDON A BIT BLOODY EASY, DIDN'T WE?
YEAH, I THOUGHT THEY'D BE WATCHIN' OUT FOR THE CAR. ODD, THAT.
eh?
THAT'S IF THEY EVEN KNOW.
LOOK, JUST 'COS THIS McNAB SAYS HALF THE MET'S TRYNNA FIND YOU, DOESN'T MEAN THEY ARE. ALL RIGHT, SO THOSE OTHER COPPERS TRIED TO STOP YOU--YOU'VE GOT A FUCKIN' GUN ON YOU, OF COURSE THEY'RE GONNA STOP YOU...
BUT WHAT IF THE SHOOTIN' AIN'T BEEN REPORTED OFFICIALLY? WHAT IF IT'S ONLY McNAB AN' HIS ANIMALS WHO KNOW? AN' THEY'RE THE ONES WHO RESPOND WHEN THE CALL ABOUT YOU COMES IN?
WHAT, YOU THINK--
McNAB'S BENT, YOU'VE ONLY GOTTA LOOK AT HIM.
HE'S EXACTLY THE KIND OF SCROTE I'D EXPECT TO BE MIXED UP WITH THE COOPERS--AN' EXACTLY THE KIND OF SCROTE OL' HARRY WOULD CALL IF HE WANTED THIS SORTED WITH A MINIMUM OF FUSS...
WHAT'S THE STATE'VE PLAY DOWN THE EAST END AT THE MINUTE, ANYWAY?
BIT BLEEDIN' MENTAL.

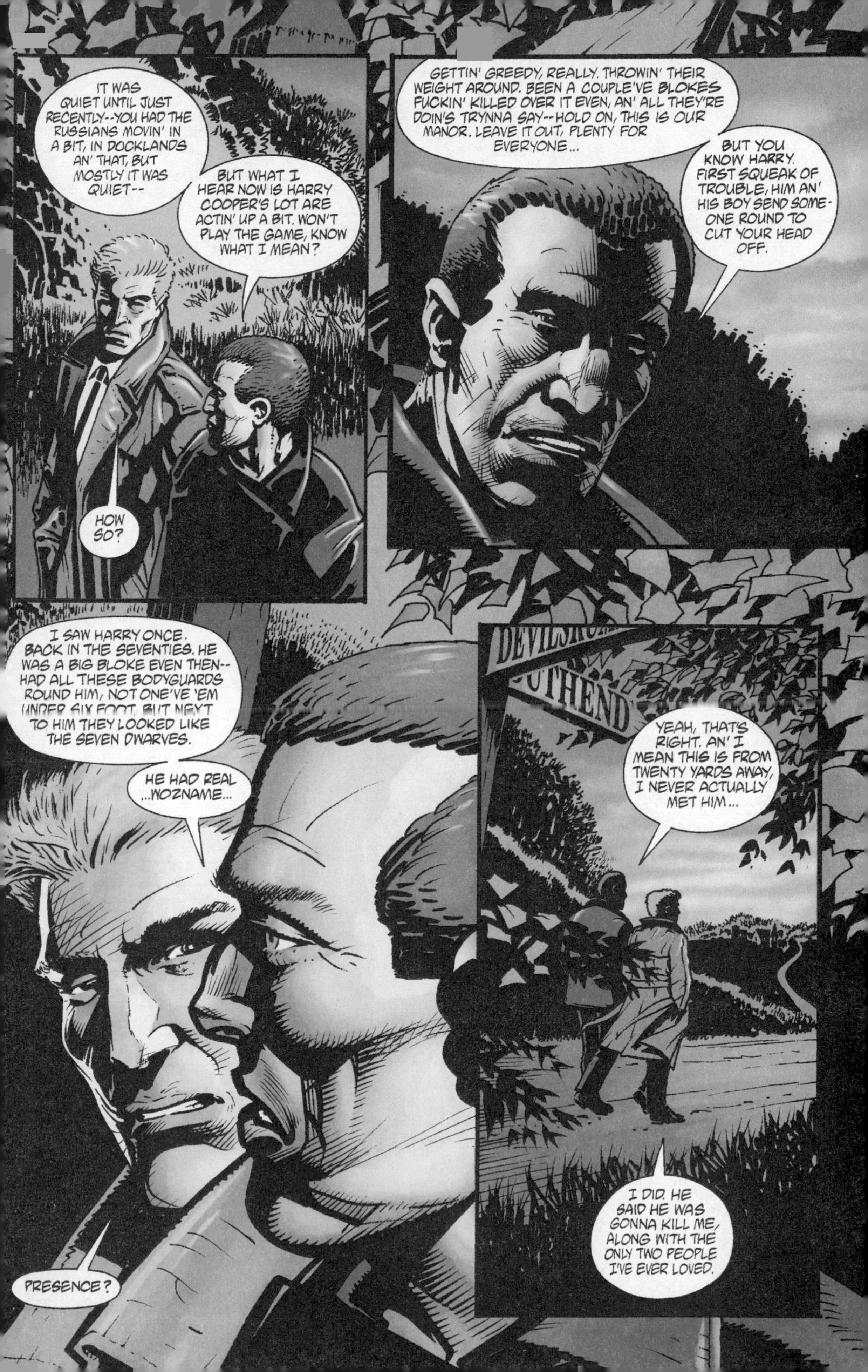
IT WAS QUIET UNTIL JUST RECENTLY--YOU HAD THE RUSSIANS MOVIN' IN A BIT, IN DOCKLANDS AN' THAT, BUT MOSTLY IT WAS QUIET--
BUT WHAT I HEAR NOW IS HARRY COOPER'S LOT ARE ACTIN' UP A BIT. WON'T PLAY THE GAME, KNOW WHAT I MEAN?
HOW SO?
GETTIN' GREEDY, REALLY. THROWIN' THEIR WEIGHT AROUND. BEEN A COUPLE'VE BLOKES FUCKIN' KILLED OVER IT EVEN, AN' ALL THEY'RE DOIN'S TRYNNA SAY--HOLD ON, THIS IS OUR MANOR. LEAVE IT OUT, PLENTY FOR EVERYONE...
BUT YOU KNOW HARRY. FIRST SQUEAK OF TROUBLE, HIM AN' HIS BOY SEND SOME-ONE ROUND TO CUT YOUR HEAD OFF.
I SAW HARRY ONCE. BACK IN THE SEVENTIES. HE WAS A BIG BLOKE EVEN THEN--HAD ALL THESE BODYGUARDS ROUND HIM, NOT ONE'VE 'EM UNDER SIX FOOT, BUT NEXT TO HIM THEY LOOKED LIKE THE SEVEN DWARVES.
HE HAD REAL ...WOZNAME...
PRESENCE?
YEAH, THAT'S RIGHT. AN' I MEAN THIS IS FROM TWENTY YARDS AWAY, I NEVER ACTUALLY MET HIM...
I DID. HE SAID HE WAS GONNA KILL ME, ALONG WITH THE ONLY TWO PEOPLE I'VE EVER LOVED.

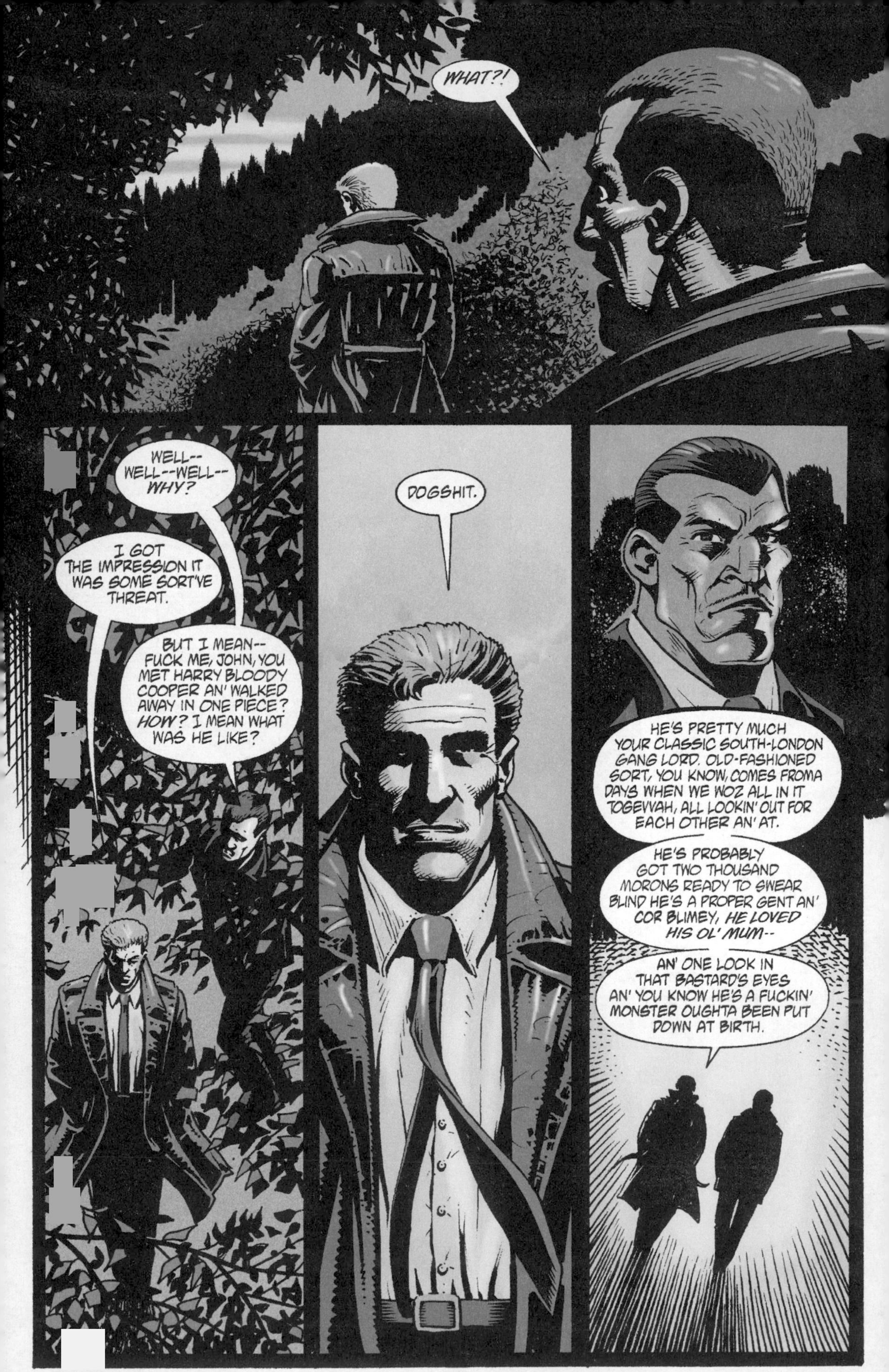
WHAT?!
WELL--WELL--WELL--WHY?
I GOT THE IMPRESSION IT WAS SOME SORT'VE THREAT.
BUT I MEAN--FUCK ME, JOHN, YOU MET HARRY BLOODY COOPER AN' WALKED AWAY IN ONE PIECE? HOW? I MEAN WHAT WAS HE LIKE?
DOGSHIT.
HE'S PRETTY MUCH YOUR CLASSIC SOUTH-LONDON GANG LORD. OLD-FASHIONED SORT, YOU KNOW, COMES FROMA DAYS WHEN WE WOZ ALL IN IT TOGEVVAH, ALL LOOKIN' OUT FOR EACH OTHER AN' AT.
HE'S PROBABLY GOT TWO THOUSAND MORONS READY TO SWEAR BLIND HE'S A PROPER GENT AN' COR BLIMEY, HE LOVED HIS OL' MUM--
AN' ONE LOOK IN THAT BASTARD'S EYES AN' YOU KNOW HE'S A FUCKIN' MONSTER OUGHTA BEEN PUT DOWN AT BIRTH.

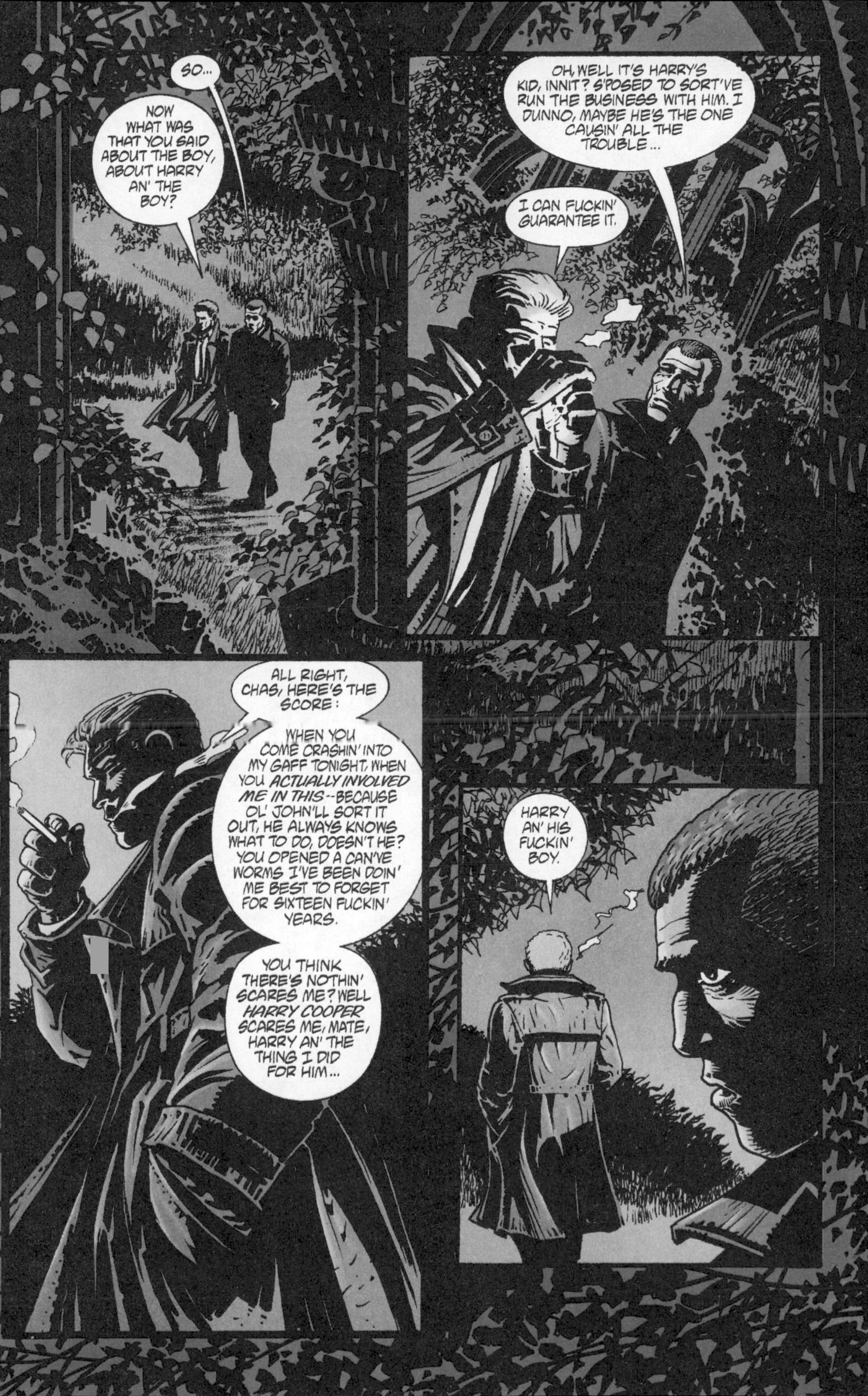
SO...
NOW WHAT WAS THAT YOU SAID ABOUT THE BOY, ABOUT HARRY AN' THE BOY?
OH, WELL IT'S HARRY'S KID, INNIT? S'POSED TO SORT'VE RUN THE BUSINESS WITH HIM. I DUNNO, MAYBE HE'S THE ONE CAUSIN' ALL THE TROUBLE...
I CAN FUCKIN' GUARANTEE IT.
ALL RIGHT, CHAS, HERE'S THE SCORE:
WHEN YOU COME CRASHIN' INTO MY GAFF TONIGHT, WHEN YOU ACTUALLY INVOLVED ME IN THIS--BECAUSE OL' JOHN'LL SORT IT OUT, HE ALWAYS KNOWS WHAT TO DO, DOESN'T HE? YOU OPENED A CAN'VE WORMS I'VE BEEN DOIN' ME BEST TO FORGET FOR SIXTEEN FUCKIN' YEARS.
YOU THINK THERE'S NOTHIN' SCARES ME? WELL HARRY COOPER SCARES ME, MATE, HARRY AN' THE THING I DID FOR HIM...
HARRY AN' HIS FUCKIN' BOY.

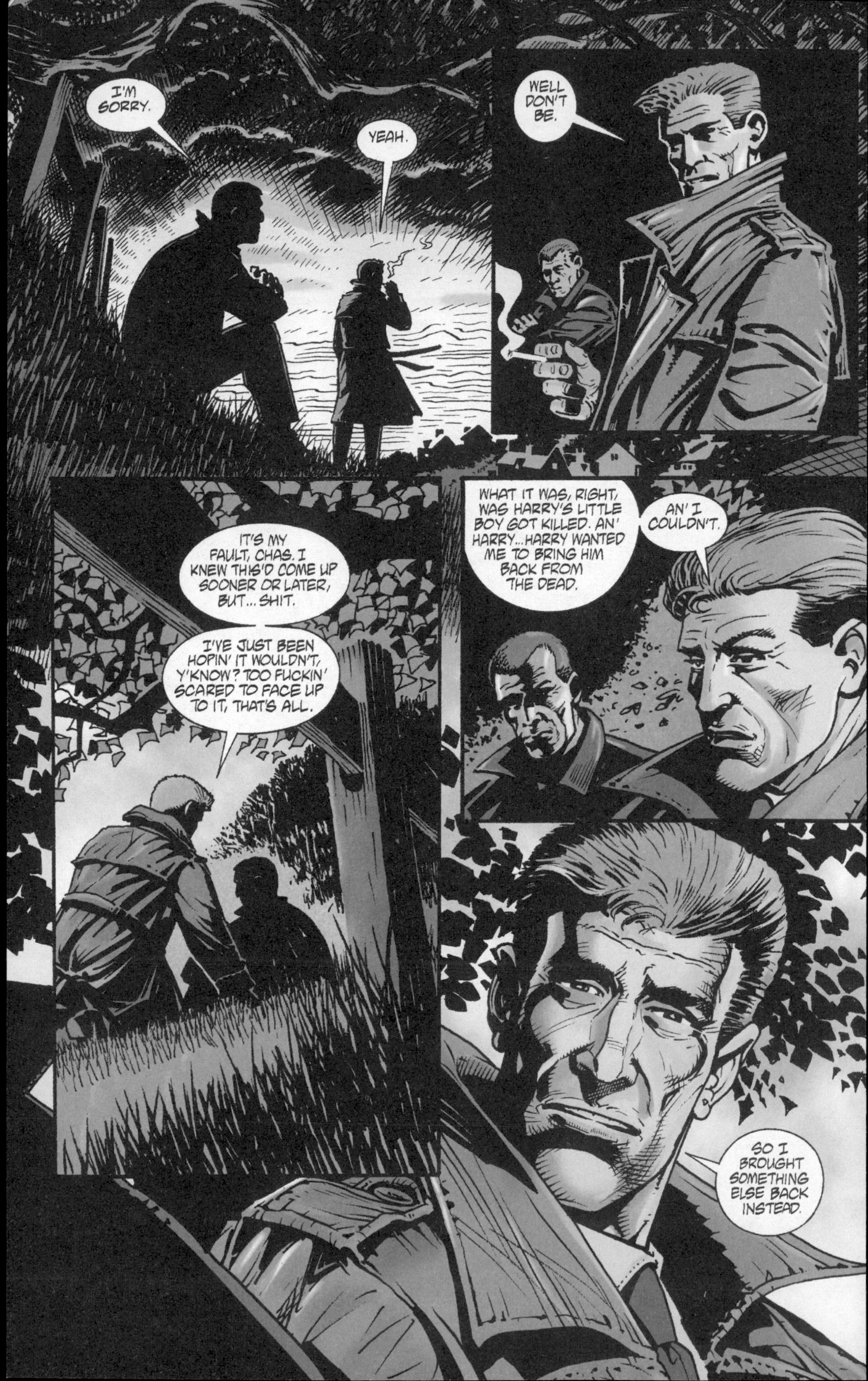
I'M SORRY.
YEAH.
WELL DON'T BE.
IT'S MY FAULT, CHAS. I KNEW THIS'D COME UP SOONER OR LATER, BUT... SHIT.
I'VE JUST BEEN HOPIN' IT WOULDN'T, Y'KNOW? TOO FUCKIN' SCARED TO FACE UP TO IT, THAT'S ALL.
WHAT IT WAS, RIGHT, WAS HARRY'S LITTLE BOY GOT KILLED. AN' HARRY...HARRY WANTED ME TO BRING HIM BACK FROM THE DEAD.
AN' I COULDN'T.
SO I BROUGHT SOMETHING ELSE BACK INSTEAD.

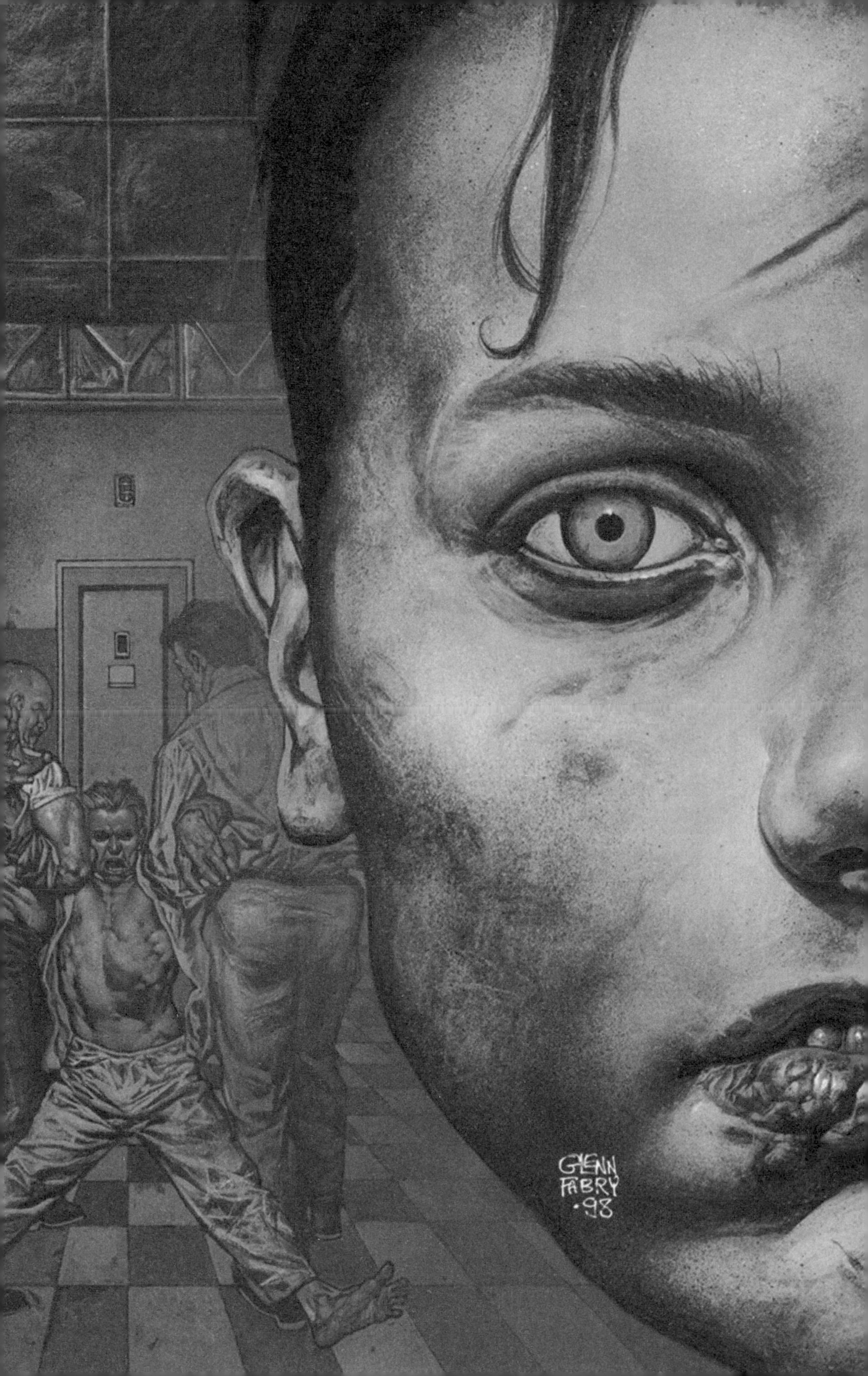
GLENN FABRY ·98

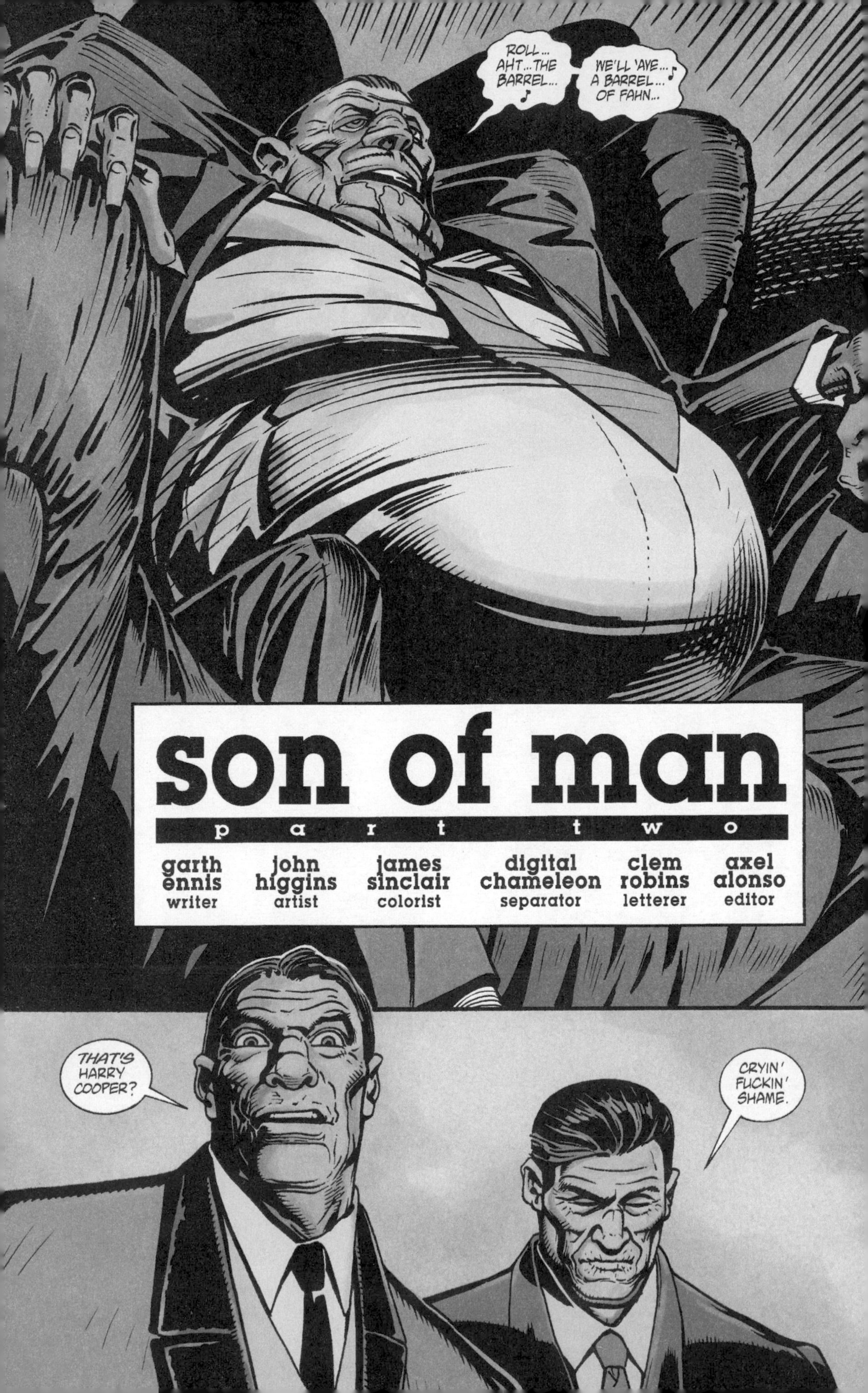

ROLL... AHT... THE BARREL... ♪
WE'LL 'AYE... A BARREL... ♪ OF FAHN...
son of man
part two
garth ennis writer
john higgins artist
james sinclair colorist
digital chameleon separator
clem robins letterer
axel alonso editor
THAT'S HARRY COOPER?
CRYIN' FUCKIN' SHAME.

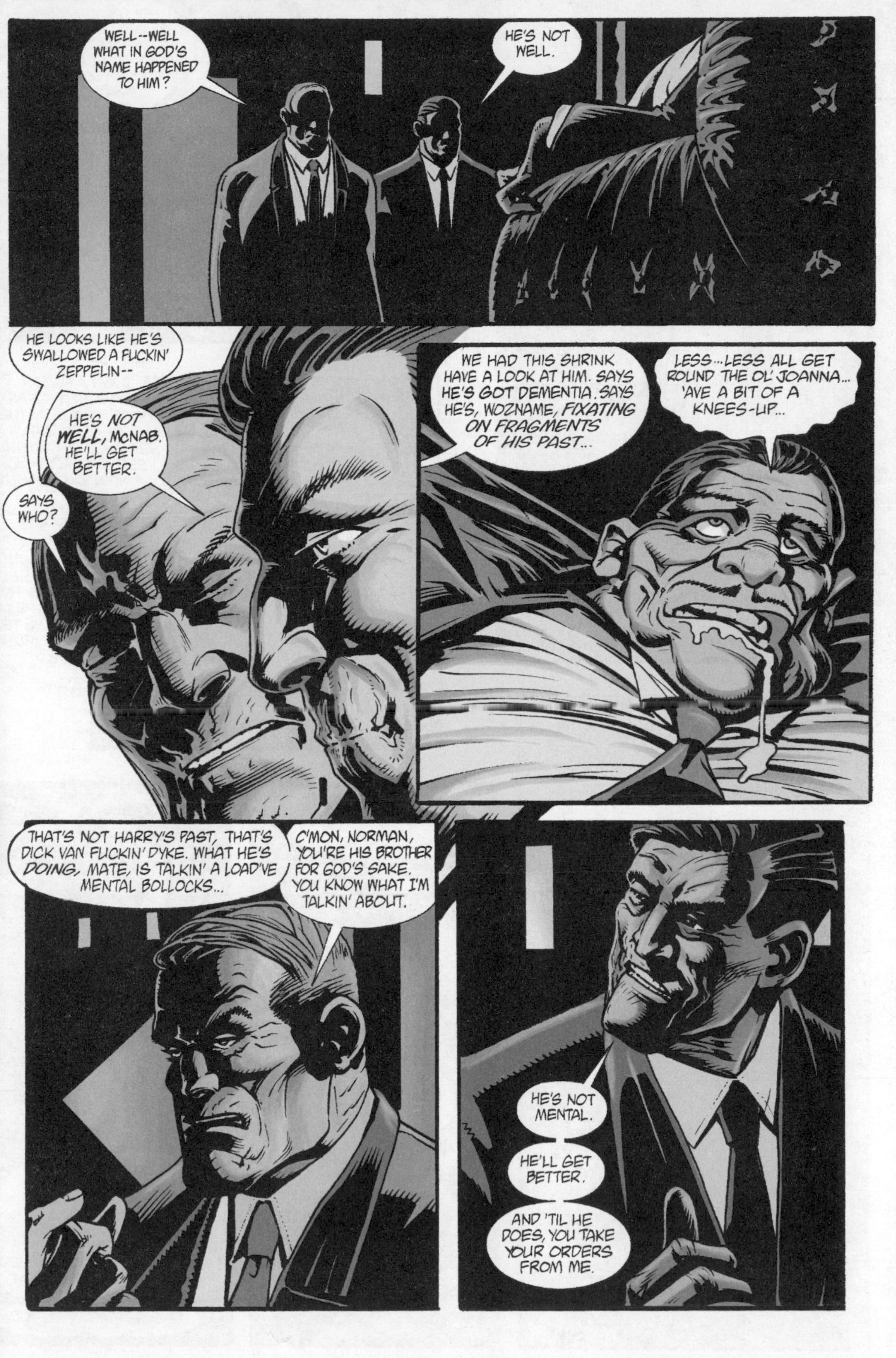
WELL--WELL WHAT IN GOD'S NAME HAPPENED TO HIM?
HE'S NOT WELL.
HE LOOKS LIKE HE'S SWALLOWED A FUCKIN' ZEPPELIN--
HE'S *NOT* **WELL**, McNAB. HE'LL GET BETTER.
SAYS WHO?
WE HAD THIS SHRINK HAVE A LOOK AT HIM. SAYS HE'S GOT DEMENTIA. SAYS HE'S, WOZNAME, *FIXATING ON FRAGMENTS OF HIS PAST*...
LESS...LESS ALL GET ROUND THE OL' JOANNA... 'AVE A BIT OF A KNEES-UP...
THAT'S NOT HARRY'S PAST, THAT'S DICK VAN FUCKIN' DYKE. WHAT HE'S *DOING*, MATE, IS TALKIN' A LOAD'VE MENTAL BOLLOCKS...
C'MON, NORMAN, YOU'RE HIS BROTHER FOR GOD'S SAKE. YOU KNOW WHAT I'M TALKIN' ABOUT.
HE'S NOT MENTAL.
HE'LL GET BETTER.
AND 'TIL HE DOES, YOU TAKE YOUR ORDERS FROM ME.

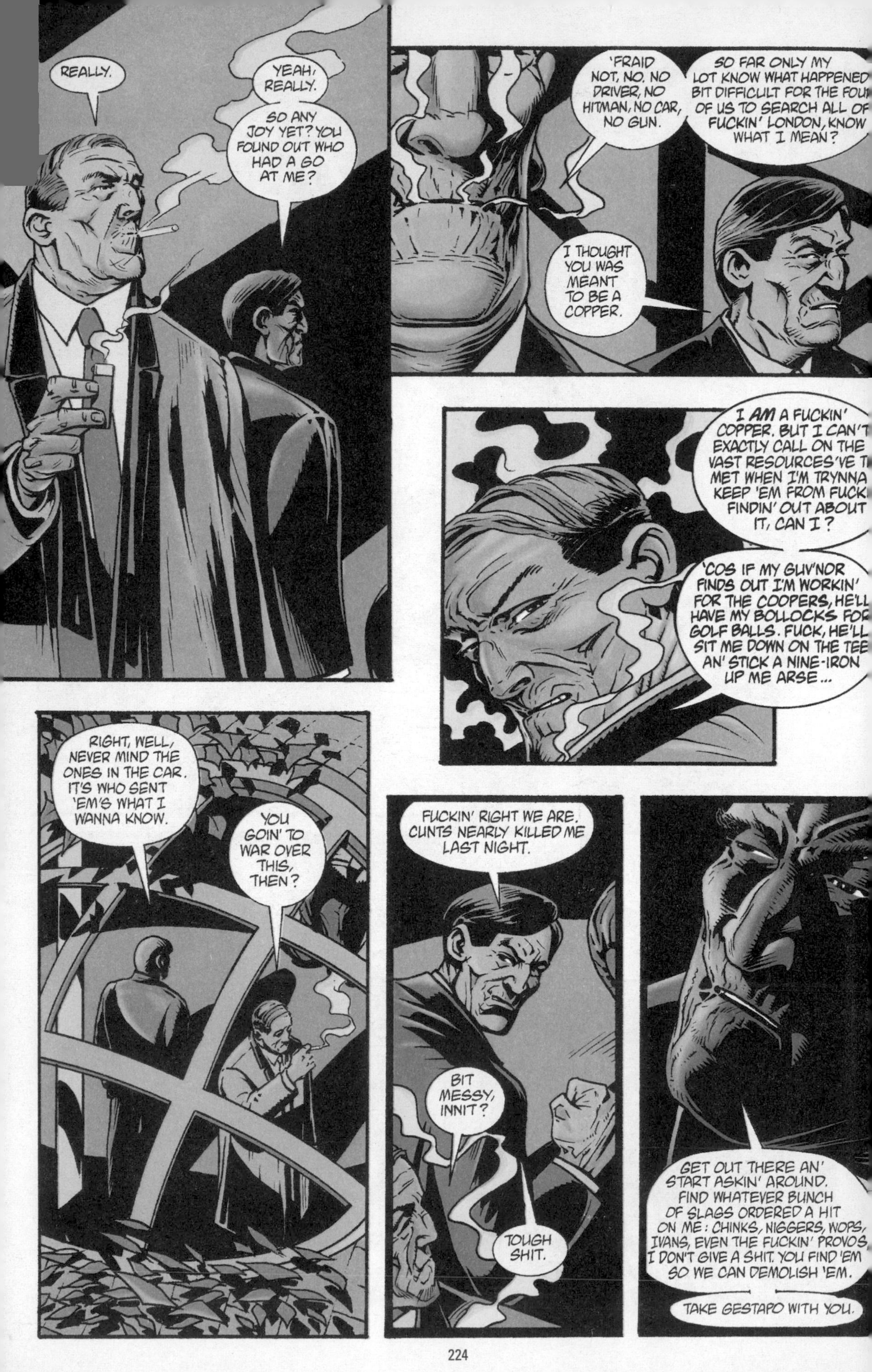
REALLY.
YEAH, REALLY.
SO ANY JOY YET? YOU FOUND OUT WHO HAD A GO AT ME?
'FRAID NOT, NO. NO DRIVER, NO HITMAN, NO CAR, NO GUN.
SO FAR ONLY MY LOT KNOW WHAT HAPPENED. BIT DIFFICULT FOR THE FOU OF US TO SEARCH ALL OF FUCKIN' LONDON, KNOW WHAT I MEAN?
I THOUGHT YOU WAS MEANT TO BE A COPPER.
I AM A FUCKIN' COPPER. BUT I CAN'T EXACTLY CALL ON THE VAST RESOURCES'VE T MET WHEN I'M TRYNNA KEEP 'EM FROM FUCK FINDIN' OUT ABOUT IT, CAN I?
'COS IF MY GUV'NOR FINDS OUT I'M WORKIN' FOR THE COOPERS, HE'LL HAVE MY BOLLOCKS FOR GOLF BALLS. FUCK, HE'LL SIT ME DOWN ON THE TEE AN' STICK A NINE-IRON UP ME ARSE...
RIGHT, WELL, NEVER MIND THE ONES IN THE CAR. IT'S WHO SENT 'EM'S WHAT I WANNA KNOW.
YOU GOIN' TO WAR OVER THIS, THEN?
FUCKIN' RIGHT WE ARE. CUNTS NEARLY KILLED ME LAST NIGHT.
BIT MESSY, INNIT?
TOUGH SHIT.
GET OUT THERE AN' START ASKIN' AROUND. FIND WHATEVER BUNCH OF SLAGS ORDERED A HIT ON ME: CHINKS, NIGGERS, WOPS, IVANS, EVEN THE FUCKIN' PROVOS. I DON'T GIVE A SHIT. YOU FIND 'EM SO WE CAN DEMOLISH 'EM.
TAKE GESTAPO WITH YOU.

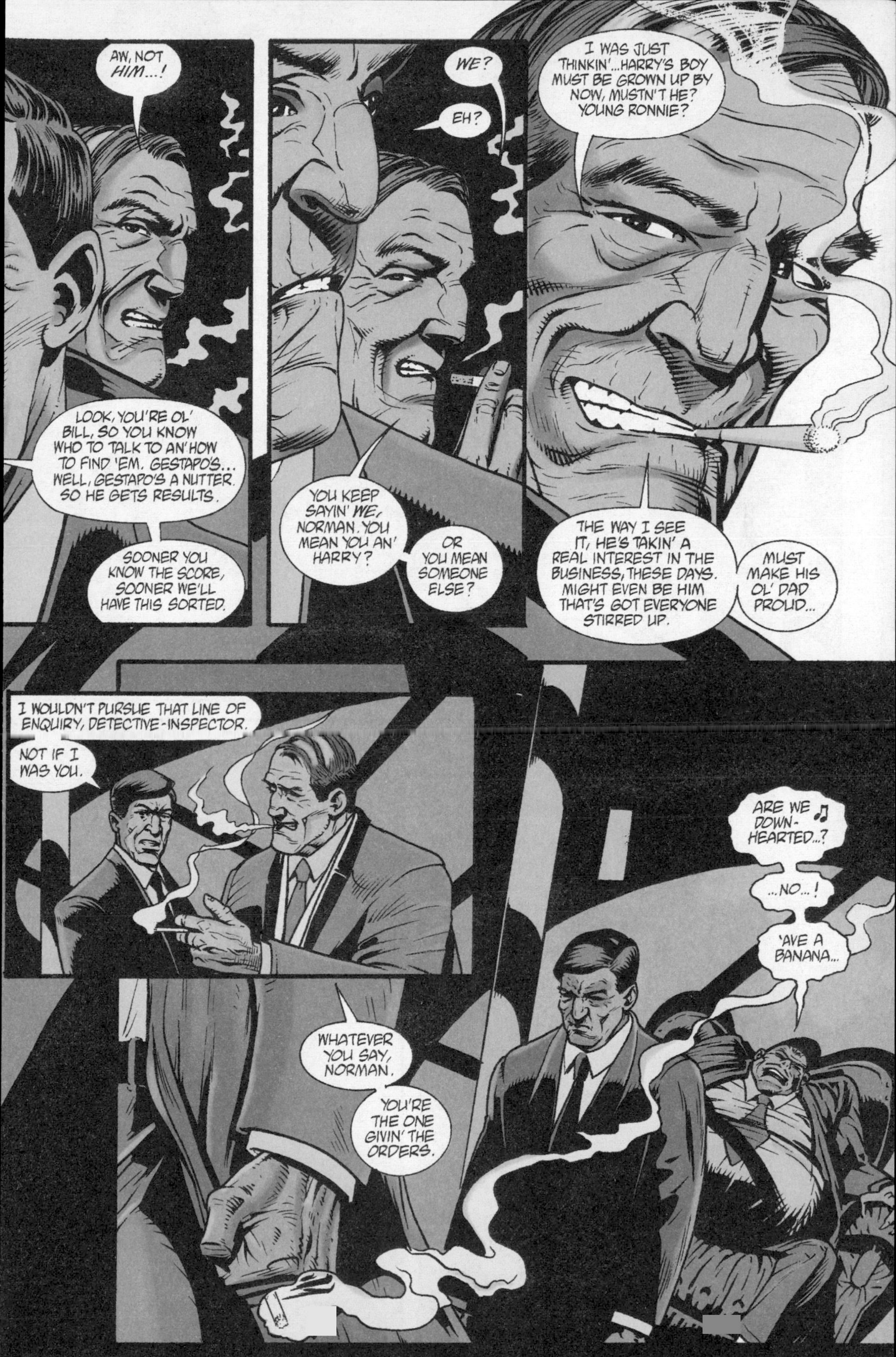
AW, NOT HIM...!
LOOK, YOU'RE OL' BILL, SO YOU KNOW WHO TO TALK TO AN' HOW TO FIND 'EM. GESTAPO'S... WELL, GESTAPO'S A NUTTER. SO HE GETS RESULTS.
SOONER YOU KNOW THE SCORE, SOONER WE'LL HAVE THIS SORTED.
WE?
EH?
YOU KEEP SAYIN' WE, NORMAN. YOU MEAN YOU AN' HARRY?
OR YOU MEAN SOMEONE ELSE?
I WAS JUST THINKIN'...HARRY'S BOY MUST BE GROWN UP BY NOW, MUSTN'T HE? YOUNG RONNIE?
THE WAY I SEE IT, HE'S TAKIN' A REAL INTEREST IN THE BUSINESS, THESE DAYS. MIGHT EVEN BE HIM THAT'S GOT EVERYONE STIRRED UP.
MUST MAKE HIS OL' DAD PROUD...
I WOULDN'T PURSUE THAT LINE OF ENQUIRY, DETECTIVE-INSPECTOR.
NOT IF I WAS YOU.
WHATEVER YOU SAY, NORMAN.
YOU'RE THE ONE GIVIN' THE ORDERS.
ARE WE ♫ DOWN-HEARTED...?
...NO...!
'AVE A BANANA...

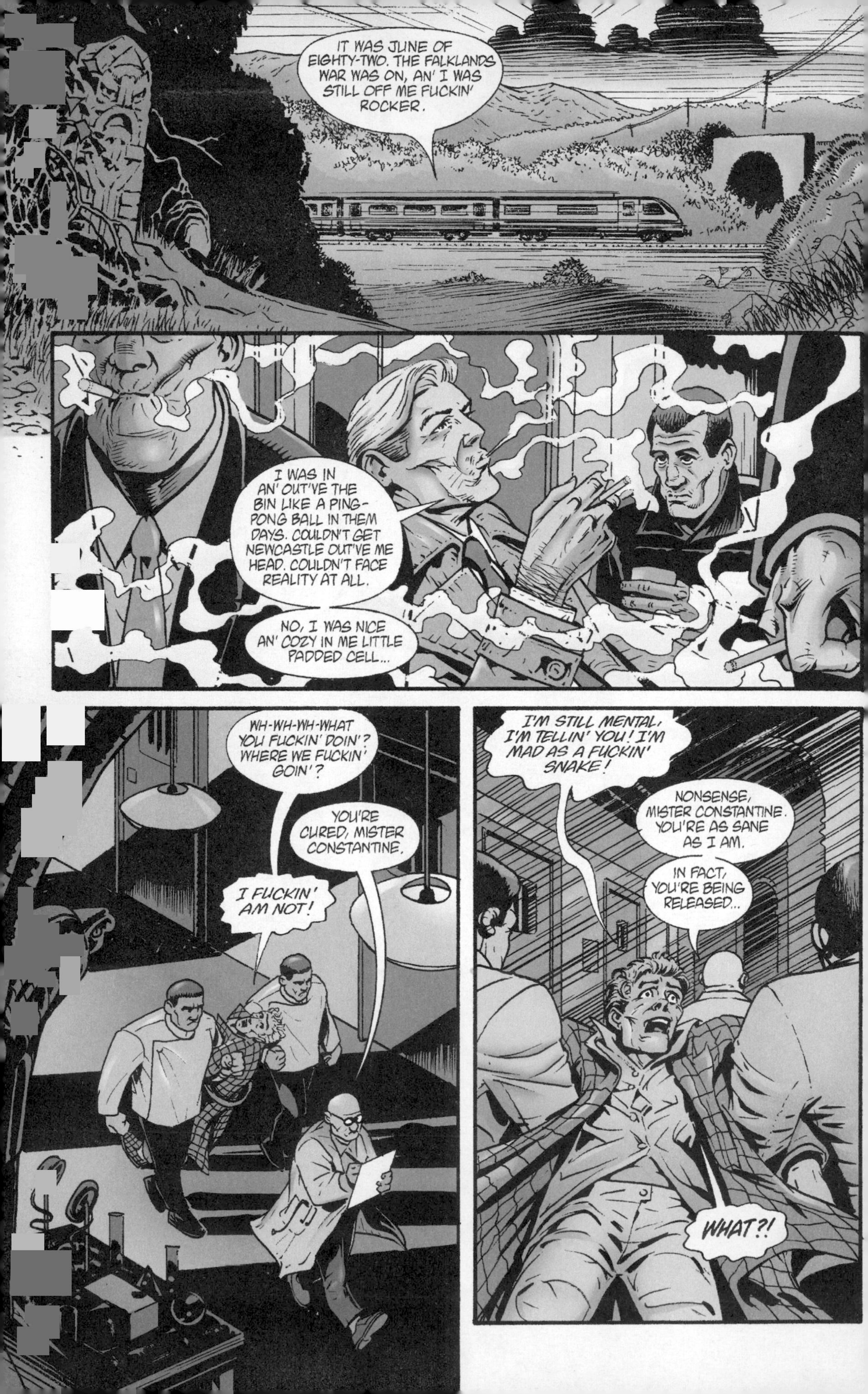
IT WAS JUNE OF EIGHTY-TWO. THE FALKLANDS WAR WAS ON, AN' I WAS STILL OFF ME FUCKIN' ROCKER.
I WAS IN AN' OUT'VE THE BIN LIKE A PING-PONG BALL IN THEM DAYS. COULDN'T GET NEWCASTLE OUT'VE ME HEAD. COULDN'T FACE REALITY AT ALL.
NO, I WAS NICE AN' COZY IN ME LITTLE PADDED CELL...
WH-WH-WH-WHAT YOU FUCKIN' DOIN'? WHERE WE FUCKIN' GOIN'?
YOU'RE CURED, MISTER CONSTANTINE.
I FUCKIN' AM NOT!
I'M STILL MENTAL, I'M TELLIN' YOU! I'M MAD AS A FUCKIN' SNAKE!
NONSENSE, MISTER CONSTANTINE. YOU'RE AS SANE AS I AM.
IN FACT, YOU'RE BEING RELEASED...
WHAT?!

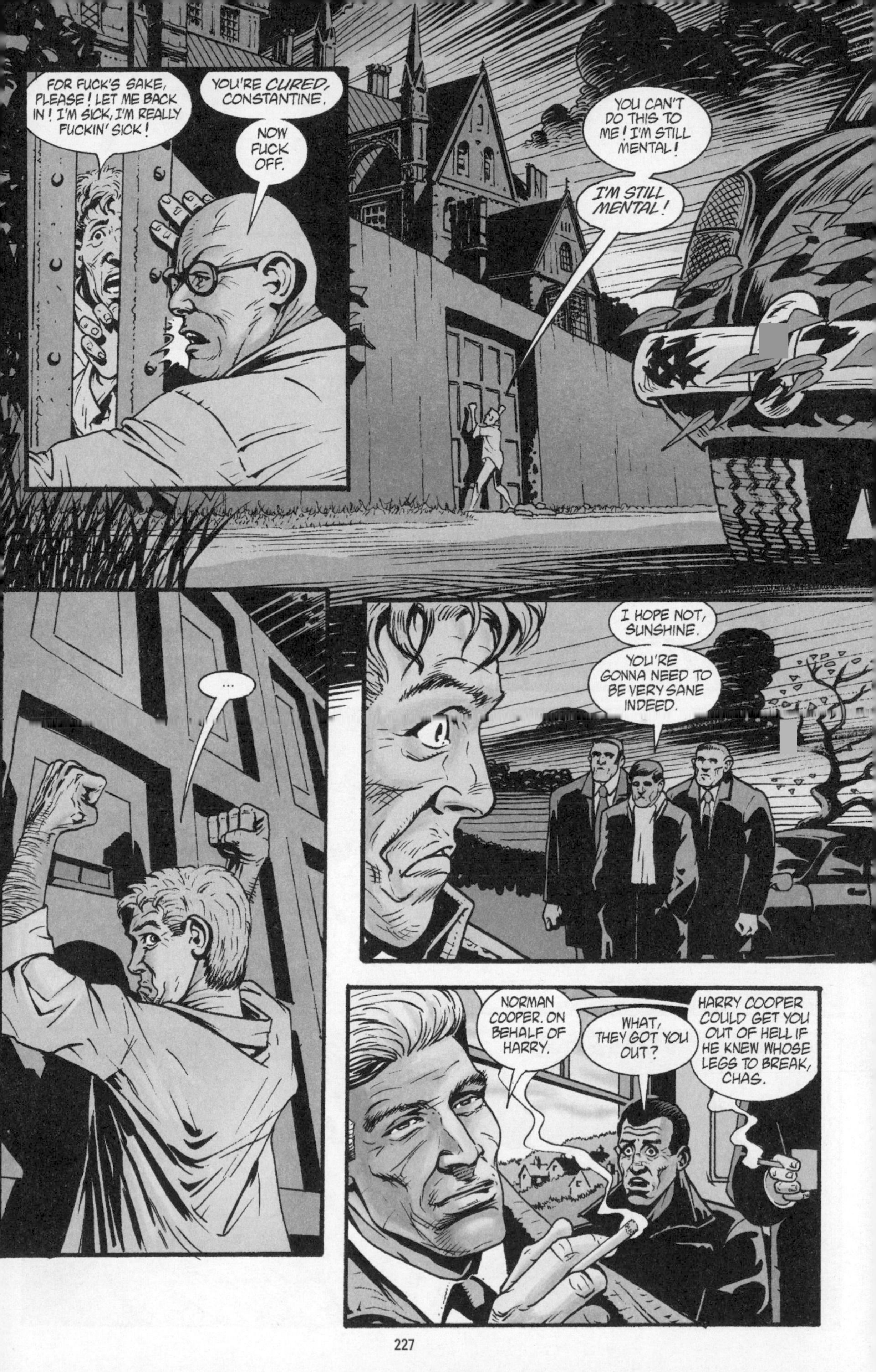
FOR FUCK'S SAKE, PLEASE! LET ME BACK IN! I'M SICK, I'M REALLY FUCKIN' SICK!
YOU'RE CURED, CONSTANTINE.
NOW FUCK OFF.
YOU CAN'T DO THIS TO ME! I'M STILL MENTAL!
I'M STILL MENTAL!
...
I HOPE NOT, SUNSHINE.
YOU'RE GONNA NEED TO BE VERY SANE INDEED.
NORMAN COOPER. ON BEHALF OF HARRY.
WHAT, THEY GOT YOU OUT?
HARRY COOPER COULD GET YOU OUT OF HELL IF HE KNEW WHOSE LEGS TO BREAK, CHAS.

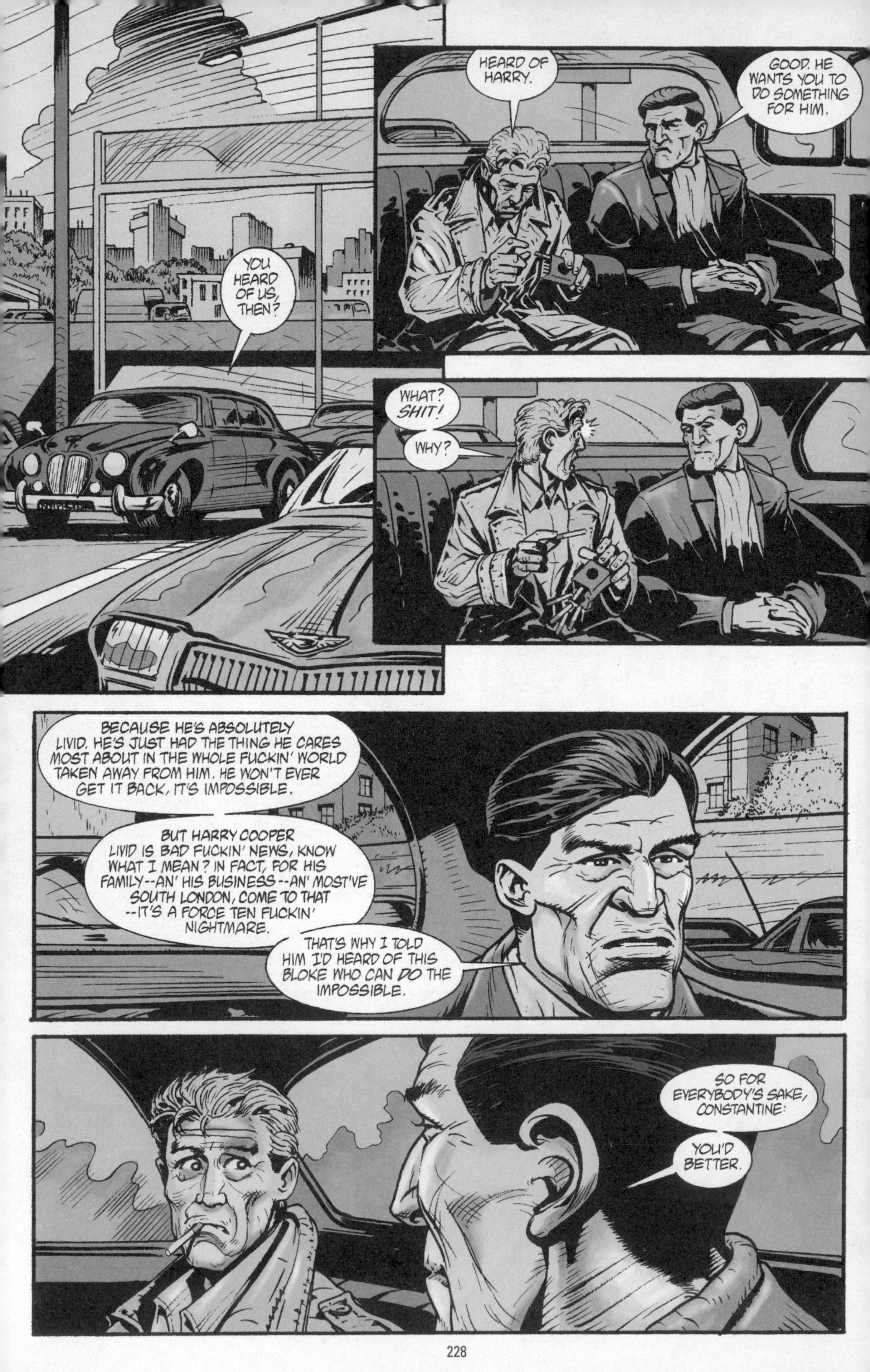
YOU HEARD OF US, THEN?
HEARD OF HARRY.
GOOD. HE WANTS YOU TO DO SOMETHING FOR HIM.
WHAT? SHIT!
WHY?
BECAUSE HE'S ABSOLUTELY LIVID. HE'S JUST HAD THE THING HE CARES MOST ABOUT IN THE WHOLE FUCKIN' WORLD TAKEN AWAY FROM HIM. HE WON'T EVER GET IT BACK, IT'S IMPOSSIBLE.
BUT HARRY COOPER LIVID IS BAD FUCKIN' NEWS, KNOW WHAT I MEAN? IN FACT, FOR HIS FAMILY--AN' HIS BUSINESS--AN' MOST'VE SOUTH LONDON, COME TO THAT --IT'S A FORCE TEN FUCKIN' NIGHTMARE.
THAT'S WHY I TOLD HIM I'D HEARD OF THIS BLOKE WHO CAN DO THE IMPOSSIBLE.
SO FOR EVERYBODY'S SAKE, CONSTANTINE:
YOU'D BETTER.

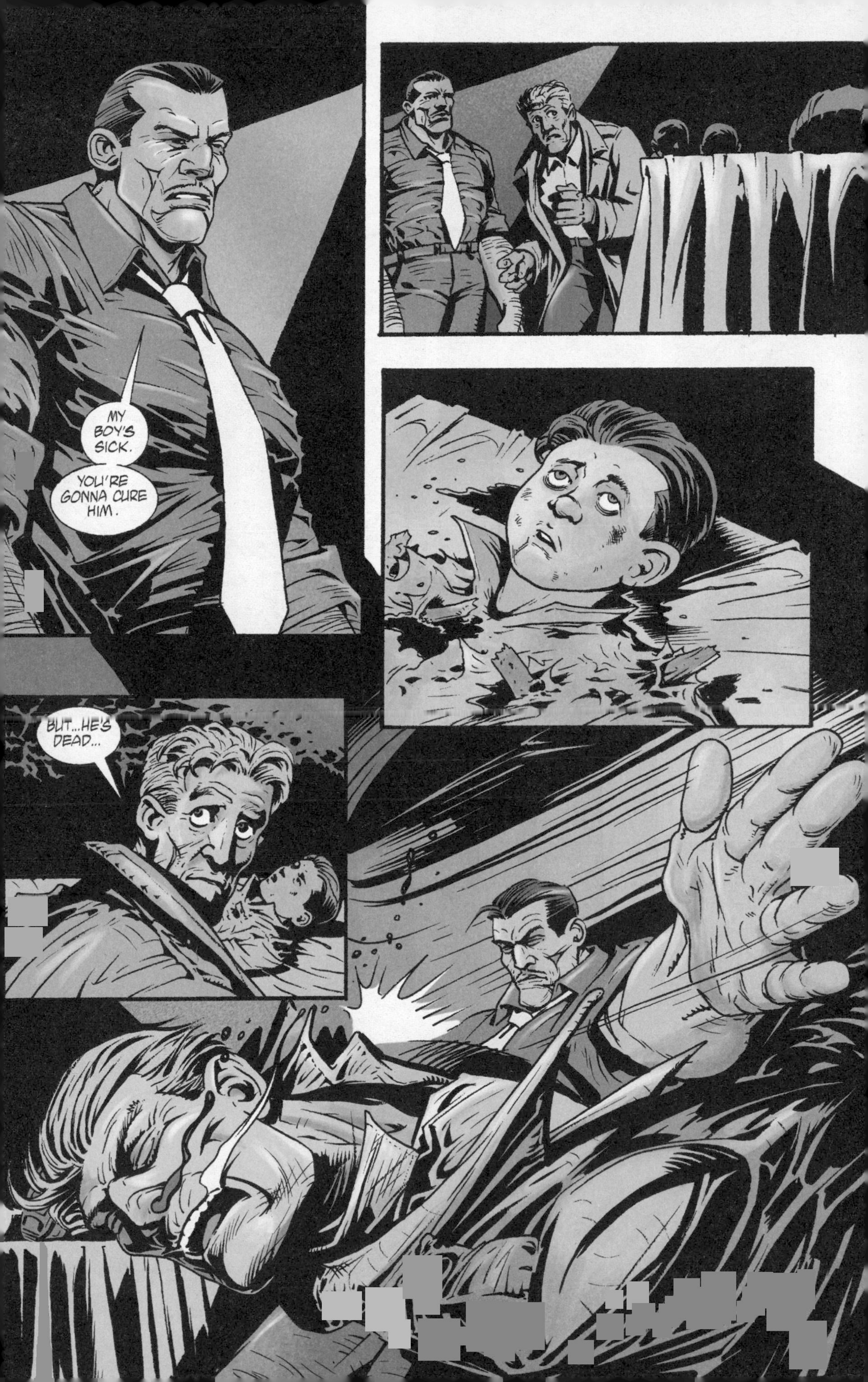
MY BOY'S SICK.
YOU'RE GONNA CURE HIM.
BUT...HE'S DEAD...

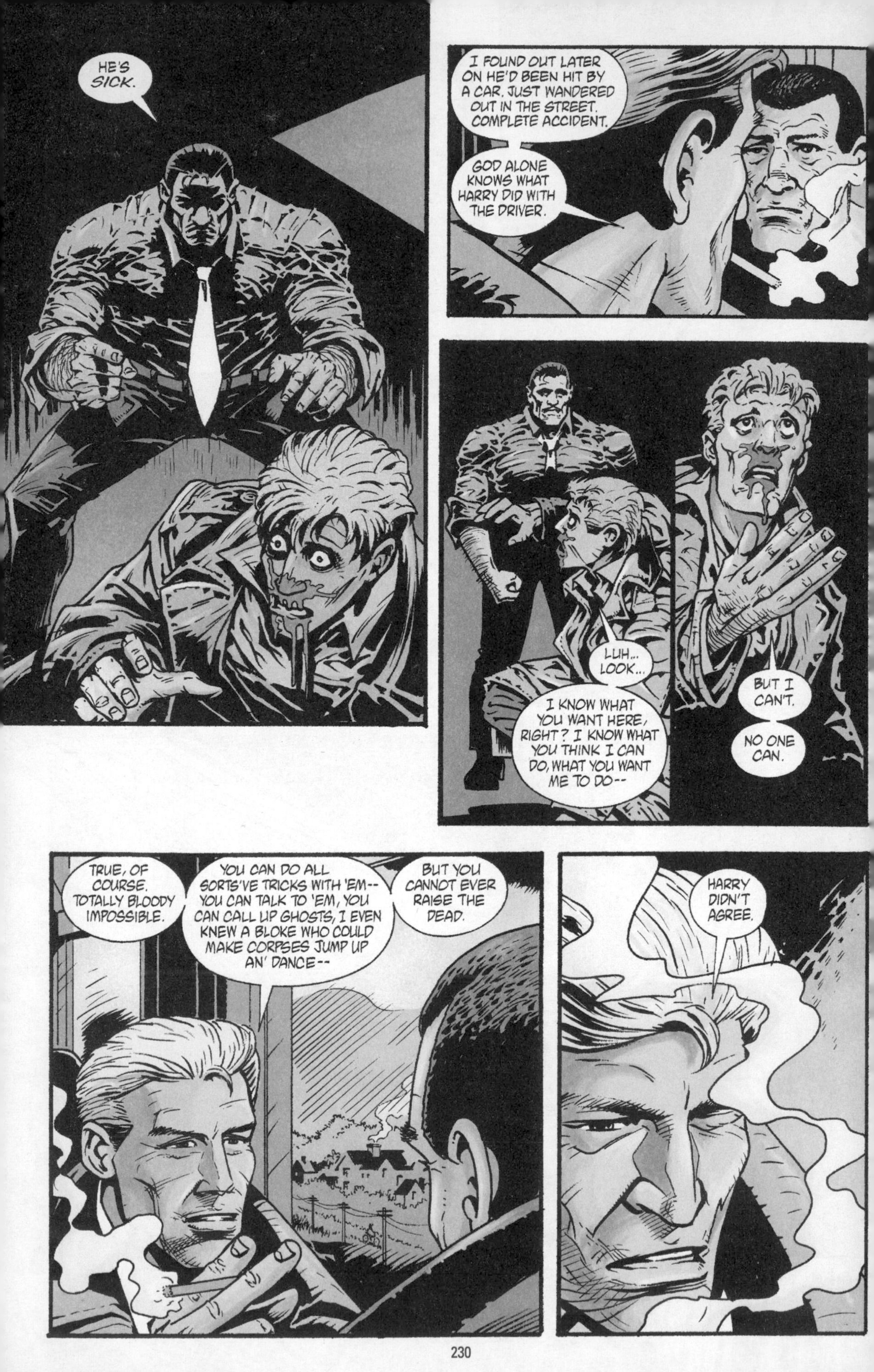
HE'S SICK.
I FOUND OUT LATER ON HE'D BEEN HIT BY A CAR. JUST WANDERED OUT IN THE STREET. COMPLETE ACCIDENT.
GOD ALONE KNOWS WHAT HARRY DID WITH THE DRIVER.
LUH... LOOK...
I KNOW WHAT YOU WANT HERE, RIGHT? I KNOW WHAT YOU THINK I CAN DO, WHAT YOU WANT ME TO DO--
BUT I CAN'T.
NO ONE CAN.
TRUE, OF COURSE. TOTALLY BLOODY IMPOSSIBLE.
YOU CAN DO ALL SORTS'VE TRICKS WITH 'EM--YOU CAN TALK TO 'EM, YOU CAN CALL UP GHOSTS, I EVEN KNEW A BLOKE WHO COULD MAKE CORPSES JUMP UP AN' DANCE--
BUT YOU CANNOT EVER RAISE THE DEAD.
HARRY DIDN'T AGREE.

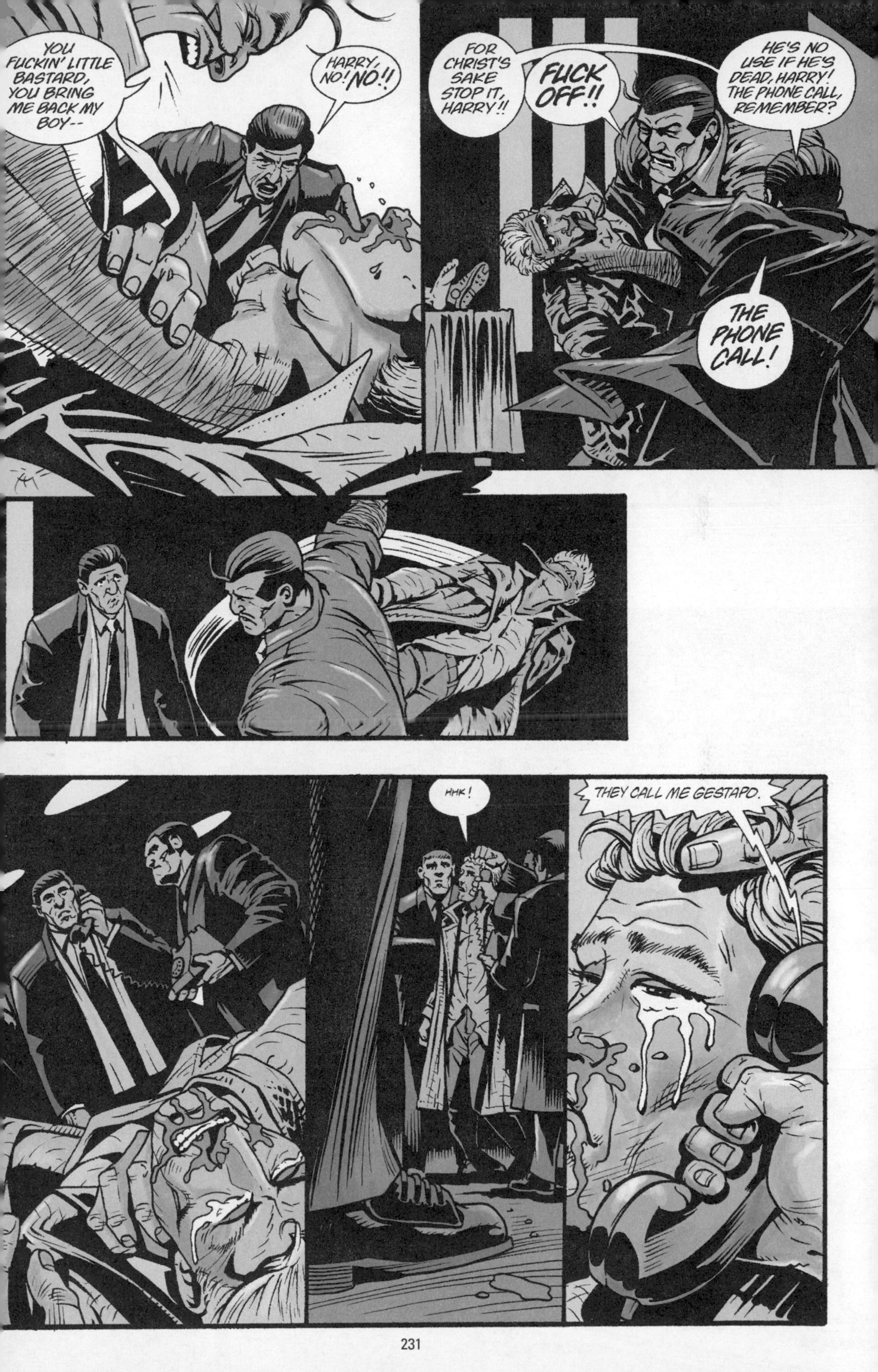
YOU FUCKIN' LITTLE BASTARD, YOU BRING ME BACK MY BOY--
HARRY, NO! NO!!
FOR CHRIST'S SAKE STOP IT, HARRY!!
FUCK OFF!!
HE'S NO USE IF HE'S DEAD, HARRY! THE PHONE CALL, REMEMBER?
THE PHONE CALL!
HHK!
THEY CALL ME GESTAPO.

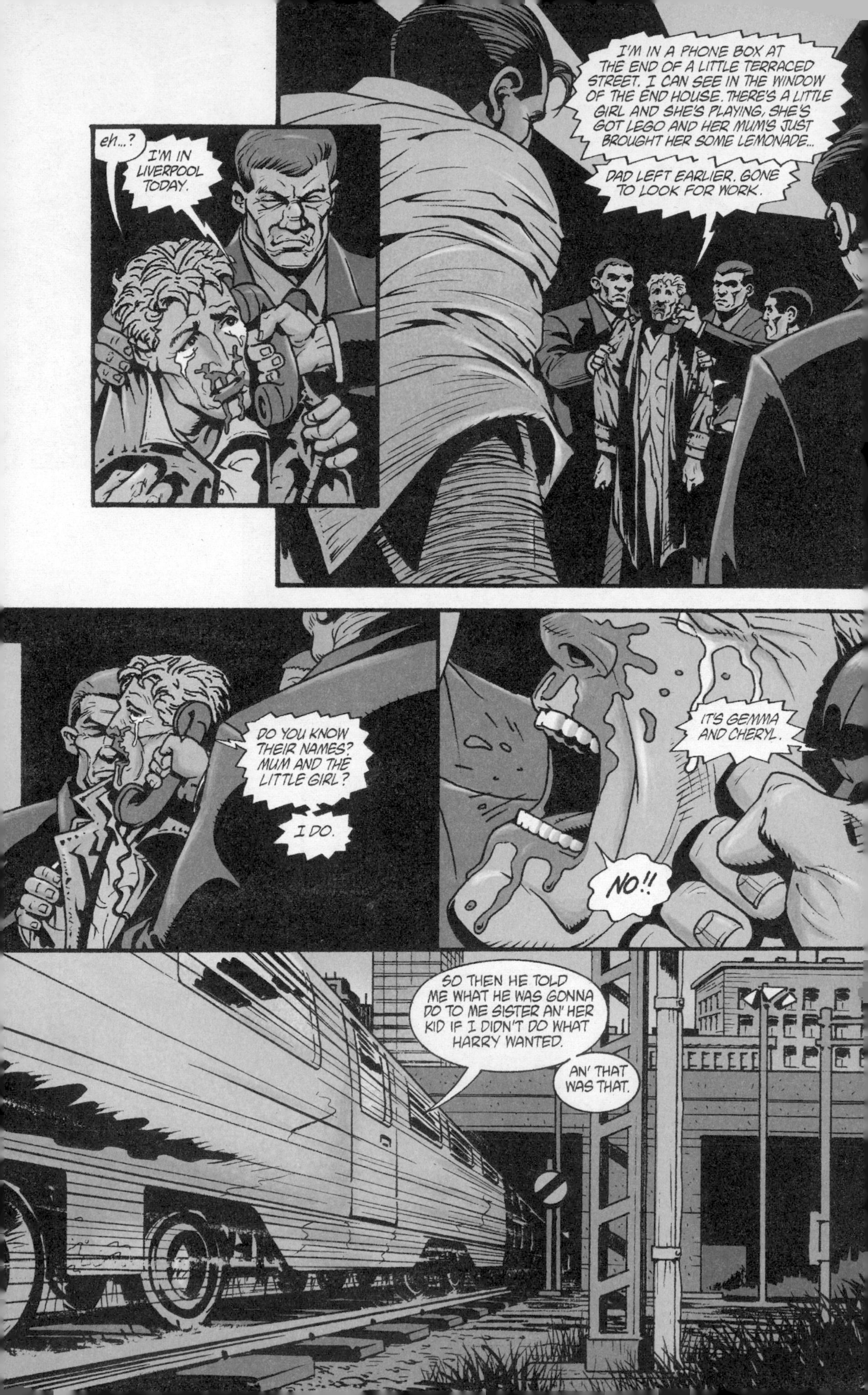
I'M IN A PHONE BOX AT THE END OF A LITTLE TERRACED STREET. I CAN SEE IN THE WINDOW OF THE END HOUSE. THERE'S A LITTLE GIRL AND SHE'S PLAYING, SHE'S GOT LEGO AND HER MUM'S JUST BROUGHT HER SOME LEMONADE...
eh...?
I'M IN LIVERPOOL TODAY.
DAD LEFT EARLIER. GONE TO LOOK FOR WORK.
DO YOU KNOW THEIR NAMES? MUM AND THE LITTLE GIRL?
I DO.
IT'S GEMMA AND CHERYL.
NO!!
SO THEN HE TOLD ME WHAT HE WAS GONNA DO TO ME SISTER AN' HER KID IF I DIDN'T DO WHAT HARRY WANTED.
AN' THAT WAS THAT.

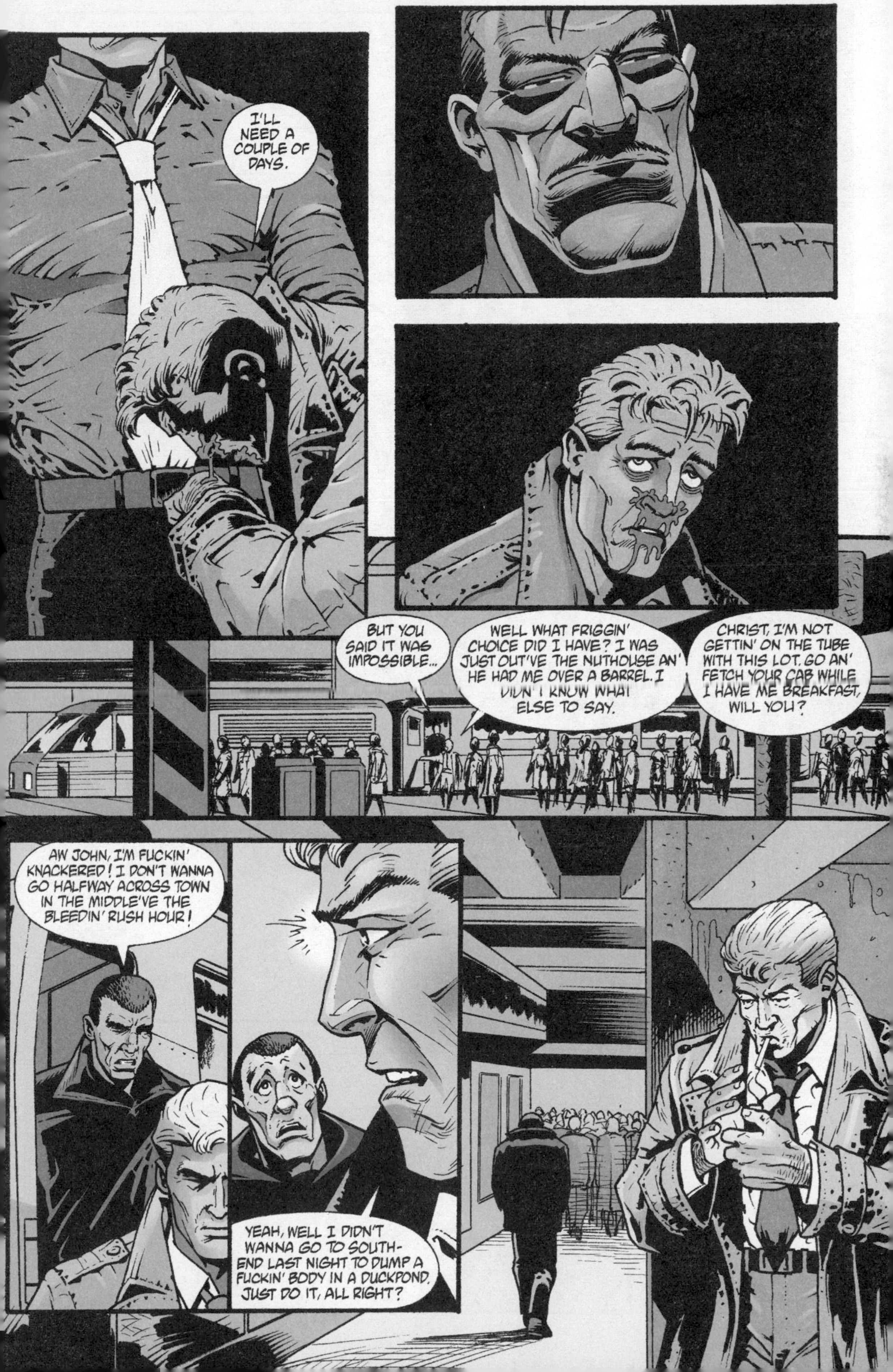
I'LL NEED A COUPLE OF DAYS.
BUT YOU SAID IT WAS IMPOSSIBLE...
WELL WHAT FRIGGIN' CHOICE DID I HAVE? I WAS JUST OUT'VE THE NUTHOUSE AN' HE HAD ME OVER A BARREL. I DIDN'T KNOW WHAT ELSE TO SAY.
CHRIST, I'M NOT GETTIN' ON THE TUBE WITH THIS LOT. GO AN' FETCH YOUR CAB WHILE I HAVE ME BREAKFAST, WILL YOU?
AW JOHN, I'M FUCKIN' KNACKERED! I DON'T WANNA GO HALFWAY ACROSS TOWN IN THE MIDDLE'VE THE BLEEDIN' RUSH HOUR!
YEAH, WELL I DIDN'T WANNA GO TO SOUTH-END LAST NIGHT TO DUMP A FUCKIN' BODY IN A DUCKPOND. JUST DO IT, ALL RIGHT?

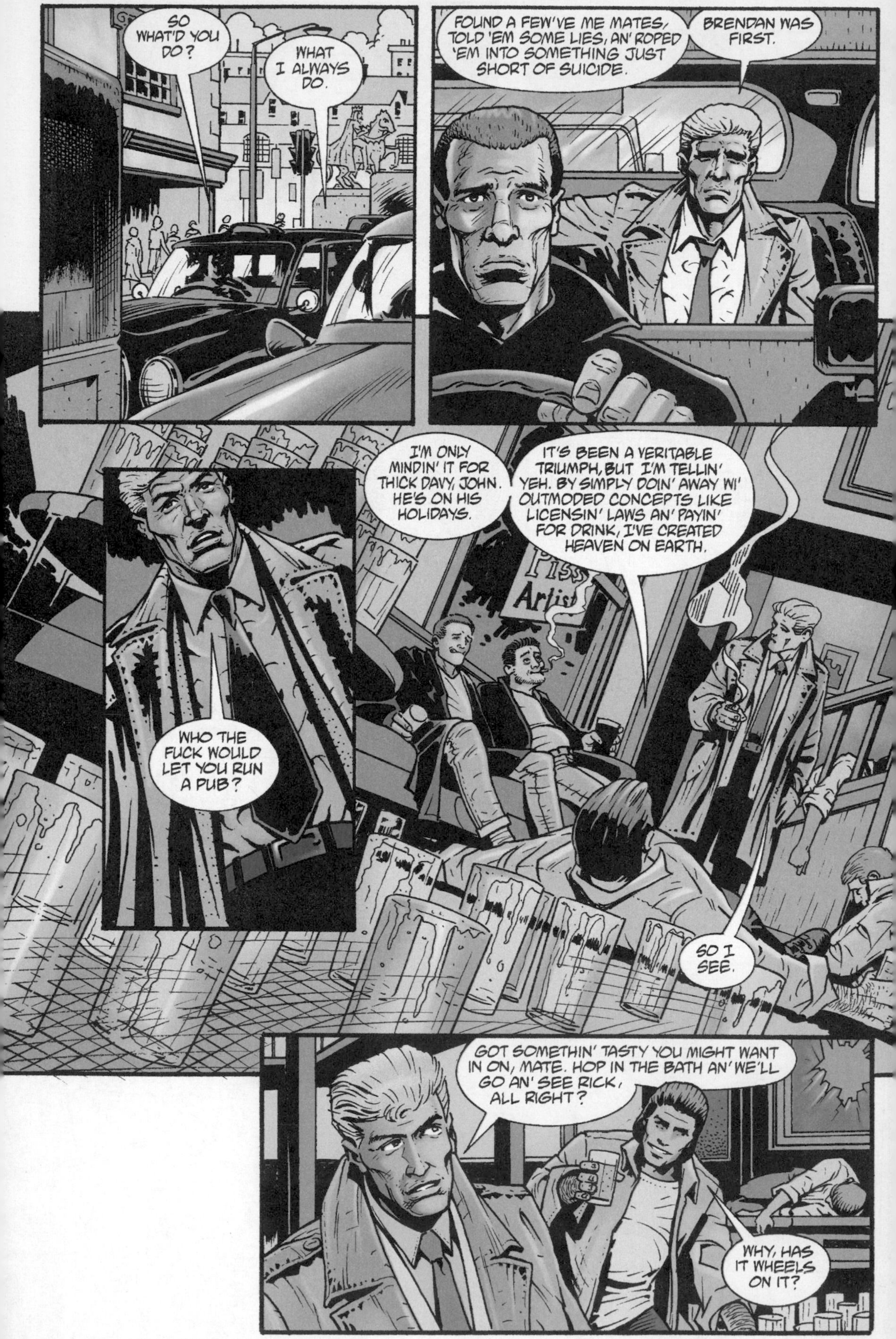
SO WHAT'D YOU DO?
WHAT I ALWAYS DO.
FOUND A FEW'VE ME MATES, TOLD 'EM SOME LIES, AN' ROPED 'EM INTO SOMETHING JUST SHORT OF SUICIDE.
BRENDAN WAS FIRST.
WHO THE FUCK WOULD LET YOU RUN A PUB?
I'M ONLY MINDIN' IT FOR THICK DAVY, JOHN. HE'S ON HIS HOLIDAYS.
IT'S BEEN A VERITABLE TRIUMPH, BUT I'M TELLIN' YEH. BY SIMPLY DOIN' AWAY WI' OUTMODED CONCEPTS LIKE LICENSIN' LAWS AN' PAYIN' FOR DRINK, I'VE CREATED HEAVEN ON EARTH.
Piss Artist
SO I SEE.
GOT SOMETHIN' TASTY YOU MIGHT WANT IN ON, MATE. HOP IN THE BATH AN' WE'LL GO AN' SEE RICK, ALL RIGHT?
WHY, HAS IT WHEELS ON IT?

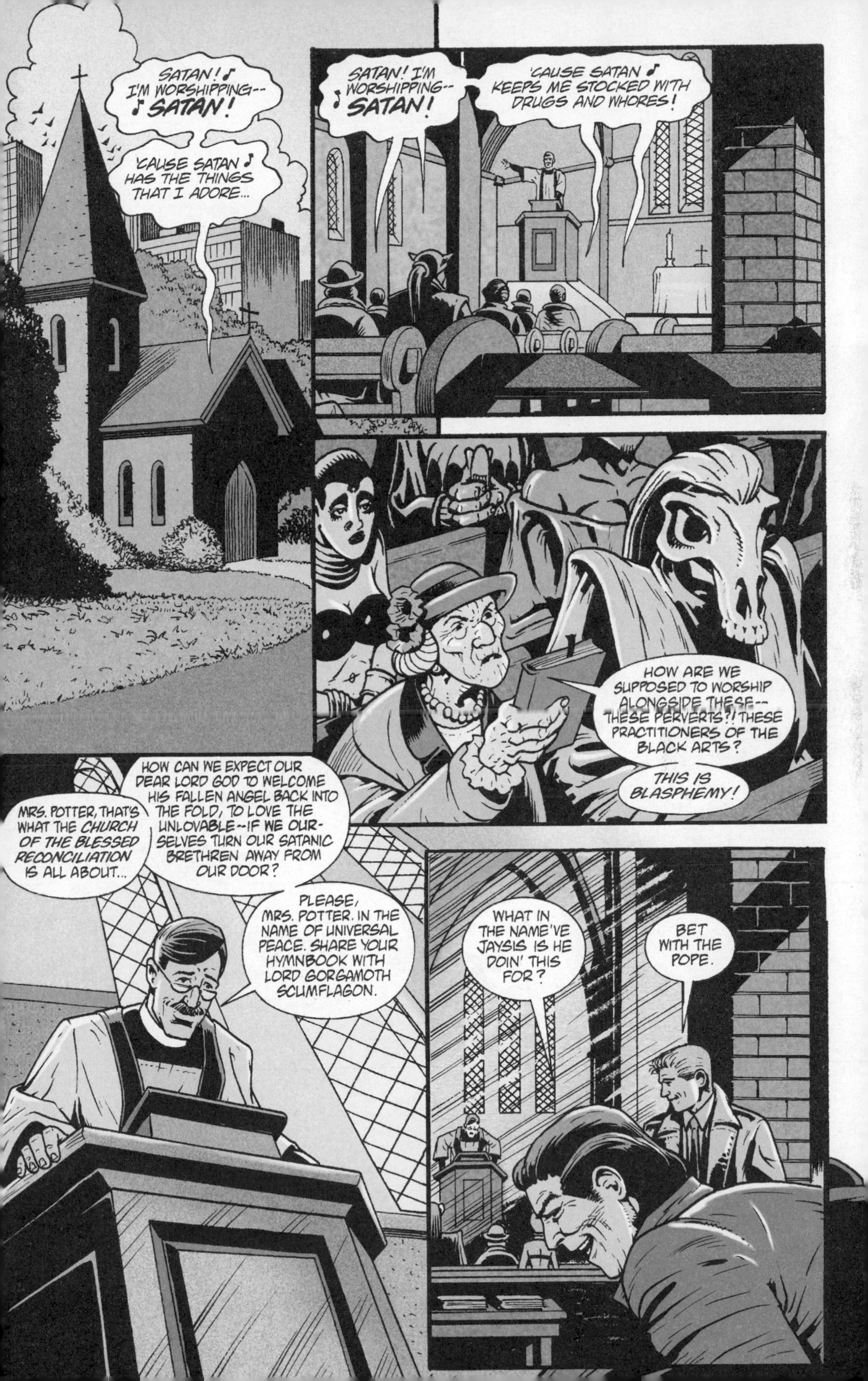

SATAN! ♪ I'M WORSHIPPING-- ♪ SATAN!
'CAUSE SATAN ♪ HAS THE THINGS THAT I ADORE...
SATAN! I'M WORSHIPPING-- ♪ SATAN!
'CAUSE SATAN ♪ KEEPS ME STOCKED WITH DRUGS AND WHORES!
HOW ARE WE SUPPOSED TO WORSHIP ALONGSIDE THESE-- THESE PERVERTS?! THESE PRACTITIONERS OF THE BLACK ARTS?
THIS IS BLASPHEMY!
MRS. POTTER, THAT'S WHAT THE CHURCH OF THE BLESSED RECONCILIATION IS ALL ABOUT...
HOW CAN WE EXPECT OUR DEAR LORD GOD TO WELCOME HIS FALLEN ANGEL BACK INTO THE FOLD, TO LOVE THE UNLOVABLE--IF WE OURSELVES TURN OUR SATANIC BRETHREN AWAY FROM OUR DOOR?
PLEASE, MRS. POTTER. IN THE NAME OF UNIVERSAL PEACE. SHARE YOUR HYMNBOOK WITH LORD GORGAMOTH SCUMFLAGON.
WHAT IN THE NAME'VE JAYSIS IS HE DOIN' THIS FOR?
BET WITH THE POPE.

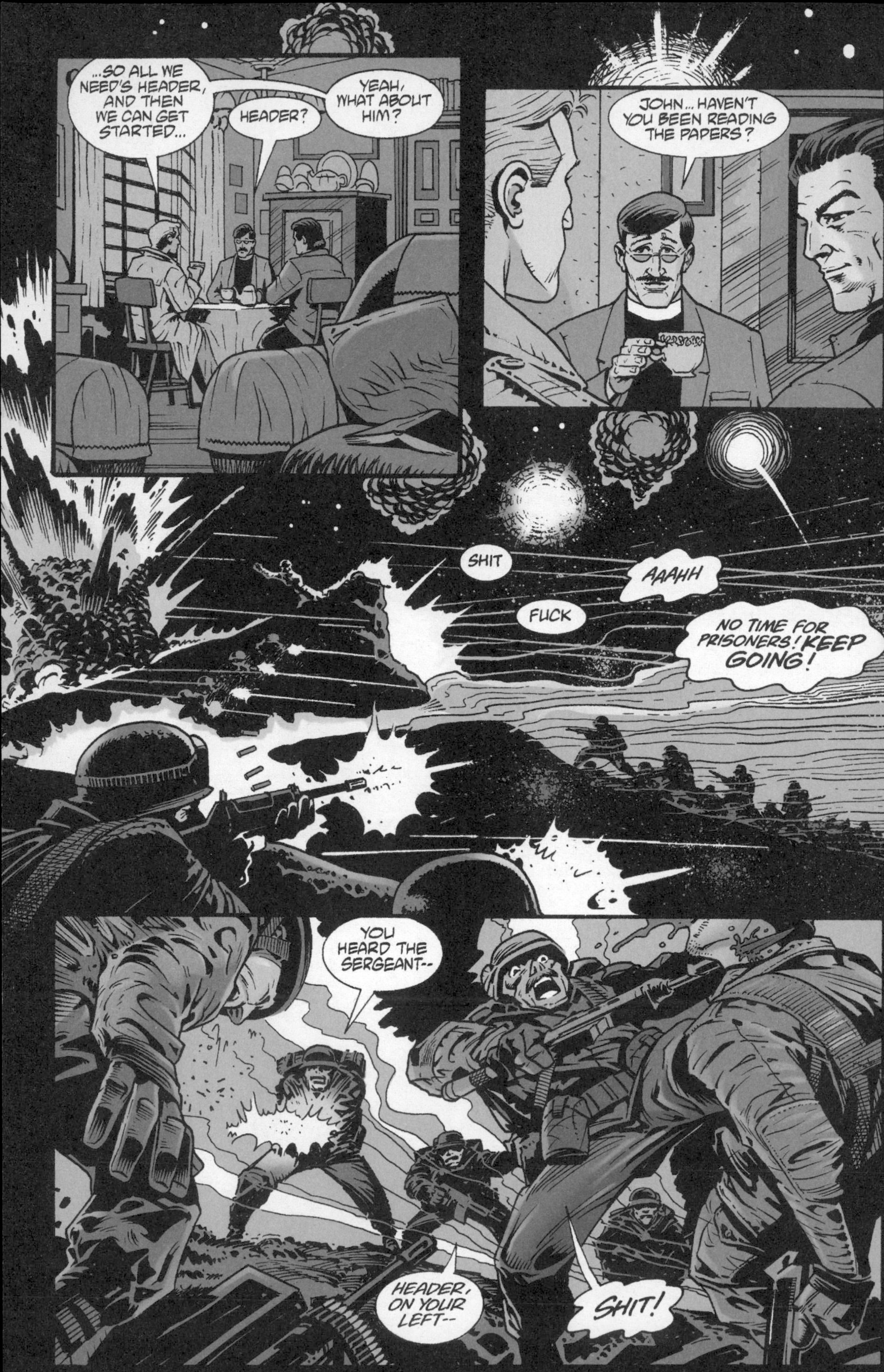
...SO ALL WE NEED'S HEADER, AND THEN WE CAN GET STARTED...
HEADER?
YEAH, WHAT ABOUT HIM?
JOHN... HAVEN'T YOU BEEN READING THE PAPERS?
SHIT
AAAHH
FUCK
NO TIME FOR PRISONERS! KEEP GOING!
YOU HEARD THE SERGEANT--
HEADER, ON YOUR LEFT--
SHIT!

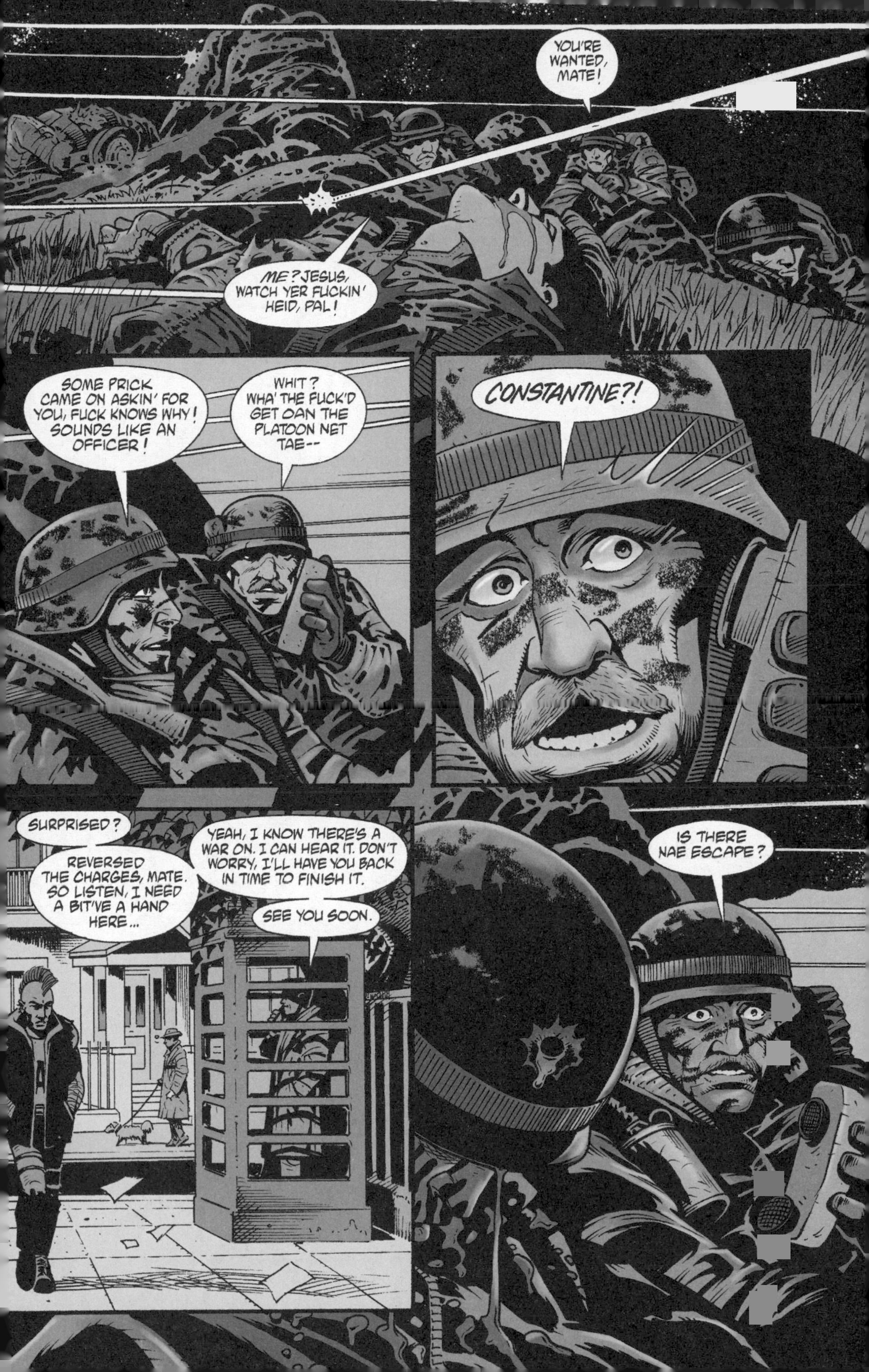
YOU'RE WANTED, MATE!
ME? JESUS, WATCH YER FUCKIN' HEID, PAL!
SOME PRICK CAME ON ASKIN' FOR YOU, FUCK KNOWS WHY! SOUNDS LIKE AN OFFICER!
WHIT? WHA' THE FUCK'D GET OAN THE PLATOON NET TAE--
CONSTANTINE?!
SURPRISED?
REVERSED THE CHARGES, MATE. SO LISTEN, I NEED A BIT'VE A HAND HERE...
YEAH, I KNOW THERE'S A WAR ON. I CAN HEAR IT. DON'T WORRY, I'LL HAVE YOU BACK IN TIME TO FINISH IT.
SEE YOU SOON.
IS THERE NAE ESCAPE?

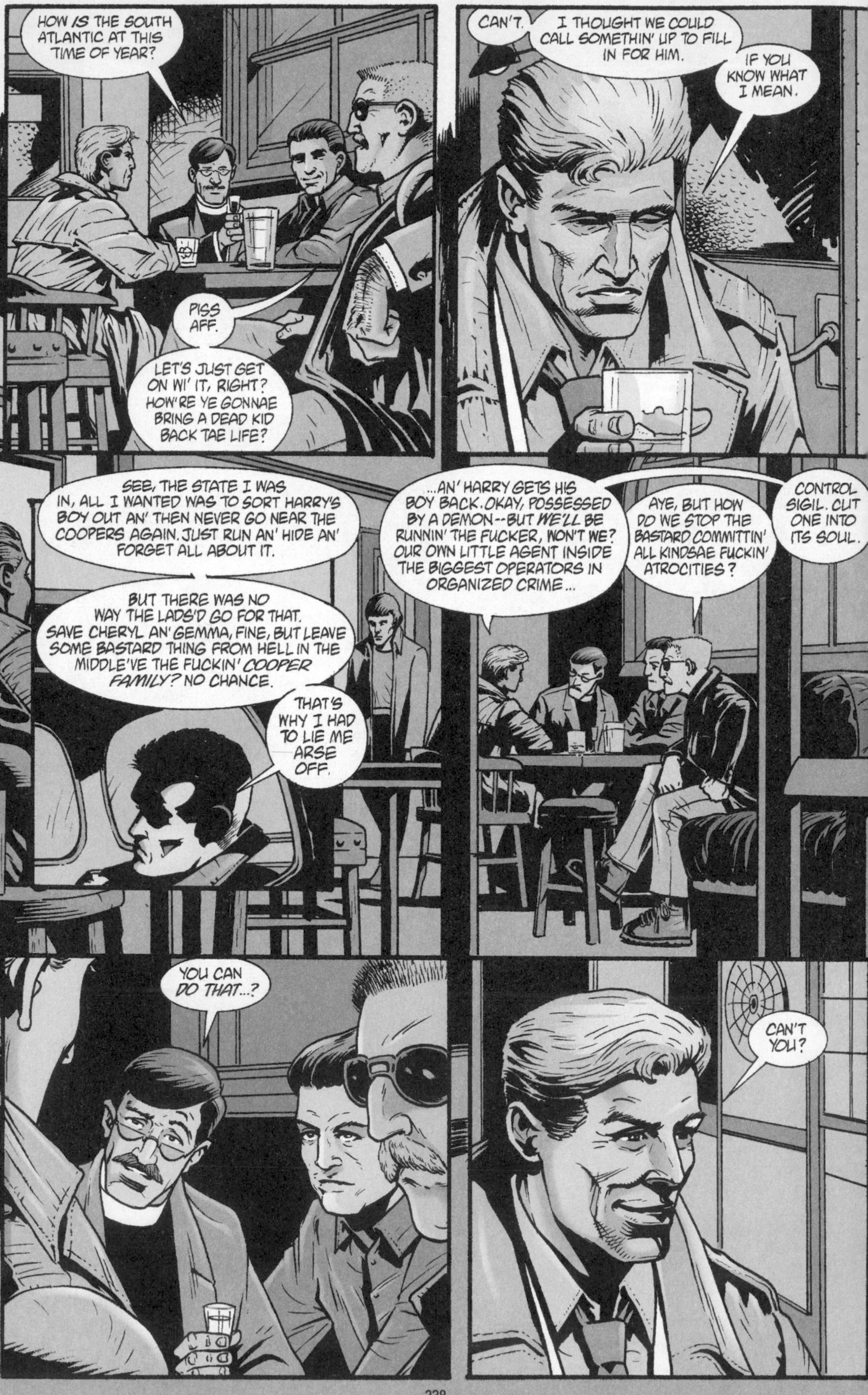
HOW IS THE SOUTH ATLANTIC AT THIS TIME OF YEAR?
PISS AFF.
LET'S JUST GET ON WI' IT, RIGHT? HOW'RE YE GONNAE BRING A DEAD KID BACK TAE LIFE?
CAN'T.
I THOUGHT WE COULD CALL SOMETHIN' UP TO FILL IN FOR HIM.
IF YOU KNOW WHAT I MEAN.
SEE, THE STATE I WAS IN, ALL I WANTED WAS TO SORT HARRY'S BOY OUT AN' THEN NEVER GO NEAR THE COOPERS AGAIN. JUST RUN AN' HIDE AN' FORGET ALL ABOUT IT.
BUT THERE WAS NO WAY THE LADS'D GO FOR THAT. SAVE CHERYL AN' GEMMA, FINE, BUT LEAVE SOME BASTARD THING FROM HELL IN THE MIDDLE'VE THE FUCKIN' COOPER FAMILY? NO CHANCE.
THAT'S WHY I HAD TO LIE ME ARSE OFF.
...AN' HARRY GETS HIS BOY BACK. OKAY, POSSESSED BY A DEMON--BUT WE'LL BE RUNNIN' THE FUCKER, WON'T WE? OUR OWN LITTLE AGENT INSIDE THE BIGGEST OPERATORS IN ORGANIZED CRIME...
AYE, BUT HOW DO WE STOP THE BASTARD COMMITTIN' ALL KINDSAE FUCKIN' ATROCITIES?
CONTROL SIGIL. CUT ONE INTO ITS SOUL.
YOU CAN DO THAT...?
CAN'T YOU?

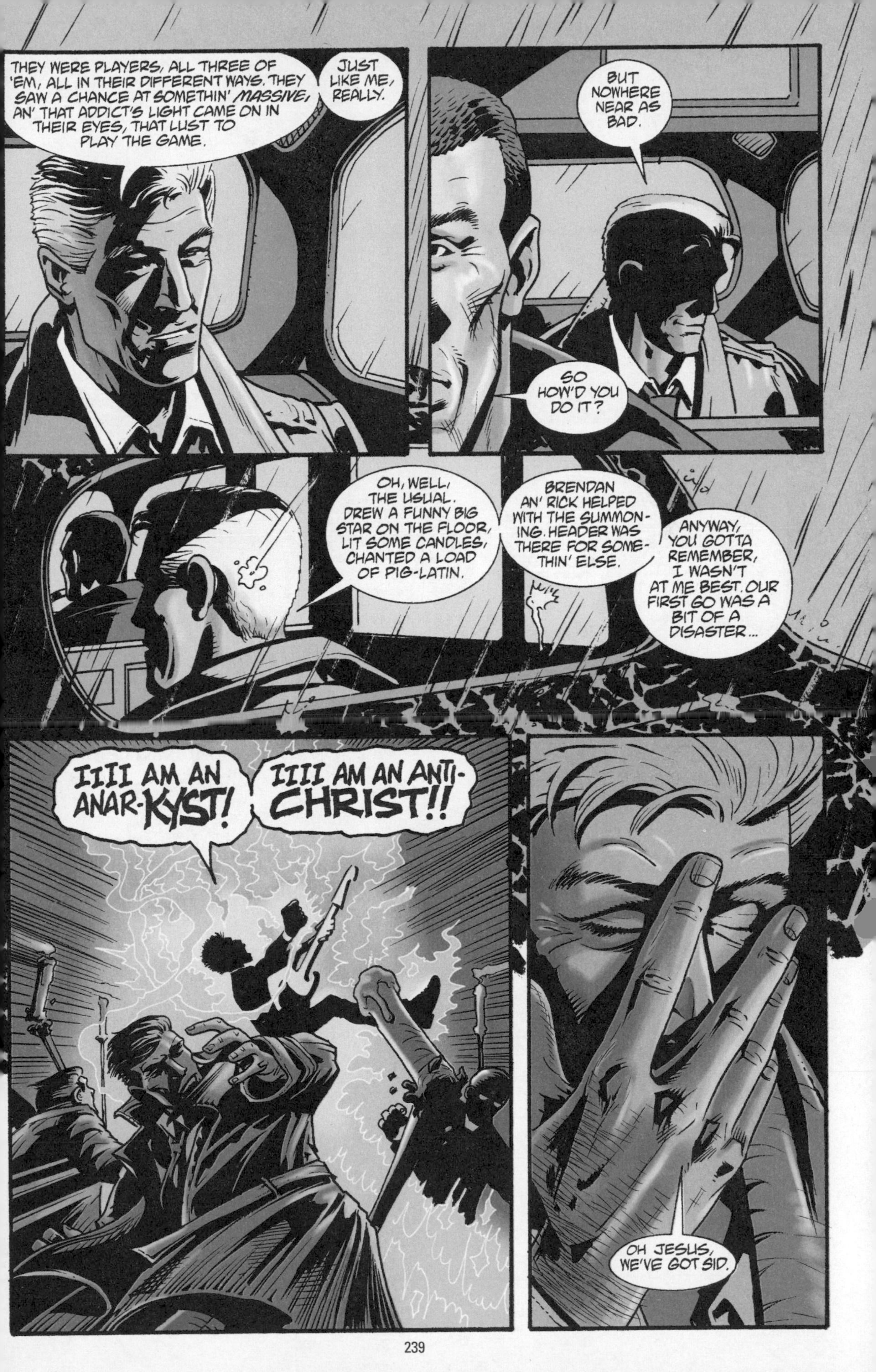
THEY WERE PLAYERS, ALL THREE OF 'EM, ALL IN THEIR DIFFERENT WAYS. THEY SAW A CHANCE AT SOMETHIN' MASSIVE, AN' THAT ADDICT'S LIGHT CAME ON IN THEIR EYES, THAT LUST TO PLAY THE GAME.
JUST LIKE ME, REALLY.
BUT NOWHERE NEAR AS BAD.
SO HOW'D YOU DO IT?
OH, WELL, THE USUAL. DREW A FUNNY BIG STAR ON THE FLOOR, LIT SOME CANDLES, CHANTED A LOAD OF PIG-LATIN.
BRENDAN AN' RICK HELPED WITH THE SUMMONING. HEADER WAS THERE FOR SOMETHIN' ELSE.
ANYWAY, YOU GOTTA REMEMBER, I WASN'T AT ME BEST. OUR FIRST GO WAS A BIT OF A DISASTER...
IIII AM AN ANAR-KYST!
IIII AM AN ANTI-CHRIST!!
OH JESUS, WE'VE GOT SID.

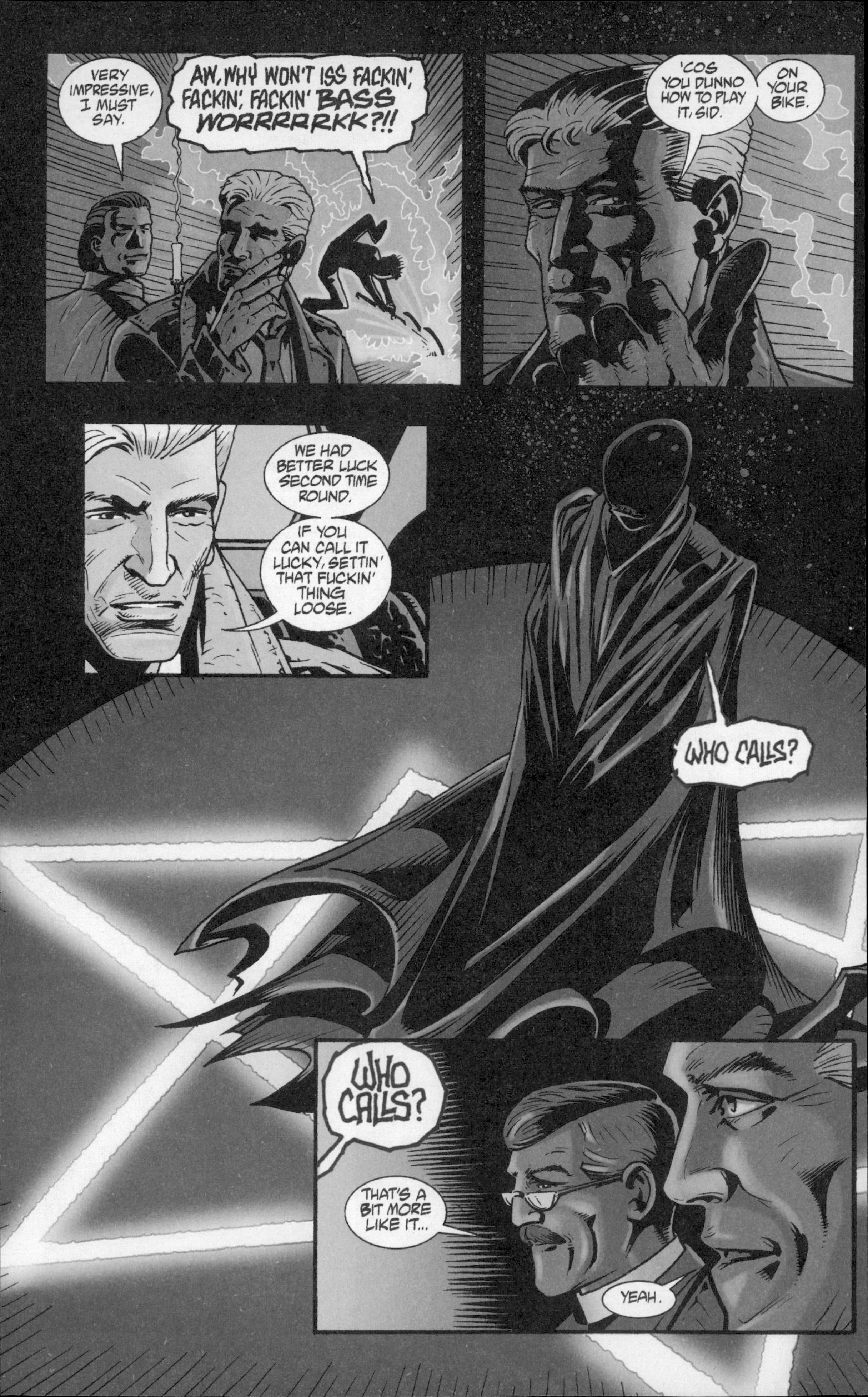
VERY IMPRESSIVE, I MUST SAY.
AW, WHY WON'T ISS FACKIN', FACKIN', FACKIN' BASS WORRRRRKK?!!
'COS YOU DUNNO HOW TO PLAY IT, SID.
ON YOUR BIKE.
WE HAD BETTER LUCK SECOND TIME ROUND.
IF YOU CAN CALL IT LUCKY, SETTIN' THAT FUCKIN' THING LOOSE.
WHO CALLS?
WHO CALLS?
THAT'S A BIT MORE LIKE IT...
YEAH.

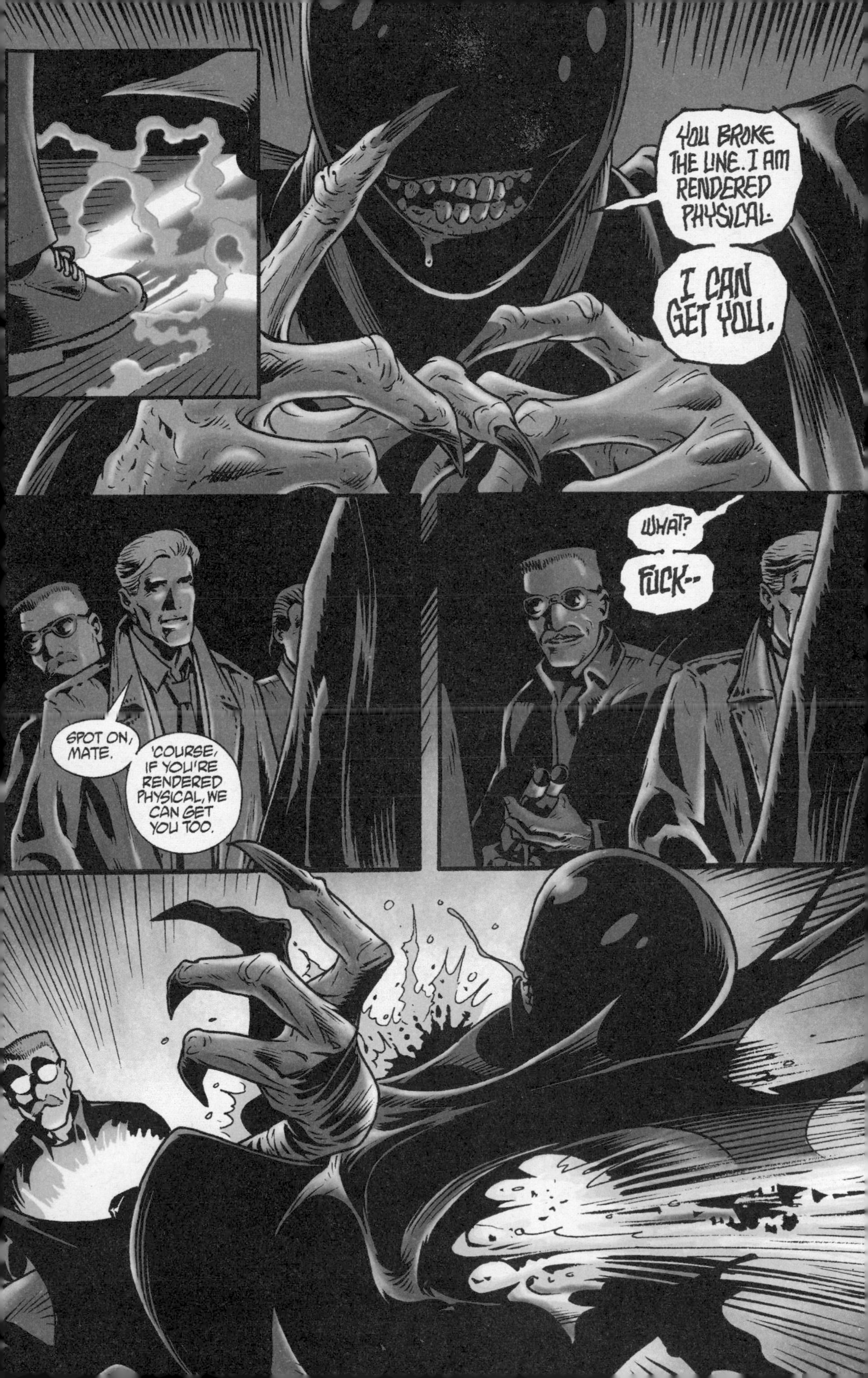
YOU BROKE THE LINE. I AM RENDERED PHYSICAL.
I CAN GET YOU.
SPOT ON, MATE.
'COURSE, IF YOU'RE RENDERED PHYSICAL, WE CAN GET YOU TOO.
WHAT?
FUCK--

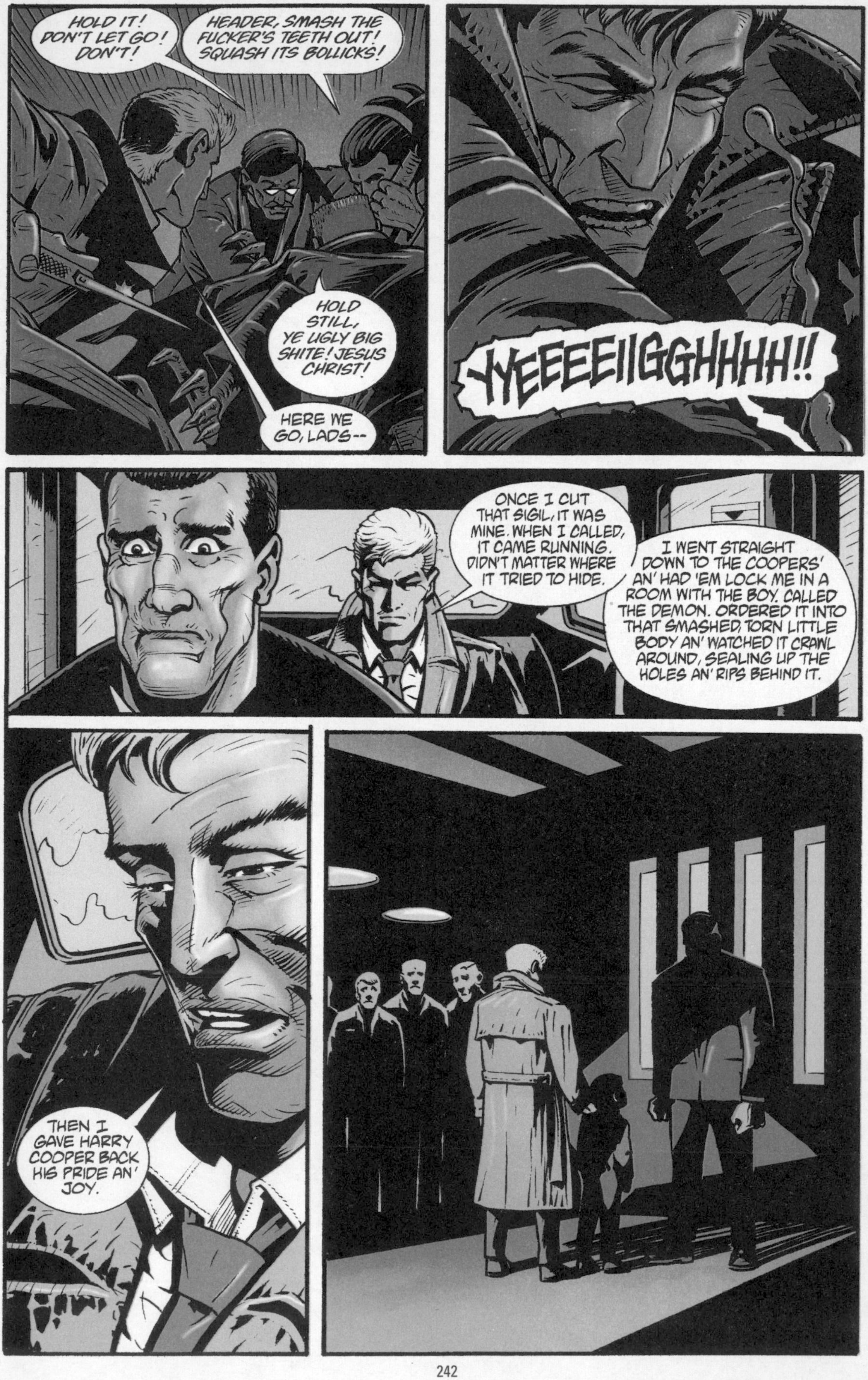
HOLD IT! DON'T LET GO! DON'T!
HEADER, SMASH THE FUCKER'S TEETH OUT! SQUASH ITS BOLLICKS!
HOLD STILL, YE UGLY BIG SHITE! JESUS CHRIST!
HERE WE GO, LADS--
YYEEEEIIGGHHHH!!
ONCE I CUT THAT SIGIL, IT WAS MINE. WHEN I CALLED, IT CAME RUNNING. DIDN'T MATTER WHERE IT TRIED TO HIDE.
I WENT STRAIGHT DOWN TO THE COOPERS' AN' HAD 'EM LOCK ME IN A ROOM WITH THE BOY. CALLED THE DEMON. ORDERED IT INTO THAT SMASHED, TORN LITTLE BODY AN' WATCHED IT CRAWL AROUND, SEALING UP THE HOLES AN' RIPS BEHIND IT.
THEN I GAVE HARRY COOPER BACK HIS PRIDE AN' JOY.

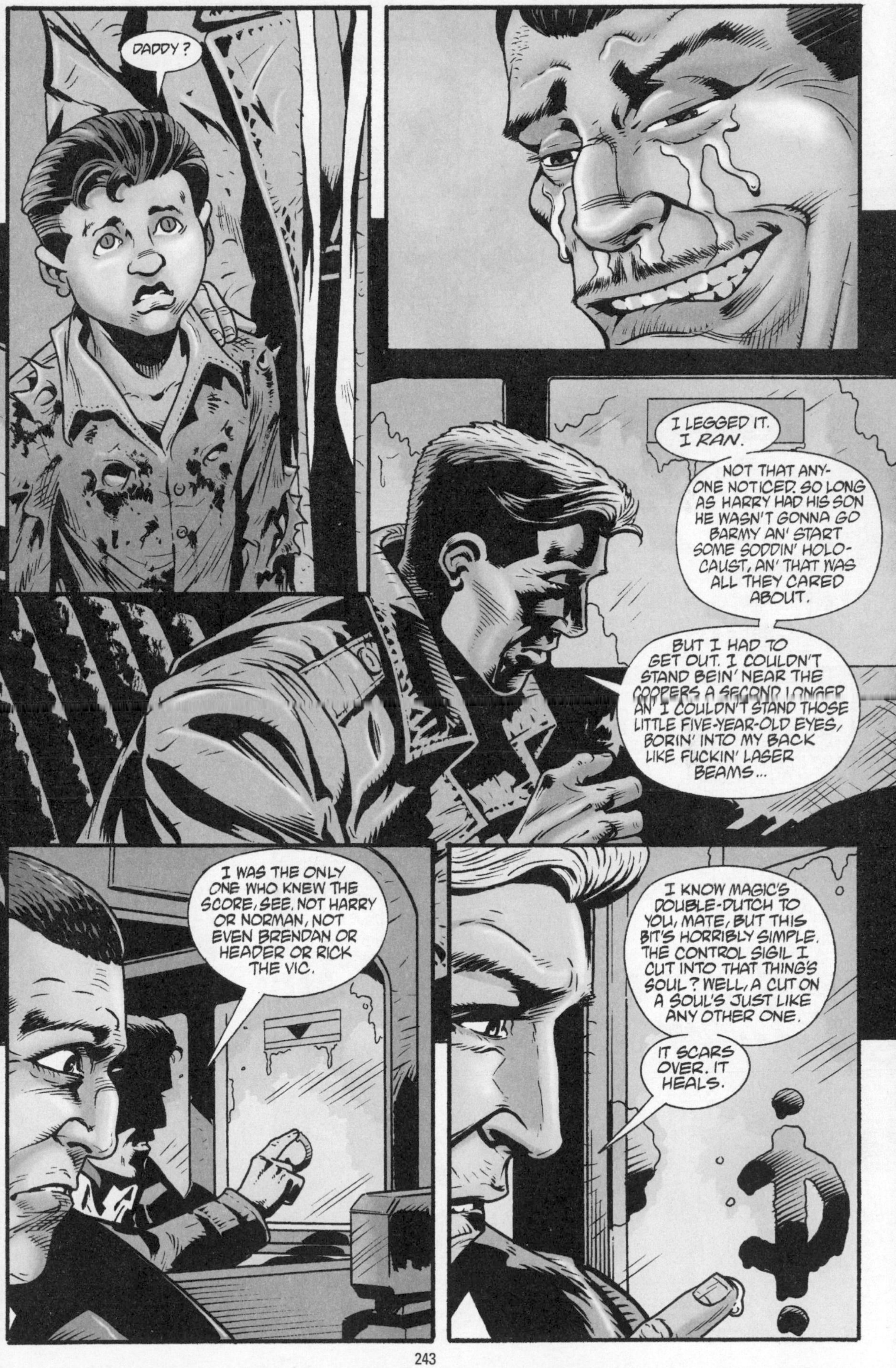
DADDY?
I LEGGED IT. I RAN.
NOT THAT ANY-ONE NOTICED. SO LONG AS HARRY HAD HIS SON HE WASN'T GONNA GO BARMY AN' START SOME SODDIN' HOLO-CAUST, AN' THAT WAS ALL THEY CARED ABOUT.
BUT I HAD TO GET OUT. I COULDN'T STAND BEIN' NEAR THE COPPERS A SECOND LONGER AN' I COULDN'T STAND THOSE LITTLE FIVE-YEAR-OLD EYES, BORIN' INTO MY BACK LIKE FUCKIN' LASER BEAMS...
I WAS THE ONLY ONE WHO KNEW THE SCORE, SEE. NOT HARRY OR NORMAN, NOT EVEN BRENDAN OR HEADER OR RICK THE VIC.
I KNOW MAGIC'S DOUBLE-DUTCH TO YOU, MATE, BUT THIS BIT'S HORRIBLY SIMPLE. THE CONTROL SIGIL I CUT INTO THAT THING'S SOUL? WELL, A CUT ON A SOUL'S JUST LIKE ANY OTHER ONE.
IT SCARS OVER. IT HEALS.

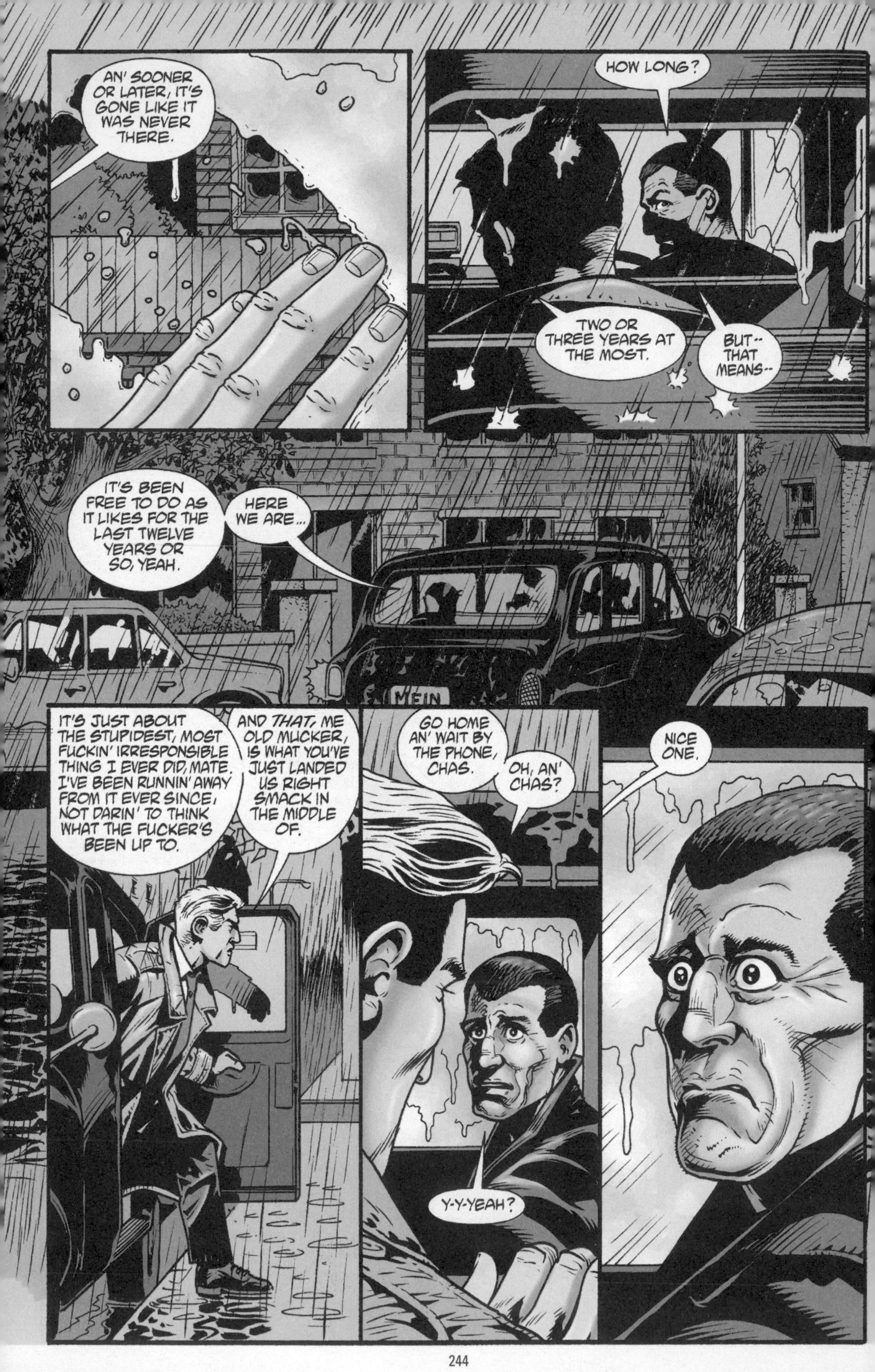
AN' SOONER OR LATER, IT'S GONE LIKE IT WAS NEVER THERE.
HOW LONG?
TWO OR THREE YEARS AT THE MOST.
BUT-- THAT MEANS--
IT'S BEEN FREE TO DO AS IT LIKES FOR THE LAST TWELVE YEARS OR SO, YEAH.
HERE WE ARE...
MEIN
IT'S JUST ABOUT THE STUPIDEST, MOST FUCKIN' IRRESPONSIBLE THING I EVER DID, MATE. I'VE BEEN RUNNIN' AWAY FROM IT EVER SINCE, NOT DARIN' TO THINK WHAT THE FUCKER'S BEEN UP TO.
AND THAT, ME OLD MUCKER, IS WHAT YOU'VE JUST LANDED US RIGHT SMACK IN THE MIDDLE OF.
GO HOME AN' WAIT BY THE PHONE, CHAS.
OH, AN' CHAS?
Y-Y-YEAH?
NICE ONE.

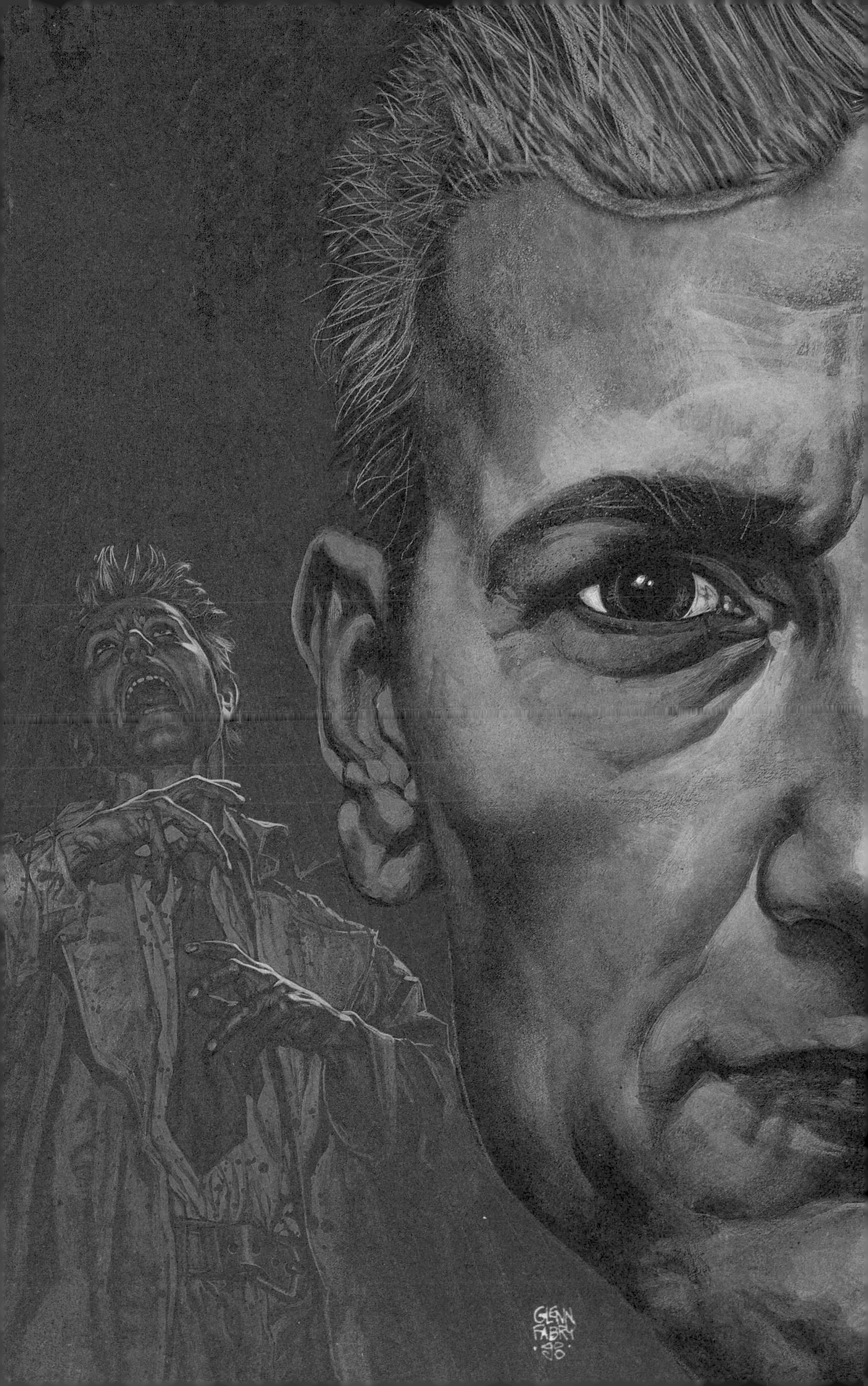
GLENN FABRY

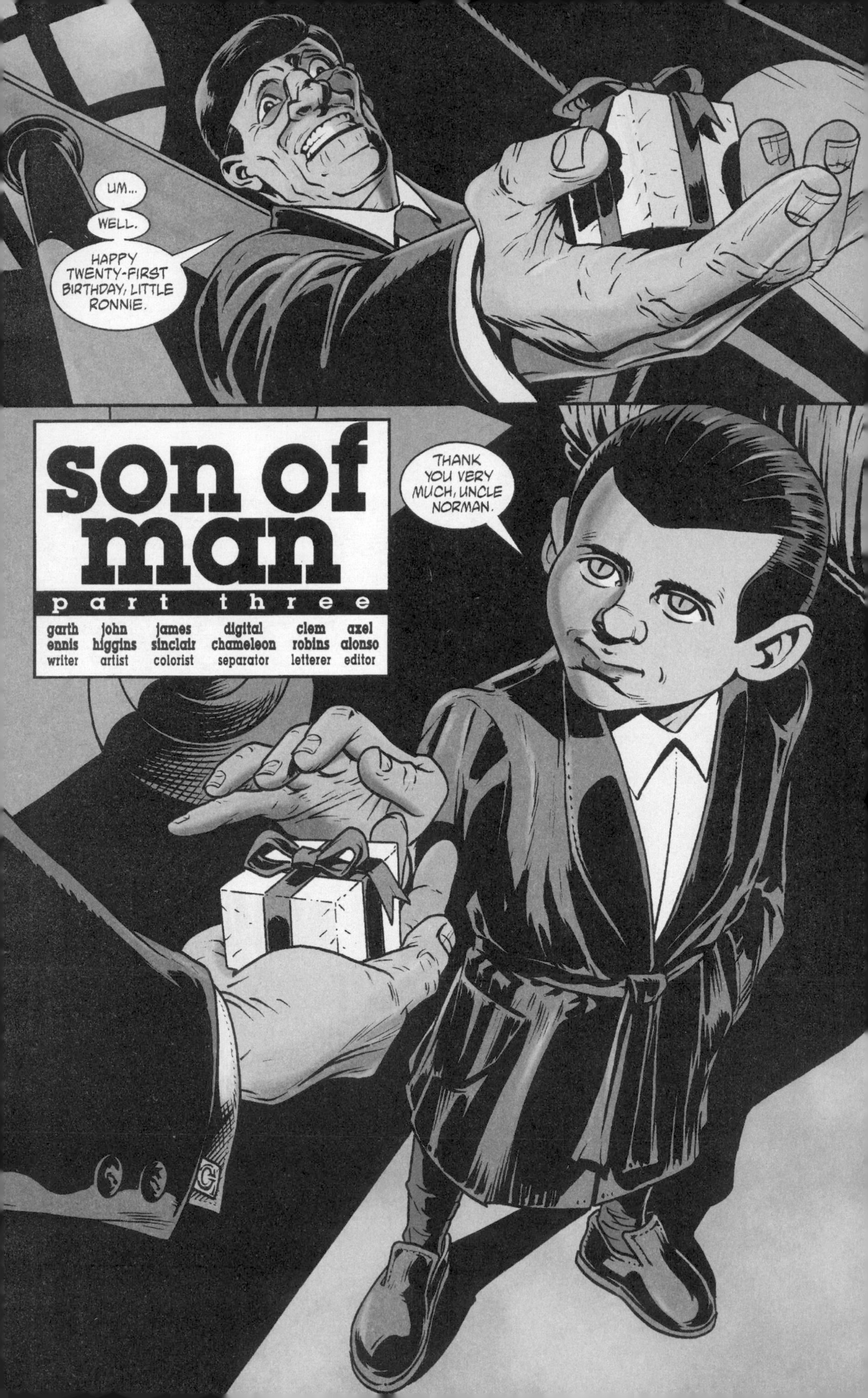
UM...
WELL.
HAPPY TWENTY-FIRST BIRTHDAY, LITTLE RONNIE.
son of man
part three
garth ennis writer
john higgins artist
james sinclair colorist
digital chameleon separator
clem robins letterer
axel alonso editor
THANK YOU VERY MUCH, UNCLE NORMAN.

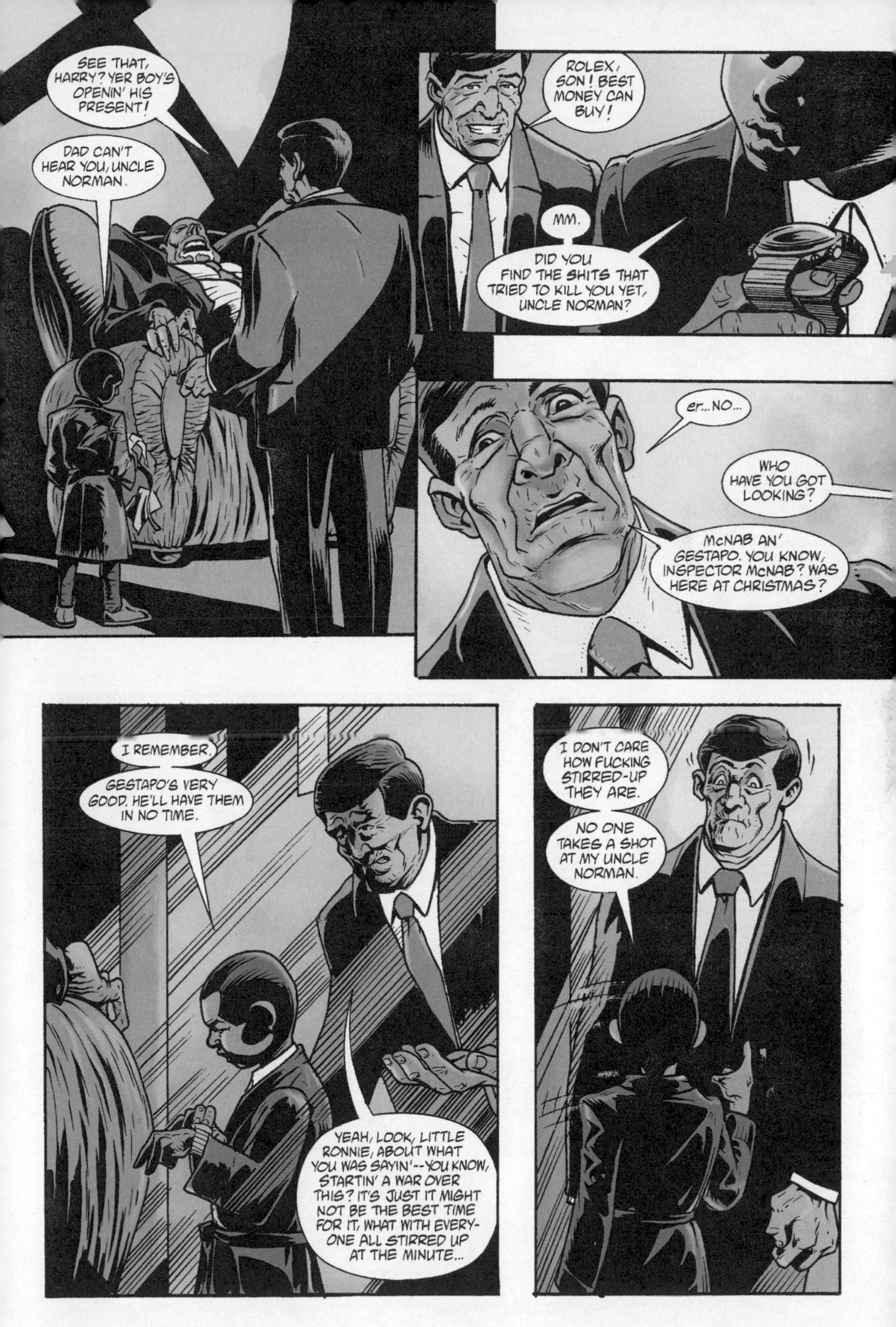
SEE THAT, HARRY? YER BOY'S OPENIN' HIS PRESENT!
DAD CAN'T HEAR YOU, UNCLE NORMAN.
ROLEX, SON! BEST MONEY CAN BUY!
MM.
DID YOU FIND THE SHITS THAT TRIED TO KILL YOU YET, UNCLE NORMAN?
er...NO...
WHO HAVE YOU GOT LOOKING?
McNAB AN' GESTAPO. YOU KNOW, INSPECTOR McNAB? WAS HERE AT CHRISTMAS?
I REMEMBER.
GESTAPO'S VERY GOOD. HE'LL HAVE THEM IN NO TIME.
YEAH, LOOK, LITTLE RONNIE, ABOUT WHAT YOU WAS SAYIN'--YOU KNOW, STARTIN' A WAR OVER THIS? IT'S JUST IT MIGHT NOT BE THE BEST TIME FOR IT, WHAT WITH EVERY-ONE ALL STIRRED UP AT THE MINUTE...
I DON'T CARE HOW FUCKING STIRRED-UP THEY ARE.
NO ONE TAKES A SHOT AT MY UNCLE NORMAN.

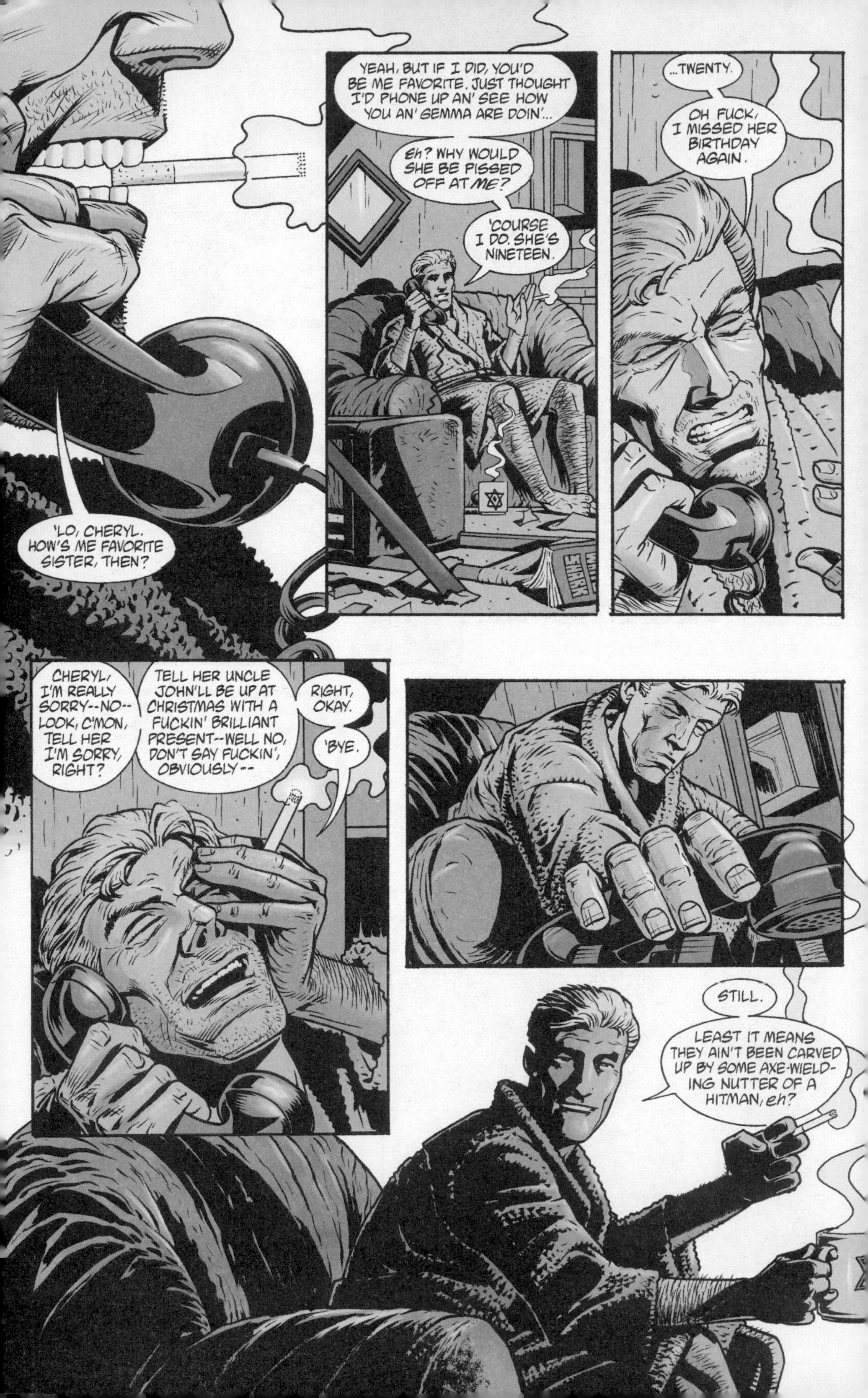
'LO, CHERYL. HOW'S ME FAVORITE SISTER, THEN?
YEAH, BUT IF I DID, YOU'D BE ME FAVORITE. JUST THOUGHT I'D PHONE UP AN' SEE HOW YOU AN' GEMMA ARE DOIN'...
EH? WHY WOULD SHE BE PISSED OFF AT ME?
'COURSE I DO. SHE'S NINETEEN.
...TWENTY.
OH FUCK, I MISSED HER BIRTHDAY AGAIN.
CHERYL, I'M REALLY SORRY--NO--LOOK, C'MON, TELL HER I'M SORRY, RIGHT?
TELL HER UNCLE JOHN'LL BE UP AT CHRISTMAS WITH A FUCKIN' BRILLIANT PRESENT--WELL NO, DON'T SAY FUCKIN', OBVIOUSLY--
RIGHT, OKAY.
'BYE.
STILL.
LEAST IT MEANS THEY AIN'T BEEN CARVED UP BY SOME AXE-WIELDING NUTTER OF A HITMAN, EH?

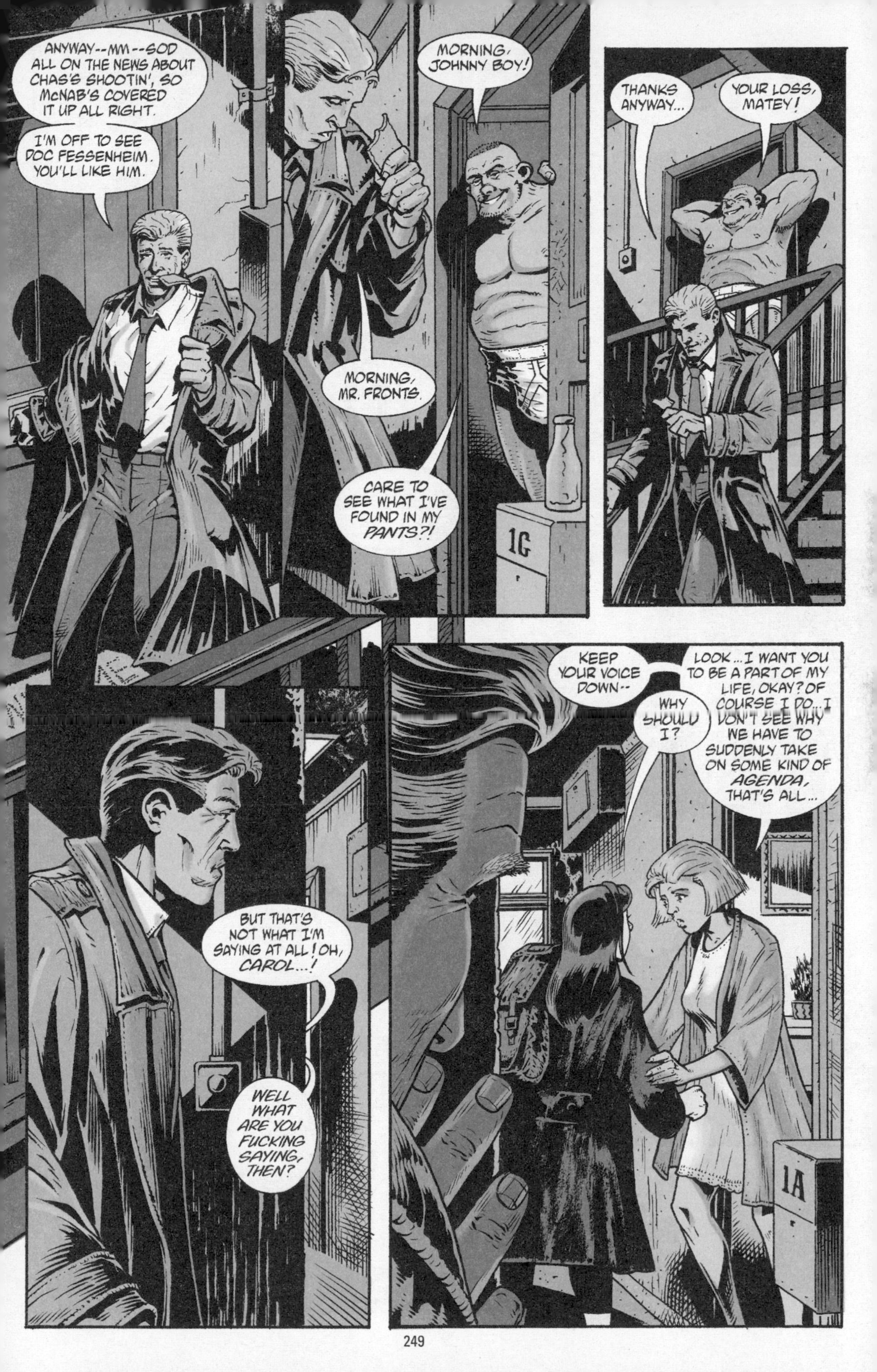

ANYWAY--MM--SOD ALL ON THE NEWS ABOUT CHAS'S SHOOTIN', SO McNAB'S COVERED IT UP ALL RIGHT.
I'M OFF TO SEE DOC FESSENHEIM. YOU'LL LIKE HIM.
MORNING, JOHNNY BOY!
MORNING, MR. FRONTS.
CARE TO SEE WHAT I'VE FOUND IN MY PANTS?!
1G
THANKS ANYWAY...
YOUR LOSS, MATEY!
BUT THAT'S NOT WHAT I'M SAYING AT ALL! OH, CAROL...!
WELL WHAT ARE YOU FUCKING SAYING, THEN?
KEEP YOUR VOICE DOWN--
WHY SHOULD I?
LOOK... I WANT YOU TO BE A PART OF MY LIFE, OKAY? OF COURSE I DO... I DON'T SEE WHY WE HAVE TO SUDDENLY TAKE ON SOME KIND OF AGENDA, THAT'S ALL...
1A

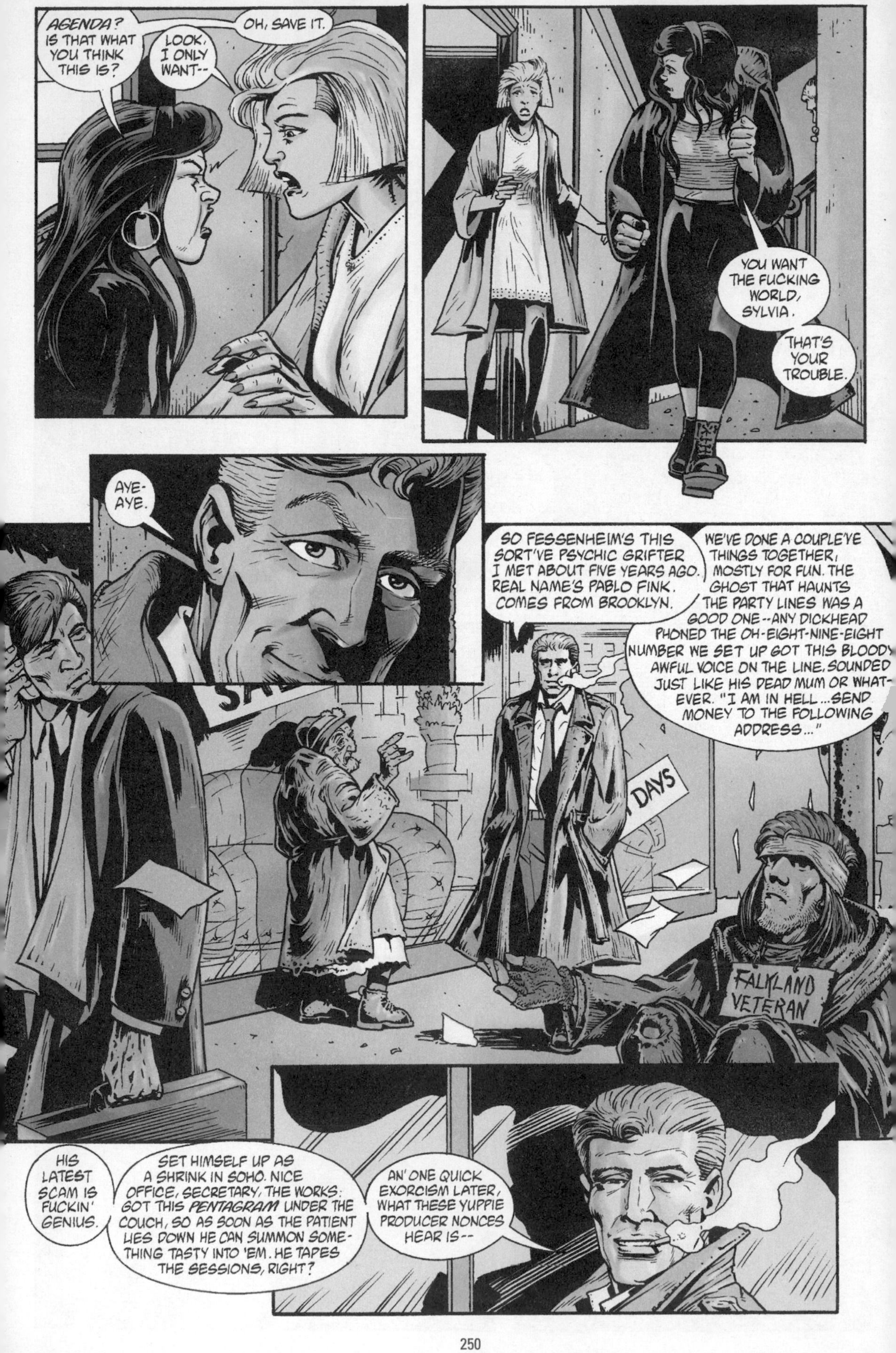
AGENDA? IS THAT WHAT YOU THINK THIS IS?
LOOK, I ONLY WANT--
OH, SAVE IT.
YOU WANT THE FUCKING WORLD, SYLVIA.
THAT'S YOUR TROUBLE.
AYE-AYE.
SO FESSENHEIM'S THIS SORT'VE PSYCHIC GRIFTER I MET ABOUT FIVE YEARS AGO. REAL NAME'S PABLO FINK. COMES FROM BROOKLYN.
WE'VE DONE A COUPLE'VE THINGS TOGETHER, MOSTLY FOR FUN. THE GHOST THAT HAUNTS THE PARTY LINES WAS A GOOD ONE--ANY DICKHEAD PHONED THE OH-EIGHT-NINE-EIGHT NUMBER WE SET UP GOT THIS BLOODY AWFUL VOICE ON THE LINE, SOUNDED JUST LIKE HIS DEAD MUM OR WHAT-EVER. "I AM IN HELL...SEND MONEY TO THE FOLLOWING ADDRESS..."
DAYS
FALKLAND VETERAN
HIS LATEST SCAM IS FUCKIN' GENIUS.
SET HIMSELF UP AS A SHRINK IN SOHO. NICE OFFICE, SECRETARY, THE WORKS. GOT THIS PENTAGRAM UNDER THE COUCH, SO AS SOON AS THE PATIENT LIES DOWN HE CAN SUMMON SOME-THING TASTY INTO 'EM. HE TAPES THE SESSIONS, RIGHT?
AN' ONE QUICK EXORCISM LATER, WHAT THESE YUPPIE PRODUCER NONCES HEAR IS--

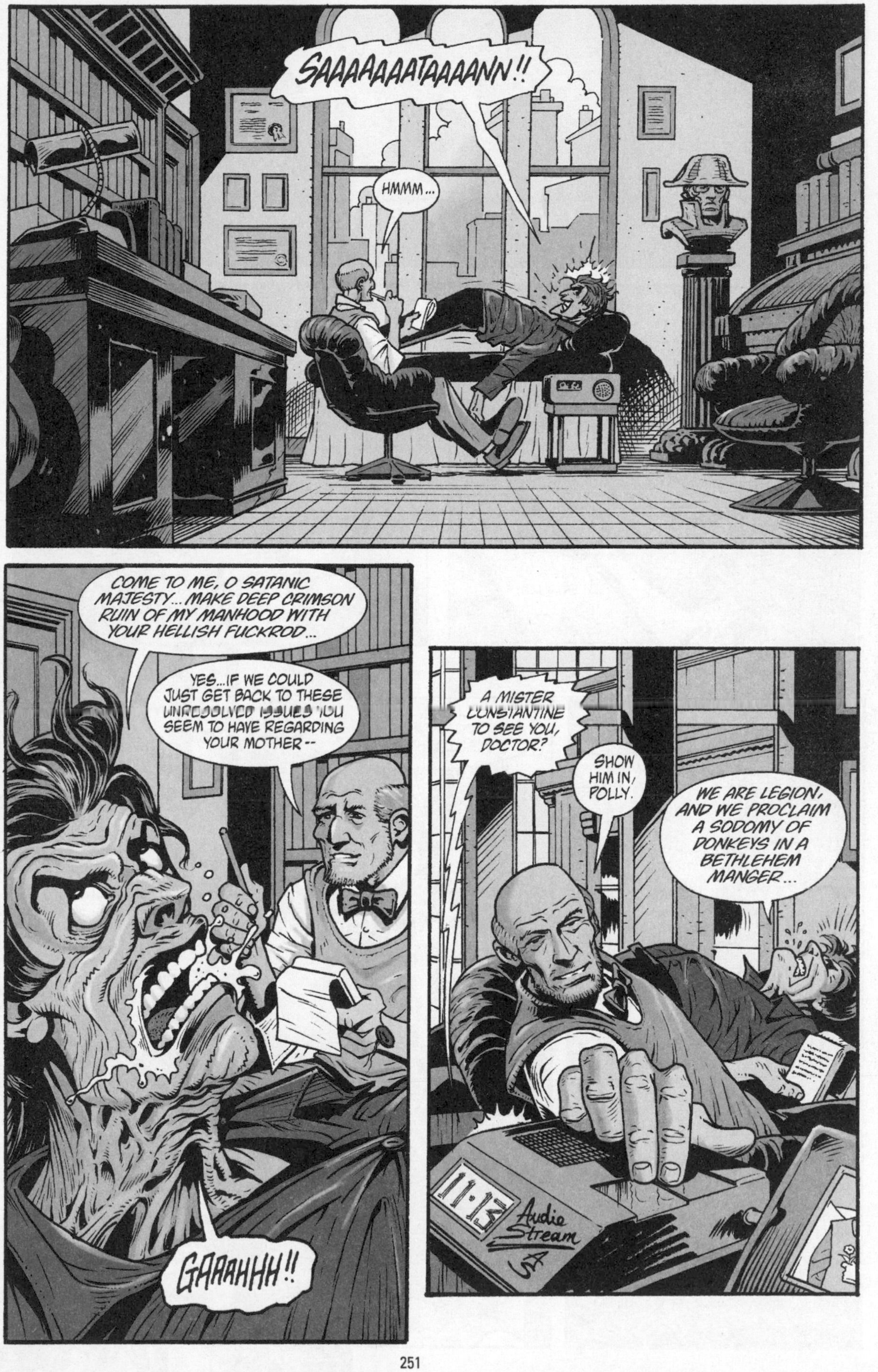
SAAAAAAATAAAANN!!
HMMM...
COME TO ME, O SATANIC MAJESTY... MAKE DEEP CRIMSON RUIN OF MY MANHOOD WITH YOUR HELLISH FUCKROD...
YES...IF WE COULD JUST GET BACK TO THESE UNRESOLVED ISSUES YOU SEEM TO HAVE REGARDING YOUR MOTHER--
GARRHHH!!
A MISTER CONSTANTINE TO SEE YOU, DOCTOR?
SHOW HIM IN, POLLY.
WE ARE LEGION, AND WE PROCLAIM A SODOMY OF DONKEYS IN A BETHLEHEM MANGER...
11:13
Audie Stream

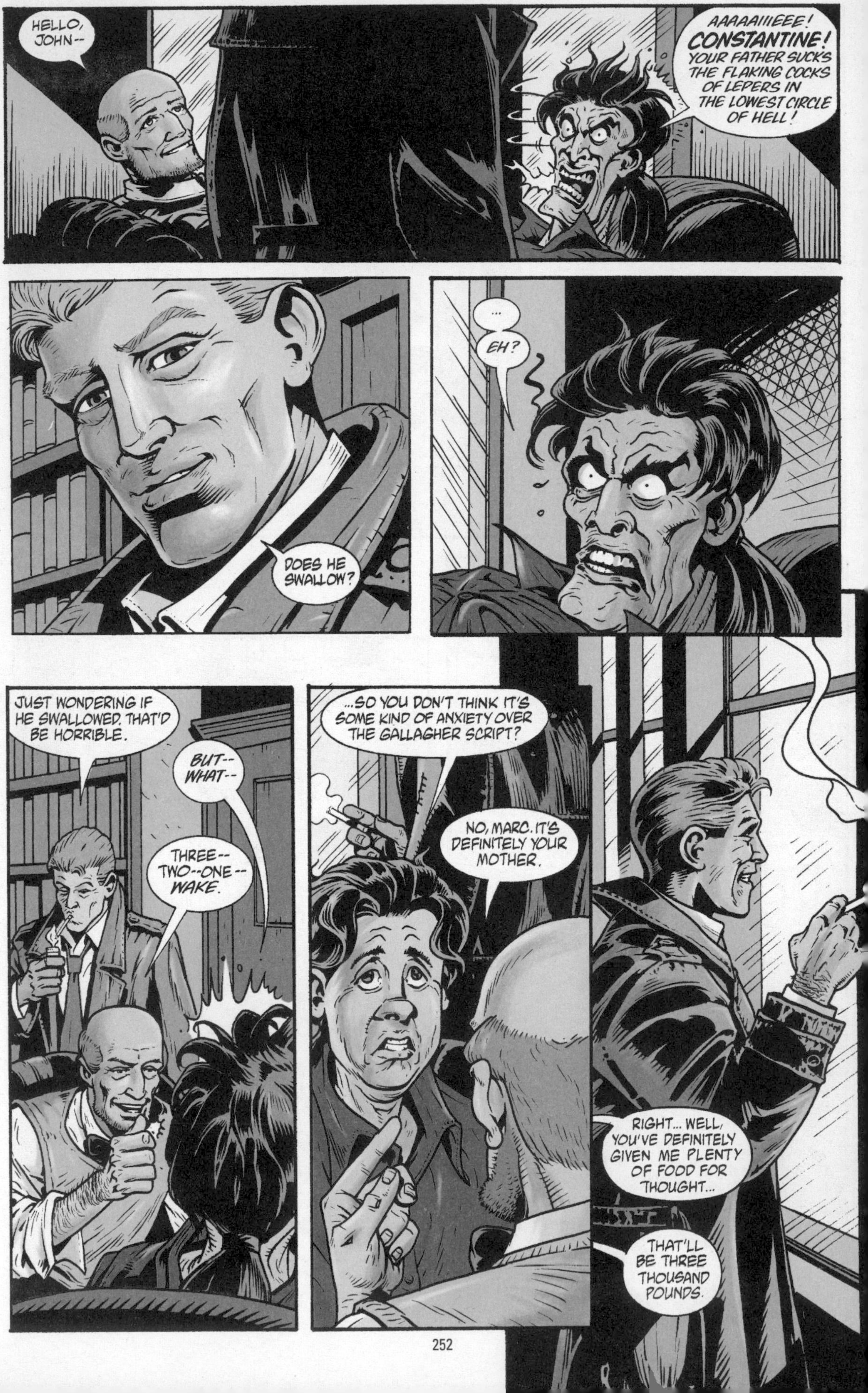
HELLO, JOHN--
AAAAAIIIEEE! CONSTANTINE! YOUR FATHER SUCKS THE FLAKING COCKS OF LEPERS IN THE LOWEST CIRCLE OF HELL!
DOES HE SWALLOW?
...
EH?
JUST WONDERING IF HE SWALLOWED. THAT'D BE HORRIBLE.
BUT-- WHAT--
THREE-- TWO--ONE-- WAKE.
...SO YOU DON'T THINK IT'S SOME KIND OF ANXIETY OVER THE GALLAGHER SCRIPT?
NO, MARC. IT'S DEFINITELY YOUR MOTHER.
RIGHT... WELL, YOU'VE DEFINITELY GIVEN ME PLENTY OF FOOD FOR THOUGHT...
THAT'LL BE THREE THOUSAND POUNDS.

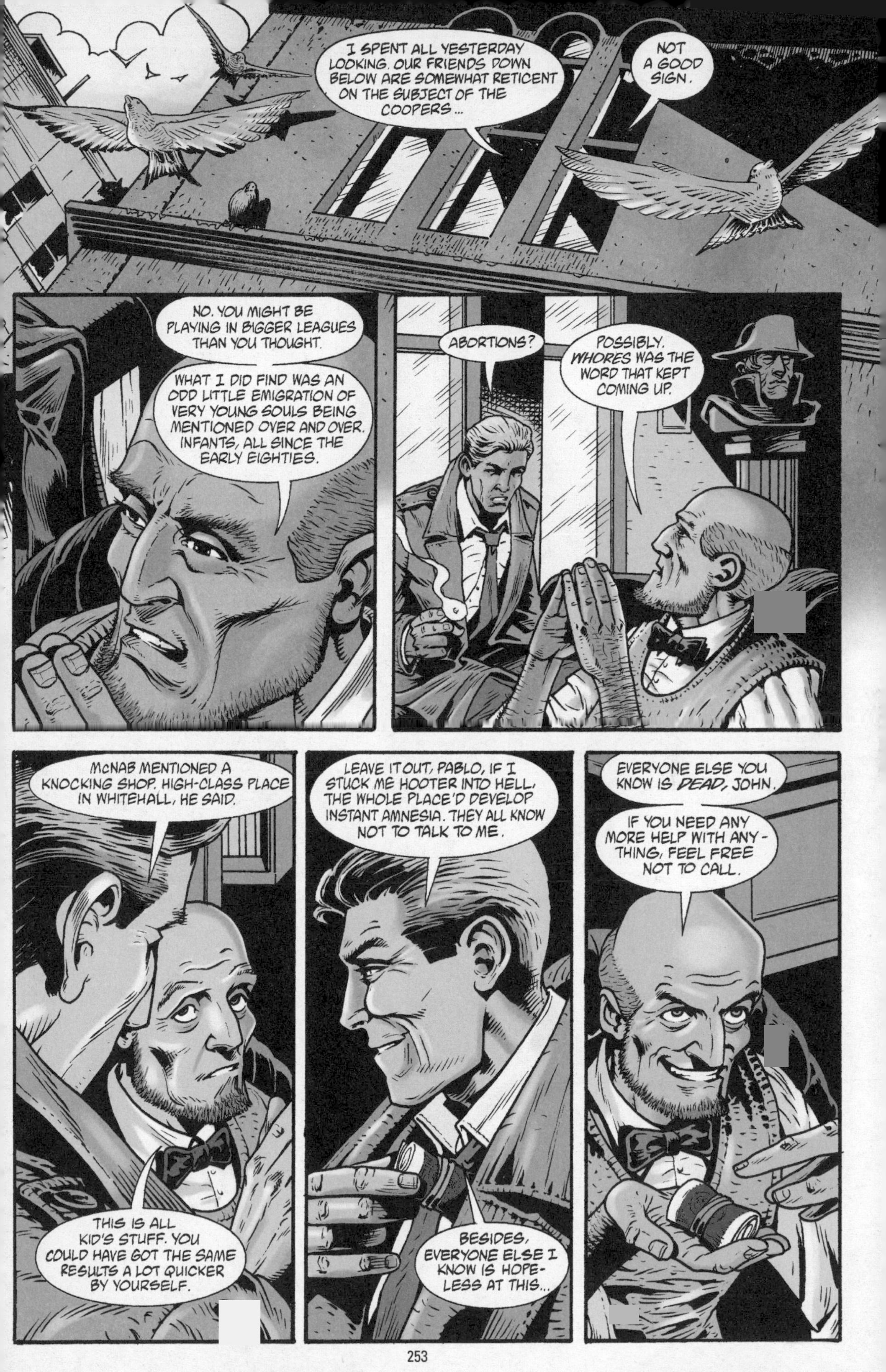

I SPENT ALL YESTERDAY LOOKING. OUR FRIENDS DOWN BELOW ARE SOMEWHAT RETICENT ON THE SUBJECT OF THE COOPERS...
NOT A GOOD SIGN.
NO. YOU MIGHT BE PLAYING IN BIGGER LEAGUES THAN YOU THOUGHT.
WHAT I DID FIND WAS AN ODD LITTLE EMIGRATION OF VERY YOUNG SOULS BEING MENTIONED OVER AND OVER. INFANTS, ALL SINCE THE EARLY EIGHTIES.
ABORTIONS?
POSSIBLY. WHORES WAS THE WORD THAT KEPT COMING UP.
McNAB MENTIONED A KNOCKING SHOP. HIGH-CLASS PLACE IN WHITEHALL, HE SAID.
THIS IS ALL KID'S STUFF. YOU COULD HAVE GOT THE SAME RESULTS A LOT QUICKER BY YOURSELF.
LEAVE IT OUT, PABLO, IF I STUCK ME HOOTER INTO HELL, THE WHOLE PLACE'D DEVELOP INSTANT AMNESIA. THEY ALL KNOW NOT TO TALK TO ME.
BESIDES, EVERYONE ELSE I KNOW IS HOPE-LESS AT THIS...
EVERYONE ELSE YOU KNOW IS DEAD, JOHN.
IF YOU NEED ANY MORE HELP WITH ANY-THING, FEEL FREE NOT TO CALL.

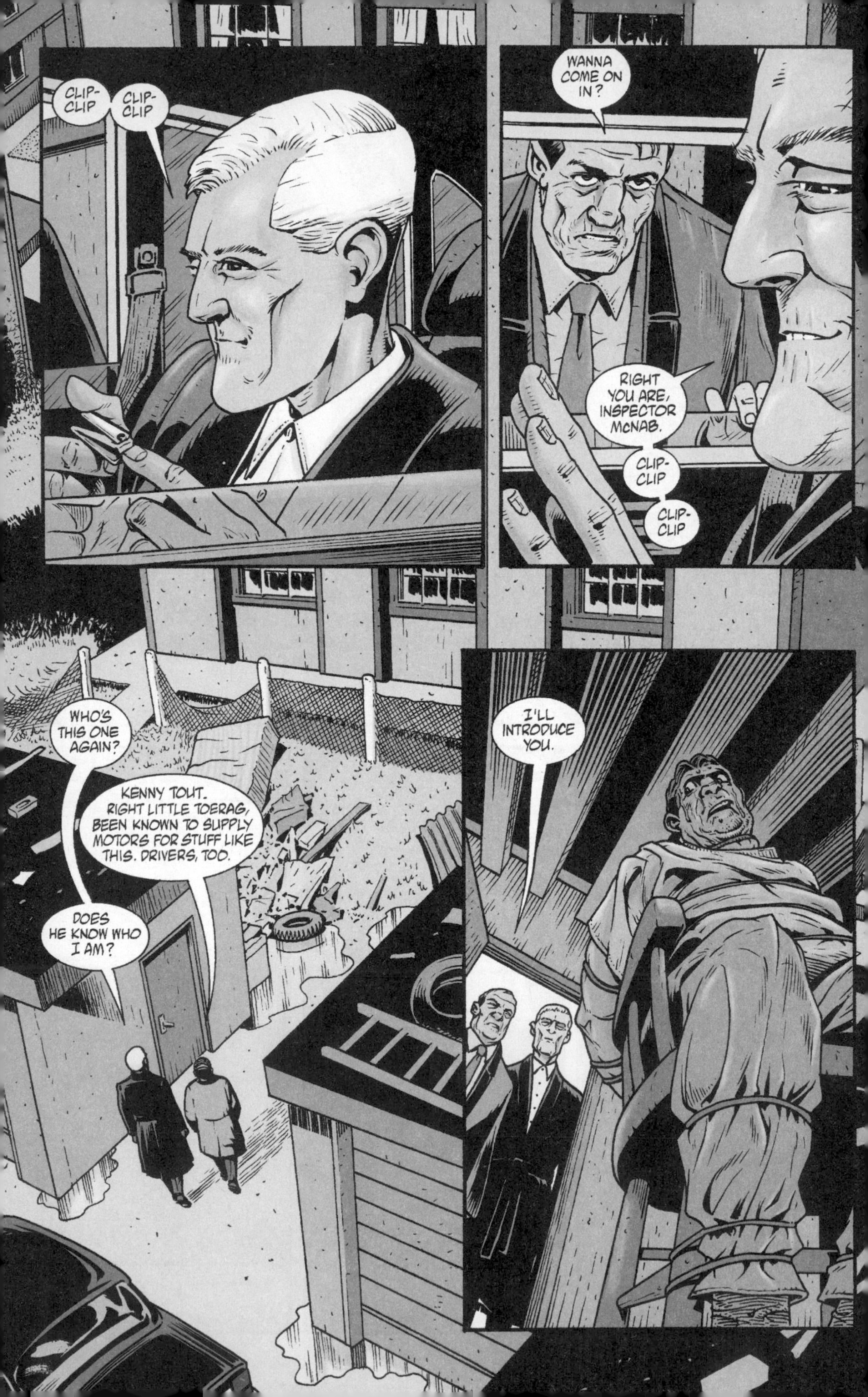
CLIP-CLIP
CLIP-CLIP
WANNA COME ON IN?
RIGHT YOU ARE, INSPECTOR McNAB.
CLIP-CLIP
CLIP-CLIP
WHO'S THIS ONE AGAIN?
KENNY TOUT. RIGHT LITTLE TOERAG, BEEN KNOWN TO SUPPLY MOTORS FOR STUFF LIKE THIS. DRIVERS, TOO.
DOES HE KNOW WHO I AM?
I'LL INTRODUCE YOU.

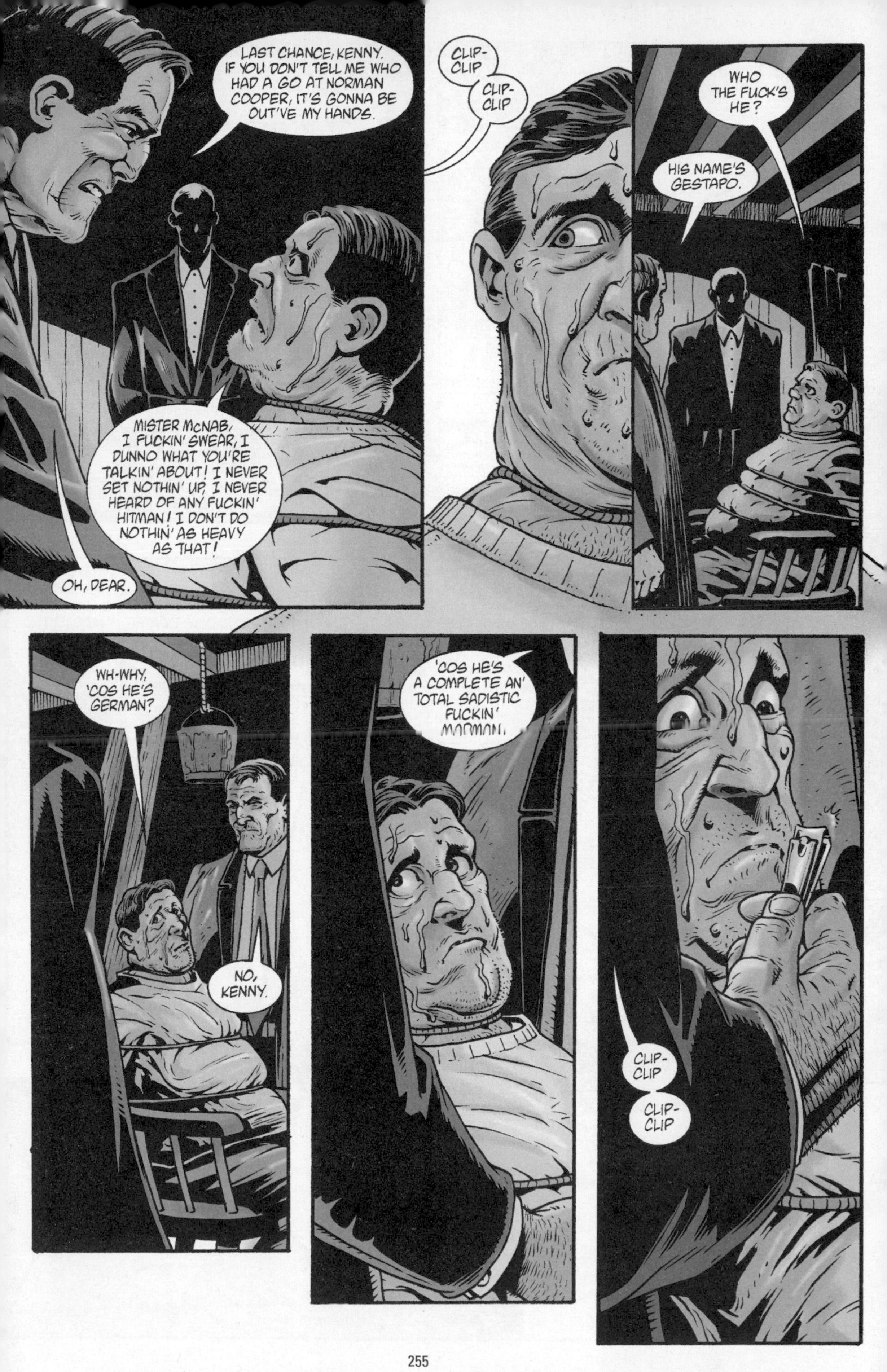
LAST CHANCE, KENNY. IF YOU DON'T TELL ME WHO HAD A GO AT NORMAN COOPER, IT'S GONNA BE OUT'VE MY HANDS.
MISTER McNAB, I FUCKIN' SWEAR, I DUNNO WHAT YOU'RE TALKIN' ABOUT! I NEVER SET NOTHIN' UP, I NEVER HEARD OF ANY FUCKIN' HITMAN! I DON'T DO NOTHIN' AS HEAVY AS THAT!
OH, DEAR.
CLIP-CLIP
CLIP-CLIP
WHO THE FUCK'S HE?
HIS NAME'S GESTAPO.
WH-WHY, 'COS HE'S GERMAN?
NO, KENNY.
'COS HE'S A COMPLETE AN' TOTAL SADISTIC FUCKIN'
CLIP-CLIP
CLIP-CLIP

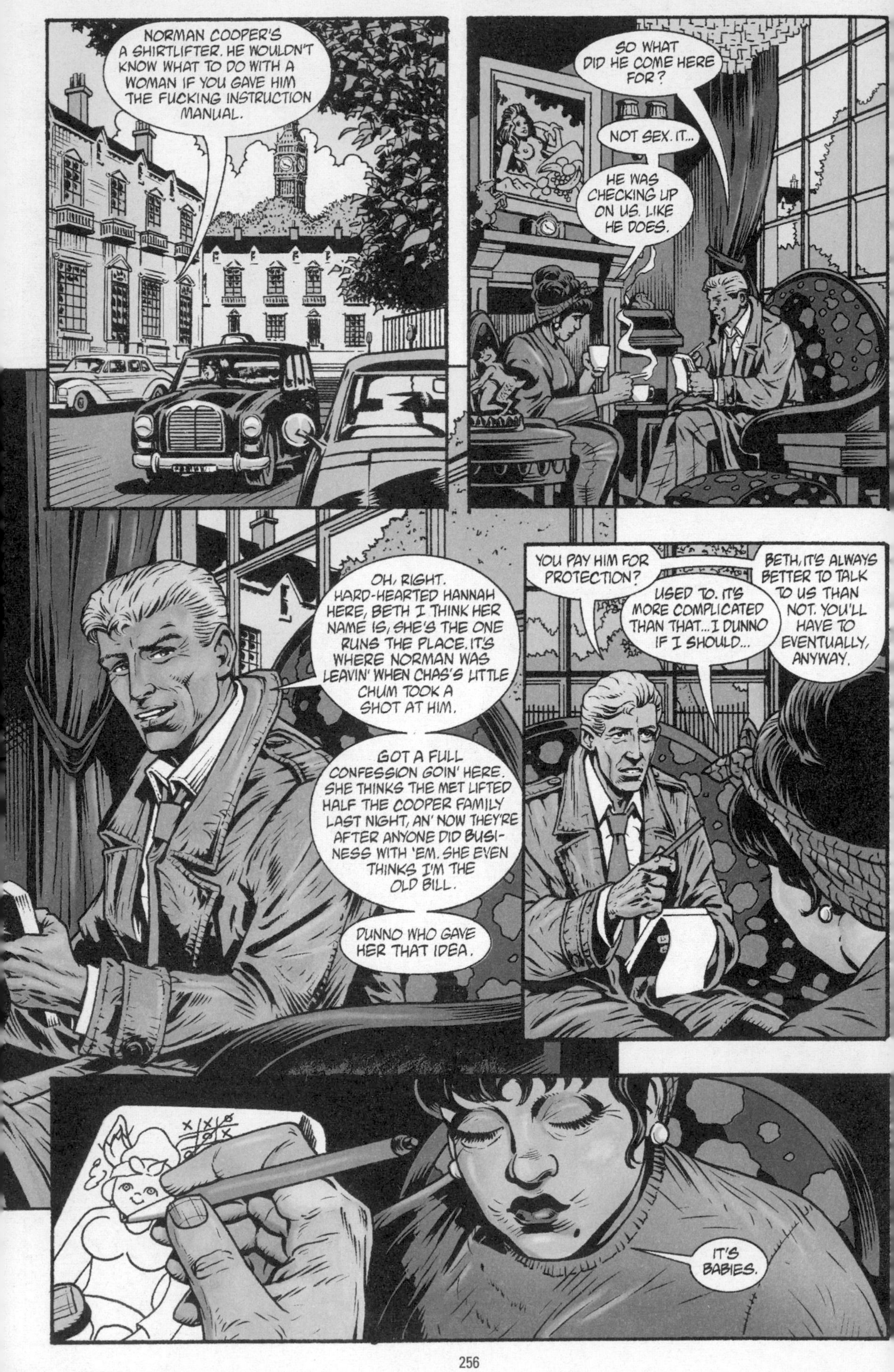
NORMAN COOPER'S A SHIRTLIFTER. HE WOULDN'T KNOW WHAT TO DO WITH A WOMAN IF YOU GAVE HIM THE FUCKING INSTRUCTION MANUAL.
SO WHAT DID HE COME HERE FOR?
NOT SEX. IT...
HE WAS CHECKING UP ON US. LIKE HE DOES.
OH, RIGHT. HARD-HEARTED HANNAH HERE, BETH I THINK HER NAME IS, SHE'S THE ONE RUNS THE PLACE. IT'S WHERE NORMAN WAS LEAVIN' WHEN CHAS'S LITTLE CHUM TOOK A SHOT AT HIM.
GOT A FULL CONFESSION GOIN' HERE. SHE THINKS THE MET LIFTED HALF THE COOPER FAMILY LAST NIGHT, AN' NOW THEY'RE AFTER ANYONE DID BUSINESS WITH 'EM. SHE EVEN THINKS I'M THE OLD BILL.
DUNNO WHO GAVE HER THAT IDEA.
YOU PAY HIM FOR PROTECTION?
USED TO. IT'S MORE COMPLICATED THAN THAT... I DUNNO IF I SHOULD...
BETH, IT'S ALWAYS BETTER TO TALK TO US THAN NOT. YOU'LL HAVE TO EVENTUALLY, ANYWAY.
IT'S BABIES.

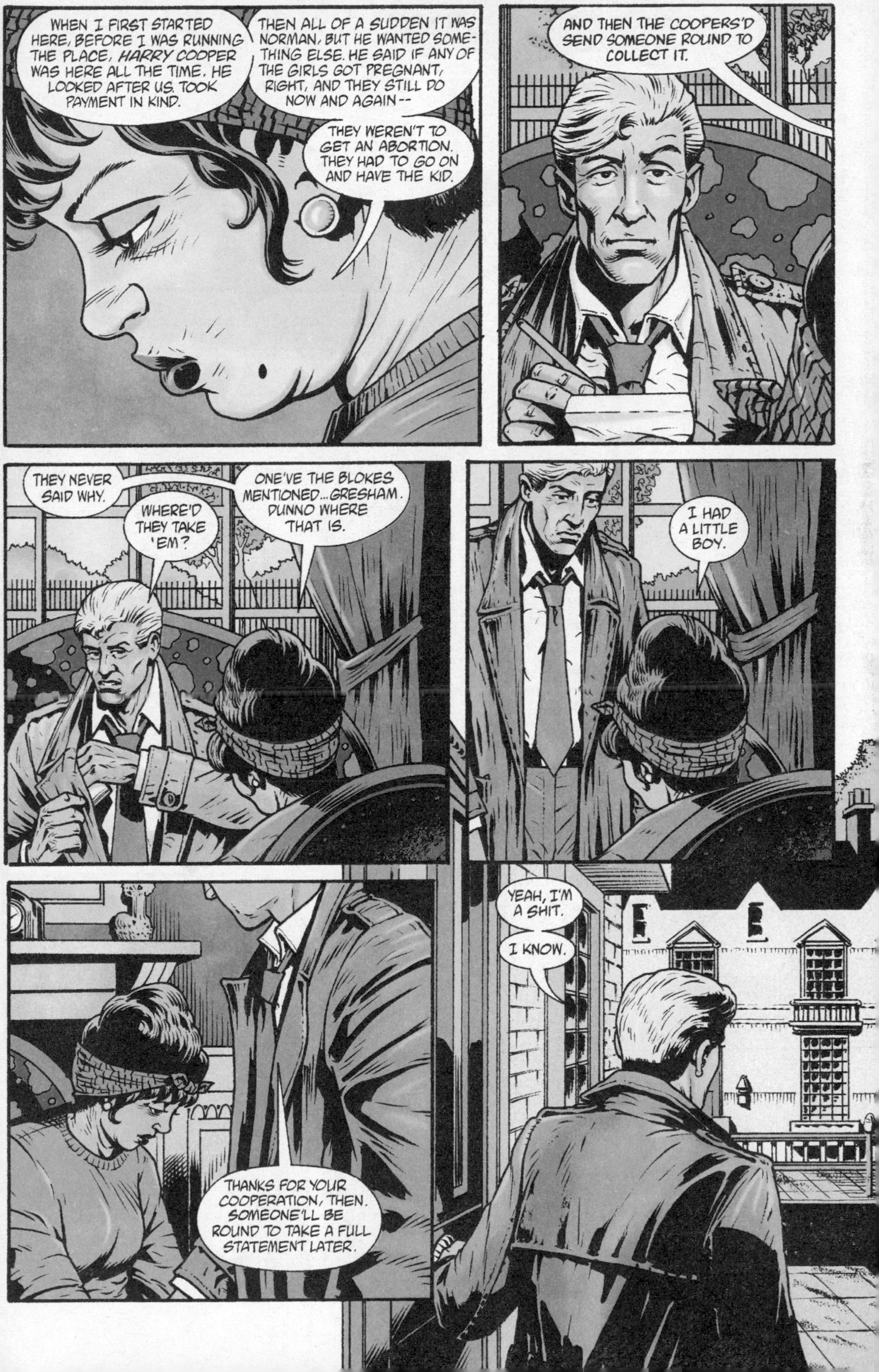
WHEN I FIRST STARTED HERE, BEFORE I WAS RUNNING THE PLACE, HARRY COOPER WAS HERE ALL THE TIME. HE LOOKED AFTER US. TOOK PAYMENT IN KIND.
THEN ALL OF A SUDDEN IT WAS NORMAN, BUT HE WANTED SOMETHING ELSE. HE SAID IF ANY OF THE GIRLS GOT PREGNANT, RIGHT, AND THEY STILL DO NOW AND AGAIN--
THEY WEREN'T TO GET AN ABORTION. THEY HAD TO GO ON AND HAVE THE KID.
AND THEN THE COOPERS'D SEND SOMEONE ROUND TO COLLECT IT.
THEY NEVER SAID WHY.
WHERE'D THEY TAKE 'EM?
ONE'VE THE BLOKES MENTIONED...GRESHAM. DUNNO WHERE THAT IS.
I HAD A LITTLE BOY.
THANKS FOR YOUR COOPERATION, THEN. SOMEONE'LL BE ROUND TO TAKE A FULL STATEMENT LATER.
YEAH, I'M A SHIT.
I KNOW.

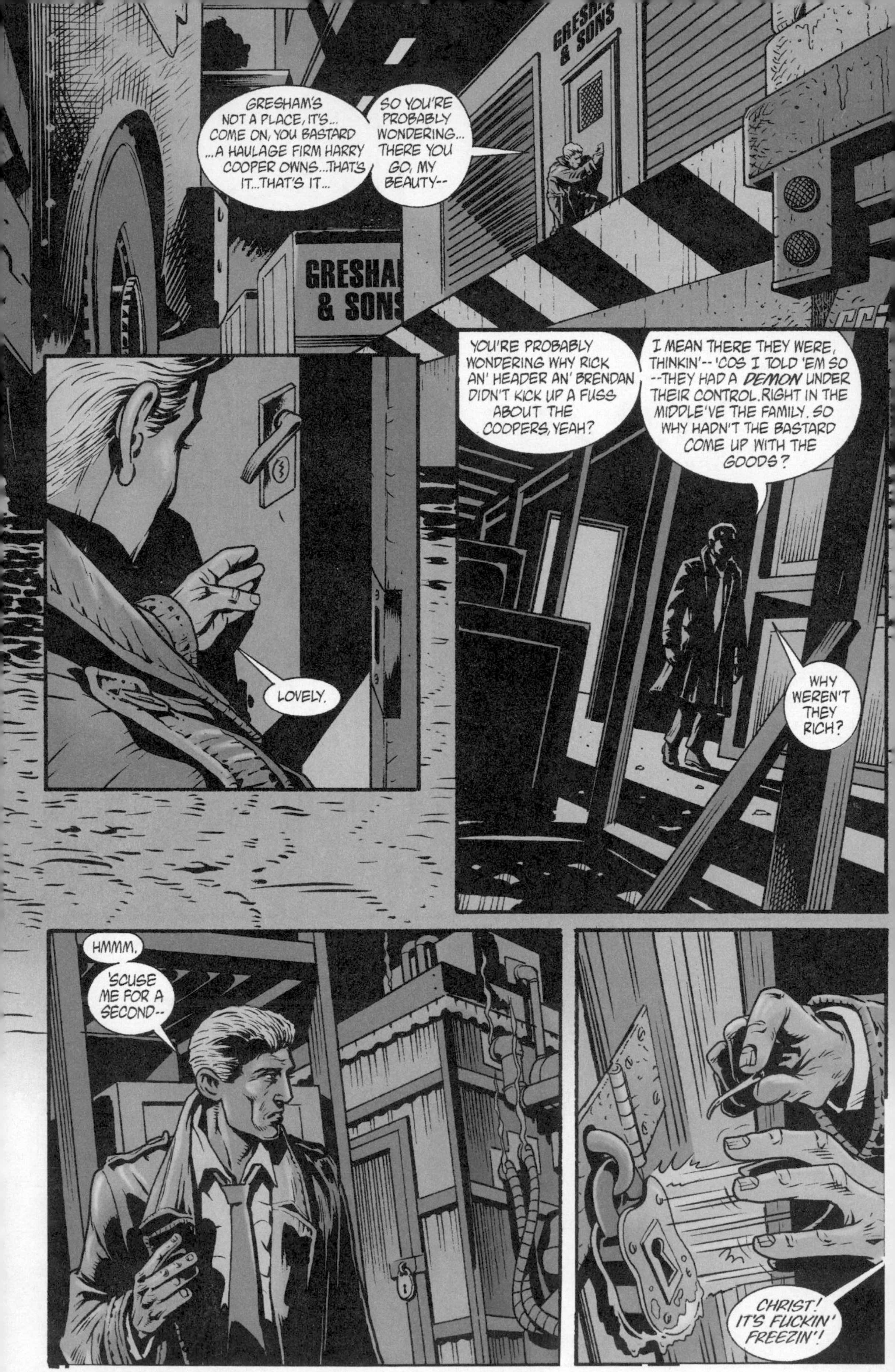
GRESHAM & SONS
GRESHAM'S NOT A PLACE, IT'S... COME ON, YOU BASTARD ...A HAULAGE FIRM HARRY COOPER OWNS...THAT'S IT...THAT'S IT...
SO YOU'RE PROBABLY WONDERING... THERE YOU GO, MY BEAUTY--
GRESHA & SONS
LOVELY.
YOU'RE PROBABLY WONDERING WHY RICK AN' HEADER AN' BRENDAN DIDN'T KICK UP A FUSS ABOUT THE COOPERS, YEAH?
I MEAN THERE THEY WERE, THINKIN'-- 'COS I TOLD 'EM SO --THEY HAD A *DEMON* UNDER THEIR CONTROL. RIGHT IN THE MIDDLE'VE THE FAMILY. SO WHY HADN'T THE BASTARD COME UP WITH THE GOODS?
WHY WEREN'T THEY RICH?
HMMM.
'SCUSE ME FOR A SECOND--
CHRIST! IT'S FUCKIN' FREEZIN'!

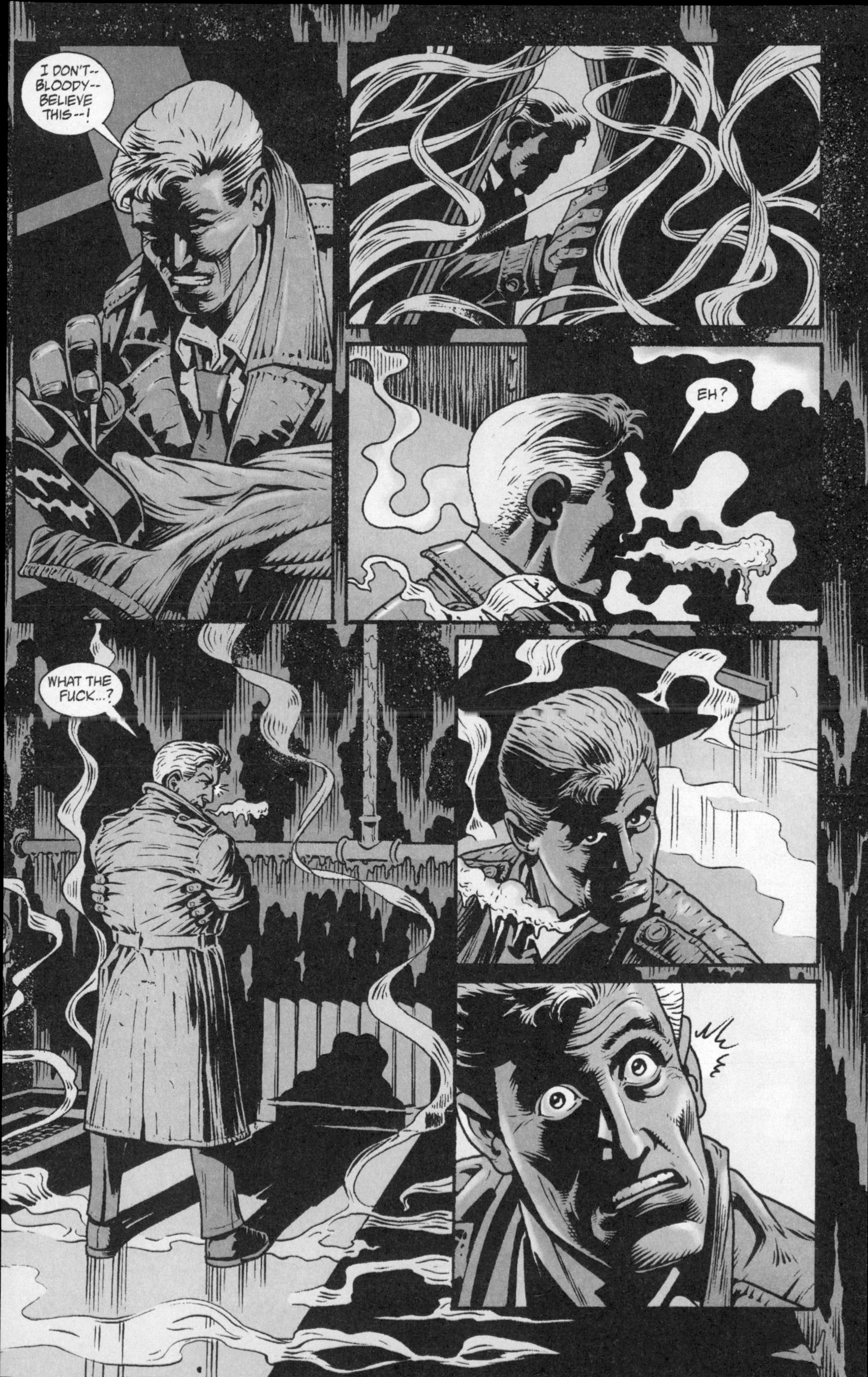

I DON'T-- BLOODY-- BELIEVE THIS--!
EH?
WHAT THE FUCK...?

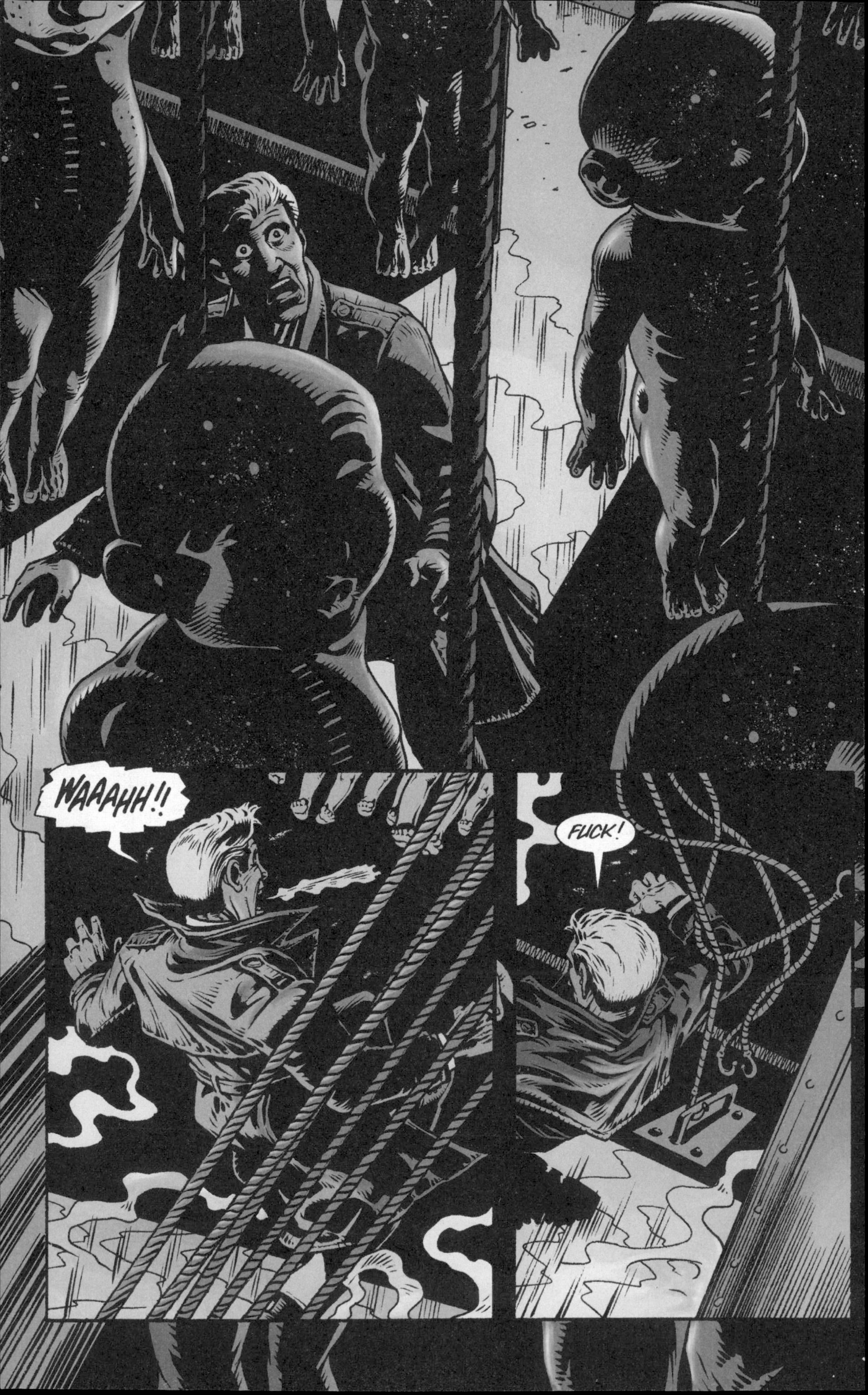
WAAAHH!!
FUCK!

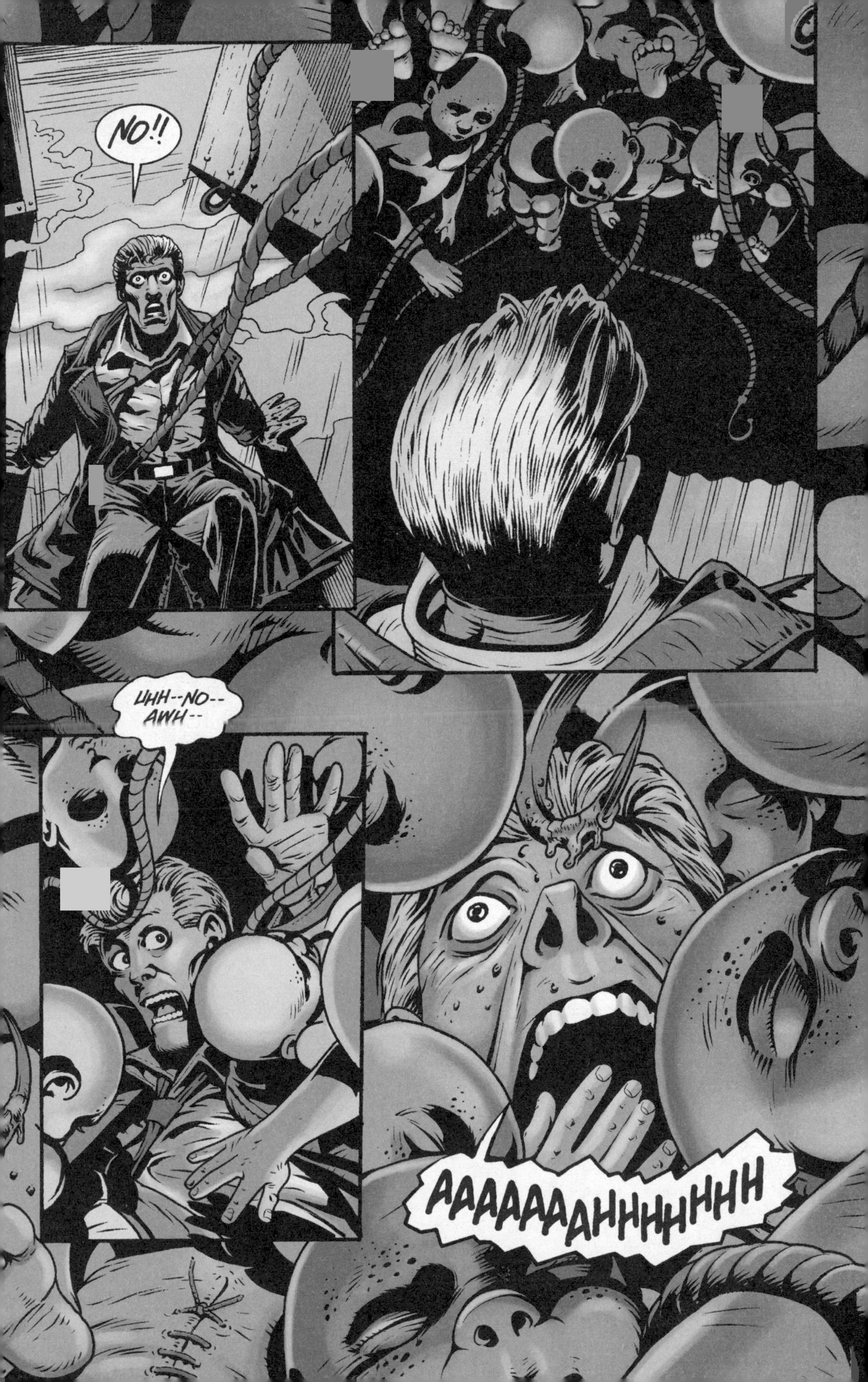
NO!!
UHH--NO--
AWH--
AAAAAAAHHHHHHH

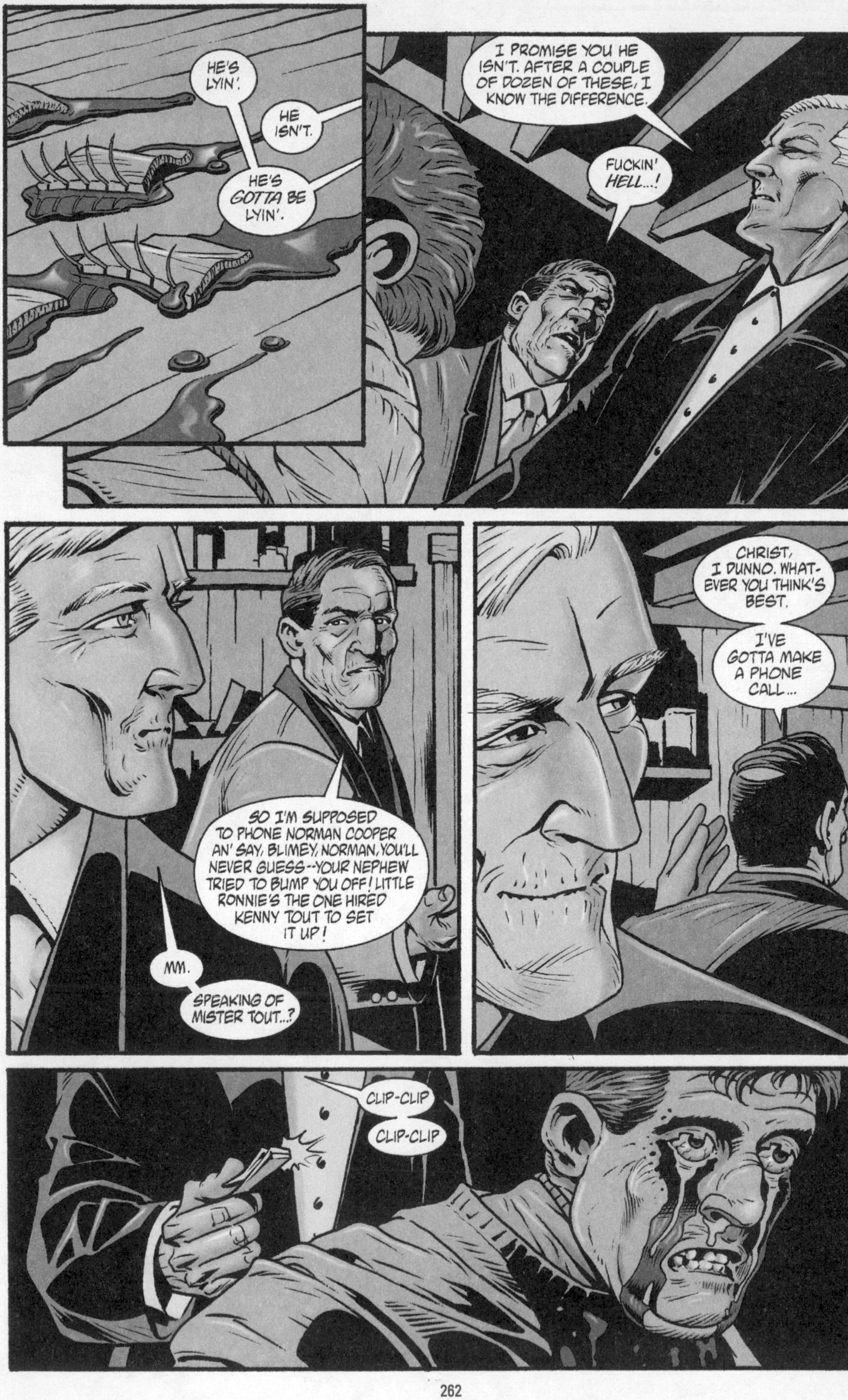
HE'S LYIN'.
HE ISN'T.
HE'S GOTTA BE LYIN'.
I PROMISE YOU HE ISN'T. AFTER A COUPLE OF DOZEN OF THESE, I KNOW THE DIFFERENCE.
FUCKIN' HELL...!
SO I'M SUPPOSED TO PHONE NORMAN COOPER AN' SAY, BLIMEY, NORMAN, YOU'LL NEVER GUESS--YOUR NEPHEW TRIED TO BUMP YOU OFF! LITTLE RONNIE'S THE ONE HIRED KENNY TOUT TO SET IT UP!
MM.
SPEAKING OF MISTER TOUT...?
CHRIST, I DUNNO. WHATEVER YOU THINK'S BEST.
I'VE GOTTA MAKE A PHONE CALL...
CLIP-CLIP
CLIP-CLIP

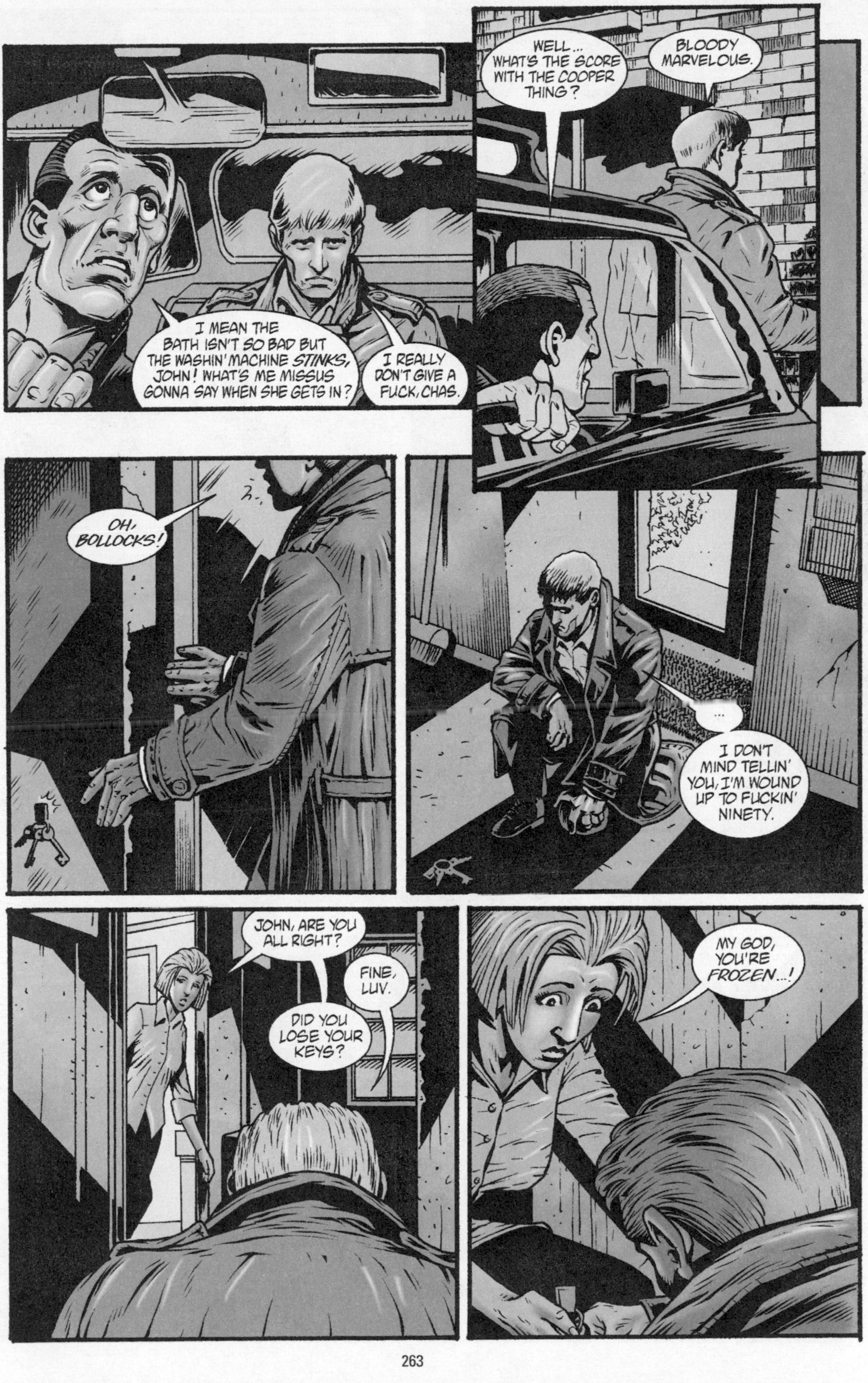
I MEAN THE BATH ISN'T SO BAD BUT THE WASHIN' MACHINE *STINKS*, JOHN! WHAT'S ME MISSUS GONNA SAY WHEN SHE GETS IN?
I REALLY DON'T GIVE A FUCK, CHAS.
WELL... WHAT'S THE SCORE WITH THE COOPER THING?
BLOODY MARVELOUS.
OH, BOLLOCKS!
...
I DON'T MIND TELLIN' YOU, I'M WOUND UP TO FUCKIN' NINETY.
JOHN, ARE YOU ALL RIGHT?
FINE, LUV.
DID YOU LOSE YOUR KEYS?
MY GOD, YOU'RE *FROZEN...!*

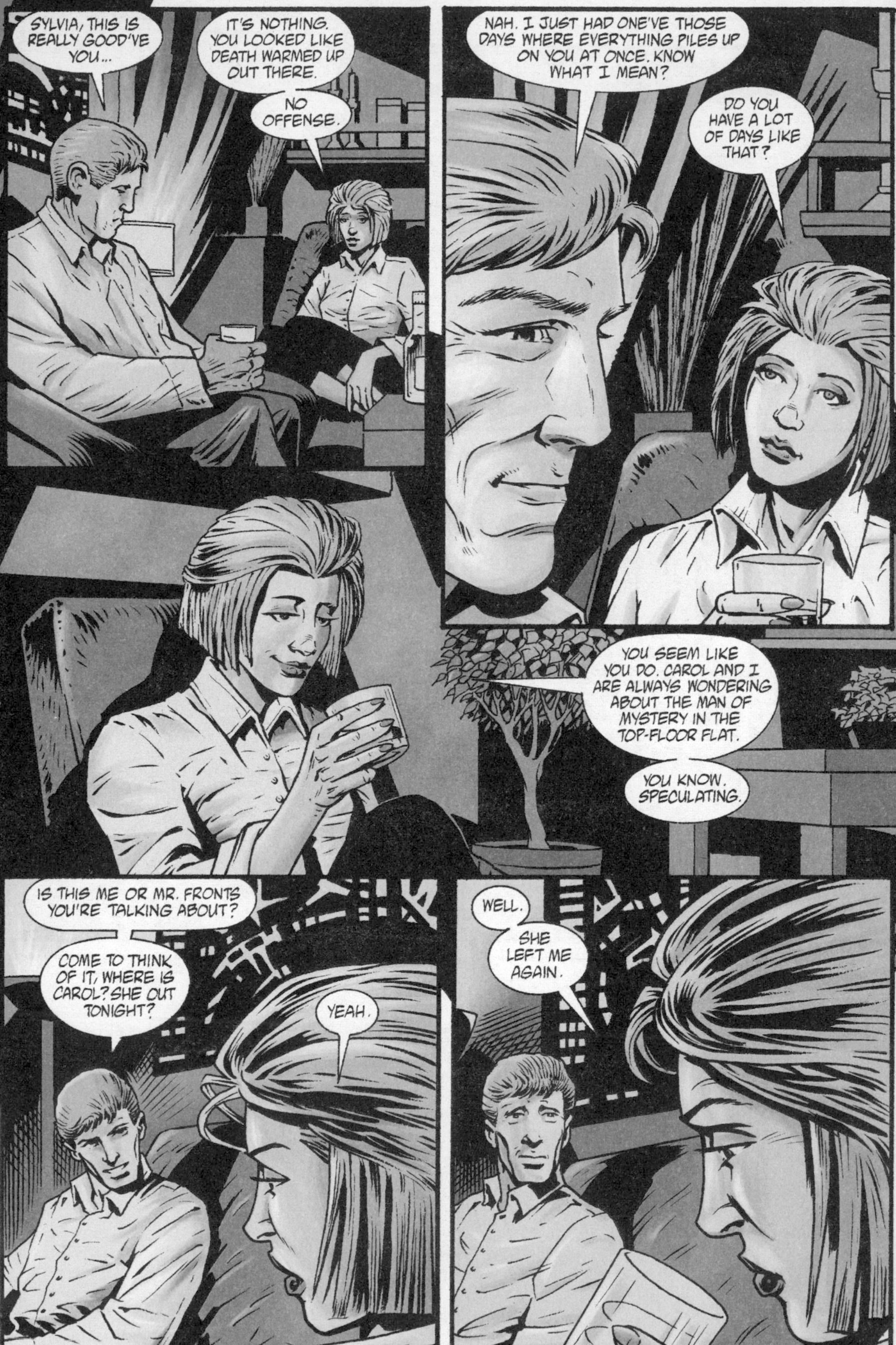
SYLVIA, THIS IS REALLY GOOD'VE YOU...
IT'S NOTHING. YOU LOOKED LIKE DEATH WARMED UP OUT THERE.
NO OFFENSE.
NAH. I JUST HAD ONE'VE THOSE DAYS WHERE EVERYTHING PILES UP ON YOU AT ONCE. KNOW WHAT I MEAN?
DO YOU HAVE A LOT OF DAYS LIKE THAT?
YOU SEEM LIKE YOU DO. CAROL AND I ARE ALWAYS WONDERING ABOUT THE MAN OF MYSTERY IN THE TOP-FLOOR FLAT.
YOU KNOW. SPECULATING.
IS THIS ME OR MR. FRONTS YOU'RE TALKING ABOUT?
COME TO THINK OF IT, WHERE IS CAROL? SHE OUT TONIGHT?
YEAH.
WELL.
SHE LEFT ME AGAIN.

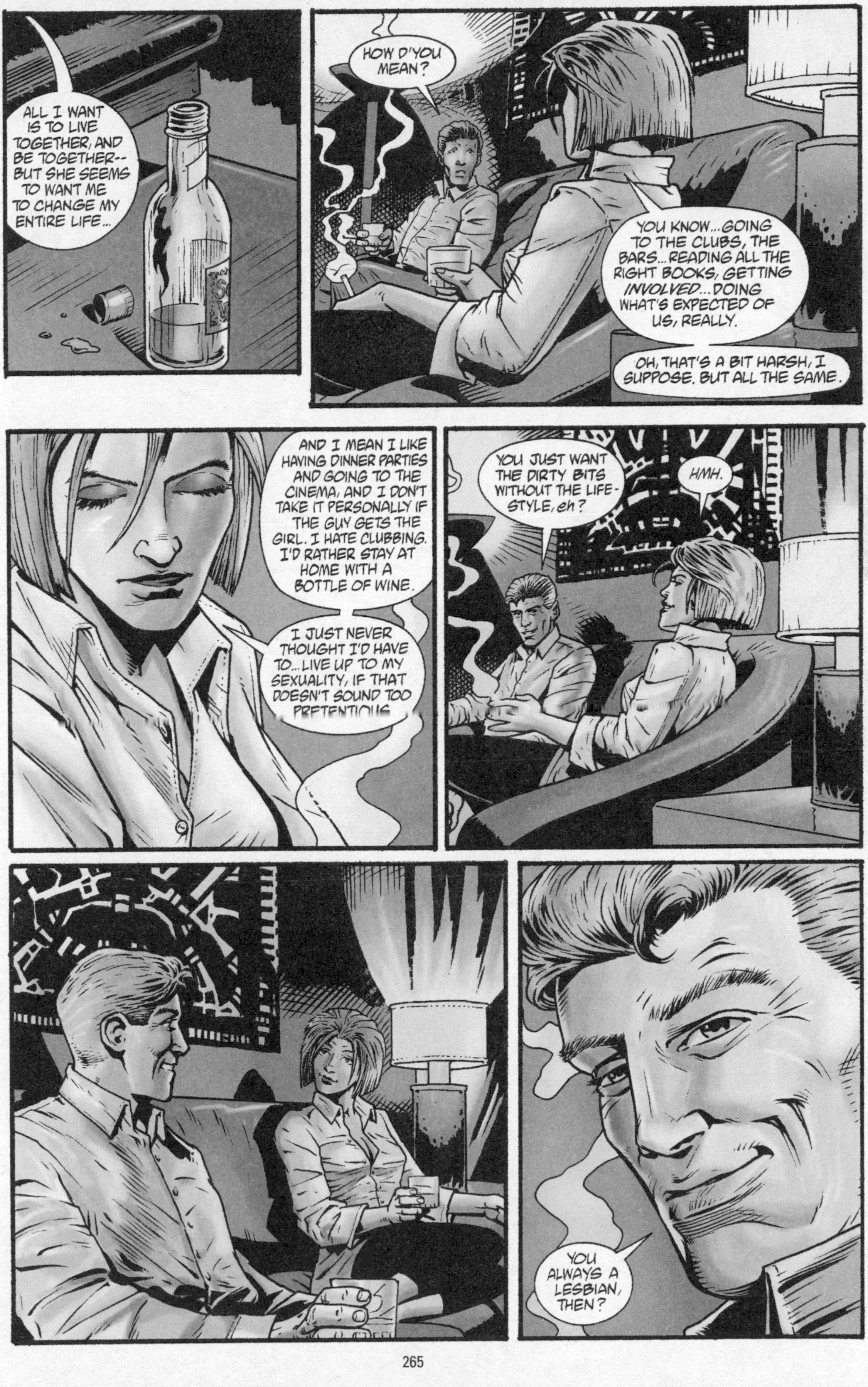

ALL I WANT IS TO LIVE TOGETHER, AND BE TOGETHER-- BUT SHE SEEMS TO WANT ME TO CHANGE MY ENTIRE LIFE...
HOW D'YOU MEAN?
YOU KNOW...GOING TO THE CLUBS, THE BARS...READING ALL THE RIGHT BOOKS, GETTING *INVOLVED*...DOING WHAT'S EXPECTED OF US, REALLY.
OH, THAT'S A BIT HARSH, I SUPPOSE. BUT ALL THE SAME.
AND I MEAN I LIKE HAVING DINNER PARTIES AND GOING TO THE CINEMA, AND I DON'T TAKE IT PERSONALLY IF THE GUY GETS THE GIRL. I HATE CLUBBING. I'D RATHER STAY AT HOME WITH A BOTTLE OF WINE.
I JUST NEVER THOUGHT I'D HAVE TO...LIVE UP TO MY SEXUALITY, IF THAT DOESN'T SOUND TOO PRETENTIOUS.
YOU JUST WANT THE DIRTY BITS WITHOUT THE LIFE-STYLE, *eh*?
HMH.
YOU ALWAYS A LESBIAN, THEN?

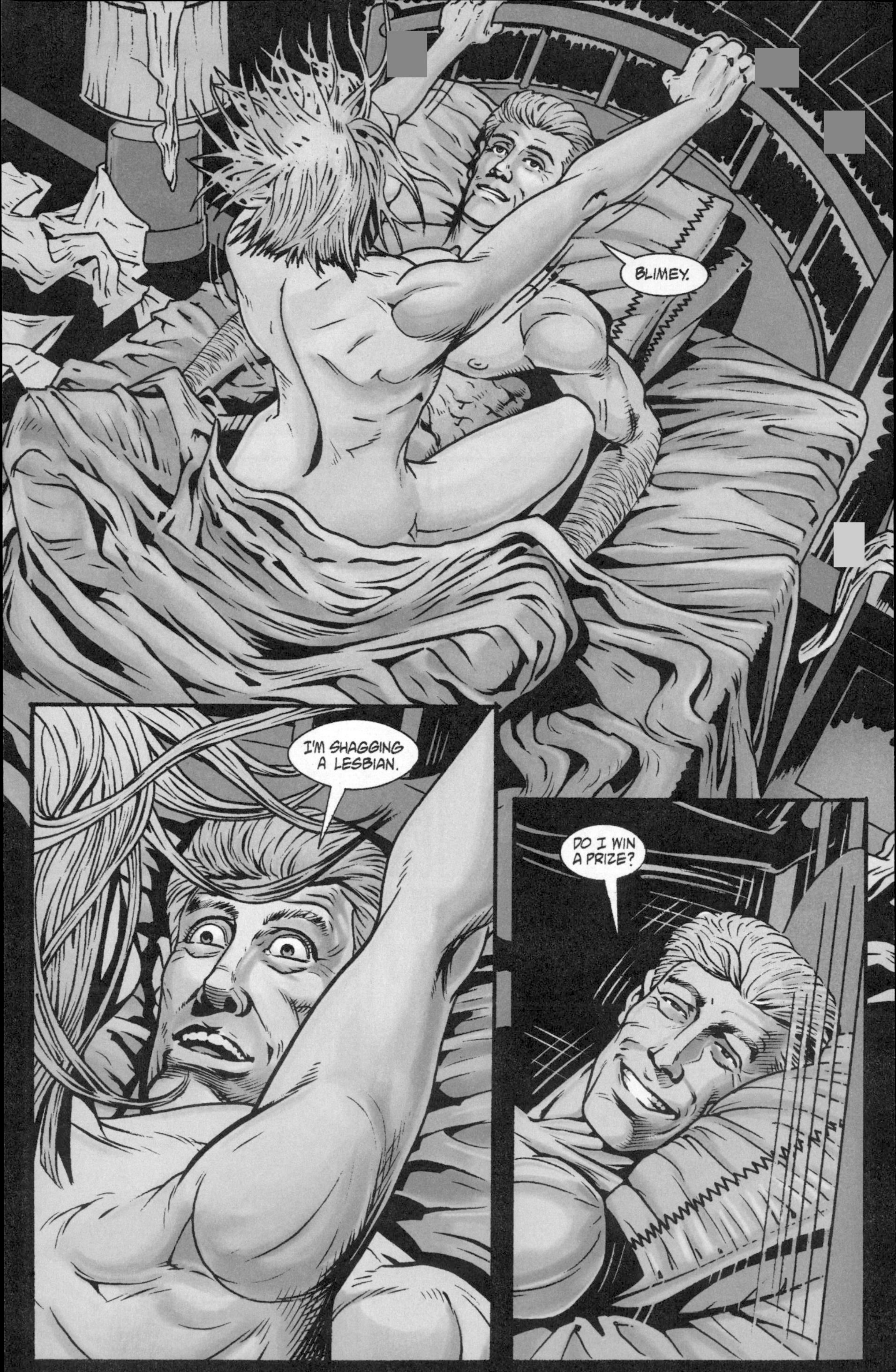
BLIMEY.
I'M SHAGGING A LESBIAN.
DO I WIN A PRIZE?

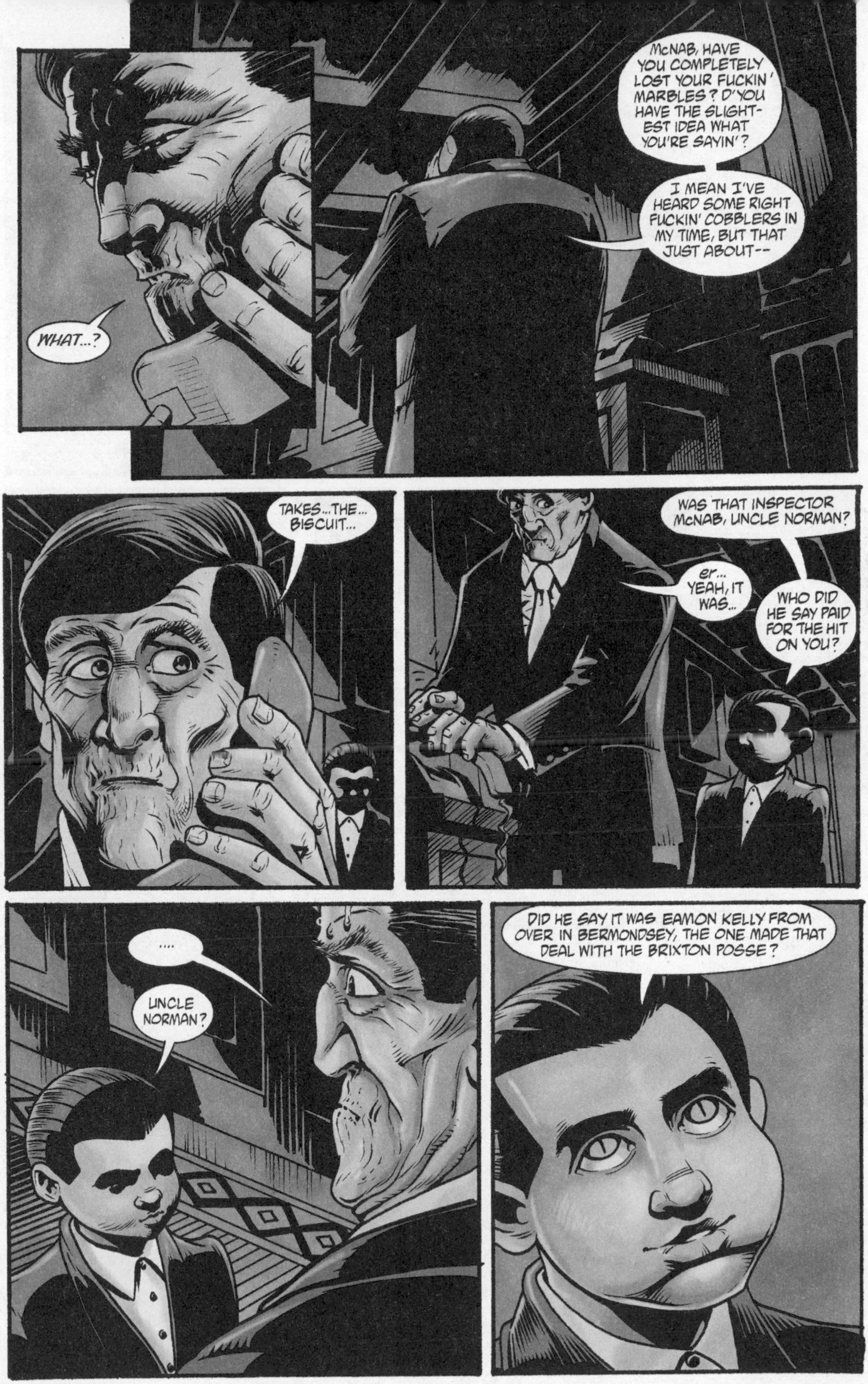
McNAB, HAVE YOU COMPLETELY LOST YOUR FUCKIN' MARBLES? D'YOU HAVE THE SLIGHT-EST IDEA WHAT YOU'RE SAYIN'?
I MEAN I'VE HEARD SOME RIGHT FUCKIN' COBBLERS IN MY TIME, BUT THAT JUST ABOUT--
WHAT...?
TAKES...THE... BISCUIT...
WAS THAT INSPECTOR McNAB, UNCLE NORMAN?
er... YEAH, IT WAS...
WHO DID HE SAY PAID FOR THE HIT ON YOU?
....
UNCLE NORMAN?
DID HE SAY IT WAS EAMON KELLY FROM OVER IN BERMONDSEY, THE ONE MADE THAT DEAL WITH THE BRIXTON POSSE?

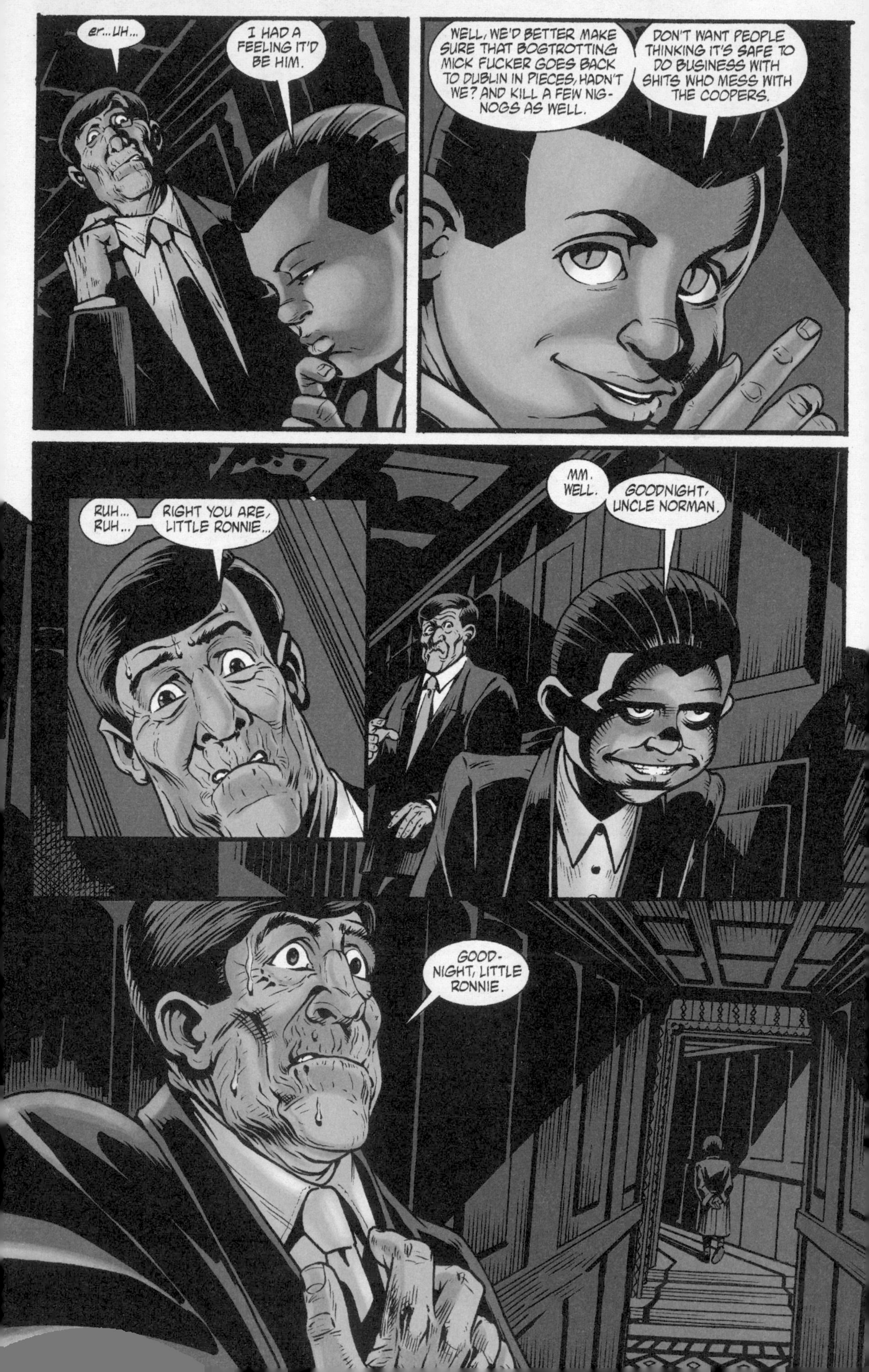
er...UH...
I HAD A FEELING IT'D BE HIM.
WELL, WE'D BETTER MAKE SURE THAT BOGTROTTING MICK FUCKER GOES BACK TO DUBLIN IN PIECES, HADN'T WE? AND KILL A FEW NIG-NOGS AS WELL.
DON'T WANT PEOPLE THINKING IT'S SAFE TO DO BUSINESS WITH SHITS WHO MESS WITH THE COOPERS.
RUH... RUH...
RIGHT YOU ARE, LITTLE RONNIE...
MM. WELL.
GOODNIGHT, UNCLE NORMAN.
GOOD-NIGHT, LITTLE RONNIE.

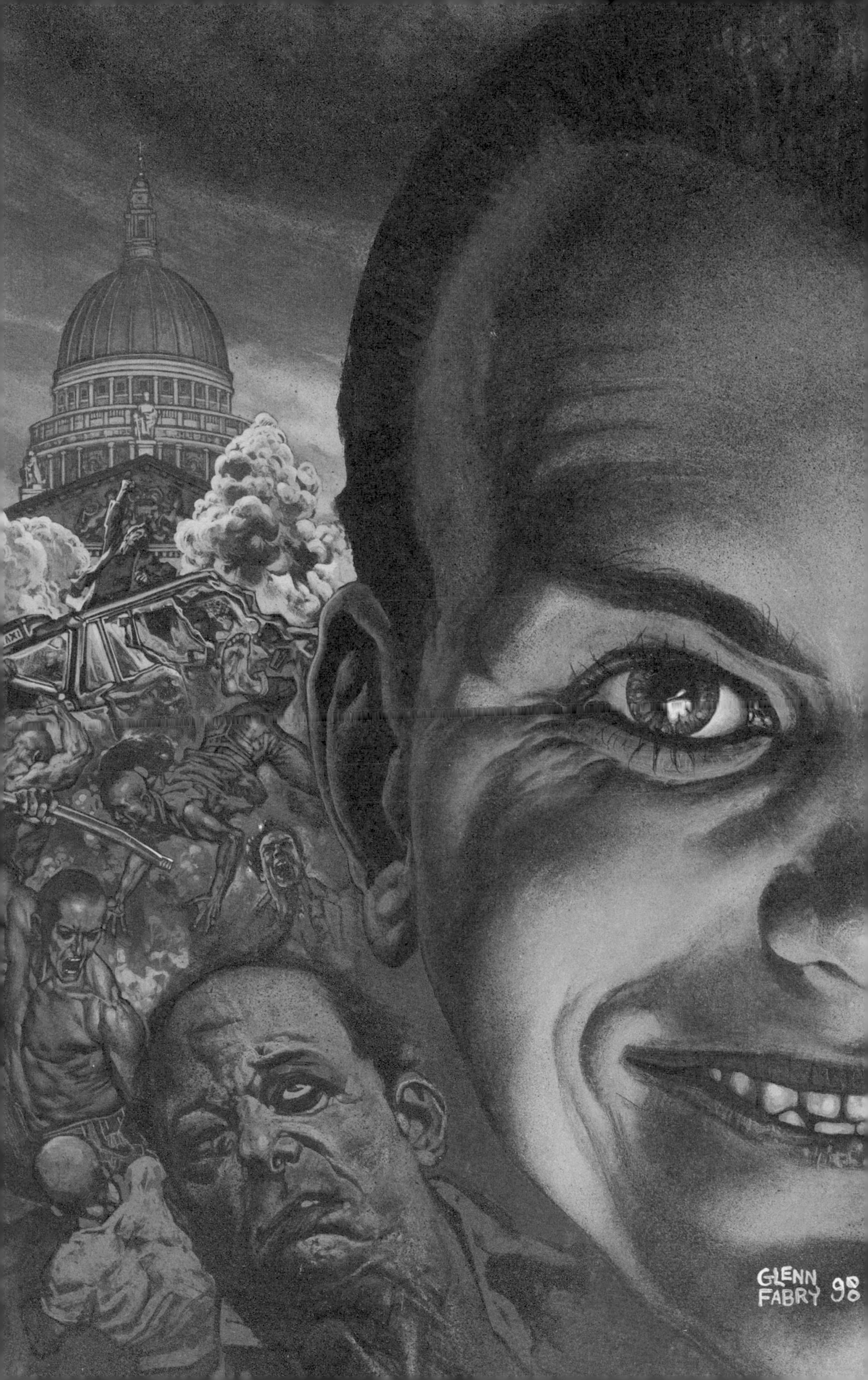
TAXI
GLENN FABRY 90

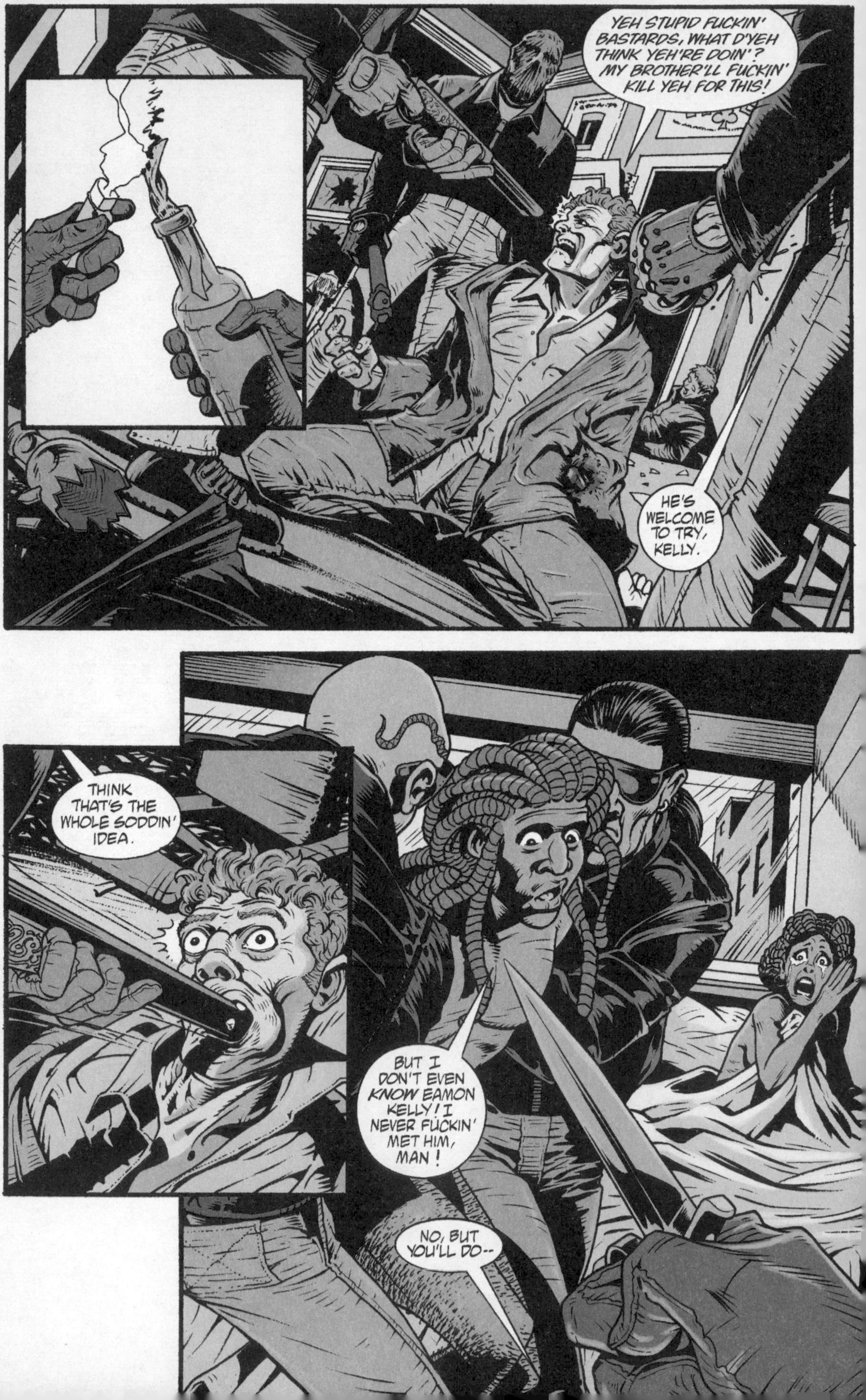
YEH STUPID FUCKIN' BASTARDS, WHAT D'YEH THINK YEH'RE DOIN'? MY BROTHER'LL FUCKIN' KILL YEH FOR THIS!
HE'S WELCOME TO TRY, KELLY.
THINK THAT'S THE WHOLE SODDIN' IDEA.
BUT I DON'T EVEN KNOW EAMON KELLY! I NEVER FUCKIN' MET HIM, MAN!
NO, BUT YOU'LL DO--

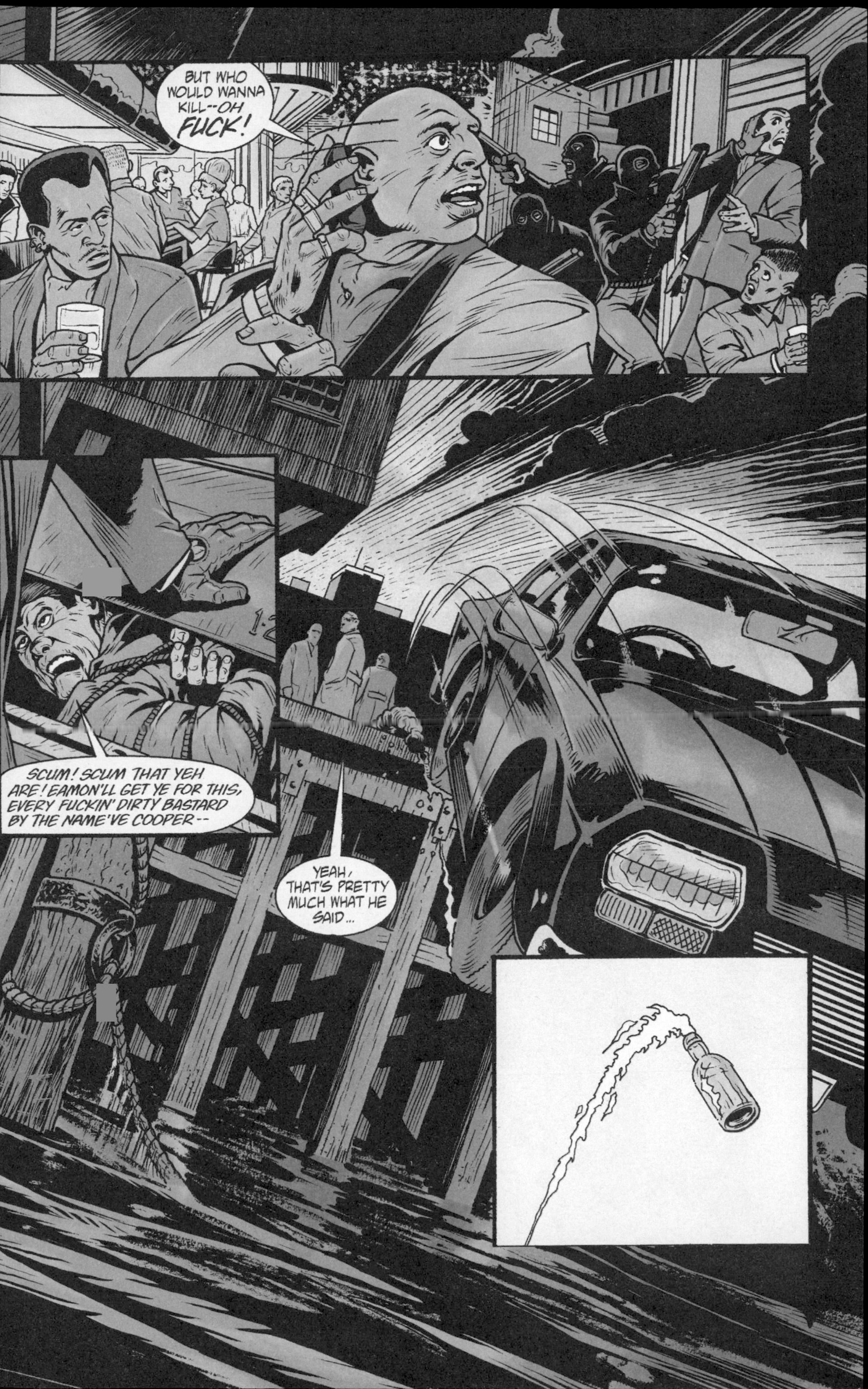
BUT WHO WOULD WANNA KILL--OH FUCK!
SCUM! SCUM THAT YEH ARE! EAMON'LL GET YE FOR THIS, EVERY FUCKIN' DIRTY BASTARD BY THE NAME'VE COOPER--
YEAH, THAT'S PRETTY MUCH WHAT HE SAID...

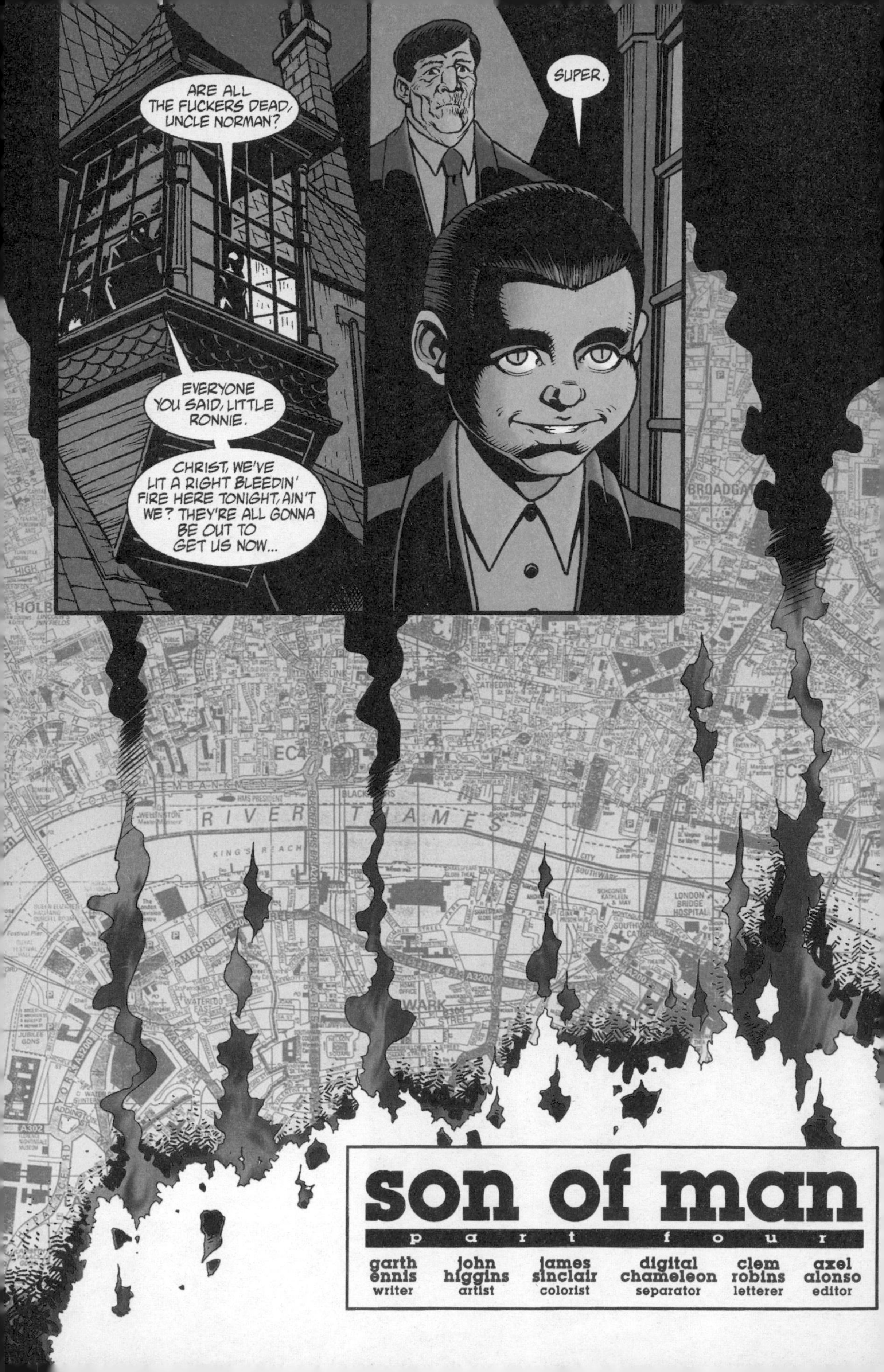
ARE ALL THE FUCKERS DEAD, UNCLE NORMAN?
EVERYONE YOU SAID, LITTLE RONNIE.
CHRIST, WE'VE LIT A RIGHT BLEEDIN' FIRE HERE TONIGHT, AIN'T WE? THEY'RE ALL GONNA BE OUT TO GET US NOW...
SUPER.
RIVER THAMES
son of man
part four
garth ennis writer
john higgins artist
james sinclair colorist
digital chameleon separator
clem robins letterer
axel alonso editor

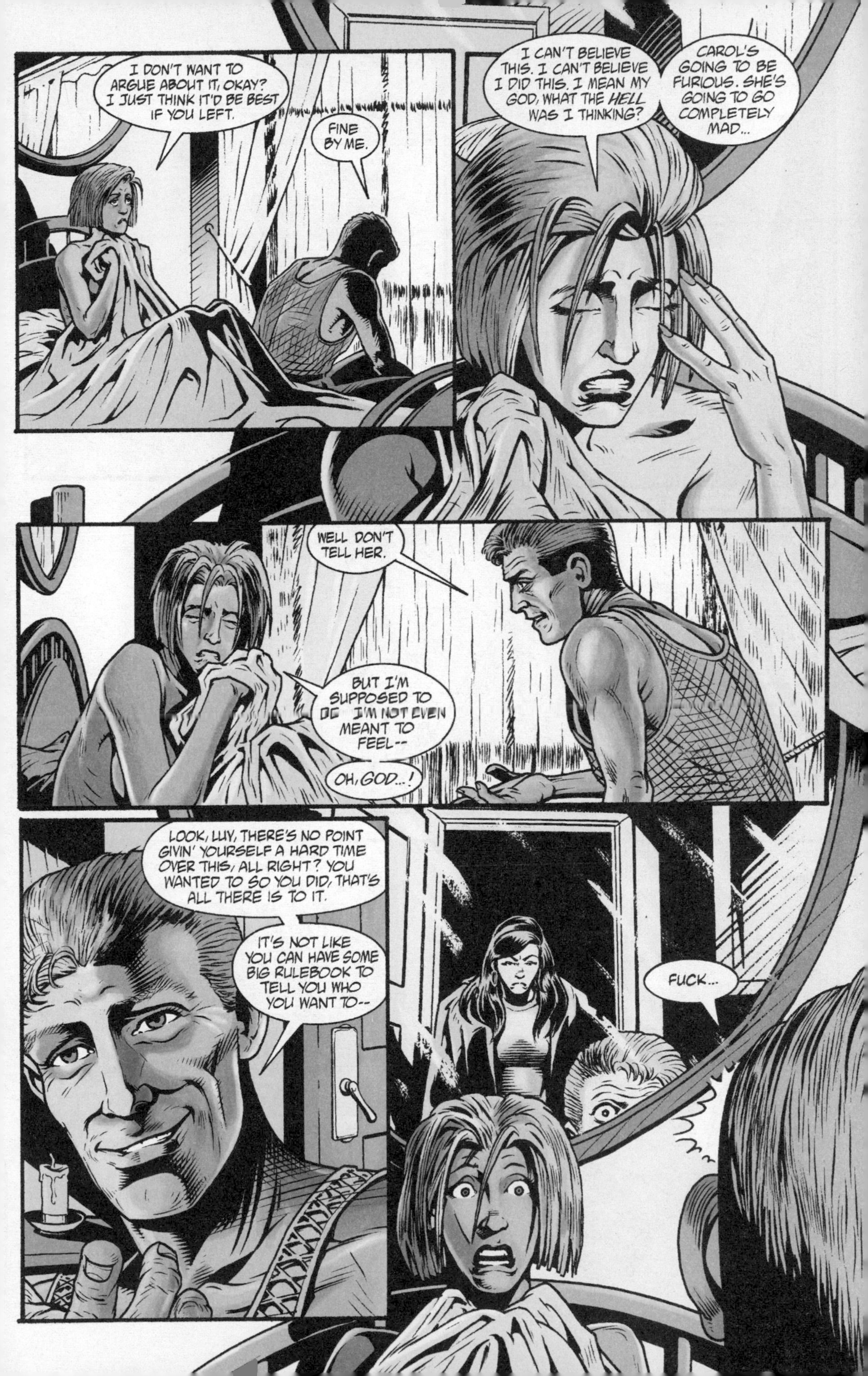
I DON'T WANT TO ARGUE ABOUT IT, OKAY? I JUST THINK IT'D BE BEST IF YOU LEFT.
FINE BY ME.
I CAN'T BELIEVE THIS. I CAN'T BELIEVE I DID THIS. I MEAN MY GOD, WHAT THE *HELL* WAS I THINKING?
CAROL'S GOING TO BE FURIOUS. SHE'S GOING TO GO COMPLETELY MAD...
WELL DON'T TELL HER.
BUT I'M SUPPOSED TO BE-- I'M NOT EVEN MEANT TO FEEL--
OH, GOD...!
LOOK, LUV, THERE'S NO POINT GIVIN' YOURSELF A HARD TIME OVER THIS, ALL RIGHT? YOU WANTED TO SO YOU DID, THAT'S ALL THERE IS TO IT.
IT'S NOT LIKE YOU CAN HAVE SOME BIG RULEBOOK TO TELL YOU WHO YOU WANT TO--
FUCK...

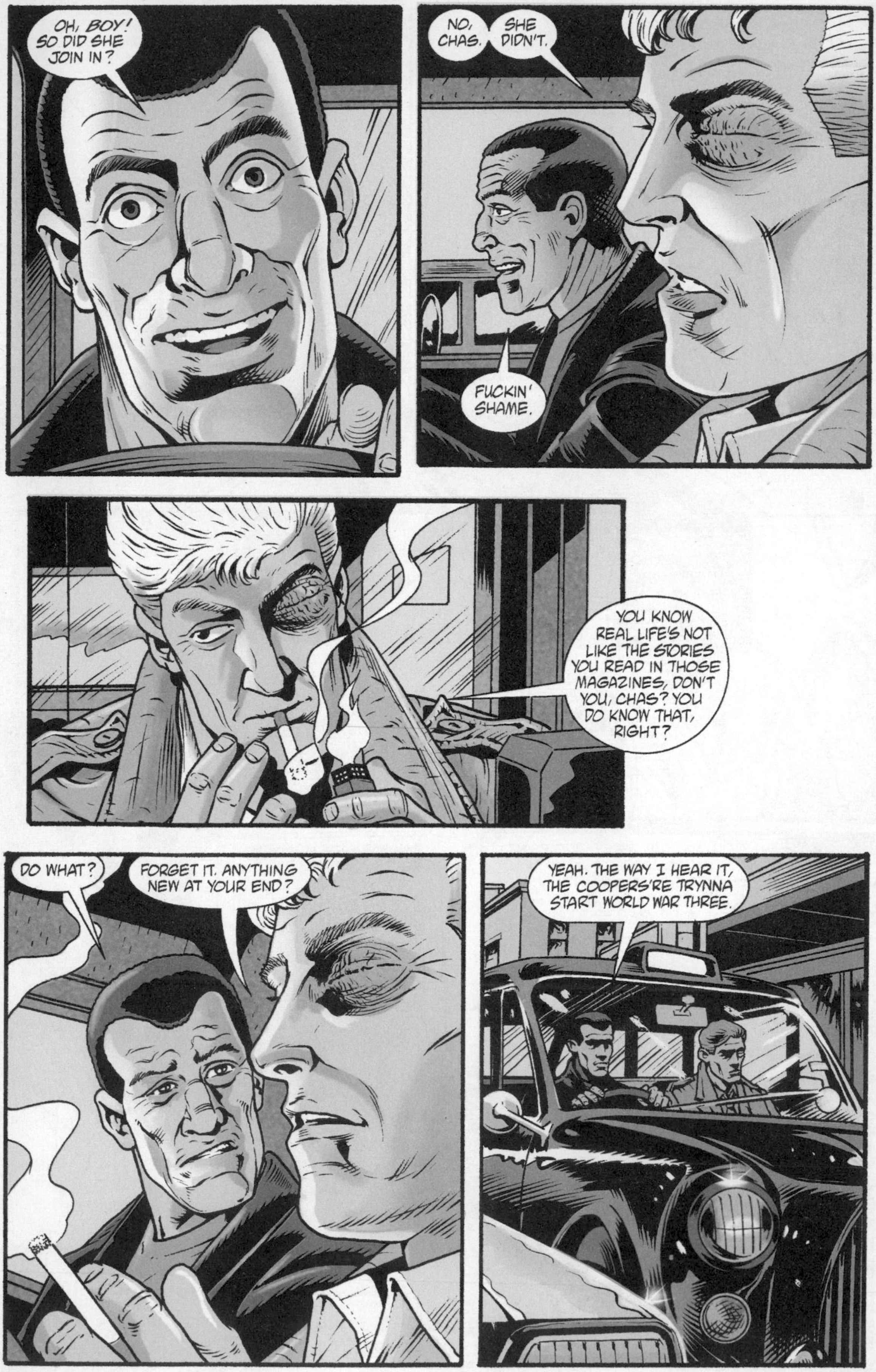
OH, BOY! SO DID SHE JOIN IN?
NO, CHAS.
SHE DIDN'T.
FUCKIN' SHAME.
YOU KNOW REAL LIFE'S NOT LIKE THE STORIES YOU READ IN THOSE MAGAZINES, DON'T YOU, CHAS? YOU DO KNOW THAT, RIGHT?
DO WHAT?
FORGET IT. ANYTHING NEW AT YOUR END?
YEAH. THE WAY I HEAR IT, THE COOPERS'RE TRYNNA START WORLD WAR THREE.

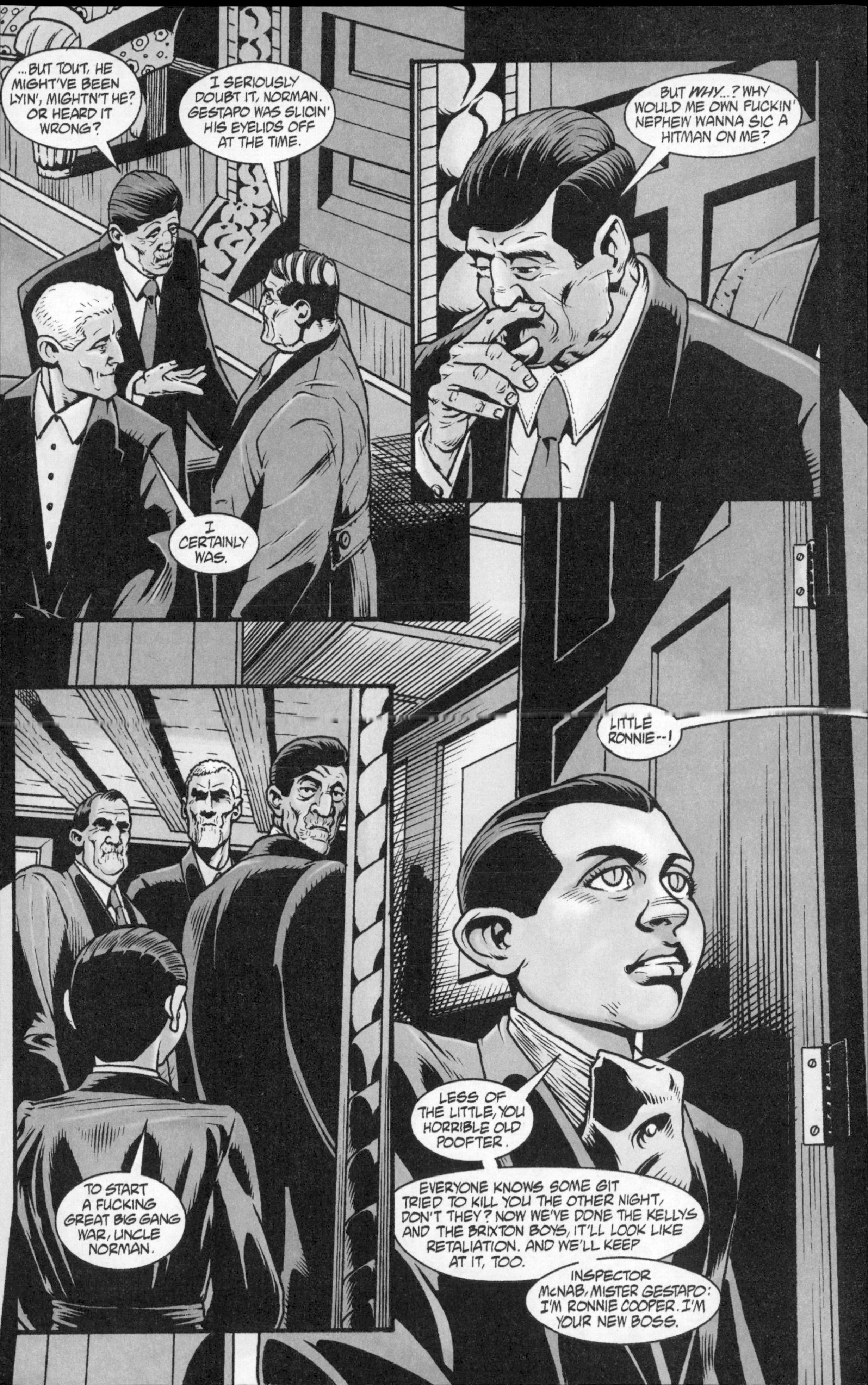
...BUT TOUT, HE MIGHT'VE BEEN LYIN', MIGHTN'T HE? OR HEARD IT WRONG?
I SERIOUSLY DOUBT IT, NORMAN. GESTAPO WAS SLICIN' HIS EYELIDS OFF AT THE TIME.
I CERTAINLY WAS.
BUT WHY...? WHY WOULD ME OWN FUCKIN' NEPHEW WANNA SIC A HITMAN ON ME?
TO START A FUCKING GREAT BIG GANG WAR, UNCLE NORMAN.
LITTLE RONNIE--!
LESS OF THE LITTLE, YOU HORRIBLE OLD POOFTER.
EVERYONE KNOWS SOME GIT TRIED TO KILL YOU THE OTHER NIGHT, DON'T THEY? NOW WE'VE DONE THE KELLYS AND THE BRIXTON BOYS, IT'LL LOOK LIKE RETALIATION. AND WE'LL KEEP AT IT, TOO.
INSPECTOR McNAB, MISTER GESTAPO: I'M RONNIE COOPER. I'M YOUR NEW BOSS.

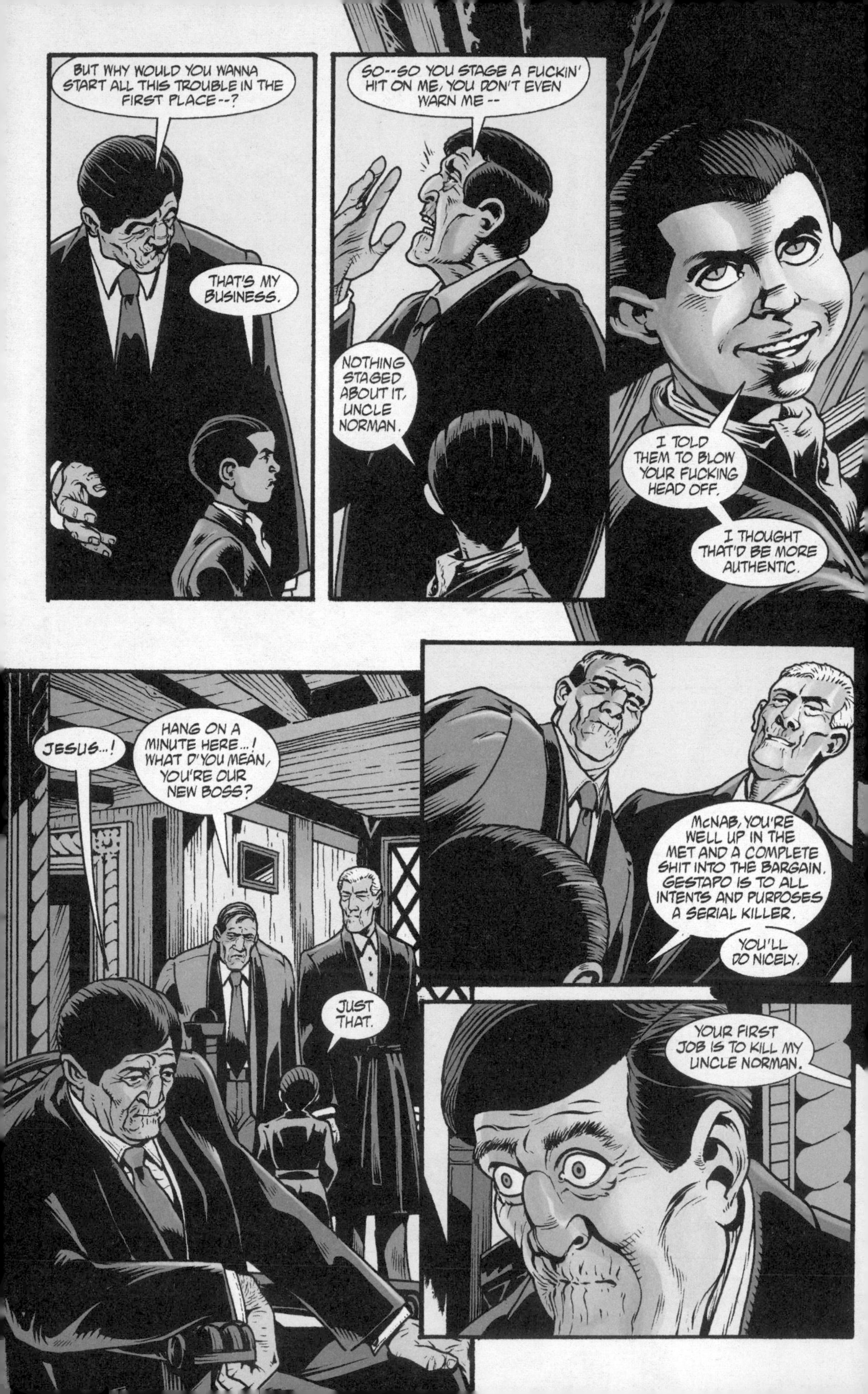
BUT WHY WOULD YOU WANNA START ALL THIS TROUBLE IN THE FIRST PLACE--?
THAT'S MY BUSINESS.
SO--SO YOU STAGE A FUCKIN' HIT ON ME, YOU DON'T EVEN WARN ME--
NOTHING STAGED ABOUT IT, UNCLE NORMAN.
I TOLD THEM TO BLOW YOUR FUCKING HEAD OFF.
I THOUGHT THAT'D BE MORE AUTHENTIC.
JESUS...!
HANG ON A MINUTE HERE...! WHAT D'YOU MEAN, YOU'RE OUR NEW BOSS?
JUST THAT.
McNAB, YOU'RE WELL UP IN THE MET AND A COMPLETE SHIT INTO THE BARGAIN. GESTAPO IS TO ALL INTENTS AND PURPOSES A SERIAL KILLER.
YOU'LL DO NICELY.
YOUR FIRST JOB IS TO KILL MY UNCLE NORMAN.

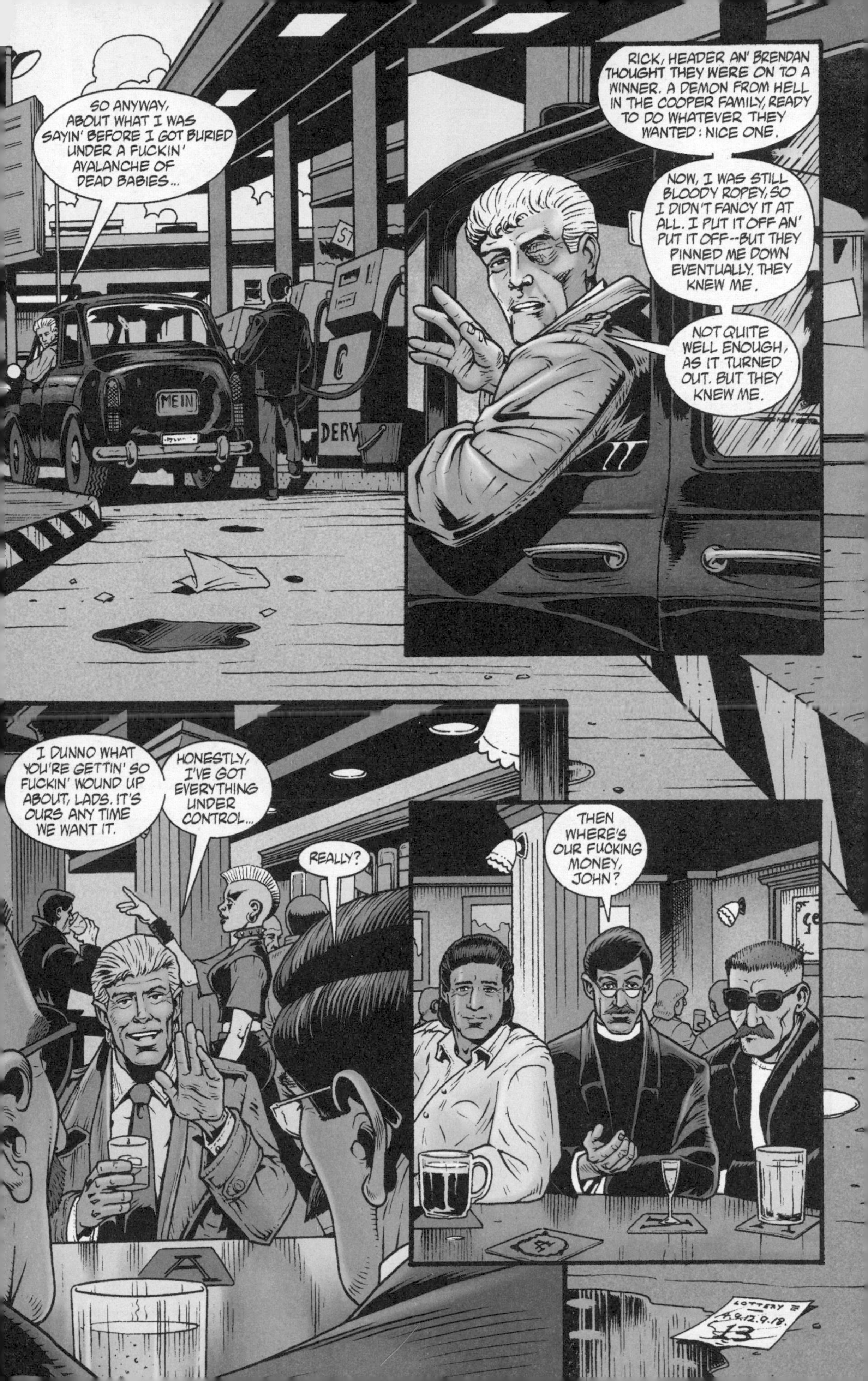
SO ANYWAY, ABOUT WHAT I WAS SAYIN' BEFORE I GOT BURIED UNDER A FUCKIN' AVALANCHE OF DEAD BABIES...
MEIN
DERV
RICK, HEADER AN' BRENDAN THOUGHT THEY WERE ON TO A WINNER. A DEMON FROM HELL IN THE COOPER FAMILY, READY TO DO WHATEVER THEY WANTED: NICE ONE.
NOW, I WAS STILL BLOODY ROPEY, SO I DIDN'T FANCY IT AT ALL. I PUT IT OFF AN' PUT IT OFF--BUT THEY PINNED ME DOWN EVENTUALLY. THEY KNEW ME.
NOT QUITE WELL ENOUGH, AS IT TURNED OUT. BUT THEY KNEW ME.
I DUNNO WHAT YOU'RE GETTIN' SO FUCKIN' WOUND UP ABOUT, LADS. IT'S OURS ANY TIME WE WANT IT.
HONESTLY, I'VE GOT EVERYTHING UNDER CONTROL...
REALLY?
THEN WHERE'S OUR FUCKING MONEY, JOHN?
LOTTERY
13

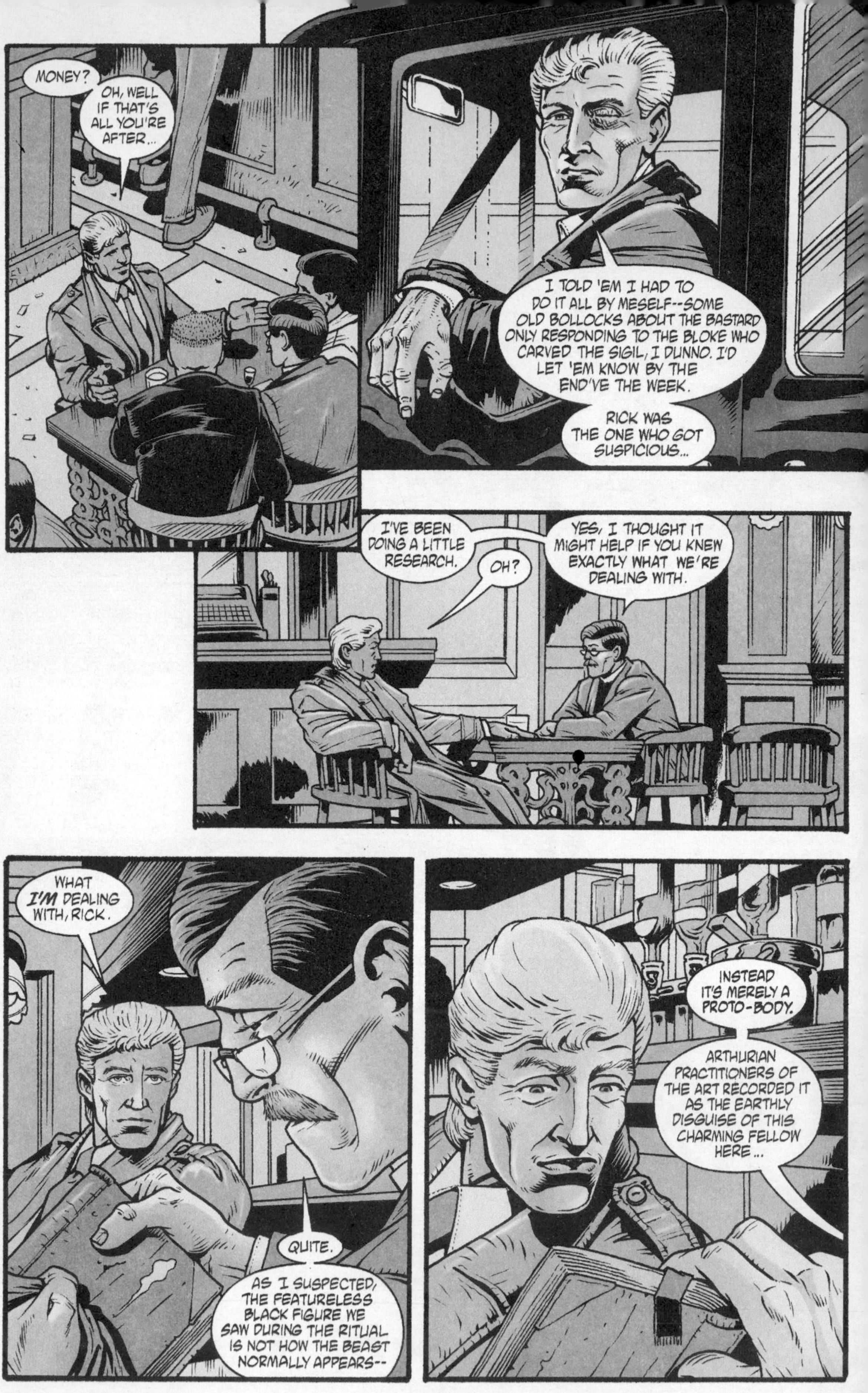
MONEY?
OH, WELL IF THAT'S ALL YOU'RE AFTER...
I TOLD 'EM I HAD TO DO IT ALL BY MESELF--SOME OLD BOLLOCKS ABOUT THE BASTARD ONLY RESPONDING TO THE BLOKE WHO CARVED THE SIGIL, I DUNNO. I'D LET 'EM KNOW BY THE END'VE THE WEEK.
RICK WAS THE ONE WHO GOT SUSPICIOUS...
I'VE BEEN DOING A LITTLE RESEARCH.
OH?
YES, I THOUGHT IT MIGHT HELP IF YOU KNEW EXACTLY WHAT WE'RE DEALING WITH.
WHAT *I'M* DEALING WITH, RICK.
QUITE.
AS I SUSPECTED, THE FEATURELESS BLACK FIGURE WE SAW DURING THE RITUAL IS NOT HOW THE BEAST NORMALLY APPEARS--
INSTEAD IT'S MERELY A PROTO-BODY.
ARTHURIAN PRACTITIONERS OF THE ART RECORDED IT AS THE EARTHLY DISGUISE OF THIS CHARMING FELLOW HERE...

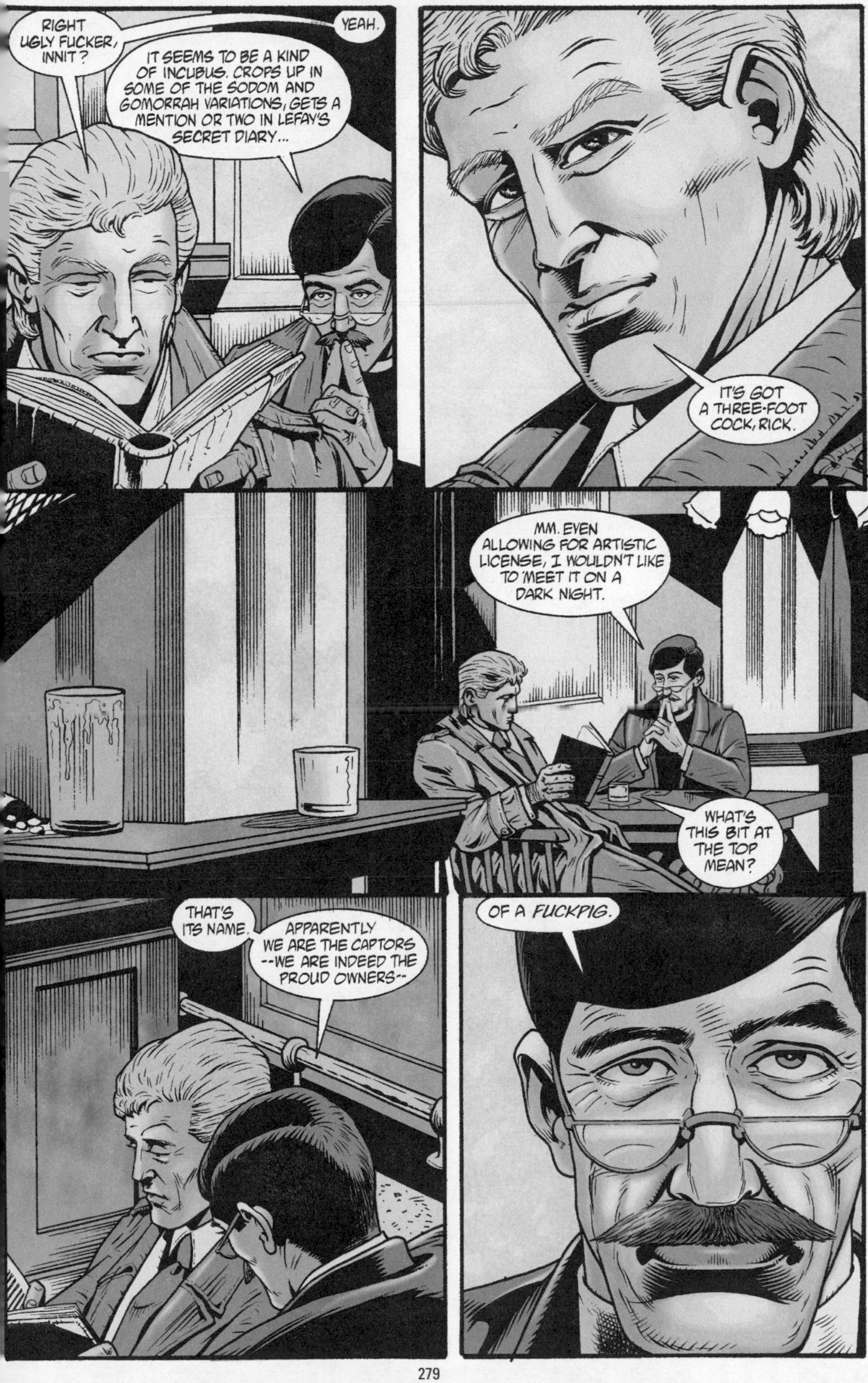
RIGHT UGLY FUCKER, INNIT?
YEAH.
IT SEEMS TO BE A KIND OF INCUBUS. CROPS UP IN SOME OF THE SODOM AND GOMORRAH VARIATIONS, GETS A MENTION OR TWO IN LEFAY'S SECRET DIARY...
IT'S GOT A THREE-FOOT COCK, RICK.
MM. EVEN ALLOWING FOR ARTISTIC LICENSE, I WOULDN'T LIKE TO MEET IT ON A DARK NIGHT.
WHAT'S THIS BIT AT THE TOP MEAN?
THAT'S ITS NAME.
APPARENTLY WE ARE THE CAPTORS --WE ARE INDEED THE PROUD OWNERS--
OF A *FUCKPIG*.

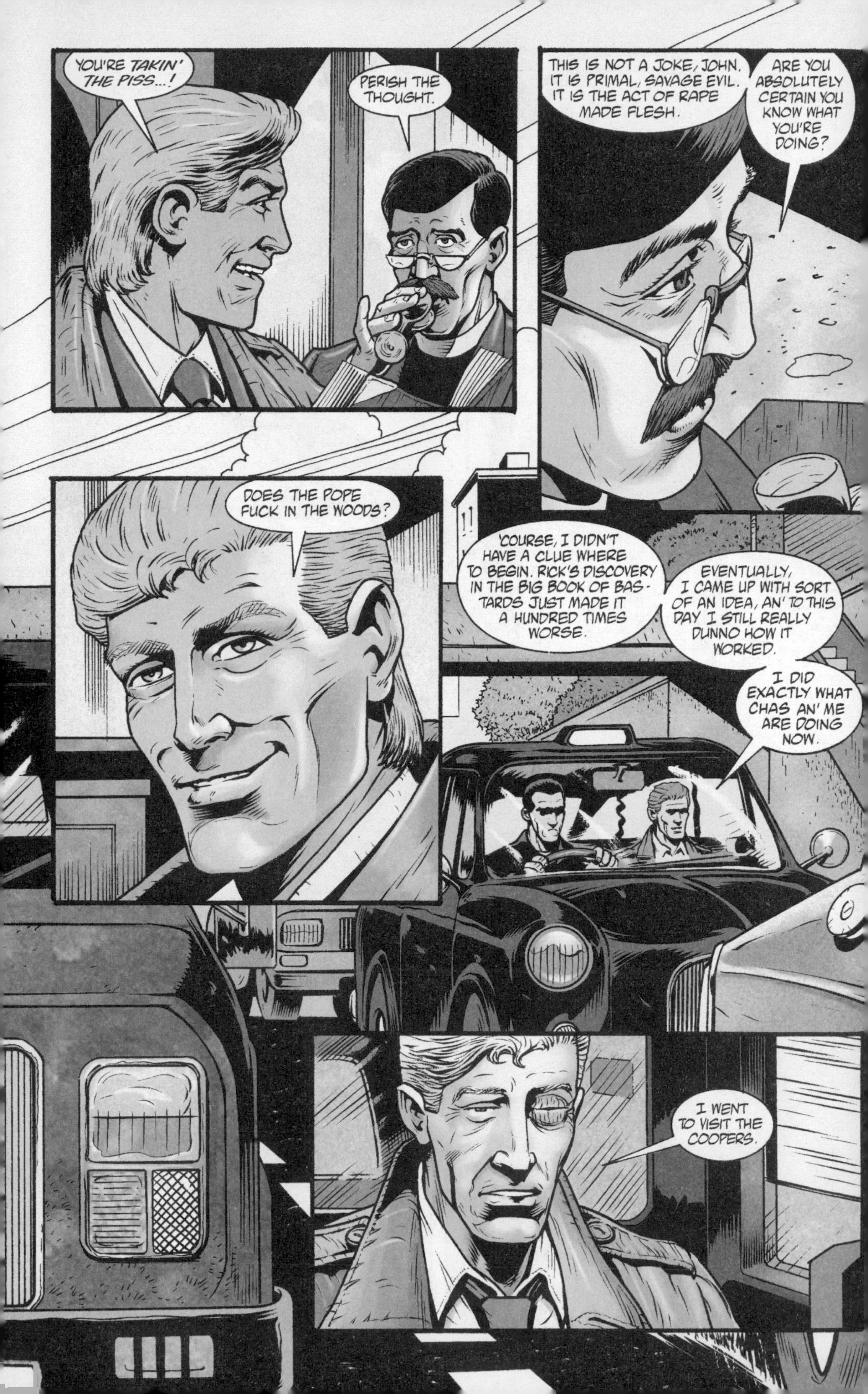
YOU'RE TAKIN' THE PISS...!
PERISH THE THOUGHT.
THIS IS NOT A JOKE, JOHN. IT IS PRIMAL, SAVAGE EVIL. IT IS THE ACT OF RAPE MADE FLESH.
ARE YOU ABSOLUTELY CERTAIN YOU KNOW WHAT YOU'RE DOING?
DOES THE POPE FUCK IN THE WOODS?
'COURSE, I DIDN'T HAVE A CLUE WHERE TO BEGIN. RICK'S DISCOVERY IN THE BIG BOOK OF BAS-TARDS JUST MADE IT A HUNDRED TIMES WORSE.
EVENTUALLY, I CAME UP WITH SORT OF AN IDEA, AN' TO THIS DAY I STILL REALLY DUNNO HOW IT WORKED.
I DID EXACTLY WHAT CHAS AN' ME ARE DOING NOW.
I WENT TO VISIT THE COOPERS.

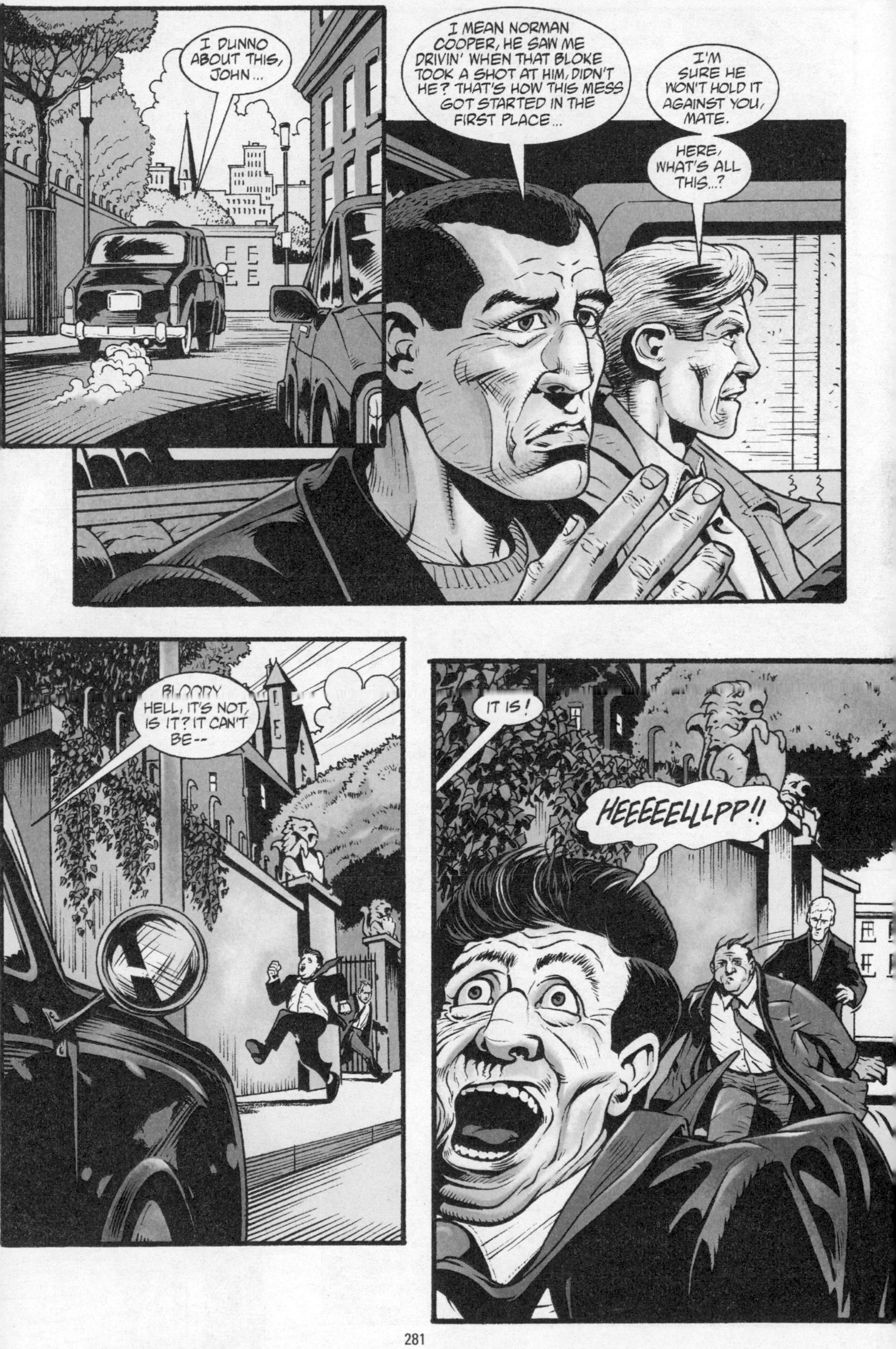
I DUNNO ABOUT THIS, JOHN...
I MEAN NORMAN COOPER, HE SAW ME DRIVIN' WHEN THAT BLOKE TOOK A SHOT AT HIM, DIDN'T HE? THAT'S HOW THIS MESS GOT STARTED IN THE FIRST PLACE...
I'M SURE HE WON'T HOLD IT AGAINST YOU, MATE.
HERE, WHAT'S ALL THIS...?
BLOODY HELL, IT'S NOT, IS IT? IT CAN'T BE--
IT IS!
HEEEEELLLPP!!

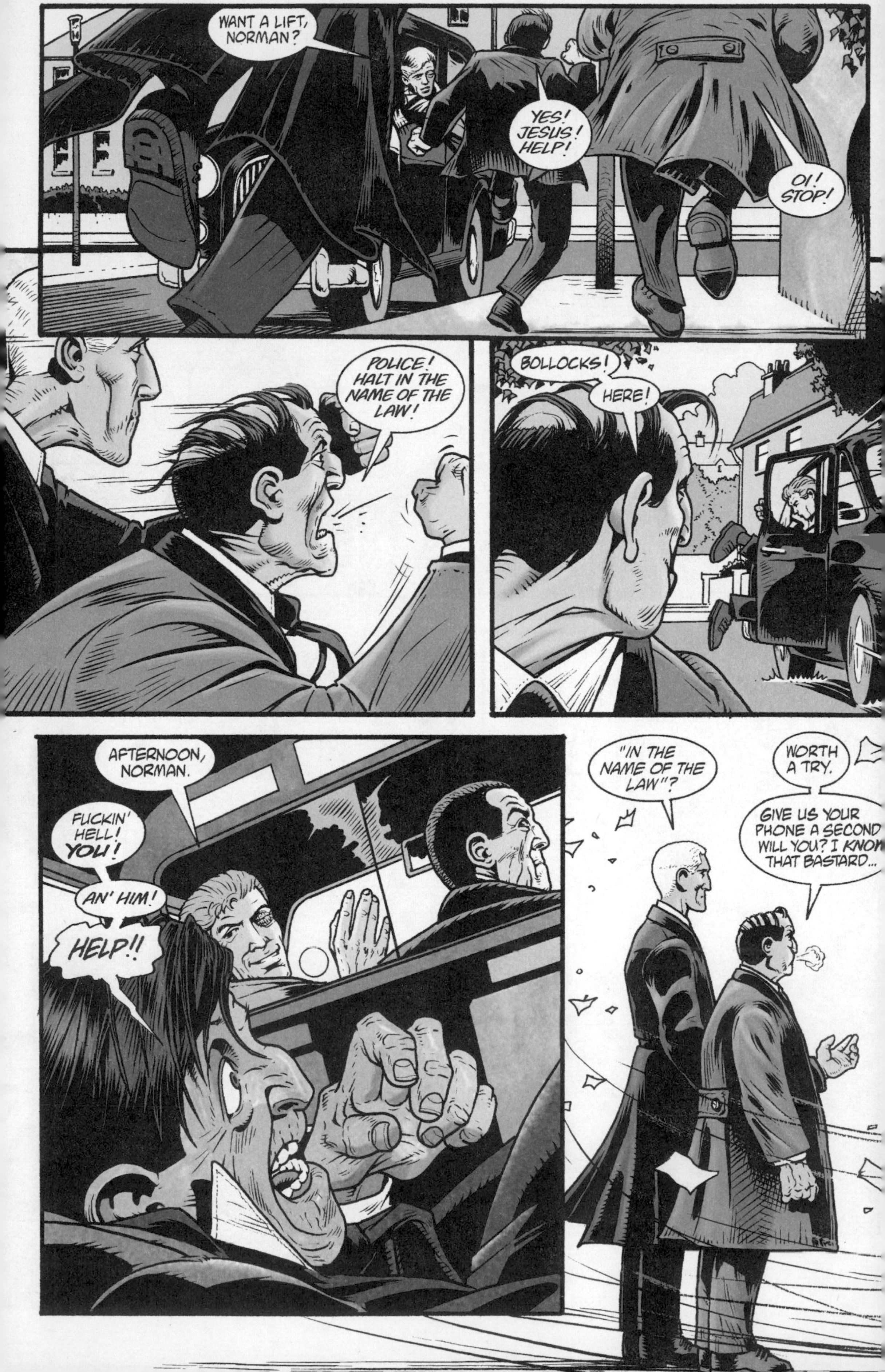
WANT A LIFT, NORMAN?
YES! JESUS! HELP!
OI! STOP!
POLICE! HALT IN THE NAME OF THE LAW!
BOLLOCKS!
HERE!
AFTERNOON, NORMAN.
FUCKIN' HELL! YOU!
AN' HIM!
HELP!!
"IN THE NAME OF THE LAW"?
WORTH A TRY.
GIVE US YOUR PHONE A SECOND WILL YOU? I KNOW THAT BASTARD...

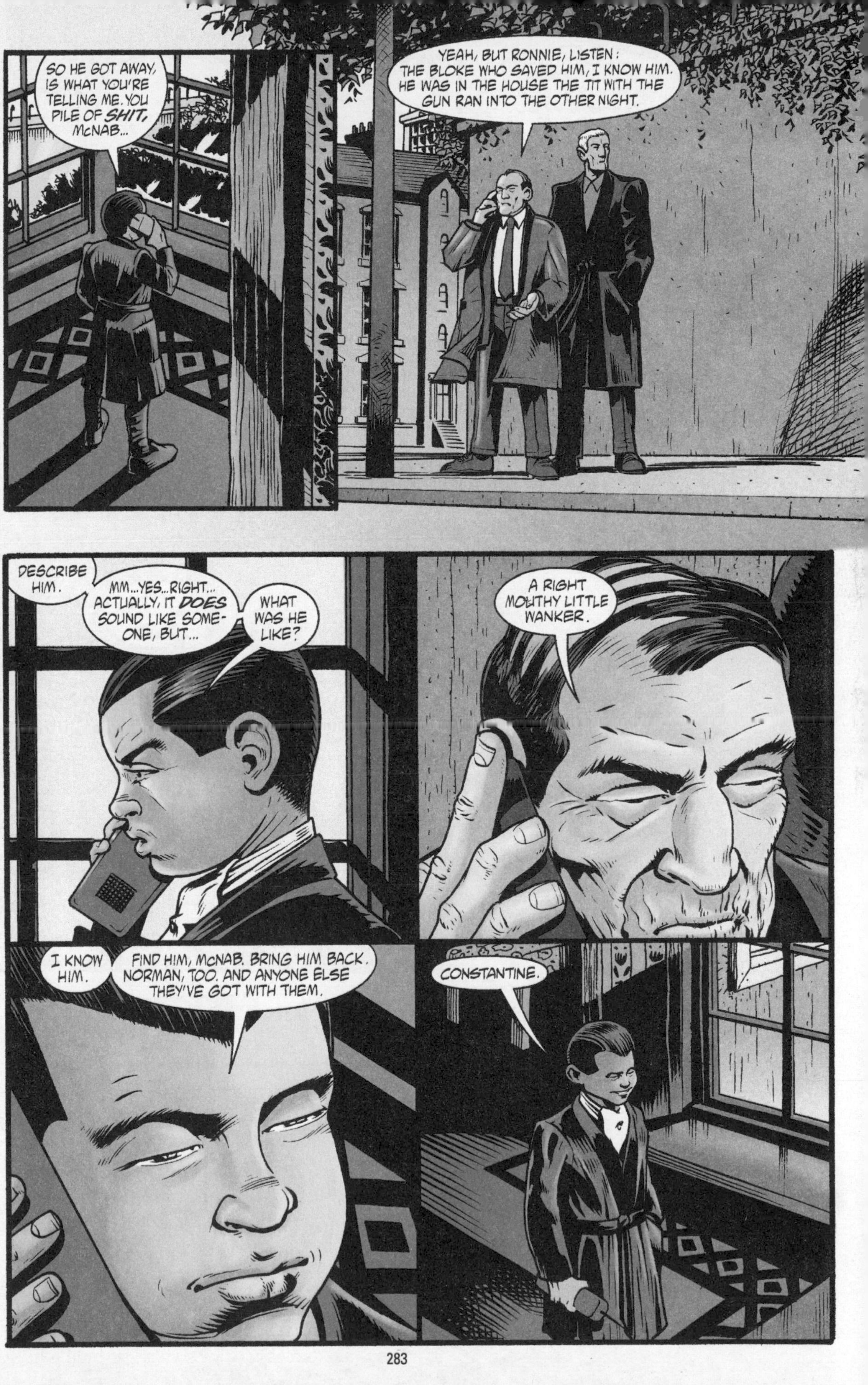
SO HE GOT AWAY, IS WHAT YOU'RE TELLING ME. YOU PILE OF SHIT, McNAB...
YEAH, BUT RONNIE, LISTEN: THE BLOKE WHO SAVED HIM, I KNOW HIM. HE WAS IN THE HOUSE THE TIT WITH THE GUN RAN INTO THE OTHER NIGHT.
DESCRIBE HIM.
MM...YES...RIGHT... ACTUALLY, IT DOES SOUND LIKE SOME-ONE, BUT...
WHAT WAS HE LIKE?
A RIGHT MOUTHY LITTLE WANKER.
I KNOW HIM.
FIND HIM, McNAB. BRING HIM BACK. NORMAN, TOO. AND ANYONE ELSE THEY'VE GOT WITH THEM.
CONSTANTINE.

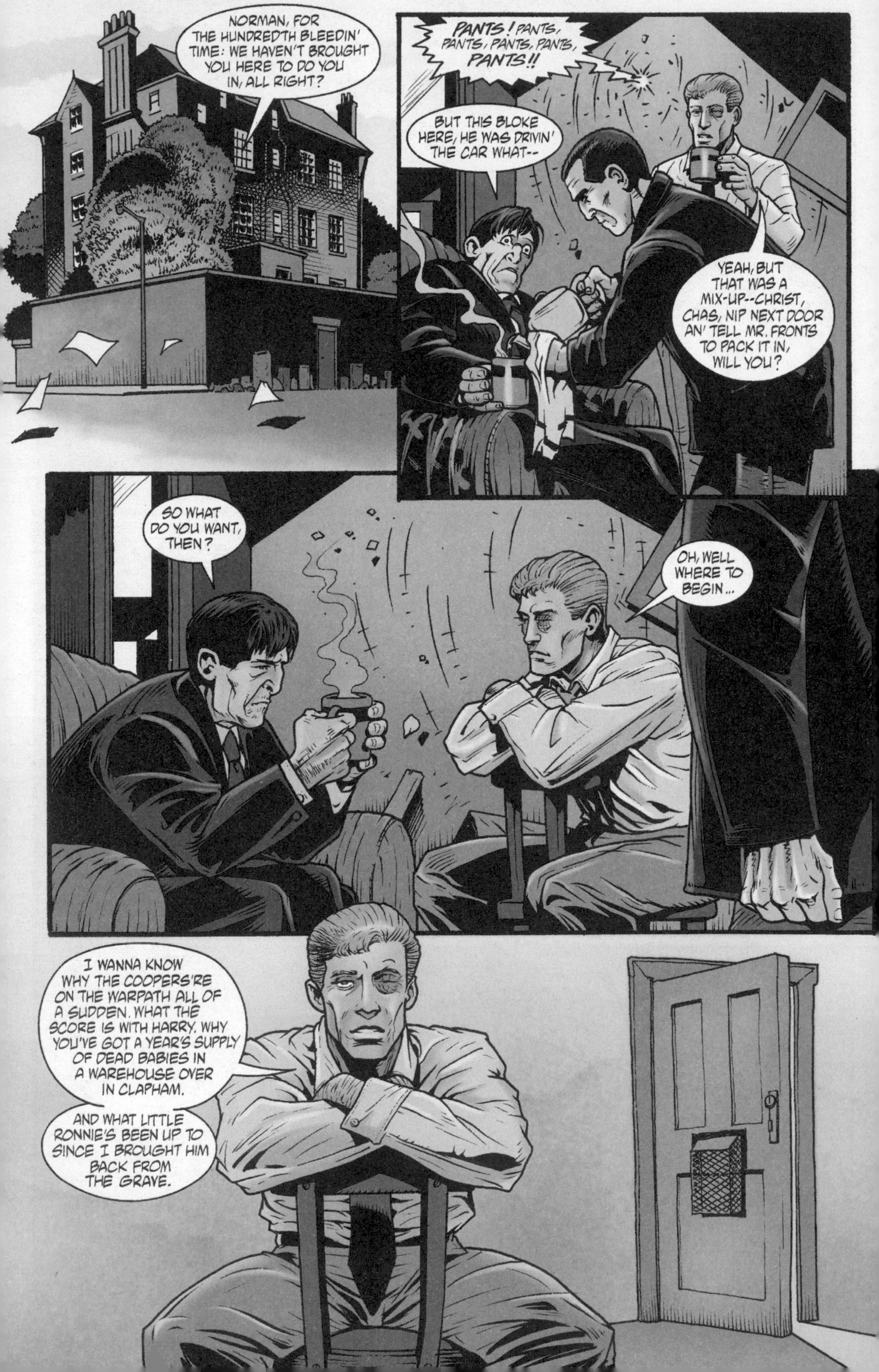
NORMAN, FOR THE HUNDREDTH BLEEDIN' TIME: WE HAVEN'T BROUGHT YOU HERE TO DO YOU IN, ALL RIGHT?
PANTS! PANTS, PANTS, PANTS, PANTS, PANTS!!
BUT THIS BLOKE HERE, HE WAS DRIVIN' THE CAR WHAT--
YEAH, BUT THAT WAS A MIX-UP--CHRIST, CHAS, NIP NEXT DOOR AN' TELL MR. FRONTS TO PACK IT IN, WILL YOU?
SO WHAT DO YOU WANT, THEN?
OH, WELL WHERE TO BEGIN...
I WANNA KNOW WHY THE COOPERS'RE ON THE WARPATH ALL OF A SUDDEN. WHAT THE SCORE IS WITH HARRY. WHY YOU'VE GOT A YEAR'S SUPPLY OF DEAD BABIES IN A WAREHOUSE OVER IN CLAPHAM.
AND WHAT LITTLE RONNIE'S BEEN UP TO SINCE I BROUGHT HIM BACK FROM THE GRAVE.

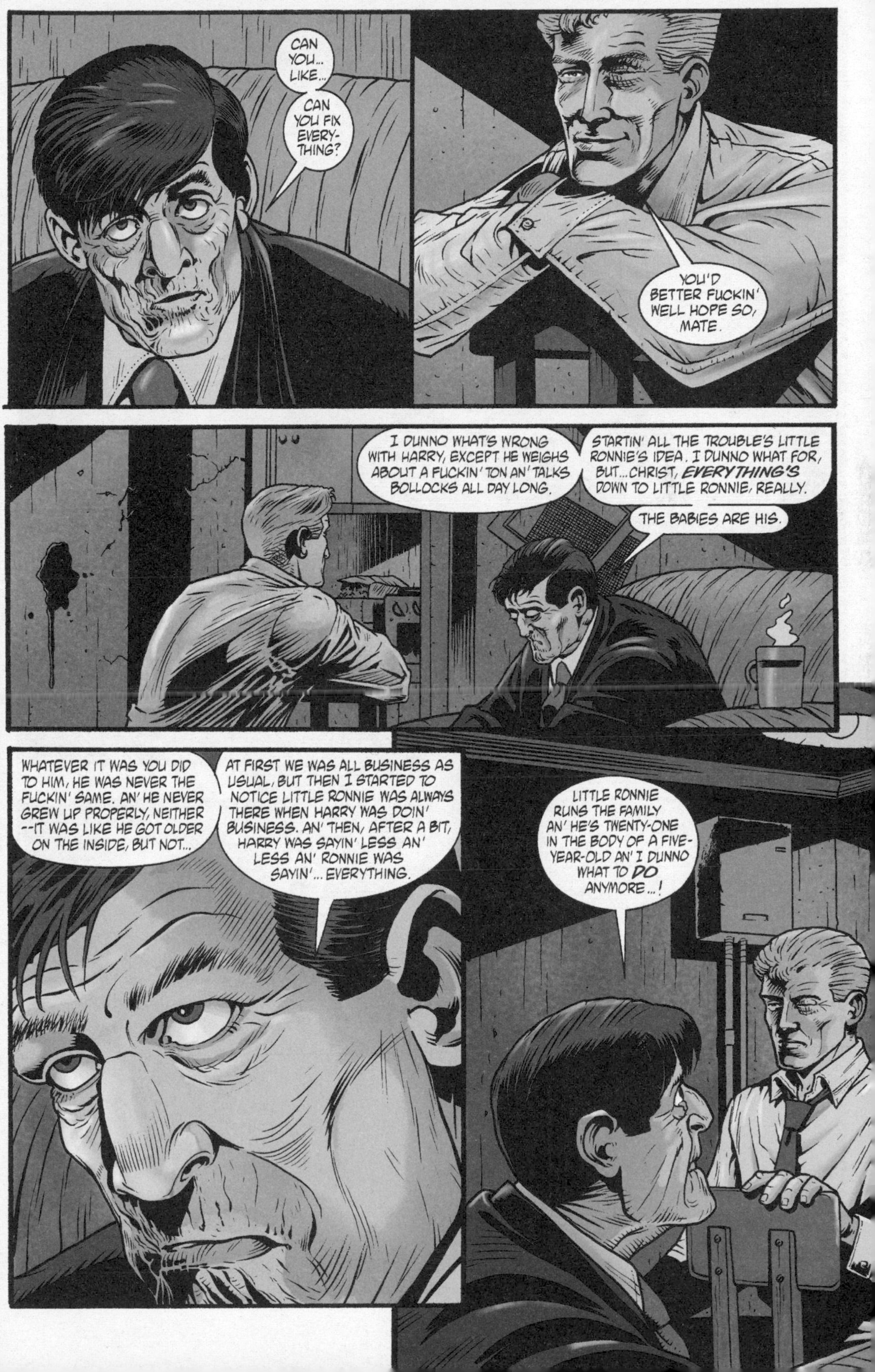
CAN YOU... LIKE...
CAN YOU FIX EVERYTHING?
YOU'D BETTER FUCKIN' WELL HOPE SO, MATE.
I DUNNO WHAT'S WRONG WITH HARRY, EXCEPT HE WEIGHS ABOUT A FUCKIN' TON AN' TALKS BOLLOCKS ALL DAY LONG.
STARTIN' ALL THE TROUBLE'S LITTLE RONNIE'S IDEA. I DUNNO WHAT FOR, BUT... CHRIST, EVERYTHING'S DOWN TO LITTLE RONNIE, REALLY.
THE BABIES ARE HIS.
WHATEVER IT WAS YOU DID TO HIM, HE WAS NEVER THE FUCKIN' SAME. AN' HE NEVER GREW UP PROPERLY, NEITHER --IT WAS LIKE HE GOT OLDER ON THE INSIDE, BUT NOT...
AT FIRST WE WAS ALL BUSINESS AS USUAL, BUT THEN I STARTED TO NOTICE LITTLE RONNIE WAS ALWAYS THERE WHEN HARRY WAS DOIN' BUSINESS. AN' THEN, AFTER A BIT, HARRY WAS SAYIN' LESS AN' LESS AN' RONNIE WAS SAYIN'... EVERYTHING.
LITTLE RONNIE RUNS THE FAMILY AN' HE'S TWENTY-ONE IN THE BODY OF A FIVE-YEAR-OLD AN' I DUNNO WHAT TO DO ANYMORE...!

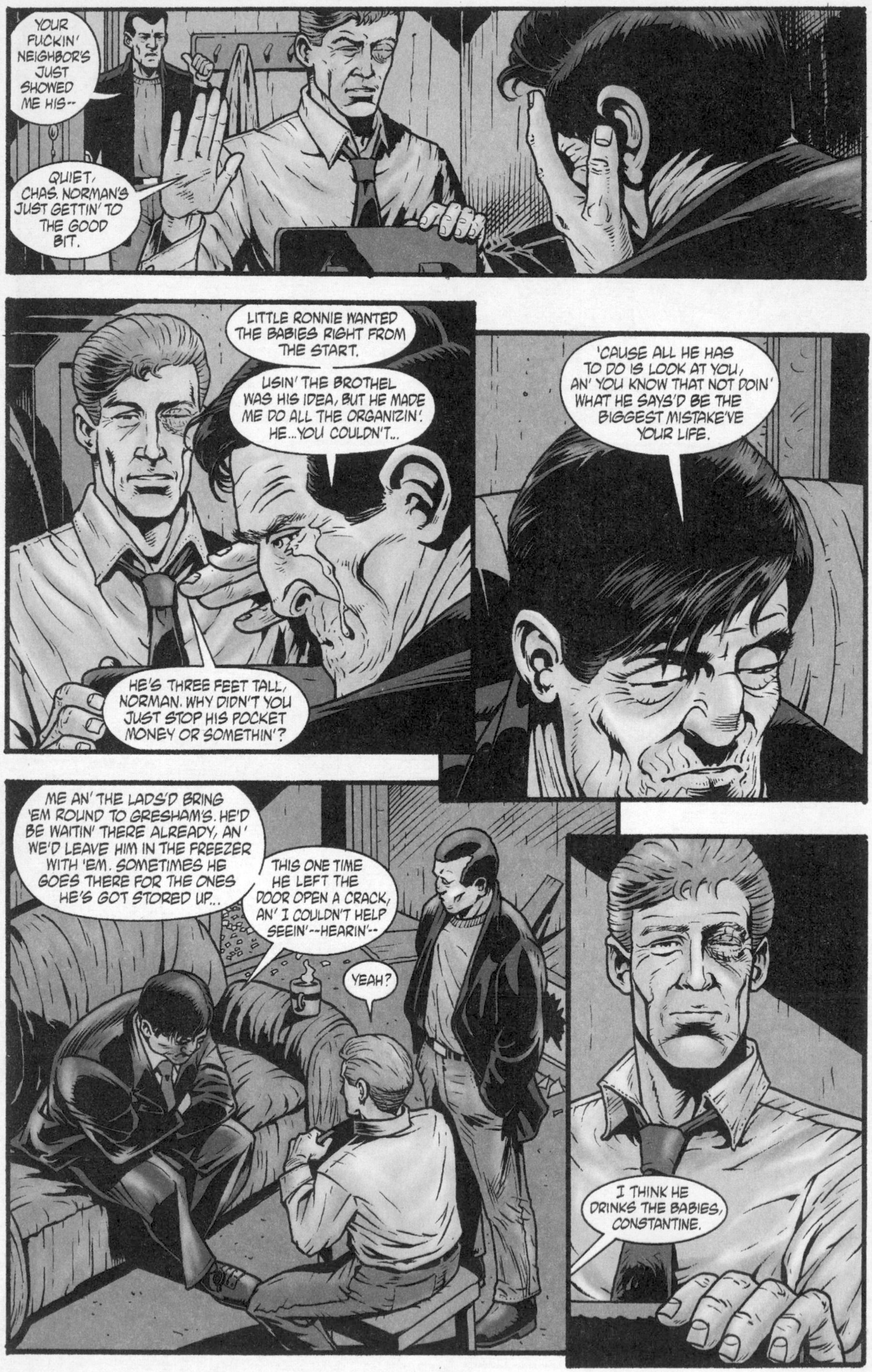
YOUR FUCKIN' NEIGHBOR'S JUST SHOWED ME HIS--
QUIET, CHAS. NORMAN'S JUST GETTIN' TO THE GOOD BIT.
LITTLE RONNIE WANTED THE BABIES RIGHT FROM THE START.
USIN' THE BROTHEL WAS HIS IDEA, BUT HE MADE ME DO ALL THE ORGANIZIN'. HE...YOU COULDN'T...
HE'S THREE FEET TALL, NORMAN. WHY DIDN'T YOU JUST STOP HIS POCKET MONEY OR SOMETHIN'?
'CAUSE ALL HE HAS TO DO IS LOOK AT YOU, AN' YOU KNOW THAT NOT DOIN' WHAT HE SAYS'D BE THE BIGGEST MISTAKE'VE YOUR LIFE.
ME AN' THE LADS'D BRING 'EM ROUND TO GRESHAM'S. HE'D BE WAITIN' THERE ALREADY, AN' WE'D LEAVE HIM IN THE FREEZER WITH 'EM. SOMETIMES HE GOES THERE FOR THE ONES HE'S GOT STORED UP...
THIS ONE TIME HE LEFT THE DOOR OPEN A CRACK, AN' I COULDN'T HELP SEEIN'--HEARIN'--
YEAH?
I THINK HE DRINKS THE BABIES, CONSTANTINE.

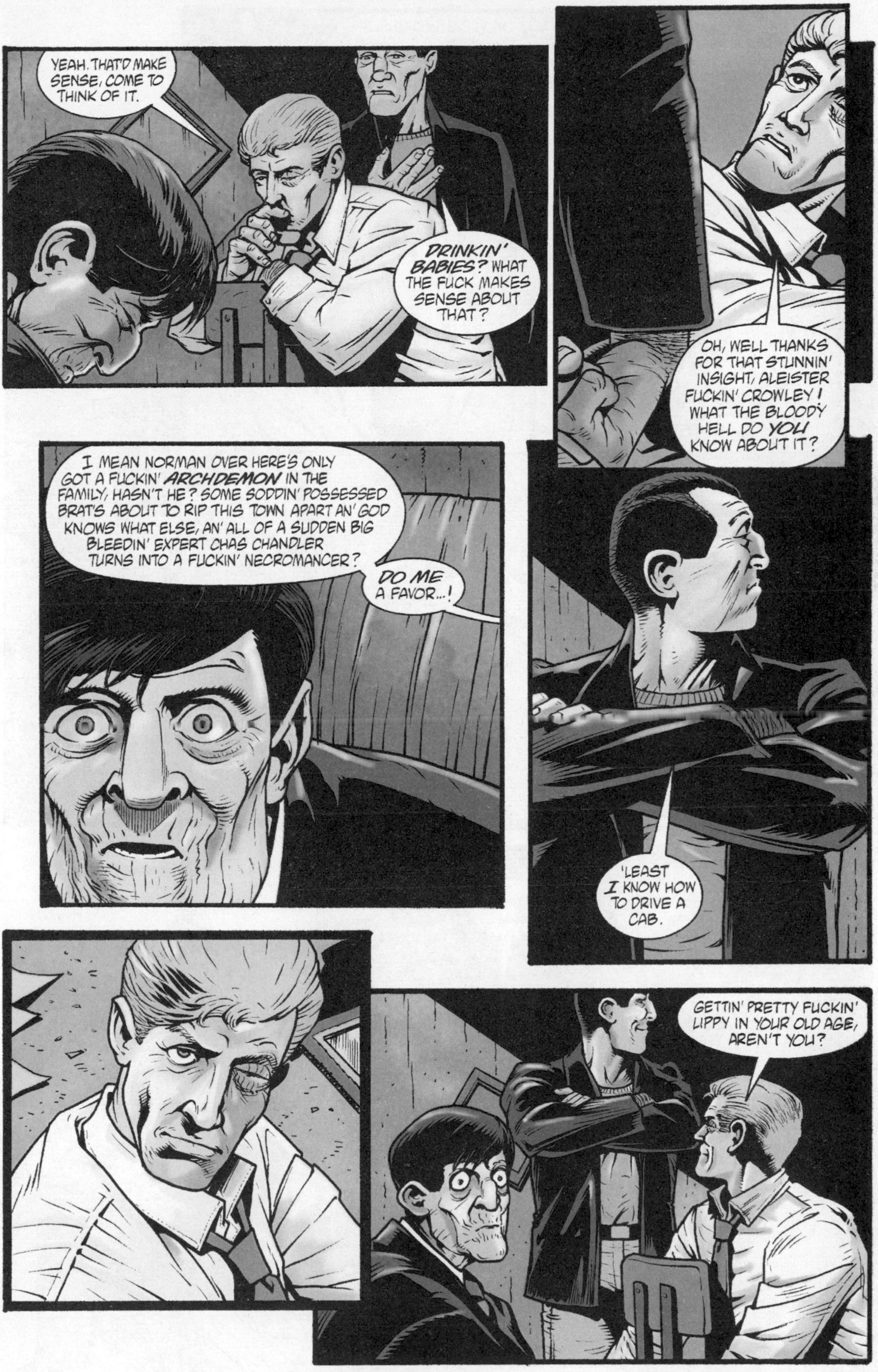
YEAH. THAT'D MAKE SENSE, COME TO THINK OF IT.
DRINKIN' BABIES? WHAT THE FUCK MAKES SENSE ABOUT THAT?
OH, WELL THANKS FOR THAT STUNNIN' INSIGHT, ALEISTER FUCKIN' CROWLEY! WHAT THE BLOODY HELL DO YOU KNOW ABOUT IT?
I MEAN NORMAN OVER HERE'S ONLY GOT A FUCKIN' ARCHDEMON IN THE FAMILY, HASN'T HE? SOME SODDIN' POSSESSED BRAT'S ABOUT TO RIP THIS TOWN APART AN' GOD KNOWS WHAT ELSE, AN' ALL OF A SUDDEN BIG BLEEDIN' EXPERT CHAS CHANDLER TURNS INTO A FUCKIN' NECROMANCER?
DO ME A FAVOR...!
'LEAST I KNOW HOW TO DRIVE A CAB.
GETTIN' PRETTY FUCKIN' LIPPY IN YOUR OLD AGE, AREN'T YOU?

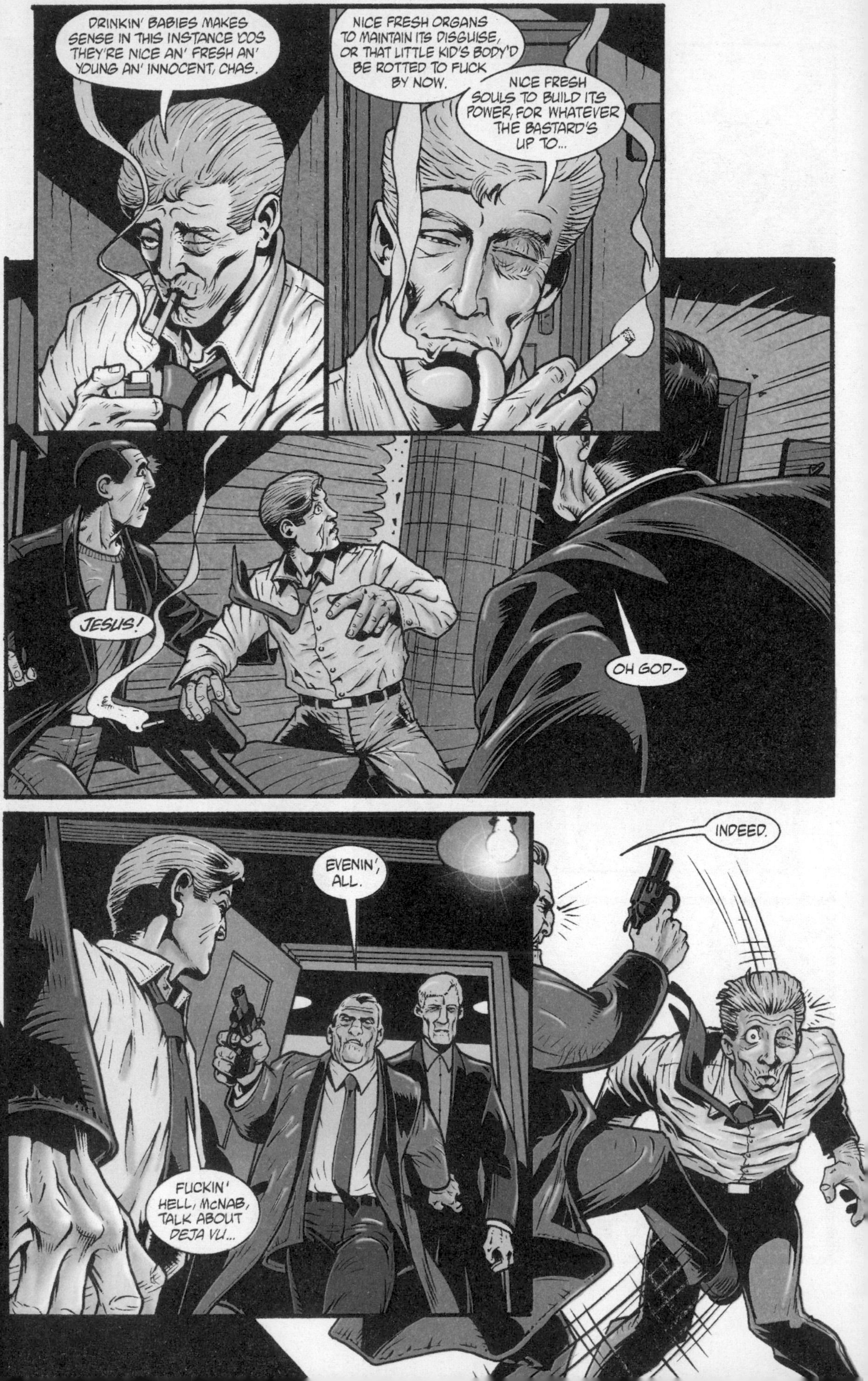
DRINKIN' BABIES MAKES SENSE IN THIS INSTANCE 'COS THEY'RE NICE AN' FRESH AN' YOUNG AN' INNOCENT, CHAS.
NICE FRESH ORGANS TO MAINTAIN ITS DISGUISE, OR THAT LITTLE KID'S BODY'D BE ROTTED TO FUCK BY NOW.
NICE FRESH SOULS TO BUILD ITS POWER, FOR WHATEVER THE BASTARD'S UP TO...
JESUS!
OH GOD--
EVENIN', ALL.
FUCKIN' HELL, McNAB, TALK ABOUT DEJA VU...
INDEED.

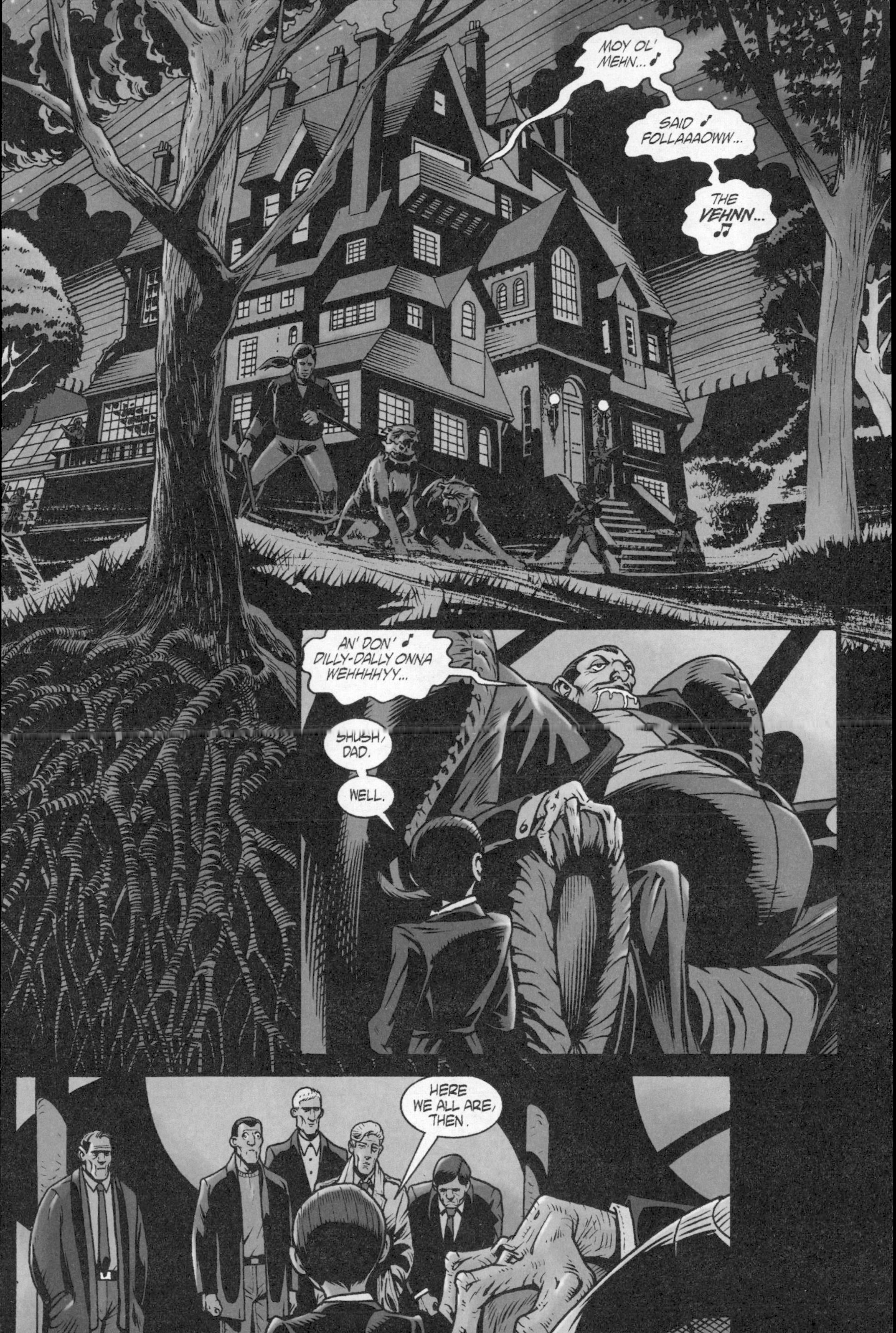
MOY OL' MEHN...♪
SAID ♪ FOLLAAAOWW...
THE VEHNN... ♫
AN' DON' ♪ DILLY-DALLY ONNA WEHHHHYY...
SHUSH, DAD.
WELL.
HERE WE ALL ARE, THEN.

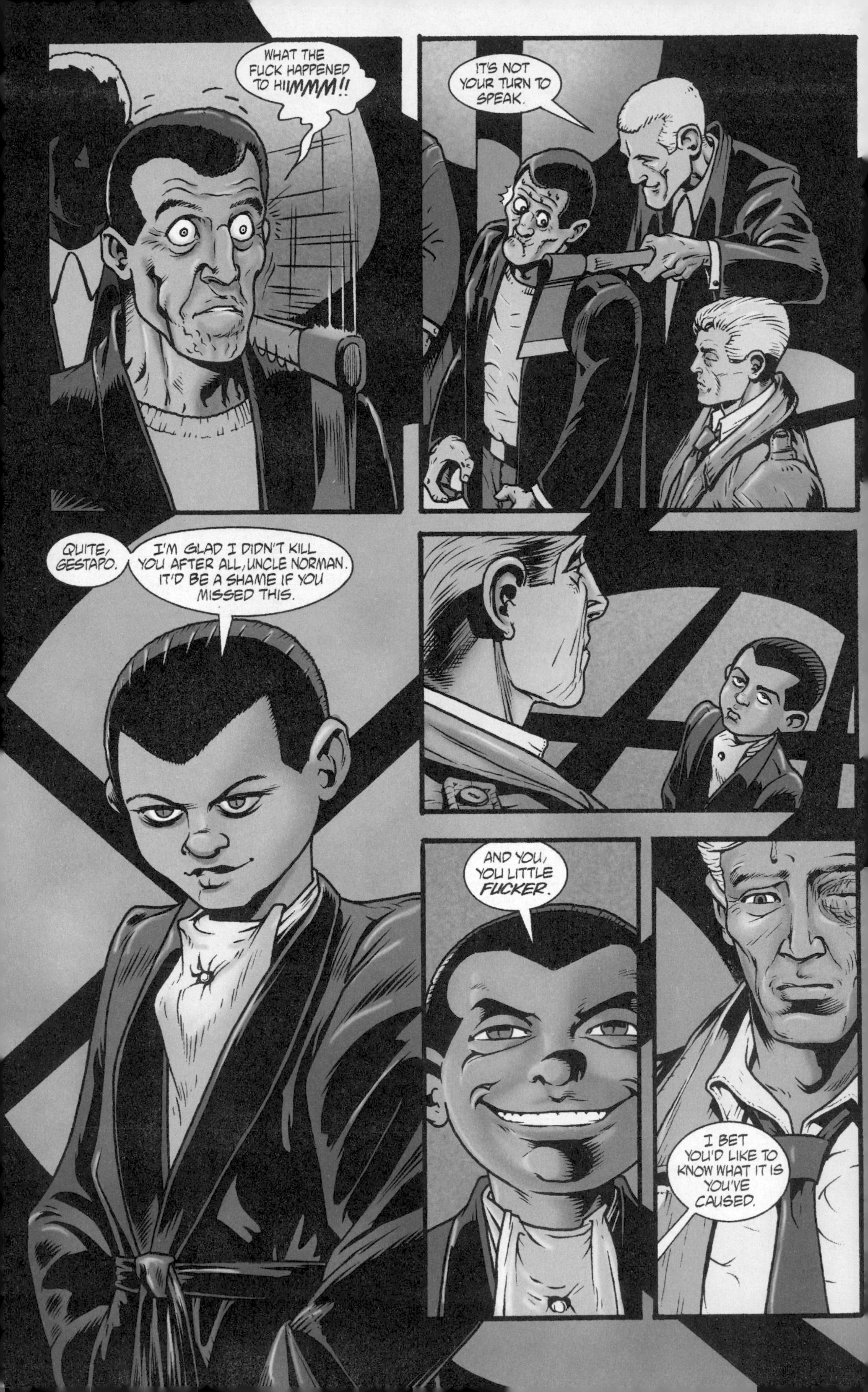
WHAT THE FUCK HAPPENED TO HIIMMM!!
IT'S NOT YOUR TURN TO SPEAK.
QUITE, GESTAPO.
I'M GLAD I DIDN'T KILL YOU AFTER ALL, UNCLE NORMAN. IT'D BE A SHAME IF YOU MISSED THIS.
AND YOU, YOU LITTLE FUCKER.
I BET YOU'D LIKE TO KNOW WHAT IT IS YOU'VE CAUSED.

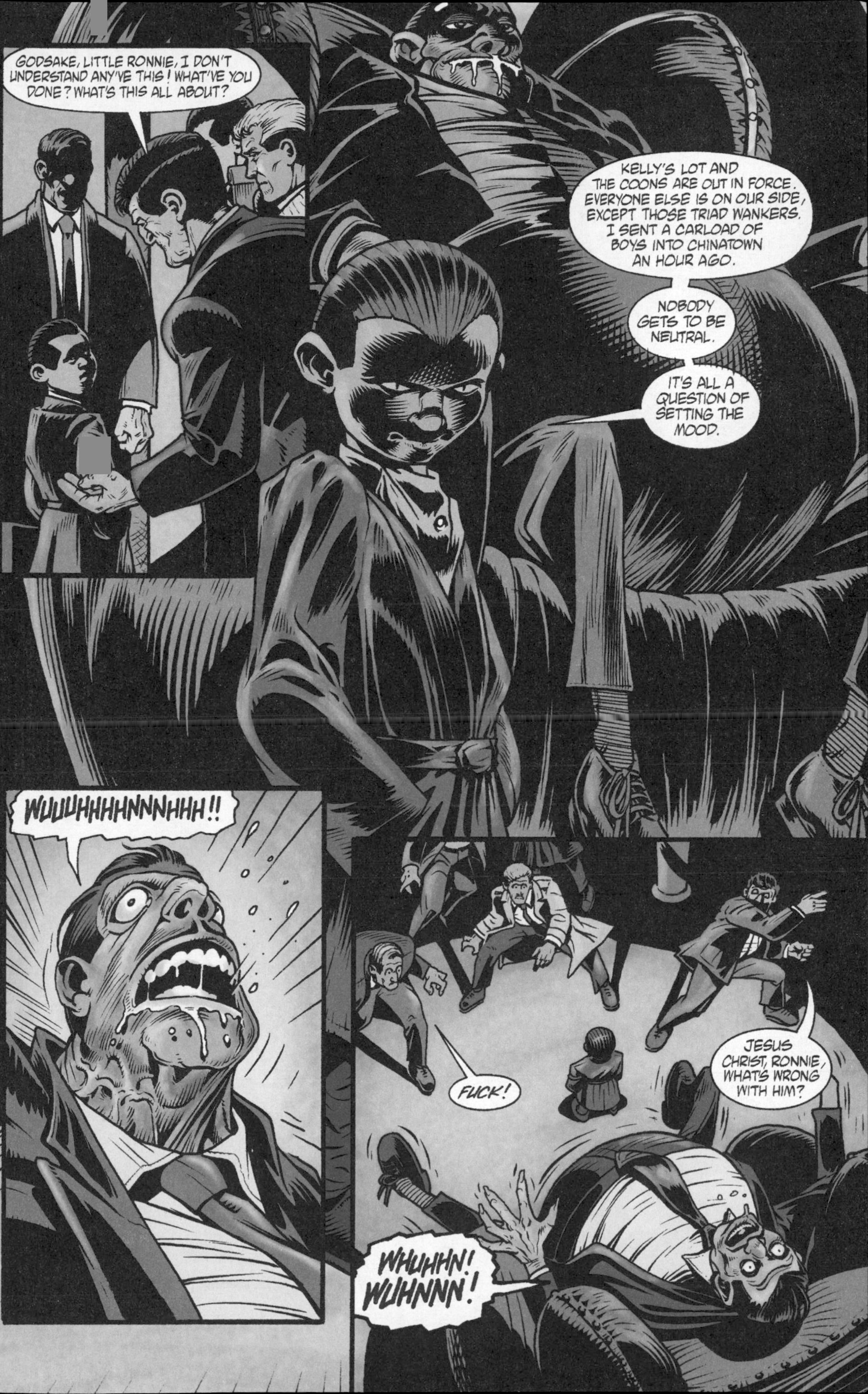
GODSAKE, LITTLE RONNIE, I DON'T UNDERSTAND ANY'VE THIS! WHAT'VE YOU DONE? WHAT'S THIS ALL ABOUT?
KELLY'S LOT AND THE COONS ARE OUT IN FORCE. EVERYONE ELSE IS ON OUR SIDE, EXCEPT THOSE TRIAD WANKERS. I SENT A CARLOAD OF BOYS INTO CHINATOWN AN HOUR AGO.
NOBODY GETS TO BE NEUTRAL.
IT'S ALL A QUESTION OF SETTING THE MOOD.
WUUUHHHHNNNHHH!!
FUCK!
JESUS CHRIST, RONNIE, WHAT'S WRONG WITH HIM?
WHUHHN! WUHNNN!

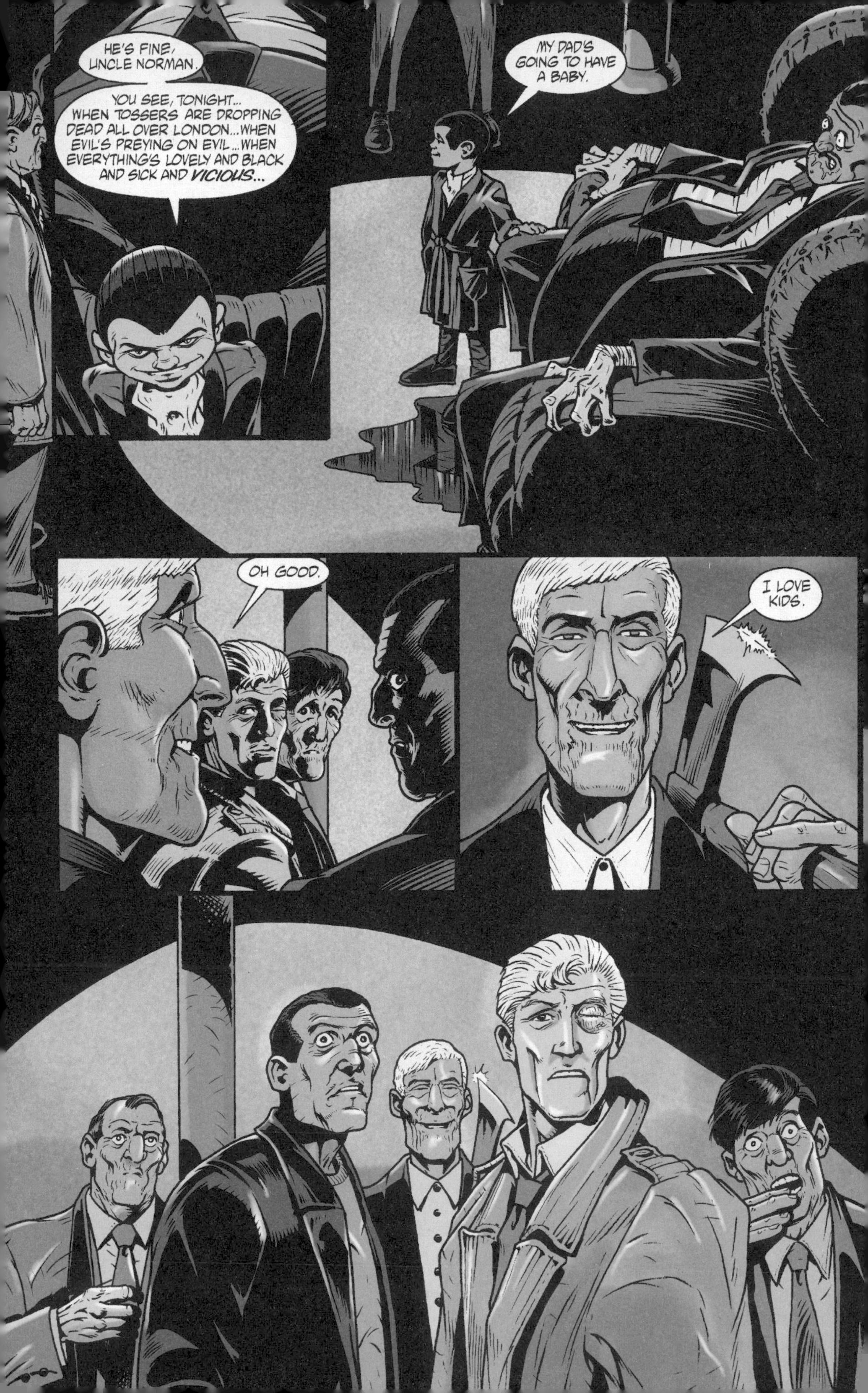
HE'S FINE, UNCLE NORMAN.
YOU SEE, TONIGHT... WHEN TOSSERS ARE DROPPING DEAD ALL OVER LONDON...WHEN EVIL'S PREYING ON EVIL...WHEN EVERYTHING'S LOVELY AND BLACK AND SICK AND VICIOUS...
MY DAD'S GOING TO HAVE A BABY.
OH GOOD.
I LOVE KIDS.

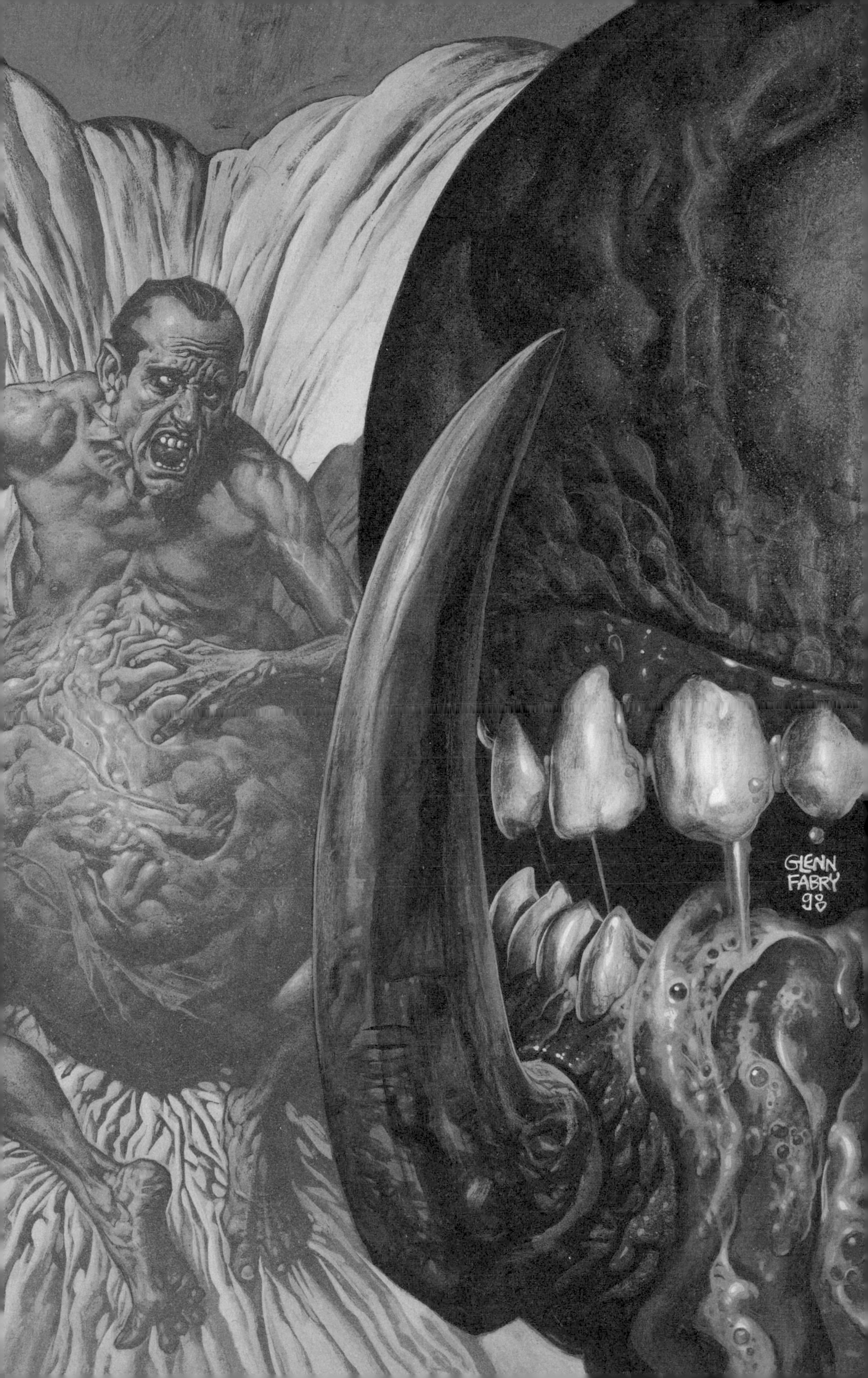
GLENN
FABRY
98

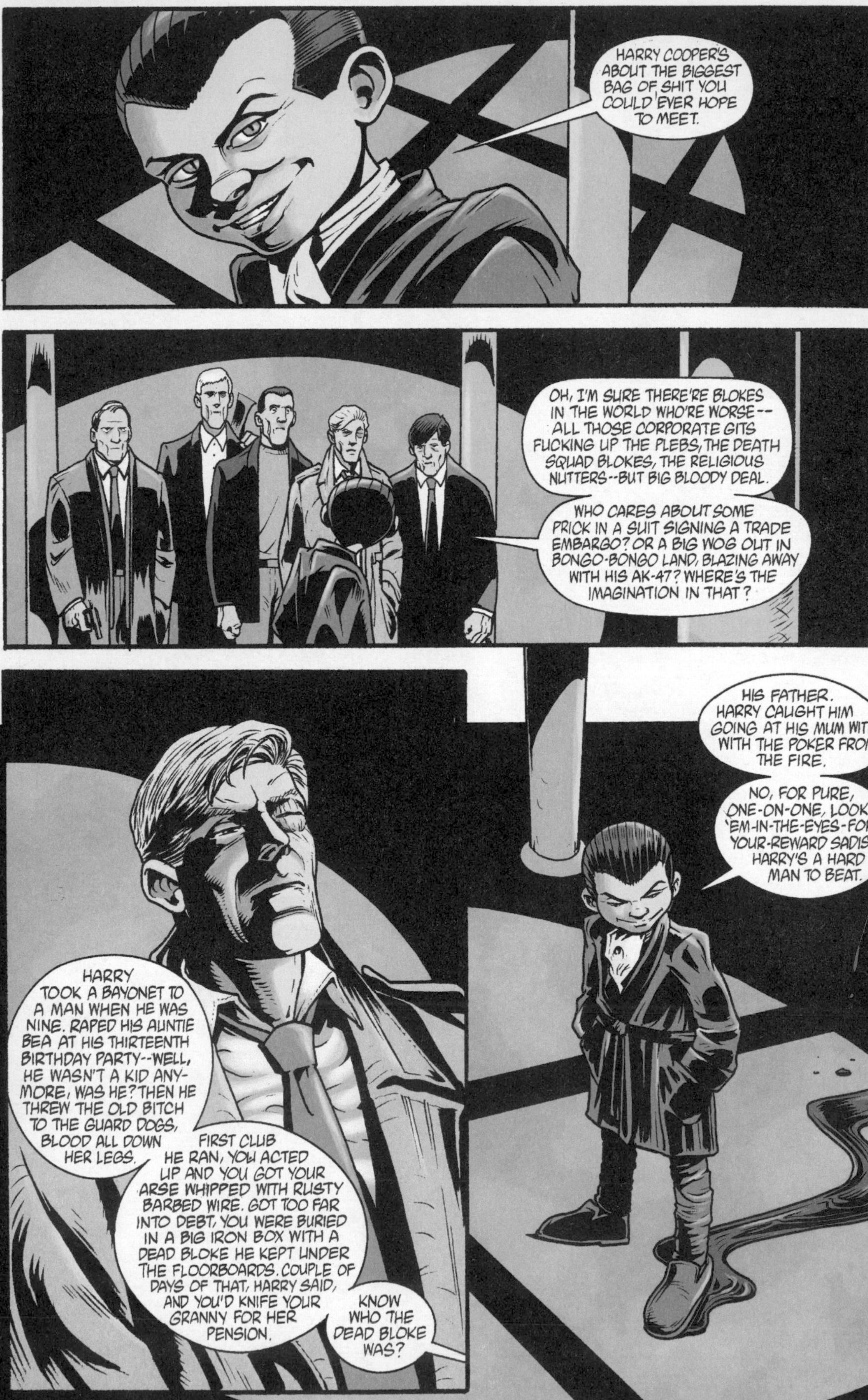
HARRY COOPER'S ABOUT THE BIGGEST BAG OF SHIT YOU COULD EVER HOPE TO MEET.
OH, I'M SURE THERE'RE BLOKES IN THE WORLD WHO'RE WORSE--ALL THOSE CORPORATE GITS FUCKING UP THE PLEBS, THE DEATH SQUAD BLOKES, THE RELIGIOUS NUTTERS--BUT BIG BLOODY DEAL.
WHO CARES ABOUT SOME PRICK IN A SUIT SIGNING A TRADE EMBARGO? OR A BIG WOG OUT IN BONGO-BONGO LAND, BLAZING AWAY WITH HIS AK-47? WHERE'S THE IMAGINATION IN THAT?
NO, FOR PURE, ONE-ON-ONE, LOOK-'EM-IN-THE-EYES-FOR-YOUR-REWARD SADISM, HARRY'S A HARD MAN TO BEAT.
HARRY TOOK A BAYONET TO A MAN WHEN HE WAS NINE. RAPED HIS AUNTIE BEA AT HIS THIRTEENTH BIRTHDAY PARTY--WELL, HE WASN'T A KID ANY-MORE, WAS HE? THEN HE THREW THE OLD BITCH TO THE GUARD DOGS, BLOOD ALL DOWN HER LEGS.
FIRST CLUB HE RAN, YOU ACTED UP AND YOU GOT YOUR ARSE WHIPPED WITH RUSTY BARBED WIRE. GOT TOO FAR INTO DEBT, YOU WERE BURIED IN A BIG IRON BOX WITH A DEAD BLOKE HE KEPT UNDER THE FLOORBOARDS. COUPLE OF DAYS OF THAT, HARRY SAID, AND YOU'D KNIFE YOUR GRANNY FOR HER PENSION.
KNOW WHO THE DEAD BLOKE WAS?
HIS FATHER. HARRY CAUGHT HIM GOING AT HIS MUM WITH WITH THE POKER FROM THE FIRE.

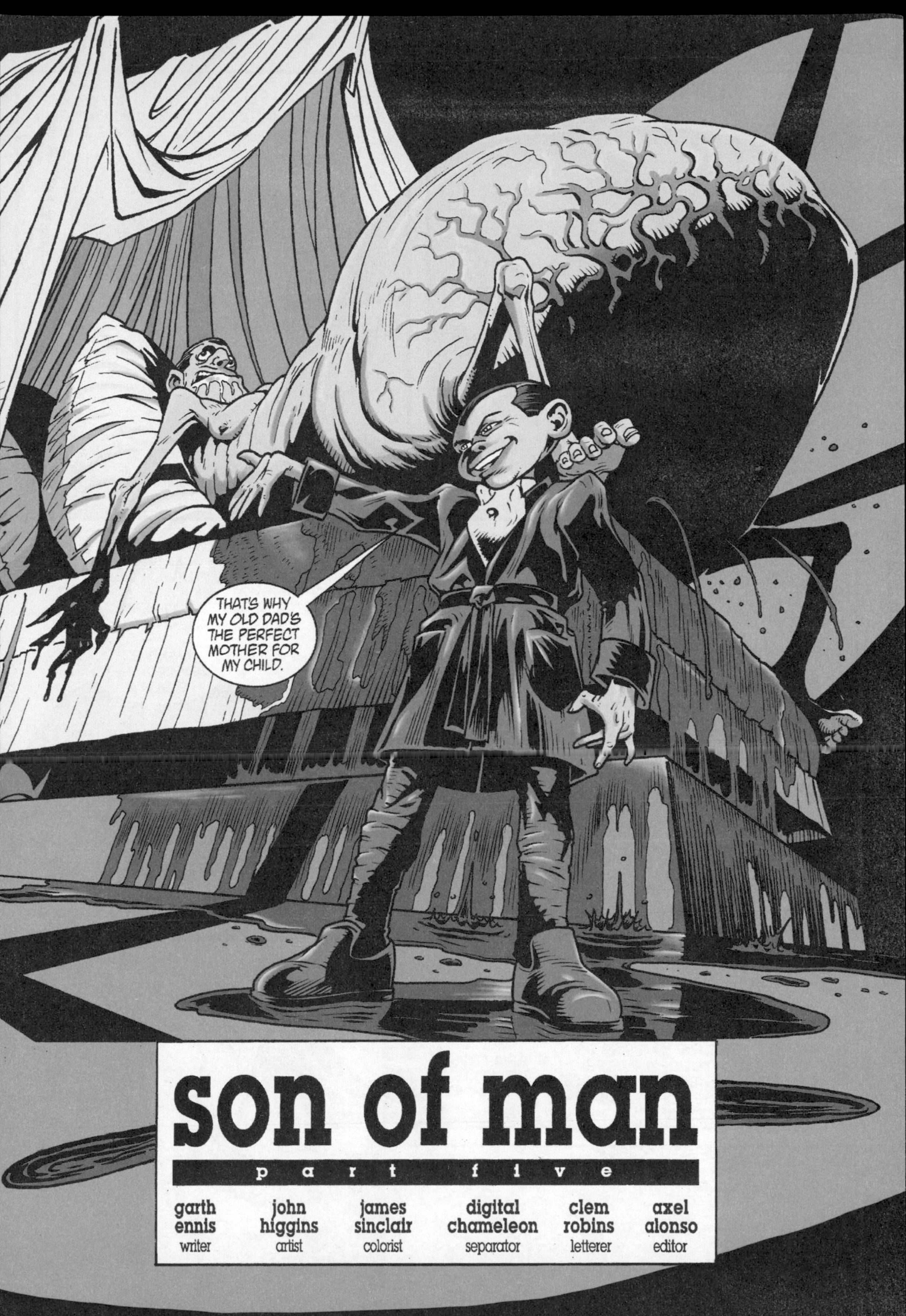
THAT'S WHY MY OLD DAD'S THE PERFECT MOTHER FOR MY CHILD.
son of man
part five
garth ennis writer
john higgins artist
james sinclair colorist
digital chameleon separator
clem robins letterer
axel alonso editor

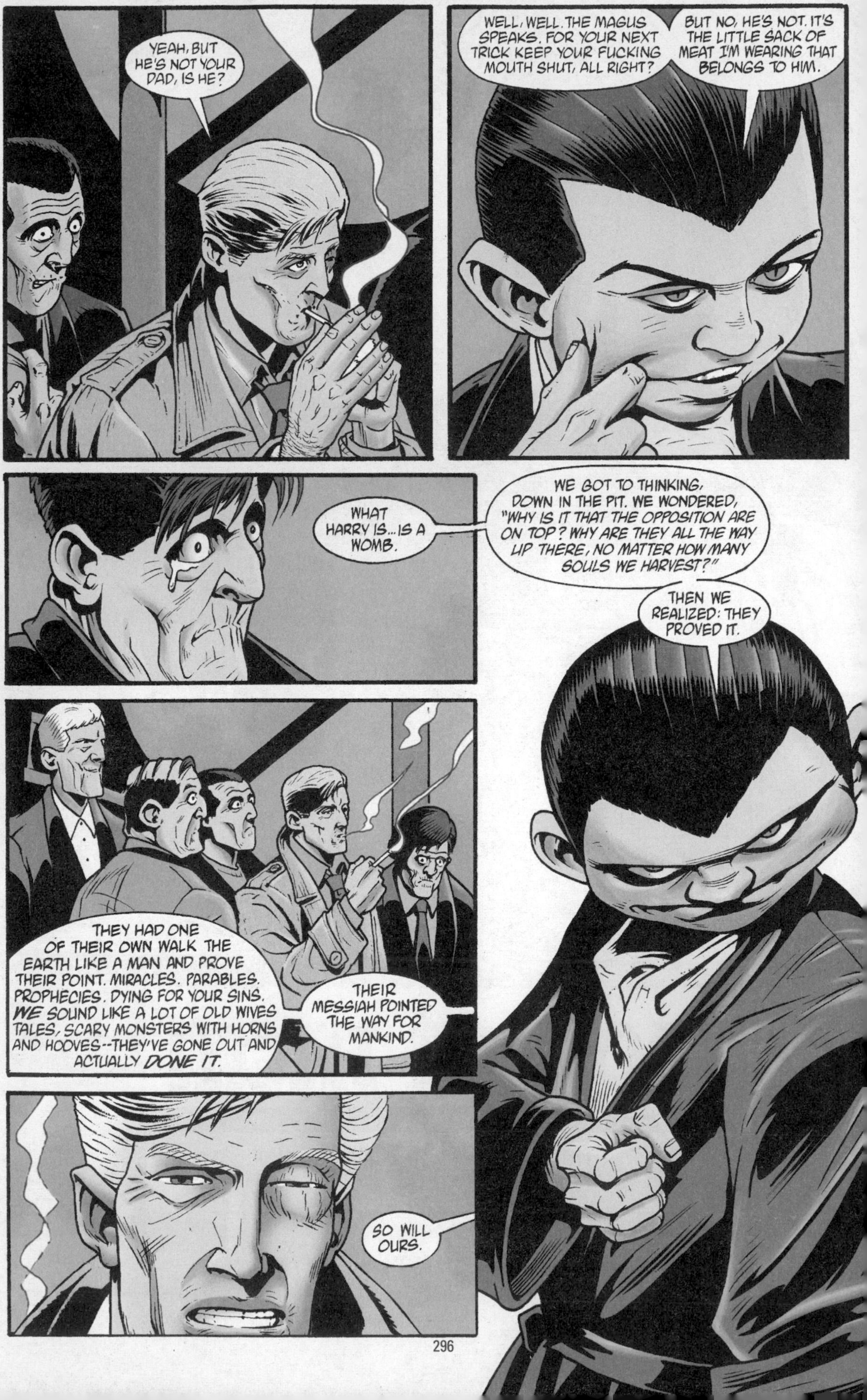
YEAH, BUT HE'S NOT YOUR DAD, IS HE?
WELL, WELL. THE MAGUS SPEAKS. FOR YOUR NEXT TRICK KEEP YOUR FUCKING MOUTH SHUT, ALL RIGHT?
BUT NO, HE'S NOT. IT'S THE LITTLE SACK OF MEAT I'M WEARING THAT BELONGS TO HIM.
WHAT HARRY IS...IS A WOMB.
WE GOT TO THINKING, DOWN IN THE PIT. WE WONDERED, "WHY IS IT THAT THE OPPOSITION ARE ON TOP? WHY ARE THEY ALL THE WAY UP THERE, NO MATTER HOW MANY SOULS WE HARVEST?"
THEN WE REALIZED: THEY PROVED IT.
THEY HAD ONE OF THEIR OWN WALK THE EARTH LIKE A MAN AND PROVE THEIR POINT. MIRACLES. PARABLES. PROPHECIES. DYING FOR YOUR SINS. *WE* SOUND LIKE A LOT OF OLD WIVES TALES, SCARY MONSTERS WITH HORNS AND HOOVES--THEY'VE GONE OUT AND ACTUALLY *DONE IT*.
THEIR MESSIAH POINTED THE WAY FOR MANKIND.
SO WILL OURS.

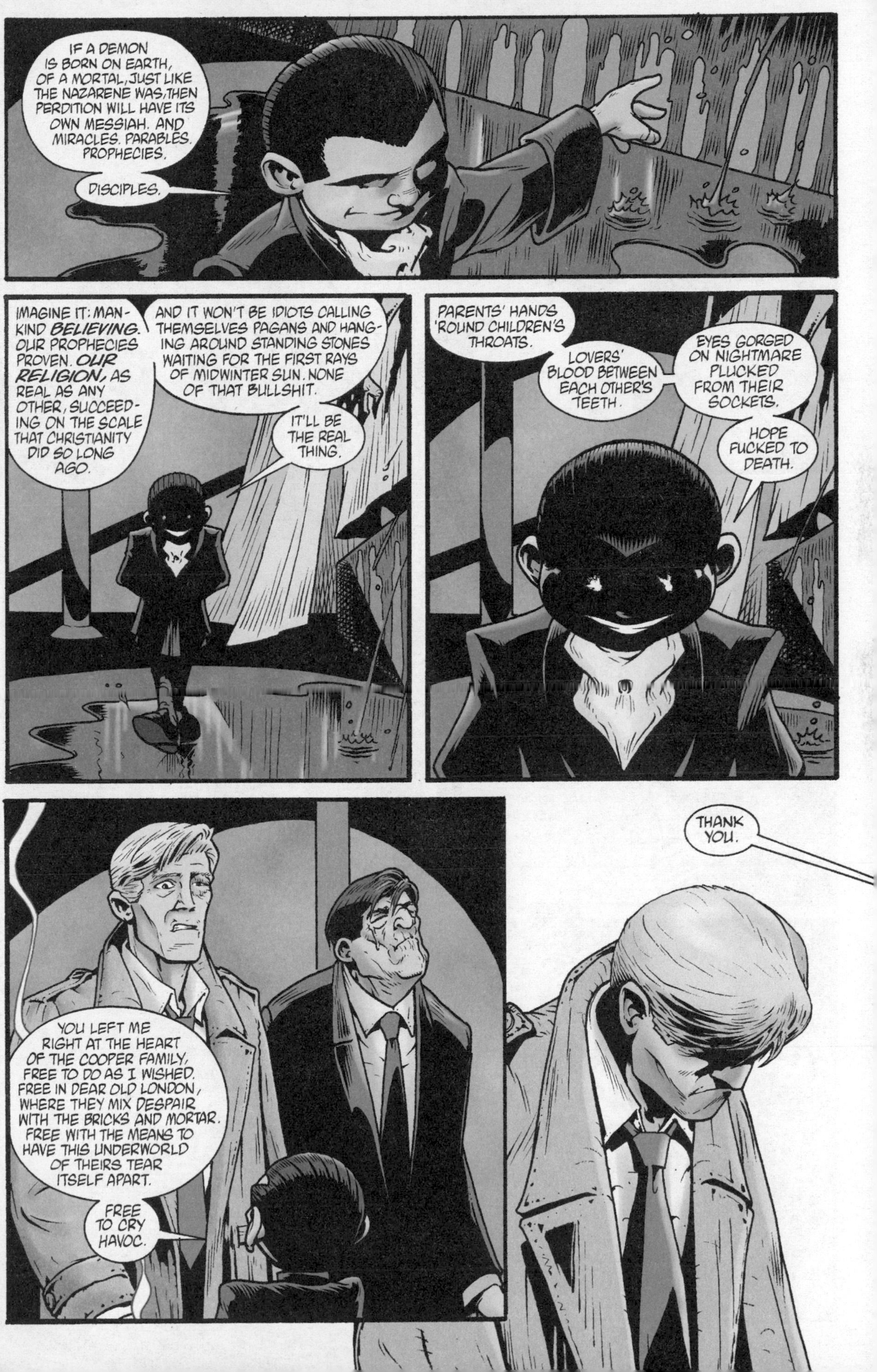
IF A DEMON IS BORN ON EARTH, OF A MORTAL, JUST LIKE THE NAZARENE WAS, THEN PERDITION WILL HAVE ITS OWN MESSIAH. AND MIRACLES. PARABLES. PROPHECIES.
DISCIPLES.
IMAGINE IT: MAN-KIND **BELIEVING**. OUR PROPHECIES PROVEN. ***OUR RELIGION,*** AS REAL AS ANY OTHER, SUCCEED-ING ON THE SCALE THAT CHRISTIANITY DID SO LONG AGO.
AND IT WON'T BE IDIOTS CALLING THEMSELVES PAGANS AND HANG-ING AROUND STANDING STONES WAITING FOR THE FIRST RAYS OF MIDWINTER SUN. NONE OF THAT BULLSHIT.
IT'LL BE THE REAL THING.
PARENTS' HANDS 'ROUND CHILDREN'S THROATS.
LOVERS' BLOOD BETWEEN EACH OTHER'S TEETH.
EYES GORGED ON NIGHTMARE PLUCKED FROM THEIR SOCKETS.
HOPE FUCKED TO DEATH.
YOU LEFT ME RIGHT AT THE HEART OF THE COOPER FAMILY, FREE TO DO AS I WISHED. FREE IN DEAR OLD LONDON, WHERE THEY MIX DESPAIR WITH THE BRICKS AND MORTAR. FREE WITH THE MEANS TO HAVE THIS UNDERWORLD OF THEIRS TEAR ITSELF APART.
FREE TO CRY HAVOC.
THANK YOU.

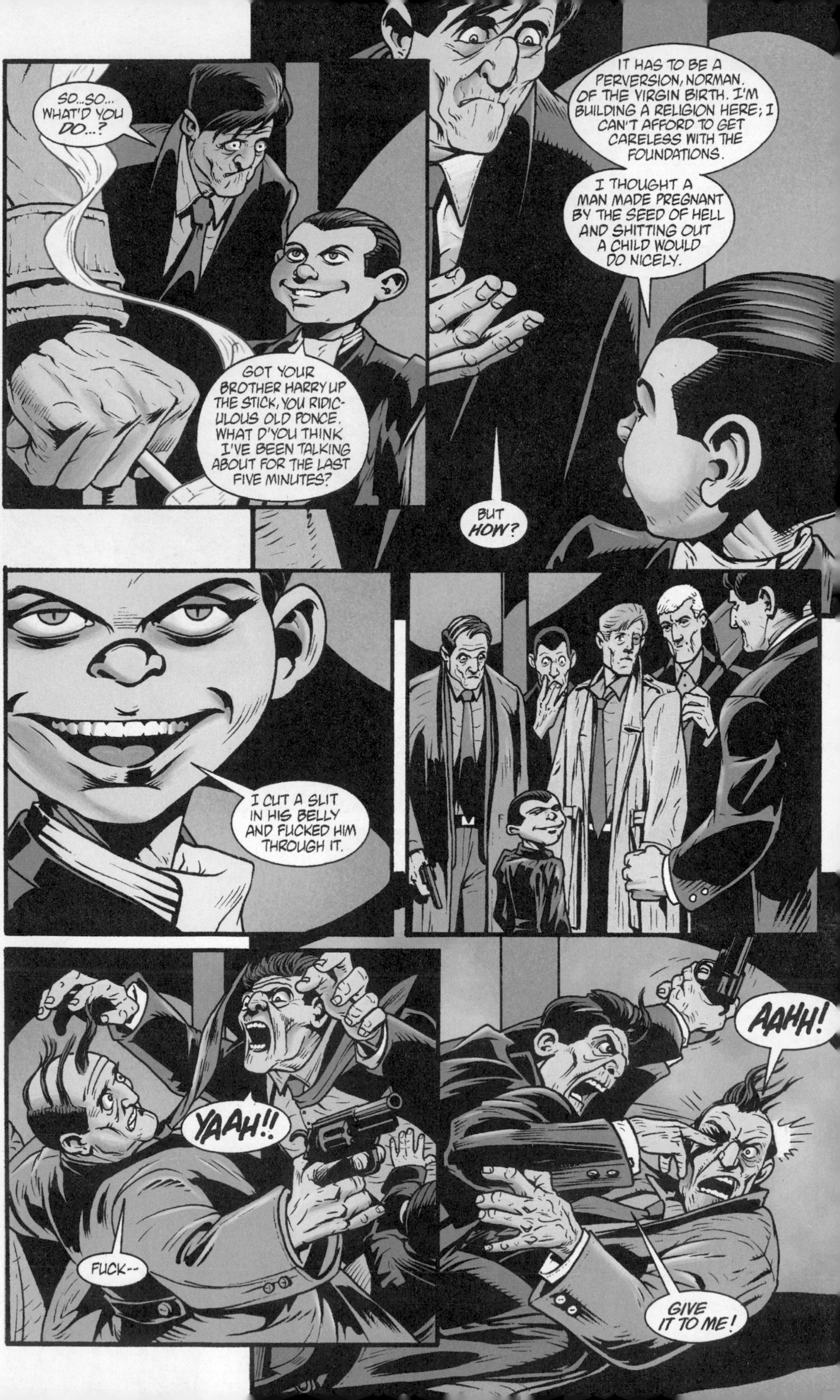
SO...SO... WHAT'D YOU DO...?
GOT YOUR BROTHER HARRY UP THE STICK, YOU RIDICULOUS OLD PONCE. WHAT D'YOU THINK I'VE BEEN TALKING ABOUT FOR THE LAST FIVE MINUTES?
BUT HOW?
IT HAS TO BE A PERVERSION, NORMAN. OF THE VIRGIN BIRTH. I'M BUILDING A RELIGION HERE; I CAN'T AFFORD TO GET CARELESS WITH THE FOUNDATIONS.
I THOUGHT A MAN MADE PREGNANT BY THE SEED OF HELL AND SHITTING OUT A CHILD WOULD DO NICELY.
I CUT A SLIT IN HIS BELLY AND FUCKED HIM THROUGH IT.
YAAH!!
FUCK--
AAHH!
GIVE IT TO ME!

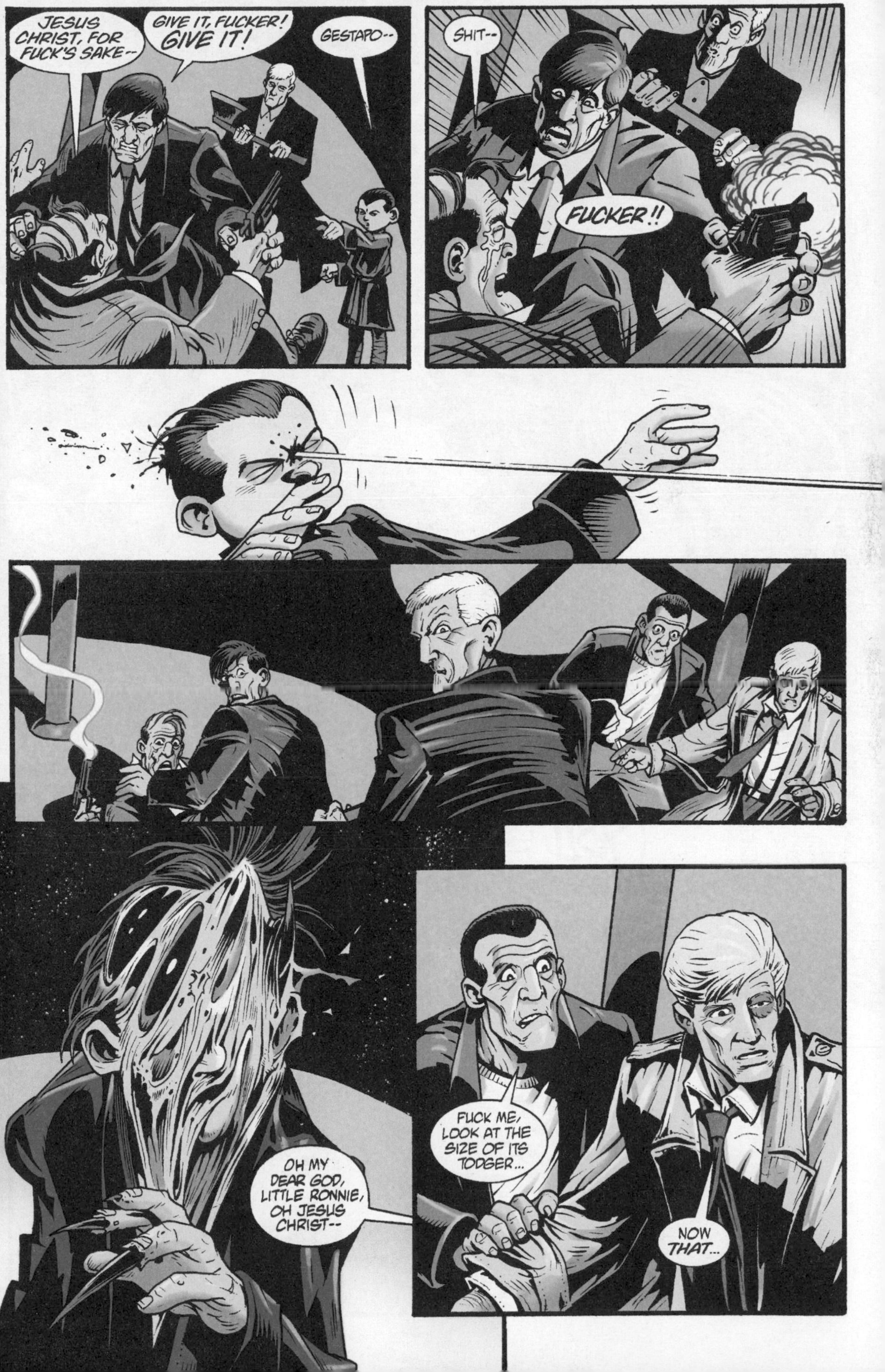
JESUS CHRIST, FOR FUCK'S SAKE--
GIVE IT, FUCKER! GIVE IT!
GESTAPO--
SHIT--
FUCKER!!
OH MY DEAR GOD, LITTLE RONNIE, OH JESUS CHRIST--
FUCK ME, LOOK AT THE SIZE OF ITS TODGER...
NOW THAT...

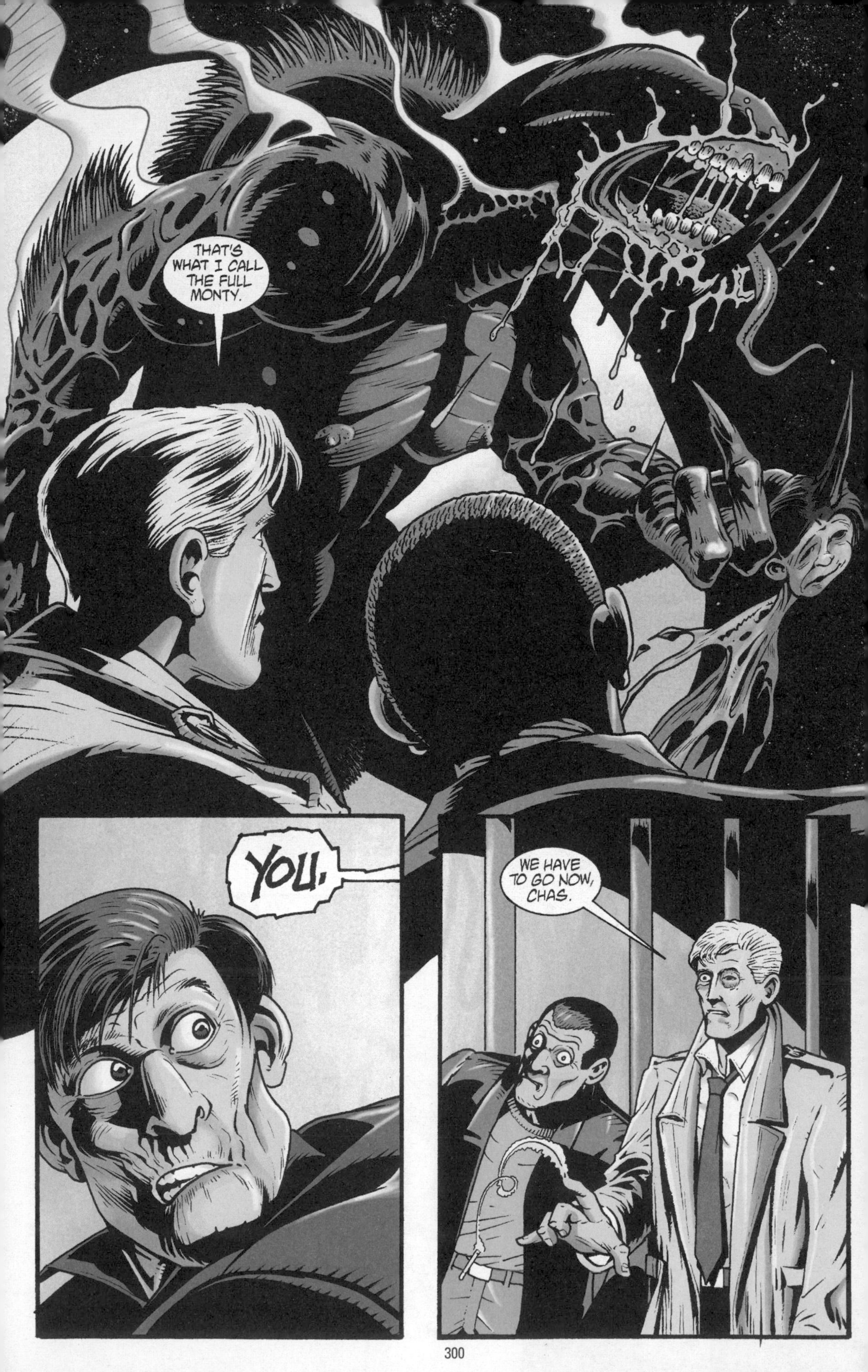
THAT'S WHAT I CALL THE FULL MONTY.
YOU.
WE HAVE TO GO NOW, CHAS.

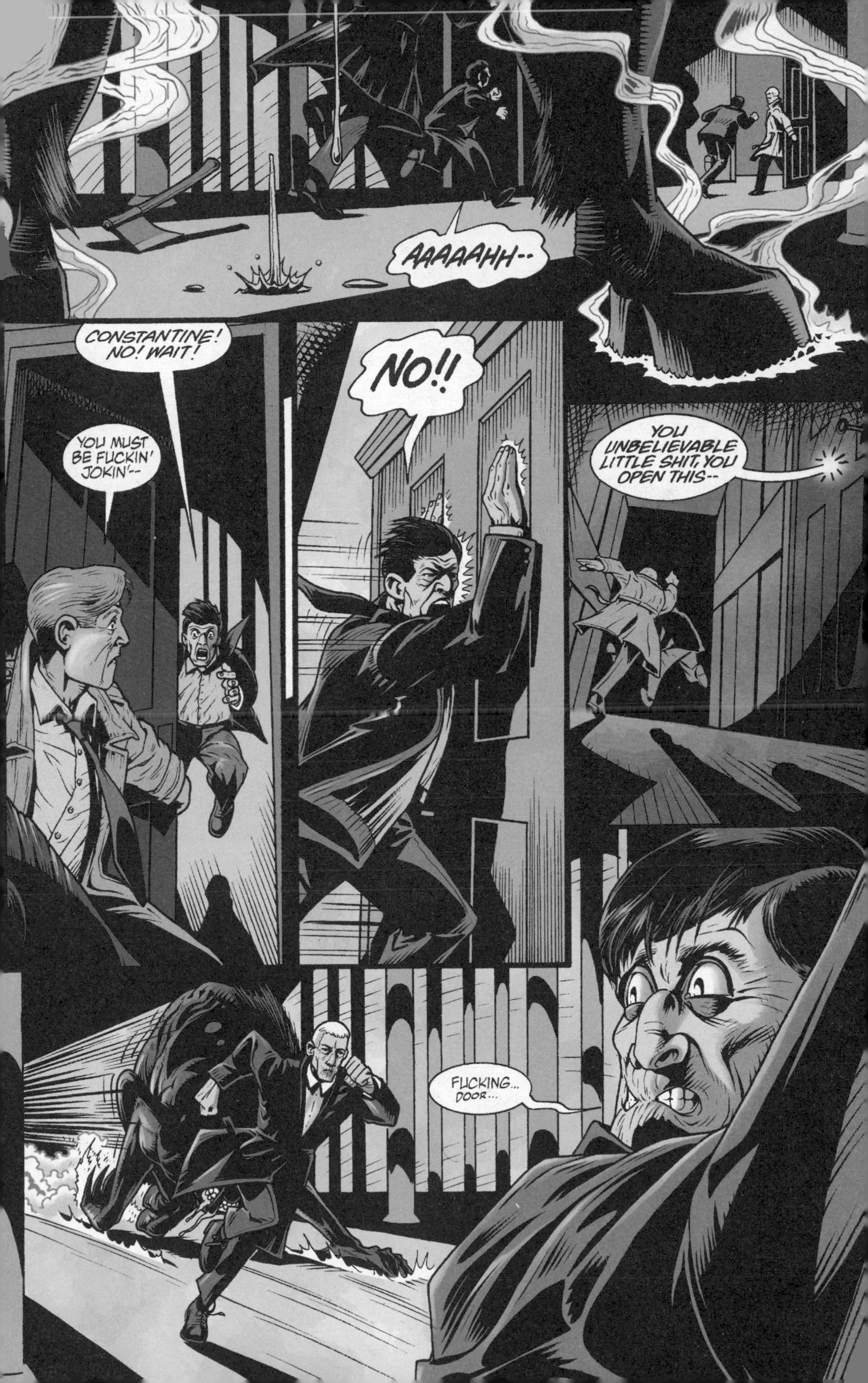
AAAAAHH--
CONSTANTINE! NO! WAIT!
YOU MUST BE FUCKIN' JOKIN'--
NO!!
YOU UNBELIEVABLE LITTLE SHIT, YOU OPEN THIS--
FUCKING... DOOR...

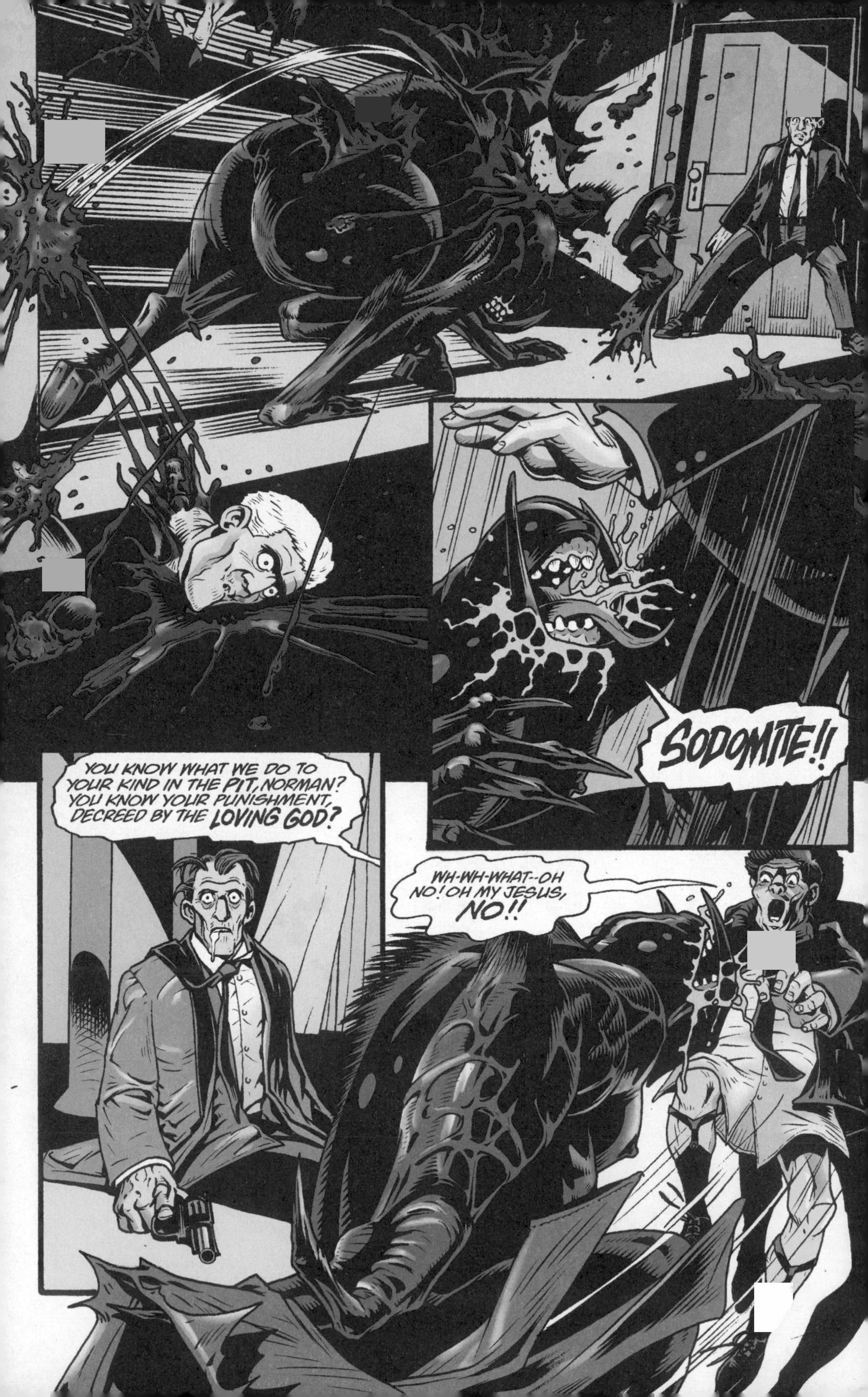
SODOMITE!!
YOU KNOW WHAT WE DO TO YOUR KIND IN THE PIT, NORMAN? YOU KNOW YOUR PUNISHMENT, DECREED BY THE LOVING GOD?
WH-WH-WHAT--OH NO! OH MY JESUS, NO!!

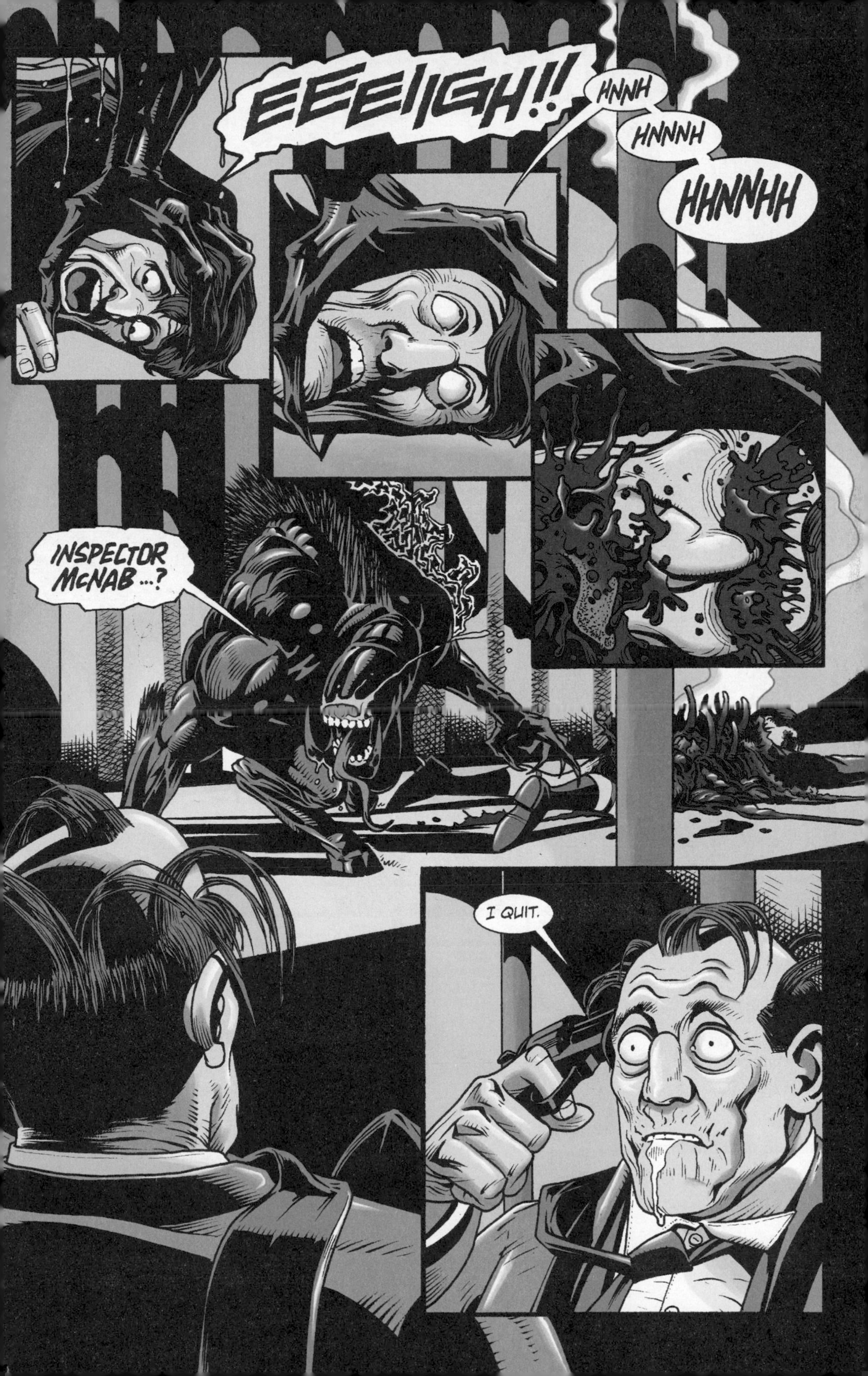
EEEEIIGH!!
HNNH
HNNNH
HHNNHH
INSPECTOR McNAB...?
I QUIT.

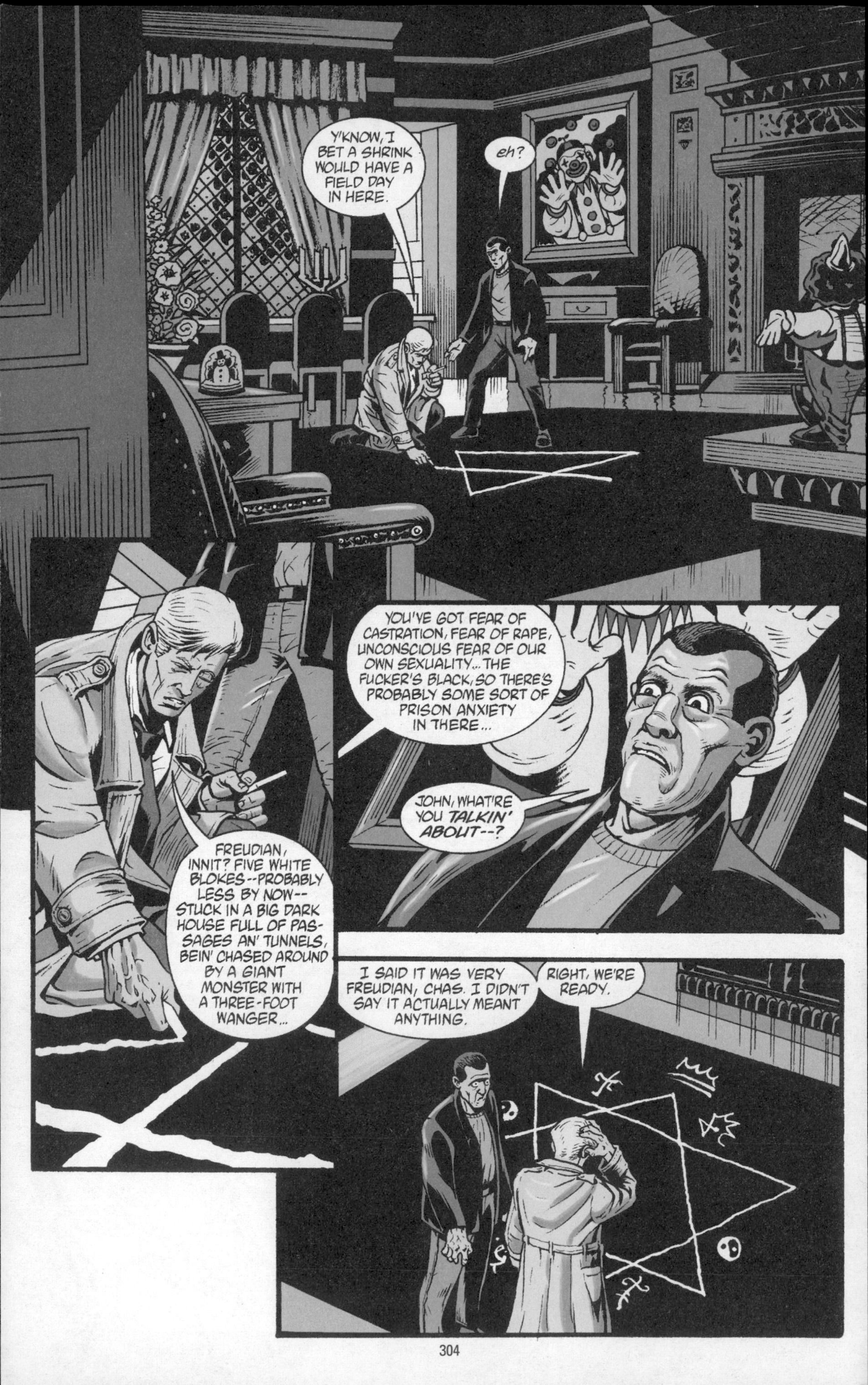
Y'KNOW, I BET A SHRINK WOULD HAVE A FIELD DAY IN HERE.
eh?
FREUDIAN, INNIT? FIVE WHITE BLOKES--PROBABLY LESS BY NOW--STUCK IN A BIG DARK HOUSE FULL OF PAS-SAGES AN' TUNNELS, BEIN' CHASED AROUND BY A GIANT MONSTER WITH A THREE-FOOT WANGER...
YOU'VE GOT FEAR OF CASTRATION, FEAR OF RAPE, UNCONSCIOUS FEAR OF OUR OWN SEXUALITY... THE FUCKER'S BLACK, SO THERE'S PROBABLY SOME SORT OF PRISON ANXIETY IN THERE...
JOHN, WHAT'RE YOU *TALKIN'* *ABOUT*--?
I SAID IT WAS VERY FREUDIAN, CHAS. I DIDN'T SAY IT ACTUALLY MEANT ANYTHING.
RIGHT, WE'RE READY.

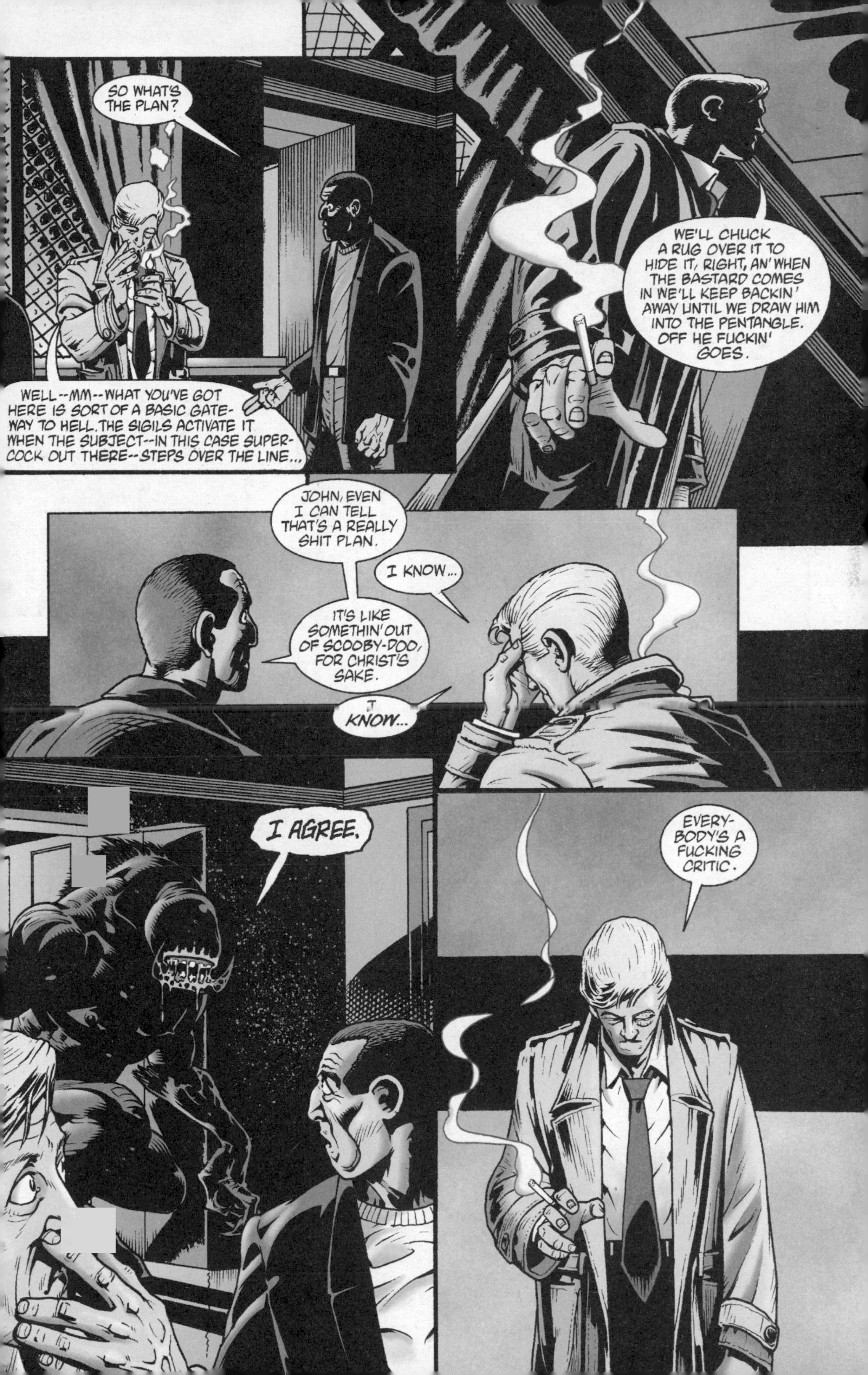
SO WHAT'S THE PLAN?
WELL--MM--WHAT YOU'VE GOT HERE IS SORT OF A BASIC GATEWAY TO HELL. THE SIGILS ACTIVATE IT WHEN THE SUBJECT--IN THIS CASE SUPER-COCK OUT THERE--STEPS OVER THE LINE...
WE'LL CHUCK A RUG OVER IT TO HIDE IT, RIGHT, AN' WHEN THE BASTARD COMES IN WE'LL KEEP BACKIN' AWAY UNTIL WE DRAW HIM INTO THE PENTANGLE. OFF HE FUCKIN' GOES.
JOHN, EVEN I CAN TELL THAT'S A REALLY SHIT PLAN.
I KNOW...
IT'S LIKE SOMETHIN' OUT OF SCOOBY-DOO, FOR CHRIST'S SAKE.
I KNOW...
I AGREE.
EVERYBODY'S A FUCKING CRITIC.

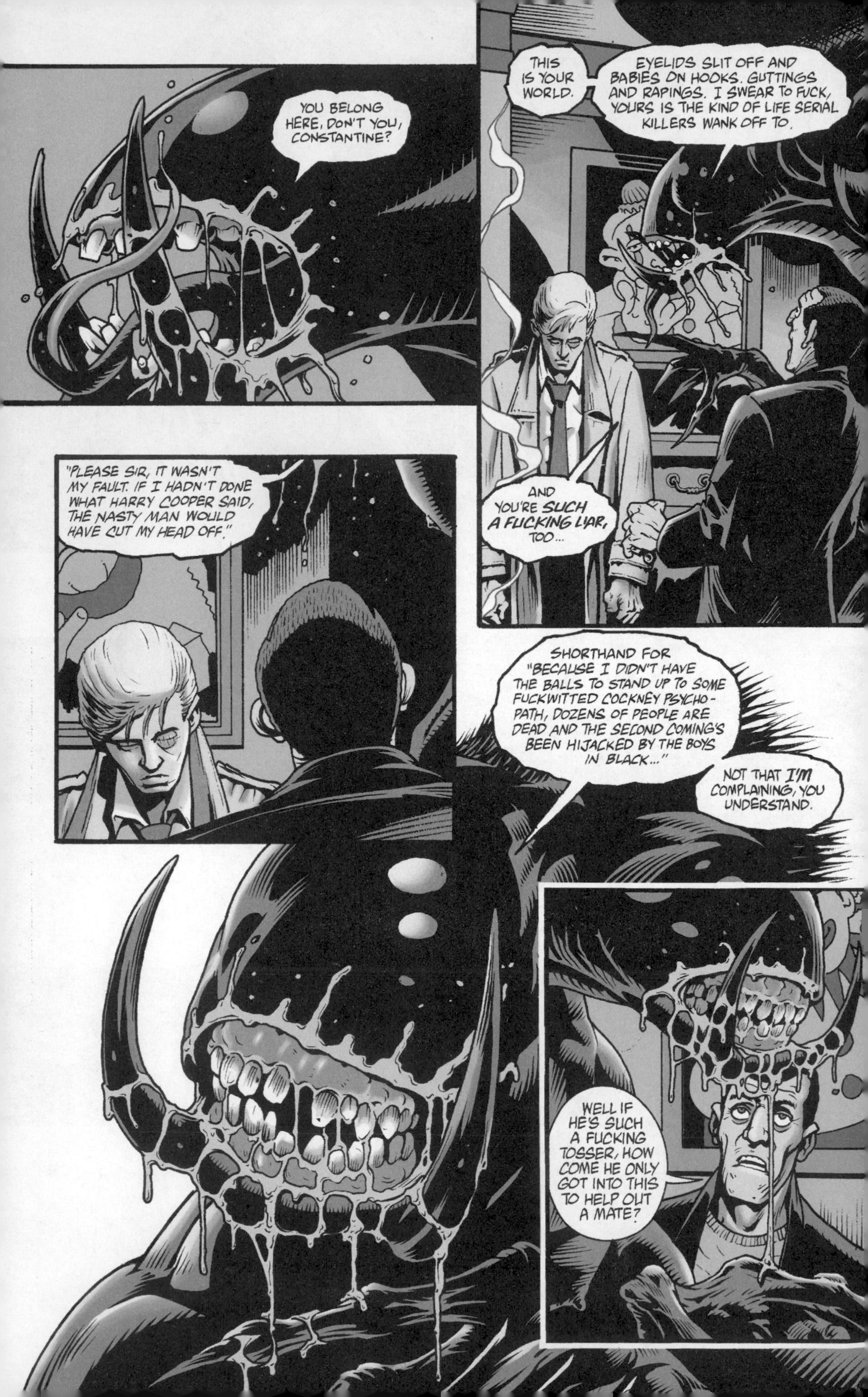
YOU BELONG HERE, DON'T YOU, CONSTANTINE?
THIS IS YOUR WORLD.
EYELIDS SLIT OFF AND BABIES ON HOOKS. GUTTINGS AND RAPINGS. I SWEAR TO FUCK, YOURS IS THE KIND OF LIFE SERIAL KILLERS WANK OFF TO.
AND YOU'RE SUCH A FUCKING LIAR, TOO...
"PLEASE SIR, IT WASN'T MY FAULT. IF I HADN'T DONE WHAT HARRY COOPER SAID, THE NASTY MAN WOULD HAVE CUT MY HEAD OFF."
SHORTHAND FOR "BECAUSE I DIDN'T HAVE THE BALLS TO STAND UP TO SOME FUCKWITTED COCKNEY PSYCHO-PATH, DOZENS OF PEOPLE ARE DEAD AND THE SECOND COMING'S BEEN HIJACKED BY THE BOYS IN BLACK..."
NOT THAT I'M COMPLAINING, YOU UNDERSTAND.
WELL IF HE'S SUCH A FUCKING TOSSER, HOW COME HE ONLY GOT INTO THIS TO HELP OUT A MATE?

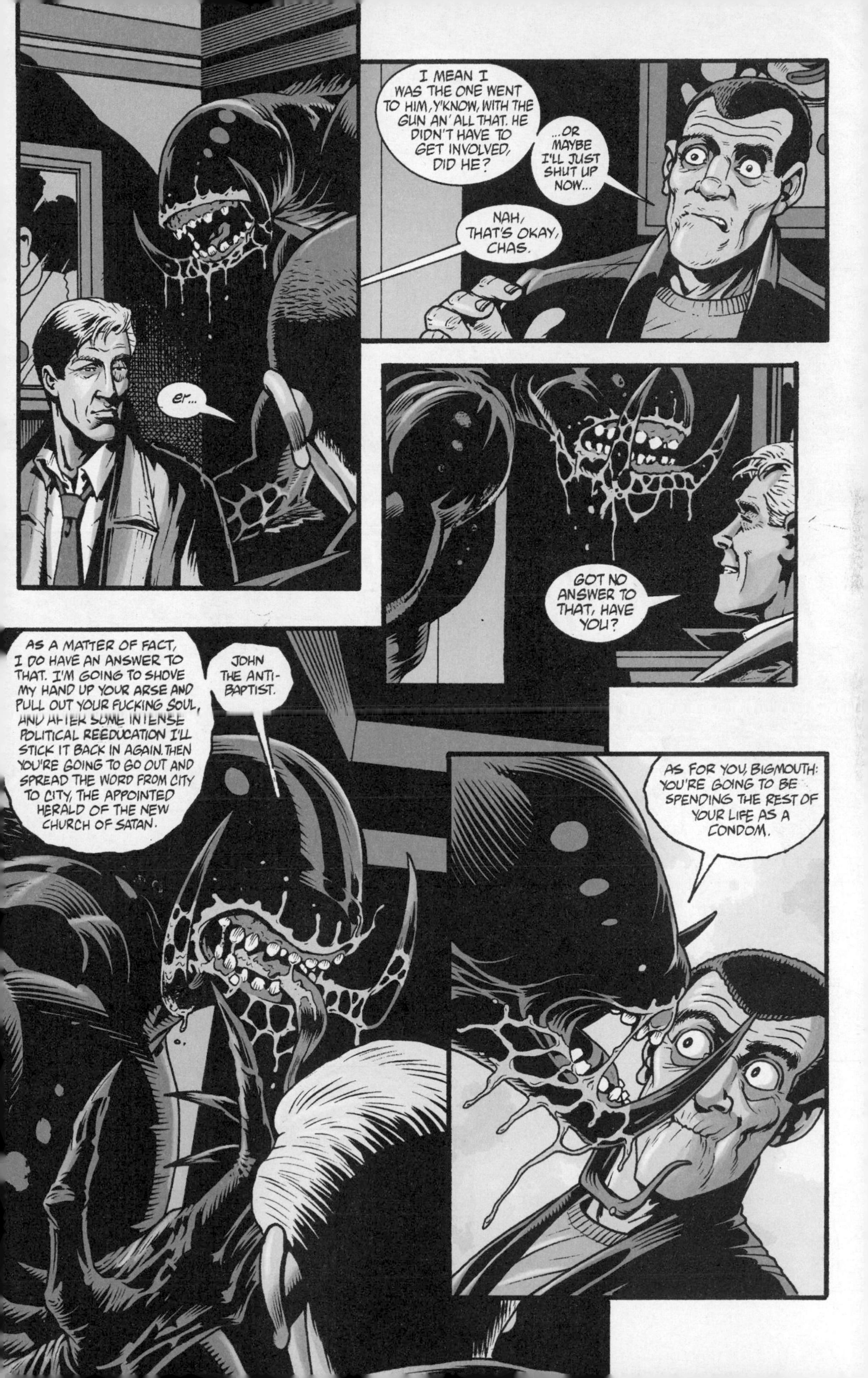
er...
I MEAN I WAS THE ONE WENT TO HIM, Y'KNOW, WITH THE GUN AN' ALL THAT. HE DIDN'T HAVE TO GET INVOLVED, DID HE?
...OR MAYBE I'LL JUST SHUT UP NOW...
NAH, THAT'S OKAY, CHAS.
GOT NO ANSWER TO THAT, HAVE YOU?
AS A MATTER OF FACT, I DO HAVE AN ANSWER TO THAT. I'M GOING TO SHOVE MY HAND UP YOUR ARSE AND PULL OUT YOUR FUCKING SOUL, AND AFTER SOME INTENSE POLITICAL REEDUCATION I'LL STICK IT BACK IN AGAIN. THEN YOU'RE GOING TO GO OUT AND SPREAD THE WORD FROM CITY TO CITY, THE APPOINTED HERALD OF THE NEW CHURCH OF SATAN.
JOHN THE ANTI-BAPTIST.
AS FOR YOU, BIGMOUTH: YOU'RE GOING TO BE SPENDING THE REST OF YOUR LIFE AS A CONDOM.

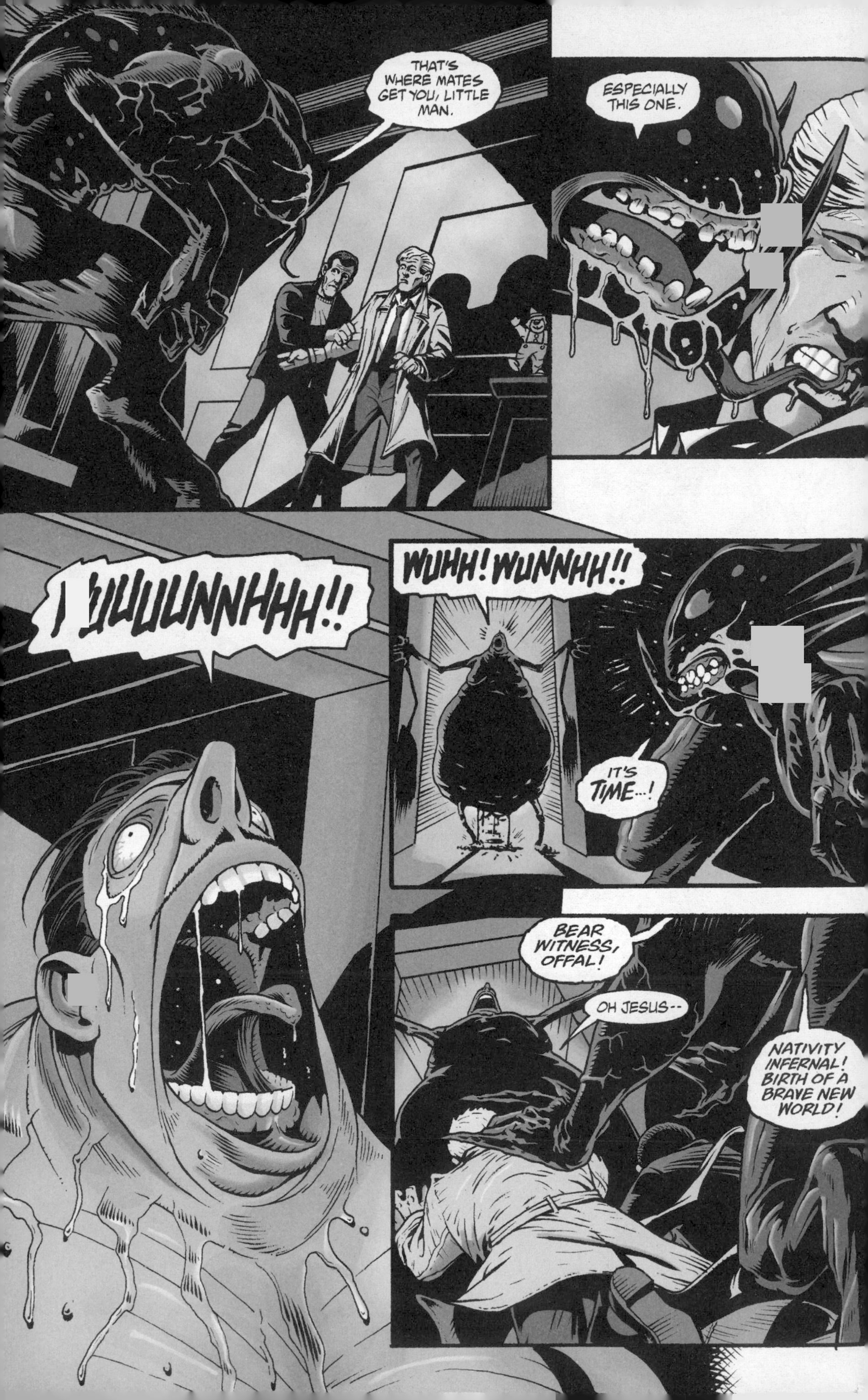
THAT'S WHERE MATES GET YOU, LITTLE MAN.
ESPECIALLY THIS ONE.
UUUUNNHHH!!
WUHH! WUNNHH!!
IT'S TIME...!
BEAR WITNESS, OFFAL!
OH JESUS--
NATIVITY INFERNAL! BIRTH OF A BRAVE NEW WORLD!

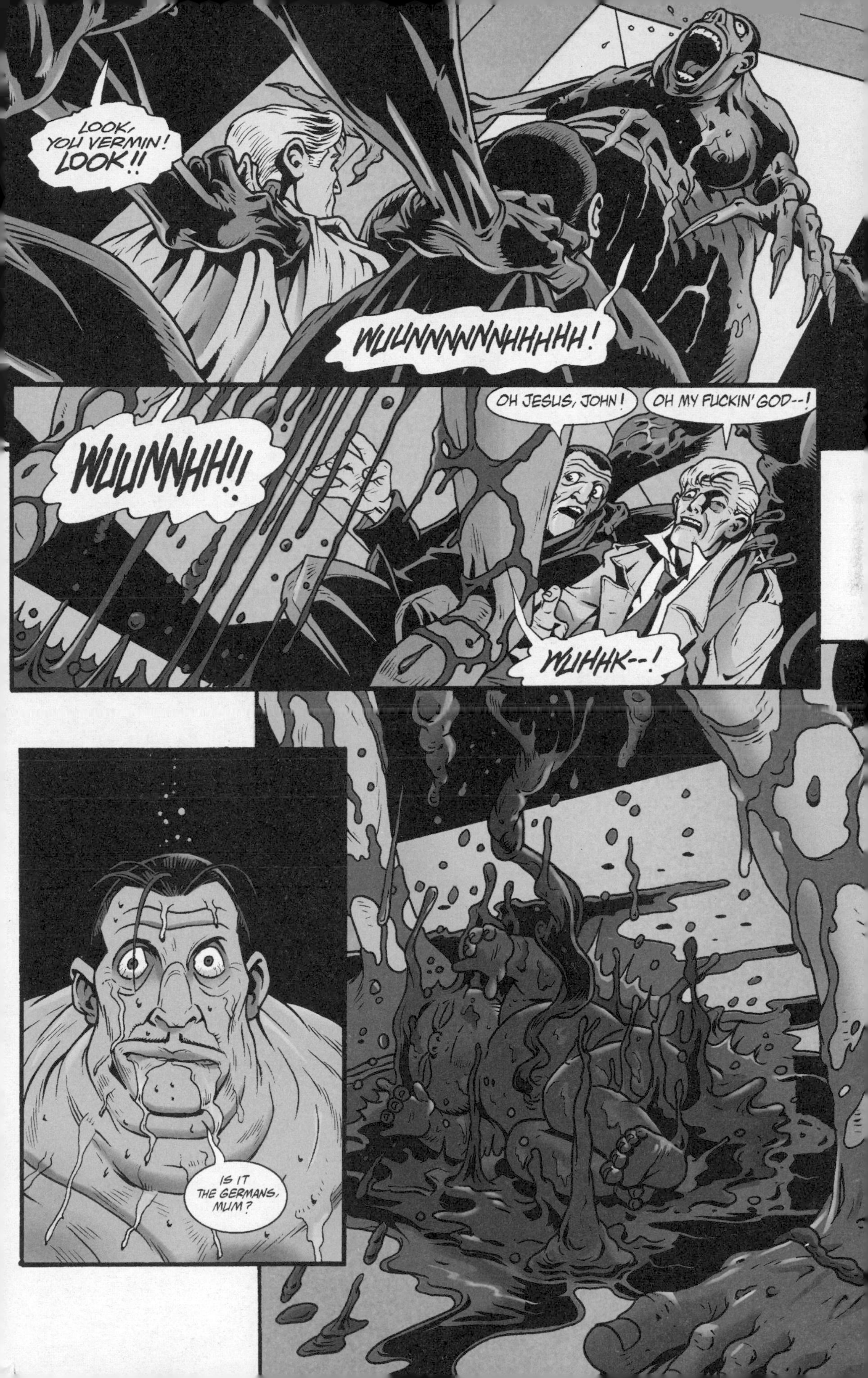
LOOK, YOU VERMIN! LOOK!!
WUUNNNNNNHHHHH!
WUUNNHH!!
OH JESUS, JOHN!
OH MY FUCKIN' GOD--!
WUHHK--!
IS IT THE GERMANS, MUM?

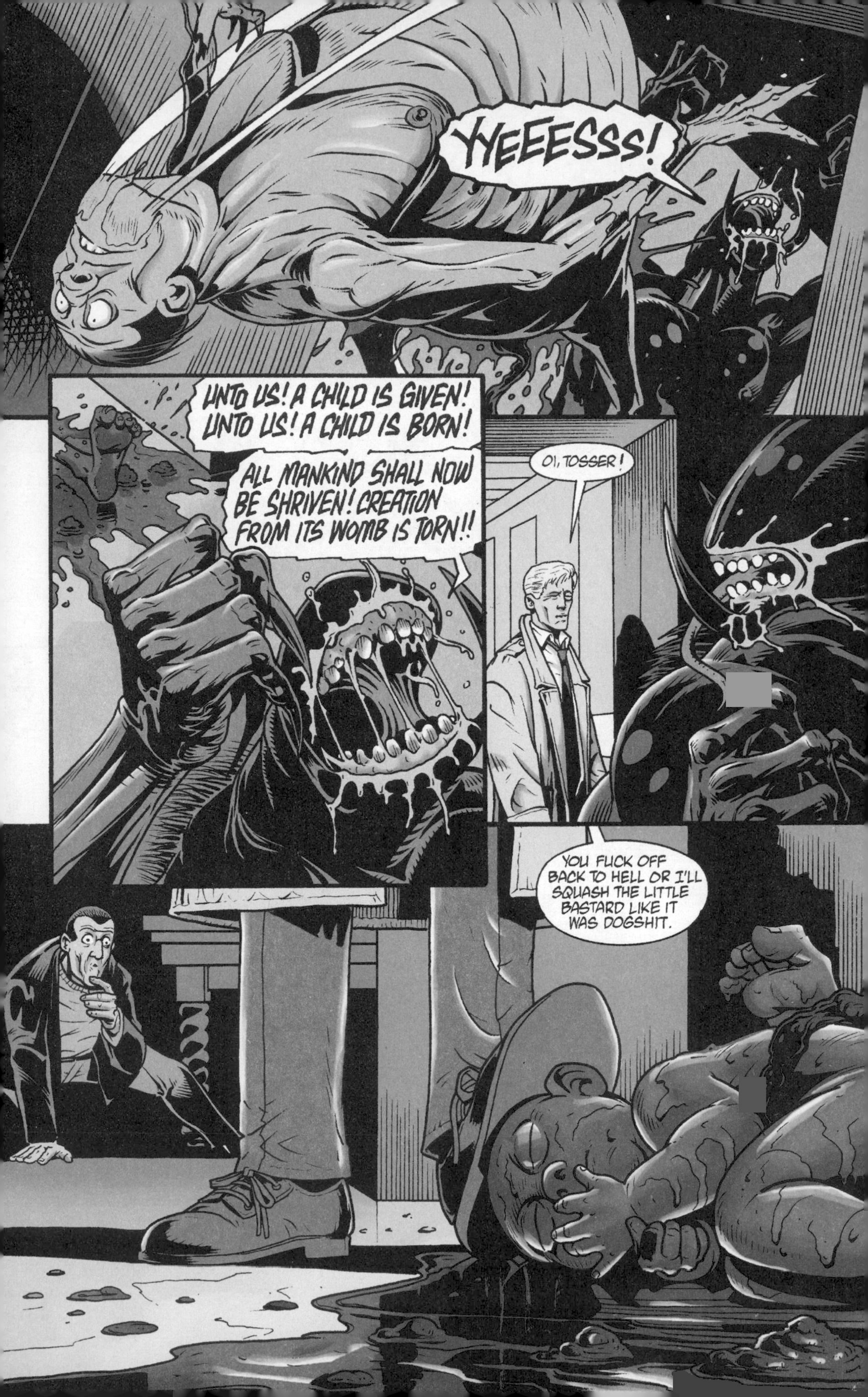
YYEEESSS!
UNTO US! A CHILD IS GIVEN! UNTO US! A CHILD IS BORN!
ALL MANKIND SHALL NOW BE SHRIVEN! CREATION FROM ITS WOMB IS TORN!!
OI, TOSSER!
YOU FUCK OFF BACK TO HELL OR I'LL SQUASH THE LITTLE BASTARD LIKE IT WAS DOGSHIT.

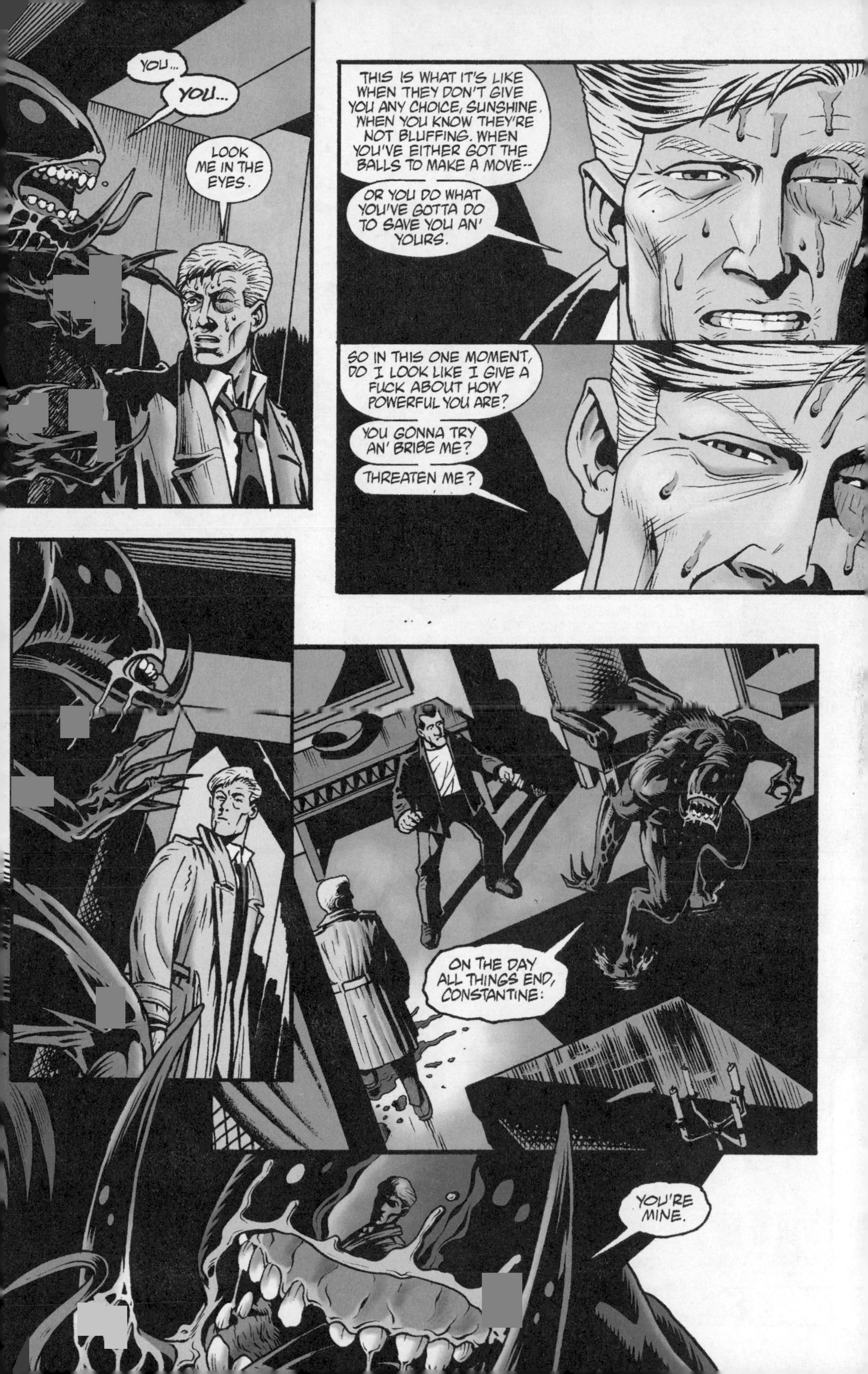
YOU...
YOU...
LOOK ME IN THE EYES.
THIS IS WHAT IT'S LIKE WHEN THEY DON'T GIVE YOU ANY CHOICE, SUNSHINE. WHEN YOU KNOW THEY'RE NOT BLUFFING. WHEN YOU'VE EITHER GOT THE BALLS TO MAKE A MOVE--
OR YOU DO WHAT YOU'VE GOTTA DO TO SAVE YOU AN' YOURS.
SO IN THIS ONE MOMENT, DO I LOOK LIKE I GIVE A FUCK ABOUT HOW POWERFUL YOU ARE?
YOU GONNA TRY AN' BRIBE ME?
THREATEN ME?
ON THE DAY ALL THINGS END, CONSTANTINE:
YOU'RE MINE.

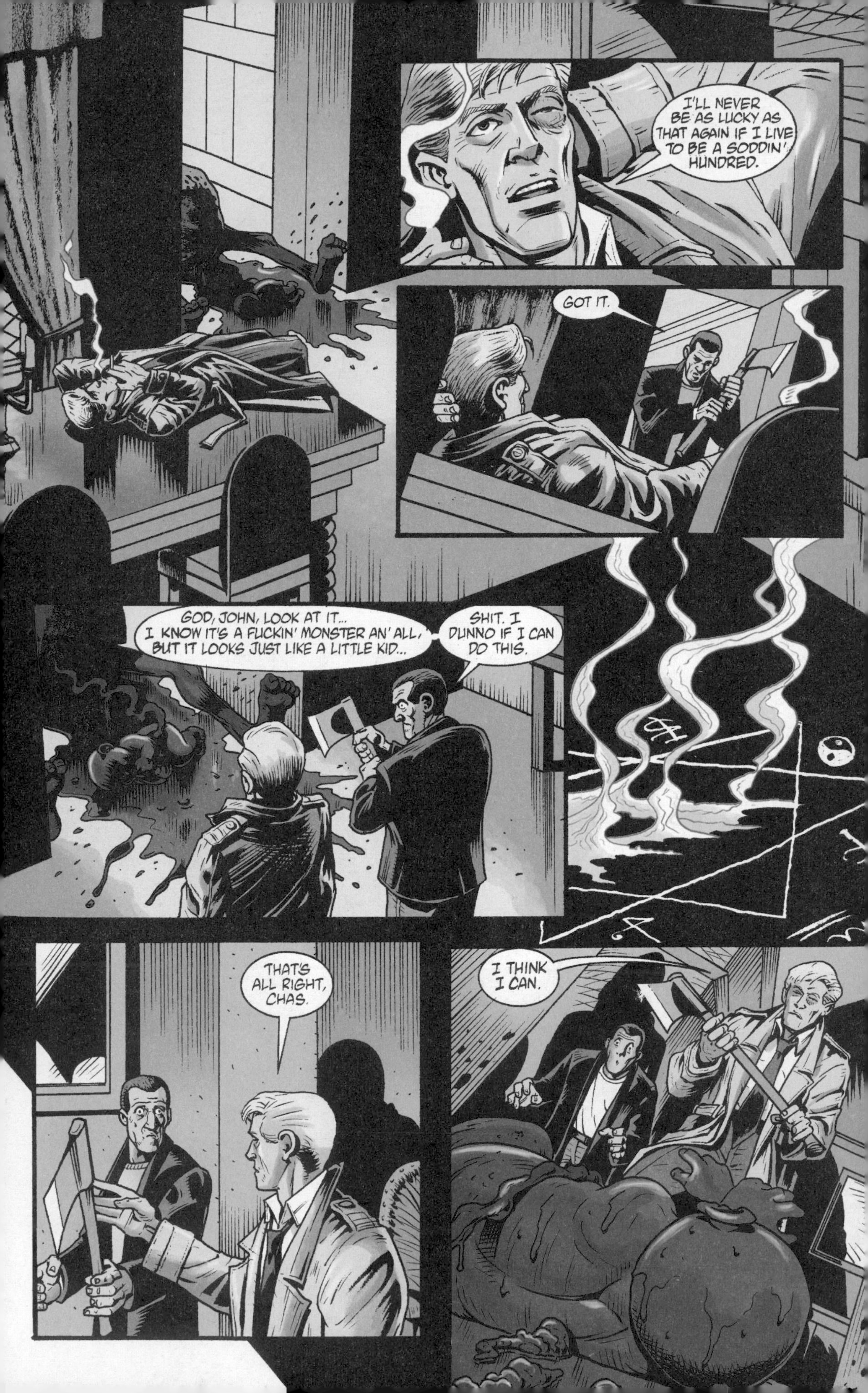
I'LL NEVER BE AS LUCKY AS THAT AGAIN IF I LIVE TO BE A SODDIN' HUNDRED.
GOT IT.
GOD, JOHN, LOOK AT IT... I KNOW IT'S A FUCKIN' MONSTER AN' ALL, BUT IT LOOKS JUST LIKE A LITTLE KID...
SHIT. I DUNNO IF I CAN DO THIS.
THAT'S ALL RIGHT, CHAS.
I THINK I CAN.

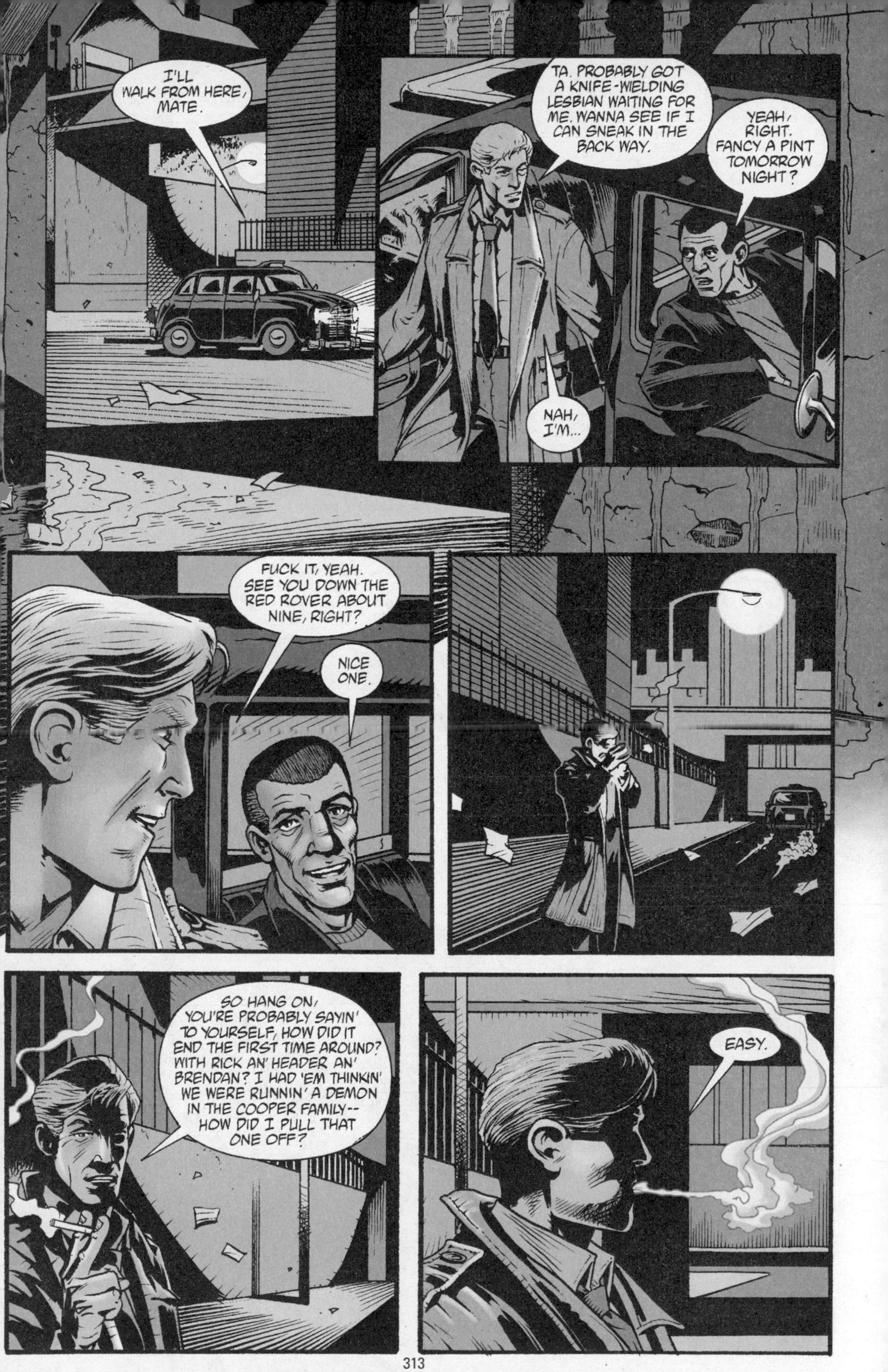
I'LL WALK FROM HERE, MATE.
TA. PROBABLY GOT A KNIFE-WIELDING LESBIAN WAITING FOR ME. WANNA SEE IF I CAN SNEAK IN THE BACK WAY.
YEAH, RIGHT. FANCY A PINT TOMORROW NIGHT?
NAH, I'M...
FUCK IT, YEAH. SEE YOU DOWN THE RED ROVER ABOUT NINE, RIGHT?
NICE ONE.
SO HANG ON, YOU'RE PROBABLY SAYIN' TO YOURSELF, HOW DID IT END THE FIRST TIME AROUND? WITH RICK AN' HEADER AN' BRENDAN? I HAD 'EM THINKIN' WE WERE RUNNIN' A DEMON IN THE COOPER FAMILY-- HOW DID I PULL THAT ONE OFF?
EASY.

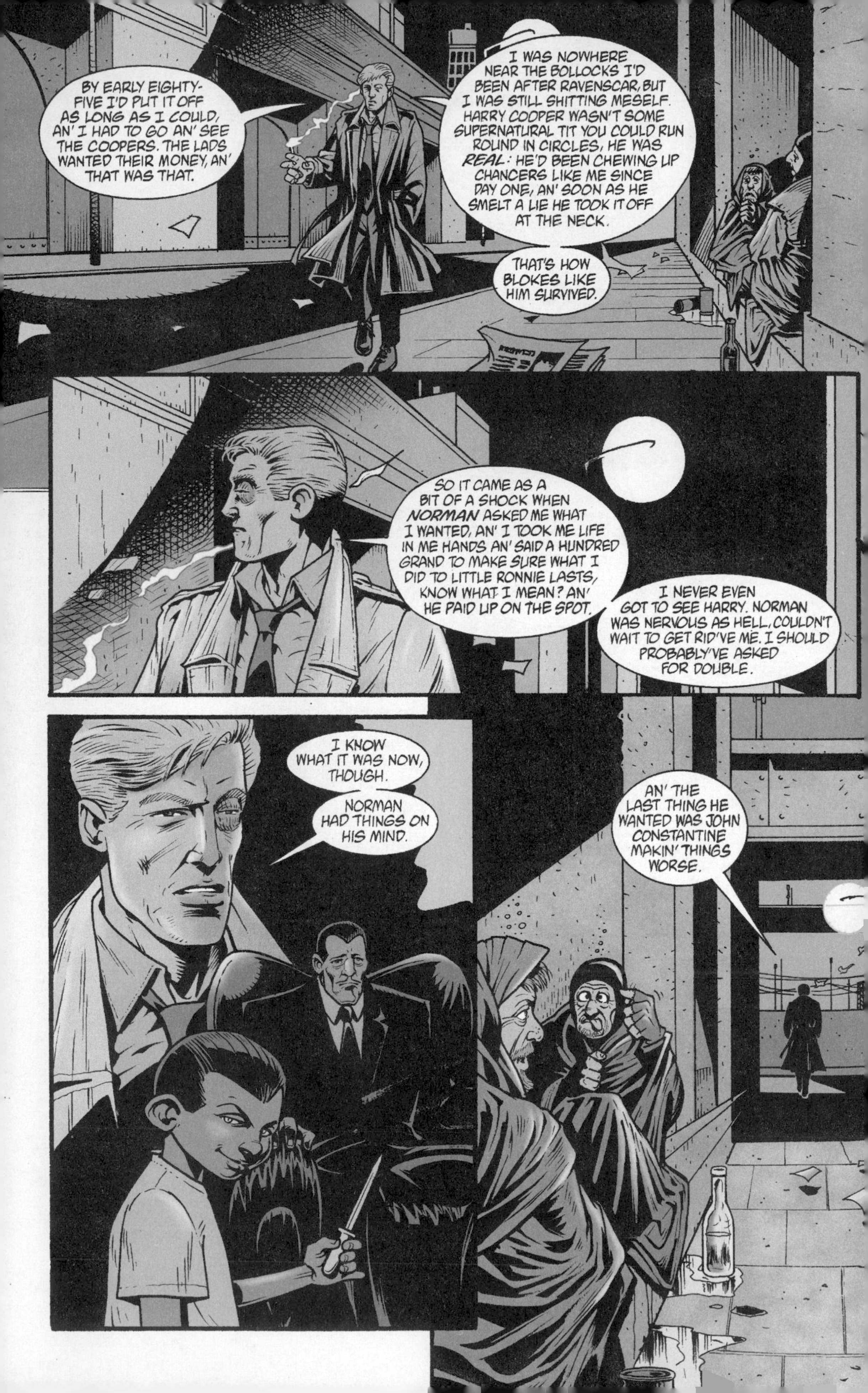
BY EARLY EIGHTY-FIVE I'D PUT IT OFF AS LONG AS I COULD, AN' I HAD TO GO AN' SEE THE COOPERS. THE LADS WANTED THEIR MONEY, AN' THAT WAS THAT.
I WAS NOWHERE NEAR THE BOLLOCKS I'D BEEN AFTER RAVENSCAR, BUT I WAS STILL SHITTING MESELF. HARRY COOPER WASN'T SOME SUPERNATURAL TIT YOU COULD RUN ROUND IN CIRCLES, HE WAS REAL: HE'D BEEN CHEWING UP CHANCERS LIKE ME SINCE DAY ONE, AN' SOON AS HE SMELT A LIE HE TOOK IT OFF AT THE NECK.
THAT'S HOW BLOKES LIKE HIM SURVIVED.
SO IT CAME AS A BIT OF A SHOCK WHEN NORMAN ASKED ME WHAT I WANTED, AN' I TOOK ME LIFE IN ME HANDS AN' SAID A HUNDRED GRAND TO MAKE SURE WHAT I DID TO LITTLE RONNIE LASTS, KNOW WHAT I MEAN? AN' HE PAID UP ON THE SPOT.
I NEVER EVEN GOT TO SEE HARRY. NORMAN WAS NERVOUS AS HELL, COULDN'T WAIT TO GET RID'VE ME. I SHOULD PROBABLY'VE ASKED FOR DOUBLE.
I KNOW WHAT IT WAS NOW, THOUGH.
NORMAN HAD THINGS ON HIS MIND.
AN' THE LAST THING HE WANTED WAS JOHN CONSTANTINE MAKIN' THINGS WORSE.

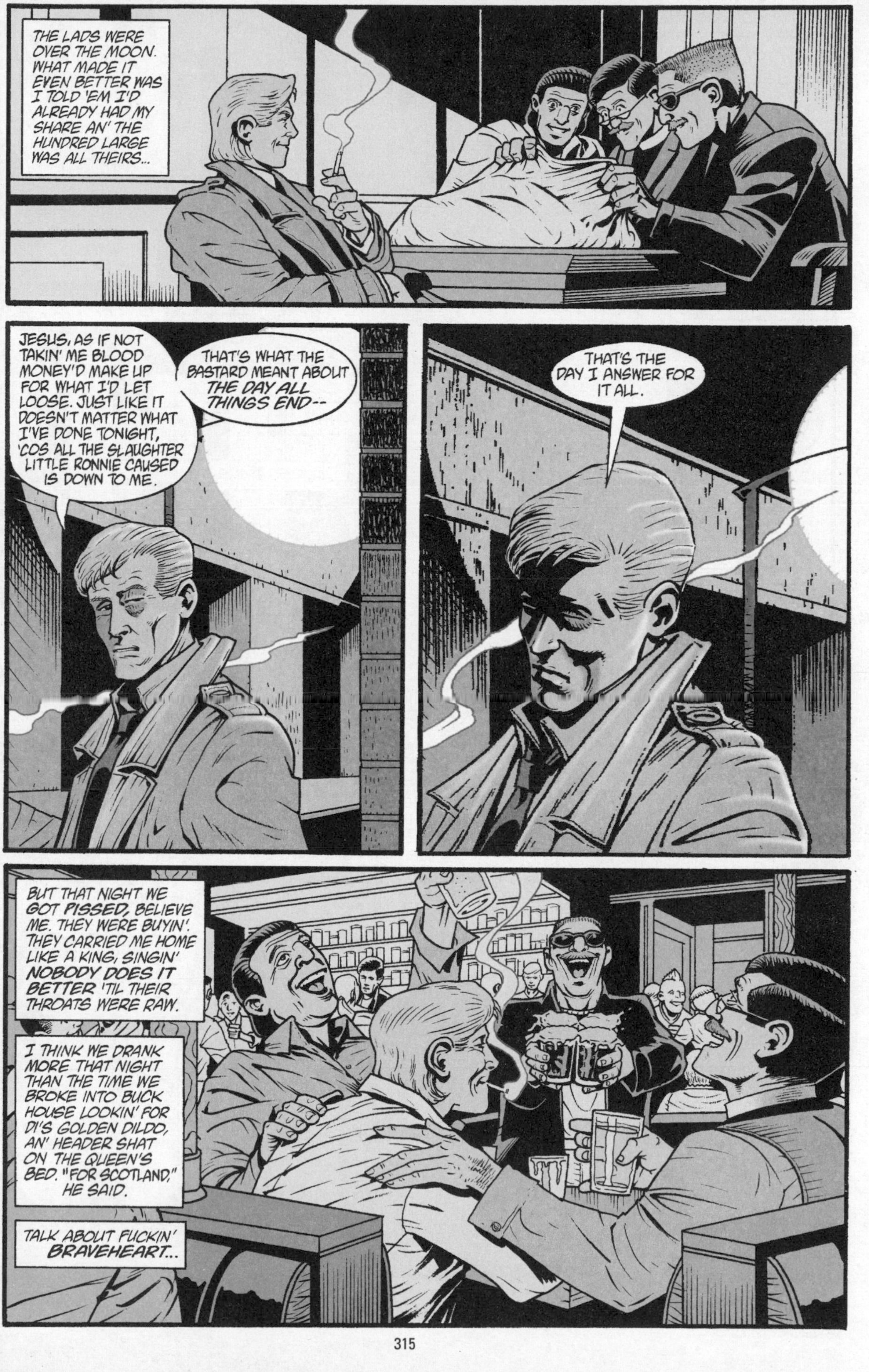
THE LADS WERE OVER THE MOON. WHAT MADE IT EVEN BETTER WAS I TOLD 'EM I'D ALREADY HAD MY SHARE AN' THE HUNDRED LARGE WAS ALL THEIRS...
JESUS, AS IF NOT TAKIN' ME BLOOD MONEY'D MAKE UP FOR WHAT I'D LET LOOSE. JUST LIKE IT DOESN'T MATTER WHAT I'VE DONE TONIGHT, 'COS ALL THE SLAUGHTER LITTLE RONNIE CAUSED IS DOWN TO ME.
THAT'S WHAT THE BASTARD MEANT ABOUT *THE DAY ALL THINGS END--*
THAT'S THE DAY I ANSWER FOR IT ALL.
BUT THAT NIGHT WE GOT **PISSED**, BELIEVE ME. THEY WERE BUYIN'. THEY CARRIED ME HOME LIKE A KING, SINGIN' **NOBODY DOES IT BETTER** 'TIL THEIR THROATS WERE RAW.
I THINK WE DRANK MORE THAT NIGHT THAN THE TIME WE BROKE INTO BUCK HOUSE LOOKIN' FOR DI'S GOLDEN DILDO, AN' HEADER SHAT ON THE QUEEN'S BED. "FOR SCOTLAND," HE SAID.
TALK ABOUT FUCKIN' **BRAVEHEART**...

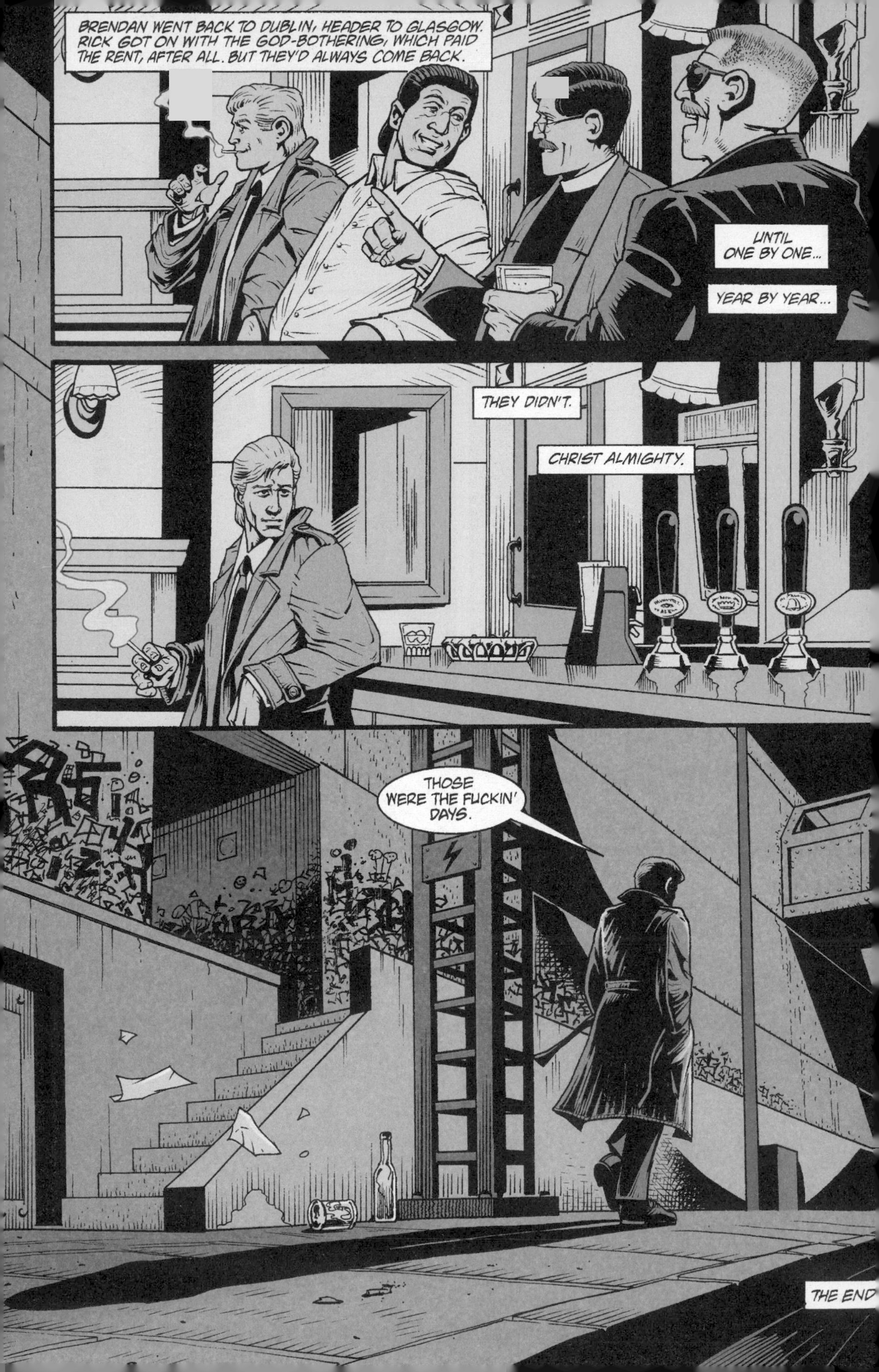
BRENDAN WENT BACK TO DUBLIN, HEADER TO GLASGOW. RICK GOT ON WITH THE GOD-BOTHERING, WHICH PAID THE RENT, AFTER ALL. BUT THEY'D ALWAYS COME BACK.
UNTIL ONE BY ONE...
YEAR BY YEAR...
THEY DIDN'T.
CHRIST ALMIGHTY.
THOSE WERE THE FUCKIN' DAYS.
THE END

Cover art by Glenn Fabry for the
JOHN CONSTANTINE, HELLBLAZER: SON OF MAN
trade paperback collection, released in 2004.

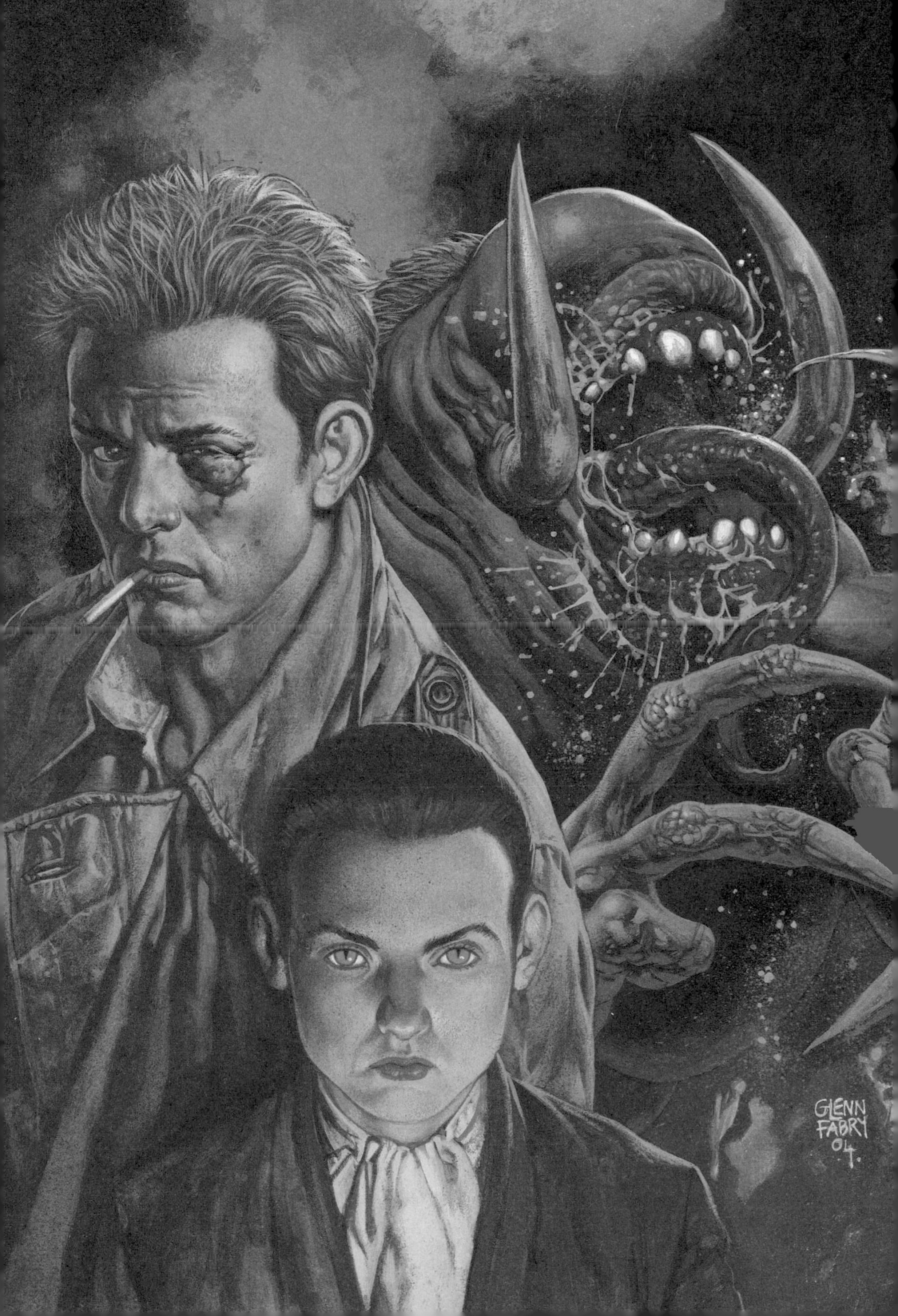
GLENN FABRY 04.

VERTIGO

FROM THE WRITER OF RED LANTERNS
PETER MILLIGAN
with GIUSEPPE CAMUNCOLI and STEFANO LANDINI

JOHN CONSTANTINE, HELLBLAZER: INDIA

JOHN CONSTANTINE, HELLBLAZER: PHANTOM PAINS

JOHN CONSTANTINE, HELLBLAZER: SCAB

JOHN CONSTANTINE, HELLBLAZER: HOOKED

JOHN CONSTANTINE, HELLBLAZER: INDIA

JOHN CONSTANTINE, HELLBLAZER: BLOODY CARNATIONS

JOHN CONSTANTINE, HELLBLAZER: PHANTOM PAINS

JOHN CONSTANTINE, HELLBLAZER: THE DEVILS TRENCHCOAT

JOHN CONSTANTINE, HELLBLAZER: DEATH AND CIGARETTES

JOHN CONSTANTINE
HELLBLAZER
MILLIGAN · CAMUNCOLI · LANDINI · SUDŽUKA

SCAB

VERTIGO

VERTIGO

"The most intense adult comic in ages."
—SPIN MAGAZINE

"Cool."
—ENTERTAINMENT WEEKLY

"Far and away the best example of the genre I have ever seen."
—THE GUARDIAN

READ THE ENTIRE SERIES!

PREACHER VOL. 3: PROUD AMERICANS

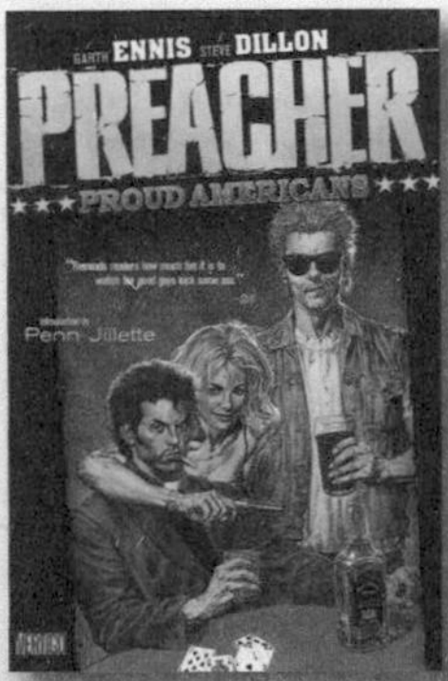
GARTH ENNIS STEVE DILLON
PREACHER
PROUD AMERICANS
Penn Jillette

PREACHER VOL. 6: WAR IN THE SUN

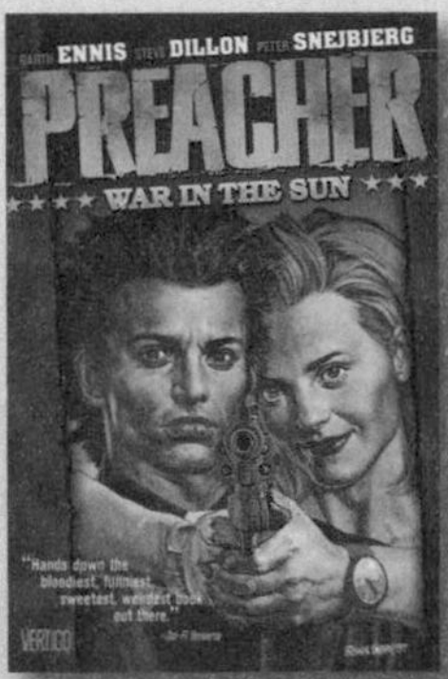
GARTH ENNIS STEVE DILLON PETER SNEJBJERG
PREACHER
WAR IN THE SUN
VERTIGO

PREACHER VOL. 1: GONE TO TEXAS

PREACHER VOL. 2: UNTIL THE END OF THE WORLD

PREACHER VOL. 3: PROUD AMERICANS

PREACHER VOL. 4: ANCIENT HISTORY

PREACHER VOL. 5: DIXIE FRIED

PREACHER VOL. 6: WAR IN THE SUN

PREACHER VOL. 7: SALVATION

PREACHER VOL. 8: ALL HELL'S A-COMING

PREACHER VOL. 9: ALAMO

GARTH ENNIS
with STEVE DILLON

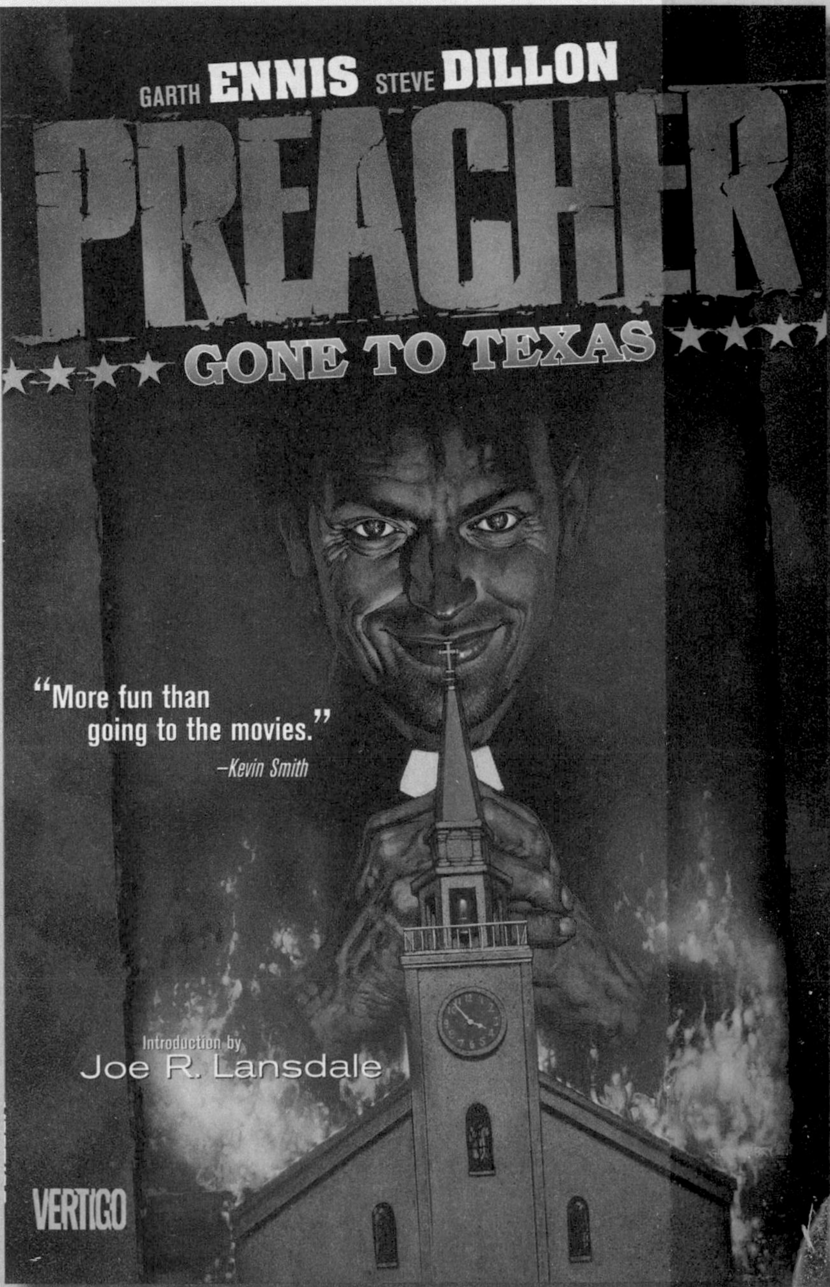
GARTH ENNIS STEVE DILLON
PREACHER
GONE TO TEXAS
"More fun than going to the movies."
–Kevin Smith
Introduction by
Joe R. Lansdale
VERTIGO

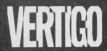